FILM CLASSICS

SPARK PUBLISHING

SPARKNOTES is a registered trademark of SparkNotes LLC

Spark Publishing
120 Fifth Avenue
New York, NY 10011
www.sparknotes.com

First edition.

Please submit all comments and questions or report errors to www.sparknotes.com/errors

ISBN-10: 1-4114-9971-9
ISBN-13: 978-1-4114-9971-3

Printed and bound in the United States

Library of Congress Cataloging-in-Publication Data

Film classics.
    p. cm.
  ISBN-13: 978-1-4114-9971-3
  ISBN-10: 1-4114-9971-9
  1. Motion pictures.
  PN1994.F43835 2006
  791.43'75—dc22

                              2005032121

CONTENTS

How to Use This Book

Film Classics provides you with key information to begin your study of classic films. We've included notes on twenty of the greatest film works of all time—films that have had a marked influence on the world of film and that are considered "classic" today. We've chosen these twenty works from a variety of genres, styles, and time periods in an effort to give you a well-rounded picture of films from the past and the present. You may have seen most or all of these films before, perhaps even several times. What *Film Classics* gives you is the inside story on how these films were made, why they're important to film study in general, and what makes them so remarkable.

We've included these features to help you get the most out of this book:

Introduction: Before diving in to the film notes, you may want to get a broader view of film in general. The Introduction will discuss the characteristics of a "classic" film, the evolution of film, and important philosophical and stylistic movements.

A Shortlist of Great Directors: A list of some of the greatest directors from the past and present, with a brief description of their characteristics and contributions to the world of film.

The Notes: The twenty notes are arranged chronologically by film release date. Trilogies are placed according to the release date of the first film in the trilogy. Each film note contains the following sections:

- **Context:** An overview that traces the director's biographical details and explores the circumstances surrounding the creation of the film.
- **Plot Overview:** A concise summary to refresh your memory and help you understand major plot points.
- **Character List:** A sketch of the film's cast in order of importance, along with a brief explanation of the role each character plays in the film.
- **Analysis of Major Characters:** In-depth studies of what makes the main characters tick.

- **Themes, Motifs, and Symbols**: The most important ideas of the film, all in one place. Themes are the fundamental and often universal ideas explored in a work of art. Motifs are recurring structures, contrasts, or filmic devices that can help to develop and inform plot and thematic development. Symbols are objects, characters, figures, musical themes, or colors used to represent abstract ideas or concepts.
- **Film Analysis**: In-depth discussion of filmic elements and what makes this particular film so remarkable.
- **Important Quotations Explained**: The most important lines from the film with explanations of why they're significant.

We hope *Film Classics* helps increase your understanding and enjoyment of these classic films. Your input makes us better. Let us know what you think or how we can improve this book at http://www.sparknotes.com/comments/.

INTRODUCTION

INTRODUCTION

WHAT MAKES A FILM "CLASSIC"?

In recent years, the true nature of the term *classic* has become obscured by media hyperbole: every film with a hint of artistic merit is immediately labeled an "instant" or "modern" classic. Although this trend likely boosts box office revenue, it detracts from film history and criticism—two serious academic fields that grant cinema the merit and significance it deserves.

In the same way that new, hip films aren't automatically classics just because they're different, unexpected, or titillating, a classic film does *not* have to be old, deeply profound, and shot in black-and-white. Few of the films included in *Film Classics* meet such criteria. Rather, all classic films exhibit certain key characteristics, such as:

- Technical achievement and innovation
- Marked influence on the craft of filmmaking
- Themes with universal appeal
- Social/cultural/political significance that defines an era
- Characteristics that epitomize a genre

All of the films presented in this book fulfill at least one of the characteristics of a classic, and one film, *Citizen Kane* (1941), fulfills them all (even the last: some critics claim the film falls into a detective/mystery genre). *Citizen Kane* demonstrates these characteristics with such admirable craft, originality, precision to detail, and innovation that it is widely recognized as the greatest American film of all time. Though some modern audiences may find the film somewhat slow and outdated, when the film is viewed in the proper context, it becomes clear how *Citizen Kane* was far ahead of its time.

Read on for more detailed explanations of why we selected the films we did for this book—and how each, in its own way, defines the idea of a "classic."

TECHNICAL ACHIEVEMENT AND INNOVATION
Each of these films exhibited unprecedented craftsmanship and cutting-edge technology for their time, paving the way for the future direction of cinema:

- *The Birth of a Nation* (1915)
- *The Matrix* trilogy (1999, 2003, 2003)
- *The Lord of the Rings* trilogy (2001, 2002, 2003)
- *Star Wars Episodes IV, V,* and *VI* (1977, 1980, 1983)

MARKED INFLUENCE ON THE CRAFT OF FILMMAKING

These four films have had a large and lasting influence on the craft of filmmaking, whether in the arena of acting, cinematography, narrative structure, or overall artistic brilliance:

- *On the Waterfront* (1954)
- *Citizen Kane* (1941)
- *8 1/2* (1963)
- *The Godfather* trilogy (1972, 1974, 1990)

THEMES WITH UNIVERSAL APPEAL

A *theme* is a fundamental and often universal idea explored in a work of art. Many films have themes that can be universally appreciated, but these four films have been selected for their unparalleled ability to evoke intense emotions and inspire deep feelings among diverse audiences:

- *Casablanca* (1943)
- *Gone With the Wind* (1939)
- *Sleeping Beauty* (1959)
- *Schindler's List* (1993)

SOCIAL/CULTURAL/POLITICAL SIGNIFICANCE THAT DEFINES AN ERA

These four films were all released in the 1970s and adeptly defined the cultural, political, and psychological climate of the turbulent post-Vietnam era:

- *A Clockwork Orange* (1971)
- *One Flew Over the Cuckoo's Nest* (1975)
- *Taxi Driver* (1976)
- *Apocalypse Now* (1979)

CHARACTERISTICS THAT EPITOMIZE A GENRE

A *genre* is a collection of conventions (plot, subject, theme, location, and style) that ultimately identify a film as a certain type to audiences and filmmakers. These four films certainly fulfill the characteristics of a classic but are perhaps best viewed as epitomizing their respective genres: the thriller, the romantic comedy, the detective film/film noir, and animated film:

- *Vertigo* (1958)
- *Annie Hall* (1977)
- *Chinatown* (1974)
- *Spirited Away* (2002)

THE EVOLUTION OF FILM

Scientifically speaking, motion pictures are little more than a technological advancement in the field of photography. Although numerous inventors contributed to the development of motion picture cameras, **Auguste and Louis Lumière** are generally credited as the forefathers of cinema. They invented their **Cinematographe**—a camera, printer, and projector all wrapped up in one—in 1895, and they held the first public screening of their films on December 28 of that year.

The earliest films rarely attempted to convey stories; inventors were so impressed with their technology that they simply recorded daily occurrences around them. Modern techniques of editing, narrative, and cinematography developed later, over a period of many years. A magician named **Georges Méliès** first recognized film's potential for special effects and used invisible cuts to stage remarkable transformations on elaborate sets. **Edwin Porter** contributed to the evolution of editing. It is **D. W. Griffith**, however, who mastered the principles of cinematic storytelling with *The Birth of a Nation* in 1915, a film that incorporated crosscutting, parallel editing, and complex narratives to create a highly compelling story. Although film has since undergone radical technological and stylistic changes, the most fundamental of these principles remain intact today.

THE ARRIVAL OF SOUND AND COLOR

After the development of the Lumière brothers' Cinematographe, motion picture technology went through various small changes and refinements. Film's first *major* innovation arrived with the advent of **synchronous sound** in 1927. Rather than watching silent films accompanied by musicians offstage, audiences were able to actually hear actors' voices when they spoke and sang. Early technology was crude at best, and any camera movement on set would be heard and recorded by microphones—synchronous sound means that the film and the sound are recorded at the same time. As a result, the early "talkies" were visually quite dull and lifeless.

This setback was temporary, however, and the visual element of cinema received another boost in 1937 with the arrival of **Technicolor film**. Films shot in color were highly popular and drew audiences to theaters in droves; soon afterward, the television age (1950s) sent them right back into their homes. Filmmakers had to figure out new ways to make films attractive, exciting, and unique. Filmmakers developed new formats to lure audiences back to the movies but had only mixed success. These new formats included the following:

- **Wide-screen**: a new film format developed in the 1950s to replace the square shape of the standard film frame (which resembled a television screen) with one that is more rectangular in shape
- **3-D**: a method of projecting two images onto a screen—one for a viewer's left eye and one for the right eye—that, when viewed through special glasses, creates an image with depth, such as in *Jaws 3–D* (1983)
- **CinemaScope**: an innovation in motion picture projection that used a new kind of lens (called an *anamorphic* lens) to create panoramic images more than twice as wide as the standard 1.33:1 aspect ratio (the ratio of width to height of the frame), such as in *Oklahoma!* (1955)

THE INFLUENCE OF SPECIAL EFFECTS AND COMPUTERS
Since the 1960s, two major innovations have shaped the landscape of film. The first is the arena of **special effects**, which continues to grow in sophistication and popularity with each passing decade. It has given birth to a wide array of tools, including the following:

- **Digital compositing**: the process of using a computer to layer various video images on top of one another, such as in *The Matrix* (1999)
- **Computer-generated imagery (CGI)**: props, sets, and characters that are created solely by computer, such as in *Star Wars Episodes I, II,* and *III* (1999, 2002, 2005)
- **Motion-control photography**: the use of computers to control each and every movement of the camera with perfect precision, usually for the purpose of creating identical images for later digital compositing, such as in *Fight Club* (1999)

The second innovation arrived in the 1990s with **computer-based online editing**. Until this era, films were spliced together by hand in a lengthy, tedious process. Now, the vast majority of films are edited on computer, where cuts and transitions can be rendered instantly. This technology, combined with the increasing affordability of digital video cameras, has led to what is often called the "democratization of film," in which younger filmmakers with limited budgets are able to make movies more easily than ever before.

PHILOSOPHICAL AND STYLISTIC MOVEMENTS

Although various philosophical and stylistic movements have emerged during film's relatively brief history, they've generally erupted in sporadic, short-lived bursts and have remained on the fringe of film culture. The influence of these movements, however, has been vast and powerful, and the most significant are worth mentioning here.

GERMAN EXPRESSIONISM (1919–1926)

After World War I, the Germans were struggling to find a place in the international film market. That all changed with the ominous film *The Cabinet of Dr. Caligari* (1920). Working on a shoestring budget, the filmmakers used dark shadows, graphic compositions, and stylized makeup and set design to reflect the Expressionist movement of art, which sought to convey the psychological state of the artist rather than portray the subject objectively. The movement enjoyed widespread acclaim, greatly influenced the film noir and horror genres, and left an indelible mark on classics such as *Citizen Kane* (1941).

ITALIAN NEOREALISM (1942–1954)

During Mussolini's reign, much of popular Italian cinema was artificial and decadent, portraying the lives of the upper class in sentimental melodramas. After the war, however, with studio settings destroyed and the economy in ruins, a new movement emerged. The neorealists sought to capture life as it really was, shooting on the streets with nonprofessional actors to create a sense of realism. These films focused on the lives of the average working-class citizen, and the traditional narrative was replaced with open-ended stories, often with ambiguous conclusions. Examples of neorealist films from Italy at this time are *Shoeshine* (1946) and *The Bicycle Thief* (1948), directed by Vittorio De Sica, and *Open City* (1945) and *Paisan* (1946), directed by Roberto Rossellini.

THE FRENCH NEW WAVE (1959–1964)

While various "new wave" movements emerged around the globe after World War II, the most influential came from a small group of film critics in France. These critics lambasted contemporary French films as dull and lacking artistry but professed great admiration for the *auteurs* of mainstream Hollywood—directors such as Alfred Hitchcock, Howard Hawks, and Orson Welles.

When these critics started making films themselves, however, they developed a style all their own. Limited by small budgets, they filmed in the streets instead of studios, rarely used lights, and often employed nonprofessional actors, much like the Italian neorealists. New, lightweight cameras allowed them to shoot hand-held, creating a documentary feel with much camera movement. Even more distinctive were the stories themselves, which contained loose plot construction, radical shifts in tone, self-referential humor, and anti-establishment characters who often drifted aimlessly rather than pursuing clear goals. Two well-known examples from this period are *Breathless* (1960), directed by Jean-Luc Godard, and *Shoot the Piano Player* (1960), directed by François Truffaut.

THE NEW HOLLYWOOD (1969–1980)

In the late 1960s, mainstream Hollywood fare was no longer attracting audiences, and box office revenue was lagging. Eager producers turned to cheap, quirky films by young filmmakers that appealed to the counterculture spirit of the times. Beginning with the psychedelic road-trip movie *Easy Rider* (1969), a new type of film emerged that revolutionized Hollywood. Filmmakers such as Martin Scorsese, Robert Altman, and Terrence Malick crafted low-budget, personal movies with independent voices and challenging themes.

The success of these films led Hollywood to embrace more stylistically divergent and innovative projects, paving the way for the careers of Francis Ford Coppola, Steven Spielberg, and George Lucas. Ironically, it was the success of Spielberg's *Jaws* (1975) and Lucas's *Star Wars* (1977) that eventually led Hollywood to abandon independent cinema for bigger, slicker, and less risky films with guaranteed box office appeal.

DOGME 95 (1995–2002)

Of all the movements in film's history, none was as rigid in its practice and revolutionary in its ideals as Dogme 95. It was created in 1995 by Danish filmmakers Lars von Trier and Thomas Vinterberg, who sought to restore truth and integrity to cinema by stripping it of the "cosmetic" veneer provided by technology. In practice, this means adhering to ten rules known collectively as "The Vow of Chastity," which include:

1. Shooting only on location, with no props or sets brought in
2. Using no nondiagetic sound (sound not inherent in the filmmaking process)
3. Using only a hand-held camera
4. Shooting only in color
5. Doing no manipulation of images using special lenses or filters
6. Including no "superficial action," such as use of weapons
7. Setting the film in the present time and place
8. Creating a work that is not considered a genre film
9. Using only Academy 35 mm film
10. Receiving no credit for the director of the work

Partly because of such strict guidelines, only thirty-one Dogme 95–certified films were made before 2002, when the movement was declared finished. However, a handful of Dogme 95 films (including *The Celebration* in 1998 and *Italian for Beginners* in 2001) won prestigious awards and encouraged audiences and filmmakers alike to embrace low-budget filmmaking and the democratization of film.

A Shortlist of Great Directors

Films are only as good as the vision behind them, and great directors can make even killer sharks and campy gangsters resonate deeply with viewers. This list represents just a handful of some of the greatest directors from the past and present, along with the films for which they are most well known. The directors are arranged by their year of birth.

Alfred Hitchcock (1899–1980)
Vertigo (1958), *Psycho* (1960)
Directed more than fifty thrillers in his lifetime and was dubbed "The Master of Suspense." Hitchcock was known for his technical innovation, masterful camera work, and the cameo appearances he made in his films.

Elia Kazan (1909–2003)
On the Waterfront (1954), *A Streetcar Named Desire* (1951)
Considered the preeminent "actor's director" of his time. Kazan cofounded the Actors Studio in 1947, which taught "The Method," a revolutionary system of acting made popular by Marlon Brando and James Dean.

Akira Kurosawa (1910–1998)
The Seven Samurai (1954), *Rashomon* (1950)
Worked in a wide array of genres but captured the attention of Western audiences with his Japanese historical epics. Kurosawa was greatly admired by Francis Ford Coppola and George Lucas, and many of his films have been remade in Hollywood.

Orson Welles (1915–1985)
Citizen Kane (1941), *Touch of Evil* (1958)
An accomplished writer, director, and actor. Most of Welles's films were box office failures, and his work was never fully appreciated in his own time.

Stanley Kubrick (1928–1999)
A Clockwork Orange (1971), *Dr. Strangelove* (1964)
Drawn to controversial and challenging projects. Kubrick imbued his work with a trademark style that included startling compositions, photographic innovation, and often stark, melancholy tones.

Jean-Luc Godard (1930–), *Breathless* (1960), and
François Truffaut (1932–1984), *The 400 Blows* (1959)
The most celebrated and influential of the French New Wave directors. Godard's and Truffaut's groundbreaking work has been emulated in numerous American films, and it has influenced the style of such directors as Quentin Tarantino.

Francis Ford Coppola (1939–)
The Godfather trilogy (1972, 1974, 1990), *Apocalypse Now* (1979)
The preeminent director of the 1970s New Hollywood, personally winning seven Academy Awards in a five-year period. Though his ambitious projects and notorious perfectionism sent studios reeling, Coppola won both critical praise and box-office success for most of his films.

Martin Scorsese (1942–)
Taxi Driver (1976), *Raging Bull* (1980)
Combined the dark, gritty, and violent landscape of the gangster genre with themes of existential isolation, moral ambivalence, and repressive social forces to craft some of the most influential films of the last three decades.

Stephen Spielberg (1946–)
Jaws (1975), *Schindler's List* (1993)
Invented the modern blockbuster with his film *Jaws*. Spielberg went on to make consistently entertaining and acclaimed films in almost every genre, from historical World War II epics to sci-fi action films.

Quentin Tarantino (1963–)
Reservoir Dogs (1992), *Pulp Fiction* (1994)
Became an overnight sensation for his exhilarating *Pulp Fiction*. Although Tarantino has made only a handful of feature-length films, his cinematic style, which includes witty dialogue, inventive narrative structures, and recycled elements from B-movies, has influenced much of modern filmmaking.

THE BIRTH OF A NATION

A NATION

(1915)

CONTEXT

David Wark (D.W.) Griffith's *The Birth of a Nation* (1915) is perhaps the most influential film in the history of American cinema. Griffith's film is an epic demonstration of the developing "language" of cinema, so assured and complete that in some ways films have changed very little in the ninety years since *The Birth of a Nation*'s release. In terms of its sheer length and scale—the film is three hours long and features a cast of hundreds—*The Birth of a Nation* far surpassed all earlier films, changing forever a medium in which viewers were accustomed to seeing one- or two-reel films of between fifteen and thirty minutes. In creating this film, Griffith essentially invented the concept of the feature motion picture.

Yet, for the film industry, Griffith's masterpiece is both a source of pride and a mark of shame, because *The Birth of a Nation* is explicitly and brutally racist. Griffith blames the entirety of America's problems from before the Civil War to the film's present on African Americans, citing then-president Woodrow Wilson's writings in *A History of the American People* for academic support. From beginning to end, the film is pervaded by the belief that African Americans are less human than Anglo-Americans. In this respect, the film has no gray area: the Ku Klux Klan members are the heroes, appropriating the concepts of honor and nobility to suit their racist ends. The challenge for viewers and film historians alike has been how to approach this film that combines such stunning and innovative artistry with such noxious political and moral ideas. Often, film historians portray the golden age of early cinema with nostalgia, so the blatant racism in this landmark film often comes as a shock to students of film when they first encounter it. Above all, students are left wondering about the nature of this gifted producer and director who seems to be so forward-looking and so backward at the same time.

Born in 1875 on a rural Kentucky farm, Griffith was the sixth of seven children of a cantankerous Confederate Army war hero, Jacob "Roaring Jake" Griffith. Having grown up poor, Griffith forewent a complete education to help his family make ends meet. Nonetheless, he read widely, immersing himself in a romantic vision of the prewar South, aided in part by the nostalgic stories of bitter relatives who were hampered by Reconstruction-era policies. Griffith, having fallen in love with Victorian authors and the work of the great Romantic Sir Walter Scott, who glorified the values of nobility and chivalry, decided to become a writer himself. After assisting his family, Griffith kicked around the country as a bit actor, living in squalor and working odd jobs. His tall, strong, good looks helped him win parts, despite his lack of training as an actor. During his acting career, Griffith dreamed of becoming a playwright rather than a filmmaker. To his mind (and for much of the public at the time) films were the lowest form of entertainment—and they certainly weren't art. Nickelodeons—the earliest movie theaters—were generally associated with the grubby alleys where recent immigrants were forced to live. Racists and city-fearers thought of films as subhuman, cheap entertainment. Griffith's attitude toward film eventually underwent a complete revolution, but this change took place only gradually.

At age thirty, with only a few successes behind him and a new stage-actress wife, Linda Arvidson, to support, Griffith took a job acting in a two-reel film at Thomas Edison's studios. He had tried to sell a script to Edison and been rejected, but the studio's director hired him as an actor because of his good looks. Later, Griffith tried to sell a script to the rival studio American Mutoscope & Biograph Company and met with the same result—the studio rejected his script but hired him as an actor based on his appearance. When Griffith began work at Biograph, the studio was in dire straits, deep in debt and hard-pressed to meet the public's demand for new films. Griffith was soon able to obtain a position as a director because of his work ethic and evident facility with the new medium. In June 1908, Griffith directed his first short, *The Adventures of Dollie*, earning a weekly base salary of $50 plus commission as stipulated by his director's contract. Thereafter, he churned out one- and two-reelers at a phenomenal rate. By 1913, Griffith had directed at least 450 one- and two-reelers for Biograph, saving the company from financial ruin. During those years, through trial and error, he formulated a directing style that made him one of cinema's first auteurs. Throughout this time, he pushed constantly for longer films with more complex stories.

Griffith lost his directorial position with Biograph after directing his longest and most expensive film, 1913's *Judith of Bethulia*, an epic spectacle far more ambitious than any previous American film. But the merger of two film companies, Mutual and Reliance-Majestic, opened up a position with more responsibility for Griffith in the developing California film industry based in Hollywood. Griffith left New York's Biograph with a splash. At the time, short films carried no directorial credits, so few outside the industry knew of Griffith. Griffith rectified the situation by buying a full-page ad in the *New York Dramatic Mirror* listing over 150 of the films he had directed, declaring himself a genius in the new medium.

Eventually, Griffith and film producer Harry Aitken created a new company, Epoch, solely for the production and distribution of their newest project, *The Birth of a Nation*. The film represented a turning point both in Griffith's directorial career and in cinema. Most of the shooting was done in secret with no complete script, and the film cost eleven times more than any conventional film produced thus far. Griffith gambled his life savings on the project, as well as much of his friends' money. Based on the play *The Clansman* by the Reverend Thomas Dixon, a Baptist minister in North Carolina, *The Birth of a Nation* interwove complex narratives with fifteen times as many shots as the longest films from that era. *The Birth of a Nation* took fifteen weeks to rehearse and shoot and three months to edit, whereas just a few years earlier, Griffith was cranking out at least one film a week.

The film's public opening in New York was a colossal publicity event. Times Square's Liberty Theater charged $2 per ticket (an exorbitant price at the time), and huge billboards of Klan nightriders welcomed special trains that brought in patrons for the screening. President and historian Woodrow Wilson, an old Princeton classmate of Dixon's, endorsed *The Birth of a Nation,* and it became the first film screened in the White House. The film contributed to the revival of a much stronger, more modern Ku Klux Klan, which had effectively dissolved in 1869. *The Birth of a Nation* toured the world, meeting with riots and protests in some cities, while some states prohibited screenings. The film's first run brought in over $10 million, and while its box office total has never been precisely tabulated, *The Birth of a Nation* clearly held the world record for over two decades. The NAACP, having formed only in 1909, mobilized its forces in protests and pointed letter-writing campaigns. They were assisted by prominent liberals, such as activist Jane Addams, as well as by several Ivy League presidents. Indeed, protestors succeeded in forcing two of the most atrocious scenes to be cut. The film touched a nerve, splitting America apart by tapping into deep wounds that had never healed and exposing unspoken prejudices to a surprising extent. It also shocked the film industry, which was certain that Griffith's financial excess would be greeted with box-office disaster.

PLOT OVERVIEW

The plot of *The Birth of a Nation* revolves around two families living on either side of the Mason-Dixon Line who become friends when their sons board together at school. The Stonemans, the Northern family, live in Washington, D.C., and own a rural getaway in Pennsylvania. The Honorable Austin Stoneman, an abolitionist politician, presides over his family, which includes a delicate daughter named Elsie, a dandy prankster named Phil, and a younger brother named Tod. The Camerons, the Southern family, preside over a modest but idyllic plantation in Piedmont, South Carolina, where slaves pick cotton in satisfaction and happily dance to entertain their masters. Margaret is the refined older sister, while Flora, the younger sister, is dreamy and innocent. Of the three Cameron brothers, Ben develops into the main character, defending the South's ideals at all costs. His two younger brothers are Wade and Duke.

PART I: THE CIVIL WAR

The film is divided roughly into halves, with subsections drawing from a historical chronology of the Civil War. After an initial prologue that blames the Civil War and Reconstruction on the introduction of Africans to America, the Stoneman boys travel south during the antebellum period to visit their old pals. Romances develop: Phil falls for Margaret, and Ben falls for a daguerreotype of Elsie. Ben carries this picture of Elsie with him until he finally meets her. Later, Dr. Cameron reads his family a newspaper article stating that the South will secede from the Union if the North carries the next elections. After the Stonemans leave, war breaks out, interrupting relations between the families. One of Griffith's historical facsimiles, or fictional documentations of actual events (which will later include General Lee's surrender and Lincoln's assassination), shows Lincoln signing for the first wave of volunteers.

Epic battles follow, spanning three years and showing the devastation the war wrecks throughout the country, especially in the South. Exceptionally produced battle sequences focus on both personal details and the bloody scale of the depredation. First, a festive Piedmont ball celebrates the South's early victory at Bull Run, and so the three Cameron brothers head off to fight in good spirits. Griffith then spans two and a half years with one cut, and Ben, battleworn and still in the field, reads letters from home. A predominantly black militia ransacks the defenseless Cameron home, while Ben dreams of Elsie. Tragically, the two youngest sons of each family, Tod and Duke, suffer fatal wounds at the same moment on the battlefield, dying in each other's arms. General Sherman begins his infamous march, destroying Georgia as he moves forward. Wade Cameron dies in Atlanta, and the Union succeeds in pinching off what's left of the Confederacy's meager food supply.

As the drama heightens, the two oldest brothers meet in battle. Though Ben's undermanned, underfed, and ravaged platoon cannot possibly win, he heroically upholds the honor of the South. Risking his life and suffering a head wound, he maniacally sprints to the Union trench and jams a Confederate flag down the gullet of a cannon. Retreating to his own trench, he again risks his life to save a wounded Union soldier while Phil's troops cheer. Eventually taken to a Union hospital in Washington, D.C., Ben finally meets Elsie, who is volunteering there. Mrs. Cameron travels to visit Ben and, upon learning he has been condemned to death under a bogus charge of spying, personally appeals to President Lincoln, who graciously pardons Ben. On April 9, 1865, Lee surrenders to Grant, and Ben leaves for home. He returns to find his home in disrepair, with little food and all the good clothing sold. He embraces Flora. Meanwhile, the elder Stoneman tries to convince Lincoln to rule mercilessly over the vanquished South, but Lincoln refuses, preferring instead diplomatic restitution. Five days later, Lincoln is assassinated at Ford's Theater, a historical event that in this movie is witnessed by Phil and Elsie Stoneman, who are at the theater that night. The Camerons deeply mourn the loss of their "best friend," and Stoneman assumes power, ending the first part of the film on a decidedly bleak and somber note.

PART II: RECONSTRUCTION

In Griffith's version of the postwar era, all blacks who aren't "faithful souls" team up with carpetbaggers from the North to loot, pillage, and degrade the time-honored traditions of Southern culture. Stoneman, a champion of black equality in the South, forces Senator Charles Sumner (a historical figure) to acknowledge the legitimacy of Stoneman's mulatto protégé, Silas Lynch, who secretly lusts after

Elsie and is sent down to organize the emancipated slaves. Head-quartered in Piedmont, Lynch instigates former slaves to rise up against Southern whites in vengeance, teams effectively with the carpetbaggers, and essentially oversees mob rule. Stoneman, in ill health, visits, bringing Elsie with him. Ben refuses to shake Lynch's hand. The two pairs of interfamily lovebirds try to restart their romances with genteel garden walks, but memories of the war make reuniting difficult. Margaret imagines a picture of Wade laid waste on a battlefield and can no longer speak to Phil. Silas Lynch spies on Ben and Elsie, who eventually succumb to their love.

In response to a horrific Election Day in which Lynch's black supremacists intimidate the whites on the streets and in the South Carolina legislature, Ben searches his soul and finds inspiration in white children frightening black children by pretending to be ghosts and hiding under white sheets. The Ku Klux Klan is born. Southern women secretly make hundreds of thousands of uniforms bearing a woven St. Andrews Cross, and the "Night Riders" start a new war against Lynch's militia. Ben's involvement in the Klan crushes Elsie, but she does not sell him out. Flora consoles Elsie and then skips off into the woods to fetch water from a spring. There, Gus, a newly promoted black officer, approaches Flora and proffers marriage. Flora slaps him, and Gus begins to chase her through the forest. Ben follows behind in search of Flora, having been told of her errand. Gus reassures Flora that he intends her no harm, but Flora finds herself pinned on the edge of a cliff. Threatening to jump rather than be touched by Gus, she either accidentally falls or intentionally jumps off the cliff, where shortly after she dies in Ben's arms. A search commences for the fearful Gus. After a complex chase sequence, the Klan eventually catches Gus and lynches him. They dump his body at Silas Lynch's door.

When Lynch discovers the body the next morning, the film's climax begins. The black militia with its white sympathizers fight against the Klan. Some of the Camerons are captured, but they are freed by faithful blacks. In flight, Dr. Cameron, Phil, and Margaret come across a tiny shack in the woods owned by Union veterans, who invite them in and make peace with the Camerons over their common hatred for renegade blacks. Elsie runs to Lynch for help, but he tries to force her to marry him, promising to make her queen of his "Black Empire." When Austin Stoneman interrupts, Lynch confides to him that he wants to marry his daughter. Exposing his own hypocrisy, Stoneman is repulsed. The noble and well-supported Klan begins its lengthy and heroic mission to rescue Elsie and the group in the cabin, now besieged by the black militia. The Klan triumphs in both battles, saving one Union veteran the horror of bashing his own child's head to save the child from the black militia. Both couples are restored and united in marriage, white supremacists strip power from blacks through intimidation tactics, and, in a religious coda meant to symbolize the second coming of the "Prince of Peace," Jesus and his angels in the City of God stand in approval over the scene.

Character List

Colonel Ben Cameron—Played by Henry Walthall The noble savior of the South, proud founder of the Ku Klux Klan, and protagonist of the film. A genteel, intelligent family man, Ben, "the Little Colonel," rises to great achievement when blacks threaten the honor of the South. His character has the greatest emotional range. He smiles broadly, cultivates a special, caring relationship with his youngest sister, and pats and touches his slaves affectionately (Griffith's code for graciousness). But when war comes, he seethes with patriotic anger against the threat posed to traditional plantation life, expressing this anger by tossing his body around and writhing feverishly. Later, he fumes with racist hatred.

Elsie Stoneman—Played by Lillian Gish The idealistic, loyal daughter of the abolitionist leader Austin Stoneman. Elsie lovingly dotes on her family and often kneels deferentially at her father's feet. Her fragile daguerreotype image helps Ben Cameron through the war. The audiences of 1915 would have been intimately familiar with Elsie's pale white skin and deep-eyed expressions of innocence, for Gish was the superstar stage and screen actress of her time. Like today's film celebrities, Gish conjured up a "type" for filmgoers: a frail, ethereal, pure-hearted beauty. Elsie's presence floats angelically over the film.

The Honorable Austin Stoneman —Played by Ralph Lewis The abolitionist leader from the North who wields power over Reconstruction after Lincoln's assassination, and the antagonist of the film. A bookish man who often holds meetings in his library, Stoneman is portrayed as physically flawed and lacking in moral character. He limps and walks with a cane, wears a wig, and lusts after his mulatto housekeeper.

Silas Lynch—Played by George Siegmann The mulatto politician and overseer of day-to-day operations during Reconstruction who becomes South Carolina's Lieutenant Governor. Portrayed as evil from the start because of his mixed-race parentage, Lynch often spies on Elsie or lusts after other women, giving sideways glances and clutching his hat anxiously. His character represents the stereotype of savage sexuality in people of African heritage.

Flora Cameron—Played by Mae Marsh as a teen and by Violet Wilkey as a child   The excitable, youngest Cameron sister who grows into a teenager during the course of the film. Often called "Little Sister," Flora is at first impishly playful. As she matures over the course of the war, she serves as a metaphor for the sea changes swamping the South. She adores her older brother, Ben, and faces the ravages of the war bravely with an increasingly haggard appearance and a careworn face.

Margaret Cameron—Played by Miriam Cooper   The elder Cameron sister who eventually falls for Phil Stoneman. Trained in the etiquette of the old South, Margaret, a quiet, round-faced flower, moves with dignity. Her facial expressions are small and subtle but reveal a great deal of emotion behind her reserved façade.

Phil Stoneman—Played by Elmer Clifton   The eldest Stoneman brother who takes a liking to Margaret Cameron. A respectful, top-hatted, mustached man with a quiet dignity, Phil slowly courts Margaret. In battle, he rises to become one of the most successful Union leaders.

Tod Stoneman—Played by Robert Harron   The youngest Stoneman brother. Tod enlivens the screen as a wildly expressive, playful fop. Thin and energetic, Tod stands in strong contrast to the reserved demeanor of his older brother. Upon his visit to Piedmont, he resumes his boyish roughhousing with Duke.

Gus—Played in blackface by white actor Walter Long   An emancipated slave who lusts after Flora. Gus becomes an enemy of the Klan after pursuing Flora to her death.

Dr. Cameron—Played by Spottiswoode Aitken The aging head of the Cameron family. Dr. Cameron is thin, white-haired, and reserved. He reads the newspapers to his family, disseminating national information. Essentially powerless in the war, he nevertheless reigns over his family with patriarchal beneficence.

Wade Cameron—Played by George Beranger The mustached, middle Cameron brother. Wade is little seen before he goes off to war. His death serves as another harsh reminder of war for the Camerons, who mourn him back at home.

Duke Cameron—Played by Maxfield Stanley The youngest Cameron brother. Duke returns Tod Stoneman's affection and playfulness, and his vibrancy around the Cameron homestead emphasizes his youth.

Mrs. Cameron—Played by Josephine Crowell The stout, stoic wife of Dr. Cameron. Mrs. Cameron, with her tightly pulled-back hair, silently serves as a pillar of support for the Cameron girls at home. Mostly, she worries and mourns, especially over the loss of her three sons "to the cause."

President Abraham Lincoln—Played by Joseph Henabery A god among men, referred to as the "Great Heart." Lincoln genuinely acts for the benefit of all. When he rises from his chair, he stands above the surrounding representatives, who stay back at a detached, respectful distance. His tall stature indicates his moral superiority. Lincoln moves slowly and with dignity and looks in the distance as if he's seeing far into the future. His death signals a devastating turning point for the South.

Lydia Brown—Played in blackface by white actress Mary Alden The Stonemans' housekeeper. A lustful mulatto, Lydia becomes sexually aroused whenever she overhears strong orders being given in Stoneman's library. She licks her fingers, beats her breast, and eventually becomes Stoneman's mistress.

Mammy—Played in blackface by white actress Jenny Lee The faithful servant to the Camerons. A large, rotund housekeeper, Mammy moans loudly and makes broad gestures.

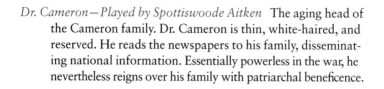

BIRTH OF A NATION

ANALYSIS OF MAJOR CHARACTERS

COLONEL BEN CAMERON

In Ben Cameron, Griffith created a born leader who exerts his dominance in both public and family life. Indeed, little power is exerted by his father and his two younger brothers. Ben's willingness to martyr himself to any cause defines his actions over the course of the film. He inspires others with his beliefs, whether he's recounting outrages to a group of colleagues, commanding a troop in battle, or riding the lead horse in a daring rescue attempt. Henry Walthall portrays Ben as a man of principles, a trait largely unseen in the other characters. In moments alone, he wrestles with his inner struggles. The details in Walthall's portrayal of Ben make his character stand out. From his quivering finger pointing out newspaper stories to his sudden collapse into convulsive tears over Flora's body, Ben becomes a multidimensional figure. The richness of his character is magnified by his unconscionable racist agenda. His scenes with Flora are quite moving, and his bruised dignity as he walks the ravaged streets of Piedmont is extremely powerful. Ben's well-defined humanity makes his vicious racism all the more painful to watch.

ELSIE STONEMAN

Elsie's selflessness brings her heartache when she is forced to choose between the two men she loves—her father and Ben Cameron. When a Klan outfit falls out of Ben's coat, Elsie chooses loyalty to her father but ultimately succumbs to her love for Ben. Elsie is pure and delicate, portrayed as an angel in a daguerreotype image, or in a lily-white nightgown wearing a headpiece of flowers. Her innocence stands in strong contrast to the sexuality of the lustful blacks and mulattos of the film. Elsie is an idealized, sentimental figure who symbolizes the purity and beauty that soldiers and families on both sides of the conflict are fighting to defend. In choosing Ben, Elsie presents the South as having been on the side of righteousness all along.

Flora Cameron

Flora, whose childhood is cut short by the brutality of the Civil War, faces new struggles head-on. She responds to each challenge with a noble heart, a sense of humor, and a bottomless reservoir of emotion. Instead of holding onto her momentary depression when she gives away her last good clothes, she smoothes down what clothing she still has and giggles with glee at the imaginative potential of play-acting in them. Instead of moping at the degradation of her homestead, she improvises a new costume for Ben's return home. Most important, instead of being holed up inside by the threat of the black militias, she gladly and innocently tramps out into the woods to fetch water, where she behaves fearlessly in response to Gus's advances. Her playful spirit and intensity represent another facet of the South's character: a refusal to surrender personal and cultural identity. Her premature death leaves Flora unsullied by the middling changes imposed by the North.

The Honorable Austin Stoneman

Griffith purportedly based Stoneman on real-life Pennsylvania Republican Thaddeus Stevens, who led the House of Representatives' radical Reconstructionists and opposed Lincoln's more moderate plans. Stoneman embodies the Union's weakening will and its misguided social reforms. His vanity makes him easily susceptible to temptation, so he "unnaturally" supports Silas Lynch, disagrees with Abraham Lincoln's policy of clemency for the South, and openly succumbs to his lust for his housekeeper. When Silas Lynch assumes power and subsequently becomes embroiled with the Ku Klux Klan, the basic premise of the reformers—that black men are equal to white men—is exposed as something they don't truly believe in. Stoneman's hypocrisy is revealed when he responds with revulsion to Lynch's suggestion of marriage with Elsie. As a consequence of his weakness, Stoneman's health deteriorates and he gradually fades from relevance.

Silas Lynch

Silas Lynch is the ultimate villain in Griffith's melodrama. The film climaxes with Lynch literally drunk on the excesses of power. He swoons from alcohol, reels with anger and bloodlust, and stops short of raping Elsie only when her father suddenly enters. The fact that Lynch first appears in the second part of the film, just after Lincoln's assassination, helps to establish him an evil, otherworldly antithesis to Lincoln and the values for which Lincoln stood. The biracial Lynch symbolizes the "disunion" referred to in the film's first frame ("The bringing of the African to America planted the first seed of disunion"). He is both a literal and a figurative embodiment of relations between blacks and whites, which are depicted as inherently corrupt and ungodly. As the second part of the film progresses, Lynch's motivations are revealed to be greedy and contrary to the ideals of the South or of any unified nation. He is a divider, not a uniter.

THEMES, MOTIFS, AND SYMBOLS

THEMES

THE PERSEVERANCE OF SOUTHERN HONOR

Though the South ultimately loses the Civil War, Griffith exploits every opportunity to present the Southern forces as heroic underdogs. Because the South embodies honor and nobility, every defeat the South suffers is redeemed by the courage and grace the Southerners display. Ben Cameron's troops are defeated only because they haven't eaten in days and the Northern army greatly outnumbers them. Even under these extraordinary circumstances, his troops manage to take two entrenchments and willingly risk their lives in a final attack, in which Ben jams the Confederate flag into a Union cannon. The North stays behind their own lines, safe in their numbers. Ben, meanwhile, comforts a fallen foe and survives a wound to his head. Though the South loses the battle, its honor and glory are maintained and impressed upon the minds of the Northern invaders. In this sense, Southern honor goes far beyond the battle scenes, motivating everything the Southerners do. When Flora falls to her death, this too is described in the intertitle as a preservation of Southern honor: "For her who had learned the stern lesson of honor, we should not grieve that she found sweeter the opal gates of death."

THE NATURE OF PROPER COURTING

The Birth of a Nation features a number of developing personal relationships—Ben and Elsie, Phil and Margaret, Stoneman and Lydia—as well as relationships that are pursued but never consummated in any way—Lynch and Elsie, Gus and Flora. The film separates the relationships into two distinct kinds: those borne from a divine plan and those borne from evil. The film condemns relationships based on physical attraction. Stoneman becomes sexually intimate with Lydia after glimpsing and then touching her naked shoulder, and Lynch lusts after Elsie. The film also condemns any biracial relationship. Gus's pursuit of Flora violates this code and is thus depicted as disgusting and horrifying. Both Gus and Lynch propose marriage to the objects of their desire at a rushed pace, which, in contrast to the protracted courtships of the good characters, is a symptom of an unnatural relationship.

The film suggests that proper relationships take time to develop and require gentleness. Ben sees a photograph of Elsie and dreams of her for two and a half years. Ultimately, it takes a war injury to bring them together. Phil and Margaret forge an instant connection when they are first introduced: they pursue gentle flirtations but respect traditional mores enough to leave it at that. Longing eye-to-eye stares, as opposed to ogling each other furtively, and warm handshakes held a few beats too long communicate their honest desire for each other. Time is the true test of love, and so, despite the pain of differing experiences during the war, each couple rekindles its antebellum love during Reconstruction.

The Manifold Tragedies of War

The Birth of a Nation depicts the tragedies of the Civil War beyond the battlefield. Boyhood chums are split apart and reunited only in death. Blossoming loves end abruptly. War turns governments against each other and makes leaders prime targets for the expression of discontent. Even after the war, Ben Cameron's soul remains tortured. At one point in the film, Griffith and Bitzer present a tableaux in homage to the Civil War photographs of Mathew Brady, in which piles of dead men stretch off into the distance, having found "War's peace." The film effectively demonstrates that once two armies are on a battlefield together, the reasons for being there become irrelevant. Each man must fight for his life, no matter whom he's fighting against.

Motifs

The Street in Piedmont

The film frequently returns to the street in front of the Cameron house in Piedmont, South Carolina. Each time we see the street, its appearance changes, mirroring the political and social mood of a given moment. When times are good, the street feels lighter: flowers are in bloom, families gather on front steps, the sun shines, and the street fills with horse carts, respectful slaves, and playful pets. The breeze brings life to characters' faces as strands of hair dance back and forth over their eyes. Ben walks proudly and opens white fences, while others pick flowers and give them as gifts. In this harmonious Southern world, the Camerons brim with familial love and devotion.

When the passion of war fuels the town and the South starts off strong, the street transforms into a scene of passionate release. Bonfires light the street, and silhouetted revelers run up and down the block, jumping and waving flags. When Ben returns home from the war, however, his formerly bustling street has been transformed. The homes are broken and burned, the bushes are trampled, and nobody but Ben walks on the street.

THE SOUTHERN LANDSCAPE

Griffith loved the rolling natural landscapes of the South and therefore set many of his most tender moments there. Both relationships that end in marriage blossom during strolls through the flowering trees, soft hills, and lazy shores of the South. Away from social and political stresses, these idyllic landscapes become paradise on earth. Doves and squirrels frolic, and women stroll with parasols, arm-in-arm with their men. In one scene, an agonized Ben retreats to a picturesque hillside and sweeps his arms over the vast river below. The preservation of Southern ideals begins with the land.

IRIS SHOTS

Griffith and his cameraman Billy Bitzer employ the use of irises in *The Birth of a Nation* repeatedly. An iris is a black mask placed over the frame that creates a circular field of view as opposed to the traditional, rectangular frame. An iris can narrow to a small point, leaving most of the frame black, or it can open up nearly as wide as the frame itself. An iris acts as a spotlight, thereby highlighting a select portion of the frame. It can also function as a zoom lens or telescope surrogate, narrowing the audience's field of vision to one point (or, conversely, widening it out from one point), as in the shots of John Wilkes Booth lurking in Ford's Theater. In 1910, the iris reminded audiences of the ovular frames of photographs, cameos, and brooches, especially when combined with a soft-focus shot, in which a face looks healthier because wrinkles and signs of age are less visible. The iris shot of Elsie as Ben Cameron awakens in the hospital serves a variety of functions: it highlights her as a "vision" of his semiconscious state, it emphasizes her beauty, it singles her out as the most important thing in the room, and it serves as a visual reminder of the daguerreotype in which Ben first saw her face.

SYMBOLS

QUALITY OF CLOTHING

Costumes are essential parts of how characters are realized in *The Birth of a Nation*. When "renegade" blacks rampage the Cameron home, one man featured on camera wears only a torn scrap of shirt, exposing his bulging muscles. The man's clothes effectively symbolize his savagery. Likewise, in the South Carolina legislature, the newly elected black representatives kick their shoes off and throw their bare feet up on the desk. When Ben returns home to Piedmont to a degraded plantation, Flora wants to greet him with her best dress, but the Camerons have little left. She improvises a white fur draping out of cotton from the fields ("Southern ermine," quips the intertitle). This costuming symbolizes not only her bravery but also the devastated economic condition of the South, which has nothing left except its honor.

ABRAHAM LINCOLN

Contrary to what one might expect from a pro-Southern telling of the Civil War, *The Birth of a Nation* portrays Lincoln with respect, associating him with near-divine goodness and gravity. The film's characters treat Lincoln almost as a Christ figure. Mrs. Cameron, for example, appeals to him to save her son's life, as a supplicant would appeal to Jesus for healing in the Bible. Congressional representatives who meet with Lincoln always agree with him and treat him with reverence, with Austin Stoneman as the lone exception. Lincoln's life becomes a symbol of hope for a peaceful reunification process. In the five days between Lee's surrender to Grant and Lincoln's assassination, the South begins to rebuild itself with hope and dignity. Southerners react to his assassination as if it were a crucifixion, and as soon as Lincoln dies, criminals from the North immediately overrun the South.

ANIMALS

The way each character treats animals corresponds to a certain quality in his or her personality. While Silas Lynch throttles a dog by the throat and tosses it aside, Elsie and Ben caress a white dove, the greatest symbol of purity and inner peace. Flora plays with a squirrel in the forest, a symbol of her communion with the lush natural landscape of the South. When the film introduces Dr. Cameron, he tickles a pair of puppies lying by his feet, which suggests his paternal gentility. The puppies also serve a further symbolic purpose: one is white and one is black. A character off-screen drops a kitten into the mix and stirs up the placidity of the scene, suggesting that everything was fine between white and black until outsiders dropped in from the North.

FILM ANALYSIS

DIRECTING: THE "LANGUAGE" OF THE CINEMA

While *The Birth of a Nation* deserves its place in film history for the way it changed the language of cinema, it is important to note that D. W. Griffith didn't invent every technique used in *The Birth of a Nation*. The burgeoning film industry of the early 1900s spawned a number of innovative directors who created many of these techniques, among them Griffith's primary collaborator, Billy Bitzer. However, Griffith's films were the most popular of the era, and he was more prolific than any of his colleagues. Moreover, Griffith frequently improved upon techniques that others had invented. *The Birth of a Nation* represents the culmination of visual strategies to communicate narrative that the film industry had been working on for the first twenty years of its existence. Countless directors after Griffith owe their technical knowledge of filmmaking to the cohesiveness of *The Birth of a Nation*.

CAMERA ANGLES AND DISTANCE

Before *The Birth of a Nation*, films were made under the assumption that if audience members paid to see a star, they would probably want to see the whole person. But Griffith realized that by moving the camera closer to his subject into a close-up, more intimate details were revealed on the subject's face, personalizing the character's expression in a much more valuable way. When contrasted with close-ups, long shots had added value. One of the most celebrated shots in the film starts with a relatively tight, intimate view of a mother and her children weeping on a hillside. Without a cut, via the opening of an iris and a pan (a horizontal movement of the camera), Griffith slowly reveals what the family watches: General Sherman's devastating march. Griffith successfully ties the personal to the historical in one shot. Additionally, actions occur on multiple planes, and the viewer is trusted to process action occurring simultaneously in the foreground, the middle ground, and the background. This occurs not only in battle scenes but in busy interiors as well, heightening the documentary authenticity of the sequences. Finally, Griffith masters the use of dissolve as scene transition. From a fixed camera position, dissolving from an empty courtroom to a courtroom full of newly elected black representatives, Griffith suggests that they overran the court and sullied the entire room and its traditions.

FLASHBACKS

Griffith invented what today is called the flashback, though he called it the "switchback." In a flashback, a brief return to a past time interrupts the forward progress of a linear narrative. *The Birth of a Nation* also makes use of parallel editing, which is a cutting back and forth between two scenes that occur simultaneously. Eager to demonstrate that films could do things that staged plays could not, Griffith mastered parallel editing. By accelerating the duration of the shots, and by making faster cuts between them, the resolution of each storyline is brought to a rousing climax through both suspense and intensity. The final sequences of the Klan rescue mission are pioneering uses of parallel editing.

INNOVATIONS

The Birth of Nation is notable for many of its innovative production strategies. Billy Bitzer was the first cinematographer to employ nighttime photography, a feat he achieved by firing magnesium flares into the night for the split-screen sequence of the sacking of Atlanta. It was the first film to use hundreds of extras to re-create battle scenes. The film also became the first to have an original score (co-scored by Griffith, who drew heavily on the motifs of classical greats). Normally a two-reeler would screen in a theater and a hired piano player would improvise general mood music so that each screening essentially had a different soundtrack. Griffith employs historical references to add documentary authenticity as well. His elaborate intertitles quote such authorities as Woodrow Wilson (even providing footnotes) and his "composition" shots re-create famous paintings or Mathew Brady photographs depicting the bleak impact of the Civil War.

PROTESTING "THE BIRTH OF A NATION"

The explicit racism of *The Birth of a Nation* provoked massive responses from individuals and organizations across the country. Early on in the film's yearlong New York City run, the NAACP succeeded in pressuring Griffith to cut a few of the most objectionable scenes. One of these scenes portrays black men as savages possessed

BIRTH OF A NATION

by animalistic lust, sexually assaulting white women. Another depicts Gus's castration, his punishment for lusting after a white woman. The other excised element was a coda proffering the one and only solution to America's strife: to deport all black Americans back to Africa. The NAACP mobilized protests even before production on the film was complete. The Los Angeles branch called for the film to be banned in the city. Picket lines faithfully formed daily in New York City, but the film still raked in enormous profits at the box office, using reserved seating instead of general admission to create an "event" atmosphere around the release. Soon after the film's premiere, activist Jane Addams released an interview in New York newspapers in which she vehemently protested the portrayal of African Americans in *The Birth of a Nation*.

While the entire film condemns African Americans and valorizes the Ku Klux Klan, certain scenes stand out for their egregiously insulting portrayals of African Americans. For example, black representatives meeting in the South Carolina legislature are seen kicking off their shoes, sneaking shots of whiskey, openly devouring chicken, and ogling white women as soon as laws pass that allow interracial marriage. In the world of the film, mulattos are necessarily evil, while those with all-black ancestry have the choice to be either "good" (i.e., faithful to whites) or "bad" (i.e., interested in self-preservation and equality). As soon as the South loses the Civil War, renegade emancipated slaves (sometimes portrayed as savages wearing only scraps of clothing) team up with foul-hearted, ambitious Northern whites to completely overrun the noble heritage of the poor aristocratic South.

Griffith was shocked and deeply hurt by the negative reactions to his film. He truly thought he was selflessly performing an honorable function for the nation, and many Americans shared his views. In response to Addams's well-publicized commentary, he released an "educational" annotated guide to *The Birth of a Nation* called *The Rise and Fall of Free Speech in America*, drawing on academic historians to back up his commentary, albeit historians who were known for their racist predilections and sympathy for the plight of the South. Griffith was so affected by the negative response that his next major film project, *Intolerance* (1916), was conceived as a response to his detractors.

Although Griffith moved on, issues surrounding the film did not. *The Birth of a Nation* was re-released in 1924, 1931, and 1938, so it remained in the minds of film lovers and human rights activists for decades. Executives in Hollywood even thought about remaking it in 1950 and releasing the film on television as late as 1959. Each cinematic re-release was met with a new round of pickets and protests. Of course, all of this controversy generated box-office appeal, and Griffith would have been an enormously wealthy man had he not sunk his own profits into subsequent films.

ACTING: AN "ACTOR'S DIRECTOR"

Griffith was known as one of the first "actor's directors." In a day when stage actors were the true celebrities and film actors were often treated as cogs in a machine, Griffith made film actors artists of their medium. Much of his camera innovation was designed to make film more effective, more humane, and therefore more cooperative with the actors. Griffith scheduled six weeks of rehearsals into the preproduction of *The Birth of a Nation* at a time when actors normally showed up with little idea of what they were going to do and were shouted through their motions on set. Lillian Gish was already a stage actress when Griffith "discovered" her for film. The two worked together on many shorts before *The Birth of a Nation*. Early silent film acting drew its techniques from the stage, with broad, obvious gestures that were meant to be seen by everyone in the audience no matter how far away they were seated. But this acting didn't work on film. Griffith's close-ups allowed for more subtle expressions of gesture.

None of the film's prominent black roles were played by black actors, but instead by white actors in blackface who were painted with burnt cork. From the birth of cinema, American film has popularized and reproduced predominant stereotypes and perceptions that are held by society. Griffith purposely exploited as many of these stereotypes as possible in *The Birth of a Nation*. Black performers were forced into a narrow range of types, so they attempted to create complex characters within the confines of the roles they were given. Many of the black actors who worked on the film rose above stereotypes by creating resilience, humor, and humanity in their characters. This early struggle, encapsulating the historical and contemporary challenge of race relations, was the beginning of black cultural identity in American cinema.

Important Intertitles Explained

1. A Plea For The Art of the Motion Picture: We do not fear censorship, for we have no wish to offend with improprieties or obscenities, but we do demand, as a right, the liberty to show the dark side of wrong, that we may illuminate the bright side of virtue—the same liberty that is conceded to the art of the written word—that art to which we owe the Bible and the works of Shakespeare.

Griffith addresses his audience with this lofty and hefty intertitle at the beginning of the film. With it, he attempts to contextualize and defend his efforts before the film's action begins. He displays passion for the artistic potential of film here, and indeed he did more than any other director of the time to push the art form's limits. Though not an unwarranted plea on behalf of the blossoming medium, especially coming from one of its most noteworthy practitioners, it was unnecessary—the best plea would have been simply a stunning and moving film that demonstrated the art of the motion picture. By placing his film in the context of canonical written works that have held up over the passing of centuries, Griffith egotistically asserts his own film's worthiness. The unreeling of the film shows that the "dark side of wrong" comprises opportunist Northern whites and black slaves who rebel against their servitude. The "bright side of virtue," of course, consists of the Southern slave-owning gentry and the Ku Klux Klan.

2. The bringing of the African to America planted the first seed of disunion.

With this plain and bold intertitle, the story of the film begins. We see a white pilgrim on a platform praying over a group of hunched, bound, and confused black men in a public square. This image shows that New Englanders (i.e., Northerners) originally brought the slaves to America, causing all the subsequent problems presented by the film. The image of Northern abolitionists demanding freedom for slaves two hundred years later is an early strike at the character of the waffling North. It also sets out the simplified thesis of the film: the land was great and noble, with unlimited potential, until Africans were brought to America, precipitating our painful and calamitous dissolution into civil war. The evocative language of the intertitle suggests an infestation or an exponentially developing disease that branched out silently through the developing United States.

3.   On the battlefield. War claims its bitter, useless sacrifice.
      True to their promise, the chums meet again.

One of the most moving sequences of *The Birth of a Nation* follows this intertitle and illustrates the power of Griffith's mastery over melodramatic film structure, as well as his skill at making an epic subject intimate and personal. The final sentence laments the need-less tragedy of lives cut short by war. Duke Cameron is wounded in battle and falls. A bloodthirsty Union soldier sprints over to him, preparing to deliver the fatal spike from his bayonet. But then Tod Stoneman recognizes Duke, and a great change washes over his face. We see his love for his friend and the humanity of their relationship. At that same moment, Tod is struck by a bullet. He collapses, and the two friends die in each other's arms.

4.   The agony which the South endured that a nation might be
      born. The blight of war does not end when hostilities cease.

Griffith introduces the second part of the film with this intertitle, fol-lowing President Lincoln's assassination. It effectively eulogizes the old South and ennobles its dignity in the face of the humiliation brought by the North. It also manages to credit the South's persever-ance and willingness to adapt as the glue that holds the new union together. Whereas Northerners planted the "seed of disunion" by bringing over the Africans, the Southerners' great sacrifice assures that a "nation might be born."

It also introduces a mammoth sequence of six consecutive inter-titles. In the space of these titles, Griffith maintains first that he intends no reflection on any race or people of today. However, he goes on to extensively quote Woodrow Wilson's *A History of the American People*, speaking of swarms from the North, insolent Negroes, and the crushing of the "white South under the heel of the black South." The forced birth of the new "empire of the South," the Ku Klux Klan, comes from natural survivalist instincts, a response in part to Stoneman, who is labeled "the uncrowned king." The second part of the film begins in Stoneman's library, teeming with debating congressional leaders, all eager to advise the new leader. When Stoneman drops his cane, pathetic congressmen scurry to pick it up for him. Borne out of the evil of Lincoln's assassination, the lustful and shifty Silas Lynch enters.

5.   The inspiration.

The birth of the Ku Klux Klan follows this intertitle. Ben Cameron writhes in solitude on a scenic hill overlooking a gorgeous expanse of the South and wonders how he can free it again. His inspiration comes right around the corner in the form of two outnumbered white children scaring a group of black children by donning a white sheet. Immediately, the black children go running. Magically, the Ku Klux Klan forms fully in the space between two shots. Whereas we see all the struggles of the South as it suffers under Silas Lynch's rule, here the solution arrives almost out of nowhere. Ben is never shown laboring to find supporters or confused about which direction to take the group.

GONE WITH THE WIND

(1939)

CONTEXT

In a film that had four directors, at least twelve scriptwriters, and a rotation of cameramen, the one unifying vision for the production of *Gone With the Wind* belonged to its producer, David O. Selznick. Born on May 10, 1902, to pioneering movie mogul Lewis Selznick, David lived his early years in financial comfort. Lewis gave his sons lavish personal allowances, advising them to spend it all and stay broke. Selznick's family wealth vanished abruptly, taken not by the ravages of war but by his father's poor business decisions and his gambling addiction. By 1923 Lewis Selznick declared bankruptcy, spending his last years financially supported by his sons.

Selznick moved to Hollywood in 1926 and quickly got a job in MGM's story department, where he began working his way up the ranks. Just two years later he moved to Paramount Pictures, where he was hired as an executive before continuing on to become vice president in charge of production at RKO. He then returned to MGM to help produce several films, most notably *David Copperfield*, *A Tale of Two Cities*, and *Anna Karenina*. When the original head of production at MGM returned, Selznick lost the creative freedom he craved and left to form his own production company in 1935. The following year, Selznick bought the film rights to Margaret Mitchell's wildly popular novel *Gone With the Wind*.

Films about the old South were popular during the first half of the twentieth century. One of the first of these films was Edwin S. Porter's *Uncle Tom's Cabin*, and twelve years later the epic *The Birth of a Nation* electrified the country, redefining cinema as an art form. By the late 1930s, however, the genre had gone into a steep decline, and when Irving G. Thalberg, the head of production at MGM, heard the synopsis of *Gone With the Wind* he was unimpressed. "Forget it," he was famously quoted as saying after he rejected the story. "No Civil War picture ever made a nickel."

Selznick had his own reservations about the story, including the cost of screen rights and production and the difficulties of choosing a cast that wouldn't alienate the many fans of the novel. Problems continued during the shooting of the film, ranging from wars between starlets over the lead role of Scarlett to Selznick's constant rewriting of the script. The production surpassed its budget before any of the action sequences were filmed, the hours were so long that some of the cast and crew took drugs to keep going, and the once supportive press abandoned the project entirely. Selznick, however, remained unbeaten through these trials, firm in his vision of a sweeping romantic drama and determined to prove that the film the press was now calling "Selznick's Folly" would be a success.

In the end, Selznick's vision didn't fail him. After its December 1939 premiere, *Gone With the Wind* proved to be a huge critical and box office success. It was labeled a masterpiece by the very critics who had once called it a folly, and it went on to be one of the top grossing films of all time. It was nominated for thirteen Academy Awards and won eight of them, including Best Picture, Best Screenplay, Best Actress (Leigh), Best Director (Fleming), and Best Color Cinematography. In addition, the Academy bestowed upon the film a special achievement award and an honorary plaque. Hattie McDaniel also walked into film history with her win as Best Supporting Actress, the first Oscar ever won by an African American. In England, *Gone With the Wind* ran in theaters for the duration of World War II, with Scarlett serving as a symbol of resistance and liberation. For these same reasons, the Nazis banned the film.

Such success, however, could not last. Despite the film's achievements, *Gone With the Wind*'s enormous scope and budget precluded the chance of it strongly influencing other films. Even if the film had spawned an imitator, there would have been no market for it. By the end of World War II, protests over Hollywood's racial stereotyping had permanently tainted Southern films, sending their popularity into steep decline. Selznick had another success in 1940 with the film *Rebecca*, but after that he was unable to repeat the success of his two most famous films and began losing money. The creative control of producers fell as directors rose in influence, and shifting balances of power marked the end of the glory days of the studio system. Like the story of the South in the Civil War, *Gone With the Wind* proved to be the end of an era.

GONE WITH THE WIND

PLOT OVERVIEW

The film opens with Scarlett O'Hara surrounded by admirers, but she is crushed when her father, Gerald O'Hara, tells her of Ashley Wilkes's upcoming marriage to his cousin Melanie Hamilton. Scarlett's father also reminds her of the importance and permanence of the land and their home, Tara, but she is too distraught to listen to him.

At a barbeque the next day at Twelve Oaks, the neighboring plantation, Scarlett is surrounded by even more admirers, but she is overtaken by jealousy when she sees Ashley and Melanie together. The roguish Rhett Butler sees Scarlett on the staircase and expresses interest in her, but Scarlett corners Ashley in the library to confess her love for him. When Ashley says they are too different to be together and leaves, Rhett reveals he has been listening the whole time.

The war quickly follows. Scarlett agrees to marry Charles Hamilton and holds the ceremony a day after Ashley and Melanie wed. Soon after, Scarlett receives a letter informing her of Charles's death in the war. Scarlett travels to Atlanta to stay with Melanie and her aunt, and while there she meets Rhett again. Now a cynical war hero, Rhett pays $150 to dance with Scarlett at a charity ball. Those listening are shocked by the offer, but Scarlett seizes on his offer as her only chance to dance, since she is in her mourning period, and agrees. Afterward, Rhett visits her regularly.

The South begins to crumble as the war continues and deaths mount. Scarlett works as a volunteer nurse tending to wounded and dying soldiers. She still pines for Ashley, who during his leave makes Scarlett promise to look after Melanie. Atlanta is attacked by the Yankees, and in the resulting chaos Scarlett is forced to help deliver Melanie's baby when the house slave, Prissy, backs down from the task. In the streets of the besieged city, Scarlett meets up with Big Sam, Tara's former slave foreman, who tells Scarlett sketchy details of her family's fate, including the news that her mother is ill. As the Confederates retreat, Rhett helps Scarlett, Melanie, the baby, and Prissy flee the city. Rhett leaves Scarlett, giving her his gun for protection, and he leaves to join the war effort. The women return to Tara to find Scarlett's mother dead, her father helpless, and Tara in ruins. Undaunted, Scarlett ends the first part of the film resolving to do whatever she must to never go hungry again.

Part Two opens with Scarlett, her family, and the slaves picking cotton in the field. Later, when Scarlett discovers a Yankee deserter trying to loot Tara, she shoots and kills him with the gun Rhett gave her and takes the money he has stolen from others. Frank Kennedy asks Scarlett for the hand of Suellen, her sister, and Scarlett agrees to the match. Later, Scarlett discovers that the taxes on Tara have been raised to $300, an impossible amount. A despairing Scarlett once again meets Ashley in secret, declaring her love for him and asking that they run away together. Ashley replies that Scarlett could never leave because she loves the land too much.

When Tara's former overseer returns and attempts to buy the property, Scarlett refuses. Her father mounts his horse to chase the overseer away but falls off during a jump and dies. Scarlett goes to Atlanta in an attempt to charm Rhett into paying her debt, but Rhett is a Union prisoner, jailed for blockade running and war profiteering. He realizes what she's up to and tells her that his money is tied up in Europe. On the way back to Tara, Scarlett runs into Frank, whom she marries for the tax money after she lies that Suellen is engaged to someone else. Scarlett uses Frank's money to build a successful mill and shames Ashley into working there. Later, Scarlett is attacked by hobos on her way through Shanty Town to the mill, and on a revenge mission Frank is killed and Ashley is injured. Rhett, who tried to stop the men from going, protects the remaining men from any repercussions that might result from their investigation of Yankee officers by claiming they spent the night in a brothel run by Belle Watling.

Rhett asks Scarlett to marry him, and she finally says yes. After moving to Atlanta they have a daughter they name Bonnie Blue, after an early Confederate flag. Scarlett says this will be their last child because she is still in love with Ashley. Rhett leaves, though Belle convinces him to return because Bonnie needs him. Rhett and Scarlett's marital problems continue. Finally, after getting drunk one night, Rhett swears he will drive Ashley out of Scarlett's mind forever and carries Scarlett upstairs to their bedroom.

The next morning Rhett leaves, taking Bonnie with him to London. When Bonnie says she wants to go home to her mother, Rhett returns her to Scarlett and then says he's leaving again. Scarlett admits that she's pregnant and that she doesn't want the baby. Rhett says cynically that maybe she'll have an accident. Immediately, Scarlett falls down the stairs and loses the baby. Some time later, Rhett and Scarlett are sitting on their porch, discussing the possibility of a reconciliation and watching Bonnie ride her pony. Bonnie attempts a jump and dies when she fails to clear the fence. Rhett goes mad with grief and, despite the pleas of Mammy, an old slave, temporarily refuses to allow his daughter to be buried.

These events prove to be too much for Melanie, who is already weakened by fatigue and a second pregnancy. She collapses. Before dying, she asks Scarlett to look after Ashley and their child, Beau, and to be kind to Rhett. When Scarlett sees how stricken Ashley is, she realizes that she and Ashley will never be together and rushes home to tell Rhett that it's him she really loves. When she arrives, though, she finds Rhett leaving for good this time, preparing to return to Charleston. Scarlett begs him not to go and asks what she will do without him, to which Rhett replies, "Frankly, my dear, I don't give a damn." Scarlett decides to go to Tara to think of a way to get him back, reminding herself that "tomorrow is another day."

Character List

Scarlett O'Hara—Played by Vivien Leigh A headstrong Southern belle and the protagonist of the film. A self-centered, determined beauty willing to step on anyone in her way, Scarlett deeply resents anything that interferes with her own interests. Constantly seeking money and entertainment, Scarlett fights for Tara only when it becomes a part of her self-image and even then is willing to abandon it at a moment's notice for a life more free of responsibility. Seeing Ashley as a living example of the social position she craves, Scarlett finds herself madly in love with him throughout most of the film. Though attracted to Rhett, Scarlett resents his ability to see the calculating woman beneath her charming veneer.

Rhett Butler—Played by Clark Gable A Confederate rogue and major foil for the protagonist. A bold, cynical rule-breaker, Rhett claims that his heroic smuggling during the war was purely for profit and that he doesn't care what society thinks of him. Despite these assertions, he joins the fighting as a soldier and later works to carefully cultivate his relationships with his neighbors. Comfortable with his wealth and the presentation of it, Rhett tries to downplay any service he performs to those around him. Rejected by everyone in his hometown of Charleston, Rhett is drawn to Scarlett because he sees her as his soul mate in rebellion. Despite his many problems with Scarlett as a wife and mother, Rhett loves their daughter Bonnie very deeply.

Ashley Wilkes—Played by Leslie Howard A Southern gentleman and major obsession of the protagonist. A passive, blond, handsome man, Ashley is so caught up in visions of the world as he feels it should be that he never does anything to affect the world as it is. Though Ashley claims to care deeply for both Melanie and Scarlett, the way he strings both women along suggests that he cares more for the tragic romance of the situation. Unlike Rhett with his daughter, Bonnie, Ashley is rarely shown having contact with his son, Beau.

Melanie Hamilton Wilkes—Played by Olivia de Havilland Ashley's wife. A kind woman unable to turn away anyone who needs help, Melanie is well liked by a swath of society that ranges from community leaders to the local madam. Wanting to find the best in everyone, Melanie foolishly sees Scarlett as a supportive sister-in-law and defends her at every opportunity. Despite this sweet nature, Melanie is also highly practical and willing to do what must be done to save those she loves.

Mammy—Played by Hattie McDaniel A house slave who helped raise Scarlett. Big-voiced and bold, Mammy remains unafraid to firmly chide Scarlett for her misbehavior despite the little effect it has. Though very loyal to the O'Haras, Mammy eventually warms up to Rhett and becomes his firm supporter.

Gerald O'Hara—Played by Thomas Mitchell Scarlett's father. A native Irishman with a fierce love of Tara and the land surrounding it, Gerald has a reckless side he indulges through wild jumps on his horse. Though he is the unquestioned head of the house, Gerald regularly seeks his wife's counsel on how to run the plantation, and it is her death as much as the destruction of the land that finally drives him to a state of half-madness.

Ellen O'Hara—Played by Barbara O'Neil Scarlett's mother. A stately, dignified woman, Ellen has very firm views on what is and what is not proper behavior and expects to see those views maintained by others in her household. She is the emotional center of her family, and the O'Haras begin to break apart after her death.

Belle Watling—Played by Ona Munson Madam of an Atlanta brothel. A kind, no-nonsense woman who maintains self-respect despite what other people think of her, Belle loves her son and has sent him away to keep him from the vices of her profession. Belle respects and admires Melanie, cares deeply for Rhett, and works to look out for their best interests.

India Wilkes—Played by Alicia Rhett Ashley's sister. A serious, dignified young woman, India was in love with Charles Hamilton before Scarlett stole him away. Because of this action, as well as the way Scarlett continues to chase after the married Ashley, India considers Scarlett a despicable woman who thinks only of using others.

Suellen O'Hara—Played by Evelyn Keyes Scarlett's younger sister. A young woman constantly in Scarlett's shadow, Suellen deeply resents Tara and all the indignities the O'Haras must go through to keep the plantation. Suellen begins to hate her older sister after Scarlett marries Suellen's sweetheart Frank, leaving Suellen with the fear that she will die an old maid.

Franklin Kennedy—Played by Carroll Nye Scarlett's second husband. A shy, older man whom Scarlett tricks into marrying her, Frank is truly in love with Scarlett's younger sister Suellen. Frank's marriage makes his life miserable despite his part ownership in a business made even more successful by Scarlett.

Prissy—Played by Butterfly McQueen A squeaky-voiced house slave. Silly, squeamish, and inclined to exaggeration, Prissy is the film's comic relief.

Charles Hamilton—Played by Rand Brooks Melanie's brother and Scarlett's first husband. A young, rash idealist who is instantly enamored of Scarlett, Charles is completely unaware of his wife's feelings for Ashley.

Aunt Pittypat Hamilton—Played by Laura Hope Crews Melanie's aunt. A high-strung woman who despairs over her role as Scarlett's chaperone, Pittypat is regularly in need of smelling salts.

Bonnie Blue Butler—Played by Cammie King Scarlett and Rhett's daughter. An attractive woman and a skilled horse rider who loves both her parents, Bonnie is the glue that holds her parents' marriage together.

Carreen O'Hara—Played by Ann Rutherford Scarlett's youngest sister. Barely a teenager at the beginning of the film, Carreen remains optimistic and encouraging throughout the film. She cares deeply for Tara, working hard and calmly bearing the sacrifices required to maintain the plantation.

Dr. Meade—Played by Harry Davenport The local doctor in Atlanta. An intelligent, brusque man with a low tolerance for foolishness, Dr. Meade takes his responsibilities to the wounded and dying Confederate soldiers very seriously.

Jonas Wilkerson—Played by Victor Jory Tara's overseer at the beginning of the film. Thin and weasel-like, Jonas attempts to combat his feelings of inferiority by going north after the war and becoming wealthy. He later returns, marries his mistress, and attempts to buy the plantation that once fired him. Jonas becomes enraged when Scarlett refuses to consider him her equal.

Emmy Slattery—Played by Isabel Jewell Jonas's mistress and later his wife. Though Jonas gives her money and legitimacy after the war, Emmy is still considered "white trash," even by the O'Haras' slaves. Scarlett blames Emmy for her mother's death.

Mrs. Dolly Merriwether—Played by Jane Darwell An Atlanta gossip. A self-declared monitor of propriety, Mrs. Merriwether warms up to Rhett only after he begins coming to her for advice. Scarlett, not willing to make such a gesture, never escapes Mrs. Merriwether's disapproval.

Mrs. Meade—Played by Leona Roberts Dr. Meade's wife. A gossip almost equal to Mrs. Merriwether, Mrs. Meade thinks highly of Melanie. She is susceptible to moments of gullibility.

Big Sam—Played by Everett Brown A farm slave. Large and friendly, Sam remains loyal to the O'Haras even when he is no longer at Tara. Though never acknowledged for it, Sam risks his life defending Scarlett against his fellow shantytown residents.

Stuart and Brent Tarleton—Played by Fred Crane and George Reeves Twin brothers. Two of Scarlett's many admirers, Stuart and Brent predict that the coming war will be short and glorious for the South. Later, they are included among the lists of the dead.

Pork—Played by Oscar Polk A thin, nervous house slave. Pork is one of the small group of slaves who remain loyal to the O'Haras despite emancipation.

Beau Wilkes—Played by Mickey Kuhn Ashley and Melanie's young son. Beau has very few speaking lines. Beau's birth severely weakens Melanie's health and adds to Scarlett's jealousy.

ANALYSIS OF MAJOR CHARACTERS

SCARLETT O'HARA

No matter how old she gets or how many times she remarries, Scarlett remains a child at heart. As the film opens, she resents serious matters such as sickness or war, merely seeing them as impediments to having fun. Even when she grows more accepting of life's practicalities, Scarlett insists on being the center of attention. She steals from other people whenever it suits her, taking Charles from India, Frank from Suellen, and all the servants from her sisters at Tara without any thought for the feelings of others. Even Scarlett's long quest for Ashley, supposedly the great love of her life, is rooted in her desire to steal him away from another woman.

Scarlett's appeal lies in her limitless internal resources. She throws herself into the backbreaking physical toil she despises in order to keep Tara going and sells goods to the Yankees she hates in order to make her business a success, always doing whatever she must to emerge victorious. Not even the loss of her loved ones holds her back. It is only after finding out about her mother's death and her father's madness that she resolves to save Tara, and after Bonnie's death that she finally welcomes the idea of having more children. When Rhett walks out the door, leaving her without a shred of hope, she cries only for a moment before resolving to win him back, a necessary first step as she attempts to reconquer her world.

RHETT BUTLER

On the surface, Rhett Butler is a textbook example of the charming rogue. His dark, good looks and supposedly wild behavior are the source of considerable gossip among the ladies. His most common expression is one of cynical amusement, and his war heroics are illegal and leave him with a healthy profit. He views social niceties as ridiculous and says exactly what he thinks, no matter who is listening or what their reaction might be. Most important to Rhett's charm is his sexuality. Unlike the proper, repressed gentlemen and ladies that surround him, Rhett believes that sex is an important part of life that should be explored and enjoyed at every opportunity.

At heart, though, Rhett desperately wants to be accepted, not in terms of social position—though Rhett is later willing to take that route for Bonnie's sake—but in the sense that he wants to be with someone who no longer makes him feel so alone. His family's complete rejection left Rhett emotionally isolated, making him hide his soft heart and readiness to help others. Rhett sees himself in Scarlett, and he is convinced that only someone who is also a rebellious outcast would allow him to be an important part of her life. When Scarlett treats Rhett as an inferior, he focuses his affection on Bonnie, who he sees as the only person he will ever love unconditionally. Melanie Hamilton is able to see the gentler, nobler side of Rhett, and he in turn genuinely respects and admires her as he does few other people. After Bonnie and Melanie die, he loses his strength.

ASHLEY WILKES

A romantic who is crippled by his nostalgia for the Old South, Ashley spends most of the film listlessly adrift through the harsher realities of the Reconstruction Era. Unlike Scarlett, he has no ambition or goals for the future, needing to be pushed into his profession by the stronger women in his life and joining the Confederate army without feeling passionate about the war. All he can do is remember the elegance of his life as it once was and wish that he could return to those days.

To Ashley, Scarlett represents passion and strength, while Melanie's gentleness and consistent devotion remind him of all the grace and beauty of the plantations that were destroyed by the war. He insists that his honor keeps him from resolving the love triangle between the three characters, but in reality he knows the situation is vital to his continued existence. At the end of the film, after Melanie has died and Scarlett's adoration has disappeared, the viewer is left wondering whether Ashley himself will soon vanish.

MELANIE HAMILTON

At first, Melanie serves primarily as an example of everything Scarlett is not. Kind instead of cutting, quiet instead of bold, thoughtful instead of self-centered, naïve instead of wily, Melanie dies as Scarlett once again rises from the ashes. Throughout her life Melanie thinks the best of everyone, and though some consider her outlook foolish it allows her to see a side of Rhett and Belle that most are unable to. It also allows her to have a far more pleasant and affectionate relationship with Scarlett than any other character in the film.

As the film progresses, Melanie's determined kindness and perpetual calm give strength to the characters in the film. Though Scarlett is the one who always forges ahead, it is Melanie who refuses to leave anyone behind, emotionally supporting Ashley even as she soothes Scarlett's sisters and brings compassion into Rhett's life. It is Melanie's calm, cool wisdom rather than Scarlett's assertiveness that soothes the characters after the raid on the shantytown, and it is Melanie's name that Mammy calls in times of crisis. Even Scarlett realizes how much she has come to rely on the unfailing support of the woman whom she viewed as a rival for so long.

THEMES, MOTIFS, AND SYMBOLS

THEMES

THE PERMANENCE OF THE LAND

As Gerald tells Scarlett in the opening scenes of the film, the land should be cherished because it can survive humanity's recklessness. However, it is not until Scarlett escapes from Atlanta and returns to her destroyed home that she begins to believe her father. Though her entire way of life is gone, she fights to keep the land because it is all that remains of the world she lost. While she is in Atlanta making her fortune, Scarlett knows that the land will be there waiting for her. After Melanie, Bonnie, and Rhett are gone from her life, Scarlett uses the land as a starting point to help her rebuild. The South, too, lives through the horrors of war and remains unbroken, though it is forever changed. The Old South is gone, but as long as the land remains its people will always be able to start life over again.

THE REAL COST OF WAR

Shying away from scenes of dramatic battles and military heroism, *Gone With the Wind* expresses the true horrors of war by showing the destructive effect it has on people caught in the crossfire. Rather than focusing on glinting sabers or dramatic cannon fire, the film instead concentrates on the pain-twisted faces of hundreds of mutilated and dying soldiers. The cynical Rhett is commended for his wartime "heroism," but those few words of praise are quickly overshadowed by the mobs of people desperate to hear whether their loved ones are alive. Death is a frequent occurrence. Dr. Meade's family gathers close as they mourn the loss of their oldest son and brother. When the younger boy swears vengeance against the Yankees, Melanie squelches the young man's desire with a simple truth: it would do his parents no good to have both their sons dead.

SELF-RELIANCE AS THE KEY TO SUCCESS

The characters in *Gone With the Wind* are most successful when they depend on no one but themselves. Scarlett refuses to listen to other people's opinions and builds a successful business relying only on her own judgment and skills. Her insistence that Ashley be by her side is only an impediment. Melanie, too, refuses to allow the opinions of others to influence her, and while some call her judgments foolish, she dies having lived a happier life than anyone she leaves behind. Rhett, rejected by his family, builds his fortune through his own confidence and abilities. Though he remains unbeaten by war and Yankee imprisonment, his need for Scarlett's affection eventually drains him of his strength. Only at the end of the film, when he heads out on his own, does he find his feet again.

PERSONAL STRENGTH CAN LEAD TO LOSS
Though strong characters succeed through the *Gone With the Wind*, the film suggests that strength is often a person's undoing. Scarlett, who has beaten poverty, the Yankees, and public opinion, loses the man she has come to love because she is too stubborn to see that she was wrong about Ashley. Melanie, who has enough emotional strength to carry every other character in the film on her shoulders, dies when her pregnancy proves to be too much. Gerald, whose bravery made him such a skilled horseman, dies taking a final, reckless jump. The determination that made Rhett a successful smuggler and social black sheep proves to be his undoing and causes him to stay with Scarlett long after he should have let her go.

MOTIFS

DREAMS
The opening title card of *Gone With the Wind* warns that the South the film portrays is no more than "a dream remembered." Ashley, once a dignified, respectable landowner, finds it impossible to escape the dreams of the life he once lived. He is unable to accomplish anything with his life after the war and is passively dragged into a profession by the stronger, more clear-headed women in his life. This daydreaming damages other lives as well. Scarlett learns that it is Ashley's romantic dreams, not his love for her, that cause him to string Scarlett along for so many years. Melanie, weighed down by his dreaming, asks Scarlett to take care of Ashley and Beau when she dies.

OBSESSION
For the characters in *Gone With the Wind*, obsession is both a strength and an Achilles' heel. It provides Scarlett with strength as she works to restore Tara and her personal status to their former

glory. Her obsession enables her to endure backbreaking work, to kill, and to perform other acts she once thought herself incapable of doing. However, Scarlett's obsession with Ashley puts her through years of pointless emotional turmoil and masks her feelings for Rhett. Melanie's deep desire to have children gives her joy as she becomes pregnant a second time, but her obsessive need and the risks it inspires ultimately kill her. Rhett's obsessive quest to win Scarlett brings him happiness at first but leaves him drained, his bravado and self-confidence entirely diminished by Scarlett's emotional distance.

DRASTICALLY CHANGING CIRCUMSTANCES

Many of the characters in the film go through drastically changing circumstances, often more than once. Scarlett, once wealthy, loses everything in the war only to win back an even greater wealth than that which she lost. Ashley, too, loses everything in the war, and though Scarlett helps him recover financially, emotionally he is never the same. Frank Kennedy, once so poor Scarlett scoffed at his wish to marry her sister Suellen, works until he becomes wealthy enough that Scarlett wants to marry him herself. Rhett, made even wealthier by his brave smuggling during the war, is also made poor by it, as his time in prison keeps him from accessing his money tied up in foreign banks. However, Rhett ultimately uses the promise of this money to quickly regain his freedom. Life is represented as a constant uncertainty in which only the foolish become complacent with their current position in life. The truly successful are always prepared for change.

SYMBOLS

TARA

In addition to representing the land it was built on, Tara serves as a symbol of family and a sense of continuity for Scarlett, often more so than the living family she has left. After her mother dies and her father goes mad, Scarlett doesn't allow her sisters to say anything bad about Tara, admonishing them that it would be like insulting their lost parents. Tara's presence comforts Scarlett after Ashley's rejections and offers a physical defense against Jonas Wilkerson when he tries to intimidate her. When Scarlett moves to Atlanta and becomes wealthy, she doesn't forget about Tara, ensuring that it remains beautiful and well cared for. After Rhett leaves, Tara serves as the only place where Scarlett can recover from the blow and lick her wounds in peace.

RHETT'S GUN

Though it initially belongs to Rhett, the gun he gives Scarlett upon her escape from Atlanta symbolizes Scarlett's own strength and ability to stand on her own. Rhett first gives Scarlett the gun before leaving her and the other women alone in enemy territory, confident that Scarlett will be able to take care of herself with the proper resources. Later, the gun and Scarlett's courage to use it allow her to defend her home from the Yankee deserter. Scarlett's abilities and independence develop until she can shoot well at close range. This talent mirrors her outlook on life, winning her no points for elegance but leaving her able to do what's necessary in any situation.

SCARLETT'S HATS

Scarlett's lovely, frivolous hats symbolize her young, girlish side, the part of her that wants nothing more than to be entertained and to be the object of all the boys' admiration. After Charles dies she wants to defy her widow's garb by wearing a fashionable hat, just as she wants to defy her mourning period by dancing and going to parties. While in Atlanta, Rhett woos Scarlett by ordering her a hat from Paris, its purchase symbolizing a much stronger acknowledgement of Scarlett's beauty and charm than he is ever willing to offer out loud. Even near the end of the film, after Scarlett has become a shrewd, practical, and highly successful businesswoman, she still claims that putting on an attractive hat makes her forget about sensible things like bookkeeping. Scarlett still wants to be thought of as the prettiest girl at the ball.

FILM ANALYSIS

THE ENDURING POPULARITY OF "GONE WITH THE WIND"

Even the most ardent fans of *Gone With the Wind* admit that time has allowed some of the film's wrinkles to show. The film's patronizing, racist treatment of African Americans is widely acknowledged as a sweeping sentimentality for the pre–Civil War South. The plot, especially that of Part Two, contains enough dramatic deaths and emotional cliffhangers to clearly mark the film as an ancestor of today's television soap operas. The film is old-fashioned in its story, style, and cast, serving more as the end of a cinematic era than as the start of a new one. Nonetheless, it has remained a popular favorite, so much so that in 1998 American Film Institute voters chose *Gone With the Wind* as one of the greatest films of all time.

An important aspect of the film's popularity is its iconic elements, the most prominent of which is Scarlett O'Hara herself. Brave, resourceful, and unbeaten, Scarlett embodies the universal desire to achieve one's dreams in the face of adversity. Though more flawed than classic heroines, Scarlett has imperfections that make her endearing to her fans. Scarlett's rise to financial independence inspired American women who entered the workforce for the first time during World War II. Rhett, too, is a symbol of hope and recovery. Self-reliant and cynical, he is beaten down by war and love but still helps his fellow man. This spirit was embodied in the strength of people living in Europe during the 1940s. *Gone With the Wind* gave Europeans hope that they too could overcome the fear and hardships of war.

Gone With the Wind is an engaging story told well. The characters are complicated and stubborn, and their presence together creates a resonant emotional tension. The scenes of Atlanta burning and of dying Confederate soldiers remain powerful despite decades of technical advancement in film. Characters undergo quests, survive hardship, and find and lose love—traditional storytelling devices as ancient as Greek mythology.

PAGE-TO-SCREEN ADAPTATION

First published on June 30, 1936, Margaret Mitchell's novel *Gone With the Wind* won a Pulitzer Prize for fiction and became an instant bestseller worldwide. When David O. Selznick bought the film rights from Margaret Mitchell on July 30, 1936, he faced the daunting task of condensing the 1,037–page novel into a film of manageable size: the studio calculated that filming the entire book would result in a film about 168 hours long. In addition, they had to make drastic cuts without damaging what Selznick called the "chemicals," or essential elements, of the novel. Selznick feared that even filling in some of the novel's holes—such as the absence of scenes portraying Rhett's smuggling activities—would damage the film's popularity in the eyes of the public. Though large chunks of the film ended up being cut, Selznick felt that the individual scenes should be left intact, sensing that audiences would understand the need for omissions but would consider any distortion or addition to their beloved story a betrayal.

To perform this immense task, Selznick hired Pulitzer Prize-winning dramatist and film writer Sidney Howard to write the script. After receiving a barrage of suggestions from Selznick, Howard sent back a first draft that was four hundred pages long, equivalent to about six hours of film. In an attempt to pare the story down, Selznick and Howard then sat through several intense editing sessions. Many of the characters who had less impact on the narrative were cut, a list that included any of the O'Haras not living at Tara and all of Scarlett's children by her first two husbands. Seeing Scarlett's string of marriages as important to her character development, Howard fought to keep Frank Kennedy in the film despite Selznick's recommendations. Selznick had Bonnie Blue restored to the script in order to keep her tear-jerking scenes in the film. While he doubted he would be able to film it, Selznick also asked Howard to write a "night of love" for Scarlett and Rhett. Despite the editing sessions, the film still ran over their desired length of three hours, and the script was shelved.

After Clark Gable was cast as Rhett, Selznick could no longer hold off finishing the script. He hired Jo Swerling, a noted script "fixer," when Howard refused to return to Hollywood. Swerling's work did not satisfy Selznick, and he called in a group of writers to try their hand at reshaping Howard's work so it would better fit

Selznick's vision. One of these writers was the novelist F. Scott Fitzgerald, whose contribution to the script was largely judged by what he removed: several dramatic speeches were replaced by simpler and more direct lines taken straight from the novel. After Fitzgerald came Ben Hecht, who worked to simplify and tighten the now haphazard script and focus more attention on Rhett's and Scarlett's relationship. Selznick contributed to the chaos by making almost daily changes to the script, and the cast did not receive a final version of the script until after the film was completed. Despite all of these different voices, the essential "chemicals" remained, helping *Gone With the Wind* go on to become one of the biggest box-office successes of all time.

CINEMATOGRAPHY

At the time *Gone With the Wind* was being filmed, Technicolor was not widely used and carried several inherent disadvantages. The Technicolor corporation owned the heavy, cumbersome cameras required for shooting, all seven of which were rented to Selznick. Each picture was required to have a color consultant who had the power to veto any color scheme she felt was incompatible with color cinematography. In addition, technical advisors were required to assist cinematographers who had only worked with black-and-white film. Technicolor, for example, required twice as much lighting for proper illumination of a scene. Selznick had previous experience with Technicolor filming and knew that it would be vital to giving *Gone With the Wind* the visual richness necessary for an epic drama. In fact, Selznick was so determined that the film's color have as much impact as the characters' emotions that he fired the original cinematographer Lee Garmes for favoring a color scheme Selznick deemed too subdued. His replacement, Ernest Haller, succeeded in obtaining more vivid effects.

Selznick knew that using shadows was an important part of a scene's visual impact and persuaded his color consultant to shoot Scarlett and her father in silhouette on the hill at Tara. With the plantation glowing brilliantly in the distance, the resulting framing effect powerfully underscores Gerald's feelings about the importance of the land. Selznick uses this silhouetting to the same effect in the film's final scene, when Scarlett stands on the same hill as she comes home to Tara. Selznick also uses shadows to emphasize moments that focus on the relationship between characters in *Gone*

With the Wind, first seen in the form of the looming shadows Scarlett and Melanie cast on the walls of the makeshift hospital. Later, the delivery of Melanie's baby is lit only with slivers of light that appear between the window slats, the darkness making the scene more intimate and giving it a powerful simplicity.

Another technique that Selznick brought from black-and-white film to Technicolor was the use of matte painting. While a shot was filmed, the area to be painted in later was masked with black matte paint on a glass screen placed in front of the camera. Later, a full-color scale illustration of the missing portion was shot onto the rewound negatives to cover the blacked-out area with calibrated precision. Previously used only for background shots, *Gone With the Wind*'s special effects cinematographer Clarence Slifer adapted the technique to complete a number of sets that were only partially finished. Tara's side views, outhouses, and background vegetation were all matte paintings, as were portions of the Twelve Oaks plantation, the train station roof, the decorations in the Old Armory, an entire street of burning houses, and even some of the wounded soldiers lying on the ground in long shots.

PORTRAYAL OF RACE RELATIONS

The most controversial aspect of *Gone With the Wind* is the film's depiction of race relations. Though freed from the novel's positive portrayal of the Ku Klux Klan, *Gone With the Wind*'s depiction of slavery remains decidedly simplistic. Adopting historian U. B. Phillip's "plantation school" view of the institution, the film shows slaves as well-treated, blindly cheerful "darkies" loyal to their benevolent masters. Slaves are portrayed as normal employees, are rewarded with presents like the master's pocket watch if they've been appropriately loyal, and are allowed to scold the young mistress of the house as if they were a part of the family. Big Sam leaves Tara only when ordered and with extreme reluctance and later saves Scarlett at serious risk to his own life.

Although they were rarely acknowledged and there was no talk of pay after their emancipation, the former slaves show no interest in leaving Scarlett. The slaves who choose to seek their freedom are looked down on, either portrayed as unscrupulous or as gullible pawns of the political parties. Though this attitude is less sensationalistic than D. W. Griffith's far more brutal caricatures of slaves in *Birth of a Nation*, *Gone With the Wind*'s refusal to acknowledge any of the complex racial issues of either the Reconstruction Era or the 1930s only supports the stereotypes presented in Griffith's film.

More damaging than *Gone With the Wind*'s simplistic view of slavery, however, is the film's depiction of all African Americans as stupid and childlike. Mammy manages to escape the film with her dignity largely intact, but Pork, the only named male house slave, is forced to appear in scene after scene with a wide-eyed, slightly glazed expression on his face. When faced with work duties beyond those he has always performed, he immediately becomes overwhelmed and panics. Big Sam's grammar is chopped down to an extremely simplistic level, far below even that of the equally uneducated Mammy. The worst example of this negative portrayal is the young house slave Prissy. Perhaps intended as comic relief, Prissy is stupid, squeamish, a liar, and becomes hysterical over the smallest things. She is a caricature of a woman, a living holdover from the slaveholder's old claim that African Americans needed to be slaves because they weren't able to function on their own. Malcolm X notes in his biography the deep shame he felt as a child when he saw *Gone With the Wind*, specifically citing Butterfly McQueen's performance as Prissy. The National Association for the Advancement of Colored People tried to arrange a boycott of the film by black audiences and, to a lesser extent, black actors.

GONE WITH THE WIND

IMPORTANT QUOTATIONS EXPLAINED

1. GERALD: "Do you mean to tell me, Katie Scarlett O'Hara, that Tara, that land, doesn't mean anything to you? Why, land is the only thing in the world worth workin' for, worth fightin' for, worth dyin' for, because it's the only thing that lasts."

Though Scarlett is too brokenhearted to pay attention to the advice Gerald gives her during the opening scenes of the film, it is one of the few bits of shared wisdom that seems to actually have an impact on her over the course of the film. All of Scarlett's actions prove she is motivated mainly by self-interest. From her image-soothing marriage to a man she barely knows to her lifelong quest to steal Ashley from Melanie, the only clear beneficiary of anything Scarlett does is Scarlett herself. Somehow, finding Tara as a looted shell changes something in her, and she becomes willing to fight for the plantation as she will for nothing else. Scarlett is willing to forego her previous fineries and make her hands raw, working like a slave in order to keep Tara going. She is even willing to debase herself in front of Rhett—the one man who has always been able to see beneath her carefully managed surface—in order to hold on to Tara. When she becomes wealthy, she makes sure to devote enough money to see that Tara is returned to its former glory.

Gerald's words also offer an inherent hopefulness to the characters who don't have their own land. The entire structure of the Old South has collapsed beyond repair, and everything that once made their homeland what it was has vanished, as the film's title suggests. For some, like Ashley, this loss is enough to make them give up entirely, drifting along the rest of their days as they remember everything that once was. But as Gerald's words remind them, the characters in the film have not been left entirely destitute. The South itself still remains, the land damaged but not destroyed by the fighting there. As long as the people pay proper homage to the land, they can't be beaten.

2.   SCARLETT: "Sir, you are no gentleman."
     RHETT: "And you, Miss, are no lady."

This exchange, which occurs just after Rhett reveals he has over-heard Scarlett's declaration of love for Ashley, neatly summarizes both the attraction and the fatal flaw in Rhett's and Scarlett's rela-tionship. Scarlett is drawn to Rhett precisely because of how, in his daring and sexual magnetism, he is entirely different from the proper but utterly tame Southern gentlemen that surround her. His willingness to spontaneously sweep her into intense, dramatic kisses is scandalous in the eyes of society, but this is part of the passion and excitement Scarlett longs for from Ashley and from life itself. Rhett, for his part, is far more honest about the reasons behind his interest in Scarlett, often remarking on how different she is from other sim-pering Southern belles. Rhett, firmly rejected by everyone in his hometown of Charleston, has an outlook on life that has made him an outcast. He hopes that Scarlett, a woman who thinks the way he does and is unafraid to defy society, will break through his isolation.

This passion has its negative side as well. Even though Scarlett is attracted by what sets Rhett apart from more traditional gentlemen, she is at times repelled by it. Despite how boring they might be, the milder, more well-mannered men—Ashley in particular—represent the refinement and promise of Southern society before the war. These are the kind of men a proper Southern belle *should* want, and despite her actions Scarlett still thinks of herself as a proper South-ern belle. A gentleman would allow her to maintain that she is a refined lady, while Rhett insists on disabusing her of the notion at every opportunity. For the first half of the film Rhett seems to enjoy this duty, but by the end of the film he is clearly disgusted by Scarlett. He discovers that the unladylike woman he put his hopes in rejects the qualities required of a good wife: compassion, understanding, and caring. No matter what Rhett does for her, Scarlett seems to care little for him.

3.   RHETT: "Take a good look my dear. It's a historic moment. You can tell your grandchildren about how you watched the Old South fall one night."

Rhett makes this statement as he and Scarlett watch Atlanta burn. Though the destruction of Atlanta dealt a major blow to the Con-federacy, Rhett isn't making a comment on the North's military success. Instead, Rhett is talking about the end of the ideals the Old South stood for, the way of life that Ashley clings to, a South that is "no more than a dream remembered." As the characters discuss at the barbeque at the Twelve Oaks plantation, the chief advantages the South had during the war were independence and pride. It didn't matter that it had fewer resources or less military strongholds than the North. The South had a far more civilized society, and as long as they were fighting for its more graceful, dignified way of life it was impossible for the South to lose. In fact, many were so convinced of the South's security they thought the war would end in a few weeks, barely enough time for the season to change on the plantations or for the beautiful Southern belles to become lonely.

4.   RHETT: "Frankly, my dear, I don't give a damn."

These are Rhett's last words in the movie and perhaps the most memorable line of *Gone With the Wind*. This line shows as much strength of character in Rhett as Scarlett's earlier defiance does in her, and with these words Rhett himself becomes almost more heroic than Scarlett. Scarlett, despite all the hardships she faces, never fully accepts that other people are just as good and as worthy of respect and admiration as she is. Stormy and wild, she is completely convinced of her own beauty and seems to be completely irresistible to every man she meets. She shucks off her genteel upbringing with only minor hesitation, hardly ever feels guilty about what she does to others, and generally lives her life on a legendary scale. Though she does exhibit admirable determination and bravery, she remains aloof and distant, and these qualities prevent her from being a wholly accessible character.

Despite all his bravado, Rhett ultimately shows more true humanity than Scarlett does. Though he first appears in the film with a reputation and demeanor as daring and iconic as Scarlett's, his affection for Scarlett quickly reveals that his heart is his Achilles' heel. He is as powerless before Scarlett as are all the other men, but unlike Charles Hamilton and Frank Kennedy, Rhett hates his powerlessness and struggles hard against it. His struggle is long and difficult. Even as he swears he'll free himself from Scarlett, his loneliness continues to draw him to her, and he sustains the hope that she'll one day love and appreciate him as he does her. Rhett doubts, and even occasionally hates, himself for the cycle of affection and rejection he's trapped in. Certain moments in the film, such as Scarlett's scene on the staircase and Bonnie's death, reveal the extent of Rhett's sadness and pain. The film never explores Scarlett's dark feelings as deeply. When Rhett finally breaks away from his poisonous relationship with Scarlett, his decision is courageous yet heartbreaking. Rhett has shown that he can feel true pain and anguish, and his feelings are evident even in his dismissive, biting words.

5.   SCARLETT: "After all, tomorrow is another day."

Scarlett says this famous last line after Rhett summarily leaves her. Distraught, Scarlett tells herself she can't think about his leaving just now, that she must go home to Tara and find a way to get him back. This line, which Scarlett says several times in the film, exemplifies Scarlett's unwillingness to let outside influences interfere with her worldview. At times, this personality trait serves as a source of strength for Scarlett, eliminating all distractions that might keep her from achieving the goals she has set for herself. When she fights her way through the Yankee lines to get back to Tara, she succeeds by refusing to even entertain the possibility that she won't be able to make it home. Had she listened to Rhett's warnings, she wouldn't have made the journey. When she builds Frank Kennedy's small sideline into a mill of her own, she doesn't bow to well-meaning advice or any of the gossip that spreads over her ambition. As a result, her business ends up being far more profitable than Frank's ever had been.

There are times, though, when Scarlett's single-mindedness also works to her detriment. Often it keeps her from being able to effectively grasp all the implications of a situation and thereby know how best to deal with them. When the Union soldiers appear after the Shantytown raid she is so concerned with her own interests that she is the last person to know where the men have gone and the amount of danger they are truly in. Even more damaging to Scarlett is her life-long obsession with Ashley. By insisting he is the only man who could ever make her happy, Scarlett is unable to see the good in her relationship with Rhett until it is too late. Similarly, she doesn't realize how much she has relied on Melanie's emotional support until Melanie is lying on her deathbed.

CITIZEN KANE

(1941)

CONTEXT

In 1998, the American Film Institute put *Citizen Kane* at the top of its list of the one hundred greatest movies of all time. Released in 1941, it was the first movie Orson Welles co-wrote, directed, and produced. Welles was only twenty-five at the time and widely considered to be a theatrical genius. Because of Hollywood's efforts to woo him from the theaters of New York, he received an almost unprecedented amount of creative control from RKO Studios in his first contract. He was free to choose the cast as well as to write, direct, produce, edit, and act in the film he created. His budget was $500,000—a significant amount for an unproven filmmaker and an amount that Welles managed to exceed. *Citizen Kane* wound up a commercial failure, and it ultimately derailed Welles's career. History has vindicated Welles by recognizing his cinematic genius, but the story of his life makes for a cautionary tale every bit as compelling as the story of Charles Foster Kane, the fictitious protagonist of *Citizen Kane*.

George Orson Welles was born in 1915, in Kenosha, Wisconsin, and endured a difficult childhood. His parents, Richard and Beatrice, were prominent in their community, but Richard was also an alcoholic. They separated when Welles was four. Welles and his mother moved to Chicago, where he became the focus of her hopes and dreams. Welles could do no wrong in her eyes, and he developed a precocious sense of his own abilities. Beatrice died when Welles was nine, leaving him in the custody of his father and of Dr. Maurice Bernstein, a pediatrician to whom Beatrice had grown close because of their shared love of classical music and opera. When Welles was fifteen, his father died, and Welles became the sole ward of Dr. Bernstein. The instability of Welles's childhood did not thwart his talents and ambitions, and when Dr. Bernstein sent Welles to a prestigious private school, he thrived. His interest in the theater led him to begin producing plays at school, and his talent for writing, acting, producing, and directing caught the attention of the local media.

When Welles graduated, Dr. Bernstein sent him to Ireland with the hope that he would forget the theater. Instead, Welles made his theatrical debut in Dublin, then went on to appear in roles in England and America. In 1934, he made his New York theatrical debut, married Virginia Nicholson, directed his first short film, and made his first radio appearance. Around this time, Welles also met John Houseman, who became his partner and mentor. After working together for several years staging plays for the Federal Theatre Project, Houseman and Welles formed the Mercury Theatre in 1937 to produce classic plays and radio specials. From this collaboration came Mercury Theatre on the Air. On October 30, 1938, the Mercury Theatre gave its most famous broadcast, a production of *War of the Worlds*. Performing the play as if it were a newscast, Welles convinced many who tuned in that aliens were invading New Jersey. The resulting panic made Welles the most talked about actor in America.

Welles's notoriety caught the attention of Nelson Rockefeller, co-owner of RKO Studios in Hollywood. RKO was best known for its frothy comedies starring Fred Astaire and Ginger Rogers, but RKO's board of directors wanted to make the type of artistically important movies that its rivals were turning out. Rockefeller felt that Welles's theatrical genius could improve the quality of RKO's pictures and urged RKO president George J. Schaefer to lure him west. Welles initially wasn't interested, primarily because at that time movies and the people who acted in them lacked the credibility of live theater and its players. Schaefer eventually made Welles an offer he couldn't refuse: a contract that gave him almost total artistic control over a project from start to finish. This kind of contract was unprecedented and is even more remarkable because major studios of this era controlled every aspect of their product. Welles couldn't resist being the star of such a coup, and he moved to Hollywood in 1939.

Plenty of people in Hollywood hoped Welles would fail. He had made no secret of his disdain for "movie people," and many resented the fact that this inexperienced young man had been given so much creative license. Welles knew of this resentment and was determined to turn out something spectacular. He first planned to do a film based on Joseph Conrad's novel *Heart of Darkness*, but due to the extraordinary budget the project would require, the idea failed. After five months in Hollywood, Welles was viewed as a failure himself. He felt a great deal of pressure when he began working on *Citizen Kane*, the story of a powerful man who alienates everyone who loves him. Although Welles denied it, he almost certainly based the movie on the life of press magnate William Randolph Hearst, and Hearst was not happy with the result. Hearst was probably upset by having a fictionalized account made of his life, no matter how close to the truth that account was, but Welles's cruel portrayal of Hearst's mistress Marion Davies was most likely what spurred Hearst's full wrath. Hearst used his considerable influence over the media to quell any mention of *Citizen Kane*. In addition, several film executives from other studios, led by an old friend of Hearst named Louis Mayer, offered RKO a vast sum of money for the film in order to destroy it completely. It is not clear whether their gesture was one of loyalty to Hearst or one of fear of the possible backlash should Hearst decide that his Hollywood friends were snubbing him, but in any case, RKO refused to hand over the film.

Hearst's friends may have failed at keeping the movie out of theaters entirely, but Hearst's efforts did result in the movie's delay and a limited run. Hearst's crippling tactics cost the film the commercial success that would have cemented Welles's reputation as a great filmmaker. Critics praised *Citizen Kane*, but after its run ended, RKO and other studios admitted that Welles's tendency toward controversy made them reluctant to work with him. Moreover, no studio wanted to incur the wrath of the influential Hearst papers. Welles's arrogance toward the Hollywood establishment and his mean-spirited portrayal of Marion Davies, who was well-liked in Hollywood, didn't help his cause. *Citizen Kane* went on to receive nine Academy Award nominations, but won only one, for writing. The audience booed when the award was announced. Welles never made another important film.

Citizen Kane didn't receive the viewership or accolades it deserved until the 1950s, when the film's considerable innovations became clearer. The cinematographer, Gregg Toland, who went on to achieve great fame, used techniques such as deep focus, low camera angles, and optical illusions to tell Kane's story. For the first time, ceilings were visible in several scenes, created by draping black fabric over the lights and microphones that hung from the top of the sound stage. Toland's skillful application of new or rarely used techniques proved revolutionary. Some of the film's innovations that had contributed to its commercial failure, including the non-linear narrative and somber conclusion, eventually set *Citizen Kane* apart from films with more traditional structures and happy endings. Along with its remarkable cinematic achievements, what ultimately elevated *Citizen Kane* to such revered heights was the character of Kane himself. Despite the reporter's attempts to uncover the real Kane, Kane remains an enigma. The depth of Kane's isolation and loneliness results in a portrait that has haunted and will continue to haunt generations of audiences.

Plot Overview

Citizen Kane opens with the camera panning across a spooky, seemingly deserted estate in Florida called Xanadu. The camera lingers on a "No Trespassing" sign and a large "K" wrought on the gate, then gradually makes its way to the house, where it appears to pass through a lit window. A person is lying on a slab-like bed. Snowflakes suddenly fill the screen. As the camera pulls back, a snow-covered cabin comes into view. The camera pulls back more quickly to show that what we have been looking at is actually just a scene inside a snow globe in the hand of an old man. The camera focuses on the old man's mouth, which whispers one word: "Rosebud." He then drops the globe, which rolls onto the floor and shatters. Reflected in the curve of a piece of shattered glass, a door opens and a white-uniformed nurse comes into the room. She folds the old man's arms over his chest and covers his face with a sheet.

In the next scene, a newsreel entitled *News on the March* announces the death of Charles Foster Kane, a famous, once-influential newspaper publisher. The newsreel, which acts as a lengthy obituary, gives an overview of Kane's colorful life and career and introduces some of the important people and events in Kane's life. The newsreel plays in a small projection room filled with reporters. The producer of the newsreel tells the reporters he's not happy with the film because it merely recounts Kane's life, instead of revealing who Kane truly was. He notes that Kane's last word was "Rosebud" and wonders if that may hold the key to Kane's character. He decides to stall the newsreel's release and sends a reporter, Jerry Thompson, to talk to Kane's former associates to try to uncover the identity of Rosebud.

Thompson first interviews Kane's ex-wife, Susan Alexander Kane, who works as a dancer and singer in a dingy bar. Susan is drunk and uncooperative. A waiter hovers over her and tells Thompson that Susan has been unwilling to talk about Kane since he died, although she spoke of him often when he was alive. The waiter also says he asked Susan about Rosebud after Kane died and she claimed she'd never heard of Rosebud. Thompson then goes to the bank that houses the memoirs of Kane's childhood guardian, Walter Parks Thatcher. As Thompson begins to read these memoirs, the image of the page dissolves into a flashback to Kane's childhood.

A roughly chronological series of flashbacks tells Kane's life story from five different points of view. The first flashback shows how Thatcher meets Kane. Kane's mother, Mary, runs a boarding house in rural Colorado. In lieu of a payment, one of her tenants gives her some stock in what she thinks is a worthless mine; it turns out to give her ownership of the Colorado Lode, a working gold mine. Finding herself suddenly wealthy, she decides to send away her son, Charles, to be raised by her banker, Thatcher. Charles is understandably upset and whacks Thatcher with the sled he's been happily riding when Thatcher shows up to escort him away. Kane's relationship with Thatcher never improves. Vignettes from their years together show Kane engaging in questionable journalism, wasting money, and constantly enraging Thatcher.

Thompson interviews other people who were close to Kane, and these characters relate their memories of the man through flashbacks as well. Thompson speaks first with Kane's good friends and employees, Mr. Bernstein and Jedediah Leland, and has one more conversation with his ex-wife Susan. Most significantly, Thompson interviews the butler, Raymond, who remembers Kane saying "Rosebud" following a violent episode after Susan left him. Each person gives his or her own version of an abandoned, lonely boy who grows up to be an isolated, needy man. All reveal in some way that Kane is arrogant, thoughtless, morally bankrupt, desperate for attention, and incapable of giving love. These faults eventually cause Kane to lose his paper, fortune, friends, and beloved second wife, Susan. Thompson, the reporter, never does find out what Kane meant by "Rosebud." Giving up the quest, Thompson is leaving Kane's abandoned castle, Xanadu, when the camera pans a scene of workers burning some of Kane's less valuable possessions. In the fire is the sled that Kane was riding the day his mother sent him away. Painted on the sled is the name Rosebud.

CHARACTER LIST

Charles Foster Kane—Played by Orson Welles Wealthy newspaper publisher whose life is the subject of the movie. When Kane's mother comes into a seemingly limitless fortune, she sends Kane away to be raised by her banker, Thatcher. Kane resents being taken from his home and the security he felt there and never reconciles himself to that separation. As a result, Kane grows up to be an arrogant and callous man. Ultimately, his attitude alienates him from everyone who cares about him, and he loses his newspaper, his fortune, and his friends.

Jedediah Leland—Played by Joseph Cotten Kane's college friend and the first reporter on Kane's paper. Leland admires Kane's idealism about the newspaper business when they start working together. However, their principles quickly diverge, and Leland becomes more ethical as Kane becomes more unscrupulous. Over time, Kane's questionable morals and paternalistic attitude disturb Leland to such an extent that Leland eventually requests a transfer to Chicago to escape Kane. Kane ultimately fires him for writing a negative review of Susan Alexander's disastrous operatic debut.

Susan Alexander Kane—Played by Dorothy Comingore Kane's mistress, who becomes his second wife. When they meet, Susan seems soft and sweet to him, but her true nature turns out to be whiny and demanding. Kane never sees her for what she is. He pushes her to sing opera because her success would justify his interest in her, even though she's not a particularly talented singer. The more he manipulates her, the further their relationship deteriorates, and she finally leaves him. She's the original owner of the snow globe.

Mary Kane—Played by Agnes Moorehead Kane's mother. Mary gives her son away when she comes into a fortune. Trim and carefully controlled, she shows little emotion when turning Kane over to Thatcher. She's also emotionless toward her husband, Jim, and she suspects he will hurt the young Kane,

although Jim seems quite kind to him. We see so little of
Mary that we never fully understand why she abandons
Kane.

Mr. Bernstein—Played by Everett Sloane Kane's friend and
employee. Bernstein, a bespectacled Jewish man, is the only
character who loves Kane unconditionally. He completely
overlooks Kane's faults and is loyal to him regardless of the
circumstances. He wants only for Kane to be happy. He's also
the only character who understands that underneath Kane's
arrogant façade is a lost, lonely boy. He may seem to be the
quintessential yes-man, but he behaves that way out of loyalty, not out of a search for personal gain.

Walter Thatcher—Played by George Coulouris The banker who
becomes Kane's legal guardian. Although Thatcher seems to
have a genuine affection for Kane, Kane never overcomes his
resentment of Thatcher for taking him from his childhood
home. A big reason Kane goes into the newspaper business is
to harass Thatcher with front-page attacks on banking trusts,
which are Thatcher's business. Thatcher appears to be doing
his best, but he never manages to forge a bond with Kane.

Emily Monroe Norton Kane—Played by Ruth Warrick Kane's first
wife and the niece of President Monroe. While Kane ostensibly marries Emily because of her connection to the presidency, he does seem to love her genuinely. Later, she wearies
of his devotion to his paper and his friends. In one of the most
effective sequences in the movie, a montage of breakfast table
scenes traces the breakdown of their marriage over a period
of years. She and Kane separate after she finds out about his
mistress, and a few years later she is killed in a car accident
along with their only child, a son.

Jim Kane—Played by Harry Shannon Kane's father. Jim provides a
contrast to Mary's precise, emotionless actions. Rumpled and
common, he vacillates between wanting to raise his own son
and wanting the money he'll get for staying away from him.
Mary's contempt for Jim is mirrored in Kane's contemptuous
treatment of virtually everyone he comes in contact with as
he grows up.

Jerry Thompson—Played by William Alland   The reporter in charge of finding out the meaning of Kane's last word. Thompson's investigation of "Rosebud" is the catalyst for everyone's recollections in the movie, and his presence in the flashbacks provides the continuity that ties the disparate perspectives together. We see him only in shadow or with his back turned to the camera.

ANALYSIS OF MAJOR CHARACTERS

CHARLES FOSTER KANE

Kane's mother sends him away when he is only eight years old, and this abrupt separation keeps him from growing past the petulant, needy, aggressive behaviors of a pre-adolescent. Kane never develops a positive emotional attachment to his guardian, Thatcher, and he rejects Thatcher's attempts at discipline and guidance. As an adult, Kane has a great deal of wealth and power but no emotional security, and this absence of security arrests his development and fuels his resentment of authority. Because of his wealth, Kane has no motivation or incentive to subject himself to social norms. He has no reason to move beyond his resentment and his sense of himself as the center of the universe, and he never takes his place as a virtuous, productive member of society. Kane seems idealistic when he first begins to run his newspaper, but his primary reason for becoming a newspaperman is to manipulate his political and social environment in order to gain total control over it. Kane's quest for power makes him charismatic, but he eventually drives away the women and friends he attracts. As those close to him mature in a way that he cannot, they must move away from him to preserve their own selves.

Kane is not a likeable man, but Welles presents his life in a way that ultimately shrouds Kane in pathos and pity. Kane is dead when the film begins, and we learn about him only through the accounts given by his old friends and lovers. Each person has a different perception of Kane, and his or her memories are not fully reliable. A fragmented picture, not a fully fleshed-out man, is all we get. However, we know enough about Kane to know he deserves sympathy. Kane's obsessive spending and collecting reveal that he is trying to fill an empty space inside himself with objects instead of people. He buys things for the sake of having them, not because they give him any particular joy. Kane is fundamentally lonely, and, intentionally or unintentionally, he drives away everyone who cares for him. His attempts to control those he loves always fail. When his second wife

Susan prepares to leave him, he says angrily that she can't do that to him. She firmly responds, "Yes, I can," and then walks out the door.

Critics generally accept that Welles based the character of Kane on publishing magnate William Randolph Hearst and other powerful men of his time, but Welles certainly based the character on himself as well. He, like Kane, was around eight years old when he lost his mother, though Welles's mother died and Kane's mother leaves by choice. Welles's mother gave him an inflated sense of his own importance that was encouraged by his school administration and his guardian after her death. As an actor, Welles naturally imbued Charles Foster Kane with some of his own experiences and characteristics. The parallels between Kane and Welles helped Welles give a remarkable performance. Welles didn't just act the part of Kane: in many ways, Welles *was* Kane.

JEDEDIAH LELAND

Jedediah Leland doubts Kane's integrity from the early moments of their partnership. Leland is as giddy as Kane is about their newfound authority at the newspaper, but the men's ethics quickly diverge. Kane signs a noble "Declaration of Principles," which Leland asks skeptically to keep as a souvenir. He seems to have a premonition that Kane's principles will be subject to interpretation. As Kane becomes increasingly despotic, Leland questions the unethical and immoral way in which they conduct their business. Leland also views Kane's self-delusion as ridiculous, even though Kane remains oblivious to his own hypocrisy and the harm he does. When Kane's staff celebrates the fact that Kane has stolen the entire editorial staff of their rival newspaper, Leland, for the first time, openly questions whether the end justifies the means and whether loyalty can be bought. Several years later, Leland has the same disagreement with Kane, which leads Leland to request a transfer to Chicago. He feels he can become an ethical, objective reporter only if he can escape Kane's suffocating control. Just like the women in Kane's life, Leland must leave Kane to save himself.

Despite his doubts and criticisms, Leland attempts to maintain his integrity without destroying his friendship with Kane, and he sustains his faith in Kane longer than any other character in the film, with the possible exception of Bernstein. When Kane builds his wife Susan an opera house in Chicago, the city where Leland now works as the drama critic for a Kane newspaper, Leland must choose loyalty or the truth after Susan's horrendous opening night. Leland starts to write a negative review of Susan's performance, but he passes out, drunk, before he can finish it. Kane arrives at the office and indignantly finishes writing the review himself to show Leland that he can be an honest man, but when Leland wakes up, Kane bluntly fires him. Leland has little reason to think any integrity or goodness lurks within Kane, but nonetheless he mails Kane the "Declaration of Principles" Kane signed so many years ago. The gesture is a rebuke, but it is also a way of suggesting it's not too late for Kane to change. Kane tears it up, effectively slicing Leland out of his life forever.

SUSAN ALEXANDER KANE

Susan and Kane fall in love with each other under false pretenses, and though Susan eventually loses her illusions about the kind of man Kane is, Kane is never able to see Susan clearly. Susan and Kane first meet in the street: Susan has a toothache, and a passing car has splashed Kane with mud. Circumstances have diminished the social, age, and class differences between the two that may otherwise have thwarted their connection. Susan, usually screechy and overbearing, here seems soft-spoken, gentle, and naïve because of her toothache, and Kane's helpless predicament makes her laugh. She has no idea who Kane is. Kane, charmed by her unselfconsciousness, believes he has found someone who will love him unconditionally. When Susan's true nature emerges, Kane willfully ignores it. She grows bitter when he pressures her to become someone he believes is more suited to his station. Kane tries to force others to see her as he does, which nearly drives her to suicide. Kane's attempts to completely control her almost rob her of her identity, and the only way she can save herself is to leave him.

Susan's appearance in Kane's life is the fulcrum on which Kane's fortunes turn. Kane's life before meeting Susan is very different from his life after meeting her, and Susan effectively splits the movie into two parts: the world of Kane's rise and the world of his fall. Before Kane meets Susan, his story plays out in a world where he's ruthless, successful, and respected. After meeting Susan, his story becomes inseparable from their relationship and their life together. Because of his relationship with her, his marriage breaks up, his political aspirations shatter, and he loses the respect of society at large. Susan represents Kane's lost innocence and fall from grace. When Susan finally leaves him, the loss Kane feels mirrors the loss he felt when his mother left. He trashes Susan's room and finds the snow globe, which brings back long-repressed memories of his childhood. Kane has no one now that Susan is gone, and nothing to hold onto but the past.

THEMES, MOTIFS, AND SYMBOLS

THEMES

THE DIFFICULTY OF INTERPRETING A LIFE

The difficulty of interpreting a person's life once that life has ended is the central theme of *Citizen Kane*. After viewing an in-depth, filmed biography of Kane's life, the producer of the biography asks his reporters a simple question: Who, really, was Charles Foster Kane? The producer recognizes that a man isn't necessarily the sum of his achievements, possessions, or actions, but that something deeper must drive him. His clue that Kane was more than his public accomplishments is the last word Kane uttered: "Rosebud." Kane's life story unfolds in layers through the reporter Thompson's investigation and is told by a succession of people who were close to him. These various points of view are imbued with people's particular prejudices, and the recollections are ultimately ambiguous and unreliable.

Kane never gets to tell his own life story, and we must wonder how much his telling of it would differ from the reminiscences of his associates. None of these people ever really knew what drove Kane to do the things he did. Only Thatcher would have had the chance to fully understand Kane, but he was too concerned with making money to have any compassion for a lonely child. He viewed Kane through a distant, mature lens of acquisition and conservatism. The differing perspectives on Kane's life, especially in the absence of Kane's own point of view, force us to question what was truly important in the life of Charles Foster Kane as well as to ponder what constitutes a life in general. Judging by Kane's last word, the most important pieces of his life were not the things that made him newsworthy, such as his newspaper successes and political ambitions, nor his friendships and associations. Instead, as Kane's life comes to an end, he grasps at a memory from his childhood. His defining moment was the point where his life changed irrevocably for what appears to be the better, from a materialistic viewpoint, but which actually leaves him vulnerable and alone.

THE MYTH OF THE AMERICAN DREAM

Citizen Kane was one of the first movies to depict the American Dream as anything less than desirable. As a child, Kane is fully happy as he plays in the snow outside the family's home, even though his parents own a boarding house and are quite poor. He has no playmates but is content to be alone because peace and security are just inside the house's walls. When Thatcher removes Kane from this place, he's given what seems like the American dream—financial affluence and material luxury. However, Kane finds that those things don't make him happy, and the exchange of emotional security for financial security is ultimately unfulfilling. The American dream is hollow for Kane. As an adult, Kane uses his money and power not to build his own happiness but to either buy love or make others as miserable as he is. Kane's wealth isolates him from others throughout the years, and his life ends in loneliness at Xanadu. He dies surrounded only by his possessions, poor substitutions for true companions.

THE UNRELIABILITY OF MEMORY

We learn the story of Charles Foster Kane from his acquaintances' recollections, not from the memories of the protagonist himself. Bernstein, one of the most unreliable narrators, gives the first significant reference to memories when he tells the reporter, Thompson, that it's surprising what a man remembers. Bernstein's memories of Kane are colored by his unwavering admiration for him, which endured even as Kane became increasingly corrupt and withdrawn. Bernstein also tells Thompson about a girl he saw once and never forgot, an idealized, almost fictionalized fantasy that resembles Kane's idealistic memories of his childhood. Thompson later meets with Leland, who is obviously suffering from the effects of old age. At one point he claims he can't remember the name of Kane's estate (Xanadu). This lapse in memory may be pretense, but it nonetheless casts a shadow of doubt on the reliability of Leland's memories. Susan Alexander recounts her life with Kane through an alcoholic haze, which negatively affects the accuracy of her memories as well. These hazy recollections and idealizations are all that remain of Kane, a man who was once so powerful and larger-than-life. No matter how monumental his achievements, even a man like Kane will eventually be forgotten.

MOTIFS

ISOLATION

Charles Foster Kane repeatedly finds himself isolated from the world around him, whether he is young or old, happy or unhappy, alone or surrounded by others, which suggests that his final isolation is inevitable. The camerawork in *Citizen Kane* emphasizes this isolation. For example, we see Kane as a happy child playing alone in the snow, and a short time later, the camera isolates him between his mother and Mr. Thatcher as they plan to separate Kane from his home. He is still alone, but no longer happy. We next see Kane seated by himself in the center of a room ringed with dark-suited men, who watch him as he opens a gift from Thatcher. Kane's isolation follows him into adulthood, where we see him sitting on his own in his newspaper office amid a celebration in his honor. The camera locates Kane in a triangular shot between Bernstein and Leland as the two men discuss Kane's increasingly depraved tactics. The three men may be in physical proximity, but the nature of Bernstein and Leland's discussion and the way the shot frames Kane mark him as an outsider. Eventually Leland leaves Kane, and Kane barricades himself in his fortress with Susan. But Susan too leaves Kane, and in the end he dies alone, never having formed a lasting bond with anyone.

OLD AGE

Because the story of Charles Foster Kane is told by his associates after his death, the primary storytellers are men who are far past their prime, and their degeneracy lends another layer of sadness and loneliness to the film. All of these men were once vital, active, and important. Now they're bored, and society has shunted them aside. Bernstein, as chairman of the board, notes that he has nothing at all to do. Leland is in an old age home, stiff and somewhat senile. Thatcher, whose story comprises a significant source of material on Kane's life, is already dead by the time Thompson consults his memoirs. Even Kane himself, as he ages throughout the film, becomes devitalized and mechanical in his movements. His aging, ravaged state is painfully apparent in the scene where Susan leaves him and he tears up her room in anger. He moves stiffly and has difficulty venting his anger as violently as he wants to, which increases his frustration and isolates him even from his own feelings. Old age in *Citizen Kane* does not come with grace, but with defeat.

Materialism

Charles Foster Kane is a rapacious collector. At one point, in a newspaper office so filled with statues that the employees can barely move around, Bernstein notes that they have multiple, duplicate statues of Venus (the goddess of physical beauty). Kane obsessively fills his estate with possessions, and at the end of the movie the camera pans across massive rooms filled with crates to show that he never even unpacked many of his purchases. Kane's collecting is not that of a discriminating connoisseur—he buys art objects so fervently that his behavior more closely resembles the ravenous actions of a predator. After his disappointments in the political arena and with Susan's opera career, Kane builds his estate, Xanadu, to isolate himself and Susan from those who spurned his attempts at manipulation, and he fills the castle with inanimate objects. He wields complete control over the world he's created, and nothing can challenge his authority in this realm. Through his materialism Kane attempts to ameliorate the insults of the real world, where he couldn't control his mother's abandonment, Susan's failed attempt at opera, the failure of his political career, and the souring opinions of his friends. He ends up at Xanadu alone, with his possessions as his only companions. By purchasing so many extravagant goods, Kane attempts to fill a void created by all the people who left him throughout his life. Yet the only two possessions that carry meaning for Kane on his deathbed are a simple snow globe and Rosebud, the sled he remembers from his youth.

Symbols

Sleds

Two sleds appear in *Citizen Kane*. Rosebud, the sled Kane loves as a child, appears at the beginning, during one of Kane's happiest moments, and at the end, being burned with the rest of Kane's possessions after Kane dies. "Rosebud" is the last word Kane utters, which not only emphasizes how alone Kane is but also suggests Kane's inability to relate to people on an adult level. Rosebud is the most potent emblem of Kane's childhood, and the comfort and importance it represents for him are rooted in the fact that it was the last item he touched before being taken from his home. When Kane meets Thatcher, who has come to take him from his mother, Kane uses his sled to resist Thatcher by shoving it into Thatcher's body. In this sense, the sled serves as a barrier between his carefree youth and the responsibilities of adulthood and marks a turning point in the development of his character. After Thatcher's appearance, Kane's life is never again the same. Later, Thatcher gives Kane another sled, this one named Crusader—aptly named, since Kane will spend his early adulthood on a vengeful crusade against Thatcher. For the second time, Kane uses a sled (or in this case, the idea it represents) as a weapon against the man he sees as an oppressive force, but unlike Rosebud, Crusader carries no suggestion of innocence.

Reportedly, the idea of using the plot device of Rosebud came from writer Herman Mankiewicz. The story goes that he had a bicycle he adored as a child, and he never really recovered when it was stolen. Welles always thought it was a rather cheap idea, but he went along with it because it was an easy way to simplify the plot line.

Snow Globe

The snow globe that falls from Kane's hand when he dies links the end of his life to his childhood. The scene inside the snow globe is simple, peaceful, and orderly, much like Kane's life with his parents before Thatcher comes along. The snow globe also associates these qualities with Susan. Kane sees the snow globe for the first time when he meets Susan. On that same night, he's thinking about his mother, and he even speaks of her, one of only two times he mentions her throughout the film. In his mind, Susan and his mother become linked. Susan, like Kane's mother, is a simple woman, and Kane enjoys their quiet times in her small apartment where he's free from the demands of his complex life. Susan eventually leaves him, just as his mother did, and her departure likewise devastates him. As Kane trashes Susan's room in anger, he finds the snow globe, and the already-thin wall between his childhood and adulthood dissolves. Just as his mother abandoned him once, Susan has abandoned him now, and Kane is powerless to bring back either one.

Statues

Kane repeatedly fails in his attempts to control the people in his life, which perhaps explains his obsession with collecting statues and the appearance of statues throughout the film, since statues can be easily manipulated. Thatcher, threatening and oppressive when alive, is harmless as a large, imposing statue outside the bank where his memoirs are housed. When Kane travels to Europe, he collects so many statues that he begins to acquire duplicates, even though Bernstein has begged him not to buy any more. Kane's office and home overflow with statues, which he acquires without joy or discrimination. Kane has always aspired to control people, not just the world's fine art, but puts his energy into collecting statues as his power over people swiftly and fully dissolves. For Kane, statues are nothing more than images of people, easily controlled—he can place them where he wants and even ignore them if he chooses. Over his statues, Kane has power: to acquire, to own, and to control. Statues eventually replace living people in Kane's life, and he dies surrounded by these figures.

FILM ANALYSIS

THE AUTHORSHIP CONTROVERSY

Orson Welles dominates *Citizen Kane*. He produced, directed, and starred in it, and his overpowering presence both on and off screen has often overshadowed the fact that the film was actually the result of a successful collaboration between some of the greatest minds in Hollywood at that time. The greatest controversy is over who wrote the script, and this battle has colored much of the discussion of this movie over the years.

Before making *Citizen Kane*, Welles had been accustomed to taking full credit for works that were often collaborations. When Welles worked with the Mercury Theatre, the Mercury Theatre on the Air scripts were generally credited as studio productions—until the great success of the *War of the Worlds* radio broadcast. The broadcast generated so much publicity that Welles decided to take full authorship credit, even though it had actually been written by studio writer Howard Koch. The Mercury Theatre continued to encourage Welles to take credit for productions, believing that his name and reputation would bring good publicity. Welles's reputation as a theatrical genius had been growing since his adolescence, and the Mercury Theatre was more than happy to take advantage of it.

Welles eventually began to buy into his own publicity, and he conveniently disregarded the fact that he was not the sole creative genius behind his troupe's endeavors. His ego wasn't welcome when he went to Hollywood to work on *Citizen Kane*, and, not surprisingly, Hollywood wasn't willing to give Welles credit he didn't deserve. Welles met huge opposition when he tried to take full credit for creating *Citizen Kane*.

Although he played a key role in writing *Citizen Kane*, Welles did not create the script single-handedly. Much evidence suggests that the original idea for *Citizen Kane* came from Herman Mankiewicz, a battle-hardened Hollywood scriptwriter. Mankiewicz was well acquainted with William Randolph Hearst, having spent a great deal of time at Hearst's ranch in San Simeon. Charles Foster Kane, the protagonist of the film, resembles Hearst in many specific, personal ways, and such information could have come only from insider knowledge of Hearst's life, which Welles did not have. Welles did play an important role in creating the script, and few critics doubt that he drew from his personal life, in the same way that Mankiewicz drew from Hearst's life, to flesh out the character of Charles Foster Kane. Welles, however, was certainly not the only person responsible for the script's creation.

Mankiewicz collaborated with John Houseman, Welles's partner at the Mercury Theater, on the initial draft of *Citizen Kane*. Both Mankiewicz and Houseman wanted writing credit on the final version, but Welles refused. Houseman gave up when Welles dug in his heels, but Mankiewicz had the power of the Hollywood writers' union behind him. He threatened Welles with legal action in order to be listed as a writer, and Welles yielded. On Oscar night, *Citizen Kane* won the award for Best Original Screenplay, and this was the only Oscar either Welles or Mankiewicz ever received.

FILMIC ELEMENTS

Citizen Kane made cinematic advances on many fronts, and its most significant contribution to cinematography came from the use of a technique known as deep focus. Deep focus refers to having everything in the frame, even the background, in focus at the same time, as opposed to having only the people and things in the foreground in focus. The deep focus technique requires the cinematographer to combine lighting, composition, and type of camera lens to produce the desired effect. With deep focus, a filmmaker can showcase overlapping actions, and *mise-en-scène* (the physical environment in which a film takes place) becomes more critical. Effectively manipulating the *mise-en-scène* for deep focus actively engages the whole space of the frame without leaving the viewer confused. Deep focus is most effective in scenes that depict Kane's loss of control and his personal isolation because it gives the audience a clear view of the space Kane commands as well as the space over which he has no power. Gregg Toland, the cinematographer Welles chose for *Citizen Kane*, had used the technique in an earlier film he had worked on, *The Long Voyage Home*, but *Citizen Kane* marked the first time it was used so extensively or effectively. *Citizen Kane* introduced Hollywood to the creative potential of other cinematic techniques as well. One such innovation was a technique known as the "wipe," where one image is "wiped" off the screen by another. Other innovations involved unique experiments with camera angles.

Welles's chosen Mercury Theatre cast was an asset to the film and vital to the success of techniques like deep focus. These cast members were classically trained theatrical actors, and none had ever made a movie before Welles brought them to Hollywood. Their stage training, rather than being overpowering, helped them to place themselves firmly in each scene, which complements the use of deep focus. The cinematography and acting technique combined so perfectly that the total control Welles was given over casting was justified. The combination of innovative techniques, not one individual technique, is what makes *Citizen Kane* such a cinematically important film.

Citizen Kane employs creative storytelling techniques as well. Acting almost as a biopic (biographical film), *Citizen Kane* portrays a long period of time realistically, allowing the characters to age as the story goes on. Instead of being told in a linear, completely chronological manner, Kane's story unfolds in overlapping segments that add more information as each narrator adds his or her story. Telling Kane's life story entirely in flashbacks was another innovative approach to storytelling. Flashbacks had been used in earlier films, but *Citizen Kane* used them most effectively. The flashbacks are given from the perspectives of characters who are aging or forgetful, which casts doubt on the memories being discussed. In other words, these are unreliable narrators whose own opinions and interpretations affect their accuracy. The storytelling techniques succeed in painting Charles Foster Kane as an enigma, a tortured, complicated man who, in the end, leaves viewers with more questions than answers and inevitably invokes sympathy rather than contempt.

Welles's achievements in this film marked a new direction in cinema. Many critics argue that *Citizen Kane*, with its inventive use of lighting and shadow, is the first film noir, or at least the direct predecessor of noir, a genre that employs dark, moody atmosphere to augment the often violent or mysterious events taking place. *Citizen Kane* introduced Hollywood to the creative potential of cinematic technique. Even apart from the controversy the film stirred, a multitude of innovations made *Citizen Kane* the most exciting movie in the history of cinema at that time.

ACTING

The principal cast members of *Citizen Kane* were not Hollywood actors. Rather, they were theatrically trained actors Welles had assembled many years before with his partner and mentor, John Houseman. In 1934, when Welles and Houseman met, Houseman was thirty-three years old and was already highly respected in the theatrical world as an actor, director, and producer. Welles and Houseman produced plays together through the Federal Theatre Project, a program formed under the Works Project Administration (WPA) to provide employment in the cultural arena. Their first project was a daring adaptation of *Macbeth*—they used black actors and staged it as a voodoo-themed production. In 1937, they both resigned from the Federal Theatre Project after one of their plays, *The Cradle Will Rock*, was closed down by federal agents because of its leftist politics.

Shortly thereafter, Welles and Houseman founded the Mercury Theatre. The group consisted of many of the elite theater actors of that time, and they were known as the Mercury Players. Eventually, the Mercury Players included actors who went on to make a significant impact in film, such as Joseph Cotten, Everett Sloane, Ruth Warrick, and Agnes Moorehead. Welles and Houseman's ambition for the Mercury Theatre was to stage the classic plays "with their original speed and violence," as Houseman once said. Their first play, a modern adaptation of *Julius Caesar* set against the backdrop of Nazi Germany, was a great success. In 1938, Welles, who had already been working very successfully in radio, formed Mercury Theatre on the Air, a weekly radio broadcast starring his Mercury Players. At this time, radio focused more on drama than music, and the Mercury Players, with their theatrical talents, were extraordinarily well-suited for the medium. Their most famous performance was the 1938 Halloween eve broadcast of *War of the Worlds*.

The Mercury Players soon moved beyond the limitations of radio. Shortly after the *War of the Worlds* broadcast, Welles accepted his Hollywood contract and moved west. At first, he flew back to New York to do his weekly radio broadcasts, but he eventually brought the Mercury Players to Los Angeles. Welles and the Mercury Players continued with the weekly Mercury Theatre on the Air radio broadcasts as Welles worked to develop a project for RKO Studios. Welles was anxious to cast his theatrical group in his first movie, but the length of time it was taking for Welles to settle on a project took a financial toll on the actors. Some had to take other jobs. A few got roles in other films, which upset Welles—he'd wanted their debuts to be in his film. The stress ultimately led to a blowup between Welles and Houseman, and their partnership ended.

If the RKO executives had not signed away so much control to Welles, the studio undoubtedly would have objected to Welles's plan to cast his Mercury Players in the key roles in *Citizen Kane*. Then, as now, the idea of casting unknowns in a major picture met a great deal of resistance. In fact, Welles maintained that the reason an earlier project he had been developing never got off the ground was that the studio was unwilling to let him cast Lucille Ball, who at that point had never starred in a major picture. In *Citizen Kane*, however, Welles was able to cast his unknown Mercury Players, and much of the success of the film stems from how well their theatrical training worked within the dramatic framework of the movie. The fact that they were unknowns actually may have contributed to their effectiveness, since more recognizable players may have distracted viewers from the story.

BIOGRAPHY OF WILLIAM RANDOLPH HEARST

Critics generally agree that *Citizen Kane*'s protagonist, Charles Foster Kane, is based on William Randolph Hearst, who built a media empire in the late 1800s and early 1900s. Though *Citizen Kane* is fiction, the number of parallels between Kane and Hearst make the connection between the two undeniable.

William Randolph Hearst was born on April 29, 1863, in San Francisco, California to multimillionaire George Hearst and Phoebe Apperson Hearst. Hearst was an only child, and his mother adored and indulged him. Mother and son often traveled to Europe while George stayed home to oversee his empire. Hearst went to Harvard but never applied himself seriously to his studies. On the verge of flunking out for his rowdy behavior, he decided he'd like to try his hand at the newspaper business. George had taken over a small paper, the *San Francisco Examiner*, as payment for a debt, and Hearst was determined to run it. He greatly admired Joseph Pulitzer and wanted to emulate his sensationalist style of journalism. Hearst went on to purchase the *New York Journal* and wooed much of

Pulitzer's staff away from him, much as Kane purchased the staff of his paper's rival, the *Chronicle*, in the film. On this foundation Hearst built a national media empire.

Hearst let neither money nor the truth stand in the way of his quest to be the most successful newspaper publisher of all time. For him, the Cuban Revolution of 1895 offered a perfect opportunity to sell more papers. His sensationalist and often false reports from Cuba are widely credited with pushing American intervention and sparking the Spanish American War. One famous anecdote, which made its way into *Citizen Kane*, tells of Hearst ordering the legendary artist Frederic Remington to send dispatches about the war from Cuba. Remington sent Hearst a telegram saying there was no war. Hearst replied that if Remington furnished the pictures, Hearst would furnish the war. Hearst made up stories about politicians, advocated political assassinations in an editorial just a few months before McKinley was assassinated, staged crimes so his reporters could write about them, and generally took "yellow journalism" (sensationalist journalism) to new depths of irresponsibility.

Around 1918, Hearst met silent movie actress Marion Davies and began what would become a life-long affair. At the time, Hearst was married and had five sons. He and his wife, Millicent Veronica Willson, a former showgirl turned society matron, separated in 1926. Hearst and Willson never divorced, and Hearst and Davies lived together openly even though they never married. Hearst built the magnificent castle San Simeon for Davies, which was the inspiration for Xanadu in *Citizen Kane*. Hearst's estate differed from Kane's— unlike the lonely fortress Xanadu, San Simeon was full of laughter and parties. Like Kane, however, Hearst was a rapacious collector who filled his castle with possessions, without regard to aesthetics or suitability. When Hearst began to suffer financially in the late 1930s, Davies saved his enterprises by selling off a million dollars in jewelry and real estate and turning the money over to Hearst. Her actions leave no doubt about the strength of their relationship, unlike the shaky bond between Kane and Susan Alexander.

Hearst and Welles probably never met, although each certainly knew of the other. Welles surely felt that Hearst had tried to crimp his early theatrical career. The two men occupied opposite ends of the political spectrum as well. Hearst was wealthy and conservative, hated minorities, distrusted Jews, supported the Nazi party, was an isolationist and an anti-communist, loathed President Roosevelt, and hated the New Deal. Welles's first big directing job, meanwhile, was with the New York Federal Theatre Project, which was part of the New Deal and supplied acting jobs for unemployed black actors. Welles tended toward liberalism and was accustomed to accepting people for their talents rather than their religion or ethnicity. However, although Hearst and Welles were polar opposites politically and socially, both were smart, egotistical, and indulged by those around them. Welles both loathed Hearst and identified with him, and portraying Kane required him to reconcile these conflicting feelings.

Important Quotations Explained

1.   Kane: "Don't believe everything you hear on the radio. Read the *Inquirer*!"

Early in the movie, during the newsreel detailing Kane's life, Charles Foster Kane arrives from Europe to a phalanx of reporters who bombard him with questions, and this is his first reply. This quote is undoubtedly one of the lines added to the script by Welles and is a dig both at himself and at William Randolph Hearst. Just before coming to Hollywood to make movies, Welles achieved notoriety through his *War of the Worlds* radio broadcast, when he had people all over America believing that Martians were invading. He was nearly arrested during the broadcast and was investigated subsequently by the FCC. The panic that resulted from the event led to stringent new rules for radio broadcasts. Welles probably felt a certain amount of resentment toward these rules since newspapers had no such controls placed upon them and often printed material that was sensationalist and simply untrue.

    The comment's mockery of Hearst also derives from the fact that newspapers were no longer the rivals Hearst had to worry about—the advent of radio and of photo magazines threatened newspaper circulation. Because these media provided a new outlet for news and information, people read their papers more critically. Credibility became increasingly important in the news media. Just as Hearst had been able to reach into people's homes and influence them through his newspapers, Welles could now do the same through radio. However, neither Welles's radio broadcasts nor Hearst's papers could be counted on as reliable sources, simply because the men behind them were so manipulative. When Kane tells the reporters to read the *Inquirer* instead of listening to the radio, he says it with tongue firmly in cheek.

2.   Kane: "It's also my pleasure to see to it that decent hard-working people in this community aren't robbed blind by a

pack of money-mad pirates, just because they haven't anybody to look after their interests."

Kane says this in Thatcher's written reminiscences. Thatcher has come to visit Kane at the *Inquirer* to question him about his motives for attacking Thatcher's business interests. Kane has set himself up as a man of the people, even though in social and economic terms he is much closer to Thatcher than he is to the masses. Kane still thinks of Thatcher as a pirate because of the way Thatcher took him from his mother, even though Thatcher has always looked after Kane's business interests. Kane understands that what Thatcher cares about most is money, so he uses his newspaper to attack Thatcher's financial interests. Kane's actions also damage his own interests, but this is less important to him than hurting Thatcher. Thatcher can't understand why Kane acts the way he does, as Bernstein later notes. In a way, Thatcher's bewilderment is easy to understand because he was merely doing what he had been contracted to do when he took young Kane into his custody. He can't fathom why Kane should resent him.

At the same time, and in the same scene, Kane is fomenting a war that will certainly have a detrimental effect on the same people he purports to protect. However, this war will bolster Kane's finances by increasing his newspaper's circulation. This quote attests to Kane's characteristic self-delusion, an affliction that surfaces here in how he perceives his relationship with the masses and elsewhere in his relationship with Susan Alexander. In Kane's arrogance, he never considers that he might not be any more qualified to look after the interests of the American people than Thatcher is. While Thatcher's goal may be to protect the money of those who are already rich, Kane's goal is to control public opinion and the political climate. Kane is not as altruistic as he likes to think he is. Thatcher understands that and points it out to Kane, as does Leland later in the film when he brings to Kane's attention that his newspaper empire is as much a monopoly as Thatcher's financial business trusts ever were.

3.   KANE: "I run a couple of newspapers. What do you do?"

Charles Foster Kane says this to Susan Alexander during their first meeting, which comes during Leland's flashback retelling of Kane's life. For Kane, part of Susan's appeal is that she knows nothing of his fame or notoriety. Kane is thinking of his mother when he meets Susan, and his notion of Susan becomes inextricably tied up in his subconscious with memories of his lost childhood. She comes to represent unconditional love, something he doesn't think he can achieve now that he is a rich newspaper magnate. Remaking himself as a man who just runs a couple of newspapers takes Kane back to a simpler time and gives him a sense that peaceful domesticity is possible. He comes close to experiencing such tranquility in the following sequence as he sits quietly in Susan's armchair and listens while she sings and plays the piano for him.

In answer to the second part of the quote, Susan says she's a shop girl, but that's not what Kane takes from the conversation. Instead he focuses on what she says about her mother's dreams for her, and he takes those dreams up as his own. Kane finds Susan attractive in part because she represents the masses that he so longs to control. At one point he even describes her to Leland as "a cross section of the American public." Kane's desire to shape Susan according to his ideal results in the collapse of both his first marriage and his political career.

4. BERNSTEIN: "A fellow will remember a lot of things you wouldn't think he'd remember."

This quote comes at the beginning of Bernstein's recollections of his relationship with Kane, when he talks to Thompson about what "Rosebud" could possibly mean. Bernstein goes on to tell Thompson an anecdote of how, back in 1896, he was on a ferry and saw a girl on another ferry. She was wearing a white dress and holding a white parasol. Although he saw her only for a second, he says that a month hasn't gone by since then that he hasn't thought of her. Many experts on film history and on *Citizen Kane* in particular consider this the most important quote in this film, encompassing as it does the themes of loss, memory, and idealism. These abstractions mean different things to the different characters who tell the story of Kane's life, yet this quote speaks to their shared experience: all of the film's characters in some way lack control over their memories, and their recollections are clouded by their own experiences and prejudices. Thompson never gets a true picture of Charles Foster Kane because everything he learns is filtered through these imperfect memories.

Just as Bernstein lost the girl in the white dress, who is merely an idealized representation of his own youth, Kane loses his childhood, and it becomes an increasingly important touchstone in his memory even as it becomes more distant and unreal. Everyone in this film loses something, and what they lose lingers as a kind of holy grail for each of them. Kane loses his mother and childhood, Susan loses her simple life, and Leland loses his family name and the respect that accompanied it. In spite of Bernstein's successes in the business world, he still harbors an inchoate longing for a girl he never met, just as Kane, in spite of his tremendous success, longs for the life that was taken from him. At the end of his life, Kane can do nothing but idealize, through his memory of Rosebud, the youth he can never recapture.

5. THOMPSON: "I don't think any word can explain a man's life. No, I guess Rosebud is just a piece in a jigsaw puzzle—a missing piece."

Thompson says this at the very end of the film as he's leaving Xanadu to catch his train. He's been unsuccessful in his quest to find out who, or what, Rosebud is. As he walks through the rooms of Xanadu, crowded with the late Kane's possessions, he picks up a jigsaw puzzle, which prompts the metaphor. *Citizen Kane* is about the jigsaw puzzle that is a person's life, and what Thompson has been doing since the beginning of the movie is trying to put that puzzle together. Thompson even has a snapshot of sorts to work from, in the form of the newsreel seen very early in the film. In spite of the information he already has, Thompson ultimately fails in his efforts to put Kane's life together simply because he's missing one key piece: Kane himself, who is dead.

This quote relates to more than just Kane's life. The state of Kane's later relationship with Susan becomes clear when we see her putting together endless jigsaw puzzles as she sits, day after day, bored and isolated, in Xanadu's vast rooms. Although Welles always maintained that Kane was not modeled on Hearst, and, more vehemently, that Susan was not modeled on Hearst's mistress, Marion Davies, the fact is that Herman Mankiewicz, a writer of the script for *Citizen Kane*, did spend quite a bit of time at San Simeon with Marion Davies and would have known of her passion for jigsaw puzzles. The references to jigsaw puzzles supply yet more evidence for the connection between Hearst's real life and Kane's fictitious life.

CASABLANCA

(1943)

CONTEXT

The director of *Casablanca*, Michael Curtiz, was born in Budapest, Hungary, in the late 1800s. He began making films there in 1912, but left Hungary in 1919 because of political unrest. After leaving Hungary, he became a prolific filmmaker in Europe, primarily in Austria, and in 1926 the head of Warner Brothers' Burbank, California studio, Jack Warner, asked him to come to Hollywood. Over the course of his career, Curtiz made almost one hundred films for Warner Brothers, including musicals, detective stories, and horror films. Curtiz never mastered the English language, though, and his cast and crew, disgruntled by Curtiz's stubbornness and mean streak, often made fun of his linguistic mistakes, calling them "Curtizisms."

Casablanca was released in 1942, and it was an immediate success, despite Warner Brothers' fears that it would fail. The film was nominated for eight Oscars and won three, including Best Director for Curtiz. Despite the award, Curtiz never really received credit for the film's remarkable achievements. Critics viewed Curtiz as a skilled technician, but they had little praise for his artistic sensibilities. Curtiz's other films never garnered much recognition, and even the success of *Casablanca* was not enough to elevate his reputation. Most of *Casablanca*'s numerous fans wouldn't be able to identify its director by name.

Casablanca has become a legend in large part because of its two leading actors, Humphrey Bogart and Ingrid Bergman, who play Rick Blaine and Ilsa Lund, respectively. Bogart's and Bergman's portrayals of Rick and Ilsa's tortured reunion and separations are as stunning now as they were in 1942. Yet both Bogart and Bergman proved to be difficult participants in *Casablanca*. Bogart acted in four other movies in 1942, and *Casablanca* was far from his favorite. Bergman took the part of Ilsa only because she was initially denied a role she really wanted, the female lead in Hemingway's *For Whom the Bell Tolls*. When she was eventually chosen for that film, she stopped thinking about *Casablanca*, prompting the envious Paul Heinreid, who plays Victor Laszlo, to denigrate her as a careerist "tiger."

Other parts of the making of *Casablanca* are also sobering and pedestrian. The movie was filmed in a period of less than three rushed months, the actors didn't like each other or the director, and the screenwriters reworked the script on the fly. The film was one of many that Warner Brothers made during the summer of 1942, and it was hardly the most expensive or the one they anticipated to become a major hit. In short, the film was just another Hollywood studio production, a chaotic collaboration whose various parts might or might not come together successfully.

Of course, its parts did come together successfully—magnificently—but a few happy accidents are also responsible for the film's tremendous popularity and classic status. For example, composer Max Steiner created an original song to replace "As Time Goes By," a song he hated, but the scenes were not re-filmed because Bergman had already had her hair cut for her role in *For Whom the Bell Tolls*. Likewise, the screenplay for *Casablanca* evolved out of a play entitled *Everybody Comes to Rick's*, which was written in 1941, before the United States entered World War II. The play has a clear anti-Nazi slant, just as *Casablanca* does, but prior to Pearl Harbor, a movie studio in the neutral United States would probably not have made such a political movie. In this respect, the timing was perfect. *Casablanca* is an unusual World War II movie in that it isn't overly propagandistic—in other words, it doesn't go overboard in preaching about the justness of the cause and the certainty of victory. In 1942, the U.S. was suffering in the Pacific, and Allied victory seemed far from certain. *Casablanca* captures this unique moment in America's part in the conflict, when the nation was fully at war but not yet fully indoctrinated in a war ideology. Throughout the film, the war's outcome is uncertain, and Casablanca is a place of anxiety and uncertainty. This uncertainty lends the movie a genuine tension and renders the political activities of Laszlo and Rick all the more heroic.

Just the title of the film is enough to conjure up visions of a distant, longed-for past. Though perhaps not the greatest of the old Hollywood black-and-white films—that honor would probably fall to *Citizen Kane*—*Casablanca* may be the most loved. When someone says, "They don't make movies like they used to," it is a good bet that *Casablanca* is the film they're measuring against the disappointing present. Unlike many other great successes, *Casablanca*'s popularity is well deserved. The film is deeply intelligent and functions both as a political allegory about World War II and a timeless romance. While many critics respect the film for the former achievement, the film's overwhelming popularity rests squarely on the latter, and *Casablanca* remains one of the greatest love stories in movie history.

PLOT OVERVIEW

The film opens with an image of a spinning globe and the sounds of "La Marseillaise," the French national anthem. A voiceover explains the significance of the city of Casablanca, in French-ruled Morocco. During World War II, many people wanted to escape Europe for America, and Lisbon, Portugal, became the most popular port of exit. Getting to Lisbon was not easy. A tortuous refugee path brought people to Casablanca, where they would search for an exit visa for Portugal. As the narrator finishes the description, the camera shows Casablanca's bustling market. Over the radio, the French police announce that two German officers were murdered on a train and that the murderer is headed for Casablanca. Shortly thereafter, an important German officer, Major Strasser, arrives at the Casablanca airport and is greeted by the local French commander, Captain Louis Renault. Strasser asks about the couriers, and Louis says that the murderer, like everyone else, will be at Rick's that evening.

The scene shifts to Rick's Café Americain, a stylish nightclub and casino. Ugarte approaches Rick, the bar's owner, and asks if he will hold some letters of transit for him. Rick observes dryly that the murdered German couriers were carrying letters of transit, but accepts the letters and hides them in the piano played by his house musician, Sam. Signor Ferrari, owner of the rival bar, the Blue Parrot, offers to buy Rick's, but Rick says his bar isn't for sale. Yvonne, Rick's neglected lover, tries to arrange a date for that evening, but Rick dismisses her attempts to pin him down and calls a cab to send her home. Louis tells Rick he's going to make an arrest and warns Rick against protecting the couriers' killer. "I stick my neck out for nobody," Rick responds. Louis also mentions Victor Laszlo, a famous Czech nationalist, will be arriving in Casablanca and warns Rick against trying to assist Laszlo, whose political activities are a threat to Nazi Germany. In the conversation that ensues, we learn that Rick was involved in antifascist wars in the 1930s, supporting the republicans in the Spanish Civil War and the Ethiopians against Italy. Strasser's arrival cuts the conversation short. With the German officer present, Louis decides the time has come to arrest the murderer of the German couriers. Cornered, Ugarte appeals to Rick for help, but Rick does nothing.

After things calm down, Laszlo enters the bar with Ilsa. They have come in search of exit visas. Strasser approaches Laszlo with hostility, and Louis politely requests that Laszlo report to his office the next day. Meanwhile, Ilsa and Sam, who recognize each other, begin to talk. At first Sam refuses Ilsa's request that he play "As Time Goes By," but eventually he relents. The music brings Rick to the piano. "I thought I told you never to play—" he begins, breaking off when he sees Ilsa. Laszlo and Louis join the group and Rick sits down for a drink, violating his rule of never drinking with customers. When the couple leaves, Rick picks up the check, breaking another personal rule.

Later that evening, Rick drinks alone after the bar closes. Sam plays "As Time Goes By" again, and Rick thinks about the past. In a flashback, we see a happier, less haggard Rick in Paris with Ilsa by his side. They drive through the city, ride a boat down the Seine, pop open a bottle of champagne, and dance at a club. Although they are clearly in love, they avoid all questions about each other's pasts. When they hear word that the German army is approaching Paris, Rick knows he will have to leave the city. Rick proposes to Ilsa, who tries her best to hide her anguish, saying she doesn't plan that far in advance. Rick isn't worried, however. He thinks they'll leave together the next day for Marseille. At the train station the next day, Rick waits in the pouring rain, but Ilsa is nowhere to be found. Sam arrives and shows Rick a note. The note is from Ilsa and says that she can never see him again.

At this point, the flashback ends, and the scene shifts back to Casablanca. Ilsa enters the bar. She wants to explain what happened in Paris, but Rick is drunk and angry, and Ilsa leaves.

The next day, Ilsa and Laszlo go to Louis's office, where Strasser tells Laszlo he will never escape Casablanca alive. The couple then goes to the Blue Parrot to visit Signor Ferrari and arrive just as Rick is leaving. As Laszlo talks with Ferrari, Ilsa tells Rick that Laszlo is her husband and has been for years, even when she and Rick were together in Paris. Ferrari says he can obtain a visa for Ilsa but not for Laszlo. The couple decides not to split up. Ferrari suggests they speak to Rick, whom he suspects is holding Ugarte's stolen letters of transit.

That evening at Rick's, a young Bulgarian woman, Mrs. Brandel, approaches Rick to ask if Louis is "trustworthy." Louis, as Rick knows, has a habit of offering female refugees exit visas in exchange for sex. Rick says Louis's word is good, but, not wanting to let Mrs.

Brandel's new marriage be harmed, he arranges for her husband to win big at the roulette table so they can buy a visa on their own. Later, Laszlo asks to speak to Rick. He offers to buy the letters of transit, but Rick says he'll never sell them. When Laszlo asks why, Rick replies, "Ask your wife."

German soldiers have gathered around Sam's piano and are singing the German national anthem. Laszlo tells the band to play "La Marseillaise," the French national anthem, and leads the patrons of the bar in a stirring rendition of the song, which drowns out the Germans. Strasser is furious and demands that Louis shut down Rick's. Louis closes Rick's on the pretext that gambling takes place there, even as he accepts his evening's winnings.

Back at their hotel, Laszlo asks Ilsa if there is anything she wants to tell him about Paris, and she replies "No." Husband and wife reaffirm their love for each other. As Victor leaves for a meeting of the underground resistance, Ilsa leaves too and surprises Rick by showing up in his apartment. She pleads with him for the letters of transit, urging him to put aside his personal feelings for something more important. When Rick still refuses, she pulls a gun on him. Rick dares her to shoot, but Ilsa cannot. Instead, she breaks down in tears and claims she still loves Rick. They embrace.

Later, Ilsa explains what happened in Paris. After she married Laszlo, he had to return to Prague, where he was arrested and put in a concentration camp. Months later, she heard he was killed in an escape attempt. She met Rick shortly thereafter. Ilsa learned Laszlo was still alive just when she and Rick were about to leave Paris together. Laszlo needed her, and she decided to stay with him. She didn't tell Rick because she knew he wouldn't leave Paris if he found out, and then the Gestapo would arrest him. Her story finished, Ilsa says she'll never be able to leave Rick a second time, but she begs that he help Laszlo escape. As for whether she will go with Laszlo or stay with Rick, she says she doesn't know what's right anymore and tells Rick, "You have to think for both of us."

Later that evening, Laszlo claims to know that Rick loves Ilsa and asks for the letters of transit for her sake. Just then the German soldiers burst into Rick's and arrest Laszlo. The next day, Rick pleads with Louis to release Laszlo, saying that Laszlo can be arrested on a more serious charge, possession of the stolen letters of transit. Rick also tells Louis that he plans to use the letters to escape with Ilsa. That afternoon, Rick sells his club to Ferrari. That evening, back at Rick's, as he hands the letters to Laszlo, Louis emerges from the shadows to make the arrest. Just as suddenly, Rick pulls out a gun and points it at Louis. He orders Louis to call the airport to make sure that evening's flight to Lisbon will take off as planned. Louis pretends to call the airport, but actually calls Strasser.

At the airport, Rick makes Louis fill in the letters of transit for Mr. and Mrs. Victor Laszlo. Ilsa objects, but Rick says he did the thinking for both of them and decided that for Laszlo to continue doing his work, he needs Ilsa by his side. Rick tells Laszlo that Ilsa visited him last night and pretended to still love him to get the letters. He knew she was lying, Rick says, because it was over a long time ago. As Rick is talking, Ilsa sobs in the background.

After goodbyes, the Laszlos board the plane. Just then Strasser arrives. He calls the radio tower to prevent the plane's taking off, but Rick shoots him, and the plane leaves. The French police arrive, and Louis, who has seen everything, orders, "Round up the usual suspects." As the cops drive off, Louis congratulates Rick on becoming a patriot and then becomes a patriot himself, symbolized by his throwing out a bottle of Vichy water (water produced in the unoccupied region of France that persecuted Jews and tried to win Nazi favor). Rick and Louis walk along the runway together. Louis says he can arrange for Rick to escape to Brazzaville, another French colony in Africa, and then announces he will go, too. The movie ends with Rick saying the famous final line, "Louis, I think this is the beginning of a beautiful friendship." "La Marseillaise" plays in the background.

Character List

Richard "Rick" Blaine—Played by Humphrey Bogart The owner of Rick's Café Americain and the film's protagonist. When we first meet Rick, he is a jaded bar owner in Casablanca who wears a dour expression as he drinks and plays chess alone. He constantly proclaims his freedom from all bonds, be they political or personal. After Ilsa enters the picture, he undergoes a considerable change. In a flashback, we see Rick in Paris. He is in love with Ilsa and visibly happy, and he is devastated when she doesn't show up at the train station. Rick never turns back into the lighthearted lover he was in Paris, but he does overcome his cynicism and apathy to become a self-sacrificing idealist, committed to helping the Allied cause in World War II.

Ilsa Lund—Played by Ingrid Bergman A Norwegian beauty who is Victor Laszlo's wife and Rick's former lover. A devoted wife, Ilsa refuses an exit visa when Laszlo is unable to obtain one as well, saying she prefers to wait with him and leave Casablanca together. In Paris, Ilsa had fallen in love with Rick, because at the time she had believed Laszlo was dead. When she learned her husband was still alive, she sent a note to Rick at the train station, saying she could never see him again. Despite her obvious commitment to her husband and her confessions of love to Rick both in Paris and later in Casablanca, she rarely displays much passion. Ultimately, the letter may be the best insight into her personality. She can be so cold and distant that reading her true thoughts or feelings can be almost impossible.

Victor Laszlo—Played by Paul Henreid A Czech nationalist writer and anti-Nazi partisan. Laszlo is a committed political leader who sees defeating the Nazis as his *raison d'être*. He endured time in a concentration camp, but he remains enthusiastic, courageous, and outspoken. Victor is a devoted husband to Ilsa and is willing to sacrifice himself to ensure her safety.

Captain Louis Renault—Played by Claude Rains Vichy France's prefect of police in Casablanca. If Laszlo represents pure political idealism, Louis represents the very opposite—unscrupulous cynicism. Louis, like the Vichy government he serves and represents, has given up caring about right and wrong, and his only loyalty is to the winning side. (The Vichy government cooperated with the Germans during World War II.) Louis is a hypocrite, castigating Rick for allowing gambling in his bar just as he pockets his earnings for the evening. Despite his self-serving behavior and seeming amorality, Louis is always a good friend to Rick and shows signs of being a decent person at heart. At the end of the movie, this seed of decency blooms into genuine political action, as he refuses to arrest Rick and decides to join his friend in exile from Casablanca. Louis approaches everything with wit, and many of the film's best lines are his.

Major Heinrich Strasser—Played by Conrad Veidt A Nazi commander sent to Casablanca to capture Laszlo. Strasser is a stereotypical Nazi villain, ruthlessly cruel and robotically efficient. From the moment of his arrival in Casablanca, he is all business, immediately inquiring about the murderers of the German couriers. He is willing to resort to cruelty in punishing his enemies and is determined to prevent Laszlo from leaving Casablanca at all costs. Unlike Nazis depicted in other films, Strasser is never overtly sadistic. Despite his unpleasant demeanor, he is always civil and polite.

Signor Ferrari—Played by Sydney Greenstreet The owner of the Blue Parrot. Like Rick's Café Americain, the Blue Parrot is a Casablanca bar, though it is noticeably less popular. At the beginning of the film, Ferrari offers to buy Rick's Café and the services of the pianist Sam. Rick initially refuses both offers, but when he decides to leave Casablanca, he does sell out to Ferrari. In addition to running the Blue Parrot, Ferrari is involved in the Casablanca black market and sells, among other things, exit visas. Although Ferrari is mostly concerned with making money, he is at heart a good person, which he demonstrates when he suggests that Laszlo approach Rick about the letters of transit.

Ugarte—Played by Peter Lorre   A member of Casablanca's criminal underworld. Ugarte's business is selling letters of transit to refugees. He may be helping them escape to Lisbon, but his aim is profit, not charity. Ugarte murders the German couriers to obtain the valuable letters of transit, which he plans to sell to Laszlo for a considerable fee. He is arrested before he can complete the sale.

Yvonne—Played by Madeleine LeBeau   A French woman who hangs out at Rick's. At the beginning of the movie, Yvonne is Rick's neglected, miserable lover. After being ignored by Rick one night, she shows up at the bar with a German soldier the very next evening. Her one redeeming moment comes during the singing of "La Marseillaise," when she shows herself to be a loyal patriot.

Sam—Played by Dooley Wilson   The pianist at Rick's Café. Sam is a warm-hearted, agreeable musician and a fiercely loyal friend to Rick. In Casablanca, he is Rick's only link to the past, since the two were together in Paris as well. When Rick drinks himself into a depressive stupor, he generally wants to be alone, but he doesn't seem to mind Sam's presence. At times, Sam seems like Rick's older brother or guardian. He looks out for Rick by trying to deny Ilsa's request that he play "As Time Goes By," and he cautions Rick about drinking too much. While Sam is a vivid presence in the scenes in which he is featured, his character is never fully developed.

Annina Brandel—Played by Joy Page   A young Bulgarian newlywed who desperately wants to escape to America. Mrs. Brandel comes to Rick to ask about Louis's reliability. Louis has offered to give her and her husband exit visas to leave Casablanca in exchange for sexual favors, and she fears that this is their only option. Her plight brings out the idealist in Rick, who arranges for Mr. Brandel to win big at the roulette table, scoring enough money to purchase the exit visas. In this way, Rick allows the Brandels to leave Casablanca with their marriage uncorrupted.

Jan Brandel—Played by Helmut Dantine Annina's husband, who wants to escape to America with his wife. Unaware that Louis has made Annina a proposal, Mr. Brandel believes that the only hope of escaping Casablanca is by winning big at the roulette table. Because of Rick's generosity, this is exactly what happens.

Berger—Played by John Qualen A Norwegian member of the Casablanca underground.

Carl—Played by S. Z. Sakall A waiter at Rick's Café. Carl is an amiable staff member who also participates in the Casablanca anti-Nazi underground. He sees through Rick's cynicism and considers him a decent, generous man.

Sacha—Played by Leonid Kinskey The bartender at Rick's Café. Sacha is more playful, nosy, and cynical than Carl, but like his coworker, he is a member of the underground and can see Rick's essential generosity and goodness.

Pickpocket—Played by Curt Bois A Casablanca street criminal. The pickpocket reveals the seedy, street-hustling, outlaw nature of Casablanca. He warns people to be careful and alert, then leaves with their wallets.

Singer—Played by Corinna Mura A guitarist and singer at Rick's. The singer's performances entertain customers, and they also give them cover to make black market purchases and obtain illegal exit visas. Laszlo and Berger are able to discuss such a sale during her performance.

Abdul—Played by Dan Seymour The doorman at Rick's Café.

Italian Officer Tonelli—Played by Charles La Torre An officer who strives unsuccessfully to catch Major Strasser's attention. Tonelli comes across as hapless and buffoonish.

Emile—Played by Marcel Dalio The croupier (the person who runs the gambling table) at Rick's Café. Emile watches Rick carefully for clues about who should and should not win at the table. When Rick arranges for Mr. Brandel to win at roulette, he does so by giving Emile a subtle signal.

CASABLANCA

Analysis of Major Characters

Rick Blaine

Rick Blaine, the cynical owner of Rick's Café Americain, often appears too jaded to be impressed or moved by anyone. He refuses to accept drinks from customers, treats his lover Yvonne without affection or respect, and seems not to care that a war is being waged around him or that desperate refugees have flocked to Casablanca. He makes a point of broadcasting his aloofness, stating on several occasions, "I stick my neck out for nobody." However, another Rick lurks behind his façade of cynicism. Near the beginning of the film, he refuses entry to the bar's private back room to a member of the Deutsche Bank, even though other, less prominent people are allowed in—a clue that despite his proclaimed apathy, his political sympathies lie with the Allies. He also criticizes the criminal Ugarte for charging refugees too much for exit visas. Shortly thereafter, Louis calls him a sentimentalist, and we learn that before coming to Casablanca, Rick was involved in political causes, supporting losing sides against fascist aggressors in Spain and Ethiopia. From the opening scene, Rick shows himself to be a mysterious and complicated man—terse, solitary, and self-involved, but also generous, discriminating, and perhaps a political partisan.

When Ilsa arrives in Casablanca, we start to understand some of Rick's mysterious past. In a flashback to his time in Paris, we see a younger, happier, lighter Rick in love with Ilsa. As though to emphasize how different he is in Paris, he is called Richard, not Rick, in all the flashback scenes. Though Rick and Ilsa plan to leave Paris together after the Nazis' arrival, Ilsa stands Rick up at the train station, and this painful separation helps explain how the optimistic Richard became the aloof, cynical Rick we see at the beginning of the film. Rick is not coldhearted, but he suffers from heartbreak. When Ilsa appears at the bar, Rick initially reacts angrily and refuses to give her and Laszlo the letters of transit. By the end of the film, he acts heroically, sacrificing both a possible future with Ilsa and his comfortable life in Casablanca so that Laszlo can escape with Ilsa and continue his important political work. In effect, three Ricks appear in the movie. In Paris, he is a romantic innocent; in Casablanca, a jaded, hard-hearted capitalist; and by the end of the film, a committed, self-sacrificing idealist. Ultimately, Rick's story remains incomplete. A dark mystery from Rick's past prevents him from returning to his native America, and though we learn much about him, we never learn why he can't go home.

ILSA LUND

Ilsa is fiercely loyal to her husband, Laszlo, and the political cause—resistance to the Nazis—he represents, but the truth of her sentiments is constantly suspect. She claims to love Laszlo, but she also claims to be in love with Rick, both in Paris and in Casablanca. We might suspect that Rick is her great passion and that only circumstance and political necessity prevent their union, but Ilsa never makes the distinction clear. She has good reason to tell Rick she loves him in Casablanca, since she needs the letters of transit he holds. Her motives are always shadowy because she always has possible, logical ulterior motives, and she maintains a cold detachment that prevents her from being understood. The letter she sent to Rick in Paris so many years ago, saying she could never see him again, is evidence of her ability to shield her true feelings from those who love her the most.

Ilsa clearly has suffered from the whims of fortune more than any other character in *Casablanca*. First, her husband is arrested and rumored to be dead. When he reappears, she must run with him throughout Europe with the Nazis always on their heels. She meets Rick and falls in love, only to have to leave him, then meets him and perhaps falls in love with him again, only to leave him once more. No matter whom she truly loves, she has not had an easy life, and her fate is the most tragic in the film. At the airport we can see that for Ilsa, the possibility of a happy ending does not exist. Ilsa herself may not even know what her own happiness would entail.

VICTOR LASZLO

Of the major characters in *Casablanca*, Laszlo is the least complex. He is the pure embodiment of the noble hero, as a good as any man can be. Laszlo is handsome, confident, idealistic, outspoken, unwavering, and impassioned. He is married to the beautiful Ilsa, and he loves his wife so much that when he learns about Ilsa and Rick, he claims to understand. He is willing to sacrifice himself so that Ilsa can escape Casablanca safely. Yet Laszlo's true love is politics. The desire to defeat the Nazis is the prime motivation for all his actions. Despite the difficulties of his political struggle, he considers himself privileged to struggle through it. Laszlo is a symbol of the resistance. He represents unwavering commitment, a quality that makes him as valuable to the Allies as he is dangerous to the Nazis.

Captain Louis Renault

Like Rick, Louis undergoes a transformation from cynicism to idealism, though in his case this change is less dramatic and more humorous. *Casablanca* is an intense film, and Louis supplies some levity, including most of the comic lines. Like the Vichy government he represents, which courted the Nazis for favors and better treatment, Louis is not a man of strong conviction, but a friend to whoever is in power at the time. He works with Strasser, but never with Strasser's sense of urgency or conviction. What he does for Strasser is meant to convey a veneer of loyalty. He arrests Ugarte, closes Rick's bar, and arrests Laszlo simply to impress his German superior. Louis himself seems not to care one way or the other. Louis demonstrates his sporting ambivalence about Laszlo's fate when he bets with Rick about whether or not Laszlo will escape Casablanca.

For a while, Louis seems to care about nothing and no one but himself. A hedonist, he takes advantage of pretty female refugees and regularly receives fixed winnings from Rick's casino. The gambling is illegal, but until Strasser pressures him to close the casino, Louis looks the other way. But Louis's obvious affection for Rick belies his seeming self-involvement. Although he tells Rick not to count on his friendship, he can't hide his feelings for his friend. He expresses this fondness early in the film when he says that if he were a woman, he would be in love with Rick. Later he commends Rick for being the only one in Casablanca with "less scruples than I." At the end of the film, the men cement their friendship when both commit themselves to the Allied cause. Rick commits by allowing Ilsa and Laszlo to escape Casablanca and by killing Strasser, while Louis does it by disavowing his relationship with the collaborationist Vichy government and deciding to escape Casablanca with Rick. Ever the follower, Louis copies Rick when he, too, has become a self-sacrificing idealist.

THEMES, MOTIFS, AND SYMBOLS

THEMES

THE DIFFICULTY OF NEUTRALITY

In love and in war, neutrality is difficult for Rick, Ilsa, and Louis to maintain. Rick makes a point of not being involved in politics. He refuses to discuss the war, shuts up Carl's attempts to tell him about meetings of the underground, and does everything in his power to present himself as nonpartisan. Later on, though, just as the United States abandoned neutrality in December 1941, Rick shifts from neutrality to commitment. His sympathy for the Allies has always been evident in small acts, such as his refusal to allow the Deutsche Bank employee entry into the back room of his casino, but his partisanship grows more overt as the film proceeds. Louis undergoes a similar transformation, and by the end of the film, neutrality seems an untenable position. Rick's Café, as well as Casablanca itself, is an oasis in the desert, a paradise far removed from the troubles of the world. Yet the underground and black market activities that take place at Rick's belie these qualities. The battle of German and French anthems that erupts in the bar shows that Rick's actually teems with political passion.

When Ilsa visits Rick in his apartment and confesses that she still loves him, she does her best to be neutral in the undeclared war between the two men who love her. For as long as she can, she tries to deny the dilemma she faces. When she finally acknowledges the dilemma and realizes she has to decide between Rick and Laszlo, she leaves the choice in Rick's hands. No clean, painless resolution is possible, and a choice must be made. In war as in love, *Casablanca* suggests, neutrality is unsustainable.

THE IMPOSSIBILITY OF ESCAPING THE PAST

The first words of "As Time Go By" announce, "You must remember this," and in *Casablanca*, Rick, Ilsa, and Louis cannot escape the past and their memories. Even when characters try to flee from the past, and many do, the past catches up with them. On two occasions, Ilsa believes she has lost men in her life, only to have them reappear at the most inconvenient times. In Casablanca, Rick has created a lifestyle for himself that he believes will allow him to forget his painful memories, but the war and the flock of refugees hoping to escape to America remind him of an event or events from his mysterious life that prevent his return home. Likewise, Ilsa's arrival in Casablanca reminds Rick of their painful love story, the memory of which he has been trying to erase. The only character who suggests that the past can be escaped is Louis, who seems able to switch alliances breezily. Yet even Louis eventually acknowledges that his decisions have consequences. He recognizes that he must flee Casablanca because there is no escaping the way he helped Rick. He might want to ignore the past, but in this case he cannot.

THE POWER OF LADY LUCK

Luck figures prominently in *Casablanca*, especially in Rick's Café. One of the bar's most popular activities is gambling, and one of Sam's most popular songs is "Knock on Wood." Mr. and Mrs. Brandel, the young Bulgarian couple, demonstrate how luck functions in the movie. "How is lady luck treating you?" Louis asks Mrs. Brandel as Mr. Brandel gambles at the roulette table. Mr. Brandel is trying to win enough money to buy two exit visas. For Louis, luck is the force that brings a beautiful woman like Mrs. Brandel to him and allows him to try to take advantage of her desperate situation. For him, luck is a lady, a sexualized concept that implies both seduction and powerlessness. Rick has a different view of luck, and he intervenes to help the unlucky Brandels, rigging the roulette game so the couple hits the jackpot twice, "miraculously" gaining the amount they need. When Mrs. Brandel approaches Rick to thank him for his generous deed, he dismisses her thanks by saying her husband is "just a lucky guy." This line has a double meaning. The literal meaning is that Brandel is just a lucky guy at the roulette table, which obviously isn't true. The metaphorical, and true, meaning is that he is lucky to have such a courageous, loving wife.

Particular people in *Casablanca* can bring both good and bad luck to each other. When Ilsa and Sam first speak, Sam tells Ilsa she should stay away from Rick because she's "bad luck" to him. But this statement isn't entirely true. Ilsa broke Rick's heart so tremendously that over a year later he still hasn't recovered, but, in this case, heartbreak has nothing to do with luck. "Luck" is simply a word used to cover up a more painful truth. Luck in *Casablanca* is also not entirely free of human influence. Ugarte is arrested while gambling, which suggests that he is unlucky to have been caught. The truth is that his own actions of murdering and stealing, rather than bad fortune, are the cause of his arrest.

MOTIFS

EXILE AND TRAVEL

The city of Casablanca is filled with foreigners, most of whom are exiles. Among the characters in the film, only the doorman Abdul is actually Moroccan. Though some characters, such as the colonialist French or the conquering Germans, are not in Casablanca as exiles, the majority are. Rick appears at first to be just another disenchanted American expatriate, but he is actually an exile from America, to which he cannot return, and also from France, where he cannot return as long as the Germans still occupy it. An exile is someone who can never return home. Along with the idea of exile comes the idea of travel. The movie opens with a montage of various means of transport, including ships, trains, cars, and planes, that refugees use on their way to Casablanca. These images of hurried travel contrast with images of leisurely voyage, such as a car ride through Paris and a boat ride down the Seine, both of which Rick and Ilsa share during the Paris flashback. Travel can be both a means, as in the case of the refugee, and an end in itself, as in the case of a tourist, but for the exile, it is never-ending. Unlike both the refugee going to a new home and the tourist soon to return home, the exile is perpetually homeless, traveling forever.

DREAMING OF AMERICA IN AFRICA

Related to the motif of exile is the motif of America, which is where all of Casablanca's refugees hope to go. If Casablanca is the oasis in the desert, America is the promised land on the desert's far side. America offers itself not as a place of temporary exile, but as a new home, even for foreigners. The difference between the refugee and the perpetual exile is determined by the ability to go to America, because America represents the final stop on the refugee path, where exile ends and an actual new life begins. Only Rick cannot go to America. Instead, he must remain in Africa. At the end of the film, he leaves Casablanca, which is on the eastern edge of Africa, for Brazzaville, which lies at the country's heart. Neither desert nor promised land, Brazzaville is pure jungle. If America represents what is known and desired, Brazzaville represents all that is uncertain. For Rick, the journey has just begun.

SPOTLIGHT

The spotlight that shines from a tall tower and lights up the city of Casablanca reminds people that they are always being watched. The spotlight is a constant presence at Rick's, regularly circling past the front doors. The spotlight first swings past the doors immediately after Louis has assured Strasser that the murderer of the German couriers will be found at Rick's, as if to stress the relationship between government authority and the invasive, spying light. The spotlight crosses Laszlo's path as he leaves Rick's with Ilsa, underscoring the fragility of Laszlo's safety and the fact that he is constantly being watched. Later that evening, Ilsa returns to Rick's and opens the front door just as the spotlight passes by, backlighting her brilliantly in the doorframe. This dramatic image is important for several reasons. First, it marks the first time the light actually pierces the front doors and enters Rick's. The image also makes Ilsa look like an angel, and lets us see her as her lovers see her. The use of light here is also a meta-filmic comment about the artificiality of the cinematic lighting. The spotlight reappears as Rick gazes out his window after he and Ilsa kiss in his apartment. Even Rick and Ilsa's romance, the device suggests, is being watched, and the war has completely altered the conditions of their love. This change could partly explain Rick's self-sacrifice at the end of the film. In order for Ilsa to escape the eye of the spotlight, Rick realizes, he must let her escape to America.

SYMBOLS

SAM'S PIANO

Sam's piano is the symbolic heart and soul of Rick's Café. All the guests want to sit beside it, in part because they want to be close to Sam, who is one of the most untainted characters in the film. The piano itself suggests purity, which may be why Louis doesn't even think to look there for the missing letters of transit. The music from the piano functions as an opiate, a drug that allows visitors to forget their worries. All is well at Rick's, at least on the surface, when Sam is playing. Sam's resumed playing after Ugarte's arrest, for instance, signals that everything has returned to normal, while his closing down of the piano when Rick and Ilsa first see each other signals that the club's peaceful innocence has been interrupted by painful memories. When the German soldiers take over the piano to play their national anthem, the bar's patrons rise in revolt and defiantly sing "La Marseillaise." More than the arrest of Ugarte, this singing proves the biggest disturbance in the bar, and Louis is forced to shut the place down.

The piano is also a symbol of Rick's heart. Rick forbids the playing of "As Time Goes By" so he doesn't have to wallow in the painful memory of Ilsa and Paris. Like many of his guests, he prefers to forget his pain. When Ilsa requests the song, Sam claims not to remember it, but at her insistence he goes ahead and plays, initiating the re-acquaintance of the former lovers. Sam awakens the song on the piano, and Rick's heart wakes painfully as well. For a while he suffers tremendously, but eventually he seems to come to grips with his aching heart and painful past and to reemerge a better person. Rick will leave Casablanca, but Sam and his piano will stay behind. Having regained his real heart, Rick is free to abandon the piano.

LASZLO

Laszlo is both a character and a symbol in *Casablanca*. His symbolic elements are rooted in his upstanding, moral personality. Before Laszlo arrives in Casablanca, Rick stirs from apathy at the mention of his name. Laszlo is a symbol of resistance to the Nazis, and his personal conflict of whether or not he can escape Casablanca represents a much larger struggle for power and control. The Nazis officially control the city, but the underground resistance has the support of the majority of the people. The balance of power teeters precariously between the two groups. Laszlo's ability to escape Casablanca will be a sign as to which group may ultimately prevail. That Laszlo was able to escape from a concentration camp and then make his way to Casablanca indicates that the Nazi control over the European mainland is not absolute. If Laszlo can find his way to America, his escape will be a symbol of the power of resistance to Nazi rule. What happens to Laszlo himself is important, but the implications of his fate make up *Casablanca*'s broader themes.

THE PLANE TO LISBON AND THE LETTERS OF TRANSIT

The plane to Lisbon is the best way to leave Casablanca, and it represents the possibility of escape from war-torn Europe and the first, most difficult step of the journey to America and freedom. The letters of transit are the golden tickets out, the exit visas that cannot be refused. Throughout the movie these letters are what everyone wants, and whoever controls or holds the letters has tremendous power. As *Casablanca* proceeds, the power shifts hands. At first, the civic authority of Casablanca, in the person of Louis, controls the plane's flights, and Rick, who possesses the letters, wields this power and has control of people's fates. Later, Rick transfers the letters to Ilsa and Laszlo, allowing them to depart on the plane. As a result of this exchange, the escaping refugees gain a powerful status as political symbols, while Louis and Rick's own power in Casablanca is weakened. The two self-sacrificing heroes have no choice but to leave the city and start over elsewhere.

FILM ANALYSIS

"CASABLANCA": A CLASSIC HOLLYWOOD FILM WITH AN UN-CLASSIC ENDING

Along with *Gone with the Wind* and *Citizen Kane*, *Casablanca* is probably the greatest example of the classic Hollywood film. Shot entirely on Hollywood sets, using studio actors, directors, and writers, *Casablanca* perfectly displays the art of collaborative studio production, rather than the vision of a single, independent auteur. With its black-and-white earnestness, hardboiled male lead, and beautiful, demure heroine, it is a paradigmatic film from Hollywood's golden age. The story itself is straightforward, but the film is hardly simplistic, partly because of its unresolvable central conflict and partly because it functions as both a realistic movie and a political allegory. The film's lasting enchantment is due to its dramatic conclusion.

Casablanca may be a classic Hollywood film, but it lacks a classic Hollywood ending, in which everyone rides happily into the sunset. For *Casablanca* to fit this outline, Ilsa would have to declare her love for either Laszlo or Rick and leave with her choice, and the rejected male would let her go without a struggle because his love was so great that above all else he wished for her happiness. *Casablanca*'s ending resembles the classic ending, but it has been twisted and complicated.

In the standard Hollywood film, no conflict would arise between the political and the personal. Love and political idealism would go hand in hand, and no painful choices would be necessary. The conclusion of *Casablanca* involves much more than the triumph of the idealistic values of sacrifice and restraint, and *Casablanca* is much more than pro-Allied propaganda. If the film concluded with the simple message that victory requires sacrifice, then the ending would be a happy one. Rick's decision to let Ilsa leave with Laszlo would privilege long-term concerns over short-term ones. In exchange for love today, victory and freedom will prevail in the future. Laszlo may think of his actions similarly. He will sacrifice himself today by suffering imprisonment in concentration camps and constantly running, in exchange for a better future. Such calculations are consistent with the classic Hollywood happy ending, and, indeed, Laszlo does get the girl in the end, just as we might expect.

For Rick and Ilsa, however, the conclusion is neither as happy nor as simple. Not only do the lovers have to split up a second time, but neither truly knows what the other is thinking. Laszlo undoubtedly loves Ilsa, but Rick's and Ilsa's feelings aren't so clear. The film demonstrates the moral value of sacrifice and the triumph of the political over personal desire, but the final scene is full of ambiguity. Ilsa's true preference for Rick or Laszlo remains a mystery. She suggests that her preference is for Rick when she visits him in his apartment to ask for the letters of transit, but her potential ulterior motive, to do what it takes to get the letters so her true love, Laszlo, can flee to safety, adds an element of doubt to what she says and does. In the final scene at the airport, Ilsa may fail to declare her love for Rick because Laszlo is never far from earshot, but she may also refrain from declaring her love because she doesn't want to lie again. She leaves with Laszlo in the end, but in a way, Rick has forced this decision on her, and which of them she truly loves remains a mystery.

Rick's feelings are almost equally ambiguous. He seems to truly love Ilsa, and his final gesture, when he not only lets Laszlo and Ilsa leave together but tries to patch things up between them by telling Laszlo about Ilsa's visit the previous evening, seems a courageous act of self-sacrifice. Yet we can't know with any certainty that Rick hasn't gotten over Ilsa. Perhaps he realized he couldn't compete against the war hero Laszlo and gave up on her, or perhaps all he really needed from Ilsa before he could move on was to hear her say she still loved him. Rick's final gesture could also be in part an act of revenge, payback for Ilsa's having abandoned him. Perhaps Rick wants to send her into a life of loneliness and solitary whiskey drinking, the same life that he himself has been leading ever since being abandoned at the Paris train station a year earlier.

Rick finds some consolation in his friendship with Louis. Rick is not substituting one relationship with another here—he is substituting one *type* of relationship with another. Ilsa and Rick's relationship is one based in romantic love, while Rick and Louis's relationship has been and still is one of expediency and political alliance, even if they have now added an element of genuine personal affection. Rick's substitution of Louis for Ilsa at the end of the film underscores the idea in *Casablanca* that politics trump romantic love, and the public is of greater significance than the personal.

We can only speculate on Rick's and Ilsa's true feelings and motives, and the point is that the ending remains a mystery. It is neither happy nor sad, but both at once, and far from the kind of ending one might expect from a typical 1940s Hollywood film.

ACTING

Though the ambiguous conclusion is part of what makes *Casablanca* such a remarkable film, not all of the ambiguity was intentional. During the filming, director Michael Curtiz and the writers could not agree on an ending. As Ingrid Bergman acted the part of Ilsa, she repeatedly asked for a clarification as to which man she truly loved, but no one gave her a straight answer. Bergman made the best of this frustrating situation by making this uncertainty fundamental to Ilsa's character. Ilsa is reunited twice with old lovers at the most inopportune times, and she has become shut off from her own feelings. The real choice at the conclusion is hers, but she elects to place it in Rick's hands. When she tells Rick to think for both of them, she absolves herself of having to take responsibility for her fate. Rather than take action, for which she would have to accept responsibility, she abandons herself to the whims of fortune. If Rick chooses wrongly, the fault will be his, not hers.

Bergman portrays Ilsa as stony-faced and almost cold, but Ilsa suffers most of all the principal characters. Although Ilsa gets a chance at both love and freedom in the end, she has not chosen her own fate. Her inability to steer her destiny is the result of her choice to let Rick decide, and in this decision, we see in her a dark, tragic fatalism. The romance of *Casablanca* is undeniable. The male characters are able to love completely and convincingly without appearing maudlin or sappy. Throughout the film Laszlo is an unapologetic optimist, and by the conclusion, Rick and Louis can envision brighter days ahead. Ilsa reveals herself to be a character of a different sort. Only in the final scenes do we even begin to grasp the full extent of her tremendous despair. Her dark fatalism makes *Casablanca* much more than a romantic tale set during a time when happy endings were not possible, and the fact that Bergman actually had to struggle to figure out who should be the object of Ilsa's true devotion renders Ilsa's despair and indecision all the more realistic and affective.

SOUNDTRACK

Casablanca is a tale of two songs. The first song, "La Marseillaise," is the French national anthem, written during the era of the French Revolution about fighting for freedom from political repression. In *Casablanca*, it represents a free France, and, by extension, the Allied side in World War II. The song plays many times throughout *Casablanca*, most significantly when almost all the patrons at Rick's join in a stirring rendition intended to overwhelm the sound of the Nazi anthem that a few German soldiers are singing. In this dramatic scene, World War II shifts from geopolitical contest to ideological and cultural battle. The war is not only between the Allies and the Axis, but also between the ideals of the French Revolution, *liberté*, *egalité*, *fraternité* (liberty, equality, brotherhood), and the rights of man, and the darker obsessions of the Nazis, including evil, tyranny, and death. In this scene, the patrons of Rick's show themselves to be fiercely pro-Allies. Even the cynically promiscuous Yvonne, who just that evening has shown up with a new German beau, sings with passion and conviction.

"La Marseillaise" may win an easy battle with the Nazi anthem, but it has a harder time defeating the other song that is central to *Casablanca*, "As Time Goes By." In World War II, the conflict is between the Axis and Allies, while in *Casablanca*, the struggle is between the public and private. Whenever "La Marseillaise" plays, including as a voiceover describing the plight of political refugees during World War II in the movie's opening and when Louis and Rick walk down the empty runway together with their friendship linked by a new political bond, *Casablanca* is a film about politics and war. When "As Time Goes By" plays, the film becomes the love story of Ilsa and Rick. Unlike "La Marseillaise," whose meaning never changes, "As Time Goes By" has many roles in the film, each with a different slant. In Paris, "As Time Goes By" was Rick and Ilsa's song, a symbol of their love. In Casablanca, it is a forbidden song that Rick fears will remind him of Ilsa, but which by its absence has come to represent her. When Ilsa does arrive in Casablanca, the song takes on a third meaning. Sam plays the song at both Ilsa's and Rick's request, and it suggests both halves of their relationship: the Parisian idyll and the train station betrayal, as well as the possibility of the love story beginning anew in Casablanca.

"La Marseillaise" isn't played in Rick's Café until after Sam plays "As Time Goes By," and this ordering is significant because we can see that Rick's political apathy relates to his disenchantment with all forms of commitment, both political and personal. Only after Ilsa reawakens his heart by coming to the bar can Rick become politically engaged again. At the same time, the fact that *Casablanca* begins and ends with "La Marseillaise" suggests that the political is the foundation upon which all things personal happen, including Rick and Ilsa's love story. The actual words of "As Time Goes By" argue that the one timeless truth is love, but in *Casablanca*, the political ultimately triumphs. Ilsa's return to Rick's life lasts only a few days. When she leaves Casablanca, she leaves Rick forever, but the war is still far from over for them both.

POLITICAL ALLEGORY

Casablanca is an exploration of the universal themes of love and sacrifice, but when the film was released in 1942, audiences viewed it as a political allegory about World War II. The film is set in December 1941, the month in which the Japanese attacked Pearl Harbor. That attack changed the course of American history, awakening the nation from political neutrality and thrusting it into the midst of World War II. *Casablanca* tells the story of a similar, though much smaller, awakening. At the beginning of the film, Rick is a cynical bar owner in the Moroccan city of Casablanca who drinks only by himself and doesn't care about politics. By the end of the film, he has become a self-sacrificing idealist, committed to the anti-Nazi war effort. The event that prompts this change in Rick is the appearance of Ilsa, his old flame, in Casablanca. Ilsa's arrival is unexpected and devastating, and it hits Rick just as hard as the Japanese sneak attack on Pearl Harbor hit America. Once Rick overcomes the initial pain, his moral sense is reignited. He doesn't get to live happily ever after with Ilsa, but he accepts the necessity of his sacrifice and the heartbreak that accompanies it. If Ilsa hadn't reappeared in his life, Rick would still be stuck in a life of bitterness in Casablanca. Instead, he is reawakened to the world and to himself.

The film also tells the story of another transformation, that of the local French commander of Casablanca, Captain Louis Renault. Louis begins the film as a pro-Vichy Nazi-appeaser but winds up a committed partisan of free France. American Rick and European Louis look out for each other's interests throughout the film, but only at the end does their relationship become anything more than the self-serving alliance of two cynics. "Louis, I think this is the beginning of a beautiful friendship," Rick says in the film's last line, thereby cementing not only their friendship, but also the maturing anti-Nazi coalition their friendship symbolizes. In the film's political allegory, Rick and Louis's relationship suggests the U.S.'s relationship to its allies in World War II.

While Rick and Louis find their political identity only at the end of the film, a number of other characters know where they stand from the beginning. In large part, this certainty has to do with their nationality. Victor Laszlo, the famous anti-Nazi writer, is Czech, and since Nazi Germany's first expansionist move was against Czechoslovakia, the Czechs knew of Nazi evil before anyone else. Similarly, all of the characters who support Casablanca's anti-Nazi underground are from nations that resisted German rule. They include the Norwegians Berger and Ilsa and the Russian bartender Sacha. On the other hand, many of the film's unseemly characters, such as the criminal Ugarte, the black market schemer Signor Ferrari, and the bumbling officer Tonelli, are Italian, and Italy was an ally of Germany during the war. While the Italians may not be worthy of admiration, none are as cruel and ruthless as Major Strasser, the film's archetypal Nazi villain.

IMPORTANT QUOTATIONS EXPLAINED

1. "You must remember this
    A kiss is just a kiss, a sigh is just a sigh.
    The fundamental things apply
    As time goes by.

    "And when two lovers woo
    They still say, 'I love you.'
    On that you can rely
    No matter what the future brings
    As time goes by.

    "Moonlight and love songs
    Never out of date.
    Hearts full of passion
    Jealousy and hate.
    Woman needs man
    And man must have his mate
    That no one can deny.

    "It's still the same old story
    A fight for love and glory
    A case of do or die.
    The world will always welcome lovers
    As time goes by."

The tune of "As Time Goes By" is one of *Casablanca*'s most important themes, but the words are sung only on two occasions. Sam sings the first two verses at Ilsa's request on the night of her arrival with Laszlo in Casablanca. Rick, who has forbidden the song in his bar, reacts angrily, but he catches sight of Ilsa just as he begins to reprimand Sam. The song becomes the occasion of their re-acquaintance. Later, Sam sings the last two verses during Rick's Paris flashback. As the song plays, Ilsa and Rick stand beside the piano and Rick fills glasses with champagne. Ilsa is noticeably distracted, and presumably she has already learned that Laszlo is still alive.

Rick casts a glance at Ilsa that suggests he knows something is bothering her, but he doesn't mention it in the dialogue that follows. In this case, the song marks a missed opportunity to tell the truth and prevent years of resentment.

The actual lyrics of "As Time Goes By" are also significant, since the message of the song suggests that the world is a complicated place full of continuous change, but that one thing remains constant: timeless, enduring romantic love. *Casablanca* does not accept these words at face value but puts them to the test. The passing of time is one of the film's main themes, and the question of whether love endures is one of its central questions. Before Ilsa shows up in Casablanca, Rick seems to have given up on the possibility of a pure, timeless love. Ilsa's confession of love in his apartment complicates the picture, but at the movie's finale, time, not love, triumphs. Time and history, in the form of the war, dominate the present and steer the future. If the love between Rick and Ilsa does survive, it will do so only as memory. The significance of the words of "As Time Goes By," therefore, is that they are ultimately false. The future can and does bring situations that interrupt love, and the fundamental things don't always apply.

2.   RICK: "Who are you really and what were you before?
        What did you do and what did you think?"
      ILSA: "We said no questions."
      RICK: "Here's looking at you, kid."

Rick and Ilsa exchange these words in Rick's flashback to their time together in Paris. Rick remembers this exchange the night he first sees Ilsa in Casablanca, as he drinks alone late at night in the empty bar while Sam plays "As Time Goes By." Rick remembers the days in Paris as idyllic and untroubled. The war had not yet come to the city, and Rick believed he had found true happiness with Ilsa. In the flashback, Rick is lighthearted and smiling, a person altogether different from the heavy brooder we see in Casablanca. In this dialogue, Rick wants to know all about Ilsa, but she rebuffs his questions by reminding him that they agreed not to discuss each other's pasts. This agreement protects the innocence of their relationship, but it also prevents Rick from learning the truth about Ilsa, which might have saved him years of heartbreak. Although the war has not yet come to Paris, it has already spread to Czechoslovakia, where Ilsa's husband, Laszlo, was arrested, sent to a concentration camp, and, she believes, killed. The past is too painful for her to think about, and she most likely also fears Rick's reaction to the news of her marriage.

In Casablanca, whenever Ilsa tries to explain to Rick what happened in Paris, she points out that they knew very little about each other. In effect, this reminder becomes her excuse for the emotional pain she caused him, but it is also a rebuke to Rick. She intentionally maintained his ignorance about her. At the same time, had Ilsa answered honestly, the whole tone of the memory would be different. Ilsa and Rick's simple love would be turned on its head. Rick seems to have a choice: a painful present and a perfect memory, or a complicated understanding of both. As he remembers the Paris days, Rick seems to prefer to keep the memory pure. But eventually he embraces the truth about his time with Ilsa both in Paris and in Casablanca, which is necessary if he is going to move on with his life. He recasts the memory by repeating the line "Here's looking at you, kid" at the end of the film.

3. LOUIS: "I'm shocked, shocked, to find that gambling is going on in here."

Louis makes this announcement in Rick's after the patrons' spontaneous rendition of "La Marseillaise" angers Strasser and he demands that Rick's be shut down. Louis must find some excuse to carry out the order, and gambling is what he comes up with. Louis is the film's great wit, and this is probably his best line. He delivers it with a straight face—then politely accepts his gambling winnings from that evening. Louis brings levity and comic relief to an ensemble of intense, brooding characters: Laszlo, the passionate politician; Ilsa, trapped in a heart-wrenching conflict; Rick, the silently suffering sentimentalist; and Strasser, the determined villain. In Casablanca, not all characters suffer from the anxiety of the war, and Louis lives a pleasant life of easygoing hedonism and harmless corruption.

Petty crime is everywhere in Casablanca, and this line serves as its official stamp of approval. It also reveals something fundamental about Louis's character. A gambler himself, he has known for some time that gambling takes place at Rick's. Not only does Louis shut down Rick's with his deadpan announcement, but he also effectively reminds us that he always could have shut down the bar in the past, but never did. Ironically, by flexing his muscle at this moment, and at the request of Strasser, Louis shows where his true loyalties lie. Had Strasser not said a word, Louis would have done nothing, as he always had before. Moreover, Louis knows that gambling is not the only illegal activity to go on at Rick's. Rick's is also a place where stolen letters of transit are sold and where members of the underground resistance meet to discuss their plans without arousing suspicion. That Louis uses gambling, rather than political activities, as the excuse to shut down Rick's is significant. Louis's eventual rejection of Vichy and collaboration is anticipated by this statement. At the height of Louis's moral hypocrisy, he reveals the seeds of his political idealism.

4.   RICK: "Ilsa, I'm no good at being noble, but it doesn't take much to see that the problems of three little people don't amount to a hill of beans in this crazy world. Someday you'll understand that. Now, now. Here's looking at you, kid."

Rick says these words to Ilsa at the airport during the final scene. As the scene unwinds, who exactly will depart Casablanca that night and which man, Rick or Laszlo, will wind up with Ilsa remain unclear. Just before Rick says these words, he states clearly his decision: Ilsa and Laszlo will leave together on the plane, and Rick will remain in Casablanca. With these lines, which culminate the most dramatic exchange of dialogue in the film, Rick recasts the entire question. The real concern, he suggests, is not which man will get the woman. In the larger scheme of things, such a concern doesn't matter. A war is raging is Europe, and the happiness of these three people is insignificant.

These lines are the clearest statement of *Casablanca*'s moral resolution: the triumph of the political over the personal. But Rick is saying more than just this. Although Rick calls himself, Ilsa, and Laszlo "little people," he also recognizes that Laszlo is something more. These lines are not a cry of despair but a recognition of the fact that large political considerations trump the individual concerns of lovers. Laszlo must survive in order to continue his political work. Ilsa must accompany him, not necessarily because she loves him, but because he loves her, and her presence will make him more effective politically. Through the personal sacrifice these words imply, Rick catapults himself from the realm of "little people" into the sphere of large causes. Like Laszlo, Rick becomes a partisan, a warrior, and a hero, and he seems to realize that whereas Laszlo's heroism is amplified by Ilsa's presence, Rick himself functions best on his own.

While Rick claims heroism for himself with these words, he denies the same privilege to Ilsa. Rick claims to have learned that their love means nothing, but Ilsa, he says, can't understand that yet. Only in the future will she figure it out. At best, her actions are passively, or accidentally, heroic. Those who see Rick as exacting some sort of revenge against Ilsa in the finale will find some proof in this scene, as Rick seems to write off as insignificant or foolish any heartbreak Ilsa may feel. He, of all people, should understand how devastating a broken heart can be, and in asking Ilsa to calmly accept and understand his decision, he is asking the impossible. Rick tries to comfort the heartbroken Ilsa with the words "Now, now," but he also calls attention to their differing priorities. She still believes in the importance of love, while he understands that some things are even greater. Shortly after this speech, Rick tells Laszlo that Ilsa visited him the previous evening and pretended still to be in love with him to get the letters. Rick prefers the certainty of being noble to the uncertainty of love, despite the ambiguities of each person's true feelings. In making the choice to let Ilsa go, he rebukes Ilsa, who, unlike Laszlo and Rick, seems still to consider love the higher value.

At the speech's finale, Rick repeats his favorite phrase of affection: "Here's looking at you, kid." The repetition of this phrase, like the consoling words "Now, now," suggests that love continues to endure, despite the circumstantial barriers that keep Ilsa and Rick apart. At the same time, the phrase takes on a new resonance. "Here's looking at you, kid," when Rick said it in Paris, implied a childlike sense of an interminable present, when the looking promised to last forever. The playful "kid" at the end suggests the innocence of Rick and Ilsa's love. In this final statement, we understand Rick to be saying, "Here's looking at you *for the last time*." The "kid" comes across as ironic, for the events of the past two years have forced both characters to see the world for what it is, a lawless and often hostile place that leaves no room for childish innocence or ignorance. Rick is not only saying goodbye to Ilsa here, but to the child within himself. His act of self-sacrifice is his political coming of age, just like that of his nation as it decided to enter World War II.

5. RICK: "Louis, I think this is the beginning of a beautiful friendship."

This sentence, spoken by Rick, concludes *Casablanca*. Rick says this to Louis after the plane carrying Ilsa and Laszlo to Lisbon has departed, Strasser has been killed, and Louis has abandoned his cynical neutrality to embrace the Allied cause. As Louis and Rick walk side by side down the airport's empty runway, we see that their fates are linked, most overtly in their shared decision to leave Casablanca for Brazzaville, in French Congo. Their fates are linked in other ways as well. On the one hand, friendship with Louis is a consolation to Rick after Ilsa's departure. However, the words speak of hope, not resignation. Both Rick and Louis have earned a new beginning. The friendship between Louis and Rick is not itself new, and their mutual affection has been evident throughout the film. Rick's calling this a "beginning," therefore, implies that the terms of the friendship have changed. Whereas the two were once joined by bonds of self-interest and generally interacted out of necessity, now they share a political bond. Political idealism, in the form of active resistance to Nazi rule and the consolidation of the American-French alliance, has replaced casino kickbacks as the cement of their relationship.

ON THE WATERFRONT

(1954)

CONTEXT

Elia Kazan (1909–2003) was born as Elia Kazanjioglou to Greek parents in Constantinople, which today is Istanbul, Turkey. When he was four years old, his family emigrated to New York City during the early-twentieth-century wave of immigration. Kazan's father, George, a rug merchant, expected him to inherit the family business. Kazan's mother, Athena, however, encouraged Kazan's independence and education in New York's public schools. After graduating from Williams College in Massachusetts, he went on to study drama at Yale. Fascinated by acting and directing, Kazan joined New York's influential leftist Group Theater in the 1930s. Many great actors, writers, and directors passed through this group, including Lee Strasberg and Clifford Odets. Acting on his political radicalism, Kazan officially joined a communist cell in 1934. He left the cell in 1936, disillusioned by its hypocrisies. Immersing himself in New York's theatrical stage scene on and around Broadway, Kazan became a skilled director noted for his ability to draw the best performances from his actors. In 1947, with colleagues Cheryl Crawford and Robert Lewis, Kazan co-founded the Actors Studio, a collective of innovative performers that would become one of the most important resources for film and theater talent in both mediums' histories.

The experimental methods the actors studied at Kazan's Actors Studio followed the teachings of Russian dramatist Konstantin Stanislavski, which Strasberg applied in the United States. Stanislavski's influential book, *An Actor Prepares*, was translated into English in 1936, forever changing the course of stage and screen acting. The style of acting based on his teachings became known as the Method, and its practitioners Method actors. A Method actor did not use the emoting techniques common at the time, which consisted of loud, stiff, stagy movements intended to clarify emotions and intentions for the audience. Rather, a Method actor strove to be himself and stay in the moment, responding or reacting as he would in private life. Smaller gestures, mannerisms, pauses, and hesitancies became more important than broad and clear external motions. Actors were encouraged to draw on their own selves and lives. Past memories, life experiences, pains, and pleasures were to be called up from the actors' subconscious and incorporated into their characters' psyches. In this way, characters took on depth and transcended one-sided labels such as "villain" or "damsel-in-distress." They became breathing, complex individuals with contradictory emotions and interior lives that complicated exterior expressions. Three early Method actors were Marlon Brando, James Dean, and Montgomery Clift. The fact that many of these acting philosophies are standard today remains a testament to the revolutionary power of the teachings at Kazan's Actors Studio.

Kazan directed his first stage play in 1935 and became one of Broadway's brightest lights. He was acclaimed especially for his powerful and realistic direction of the plays of Tennessee Williams, such as *A Streetcar Named Desire* (1947), and Arthur Miller, such as *Death of a Salesman* (1948).

Although Kazan directed plays and films and write novels throughout his long and fruitful life, he did most of his work from the mid-1940s until the mid-1950s, one of the most controversial eras in film history. He worked with famous playwrights, including Miller and Williams, and with notable authors, such as John Steinbeck. He directed films for producer Darryl F. Zanuck of 20th Century Fox, helping that studio cement its reputation. In the postwar decade, Kazan directed ten motion pictures, all critically acclaimed. Some of the most influential include *A Tree Grows in Brooklyn* (1945), his first film made under a nine-year contract signed with 20th Century Fox; *Gentlemen's Agreement* (1947), for which Kazan earned his first Best Director award; *A Streetcar Named Desire* (1951), adapted by Tennessee Williams from his own play; *Viva Zapata!* (1952), written by John Steinbeck; and *East of Eden* (1955), adapted from Steinbeck's novel.

Kazan made *On the Waterfront* in 1954 for Columbia Pictures. Although critics now almost universally regard *On the Waterfront* as a masterpiece of Method acting and a reflection of issues central to its time, when the film first came out a few critics were less sure. The critics agreed that the film had tremendous power, but many were leery of the new acting style and undecided about the effectiveness of Brando's slouchy inarticulateness. *On the Waterfront* was based on a series of investigative pieces published in 1949 by New York City journalist Malcolm Johnson, for which he won a Pulitzer Prize. Over time, though, the strength of the acting prevailed, and the personal struggle that each character undergoes within his or her own soul stuck with viewers and reviewers, who returned to the film time and time again. The film was a critical and financial success,

ON THE WATERFRONT

earning more than $10 million on a $1 million budget. This success allowed Kazan to form his own production company, Newtown Productions, through which he would make his next three films.

The politics of this era, however, forever altered Kazan's life. Following World War II, at the start of the cold war, many Americans feared an infiltration of Soviet Communism. In 1947, the controversial House Un-American Activities Committee (HUAC) was formed with the intention of purging the United States of any Communist influence. Hollywood's high profile and liberal makeup made it a prime target. HUAC subpoenaed many actors, screenwriters, and directors to coerce them into informing on their colleagues by "naming names"—that is, making public which of their friends now had, or formerly had, any associations with the Communist Party. HUAC subpoenaed Kazan once, and at his initial hearing he refused to divulge details. At a second hearing in 1952, however, Kazan chose to give the names of seven former colleagues from his Group Theater days. Budd Schulberg, the screenwriter of *On the Waterfront*, also cooperated with the committee.

Kazan justified his actions by saying that supporting anti-Communist efforts would protect his liberal beliefs and his country. His justifications, however, met with much criticism, particularly from two American writers, Lillian Hellman and his good friend Arthur Miller, who believed naming names was a betrayal of fellow artists. *On the Waterfront* celebrates as a hero a man who informed on mob leaders, and many people believe that Kazan made the film as a response to Hellman, Miller, and other critics. Miller's play *The Crucible*, whose hero dies rather than accuse people of being witches, of course represents the opposing view.

In 1999, when Hollywood presented Kazan with an honorary Oscar for a long and distinguished career, the film industry was bitterly divided. Some protested or refused to stand when Kazan accepted the award, believing still that his actions were calculated to save his own career and fatally damaged the careers of many Hollywood screenwriters who subsequently were blacklisted. Others—including Miller—believed that his cinematic achievements, which include many undoubted masterpieces, should stand on their own.

Kazan died in 2003 at the age of ninety-four.

PLOT OVERVIEW

On the Waterfront opens by introducing the small group of corrupt racketeers that run the docks of Hoboken, New Jersey, across the river from Manhattan. Terry Malloy, an inarticulate former prize-fighter in his late twenties, serves as a petty errand boy for the union head, Johnny Friendly. Friendly's gang uses Malloy as a decoy to draw fellow longshoreman Joey Doyle out of his apartment and onto the roof. Doyle is planning to break the bullied workers' policy of remaining "deaf and dumb" by testifying in front of the Water-front Crime Commission the next day about the corrupt methods union bosses employ to extort money and labor from the working-class longshoremen. The gangsters push Doyle off the roof to his death, implicating Malloy in the murder as an accomplice. A shocked Malloy had fooled himself into believing Doyle would only be roughed up a little.

The neighborhood gathers over Doyle's body. Pops Doyle, a longshoreman for four decades, tells everyone he had advised his son to be quiet, since his testimony would risk the jobs and lives of all the stevedores. Joey Doyle's sister Edie, a buttoned-up Catholic teacher trainee who is home visiting from her school, screams pas-sionately for justice over her brother's corpse. Finally, the local priest Father Barry kneels over Doyle, praying. Besides Edie, the entire waterfront knows what really happened, but no one will speak. At Johnny Friendly's smoky barroom hangout, Charlie "the Gent" Malloy, Terry's brother, who serves as Friendly's right-hand man, is introduced. Terry's hot temper in this scene indicates that his conscience is wrought by his role in Joey's death.

After lolling around his rooftop pigeon coop the next morning with a devoted neighborhood boy, Malloy walks to the docks for the morning shape-up. Two Waterfront Crime Commission officers seek out Malloy, who is rumored to be the last man to see Joey alive. Malloy stays mum. Edie and Father Barry appear to witness the dis-tribution of jobs for the day—any man who receives a work tab will have a job. There are many more men than there are work tabs, however, and the work-thirsty crowd surrounds the foreman, Big Mac. Big Mac throws the work tabs across the pier, causing a mad free-for-all. Malloy meets Edie when he grabs a tab that she's desperately trying to secure for her father and, upon learning who she is, gives her the tab.

Charlie asks Terry to attend a secret meeting in Father Barry's church arranged by the men who didn't get work that day. Not wanting to be a *stoolie* (short for *stool pigeon*), or informer, Terry offers weak protests. Johnny Friendly has set Terry up with a cushy job, however, so he doesn't really have a choice. No one speaks at the meeting when Father Barry asks about Joey's death. Thugs ambush the proceedings and mercilessly beat all who can't escape. Grabbing Edie's hands, Terry helps her escape. As he walks her home through a park, they awkwardly get to know each other. Edie accidentally drops her glove and Terry picks it up, suggestively sliding his hand into it. At one point, a homeless man interrupts and mentions that Terry saw Joey the night he was killed.

Terry leaves Edie sweetly and awkwardly. Pops Doyle, who witnesses the entire episode from his window and wants no daughter of his consorting with the brother of the vicious Charlie Malloy, packs Edie's bags and prepares to send her back to school. Edie defends the confused Terry and demands to stay in order to find Joey's murderer.

That evening, Edie and Terry meet accidentally on the tenement rooftop, where Terry has been caring for both his and Joey's pigeons. Curious about his sensitive side, Edie agrees to go for a drink with Terry at a local saloon, though she's never had a beer. In this raucous bar, the two have a tender, pained conversation. Edie pleads with Terry for help and he wants desperately for her to like him, but he can't help her. After a disagreement, Edie tries to leave, but a boisterous wedding celebration sweeps her up. Edie and Terry end up dancing at the party until late. Two events crush their blissful escape. First, Johnny Friendly sends a goon to find Terry and tell him to report to the boss immediately. Moments later, the Waterfront Crime Commission serves Terry with a subpoena to appear at the State House in a few days to answer questions about the death of Joey Doyle. Angry with Terry for hiding facts about his and his brother's involvement in Joey's death, Edie runs away. Terry walks home alone, but Charlie and Friendly find him. They berate him for hanging around with Joey's sister and not reporting on the meeting.

The next day at the docks, the union kills "Kayo" Dugan, a stevedore who had secretly testified at great length about Friendly's operation, by "accidentally" dropping a crate of Irish whiskey over him. Beside Dugan's body, Father Barry pledges his support to the longshoremen and demonstrates his commitment by standing firm as men throw rotten fruit and beer cans at him from above. He preaches at length from the hold that Dugan's death was a crucifixion. Torn, Terry retreats to the rooftops and the pigeons that night. Edie finds him there, and they finally kiss passionately. The next day Terry confesses to Father Barry about his involvement in Joey's death. Father Barry convinces the reluctant Terry to tell Edie. He eventually does tell her, in a momentous scene where the whistle of a steamship drowns out their conversation. Distraught, she runs away.

Back on the rooftop, a commission officer talks with Terry about his old prizefights, while at the longshoreman's shack Johnny Friendly puts pressure on Charlie to make sure his brother doesn't squeal. When Charlie and Terry ride in a cab together, their differing interests explode. Terry wants help from his brother, but Charlie wants to make sure Terry won't talk. In the passion of conflicting emotions, Charlie pulls a gun on his brother, who piteously and gently turns it away. Charlie begins to reminisce about Terry's boxing days, causing Terry to bring up the truth that Charlie forced him to throw a big fight, on Johnny Friendly's orders. He laments that he could have made something of his life, had Charlie not betrayed him. After the conversation, Terry flees to Edie's, and Charlie is taken to Johnny Friendly's. Terry breaks down Edie's door and forcibly kisses her. Through the window Terry is called down to the street, just as he had called to Joey at the beginning of the film. He and Edie run from a speeding car, only to discover Charlie hung by a hook in the gently falling rain, murdered for his failure to convince Terry to remain silent. Vowing to avenge his death, Terry runs to Johnny Friendly's bar, gun in hand. Father Barry finds him there, drunk and confused. Terry curses at Father Barry, and Father Barry punches him. He tells Terry not to play at Friendly's level, since he'll achieve only mob justice and have no legal protection. He tells Terry the only right thing to do is to testify against the corrupt union leaders, and Terry finally agrees.

The next day Terry testifies to the commission in court. On the way home, he's protected by cops and scorned by his friends. Tommy, the neighborhood kid, has killed all his pigeons. Knowing what he has to do to claim his identity and independence, he grabs Joey Doyle's jacket from Edie's apartment and walks down to the docks for the morning shape-up. With all the longshoremen looking on, Terry calls Johnny Friendly out of his tiny shack and delivers an emotional speech announcing his new goal: to break away from mob rule toward independent thought. A fight ensues between

Terry and Friendly. When the fight moves behind the shack, out of sight of the longshoremen, a pack of Friendly's goons move in and pummel Terry mercilessly. Other goons restrain the longshoremen, who are not really making an effort to help anyway. Instead, they place all their hopes on Terry. Finally, Edie and Father Barry burst through and find Terry almost comatose, the water lapping at his body. Father Barry encourages Terry to stand in order to be a model of strength for the longshoremen. Terry rises without assistance, but he wobbles violently and squints through swollen eyes. He shuffles up the ramp and staggers toward the work hangar to show he's ready for that day's honest labor. Finally, he manages to reach the hangar. All the longshoremen, truly inspired, follow their new leader. Johnny Friendly wails helplessly, alone on the docks. The longshoremen disappear into the hangar, and the garage door closes.

Character List

Terry Malloy—Played by Marlon Brando The protagonist of the film. A former prizefighter, Terry is physically strong but shuffles through most of the film with his hands in his pockets and his collar turned up. Inside, he's tender and conflicted, as is evident from his anxious physical behaviors and ineloquent speech. He communicates through long silences and seething outbursts.

Edie Doyle—Played by Eva Marie Saint The Catholic teacher-in-training who falls for Terry Malloy. Not familiar with the lifestyle on the waterfront, she exhibits bravery by choosing to stick around through a dangerous time. An almost angelic gentle soul who often rescues stray animals, she sees the good in Terry that nobody else sees. She walks cautiously and looks around curiously. In many ways, her utter innocence represents the complete opposite of Terry's street smarts.

Father Barry—Played by Karl Malden The Catholic priest whose parish consists of the longshoremen. Like Edie, Father Barry has little understanding of what happens daily on the docks. But soon he puts on his heavy overcoat, hat, and white collar, and finds the strength of his own convictions in applied practice at the docks, rather than in the safety of the church.

Johnny Friendly—Played by Lee J. Cobb The vocal and corrupt leader of the Longshoreman's Union. A tough criminal who had to claw his way to the top, Friendly cannot be described as purely evil. He demonstrates affection for Terry and Charlie, but he operates by a different set of rules. He's "friendly" to the men as long as they're on his side. If they're not, they're in big trouble. He almost always has a cigar.

Charlie "the Gent" Malloy—Played by Rod Steiger Johnny Friendly's educated right-hand man and Terry's brother. Charlie walks around in an expensive camel-hair coat that sparks derision from the longshoremen. His tense eyes betray tremendous anxiety beneath his calm, round face. Though he's a willing and calculating criminal, he's never able to hide his deep love for his brother.

Timothy J. "Kayo" Dugan—Played by Pat Henning A short, strong longshoreman who testifies to the Waterfront Crime Commission and is murdered on the job for it. Dugan's sarcasm and ability to elucidate the longshoremen's frustration single him out quickly as a representative for the longshoremen.

Pop Doyle—Played by John Hamilton The elderly stevedore father of the murdered Joey Doyle. After four decades on the docks, his face is grizzled and has patches of a white beard. He maintains a fierce, lock-jawed façade. His only concern for the duration of the film is the well-being of his daughter, Edie.

Big Mac—Played by James Westerfield The pier boss who dispatches the work tabs each morning. One of the more vocal members of Johnny Friendly's gang, Big Mac maintains a stoic facade while insulting Terry and Charlie and remains steadfastly loyal to Johnny Friendly.

Glover—Played by Leif Erickson A Waterfront Crime Commission officer. Glover fulfills his official duties in a by-the-books, workmanlike fashion, but his tall presence also radiates sensitivity. His gentle questioning of Terry on the rooftops proves his understanding of Terry's dilemma.

Luke—Played by Don Blackman An African-American longshoreman. His quiet, reflective demeanor radiates in his silent face. Good friends with Dugan, Luke respectfully returns Joey's jacket to Edie after Dugan's death.

Tommy—Played by Arthur Keegan The kid who idolizes Terry and hangs out in the pigeon coops. His attachment to Terry on the rooftops reflects Terry's near-childlike innocence when daydreaming or tending the pigeons.

Tullio—Played by former boxer Tami Mauriello One of Johnny Friendly's goons. Tullio's round, mask-like face is cold and inexpressive.

ON THE WATERFRONT

Truck—Played by former boxer Tony Galento   One of Johnny Friendly's goons. Truck harasses Father Barry during his speech over Dugan's body by throwing bananas at him . . . until Terry flattens him with an uppercut and a hook.

Barney—Played by former boxer Abe Simon   One of Johnny Friendly's goons. An enormous physical presence with an iron jaw and deep voice, Barney almost resembles a giant.

Mutt—Played by John Heldabrand   A local homeless man. Unshaven, with a tan overcoat, Mutt appears sympathetic, intelligent, and down on his luck. Well-known around the waterfront, he seems to know exactly what goes on despite his desperate straits.

Johnny's Banker—Played by Barry Macollum   Nicknamed "J.P. Morgan." A tight-faced stereotype, Johnny's Banker dresses finely in a wardrobe that includes sharp hats. Physically, he resembles a weasel in his thin wiliness.

Gilette—Played by Marty Balsam   Glover's assistant from the Waterfront Crime Commission. Shorter and less vocal than Glover, Gilette exists primarily as a sarcastic sidekick to his boss.

Joey Doyle—Played by Elia Kazan   A young longshoreman murdered for his testimony to the Waterfront Crime Commission. Joey's shadowed head from his apartment window is seen only in long shot, then his body falls from the roof to the ground. His death becomes the ghostly presence that overrides the film, as well as the spark that kick-starts all subsequent events.

Mr. Upstairs—Played by an uncredited actor   The corrupt leader who directs Johnny Friendly from afar. Mr. Upstairs's face is never shown, and we see only the plush estate (with television set and butler) where he lives.

Jimmy Collins—Played by Thomas Handley   Joey Doyle's best friend in the neighborhood. Jimmy's refusal to speak out even after his best friend's death illustrates the depth of the longshoremen's silence.

ON THE WATERFRONT

ANALYSIS OF MAJOR CHARACTERS

TERRY MALLOY

The brooding, inarticulate protagonist of *On the Waterfront* nurses a seething bundle of contradictory emotions for most of the film. Terry doesn't particularly care about work and instead devotes his dreams, energy, and care to his racing pigeons. After being pushed around for too long, however, he realizes that his actions have definite, provable results. Marlon Brando's portrayal of Terry is key to our understanding his character. Brando shuffles around and affects such mannerisms as looking away from the person with whom he's speaking, putting his hand nervously behind his head, or stuffing his hands in his pockets. Often, his focus seems misplaced, leaving us to wonder what's going on deep inside his mind. For example, he plays with his jacket's zipper while he learns what happened to Joey Doyle, and he fiddles with a piece of dust after Charlie pulls a gun in the cab. Malloy has a lot going on in the parts of his mind that we are never privy to.

As the film progresses, Brando's physicality shifts, which indicates a shift in Malloy's priorities and objectives. In Malloy's final stand on the docks, when he wears Joey Doyle's jacket, he stands more confidently, with few nervous gestures. He looks around him calmly, not fearfully as he would have earlier. He talks instead of whines. His gum-chewing is cockier. His burgeoning independence, rooted in a complex decision, infiltrates his whole being. Terry's transformation is not wholly self-induced, but rather brought on by a string of revelations and events, including his misunderstood role in Joey Doyle's death, his growing awareness of Edie's love and his love for her, Father Barry's pressing care, and the murders of Dugan and Charlie. There are so many factors working on Terry's character, in fact, that we're left wondering how much of a "choice" Terry Malloy really has after all.

EDIE DOYLE

Edie's nearly angelic soul helps Terry to reclaim his conscience. Her restraint, modesty, and acceptance open up a new place in Terry's rough-and-tumble heart. Sexuality is crucial in her involvement with Malloy, and their attraction grows, in part, because they are physical opposites: Malloy is a brawny former boxer and she's a polite church girl.

Edie's loyalty to her brother is the driving motivation for all her actions. Were it not for her steadfastness, Pops Doyle would have succeeded in sending her home, and the thugs of the gang would have succeeded in intimidating her. To Malloy, she represents a way out. Not happy with the few paths open to him on the waterfront, he could start a new life, with Edie, somewhere else. Malloy tests her genuine naïveté and faith in the good will of others when he tells her of his involvement in Joey's death. But at the end of the film she has reclaimed her faith in humanity, and she remains almost purely good to the end.

FATHER BARRY

Though his behavior changes throughout the film, Father Barry remains steadfast to one overriding mission: administering the word of God by advocating peaceful resistance. Early on, the priest appears well intentioned but of no practical use, as when he tells Edie she can find him in the church if she needs him. After visiting the docks and speaking with the workers who don't get jobs that day, he begins a slow process of toughening. In many ways, his development parallels Terry's—he becomes active rather than passive and begins to acknowledge his own potential effectiveness. Father Barry's increased cigarette smoking represents his thickening skin. He affirms his faith in his mission to guide the longshoreman with a peaceful hand when he delivers his famous "Sermon on the Docks" over Dugan's body, withstanding banana and beer can attacks to deliver his message and demonstrate the good of his word. Despite the presence and importance of Father Barry, religion does not play an overt role in the film's crucial events.

JOHNNY FRIENDLY

Once Johnny Friendly has power, he has to maintain it at all costs, and he acts out whenever someone or something challenges that power. His position as the leader of the Longshoreman Local Union requires daily muscle-flexing. In a passionate speech he gives at the bar the first time we meet him, Friendly describes his past life. Clawing for scraps and fighting to get by on the streets since his youth, an organization like the union became his only option for self-preservation. Money and power are his motivations now. When a man is on his side, as Terry is in the beginning of the film, Johnny Friendly is all smiles, quick to give out hugs, pats on the back, and extra $50 bills. When a man's goals diverge from his, however, that man instantly becomes an enemy. Since Johnny Friendly abides by the same code throughout the film, his character traits change very little, but his effect on other characters—and on the viewers—changes dramatically. Initially, Friendly comes across as powerful, and his booming speeches command respect. His disseminations of beatings become cautionary tales. However, after Terry Malloy speaks out to the Waterfront Crime Commission and effectively strips Friendly of all his power, Friendly becomes pitiable. He is nothing more than a puppet with a few of his strings cut. He flails comically, he roars ineffectively, and none of his orders stick.

CHARLIE MALLOY

Charlie Malloy negotiates a complex gauntlet of emotions and becomes a tragic figure at the end for unsuccessfully trying to bridge the gulf between two enemies. He's as loyal as a blood brother to Johnny Friendly. Friendly has promoted him to second-in-command in the organization and has made it possible for him to provide for himself handsomely. Additionally, Friendly has been a sort of father figure for both Malloys since their father was murdered and Friendly took them under his strong and binding wing. However, Charlie's love for Terry, Friendly's enemy, is palpable in their every interaction. Whether he's kidding with Terry about his cushy position on the docks or berating him for his relationship with Edie, Charlie exhibits concern for Terry's well-being. However, he doesn't consider Terry's personal wishes, which proves to be a fatal mistake. Actor Rod Steiger portrays Charlie's growing anxiety with knowing eyes and hesitant flappings of a glove in the taxicab. As the film progresses, Charlie realizes that his two sides cannot reconcile, and he becomes increasingly desperate to figure out how to maintain his loyalties to opposing parties.

ON THE WATERFRONT

THEMES, MOTIFS, AND SYMBOLS

THEMES

INFORMING AS THE CORRECT MORAL CHOICE

Terry Malloy obeys moral authority by choosing to inform on the corrupt union officials—that is, in the film he clearly makes the morally correct decision. Those on his side include a Catholic priest and a kind-hearted teacher trainee, and these endorsements increase the audience's sympathy for one side over the other. Vicious doubt and derision about his potential choice affect Terry and all his friendships throughout the film, since the men are understandably concerned about their own jobs and their own lives. The closing scene, however, changes these feelings profoundly. The entire work crew follows the bleeding Terry back to work, leaving Johnny Friendly alone, indicating that they've chosen a new leader to follow. Their group action confirms that, deep down, they all wanted Terry to do what he did. All of the previous discord, then, merely generates suspense until this mass action plays out.

The choice Terry makes to inform on the union officials echoes the choice Budd Schulberg and Elia Kazan made to inform before HUAC on former communists, but Terry achieves results that are far less morally ambiguous than the results Kazan and Schulberg achieved. Kazan and Schulberg effectively blacklisted for decades many of their creative, intelligent, and politically active peers. The only loser from Terry's decision is Johnny Friendly, a merciless bully who clearly deserves what he gets. Kazan's testimony allowed him to pursue a directing career undisturbed. However, many of his subsequent films deal with themes similar to those in *On the Waterfront*, which suggests that his HUAC decision haunted him, even in the creative realm, for at least a decade. The recurring themes also suggest that Kazan felt a need to continually assert the right of the individual's conscience over that of a mob or governmental authority. At the end of *On the Waterfront*, Terry is surrounded with people who admire and respect him. His informing has elevated him in the longshoremen's eyes, and he has no reason to doubt his decision.

Kazan, though he built a successful career, was never fully embraced by Hollywood, and his own decision to inform stranded him in morally ambiguous territory.

THE TRANSFORMING POWER OF FAITH

Edie and Father Barry, the two characters who most help Terry figure things out, have faith in something intangible. Edie maintains faith in her belief that people care about the well-being of others and want to do the right thing. Father Barry maintains faith that acting as a representative of God can help others do the right thing. They both base their actions on these beliefs, and the film validates the value of living by certain principles. Essentially, Terry redeems himself by justifying their faith. The other characters do not have faith like Edie and Father Barry do, resulting in a distinct dichotomy. On one side are Father Barry and Edie, who have faith in concepts that are completely invisible. On the other side are the corrupt union officers, who have faith in money and power, acquisitions that are measurable. Though this delineation of good versus evil threatens to be overly transparent, the ways that faith changes Terry and forces Charlie to face his own moral wavering bring new depth and texture to the idea of what it means to be faithful and faith*less*.

POWER CORRUPTS

Though the film sympathizes with Johnny Friendly and his rough upbringing, it shows that his taste for power has left him morally bankrupt. This idea that power corrupts does not apply only to Johnny Friendly, however. Mr. Upstairs, for example, turns on Johnny Friendly in an instant. In the game of power, the film says, there are no true friends, just the acquisition of more power and the defense of that power. Johnny Friendly cannot make even one decision that's not related to maintaining his power or acquiring more. Even when he stuffs $50 into Terry's shirt in a seemingly caring gesture, he is really buying Terry by obligating him to repay the favor with loyalty.

MOTIFS

THE ROOFTOP AS RETREAT FROM THE WORLD

Whenever Terry Malloy feels pressure from the outside world, he retreats to the rooftop of the tenement. The rooftop is so far away from the docks that he can pretend it's another world. On the rooftop, Terry can be a dreamer. He's closer to the clouds, and he has a view of the city—and seeing the city from afar places him somehow outside it and above it. Terry's goal is, in a sense, to stay up on the roof—that is, to be at all times the person he is when he's there. Joey Doyle spent time on the roof, too, raising pigeons, and he made a similar decision to testify to the commission. The rooftop serves as a place where characters can go to scrutinize their own morals and choices without the pressures of the world below.

CRUCIFIXION DIALOGUE

Father Barry often compares the deaths of innocent longshoremen and crucifixions, thus making their martyrdom explicit. Father Barry orders the longshoremen (as well as the viewer) to account for actions and non-actions, such as silence, that he considers sins. Joey Doyle and Dugan both died for the sins of the longshoremen, and religious imagery accompanies these deaths. Edie cradles Joey's corpse like Mary cradled Jesus' body, Father Barry rises out of the cargo hold with Dugan's body as if ascending to heaven, and Charlie's corpse hangs by a hook, all of which are visual references to Christ's body on the cross.

"D & D": DEAF AND DUMB

The longshoremen try to portray their silence as part of a code, but the film suggests that it's merely mob-approved cowardice. "D & D" runs throughout the dialogue, and the phrase is so familiar that men on all sides use it. Dugan the longshoreman and Johnny Friendly the union chief each refer to the phrase naturally. The words in the phrase suggest a kind of slavery. Those who are deaf and dumb have no articulate voice, and they are allowed to channel everything they see and feel only into work. Those who are deaf and dumb become work machines without identities. Part of Terry's transformation in the film involves shaking up the accepted pattern of abiding by the code and thinking for himself, thereby forging an identity. He thinks, therefore he is.

SYMBOLS

HUDSON RIVER

The Hudson River separates Hoboken, New Jersey, from New York City. Manhattan may as well be a thousand miles away, since the Manhattan life the longshoremen imagine is so different from daily life on the waterfront. The river is a border, an edge that the longshoremen will never be able to cross. The Hudson brings in the ships, and the edge of the Hudson is where the Longshoreman's Local Union runs its corrupt operations. Others are free to come and go, but the Hudson reigns in the stevedores. Across the Hudson, the Empire State Building looms like the Emerald City from the *Wizard of Oz*, distant and strange. It represents dreams and a different life, yet it's always glimpsed through a fog. Its sleek jutting frame contrasts dramatically with the ramshackle rooftops of Hoboken, with their discolored patches and mismatched roof levels.

Pigeons

The pigeons are cooped up in a cage. They're fragile. Their natural impulse is to fly, but they've been trained not to. They represent a different, more elemental lifestyle, flying and eating and playing and sleeping. In all of these ways, they perfectly symbolize Terry Malloy. Though he's a tough former boxer, his excessive care for these birds indicates a special affinity between them. The imagery of him actually inside the cage himself, evident when he tends the birds, suggests this affinity as well. Malloy is a dreamer, a delicate and sensitive man, and much of the conversation that Brando has with Edie about hawks and pigeons can be translated into words about each other. In many ways, Malloy essentially *is* a pigeon—that is, he lives on the rooftops. We never once see him in his apartment. His home is the roof.

The pigeons also have a negative connotation: *stool pigeon*, a slang term used to describe informers. The term comes from the combination of *stale*, a fifteenth-century English word used to describe one person who acted to catch another, and *pigeon*, which has always been used to describe someone who lets himself be swindled. A pigeon is a sucker. Every time a character uses the term *stool pigeon* or its abbreviation, *stoolie*, Terry Malloy's conflict boils to the surface.

Hooks

The sharp metallic hooks that the longshoremen use to help them load and empty pallets hang over their shoulders menacingly. These hooks represent the forces that literally hang over them in the form of Johnny Friendly's goons. Over the course of the film, Terry, Dugan, Luke, and many other longshoremen have the hawk-like talon of the hook pressing against their chests.

GLOVES

Gloves appear only twice in *On the Waterfront*, but each time the symbolism is crucial to both the reading of the scene and the film as a whole. Gloves indicate a shift in the dynamics of a scene, exposing a new layer of a character's anxiety, sexuality, or vulnerability. When Edie drops her pure white glove in the park, Terry picks it up and plays with it casually, frustrating Edie's sense of order and decorum. In a way, he is touching an extension of her, especially when he inserts his hand into the glove. The gesture is both sexual and intimate, friendly and aggressive.

Gloves appear a second time when Charlie plays with his in the taxi with Terry. Charlie is scarved and buttoned up tight in his camel-hair coat and proper hat, but he takes one glove off and fiddles with it nervously for the duration of the ride. This gesture indicates his anxiety and suggests that he is bound to face something uncomfortable. Compared with Charlie's tightly dressed body, his one naked hand suggests a small vulnerability. Part of him has slipped out of its tight wrapping, and in that sense the glove contributes to the crushing intimacy of the scene.

Film Analysis

Directing

Kazan wanted his directing in *On the Waterfront* to be invisible so that the actors' performances could be the focus of the film. Kazan and Polish-born, New York–based cinematographer Boris Kaufman eschew flashy camerawork and avoid employing extreme angles, intense close-ups, and overt camera movements. Instead, the actors often appear in two-shot (two people at midrange) or in wider shots to show the arrangements of characters. Kazan and Kaufman use the positioning of characters within a frame to suggest a power dynamic. For example, at the end of the film, when Terry Malloy runs down the ramp that connects the dock to the Longshoreman's Local Union shack, he stands literally between both camps, hanging in thin air. Johnny Friendly sits below him, as if in a netherworld, emerging from a shack floating on the water. The longshoremen stand as a unified mass on the solid ground of land. Malloy is literally and symbolically in between. Kazan and Kaufman also use suggestive framing when Father Barry is hoisted out of the hold with Dugan's corpse on the palette. In their unmoving, reverent pose, rising above all the men around them, Father Barry seems to be riding with Dugan straight into heaven as a reward for speaking his mind.

There are some moments, however, when the direction begs to be noticed and discussed. The most important incidence of style taking precedence over content is when Malloy confesses to Edie his involvement in her brother's death. Instead of letting the viewer hear this crucial conversation, Kazan allows the noise of a nearby ship's whistle to overwhelm the voices, and only a few of Malloy's words can be heard. Kazan uses this impressionistic rendering to suggest the depth of feeling and the frenzy of confused emotions underpinning the conversation. Because the feelings are more important than the actual words spoken, the scene's impact is more powerful than the impact a literal rendering would have provided. The ship's whistle and a pounding machine overwhelm Malloy's confession, emphasizing the weight his words have on Edie. She clutches her face and ears as if resisting the world around her, then flees. She

leaves Malloy alone on a pile of rocks with the Empire State Building visible in the background through the fog, representing a distant
dream and an idealized way of life. Scenes like this are rare, however, and Kazan usually allows his actors to work in an uncompli-
cated frame.

Kazan encouraged his actors to use a lot of physical touch, which
was a significant directing development. Not all the touching is
erotic—some is merely friendly or intimate. Goons and longshoremen push each other around in friendly games. Charlie and Terry sit
practically on top of each other in the taxicab scene. Charlie and
Edie touch often in the saloon with arm-taps and caresses. Father
Barry touches almost everyone he comes into contact with. Even
Johnny Friendly hugs and lifts Terry in their first scene at the bar.
Touching emphasizes the crowded environment, but it also affirms
the intimacy of all these relationships. In a stage production, where
characters might stand a few feet apart from each other as they
speak, creating naturalistic emotions is a challenge. But in Kazan's
world, people use their bodies. They bump into each other, shake
hands, hug, tap each other to demonstrate points, horse around—
they generally feel real to the viewer.

Kazan creates some of the most subtle moments of direction ever
to hit the screen. In the first shot of the film, an enormous cruise ship
fills the frame, lodged at the docks. From a grungy little shack in a
small corner of the frame, Johnny Friendly marches out with all his
men, followed by Terry Malloy. A very small group is running a
large area, a contrast that the frame emphasizes. Additionally,
Terry's "confession" to Father Barry takes place outside of the
church. Even though Terry wants to talk to Father Barry inside the
church, the machinations of the plot draw them outside to the
waterfront. This location shades the scene: Terry's confession, Kazan
is saying, is not a religious one. Merely speaking will not absolve
Terry of any sins, and only action will alleviate his guilt. Father
Barry is not a Catholic mentor to Terry but a mentor of the soul. The
waterfront becomes a living, breathing part of his confession.

MISE-EN-SCÈNE

The mise-en-scène, or physical environment in which *On the Waterfront* takes place, is not a set. Kazan and his crew filmed *On the
Waterfront* on the actual docks and piers of Hoboken, New Jersey,
in view of New York City. Kazan achieves authenticity and grit

thanks to the backdrops of the inner cargo holds of ships, the cramped, dank spaces in which the union workers live, and the seedy, smoky bars of the area. No amount of careful art direction could result in a set that comes even close to the real thing. Even many of Johnny Friendly's goons were not actors. Instead, they were actual former heavyweight boxers who were hired for their rough demeanor and imposing physical presence. Many of the longshoremen, too, were actual workers from the Hoboken docks. The background sounds on the dock—ships' whistles and chains clanging through metal loops—add to the realistic aural environment. All of these decisions result in an environment that heightens the reality and depth of the characters' struggles and emotions.

Kazan filmed *On the Waterfront* outside on the docks in what happened to be one of New York's coldest winters in years. Breaths are visible and steam up in the bone-cold air. A small detail like this suggests the brutal treatment these dock workers face daily, not only from the corrupt union officials but from the elements themselves. The visible breaths also affirm the unique existence of each character— it's difficult to lump any of these men into the background. The cold took its toll on Kazan's actors—Kazan says the hardest job of his directing was to get the actors to come out into the cold. The actors didn't have to stretch to act cold from the comforts of a climate-controlled set. With so many natural elements to the *mise-en-scène*, the actors were free to focus entirely on their characters' emotions.

The steamy hot air seeping up through the sewers or steam being released on the docks creates a misty visual atmosphere. The drifts of steam and cloud suggest the moral ambiguity of every character. When Malloy finally tracks down Father Barry to confess, for instance, they walk through an indistinct park, with steam swirling all around them, a seeming manifestation of the uncertain and frightening terrain through which they're each carefully trying to find their way.

Ironically, the profoundly intimate taxicab scene is the one major scene that was not shot on location. It was shot in half a taxi's shell in a studio—proof that the actors' skill can shine in settings both false and real.

Costumes

The characters in *On the Waterfront* do not wear much makeup or elaborate costuming. Eva Marie Saint's Edie Doyle is wind-worn in her close-ups—just being outside, it seems, is painful. She has wrinkles around her moist stung eyes and exposed cheeks. Marlon Brando's Terry Malloy wears the same simple lumberjack's coat with holes in the elbows for the duration of the film. Its checkerboard pattern helps us to identify him in any crowd and sets him apart as different. In the final scene, he's *not* wearing the jacket. Rather, he wears Joey Doyle's, signifying his acceptance of Father Barry's belief that Doyle was a true martyr. He dons the skin of a martyr to stand up for a principle himself.

Changes in costume like this are also key indicators of shifting emotions or suggested eroticism in a paranoiac, code-restricted Hollywood. After we get used to seeing Catholic teacher-in-training Edie Doyle all buttoned up in her proper overcoat, her appearance at the end of the film in a soft white slip, with her hair free of its barrettes, is surprising. Her body is presented in a new light. She now has a feminine shape, and in comparison with her formerly demure appearance, her physicality jumps right off the screen.

ACTING

Marlon Brando as Terry Malloy communicates the angst and confusion of an inarticulate speaker trying to form his own identity in familiar but newly threatening surroundings. He strives to be an individual with strong principles, and his movements reveal his struggle. He chews gum expressively, shrugs, lags behind, pulls his collar up, and stuffs his hands in his pockets. All of these nervous, almost evasive gestures and behaviors represent a stark contrast from the goons in Johnny Friendly's gang. Though they are just as verbally inexpressive, the henchmen stand strong in twos and threes, in solid hats and long overcoats, sure of what they're doing at all times. The henchmen make eye contact, while Malloy frequently looks away. Brando must convey Malloy's interior life through these physical gestures, since the script gives Malloy so little verbal eloquence.

Kazan worked with Brando at the Actors Studio, so he knew his talents and knew the benefits of improvisation in acting. Improvisation means deviating from the written script and exploring an urge, a path, a riff, or an intuition because it feels right or "in character." Improvisation can become scripted if, for example, an exploration works extraordinarily well in rehearsal. The famous "white glove" scene began as improvisation. Brando's seemingly unconscious fiddling with the glove throws off the entire rhythm of the scene and adds to the unexpected nature of each step. It creates a second dynamic. The first dynamic is their private, delicate conversation, and the second gives meaning to their physical interaction. Dropping the glove makes Edie unsure of what she wants to do with her body. Should she reach out to grab the glove, or politely await its return? She cycles unconsciously and hesitantly through various options, even as she keeps up an intimate conversation. Each parry and thrust of her initial step and Malloy's teasing counterstep sends an electric charge through the scene.

Strong acting is also notable in Charlie and Terry's scene in the taxicab. Rod Steiger and Marlon Brando are large men stuck in a cramped environment, navigating through charged emotional territory. The actors choose unconventional reactions to throw the audience off guard. Steiger's ultra-cool Charlie can't stop fiddling with his gloves, for example, and Terry doesn't flee the pistol but rather calmly turns it aside. The men speak very few words, and the words, too, are rather conventional. The actors' symphony of facial expressions makes those few words eloquent. The pauses and ellipses between and around the spoken words, combined with the expressiveness of the faces, create volumes of meaning and emotion.

The scene in the taxi was shot three times. Once the crew rolled in a two-shot, with both Brando and Steiger visible. Once the camera closed in on Brando so that Steiger wasn't seen, even though he was there with Brando as someone for Brando to interact with. However, when it came time for Steiger's close-ups, the notoriously complex Brando had to leave for a psychotherapy appointment—so Steiger did all his close-ups with an extra on the set playing Terry Malloy off-screen. That the scene is such a success is a testament to the power of the acting.

ON THE WATERFRONT

Important Quotations Explained

1. FATHER BARRY: "D & D? What's that?"
    KAYO DUGAN: "Deaf and dumb. No matter how much we hate the torpedoes, we don't rat."

This exchange takes place during the secret meeting the priest holds in the basement of the church. It illustrates the depth and longevity of the longshoremen's bind. Though they all agree, deep down, that the treatment they receive from Johnny Friendly and his goons is unfair and inhuman, speaking out about it might put them in a worse situation—that is, jobless or dead. Living by the code forced on them by the corrupt union has preserved their lives, but they live in a degraded state almost like slaves. To save their own lives, the longshoremen agree to act as if they see and hear nothing. The word *torpedoes* is slang for Johnny Friendly and his goons, who point weapons of sorts at the longshoremen every day. The goons hang out on the docks as perpetual reminders of Friendly's strength, and they have a long history of roughing people up. To *rat* means to reveal injustices or transgressions to a party that's not immediately involved, such as a lawyer or the Waterfront Crime Commission. It holds the same significance as *stool pigeon* in the slang of the stevedores.

2. EDIE: "Which side are *you* with?"
    TERRY: "Me? I'm with me—Terry."

When nameless thugs ambush the secret meeting, Terry helps Edie escape. As they walk through the park in front of the church, a hesitant Edie tries to figure out who Terry is. She can't read him because she isn't familiar with the area or the way the dock works. She doesn't know who's who. Terry's casual answer here reveals a streak of naïveté because, though he may think he's independent at this point, he's clearly a pawn of Johnny Friendly and Charlie "the Gent." He wouldn't have shown up at the meeting if he were truly on his own. As Terry's conscience swells inside him, and as he begins to act on that conscience, this statement becomes increasingly true. But at this time, his attempts to distance himself from either side are mere dreaming. Nevertheless, this dreaming reveals his awareness that he wants nothing of the life either side can offer him. Deep down, he's not a thug, but he's not a day laborer either. The film traces Terry's discovery of who that "me" really is.

3. TERRY: "Hey, you wanna hear my philosophy of life? Do it to him before he does it to you."

The night after Terry and Edie walk through the park, Edie finds Terry on the rooftop tending to the pigeons, including Joey's. Curious about his sensitive side, she agrees to go with him to a saloon, where they have an intimate and revealing conversation. Terry's statement here indicates the huge philosophical gap between him and Edie. This gap makes their developing relationship all the more powerful, because to understand each other they must attempt to understand an unfamiliar and even unsavory way of living and thinking. Terry's words summarize a lifetime of being pushed around and having to scrap for every morsel and every bit of self-confidence. In Edie's worldview, everybody cares about everybody else, while Terry visualizes a dog-eat-dog world in which people do what they have to do in order to survive.

4. TERRY: "But you know if I spill, my life ain't worth a nickel."
FATHER BARRY: "And how much is your soul worth if you don't?"

After Father Barry hears Terry's out-of-church confession about his involvement in Joey Doyle's death, he urges Terry to tell both Edie and the Waterfront Crime Commission, and he gets this response. This brief exchange effectively summarizes Terry's mounting dilemma and is the thematic crux of the film. Terry must decide whether he wants to risk his life by speaking out against larger, stronger forces, or to live the rest of his life with a secret harbored deep in his heart. Father Barry's response here indicates that Terry's duty as a human being is to tell the truth. Otherwise, he'll live a tortured existence with a cowardly soul. As a priest, Father Barry believes in a glorious afterlife, but only for those who have done their best to cleanse their souls. This conversation foreshadows Terry's final explosion on the docks in which he reclaims his conscience and forges an individual identity: "I been rattin' on *myself* all these years."

5.   TERRY: "You don't understand. I coulda had class. I
             coulda been a contender. I coulda been someone, instead of
             a bum, which is what I am, let's face it . . . It was you,
             Charlie."

Terry says this to Charlie at the end of the profoundly intimate taxi-cab conversation where the two tense brothers are alone for the first time in the film. Charlie, who cares deeply for his brother but hasn't looked out for him properly, allows himself to deny the reason for Terry's failed boxing career. He condemns mistakenly the rotten trainer who supposedly mismanaged Terry's skills. But in truth, Charlie's association with Johnny Friendly meant that the union had a boxer it could control. Through Charlie, Johnny Friendly ordered Terry to tank a big fight, guaranteeing himself a huge payoff by betting on the opponent. Even though Charlie made sure Terry got a bit of cash, Terry complains here that Charlie killed what was really at stake—his soul, his pride, and his self-esteem. This well-known quote reveals the complexity of the brothers' relationship and expresses Terry's deep inner pain that the relationship probably cannot be salvaged. The brothers love each other—but Terry now acknowledges his brother's partial responsibility for his current bind, and he finally realizes that he can escape the label of "bum" only through his own actions.

VERTIGO

(1958)

Context

Alfred Hitchcock was born to middle-class parents in London, England, fittingly on Friday the thirteenth of August 1899. When he was twenty-one, he took a job at Paramount Studios in London as a writer and illustrator of silent-movie title cards, which led to work as an art director and finally to a position as a director. He acquired the honorary title "Master of Suspense" while working on a radio adaptation of his film *The Lodger* for RKO in 1940. Hitchcock married his assistant, film editor Alma Reville, with whom he collaborated on all his work. The couple, along with their daughter Patricia, moved to the United States in 1939, where they lived for the rest of their lives.

Rebecca, Hitchcock's first American-made film, won the 1940 Academy Award for Best Picture. In 1947, seeking artistic independence, Hitchcock broke with noted Hollywood producer David O. Selznick, with whom he had worked for almost eight years, and formed his own company, Transatlantic Pictures. The company went bankrupt after producing two films that used the expensive and difficult "ten-minute take" technique, in which the entire script was shot in a series of ten-minute, uninterrupted takes. The point was to create films that appeared to have no editing, but the process was hard on actors and producers alike. Hitchcock then worked a brief stint at Warner Brothers, followed by a run at Paramount, which produced *Vertigo*. His last film for Paramount was *Psycho,* in 1960. He then moved to Universal, where he remained for the rest of his career. Hitchcock also made a foray into American television with his series *Alfred Hitchcock Presents*, which ran from 1955 to 1962 before being reformatted as *The Alfred Hitchcock Hour*, which ran for another three years. *Hitchcock* died at home in California on April 29, 1980, while working on his fifty-fourth film.

One of *Vertigo*'s main themes—the attempt to create the ideal woman—has roots in the Roman myth of Pygmalion and Galatea in which the sculptor Pygmalion uses his art to create an ivory statue of the perfect woman and then tragically falls in love with it. But the film has roots in reality as well. There are parallels between the *Vertigo* protagonist's quest for the ideal woman and Hitchcock's relationship with Grace Kelly, an actress who appeared in three of his films. Hitchcock felt that Kelly's blond beauty and distinct acting style made her the standard by which all other actresses should be judged. Her departure from the film world in the mid-1950s to marry Prince Rainier of Monaco led Hitchcock to attempt to mold other actresses in her image. Kim Novak, the blonde co-star of *Vertigo*, was one of these Grace Kelly stand-ins.

Vertigo, like all Hitchcock films, was influenced by the art-film movement of the 1920s, which stressed experimentation and strong use of imagery. Early in his career, when Hitchcock worked at the UFA studios in Berlin, Germany, he absorbed the German Expressionism of F. W. Murnau and Fritz Lang, whose method of exposing the inner life of characters through unusual camera angles, moody lighting, and exaggerated *mise-en-scène* (stage-setting) influenced much of Hitchcock's work. Hitchcock's *Vertigo*, in turn, influenced the French New Wave school of film. Filmmakers such as Alain Resnais and François Truffaut introduced elements of *Vertigo*'s plot and certain symbolic and stylistic details from the film into their own works. By the 1960s, this group had raised the status of Hitchcock to that of *auteur*, or film artist, by reverently deconstructing his work in the film journal *Les Cahiers du Cinéma*. Most notable in *Les Cahiers* are fifty hours of interviews with Hitchcock conducted by Truffaut.

The Hollywood premiere of *Vertigo* received mainly positive reviews from film trade papers. *The Hollywood Reporter* called it ". . . a picture no filmmaker should miss" and applauded Hitchcock's "pioneering techniques." *Variety* gave it a mixed review, predicting box office success but criticizing the film's first half as too slow and too long. Reviewers outside Hollywood weren't as complimentary. *Cue* panned Hitchcock's concentration on scenery, technique, and "gimmicks" and lamented what it felt, at just over two hours, was an overlong film. *The New Yorker* went so far as to call the film "farfetched nonsense," and *Time* magazine labeled it "another Hitchcock and bull story." *Vertigo* had an average box-office run. In terms of box office receipts, it ranked twenty-first in 1958, making $3.2 million domestically. In 1958, the film was nominated for the Academy Award in Art Direction and Sound. *Vertigo* returned to the screen in 1983 as part of a program to re-release Hitchcock's films, and it was carefully restored in 1996. Today, *Vertigo* is a critically acclaimed film that is still hotly debated by film critics, academics, and Hitchcock fans alike. In 1998, the American Film Institute named *Vertigo* number sixty-one on its "100 Greatest American Movies of All Time" list. The Institute also ranked the film eighteenth on both the "100 Most Thrilling American Films" and "100 Greatest Love Stories of All Time" lists.

VERTIGO

Plot Overview

While pursuing a criminal across the rooftops of San Francisco, detective Scottie Ferguson slips and finds himself dangling from the gutter of a tall building. A colleague falls to his death in an attempt to rescue Scottie as he looks on in horror. In the apartment of his ex-fiancée, Midge, Scottie discusses his career plans in light of his newly discovered acrophobia, which has prompted him to quit the police force. Scottie is contacted by college acquaintance Gavin Elster, who has heard of Scottie's accident and wishes to hire him to trail his wife Madeleine, who Elster believes is possessed by the spirit of her great-grandmother Carlotta Valdes. Scottie later learns from Elster that Carlotta committed suicide at age twenty-six—Madeleine's current age—and he fears that Madeleine, too, has suicidal tendencies. Scottie is initially skeptical but begins to follow the beautiful and mysterious Madeleine in her wanderings around San Francisco, eventually tracking her to the McKittrick Hotel, where he learns Madeleine spends time under the name Carlotta Valdes. Scottie and Midge learn the story of Carlotta Valdes and her San Francisco manor from bookstore owner and local historian Pop Leibel, and they later discover that the McKittrick hotel is in fact Carlotta's former home.

The next day, Scottie continues to trail Madeleine, this time to a spot under the Golden Gate Bridge, where he watches her throw herself into the San Francisco Bay. Scottie dives in and rescues the unconscious Madeleine and drives her to his apartment, where he undresses her and puts her to bed. When Madeleine awakens, she claims not to remember anything about her suicide attempt, so Scottie tells her that she appeared to have slipped. As they talk, they begin to fall in love. But when Scottie leaves her to answer the phone, Madeleine slips out the door and flees. The next day, Scottie is surprised to trail Madeleine back to his own apartment, where she is leaving a thank you note for him. They decide to spend the day wandering together, traveling to the giant sequoia forest at Big Basin, where Madeleine makes evasive allusions to her possession and her strange dreams about death. She describes a place in her dreams that looks like Spain, which Scottie later recognizes to be the mission at San Juan Bautista.

Scottie tells Madeleine that he can explain her strange obsessions as a repressed memory of time she must have spent at the mission. He resolves to take her to the spot to bring to rest the notion that she is possessed. When they arrive, she recognizes it all, and after professing her love for Scottie, runs agitatedly toward the bell tower. She heads up the spiral staircase with Scottie in hot pursuit. Near the top of the tower, Scottie's acrophobia strikes, and he is unable to continue the climb. He looks out the window in time to see Madeleine's body hurtle down to the rooftop of an adjoining building. Scottie flees. He is next seen at the coroner's inquest, where Gavin Elster is cleared of all responsibility for his wife's death, but where Scottie is berated by the coroner for allowing his phobia to, in effect, cause the death of an innocent person. Wracked with guilt and grief, Scottie spends the next year catatonic in a sanatorium, where Midge attempts to bring him back to reality.

After his release from the sanatorium, Scottie again wanders the streets of San Francisco, seeing hints of Madeleine in everyone. He follows one woman, who he believes looks like a brunette Madeleine, back to her apartment and questions her relentlessly about her identity. She says her name is Judy Barton, that she hails from Kansas, and that she works in a department store. Scottie invites her to dinner. As soon as he leaves to allow her to change her clothes, Judy begins to pack a suitcase. Hesitating about what to do, she sits down and composes a letter to Scottie. In it, she divulges that she had been hired by Gavin Elster to play the role of Madeleine in a plot to murder his wife. Judy reveals that when she got to the top of the bell tower, Elster was waiting with the already-dead body of his wife dressed identically to Judy, which he hurled out the window for Scottie to witness. She ends her letter by admitting her love for Scottie. After a brief hesitation, she tears up the letter.

Scottie and Judy have dinner and it is apparent that Scottie is interested in Judy only insofar as she resembles the dead Madeleine. His obsession deepens, and he insists that Judy dye her hair blonde and wear clothing identical to that worn by Madeleine. Judy initially resists, but then decides she would rather be loved by Scottie as someone else than lose his love altogether. When she returns from the beauty parlor, her transformation is complete. They kiss passionately. In the next scene, the two are preparing to go to dinner when Scottie notices that the necklace Judy puts on is Carlotta's necklace, which Madeleine wore the day she died. He realizes Judy's true identity but does not say anything right away.

Instead, Scottie tells her he wants to take a drive in the country and begins driving toward San Juan Bautista. Judy becomes increasingly hysterical as she realizes that Scottie suspects her secret. In a rage, Scottie drags Judy up the steps of the tower, confronting her with her deception. She admits her guilt but claims to still love Scottie and begs for his forgiveness. They reach the top and embrace, but are interrupted by the shadowy figure of a nun. Judy is so startled by the ghostly figure that she screams and falls from the tower to her death. Scottie is left alone in the tower, cured of his acrophobia but broken in every other respect.

Character List

John "Scottie" Ferguson—Played by James Stewart The protagonist of the film. Scottie is a former detective who quits his job when he develops severe acrophobia, or fear of heights. He is a romantic who rejects reality in favor of illusion. His obsession with the ideal woman fuels much of the action of the film.

Madeleine Elster—Played by Kim Novak The female lead of the film. "Madeleine" is actually a role played by Judy, who is impersonating Gavin Elster's wife. Romantic and ethereal, "Madeleine" is supposedly haunted by long-dead relative Carlotta Valdes and seems bent on committing suicide against her own will. Madeleine becomes Scottie's love interest and represents the ideal woman to him.

Judy Barton—Played by Kim Novak The true identity of the woman who impersonated Madeleine in the first half of the film. Judy played the role of Madeleine at the behest of her one-time lover, Gavin Elster. She is malleable, lonely, and a bit hard. She is willing to surrender her own identity so that Scottie will love her.

Midge Wood—Played by Barbara Bel Geddes Scottie's friend and ex-fiancée. Pretty and very capable, Midge is an artist who makes her living designing women's undergarments. She is a mother figure who is still in love with Scottie and represents everyday reality.

Gavin Elster—Played by Tom Helmore The film's anti-hero. Gavin is an old college acquaintance of Scottie who has married into a wealthy shipbuilding family. He is calculating and manipulative, exploiting Scottie's weakness to achieve his own goals.

VERTIGO

Coroner—Played by Henry Jones The voice of Scottie's conscience, who berates Scottie for allowing his fear of heights to
prevent him from saving Madeleine's life. The coroner's manner is clinical and unsympathetic.

Pop Leibel—Played by Konstantin Shayne Bookstore owner and
San Francisco historian. Pop represents the "old" San Francisco inhabited by Carlotta Valdes.

Doctor—Played by Raymond Bailey Psychiatrist in the sanatorium where Scottie recovers from Madeleine's death. The
doctor is the voice of reason who attempts to make sense of
Scottie's descent into madness.

Analysis of Major Characters

Scottie

The scene in Midge's apartment reveals that Scottie was a fairly average man firmly rooted in reality before his near-death experience. Scottie was a lawyer who joined the police force as a detective in hope of one day becoming chief of police. But Scottie has become acrophobic and is so disturbed by his condition that he quits his detective job. His restlessness and aimlessness are so palpable that when he takes a job sleuthing for Gavin Elster, he is perfectly positioned to get caught up in the world of dream and illusion that Elster and "Madeleine" create for him. He yearns for his life before the accident on the roof, and Madeleine's apparent possession by a figure from the past is attractive to him, despite his initial skepticism.

By the time Scottie attempts to re-create Judy in Madeleine's image, it is clear that he has become completely lost in the world of illusion and fantasy—so lost that he can no longer articulate rational reasons for his behavior. When Judy asks him what good it will do for her to "become" Madeleine, Scottie answers very genuinely that he doesn't know. And yet he is driven to make the transformation happen, even at the risk of driving away Judy. The revelation of Judy's true identity shatters Scottie's illusion. Rage at the dissolution of his dream and at Judy's trickery now possesses him.

Madeleine/Judy

The Madeleine character of *Vertigo* is a fabrication from the start, a fact that is not known until two-thirds of the way into the film when it is revealed that Judy impersonated Madeleine in a scheme to murder the real Madeleine Elster. It is a fact that unmoors viewers as it means that "Madeleine's" apparent motivations, haunted dreams, memories, and even mannerisms have been externally created by Judy in collaboration with Elster. "Madeleine" is the perfect representation of the world of romantic illusion to which Scottie is tragically attracted. It is difficult to discuss what motivates "Madeleine" because she is no more than a projection. Judy, on the other hand, is a real person, complete with imperfections, complex feelings, and motivations. Where "Madeleine" represents the unattainable ideal, Judy represents the real. The only point at which Judy and Madeleine converge is in their love for Scottie.

Judy's manners are unrefined, even a bit coarse. In short, she is the antithesis of the refined, ethereal "Madeleine." But Scottie recognizes some echo of Madeleine in Judy and relentlessly quizzes her about her identity. At first, Judy defends her true self, repeating her name, the name of her hometown in Kansas, and her occupation. In retrospect, we see that she is probably desperate to reclaim her true identity after having played the role of Madeleine for so long. When it becomes clear to Judy that Scottie will never love her for her own attributes, she consciously surrenders herself and allows him to transform her into Madeleine. Indeed, by the time her transformation is complete, it seems that rather than playing a role, Judy has actually taken on Madeleine's identity, a fact that would account for her unthinking and fatal choice of Carlotta's necklace when she dresses for dinner.

MIDGE

Where Madeleine represents a romantic, otherworldly ideal, Midge stands for its opposite. The bespectacled Midge is practical, competent, realistic, and well adjusted. An artist by training, she applies her skill to prosaic ends, creating advertisements for women's undergarments. Throughout the film, she attempts to keep Scottie's feet on the ground. First, she tries to change Scottie's mind about giving up his detective job and works on helping him overcome his acrophobia. When he begins his job trailing Madeleine, Midge attempts to unmask the improbability of the situation. Her constant attempts to make Scottie discuss the case reveal her desire to ground the mystery in reality and his unwillingness to do so. Scottie considers Midge's treatment of Madeleine's world to be a kind of blasphemy, and it becomes clear to Midge that she will find no entrance into that world. It is significant that the last shot of Midge is of her retreating down the hall of the sanatorium. She has been unable to bring Scottie out of his catatonic state and back to reality. He is now firmly entrenched in the world of illusion, beyond the reach of the "real world."

Themes, Motifs, and Symbols

Themes

Death as Both Attractive and Frightening

In the opening scene of *Vertigo*, Scottie is moments away from death as he dangles from the roof of a tall building. His fear is palpable, and while he is overcome with terror watching his comrade fall, letting go seems to be the only way out of the situation. Madeleine is the embodiment of this fear of and attraction to death. Supposedly possessed by a woman who took her own life, Madeleine wanders San Francisco, drawn to the idea of suicide and yet fearing death. One day after attempting to drown herself in the San Francisco Bay, she and Scottie wander among the ancient Sequoia trees and she expresses a dread of death. "I don't like it, knowing I have to die," she tells him, and she pleads with him to take her into the light.

This confusion of impulses manifests itself on a more figurative level when Scottie attempts to mold Judy in Madeleine's image. While Judy initially fights the annihilation of her real self—a kind of death—she eventually embraces it as a way to claim Scottie's love, saying, "I don't care anymore about me." Scottie enacts these contradictory impulses when he drags Judy to the top of the bell tower with the apparent desire to kill her, and then reacts with horror and despair when she plummets to her death.

The Impenetrable Nature of Appearances

The mask-like qualities of appearance are suggested during the opening credits of the film, which feature a woman's expressionless face and a shot first of her lips and then of her nervously darting eyes. The depths of emotion and experience in this woman are unknowable to us. In the scene in Midge's apartment, Scottie appears to be a balanced man on the mend from a traumatizing experience, but it does not take long to realize that his healthy exterior masks a burgeoning madness. And while Midge is pragmatic, unromantic, and controlled in her responses, her exterior hides the soul of a passionate person. After her failed attempt to break into Scottie's dream-world by painting her own head on Carlotta's portrait, she flies into a surprising rage, flinging paintbrushes at her own reflection in the window—an attempt to shatter the mask that Scottie sees and mistakes for her whole identity.

Madeleine's character is nothing but appearance. She is a fabrication loosely based on the legend of a dead woman, and Scottie's attempt to understand and penetrate that appearance is what leads to his downfall and the downfall of Judy/Madeleine. After assuming Madeleine's appearance at Scottie's insistence, Judy has difficulty penetrating her own mask. By the time Scottie drags her up the steps of the bell tower, she no longer has a firm grasp on her true identity and alternates between speaking as Judy and as Madeleine.

THE FOLLY OF ROMANTIC DELUSION

While Scottie's acrophobia is his most apparent Achilles' heel, his true tragic flaw is his penchant for romantic delusion. He fools himself, and is easily fooled by others, into believing in illusions that are romantically gratifying to him. Hitchcock presents Midge as a highly sympathetic character and prompts viewers to root for her in her vain attempts to woo Scottie. Midge is the antithesis of romantic delusion, firmly grounded in the real world and able to offer Scottie a mature kind of love. But this is the kind of love that Scottie rejects in favor of the illusive, dreamlike love he finds with Madeleine. And it is his decisive submission to delusion that ensures the film's tragic ending. Judy pleads with Scottie to accept her as she is, to try to move beyond the dead Madeleine, but this is something he cannot do. Judy's startled fall from the bell tower is the film's final example of the folly and danger of romantic delusion. When the shadowy figure of a nun appears behind Judy and Scottie in the tower, Judy seems to be overtaken by the romantic notion that it may be the ghost of the real Madeleine returning to the scene of the crime.

MOTIFS

POWER AND FREEDOM

Power and freedom are held up as privileges men had in the past, but presumably do not have in the present. While discussing his nostalgia for the San Francisco of the past, Gavin Elster tells Scottie that he misses the days when men had "power [and] freedom." Later, when Scottie is researching the story of Carlotta Valdes, the bookshop owner and historian Pop Leibel tells him that the wealthy man who abandoned Carlotta and kept her child was able to do so with impu-

VERTIGO

nity because men in those days had "the freedom and the power" to do such things. Scottie yearns for the time when he felt he was the master of his own destiny, before his brush with death on the rooftop. The words *freedom* and *power* again are spoken by Scottie as he drags Judy up the stairs of the bell tower.

Tunnels and Corridors

Tunnels and corridors repeatedly represent the passage to death. The first tunnel image appears when the camera reveals Scottie's perspective as he clings to the rooftop gutter. The camera shoots straight down the side of the building, creating a tunnel effect. While visiting the sequoia forest, Madeleine shares a recurring dream in which she walks ". . . down a long corridor." Nothing but darkness and death await her at the end of the corridor. She also dreams of a room in which there is a corridor-like open grave. When Midge walks away from Scottie for the last time, it is down a long sanatorium corridor that darkens around her. This passage marks a kind of death for Midge as she loses hope of rekindling her romance with Scottie.

Hitchcock turns the tunnel-to-death motif on its head in the corridor outside Judy's apartment. Judy emerges at the end of the hallway after her transformative trip to the beauty salon. Rather than retreat down the corridor, she comes forward as Madeleine in a kind of resurrection scene. The next tunnel Judy travels through is in Scottie's car, when he takes her back to San Juan Bautista to retrace the steps of her crime. As they drive toward the mission, tall trees on either side of the road combine with dusky lighting to give the impression of a tunnel.

Bouquets of Flowers

In one scene, Scottie follows Madeleine to a flower shop, where she purchases a small nosegay. Its fragile perfection is an ideal representation of Madeleine herself. The bouquet appears again several times, most notably when Madeleine stands at the edge of San Francisco Bay, plucking petals from the flowers and tossing them into the water. The destruction of the bouquet mirrors Madeleine's fixation on self-destruction as she prepares to drown herself in the bay. After Madeleine's death, Hitchcock provides a graphic depiction of Scottie's nightmare in which a brightly animated bouquet swirls about and then violently disintegrates—a symbolic representation of Madeleine's death. When Scottie spends the day with Judy before her transformation into Madeleine, he buys her a single flower to wear as a corsage, not a replica of Madeleine's signature bouquet as we might expect. It is a visual reminder that Judy does not possess the ideal perfection of Madeleine, but merely a small seed of it.

SPIRALS

Spirals evoke the literal and figurative feelings of vertigo that hound Scottie and Madeleine/Judy. The opening credits feature a spiral emerging from a woman's eye. When Scottie looks down from the roof at his fallen colleague, the dead man's limbs are splayed in the shape of a spiral, indicating that events have spiraled out of control.

As Scottie observes Madeleine in the museum sitting in front of Carlotta Valdes's portrait, the camera zooms in on the back of her head to reveal a tightly wound spiraling bun, an exact replica of the style worn by Carlotta. The spiral foreshadows the dizzying chaos into which Madeleine will lead Scottie. The most physically jarring spiral is the one formed by the winding stairs of the bell tower as revealed from Scottie's perspective. As he chases Madeleine up the stairs attempting to halt her apparent suicide, his acrophobia takes over and the camera shoots straight down the stairwell. His vertigo has made him powerless to save the woman he loves. The very structure of the film suggests a spiraling circularity: Scottie falls in love with Madeleine, loses her to death, then falls in love with Judy/Madeleine again, only to lose her to death as well.

SYMBOLS

SEQUOIA TREES

Scottie and Madeleine's visit to the forest of sequoia trees is one of Scottie's last attempts to return to a healthy worldview. He tells Madeleine that the tree's scientific name means "always green, ever living," making explicit the idea that sequoia trees symbolize life in the film. However, the trees remind Madeleine of her own mortality. In response to this immense life force, she says, "I don't like it, knowing I have to die." The couple looks at the cross-section of a felled tree, which shows how old the tree was when it was chopped down and suggests that the tree would have gone on living forever had it not been for human intervention. Madeleine's response to the trees is complex. She appears simultaneously to be afraid of dying and afraid to embrace life. Ultimately, she runs away from the forest, feeling alienated from life and wanting to die.

GREEN

The color green appears frequently throughout the film, typically in association with eerie or uncanny images. For example, when Scottie first sees Madeleine in Ernie's Restaurant, she stands out vividly from everyone else in the room because of her dramatic green stole, giving her a startling and somewhat unsettling appearance. In his apartment, as he becomes more withdrawn from the outside world and immersed in a dream world, Scottie wears a green sweater. Judy, who seems to be the ghost of Madeleine, first appears wearing a green dress. Her room is illuminated at night by the building's green neon sign, and when she emerges into Scottie's view as the fully transformed Madeleine, she is bathed in the green light, making her look even more like the specter of the dead Madeleine. Thus, while green sometimes symbolizes life, as in the sequoia forest, it also symbolizes the ghostly or uncanny. Both associations with the color green are traditional and can be seen in the earliest folktales. For example, because green can represent the spring and the rebirth of nature, it is also associated with the life after death embodied by ghosts and spirits, as in *Sir Gawain and the Green Knight*.

VERTIGO

FILM ANALYSIS

SCOTTIE AS EVERYMAN

In *Vertigo*, Hitchcock wins sympathy for Scottie almost immediately as he dangles by his fingernails from a rooftop high above the street. The camera's dizzying angle presents Scottie's point of view as he hangs helplessly over the abyss. When the camera cuts to his face, it is powerfully engaging to see Scottie's cold sweat and obvious terror. Our sympathy and identification with the protagonist are key to the film's powerful impact.

After bonding with Scottie in crisis, we then get a sense of Scottie's amiability, sense of humor, and desirability to women in the scene in Midge's apartment. The fear of heights that he exhibits in the same scene is a common phobia with which many viewers can easily identify. When it leads to Scottie's downfall, his pain can be felt all the more keenly.

These opening scenes position Scottie as an Everyman—someone with attractive character traits and some very human flaws. His career aspiration to become chief of police, his conflicted feelings about Midge, and his need to recuperate after a brush with death on the roof all serve to make him accessible and human. When he tentatively accepts a detective job from Gavin Elster, we can sympathize with his desire to feel useful and to immerse himself in his prior life as detective.

It is critical that we feel sympathy for Scottie by the time he begins to trail Madeleine because the dreamlike "detective work" scenes change every-day reality into a world that is harder to recognize or to compare to the real world. Hitchcock employs soft-focus camera work and Bernard Herrmann's swirling music to create a world that facilitates Scottie's ever-growing obsession with Madeleine. By the time Scottie and Madeleine profess their love for each other, we've been assimilated into this dream world and are as enchanted as Scottie is by Madeleine's ethereal, haunted persona and as anxious to help Madeleine escape her "possession." When Madeleine hurls herself off the bell tower of San Juan Bautista, Scottie's helplessness and anguish are ours as well.

Hitchcock tests our sympathy for Scottie as his obsession for the dead Madeleine leads him to mold Judy into Madeleine's image. But Hitchcock lessens the distastefulness of this monomaniacal behavior by first showing Scottie at his weakest and most vulnerable. Following Madeleine's death, the catatonic Scottie is placed in a sanatorium and is completely unresponsive to Midge's aid and care. The doctor reveals that Scottie suffers from "acute melancholia, together with a guilt complex." Hitchcock even makes us privy to Scottie's nightmares, which he depicts in a striking mix of cartoon and surreal photography. The dream culminates with the protagonist falling headlong into an open grave. By experiencing his dream, the viewer gains a visceral sense of Scottie's identification with Madeleine and his subconscious desire to join her in death. While Scottie's subsequent obsessiveness may still be distasteful, Hitchcock has ensured an understanding of the roots of that behavior. Hitchcock also strengthens the identification with Scottie's obsession by filming many key scenes from Scottie's perspective. When Judy emerges from her room completely transformed, the camera turns with Scottie to show what he sees: her figure bathed in a green light, her outline diffused in a ghostly glow.

By the time Scottie discovers Judy's secret past as "Madeleine" and begins his maniacal return to the top of the bell tower, our feelings are as conflicted as his. We are horrified when he drags Judy up the stairs and simultaneously root for him to conquer his acrophobia and reach the top. We share the admixture of repulsion and attraction Scottie feels toward Judy/Madeleine as she attempts to explain her role in the death of Elster's wife. Instead of providing a feeling of completion or catharsis, however, the final sequence of events resurrects the state of suspense: Judy has fallen to her death and Scottie stands in the bell tower, untroubled by acrophobia, but a shattered man in every other sense.

GREEK AND ROMAN MYTHOLOGY

Perhaps the most obvious mythological influence on the film is the Greek myth of Orpheus and Eurydice, in which the musician Orpheus loses his wife, Eurydice, to death and ventures into the underworld to rescue her, only to lose her again. *Vertigo* plays off of two central themes of this story. First, Scottie's Orpheus character attempts to save Madeleine, the Eurydice character, from drowning in the San Francisco Bay. He succeeds, only to lose her in a "suicide"

VERTIGO

off the bell tower. He then gets a second chance to save Madeleine from death, this time by recreating Judy in Madeleine's image. He achieves this resurrection, but then loses her again when she plunges from the bell tower. And just as in the Orpheus myth it is Orpheus's fault—his failure to follow the instruction not to look back at his beloved as he leads her out of Hades—that he loses Eurydice again, so in *Vertigo* it is Scottie's flaws that lead to his losses: his acrophobia causes him to lose Madeleine and it is his insistence on recreating a dead woman that leads him to lose Judy.

The Roman myth of Pygmalion and Galatea is also a clear influence on *Vertigo*. The sculptor Pygmalion (Scottie in the film) uses his art to create a sculpture of the perfect woman (*Vertigo's* Madeleine) and then tragically falls in love with his creation. George Bernard Shaw's play *Pygmalion*, which was later adapted into the musical *My Fair Lady*, also echoes here, particularly in the scenes in which Scottie, as a *Pygmalion* Professor Higgins, attempts to transform Judy, his Eliza Doolittle, into a proper lady, but without any of the comic effects of the play.

Scottie can also be seen as Tristan, the ill-fated lover of the medieval legend *Tristan and Isolde*, who marries a second woman named Isolde when the true Isolde of his passions weds another. That legend ends with the death of Tristan and the suicide of his beloved, just as *Vertigo* ends with Judy/Madeleine's accidental death and Scottie's living "death" in the wake of tragedy.

PAGE-TO-SCREEN ADAPTATION

Alfred Hitchcock was known for his deep involvement in the screenplay-writing process, a fact that accounts in part for the distinctly recognizable quality of all his films. Viewers are treated to a visual reminder of Hitchcock's presence in each film when they spot the director in one of his famous cameo appearances. Turning the novel *D'Entre les Morts* by French mystery writers Thomas Narcejac and Pierre Boileau into a screenplay for *Vertigo* proved a long, arduous, and, at times, frustrating enterprise for Hitchcock. Translated into English as *From Among the Dead*, Paramount purchased the rights to the novel in 1955, and Hitchcock set to work adapting it. His first move was to hire the popular playwright Maxwell Anderson to create a first-draft screenplay. Completely dissatisfied with what Anderson produced, Hitchcock hired his former colleague Angus MacPhail to try his hand at an adaptation. However, MacPhail's alcoholism and resulting poor health led him to quit before he had produced anything of consequence.

Hitchcock finally hired Alec Coppel, an obscure author of three novels and a play. They worked collaboratively on the script for several months, but when Coppel presented Hitchcock with a completed first draft, the director was not pleased with the work. He attempted to persuade the previously ousted Anderson to revise Coppel's script, but the writer never produced a new draft. Hitchcock then hired writer Samuel Taylor, whose agent recommended him on the basis of his deep knowledge of San Francisco, where *Vertigo* is set. Without reading either the novel or Coppel's screenplay, Taylor wrote a new draft based on Hitchcock's vision for the film. Taylor added characters, improved the dialogue, and made the controversial decision to reveal Judy's secret—the plot twist—two-thirds of the way through the film. In the end, the novel's disdain for its characters and its view of life as debasing and meaningless was transformed by Hitchcock and his writers into sympathy for and identification with the characters and the admittedly imperfect world they inhabit. When all was said and done, only the basic plot line of the novel remained.

Score/Soundtrack

Hitchcock was an admirer of composer Bernard Herrmann long before the temperamental musician agreed to write a score for one of the director's films. Herrmann finally signed on to write the music for Hitchcock's 1955 film *The Trouble with Harry*. The two discovered an easy collaboration and worked together for eleven years, until an argument over *Torn Curtain* put an end to their partnership. Herrmann wrote the bulk of the score for *Vertigo*, considered by many critics and by Herrmann himself to be his finest film score, in a little over a month. He also had been hired to conduct the orchestra for the film's soundtrack, but an American musician's strike necessitated that it be recorded in Vienna under the baton of British conductor Muir Mathieson.

Herrmann scored the swirling harps and strings that imbue most of the pivotal action sequences in the film to mirror the vertigo that dogs the protagonist. The effect is heard as Scottie hangs from the roof in the opening scene, and as Scottie drags Judy to the top of the bell tower at the end of the film. The score also includes hints of motifs used by Wagner in *Die Walküre* and in *Tristan und Isolde*—

VERTIGO

a logical choice, given the film's roots in that myth. This highly romantic score also pays homage to Latin melody and rhythm, especially in the portions of the film meant to evoke feelings of the historic San Francisco and its Spanish influences. In scenes that feature the amorous relationship between Scottie and Madeleine/Judy, the orchestration reflects their tumultuous romance by relying on swelling strings, harp, and contrabassoon.

Hitchcock places Herrmann's background music in direct opposition to music that is played deliberately as part of the action of the film. While Herrmann's score represents the forces of destiny and the mysterious dream world inhabited by Madeleine, music that Midge plays on her radio and record player represents her world and the norms and strictures of conventional society. In two instances, Hitchcock develops the characters of both Scottie and Midge by drawing our attention to Midge's music. In the scene that first depicts Scottie recuperating from his brush with death, he becomes irritated with her concern for him and complains about the music she is playing—Bach's *Sinfonia*. The music underscores the conventional life that Midge represents and that Scottie rejects. The clash between the conventional world and Madeleine's world of romance and intrigue comes to a head after Madeleine's apparent death. Scottie is catatonic in a sanatorium, where Midge vainly attempts to bring him back to reality by playing Mozart's Symphony No. 34 on a phonograph. The music again provides a clue that he no longer responds to the conventional world. Scottie is now completely lost in Madeleine's haunted dream world.

Important Quotations Explained

1. GAVIN: "Do you believe that someone out of the past, someone dead, can enter and take possession of a living being?"

Gavin Elster asks Scottie this question in his attempt to hire Scottie to trail his wife. Elster is referring to his belief that the long-dead Carlotta Valdes has taken possession of his wife, Madeleine. For the first two-thirds of the film, both Scottie and the viewer come to believe that it is indeed possible for someone dead to take possession of a living being, as Madeleine glides around San Francisco apparently haunted by Carlotta, even driven to suicide by her ghost. But Madeleine is not the only one in the film possessed by a dead person. After Madeleine's apparent suicide, Scottie, too, becomes possessed. As he wanders about the streets of San Francisco after her death, he is continually convinced that he sees Madeleine in other women. When he meets Judy, he is certain that he has found her.

Judy also spends much of the film possessed by a dead person. The Madeleine whom she impersonates comes back to "haunt" her when Scottie insists that she assume the dead Madeleine's identity in both appearance and behavior. Eventually, Judy loses herself to a kind of possession by the dead woman. As Scottie drags her up the stairs of the bell tower at the end of the film, Judy answers sometimes as herself, sometimes as Madeleine, no longer certain of her true identity. When she sees the shadowy figure of a nun at the top of the bell tower, she panics and falls, fearing the apparition may be the dead Madeleine returning to avenge her murder.

2. POP LEIBEL: "He [Carlotta's lover] threw her away. Men could do that in those days. They had the power and the freedom."

These are Pop Leibel's words as he shares the tragic story of Carlotta Valdes with Scottie and Midge, the woman who supposedly possesses Madeleine Elster. Significantly, Pop Leibel echoes the words "power" and "freedom" that were used by Gavin Elster when he spoke nostalgically with Scottie about the San Francisco of the past. This power and freedom are precisely what Gavin Elster desires, and in the murder of his wife, he achieves this desire in much the same manner as Carlotta's lover. Ironically, Judy, in playing the role of Madeleine possessed by Carlotta, eventually shares Carlotta's fate. She, too, is "thrown away" by her lover, Elster, once she has served his needs. And while Judy does not commit suicide like Carlotta, her death is the result of her submission to and exploitation by men who claim to love her—both Elster and Scottie.

3. SCOTTIE: "What are you thinking about?"
    MADELEINE: "Of all the people who were born and died while the trees went on living."
    SCOTTIE: "Their true name is *Sequoia sempervirens*— always green, ever living."
    Madeleine: "I don't like it . . . knowing I have to die."

This dialogue between Scottie and Madeleine takes place in the giant sequoia forest at Big Basin. The thematic tension between fearing death and desiring its release comes to a head here, as Madeleine apparently grapples with an irresistible drive toward suicide and a simultaneous fear of her own demise. In retrospect, it is Judy's true voice speaking here. It is in this forest that Scottie and "Madeleine" profess their love for each other. The Judy within Madeleine realizes that once she fakes her suicide, she will no longer exist for Scottie and their love affair must end. The trees' scientific name and meaning foreshadows Scottie's later preoccupation with the dead Madeleine and with keeping her "ever living."

4. JUDY: "If I let you change me, will that do it? If I do what you tell me, will you love me?"
    SCOTTIE: "Yes—yes."
    JUDY: "Alright then, I'll do it. I don't care anymore about me."

This exchange takes place in Judy's apartment after Scottie spends an entire day attempting to transform Judy into Madeleine. Judy has finally given in to the romantic delusion that has already destroyed Scottie. Until this exchange, Judy has tried to convince Scottie to love her for her true self. But it is now clear to her that he will love her only as Madeleine. Judy's surrender provides a clear understanding of what motivates her: an overwhelming desire to be accepted and loved. She is willing to delude herself and live in Scottie's world of fantasy and illusion to attain that goal. Undoubtedly, the same motivation must have originally led her to accept the role of Madeleine at Gavin Elster's request. Her conscious decision to stop caring about herself opens the door to the disintegration of Judy's identity. She so successfully adopts the persona of Madeleine that she makes the fatal mistake of putting on Madeleine's "Carlotta" necklace. By the time Scottie drags her to the top of the bell tower, she is no longer certain of her own identity, speaking to him alternately as Judy and Madeleine. Judy's willingness to abdicate her own identity and her ultimate disintegration is realized in her death at the bell tower.

5. SCOTTIE: "He made you over just like I made you over—only better. Not only the clothes and the hair, but the looks and the manners and the words . . . And then what did he do? Did he train you? Did he rehearse you? Did he tell you exactly what to do and what to say?"

Scottie spits these words at Judy as he drags her up the San Juan Bautista tower. Here he conveys the full measure of his rage, disappointment, and bitterness. For the first time, Scottie sees the parallel between himself and the evil Gavin Elster. Just as Elster trained and groomed Judy to be the Madeleine who could entrance and manipulate Scottie, so Scottie dictates all elements of Judy's appearance in order to transform her into Madeleine. The comparison of the two men here is Hitchcock's way of conveying that the seeds of evil reside in everyone, no matter how well intentioned one might be.

VERTIGO

SLEEPING
BEAUTY

(1959)

Context

Walter Elias Disney was born in Chicago on December 5, 1901, to an Irish-Canadian father and a German-American mother. The family raised Walt, his sister, and his three other brothers on a farm near Marceline, Missouri. An unusually energetic boy, Walt developed a passion for drawing at an early age, along with an equally intense passion for salesmanship. He sketched relentlessly, then sold his sketches to neighbors, friends, and family. Moving back to Chicago for high school, Disney continued to draw but also took photographs, wrote for the school paper, and attended the Academy of Fine Arts in the evenings. A thirst for adventure led him to attempt military service in 1918, but he was too young to enlist. Instead, he joined the Red Cross as an ambulance driver and official chauffeur. In 1923, Walt followed his older brother, Roy, to Hollywood, carrying with him only a few drawing implements, one completed short animated film subject, and almost no money. Securing borrowed funds, he and his brother began an animated production company in their uncle's garage. Disney's entrepreneurial spirit and inspired imagination led quickly to the development of the Disney empire.

While Walt Disney's success as a businessman is legendary, his artistic accomplishments should not be overlooked. Over the course of his career, he stretched the limits of animated film by constantly innovating and perfecting new methods of animation. Before he was twenty, Disney became the first animator to seamlessly combine live-action footage with drawn animation. In releasing the world's first fully synchronized sound cartoon, "Steamboat Willie," in 1928, Disney also introduced the public to the character of Mickey Mouse. He introduced Technicolor to his productions in the early 1930s and used a revolutionary multiplane camera technique as early as the mid-1930s. Throughout his career, Disney and his teams innovated in the realms of effects animation, special processes, multiple exposures, props, and camera tricks.

The amazing success of Disney's early films gave him unusual freedom to expand and experiment further, despite the Great Depression and World War II. In the thirties, when the nation's economy was at its lowest ebb, the budgets for his films seemed staggering—*Snow White and the Seven Dwarfs*, for example, cost an astonishing $1.4 million. Still, the studio (constructed in Burbank in

1940) tightened its belt a bit during wartime, devoting much of its money and energy to the production of government-commissioned propagandist and military training films. In the 1950s, Disney created the Disneyland theme park in California and debuted the wildly successful "Disneyland" anthology series, later renamed "Walt Disney's Wonderful World of Color." By the time the workaholic Walt Disney died on December 15, 1966, his studio had released eighty-one feature films and won forty-eight Academy Awards. Today, the corporation which bears his name continues to expand and forge ahead in the fields of computer animation and restoration.

Sleeping Beauty was Walt Disney Pictures' sixteenth animated feature and, at the time, the most expensive of his films to produce. Making the film took more than six years at an estimated cost of $6 million, a figure that was totally unheard of for an animated feature in Disney's day. The lengthy production period resulted in part from the fact that Disney was preoccupied with the creation of Disneyland and the development of future projects. He rarely visited the studio, yet much of the creative process depended on his explicit approval.

The film process for *Sleeping Beauty* employed a new film size—Super Technirama 70. The 70-millimeter filmstrip was twice as wide as the 35-millimeter usually used both then and now and captures backgrounds with stunning clarity. It also employs a 2.35:1 aspect ratio, meaning that the width of the screen runs 2.35 times as wide as its height. Even today, 1.33:1 and 1.85:1 aspect ratios are more commonly used. The super-widescreen format allowed for the radical content and design of the film to be presented in a noticeably new way, with crystal clear focus and ultra-sharp backgrounds spread over more frame area. In contrast, other famous Disney films like *Cinderella*, *Peter Pan*, and *Alice in Wonderland* employ softer geometries and softer focuses.

Background painter Eyvind Earle based his radically detailed backgrounds on medieval, pre-Renaissance, and Gothic art. Artists who influenced his designs include Pieter Breughel and Jan van Eyck, as well as other Dutch, Italian, and Greek masters. The incredible detail of the art parallels the more adult content of this film as compared with Disney's earlier animated features. *Sleeping Beauty,* unlike the Mickey Mouse films or even *Snow White,* emphasizes human characters and renders death, sadness, and longing with realistic displays of emotion. The epic widescreen style also lends to the importance of spaces in conveying the emotional temperature of a scene. Earle answered directly to Walt Disney but supervised the visual design of the film by using an assembly line to divide up the labor. For example, Frank Armitage, an acquaintance of the Mexican muralist Diego Rivera, focused on the wide, sweeping backgrounds. Marc Davis supervised Princess Aurora's and Maleficent's characters.

Beginning in 1956, widescreen blockbusters rose in popularity, a trend that Disney attempted to capitalize on with *Sleeping Beauty*. Mammoth epic films shot in widescreen format changed the film world as they appeared one after another, including *War and Peace* (directed by King Vidor, 1956), *The Ten Commandments* (Cecil B. DeMille, 1956), *Ben-Hur* (William Wyler, 1959), and *Lawrence of Arabia* (David Lean, 1962). These epic films are longer than *Sleeping Beauty*—all of them are over three and a half hours long—but given its artistic scope and ambition, *Sleeping Beauty* deserves the title of epic as well.

Sleeping Beauty also stands out among other animated films because of its score. The music of the instrumentalists and singers plays for the duration of the movie. Only in rare moments does all instrumentation or song drop out. In most cases, a moving score sweeps the film along as an undercurrent. Disney chose to adapt Tchaikovsky's music for "The Sleeping Beauty" ballet, and in choosing to draw from such a grand composer for his seemingly simple family film, Disney declared the timelessness and artistic merits of *Sleeping Beauty* and brashly placed it in a canonical tradition. Disney spared no expense for its technical production, either. George Bruns, who is also noted for composing original tunes for *Pirates of the Caribbean*, *The Jungle Book*, and the 1950s hit *The Ballad of Davy Crockett*, recorded the score in Germany with state-of-the-art equipment.

Sleeping Beauty has the distinction of being the last film that Disney personally produced. Recently, *Sleeping Beauty* became the second film to receive a thorough computer restoration, in which a team of forty computer technicians pored over all 108,000 frames of the film to clean and refurbish the colors. The print that the crew succeeded in creating, with its rich hues and subtle saturations, actually surpasses the print of the film's initial 1959 release.

Plot Overview

Sleeping Beauty opens with a shot of turning pages in a storybook, indicating the historical but fantastical nature of the subsequent tale. In the story proper, a narrator introduces King Stefan and his unnamed wife, who finally have a child after years of longing for one. Well-wishers from all over Stefan's peaceful kingdom arrive to deliver gifts and celebrate the birth. Stefan, a tall, thin, black-bearded king, invites King Hubert, a short, round, gray-bearded king from the adjacent kingdom, to the celebration. The two kings have planned a happy merger of their lands. As part of the festivities, Hubert's young son, Prince Phillip, is betrothed to the infant princess, Aurora.

Three pleasant, grandmotherly fairies from the forest arrive to bestow gifts on the baby. Flora delivers the gift of beauty, and Fauna gives Aurora the gift of song. But before feisty little Merryweather can present her gift, the evil Maleficent appears in a rush of portentous wind. In bitter response for not being invited to the celebration, the tall, horned, black-clad witch curses Aurora. She declares that the princess will prick her finger on the spindle of a spinning wheel on her sixteenth birthday and die. She then disappears in a swirl of foul purple clouds. Merryweather can't revoke the curse, but she changes the effect of the prick to a deep sleep instead of death, out of which the princess can be awakened by the kiss of true love. A distraught King Stefan orders a bonfire of all the spinning wheels in the kingdom, attempting to circumvent Maleficent's powerful curse. Saddened, he also allows the three fairies to take Aurora away from the kingdom in order to protect her. To hide her, they will raise her without their magic, as mortal peasants. They rename her Briar Rose.

Sixteen years pass mournfully in the kingdom. The day of Rose's momentous sixteenth birthday arrives. Maleficent has not yet found Aurora because, as she realizes only today, her henchmen have been searching only cradles for sixteen years. After zapping them with bolts of lightning, she commands her raven to scour the kingdom one last time looking for a sixteen-year-old. At the modest forest cottage of the three fairies, Rose's "aunts" are trying to prepare a birthday celebration. They've sent Briar Rose out to the forest to collect berries.

As Rose wanders barefoot through the springtime wood, she radiates in the glory of Flora's and Fauna's gifts of beauty and song. She hums operatically and her congenial friends, the happy animals of the forest, come out to play. Her sirenlike voice also mesmerizes a distant horse rider, who convinces his tired white steed, Samson, to search for its source. Rose stops singing to tell the animals about a vivid dream she had in which she fell in love with a prince. The passing rider has meanwhile fallen in a stream because of his horse's urgency, and a chipmunk notices that his cape, hat, and boots hang nearby to dry. The animals swipe the clothes and humorously simulate the dream-prince: an owl flutters in the cape, two hopping rabbits match steps in the boots, and the chipmunk sits on the owl's head wearing the hat.

Playing along good-naturedly, Rose dances with her forest friends, sweetly singing the *Sleeping Beauty* classic "Once Upon a Dream." Midway through the dance, the mysterious rider finds his clothes and cuts in seamlessly, dancing and singing with a shocked Rose. Confused and surely feeling the sparks of love at first sight, Rose, having been told not to speak to strangers, tries to flee. The nameless rider asks for her name. Flustered, she doesn't reveal it, yet manages to yelp out an invitation to come to her cottage that night.

Back at the cottage, the bumbling and nitpicky fairies can't bake a legitimate cake or sew a proper dress, which Rose will need to assume her rightful title as Princess Aurora. So, at Merryweather's urging, the fairies agree to make one exception to their no-magic rule and use their magic wands. A familiar Disney scene ensues, where dancing mops joyously sweep the cottage and anthropomorphic cake ingredients read their own recipe and waltz into the mixing bowl. Flora and Merryweather argue over the color of Rose's dress. Each wants it to be the color of her own dress: Merryweather's is blue and Flora's is pink. Riled, they start zapping with their wands everything in the cottage, turning it blue or pink. As a result, colorful magic dust spurts up the chimney. Maleficent's raven spots the dust and flies down to surreptitiously witness the scene of Rose's return. He watches Rose return a new woman, gaily dancing and singing, clearly in love. The fairies are forced to tell her the truth of her life, that she's a princess who is already betrothed to Prince Phillip. The news devastates Rose, who flees in tears to her room.

King Stefan and King Hubert together await sunset, the time of Aurora's prophesied return. Standing by a sumptuous feast, the anxious men argue briefly, then drink to friendship. Prince Phillip returns to the castle, devilishly tricking Hubert into agreeing to his marriage to the peasant girl instead of Aurora. Phillip rides off before Hubert realizes what has happened, heading back to Rose's cottage. But Rose, teary-eyed, has been secretly brought to Stefan's castle. Placing a gold crown upon her head, the fairies leave Aurora alone for a few moments to contemplate her future. Immediately, a glowing green ball puts Aurora in a trance and leads her through dark passages within the castle, up a staircase and into a tower, where it turns into the augured spinning wheel. Realizing their error too late, the panicked fairies follow and are able to make Aurora hesitate before touching the wheel, but Maleficent's powers are too strong. The princess touches the spindle and collapses.

The sun begins to set, and the celebration nears. But Hubert has yet to tell Stefan about Phillip's intentions, and Aurora lies comatose in an upper chamber. Unsure of how to proceed, the fairies decide to put everyone in the kingdom to sleep as well. As Flora sprinkles fairy dust over those around the throne, Hubert reveals that Phillip met his peasant girl "once upon a dream." What luck—Phillip and Aurora are already in love but they just don't know it. Phillip can break Maleficent's curse with a kiss, so the fairies regroup and fly back to the cottage. However, Maleficent and her henchmen have already captured Phillip. Expecting a peasant boy, Maleficent is overjoyed at her luck and steals the prince away.

Finding only Phillip's hat at their cottage, the fairies sneak into Maleficent's castle. Maleficent taunts Phillip, revealing the identity of his true love but refusing to release him to her for one hundred years. The fairies sneak in when Maleficent finally goes to bed, zap open the chains that bind Phillip, and arm him with a Shield of Virtue and Sword of Truth. An army of one, with three helpers, Phillip must navigate a brutal path to return to his true love. First, Maleficent's castle crumbles and goes up in flames around him. Then she makes a forest of thorns grow in front of Stefan's castle. Finally, she turns herself into a dragon to stop him. But Phillip brandishes the Sword of Truth and slays her with one thrust. Phillip awakes Aurora with a kiss, and the castle band launches into "Once Upon a Dream." As the couple dance into the clouds, Flora and Merryweather resume arguing over Aurora's dress, which changes from pink to blue over and over again, until the storybook closes. The End.

Character List

Princess Aurora / Briar Rose — Voiced by Mary Costa   The story's protagonist. Mary Costa, the voice of Aurora, spoke the lines, sang the songs, and at the time was just about the same age as her character. Given beauty, talent, and riches at birth, Aurora symbolizes all that is good, and she is the prize of Stefan's kingdom. She appears in only a few scenes midway in which she dances in the forest, cries in the cottage, and succumbs to the sleep of Maleficent's curse. However, in every scene she naturally embodies grace and humility. A live action model named Helene Stanley provided the basis for the character's graceful dancing.

Prince Phillip — Voiced by Bill Shirley   The nobleman betrothed to Aurora as a young boy who fortuitously falls in love with her as Briar Rose sixteen years later. Prince Phillip is a proud and strapping youth who willingly fights to the death in the name of love and goodness. He can dance, sing, fight, ride a horse, joke, and outwit kings. As the savior figure of the film, he embodies goodness and has no fatal flaw. He is noble, charming, and humble.

Maleficent — Voiced by Eleanor Audley   The evil witch who puts a deadly curse on Aurora and rules alone atop a craggy mountain beneath a swirling green cloud. Everything about Maleficent's ugly presence portends ill: her black and purple cloak, her sharp and angular frame, the curdling raven on her shoulder, her long yellow fingers, and the green gases that signal her appearance. Maleficent embodies pure evil. She exists to challenge the pure goodness of Aurora and Stefan's kingdom.

Flora — Voiced by Verna Felton   One of three beneficent fairies (pink dress). The unofficial leader of the three fairies, Flora and her pleasantly nattering, tiny-winged colleagues help Phillip defeat Maleficent. They seem grandmotherly one moment, but when there's business to take care of, they'll whip themselves into tiny balls of light and fiercely uphold the side of goodness.

Fauna—Voiced by Barbara Jo Allen One of three beneficent fairies (green dress). Fauna is the calmest of the three fairies, if only because she doesn't argue as much. Overall, Flora and Fauna behave somewhat similarly. They exist as a pair perhaps to make Merryweather's stocky intensity more striking. Disney initially wanted all three fairies to be exactly the same, but his animators convinced him otherwise. The similarity of Flora and Fauna may represent a compromise resulting from this argument.

Merryweather—Voiced by Barbara Luddy One of three beneficent fairies (blue dress). Merryweather is frumpier and feistier than the other two fairies, and she has to be held back on occasion from attacking Maleficent. Merryweather takes action much more often than her two colleagues, and she often speaks sharply and sarcastically, providing humor and piercing through to the truth of a given situation.

King Stefan—Voiced by Taylor Holmes Princess Aurora's tall, thin father. A pleasant, nervous man, Stefan is most easily defined in terms of what he's not. He's not a powerful presence either physically or as an authority figure, and he's not especially sharp-witted. Instead, he's an affable, timid father who reigns peacefully over a kindly, sleepy kingdom.

King Hubert—Voiced by Bill Thompson Prince Phillip's short, round father. A friendly, optimistic, blubbering man, Hubert easily trips over his words. Hubert reigns over the kingdom next to Stefan's. A congenial sort, he looks forward merrily to the celebration. He's the more boisterous of the two kings.

Maleficent's Raven—No voice credit A jet-black harbinger of doom who serves as Maleficent's right-hand man. His only role is to perform her bidding, which he does with terrifying competency. His submissive status to Maleficent is manifest by her constant reference to him as "my pet."

Maleficent's Goons—Voiced by Bill Amsbery, Candy Candido, and Pinto Colvig A collection of pigs, hawks, alligators, and other beasts. This mindless pack of helmeted louts scurry around Maleficent's gloomy castle, guarding her chambers and doing her bidding. However, with their lack of intelligence, suggested by the dull brown palette with which they're painted, they manage to foul Maleficent's plans on at least one important occasion.

The Owl—Voiced by Dal McKennon The only member of Briar Rose's forest friends who speaks to her. When Rose complains "Why do they treat me like a child?" the owl asks, "Who?" When Rose reveals "But I *have* met someone!" the owl asks, "Who?" The owl serves the same function as Maleficent's raven or Phillip's horse: to give one of the human characters someone to talk to when he or she is alone.

Singer—Voiced by Thurl Ravenscroft The drunken guitarist who entertains Stefan and Hubert as they await Aurora's return. Every chance the singer can get, he swipes some of the King's alcohol, putting it into the bowl of his instrument.

King Stefan's Wife—No voice credit Aurora's mother who is never named and has only two lines. King Stefan's wife's role in the film is limited, and she basically exists to round out the traditional setup of a kingdom. She has a gentle, caring face and clear concern for the welfare of her child. Aurora's embrace of her at the end of the film is a genuinely moving moment.

Samson—No voice credit Prince Phillip's strong white horse. Samson doesn't speak, but he understands Phillip's words and nods or neighs approvingly. When tired, he's easily bribed to continue on by the promise of food.

Narrator—Voiced by Marvin Miller An off-screen voice that introduces the tale of *Sleeping Beauty*.

ANALYSIS OF MAJOR CHARACTERS

THE GOOD FAIRIES: FLORA, FAUNA, AND MERRYWEATHER

The three good fairies are completely benign and agreeable, but they don't seem nearly powerful enough to stop Maleficent or save the Princess, a fact that produces much of the movie's suspense. They worry constantly about the Princess's welfare; they bounce pleasantly when they walk; and their tiny wings, when in motion, resemble little clapping hands. Even in flight, the fairies perpetually perform gestures of affirmation. These elderly and safe female characters behave in ways that make them appear vaguely British. For example, they make a point of having tea, and they insist on politeness. Their quaintness increases when they swirl themselves into butterfly-size balls of light to avoid detection. Disney's animators drew the fairies in such a way as to seem thoroughly unthreatening. Even tiny Merryweather's feistiness plays comically, not seriously, since her impish impulsiveness never actually achieves anything. Whenever they need to, the other two fairies easily hold her back.

The names and two-toned colored dresses (warm/cool) of the fairies further suggest the nature of their characters. Flora refers to either the Roman Goddess of Flowers or any general plant life, and her pink dress may remind us of a fragrant blooming rose. Fauna, in green, similarly refers to either the Roman Goddess of Animals or any general animal life. Her color may remind us of the lush healthy forest, free open spaces, and clear, crisp air. Merryweather's name can be broken down into just what it sounds like—good weather, which translates into positive omens. The happy spells of the fairies always rhyme. Though they occasionally bicker good-naturedly, they're selfless when it counts. True happiness comes to them only if true happiness comes to the princess.

THE EVIL FAIRY: MALEFICENT

Nothing happens to turn Maleficent evil. No back story is offered or hinted at to explain her malevolence—she has just simply *always been evil*. Since she has no past, there are no grounds for any sympathy for her. In the logic of the fairy tale, she exists to define the complete opposite of the good characters, Aurora, Phillip, and the fairies. Therefore, her motivations never change. Her experience does not follow an arc or lead to change. She shows up wanting to do hurtful things, and she dies wanting to do hurtful things. Her character is drawn so ominously that there is never any question whose side the audience should be on. Solitary, angular, and horned, Maleficent speaks in a deep, theatrically harsh voice and deploys a bitter, jealous wit to ensure that she appears completely without the capability to love or to be loved.

The film bestows on her the skill of creative spell-casting in order to present challenges for the good characters to overcome. She proclaims death to Aurora, but Merryweather skillfully changes that to a deep sleep. She casts a forest of thorny branches in front of Prince Phillip after he escapes from her castle, but the good fairies equip him with the power to slice through it. Finally, her transformation into a giant dragon makes her so threatening, so unfairly dominant, that there's no question she deserves death, right then and there.

PRINCESS AURORA/BRIAR ROSE

Though Aurora/Rose makes few appearances in the film, the viewer can be sure of one thing: She holds steadfastly to one dream, the dream of true love. She exists more as a concept than as a complex character. The filmmakers intend for her to embody the ideal woman. No amount of hiding in peasants' clothes can change her nobility and goodness. Typically, the main character of a film appears for much of the screen time and undergoes changes or rises above challenges to achieve a happy ending. In *Sleeping Beauty*, however, Aurora's unchangeable nature is exactly the point. She's pure, innocent, and good from the start, and her stalwart attachment to her beliefs guarantees her a happy ending.

Flora and Fauna give her the gifts of beauty and song, but Aurora/Rose also has other characteristics. Most significantly, she's passive. She wishes and dreams, but she can't take much action, largely because she's asleep for much of the story. This passivity is so comprehensive that after Prince Phillip awakens her, she doesn't say anything for the rest of the film. The director's intention seems to be to create a distant, iconic status for Aurora/Rose so that she appears ideal, something to be admired from afar.

PRINCE PHILLIP

According to the logic of Disney's film, Phillip represents a young girl's ideal man. He's strong, handsome, sensitive, funny, utterly faithful, and completely unrealistic. He's Aurora's perfect match because they both believe in the same concepts: love at first sight, marriage after one dance, a happy ever after. By believing so whole-heartedly in these concepts, he carries the power to break Malefi-cent's curse with one kiss. Just like Aurora, Phillip doesn't change in the film, although he is shown as a young boy, when he's betrothed to Aurora. Therefore, he's a few years older than she is and presum-ably a little bit wiser and more knowledgeable. The age difference becomes crucial to the creation of their wedding plans, because the passive Aurora can safely leave decisions and important concerns to the older, wiser man. The animators create Phillip so that the audi-ence can have complete faith in him. He'll always do the right thing, according to the moral rightness of this particular fairy tale. It's so easy to figure out what he'll do, however, that we can predict it. Phil-lip presents no big surprises. Though Aurora and Phillip seemingly defy the wishes of their elders (the fairies and Hubert), at the end they are filial, deferential children who assume their rightful place.

Themes, Motifs, and Symbols

Themes

True Love Conquers All

In the fourteenth-century world of Disney's very 1950s fairy tale, pure, innocent love possesses such tangible strength it can defeat anything, even seemingly unbeatable curses or fearsome dragons. Unlike the vague and elusive real-world concept of love, true love within the film's storybook world has definite qualities and characteristics, and its rules are easy to grasp. True love is instant and permanent. Once Briar Rose sees the mysterious stranger, she falls for him completely and irrevocably. The fairies can't faze Rose even when they tell her she's really a princess and will soon marry a prince. Instead, Rose flees to her room, distraught at the possibility that she'll never be with her true love (whose name, incidentally, she does not yet know). Second, true love has utter faith and never questions itself. As soon as Phillip and Aurora admit to themselves that they love the other, neither ever doubts his or her decision, and each assumes that their union is the only right path. For instance, as Phillip hacks his way through Maleficent's henchmen and falls off crumbling cliffs, with the future of an entire kingdom resting on his success, he never questions once why he's doing it. Once the couple is united, they will indeed live happily ever after. The final dissolve of the film transports the dancing couple from the floor of Stefan's ballroom into the clouds and serves as visual proof of the perfection of their relationship and their faith.

The success of true love matters not only to the lovers involved, but to other people as well. If Phillip and Aurora do not unite, the entire kingdom crumbles. Maleficent will reign victorious, the kingdoms of Stefan and Hubert will not merge, and chaos will presumably splinter the land, given that a giant dragon is on the loose. Since true love is rare and special, not everyone can have it. It becomes a model for others to look up to, and the glue that holds a kingdom together. Indeed, above all else, the film posits that true love conquers all. It can defeat and dismiss every obstacle, every evil, and every unloving person who comes into its path.

HOME IS WHERE THE HEART IS

Home environments provide the crucial foundation for the love and goodness that the characters in *Sleeping Beauty* value so highly. The characters who have families have love and support, even in times of strife. Stefan and his wife have each other and share a longing for their daughter, the three fairies have one another, and Hubert has his son and, presumably, a wife back in his kingdom. The only character with no other human companionship, of course, is Maleficent. The evil fairy's inability to love and be loved (she calls herself the "mistress of all evil") is suggested by her lack of proper companionship. She keeps a raven and a horde of subhuman henchmen within her castle walls, which suggests some sort of perversion. Even the loving cottage of the fairies and Briar Rose is a humans-only affair. Maleficent is also excluded from another kind of domestic relationship: that between parent and child. Stefan and Hubert are both fathers, and even the fairies raise Briar Rose for sixteen years. Maleficent has only "my pet," her raven, which is an inadequate substitute for, and a perversion of, true human family relations. A moral of the film is that families provide support and should join to create even larger families to generate even stronger support. Stefan's and Hubert's joint kingdoms will certainly prosper for generations to come.

MOTIFS

PERSISTENT MELODIES

The score of Disney's *Sleeping Beauty* is adapted from the music Tchaikovsky wrote for the ballet *The Sleeping Beauty*, which opened in St. Petersburg in 1890. Tchaikovsky incorporated musical motifs for each of the main characters, and they appear both simply and within more complex orchestral arrangements throughout the ballet. Tchaikovsky stayed very close to the storyline of *The Sleeping Beauty* as he composed his score, the result of which is a tightly woven arrangement that moves the story and its themes forward.

Almost every major character in *Sleeping Beauty* has his or her own musical reference that emphasizes his or her particular personality. Every time Maleficent appears, for example, harsh brass instruments whine, shriek, or burst suddenly from the silence, while the bows of cellos and basses slither ominously on low-register strings. Aurora skips through the forest with the dainty accompaniment of a harp, emphasizing her lightness and ethereal quality. Mary Costa, who voiced Aurora, has an operatic, upper-register singing voice that suggests childishness and Aurora's burgeoning adolescence. Prince Phillip trots in on his horse, Samson, to an orchestrated, stomping march. The characters in *Sleeping Beauty* aren't difficult to evaluate, and musical accompaniments are not needed to further an understanding of them. Instead, these repeated and consistent musical accompaniments serve as triggers of a sort, to increase the tension, movement, and cohesiveness of the film. In particular, the music that surrounds Maleficent intensifies her evil intentions and serves as a kind of foreshadowing—we know something bad is coming when Maleficent appears and we hear her ominous accompaniment. The melodies repeat themselves persistently—characters sing and whistle them, and various instruments pick them up throughout the film. This repetition gives the film a kind of solidity and simplicity. The most famous song, "Once Upon a Dream," appears so often that it is practically a major character, and it serves as the thematic thread that holds the movie together.

DREAMS AND VISIONS
Throughout *Sleeping Beauty*, characters dream of and idealize lives beyond their own. Briar Rose, for example, dreams of the eternally perfect groom. Her song, "Once Upon a Dream," literally describes the way she meets Phillip, who first hears Rose's sirenlike voice from afar, as if calling to him from a dream. Aurora appears to be dreaming as she falls into a deep sleep in the castle, though we are not privy to what she's dreaming. In addition to the dreams that characters sing about or discuss, the film presents visions—spectacles that show something past or to come, but without making clear who in the film has them. For example, when Flora and Fauna bestow their gifts upon the baby Aurora, the film illustrates each gift by dissolving into a vision. Galaxies of colors swirl, heavenly choirs praise either the gift of beauty or song, and through dissolving clouds, fluttering doves, and silver fireworks, the viewer is treated to a majestic demonstration of just how special and otherworldly these gifts are. Whether the eminences in the castle court can see the vision, however, remains uncertain. Maleficent also creates swirling visions for the captive Phillip in her dungeon. The first is of Aurora sleeping

deeply. The second is of Phillip, a hundred years older, heading back gray-haired to his castle. These visions serve to enhance the magical qualities of this fairy tale and reaffirm that, despite being drawn into the tale, the viewer remains outside of it, "reading" the story from beginning to end.

ANIMATING THE INANIMATE
Sleeping Beauty is, obviously, an animated film, but the magic of film animation is both showcased and echoed by scenes in which characters bring static or inanimate objects to life. The central plot involves Prince Phillip waking Aurora, and with her the entire kingdom, from a magical sleep, in effect reanimating the world of the film. The fairies animate items that are normally unmoving, such as mops and sacks of flour, giving them the ability to dance and clean. Every time a fairy waves her magic wand and transforms something from one thing into another, the viewer may think of Disney's team doing the same thing. Elements that are still, static, or dead are awakened, animated, reanimated, or given new life.

THE GEOGRAPHICAL TRIANGLE
Every scene in *Sleeping Beauty* takes place in one of three places, each with a distinctive terrain and its own set of values. At one point in this geographical triangle, Stefan's sun-splashed kingdom sits high atop a green hill, white-walled and positioned to catch the sunset. The forest sits at another of the three points, where the fairies' modest cottage is nestled within the depths of the shaded glen. Tall trees, forest animals, spacious greens, and healthy rivers abound in this rustic locale. And at the third point, of course, lies Maleficent's fortress, atop the purple crags of the Forbidden Mountain. It swirls in green gases and comprises a dizzying array of rotting, mossy hallways woven into an evil labyrinth that only Maleficent and her henchmen can navigate.

Most of the film's action results from a resident of one of these three places venturing into another's terrain, thereby presenting a clash of values and the instigation of some sort of conflict. For example, when Maleficent appears in Stefan's castle, she levels the curse upon Aurora that propels the plot. When the Prince rides Samson into Briar Rose's glen, they meet and spark true love at first sight. And when the fairies venture into Maleficent's fortress, they free the Prince and commence the final battle between Good and Evil. Each resident has the most power on his or her own home territory. The fairies take Aurora deep into their woods to protect her,

Maleficent kidnaps Phillip and chains him in her own dungeon to hide him, and Stefan never leaves his castle, providing the strong home base for his family, which is reunited happily at the film's close. The simplicity of this three-pronged geographical arrangement allows for rich contrasts based on which resident is in which terrain, and how arrangements of people interact in unfamiliar landscapes.

SYMBOLS

THE SPINNING WHEEL

Part of Aurora's "fall" into Maleficent's spell—her finger pricked on the spinning wheel—refers to her approaching maturity or awakening. When Rose dips her foot into the water by the river, for example, she appears to be testing it out, awakening to new, mature knowledge of the world. This maturity could ultimately mean a flowering into sexual awareness, since she is, after all, sixteen and dreaming of a Prince, or simply a general adolescent growth into adult knowledge. The film never takes a firm stand on what sort of maturity Aurora grows into, but the overall conceit of Aurora "awakening" to a man's kiss suggests that her maturity may indeed be a sexual one.

A spinning wheel often symbolizes the unstoppable revolutions of the years, and in the film it encourages the contemplation of time and how it changes things. Spinning wheels also refer to creation, since they're used to weave yarn or string into cloth. Most simplistically, the spinning wheel is a literal manifestation of the old phrase "spinning a spell," which means to curse someone. Aurora, under Maleficent's power, is made to touch the spindle—the wheel appears precisely at the crucial moment of the curse's fruition.

COLORS AND SHAPES

Sleeping Beauty establishes a palette of meaning by associating certain hues and saturations with certain qualities of character. Everything painted in black, green, scarlet, or sickly purple hues is evil. These colors mark Maleficent's clothing, her castle's interior, and the atmosphere outside of her castle. These colors are also heavily saturated, deep and harsh, and often fit into a coded shape pattern. The darker colors usually appear in less pleasing, angular shapes, such as Maleficent's sharp, lanky dress, her jagged castle jutting into the sky, or her talon-like fingers.

Aurora and her father's kingdom are painted warmly in an array of bright colors: oranges, blues, pinks, and yellows. Anything rendered in these colors in the film appears happy, friendly, relaxed, and loving. The borders around these colors are less harsh, more softly edged. Aurora's soft profile, the sumptuous feast of Hubert and Stefan, and the cuddly animals of the forest are colored in this spectrum. Every dominant color in the film corresponds to a specific person or place. Samson's white hide, Merryweather's blue dress, and Maleficent's henchmen's brownish cast all indicate something crucial about their characters.

ANIMALS

Since the prominent animals in the film do not really exist outside of their relation to a human, the role of these animals is to serve as indicators of the humans' own characteristics. The cute, friendly animals in the forest, such as the smiling owl, the pair of wide-eyed rabbits, and the loping chipmunk, are all associated with Briar Rose. Because of them, her character appears gentle, free, playful, radiating good will for all, and, most of all, innocent. Samson, the strong white horse of Prince Phillip, reinforces Phillip's nature as innately pure, a master of beasts, and powerful, but also friendly and kind to all good creatures. Finally, Maleficent's raven insinuates that she is a spying, secretive, harsh creature. This style of communication is crucial to Disney films. Before the human characters act or speak, animals or other figures give an idea of how to understand them. These characters don't have to say much. Through the colors in which they are rendered and the animals that accompany them, they are clearly coded to be read in a certain way.

SLEEPING BEAUTY

FILM ANALYSIS

THE STORY AND SCORE OF "SLEEPING BEAUTY" THROUGH THE AGES

Previous versions of the *Sleeping Beauty* fairy tale date back to the fourteenth century, in which the film is set. A fourteenth-century romance called *Perceforest* (printed in France in 1528) contains an embryonic version of the story we know today. An Italian soldier, Giambattista Basile, adapted the tale for his "Sun, Moon, and Talia" story printed in 1634. Details of these versions are shocking, even repulsive. For instance, in some of these early versions, the King, or sometimes even the Prince, impregnates the Sleeping Beauty character *as she's sleeping*, and then leaves her. She awakens not at the kiss of the Prince, but at the birth of her twin children.

The credits of the film maintain that Charles Perrault's version, "The Sleeping Beauty in the Wood," was the model for Disney's *Sleeping Beauty*. The story appears in Perrault's famous 1697 *Histories, or Stories of Past Times*. Extreme violence permeates his version, which continues the story after the Prince and the Princess are united. As Perrault tells it, the blissful couple do indeed marry and bear two children. But the Prince never tells his family about the marriage, and Sleeping Beauty never questions his decision. Soon the Prince must leave for war. He finally tells his mother about the marriage and leaves his wife under her care. But the Prince's mother hates children and practices cannibalism, and she viciously persecutes Sleeping Beauty. Moments before the mother throws her two grandchildren into a pit of venomous vipers, the Prince fortuitously returns from war and pushes his own mother into the deadly pit.

No version of the story previous to Perrault's has Sleeping Beauty awaken with the kiss of the Prince. The version penned by the Brothers Grimm called "Briar Rose," from their *Children's and Household Tales* (1812–1815), not only includes this element but ends the story when the Prince and the Princess reunite. Their tale involves no rape or cannibalism, and, therefore, despite what the credits say, the film bears the closest resemblance to this version.

Disney's version was not the first film adaptation of the Sleeping Beauty tales, nor was it the first animated version. German pioneer animator Lotte Reiniger, who was best known for shadow puppet animation, produced at least two artistically advanced animated adaptations of the Sleeping Beauty tale. One version appeared as early as 1922. Friz Freleng, who directed Bugs Bunny cartoons, made a 1942 adaptation called "Foney Fables" that incorporated elements of many old fairy tales. In the "Sleeping Beauty" segment of this cartoon, Prince Charming yells at Sleeping Beauty for sleeping in. Izzy Sparber, who directed Popeye cartoons, then entered the mix with 1947's "Wotta Knight." Bluto and Popeye fight over Olive Oyl, playing tug-of-war with her pigtails in a battle for her love.

Peter Ilyich Tchaikovsky created the score of *The Sleeping Beauty* for the Imperial Ballet at St. Petersburg's Maryinsky Theater. First performed January 3, 1890, the now-classic ballet was originally created by Ivan Vsevolozhsky and choreographed by Marius Petipa. In a legendary demonstration of passion, Tchaikovsky composed the entire score in only forty days. Walt Disney actually wanted an original score for his motion picture and spent a great deal of time attempting to develop one. In the end, however, he decided that the classical grandeur of the ballet's score, full of waltzes, did not need to be mimicked, but rather used outright. George Bruns adapted it.

VISUAL STYLE AND MISE-EN-SCÈNE

In Disney's oeuvre (body of work), *Sleeping Beauty* stands out for its strikingly divergent visual style and mise-en-scène (the physical environment of the film). Led by supervising animator Eyvind Earle, the team emphasized detail in the backgrounds and in the expressions of the characters to such an extent that the film's visual style intrigues almost as much as the fairy tale itself. The makers based the film's style on an art history canon of Dutch, Italian, and Greek masters and Medieval, Pre-renaissance, and Gothic art. The optically challenging black-and-white checkered floor in the room in which Aurora sleeps recalls Dutch and Italian masters, for instance, and the grand cathedral-esque ballroom retains the style of Gothic architecture.

Many elements of the visual style merit close examination. For instance, to create the nestled, safe seclusion of Rose's forest home, the team employed multiple, overlapping cels of animation. Painted on the deepest cel is a row of trees, and on the frontmost layer are branches from other trees. The animators tuck Briar Rose between these two layers as she walks barefoot in the woods. To further naturalize the scene and highlight the layers and depths, external light sources create diagonal shadows that softly trail shafts of light through the gaps in the clearings. The accuracy of Rose's movements through those clearings came from live action models that were filmed for study. Multiple scenes, including Briar Rose's dance in the woods, were choreographed and filmed with live action models for extra precision of human movement.

Strong verticals dominate the landscapes of the film. Deep rows of tall trees stretch out through the forest. In Stefan's castle, columns, tapestries, and hanging manuscripts stretch the enormous height of the ballroom. Maleficent's tower is a giant vertical shaft charging up into the skies. Even Briar Rose has verticals in her dress and hanging hair to emphasize her thinness in contrast to the plump fairies. These verticals emphasize the width of the 70-millimeter frame and create vast open spaces whose meaning shifts according to the context of the scene.

Important Quotations
Explained

1. NARRATOR: "In a far away land, long ago, lived a king and his fair queen. Many years had they longed for a child and finally their wish was granted. A daughter was born, and they called her Aurora. Yes, they named her after the dawn for she filled their lives with sunshine. "

At these words, spoken by an off-screen voice, the golden storybook of *Sleeping Beauty* opens. The camera then zooms in upon the still illustrations of the book's turning pages, and they begin to animate. Choral voices swell after the word "Aurora," establishing her dawning glory and simultaneously suggesting the emotional veracity and gravity of the story. The quote also suggests that the story's royal family achieves happiness and completion only when a child joins them. Without the child, the family suffers. Disney thus affirms his appeal to the traditional family of two married parents with children. The subsequent story affirms the rightness of an intact family. When Phillip returns Aurora, who has been displaced from her family for so long, he creates a larger, happier, and more profitable family as Stefan unites his kingdom with Hubert's.

The opening asserts that the story is set in a distant time, in an unnamed place. This vagueness allows viewers to stimulate their imaginations, and assures them that historical accuracy is neither of concern nor to be expected. Though the film later narrows the timeframe to the fourteenth century, viewers must reconcile this semi-mythical setting with the reality of the film's 1959 release in the United States. Walt Disney originally wished to remake *Sleeping Beauty* and re-release a new version of it every seven years, a plan that suggests not only that new versions of the film would have changed through the decades, but that the 1959 version of the film indeed relates in many ways to 1950s America.

2. PRINCE PHILLIP: "But don't you remember? We've met
    before!"
    BRIAR ROSE: "We . . . we have?"
    PRINCE PHILLIP: "Of course, you said so yourself: Once
    upon a dream!"

After the romantic initial meeting of Briar Rose and Phillip in the glen, Rose becomes confused by her attraction to this stranger. Phillip, instantly comprehending Rose's inherent goodness, understands her caution at conversing with a stranger and humorously attempts to convince her that they already have a relationship. This teasing plays into the idea that their relationship has been somewhat predetermined and that their meeting was simply a matter of time. Phillip picks up instantly on Briar Rose's belief that true love is pre-ordained, instant, and forever. They unite in idealizing a romantic relationship and play on the dream motif of the film. This exchange also establishes Phillip as the calmer half of the pair, more confident and more in control. By contrast, Briar Rose is a tittering wreck experiencing love's first tugs on her adolescent heart. Their initial meeting also foreshadows their eventual marriage, which proves Rose's dream true. Though she isn't aware of it now, she will in fact marry the Prince of her dreams, and "Once Upon a Dream" will play during their triumphant moment of reuniting.

3. FLORA: "The road to true love may be barriered by still
    many more dangers, which you alone will have to face. So
    arm thyself with this enchanted Shield of Virtue, and this
    mighty Sword of Truth, for these Weapons of Righteousness
    will triumph over evil."

Flora gives her cautionary advice just after the fairies free Phillip from his chains in Maleficent's dungeon, and just before his Dante-esque journey through the tribulations created by the resistance of evil. The quote exemplifies a somewhat inconsistent morality inherent in the fairy tale. Although Prince Phillip is pure, innocent, noble, and brave, the fairies personally arm him like a warrior with the implicit final goal of murdering Maleficent. Couching the Prince's quest within these ominous statements, Flora reassures him that any violence he may have to commit is natural. Violence becomes a duty, a right, part of his goodness rather than contrary to it. Officially blessed, he takes his Weapons of Righteousness and runs headlong into battle with Evil. Though Flora suggests that the Prince must face this noble challenge alone, the Prince doesn't overcome any obstacle without the aid of the fairies. Repeatedly, the fairies modestly minimize their own roles in the success of the Prince's quest, which shifts more focus onto the Prince's individual heroism.

4. MALEFICENT: "No, it cannot be! Now shall you deal with me, O Prince, and all the powers of hell!"

After the Prince escapes Maleficent's flaming castle and defeats her sudden forest of thorns, he stands ready to make a safe return to Stefan's castle. Maleficent must gather all her powers and appear in person for a final standoff with the Prince. The fact that Maleficent uses the word *hell* at this crucial juncture effectively shocks the audience and further cements her evil nature. Phillip, Stefan, or Aurora couldn't possibly use the word *hell*, and its appearance here proves without a doubt that Maleficent really is a member of the other side. Maleficent's use of the word *hell* suggests that the film's war between Good and Evil is actually a religious battle. If Maleficent can conjure the powers of hell, she is obviously a devil and an unbeliever, and her murder is justified. By association, too, the people opposing her must be devout, God-fearing believers.

5. FLORA: "Sword of Truth, fly swift and sure, that evil die and good endure."

As Prince Phillip teeters on a crumbling cliff, a step away from falling to his death, he is able to strike at Maleficent's dragon one last time. The quote verbalizes the joint wishes of Phillip and all the fairies in this culminating moment of battle. The normally charming rhyming spells of the grandmotherly fairies take a twisted turn here with a rhyming prophesy of death, through which Flora essentially blesses the murder of Maleficent. Spells or prophecies delivered through rhyme schemes seem familiar, as if the speaker repeats something tried-and-true, passed down through the generations. This couplet, for instance, rolls off the tongue as if long-held wisdom has been perfected into a catchy phrase. Ancient storytellers like Homer passed down their tales in rhyme schemes to make them easier to recite. The classic struggles had to be rhythmic and easily remembered, so that they stuck in the listeners' and tellers' heads. Any prophesy in rhyme suggests a resuming of some classic battle, and here suggests that Flora's words have historical veracity. She reminds the audience that this murder is both necessary and right, and that truth and goodness will emerge victorious from Phillip's one strike of truth.

8 1/2

(1961)

8 1/2

CONTEXT

Although *8 1/2* (1963) is director Federico Fellini's most widely recognized achievement, he was already internationally renowned when he began working on it in late 1960. He had directed *La Strada* (1954), which won a Best Foreign Language Film Oscar when it was released in the United States three years later, and *La Dolce Vita* (1960), which had just been released, had won the Palme d'Or ("the Golden Palm," the award for best film) at the Cannes Film Festival in 1960, and would go on to earn four Oscar nominations. Not surprisingly, as soon as Fellini began jotting his first notes for his "eighth-and-a-half" film (*8 1/2* follows six feature-length films and three short films and collaborations), production companies, costume designers, photography directors, and flocks of actresses were hanging around him, eager to stake a claim in the next hit. Cineriz, the production company that had worked with Fellini twice before, expected him to create another cinematic masterpiece. Before Fellini had even outlined the plot of the film, the machinery of its production was already in motion.

Fellini was in his early forties, already anxious about typical midlife concerns regarding family, aging, and professional virility, and he felt enormous pressure. This stress was so pervasive that the making of the film became its own principal influence. Fellini had intended the film to describe the crisis of an artist, a journalist, or even a lawyer who is tormented by matrimonial, spiritual, and creative challenges, but he didn't know how to design the story. *La Strada* and *La Dolce Vita* had given Fellini a reputation for ingenuity, and he once again wanted to create something wholly new, as if to prove that he was still in his prime. But as he witnessed the steady physical construction of the film—the sets, the cast, the lighting—he felt increasingly unsure about how he would tell its story. At one point, Fellini decided to quit. When he was in the middle of writing a letter of resignation, however, members of the crew happened to congratulate him on his imminent accomplishment, and the gesture convinced him that he could not abandon the project. Instead, he was inspired by the drama of the moment and decided that the film would be about a director who wants to escape the making of his own movie.

Although *8 1/2* draws on Fellini's directorial experience, it is also clear that Fellini modeled the personal life of the film's protagonist, Guido Anselmi, on his own. Guido's experience in the film is accented with memories of his childhood, and these sequences are consistent with Fellini's biography. Fellini was born on January 20, 1920, and grew up in Rimini, a city in northern Italy on the coast of the Adriatic Sea. His parents, his father a traveling salesman and his mother a housewife, sent him to parochial school, whose influence appears in two of *8 1/2*'s memory sequences. When Fellini was twelve, a circus visited Rimini, and when it left, Fellini went with it. He found work performing as a clown but soon returned to his parents, only to suffer a restless adolescence in the quiet city and leave home again when he was seventeen. This second time, Fellini followed a vaudeville troupe and earned his keep by writing comedy sketches for it. After the troupe performed in Florence, he stayed to write for humor magazines, then went to Milan, where he worked as a cartoonist. The dictator Benito Mussolini had banned American cartoons, so Fellini drew bootleg versions of them.

Fellini spent the years of World War II in Rome, where he avoided the military draft and continued to write pieces for humor magazines, as well as for *Cico and Pallina,* a radio drama. The woman who played Pallina was Giulietta Masina, a fledgling screen actress who would become Fellini's wife and the star of many of his films, including *La Strada* and *Nights of Cabiria* (1956). They married in October 1943 and settled in Rome. Masina continued to look for small movie roles, while Fellini spent his days on the Via Veneto, a luxurious and lively Roman street, peddling caricatures to passersby. Through Vittorio Mussolini, son of the dictator and a close friend of Fellini's, Fellini met director Roberto Rossellini. Fellini agreed to help Rossellini write his film *Open City,* which Rossellini completed in 1945.

Open City is a major film of the so-called neorealist era, which capped a celebrated tradition of Italian filmmaking that had developed since the turn of the twentieth century. The history of Italian film begins with the *Kinetografo Alberini*, a motion-picture camera patented by Filoteo Alberini in 1895—an invention overshadowed by that of the Lumière Brothers' revolutionary Cinématographe (the first widely used camera, printer, and projector) around the same time. Alberini contributed to the Italian trend toward melodramatic costume films, which soon gave way to *commedia brillante*—light comedy that drew from Italy's lavish opera tradition.

Italian realism followed, inspired by the stories and plays of Giovanni Verga, who wrote pastoral stories about common folk such as hunters and fishermen. As World War II began, the Italian market was inundated with Fascist-sponsored propaganda films. These were accompanied by "white telephone" films, whose superficial plots, mostly confined to glamorous apartment interiors, ignored the disastrous political climate. These films were the impetus to Italian neorealism, which was as much of a sociopolitical movement as a film genre.

Neorealist directors like Luchino Visconti (whose 1943 *Ossessione* inspired the "neorealist" label), Roberto Rossellini, and Vittorio De Sica, disgusted by the irresponsibility of making lighthearted films during the humanitarian crises of Mussolini's reign and the Holocaust, began to make films with socially relevant messages. In addition to having a moral philosophy, the neorealist films often used ordinary-looking or amateur actors, were shot on location with natural light, and underwent constant revisions during production that reflected the director's experience as he worked with the film. These qualities were directly opposed to the reigning philosophy of Hollywood at the time, which bubbled with superstars like Elizabeth Taylor and Cary Grant and was still carefully timing the dramatic moments of its artificial (but often thrilling) plots.

After *Open City,* Rossellini asked Fellini to collaborate with him on his 1946 film *Paisan,,* the weighty theme of which—the social plight of Italy—strayed even further from Hollywood drama and secured Fellini's reputation as an excellent screenwriter and director. During the 1950s, however, Fellini strayed from Rossellini's neorealism, trading sociopolitical virtue for artistic exploration. He did, however, continue to include ordinary actors and situations in his films and kept his scripts dynamic throughout production (which was certainly the case for *8 1/2*).

Before *8 1/2*, Fellini's most critically appreciated achievements were *La Strada*, *Nights of Cabiria*, and *La Dolce Vita*. What critics applauded in these films, as well as in *8 1/2*, was Fellini's talent for ironic social commentary, the elegance with which he merged fantasy and reality, and his sense of humor, evoked most memorably by his exaggerated characters. As in Fellini's previous films, titillating comedy pervades *8 1/2*, though its prevailing themes involve crisis and frustration. These themes, which include marital and spiritual infidelity, aging, and creative stagnancy, mirrored Fellini's own life at the time. Fellini's special intimacy with the protagonist and the plot contributes to *8 1/2*'s organically subjective style of filming, which is perhaps what critics appreciated most. Just as three major novels—Gustave Flaubert's *Madame Bovary,* Marcel Proust's *In Search of Lost Time,* and James Joyce's *A Portrait of the Artist as a Young Man*—transformed the novel by focusing on the psychology of the individual, so was *8 1/2* revolutionary in the film world for its unwavering preoccupation with Guido's thoughts. *8 1/2*'s influence has been seen in countless European and American films directed from a subjective viewpoint, such as Woody Allen's *Annie Hall* (1977). In *8 1/2*, the hero Guido's consciousness is remarkably present in every passage, not only in the fantasy or dream sequences. All sounds, sights, and actions are immediately subject to Guido's interpretation, as if his reactions are a filter between his world and Fellini's lens. No one had filmed in such a way before. For that reason, perhaps above all others, *8 1/2* became a favorite of film critics, winning the 1964 Oscar for Best Foreign Film and the first prize in the 1963 Moscow Film Festival.

8 1/2

PLOT OVERVIEW

Guido Anselmi, a forty-three-year-old film director, visits a fashionable health spa, seeking treatment for his liver trouble. A number of people from the film industry, however, have followed him there in preparation for the production of his next film. On his first night, Guido has a dream in which he escapes from a car stalled in traffic and flies into the sky, only to be yanked back down to Earth by two film industry men. Guido wakes up as a doctor enters his room. During his physical exam, his collaborator and co-screenwriter Daumier enters and alludes to his displeasure with Guido's work. Guido enters the bathroom for a moment alone, only to find a telephone ringing there.

At the spring of the health spa, the waters of which are considered an all-purpose "cure," guests line up for glasses of spring water and relax in the garden. As Guido waits for his water, he has a vision of Claudia, his leading actress, but a plain-looking nurse wakes him from his reverie by telling him to take his glass of water. As Guido turns away from the spring, he again meets Daumier, who gives Guido a sheet of notes that criticize his script. In his tired, patronizing tone, Daumier lists the script's faults and denounces the film for being uninspired. As Daumier drones on, Guido spots his old friend Mario Mezzabotta, who introduces him to his significantly younger American fiancée, Gloria Morin.

At a small train station, Guido reads Daumier's notes as he waits for his mistress, Carla, to arrive. When the train comes, he thinks for a moment that perhaps Carla didn't make the trip after all and feels relieved. He soon spots her on the other side of the train, however, burdened with an enormous cart of luggage. He takes her to a small family-owned hotel in order to avoid the attention that they would receive at his own hotel. When they arrive, Carla orders lunch, and as she enjoys a plate of chicken and chats about her husband, Guido becomes bored, reading a paper while he hums and smokes. Later, in Carla's room, Guido directs a role-playing game in which he orders Carla to pretend she is a prostitute.

As Carla sits up in bed reading cartoons and eating peaches, Guido has an eerie dream in which he meets his parents in a graveyard. They both express disappointment in him, and after Guido helps his father step into a grave, he meets his mother, who suddenly transforms into his wife, Luisa, before he wakes up. Later, back at his hotel, Guido leaves his room and shares an elevator downstairs with clergymen. When he enters the lobby, a barrage of managers, actresses, and his collaborators demand his attention, and he dismisses each one as quickly as possible until he meets Pace, his producer, who gives him a watch as a gift.

Guido attends an evening entertainment revue at the hotel, where he watches Mezzabotta dance foolishly with Gloria. Bored with the music and irritated by complex questions that an American reporter asks him, Guido spots Carla, who sits at a far table in a failed attempt to be inconspicuous. A duo of mind-reading magicians begins its show, reading the minds of the hotel guests, and Gloria becomes frightened and refuses to participate. When the magicians read Guido's mind, they produce the words *Asa nisi masa*, a mysterious and apparently nonsensical message that is significant in Guido's past. The message causes Guido to recall a scene from his young boyhood, in his grandmother's farmhouse, in which he bathes in a big tub with his cousins and is put to bed by his doting aunts and his grumbling grandmother. Guido's young female cousin sits up in bed and tells him the words to a magic spell, *Asa nisi masa*.

At about two o'clock in the morning, Guido returns to the hotel lobby, where the concierge tells him that his wife, Luisa, telephoned. As he waits for the concierge to get her on the line, Guido talks with a French actress who has been trying desperately to find out more about her part in his film. He upsets the actress by refusing to give details about his film and saying he must leave to talk to Luisa. As they talk on the phone, Guido realizes how much he misses Luisa and asks her to join him at the spa. Before he retreats to his room, he visits the production office, where he answers the questions of his collaborator Cesarino, who is working on set details, and has a quarrel with his longtime friend and fellow director Conocchia, whom Guido accuses of being obsolete. Once in his own hotel room, Guido ponders the still-unfinished story of the film and has another vision of Claudia before falling asleep.

A ringing phone wakes him up a few hours later. It is Carla, calling from her hotel to ask him to attend to her because she has developed a fever. Guido goes back to sleep and doesn't visit until the next afternoon. He finds Carla sweating and delirious, and he feels guilty for having dismissed her request. Later, he has a short meeting with the Catholic cardinal in order to discuss his film, but the cardinal asks him only whether he is married and whether he has children (he doesn't). During the meeting with the cardinal, Guido's attention is drawn to a woman some distance away, who reminds him of a gypsy woman, Saraghina, whom he knew in his youth. He then has a day-dream about the day he and other Catholic schoolboys were caught watching Saraghina dance on the beach.

Guido has coffee with Daumier, who accuses him of being naïve, and then he visits the steam baths with his fellow filmmakers, Mez-zabotta, and other familiar guests. Guido imagines the shrouded fig-ures around him as expiring invalids and has a daydream about meeting the cardinal in a chamber of the steam baths. In this fantasy, the cardinal uses Latin passages of the Bible to instruct Guido to choose the path of the church.

That evening, Guido sees Luisa at an outdoor auction being held at the hotel. He watches her for a moment before she sees him, and they greet each other warmly. They dance together tenderly before Pace announces that they are going to visit the rocket launch pad that his construction team is erecting for the film set. Luisa suddenly becomes upset, perhaps by something that a member of the produc-tion team has told her, and refuses to sit with Guido on the drive to the set. As the group of filmmakers and their friends ascend the stair-case of the launch pad, Guido consults with Rossella—his wife's close friend—about Luisa, and Rossella tells him that Luisa is con-fused and dissatisfied with him. Guido confesses that his film doesn't have anything to say, and Rossella tells him to make up his mind about his life. Back at the hotel, Guido and Luisa argue about his infidelity before going to sleep in separate beds.

The next morning, as Guido, Luisa, and Rossella have breakfast together, Carla arrives in a ridiculously embellished horse-drawn carriage and sits nearby. Guido pretends not to know her, but it is obvious to Luisa and Rossella that Carla is his mistress. Defeated, Guido retreats into a fantasy that takes place in the farmhouse of his youth, in which all the women to whom he has been attracted in his life devote themselves to his pleasure. At first, this harem seems har-monious, its women content with serving Guido. When an aging Parisian showgirl throws a fit because she is being sent upstairs (the place where women in the harem are banished upon reaching the age of thirty), however, Saraghina declares a rebellion, and Guido subdues them with a lion tamer's whip.

Later that afternoon, Guido, Luisa, and their friends watch the screen tests with the production team. While Daumier alludes to Guido's inferiority to the French novelist Stendhal, Guido fantasizes that Cesarino and his coworker Agostini hang Daumier. Luisa is furious to see that the mistress character and the wife character in Guido's film are clearly modeled after Guido's own mistress and herself. She walks out of the theater, and when Guido follows her, she says she is leaving him. Guido returns to the screen tests and reviews other actors who clearly represent his own real-life acquaintances.

Suddenly, Claudia Cardinale's press agent appears to announce her arrival. Claudia takes Guido for a drive, asks about her part in the film, and expresses her enthusiasm about working with him. Finally seeing Claudia in the flesh, Guido finds her breathtaking yet disappointing. He knows that she will be neither the answer to the questions he has about his film nor the resolution for conflicts he wants to include in the picture. They park the car on a deserted road near the spring. Guido has one last vision of the ideal Claudia as the real version sits beside him and listens to his explanation of the film, which describes a man unable to commit to anything. Just as he admits to Claudia that there is no longer a part for her in his film, Cesarino, Agostini, Pace, and Conocchia arrive. They announce that there will be a press conference at the launch pad the next day and that shooting will begin in a week.

The next afternoon, droves of cars arrive at the launch pad. Agostini and Cesarino practically drag Guido to the press conference, and aggressive journalists shout questions at him all the way to the podium, where Pace insists that he give a speech. Overwhelmed by the pressure, Guido begins to hallucinate and sees Luisa in a wedding dress, asking him whether he will ever be faithful. Then, Guido imagines that Agostini puts a gun in his pocket, and Guido crawls under the table to shoot himself in the head.

Guido cancels production of the film. Agostini directs the construction crew to dismantle the rocket launcher, and Daumier, unusually supportive, congratulates Guido on having made the right decision to give up his mediocre film. As Daumier continues talking, Guido imagines that Maurice (the mind-reading magician) tells him that his show is just beginning. Guido sees Claudia, his aunts, Saraghina, his parents, Carla, the clergymen, and other familiar characters dressed all in white and blissfully smiling, walking together on grassy sand dunes. Guido is inspired once again and describes a new film that will portray his true self, no matter how confused it is. He asks Luisa to accept him as he is, and she says she will try.

8 1/2

Maurice and Guido direct all of the characters in the film into a large circle, which Guido persuades Luisa to join, then joins himself. The line moves off the stage, leaving only a boy fife player (who resembles Guido in his youth) who leads five circus musicians. The boy directs the other musicians to leave the stage before playing a short solo and marching out of the spotlight alone.

8 1/2

Character List

Guido Anselmi—Played by Marcello Mastroianni The film's protagonist, a renowned Italian film director in the middle of making a film he hasn't finished writing. Guido feels guilty about cheating on his wife and abandoning the Catholic Church, and he is afraid of aging and creative exhaustion.

Luisa—Played by Anouk Aimée Guido's wife, who loves him despite his faults. Luisa is an intelligent, charming, and beautiful woman who rejects the artificiality of Guido's star-studded lifestyle and is fed up with his philandering and lying. She brings her friends and her sister along with her to visit Guido.

Carla—Played by Sandra Milo Guido's mistress, who has a husband of her own. Sumptuously feminine yet charmingly childish, Carla never challenges or reproaches Guido, but her tacky style and idiotic personality embarrass him. Unquestioning and never demanding, she is Luisa's foil.

Mario Mezzabotta—Played by Mario Pisu Guido's friend, who is annulling his marriage so that he can marry his new fiancée, Gloria, a friend of his daughter. To Guido, Mezzabotta is a pathetic figure who embodies the director's fears about aging.

Gloria Morin—Played by Barbara Steele Mezzabotta's waiflike young fiancée. An aspiring actress and a philosophy student, Gloria alternatively murmurs coquettish and pseudo-intellectual nonsense.

Claudia—Played by Claudia Cardinale An actress whom Guido considers for the leading role in his film. Although Claudia's beauty is ideal and her presence dreamlike, Guido realizes that her perfection will not suit his film. Claudia represents youth, purity, and healing.

8 1/2

Rossella—Played by Rossella Falk Luisa's best friend, who accompanies Luisa to visit Guido at the spa. Guido calls Rossella "grasshopper" because, like Jiminy Cricket in *Pinocchio*, she cares for and advises him. She tries to lighten the tension between Guido and Luisa. She is also a clairvoyant.

The French Actress—Played by Madeline LeBeau A famous actress whom Guido has requested to play the Carla character in his film. The actress's insistent demands to know more about the part convince Guido that she is inappropriate for the role of the easygoing Carla. Her agent's nagging for contractual details and her own nervous presence are a constant reminder of the pervasiveness of Guido's occupation.

Daumier—Played by Jean Rougeul Guido's pretentious associate screenwriter. Daumier continually appears without warning, nonchalantly describing the film's flaws. His criticism is frustrating to Guido but delightful for the audience, for it scrutinizes the direction of both Guido's film and *8 1/2* itself. The vain, arrogant Daumier is always eager to schmooze with the press and with beautiful actresses.

Saraghina—Played by Eddra (Edra) Gale A large gypsy woman who lives on the beach during Guido's boyhood. Guido and other boys visit Saraghina surreptitiously to hear her sing and dance the rumba. Saraghina plays a significant role in Guido's sexual awakening as well as his straying from the Catholic Church.

Pace—Played by Guido Alberti Guido's producer and a constant source of nagging pressure. Pace insists that production move forward regardless of its state of confusion. His young, moronic girlfriend often appears beside him, lapping ice cream.

Conocchia—Played by Mario Conocchia An old friend and creative collaborator of Guido's who threatens to quit working on the film out of frustration with Guido. Guido sometimes finds Conocchia's influences to be too outdated for the production of his film, which he wants to feel new and fresh. Conocchia's presence exacerbates Guido's fears of becoming creatively impotent himself.

Cesarino—Played by Cesarino Miceli Picardi A member of the production team and the casting director. Cesarino is a good friend of Guido's and their pleasant encounters are evidence of the comfort Guido can find in his work.

Maurice—Played by Ian Dallas A mind-reading magician and old friend of Guido's. Maurice helps Guido find his creative inspiration and encourages him to follow it. He is Daumier's foil.

The Beautiful Woman—Played by Caterina Boratto A mysterious woman who is staying at the spa's hotel. In real life, Boratto was an icon of beauty in Italy, and Italian viewers would recognize her as an old movie star. Her likeness also appears on a statue of the Virgin Mary in a memory sequence of Guido's childhood.

Bruno Agostini—Played by Bruno Agostini Another member of the production team. The same age or younger than Guido, always impeccably dressed and coldly efficient, Agostini is Conocchia's foil.

Jacqueline Bonbon—Played by Yvonne Casadei A retired Parisian cabaret dancer who, like Saraghina and the Beautiful Woman, contributes to Guido's first romantic experiences. Jacqueline is older than Guido's other love interests, and she contributes to the motif of growing old.

8 1/2

ANALYSIS OF MAJOR CHARACTERS

GUIDO ANSELMI

Forty-three-year-old Guido Anselmi is a famous film director under an enormous amount of pressure. His producer, having invested heavily in Guido's next film despite the fact that its script is still incomplete, is counting on Guido to make another success. The producer is ready and eager to begin filming. Guido, however, who was recently diagnosed with a mild liver ailment, is feeling old, and it is important to him that this film is different from the others—something new. At the same time, Guido knows that his wife, Luisa, is becoming more and more frustrated with his neglect of her, and he is afraid of losing her for good. In this way, Guido is simultaneously challenged to define the trajectory of his own life and that of the protagonist in his film.

As Guido wrestles with the questions of whether he can manage to be a true husband to Luisa and whether he can make his film really work, his associates, who have joined him at the health spa where he is staying, exacerbate the pressure he feels. The directorial suggestions of Conocchia, Guido's longtime collaborator, seem outdated and make Guido worry that his own creative virility is also becoming limited as he ages. Similarly, Mezzabotta, who looks ridiculous with his significantly younger fiancée, makes Guido anxious about aging. Although Carla, Guido's mistress, is a comfort to him, Guido is afraid that her tacky conspicuousness makes him look as foolish as Mezzabotta. Carla is the polar opposite of Guido's wife, Luisa, whom Guido truly loves. His insatiable temperament, however, prevents him from committing to one woman.

Extramarital lust and fear of aging are common midlife challenges, so even the frequent daydreaming that seems so unique under Fellini's direction is not too far out of the ordinary. Still, Guido's acute sensitivity and vivacious creativity make him an exceptional character. Whereas it is natural for one's environment to inspire associations and recall memories, mild visual stimuli as innocuous as spa-goers in a steam bath inspire Guido to create entirely new worlds that correspond with his attitude. When Guido realizes that he can use this special interpretative talent to synthesize the conflicts of his protagonist with his own challenges, his creative crisis is resolved. The ultimate success of Guido's marriage, however, remains uncertain.

LUISA

Luisa's first encounter with Guido when she comes to visit him at the hotel encapsulates her role in Guido's life and in the film. The scene opens amid the opulence that has come to characterize Guido's lifestyle: a flock of women in feathers and pearls parts for a moment, and Luisa emerges, a standout in a plain white shirt, boyish haircut, starkly framed glasses, and minimal makeup. Compared to the painted and bubbly Carla, the morosely pretentious Gloria, and the tortured French actress, Luisa is a relief with her subtle beauty and discriminating sensibility. Luisa's detached observation of the luxury auctions and jewelry boutiques around her implies that the glamour of Guido's life doesn't impress her. When Guido realizes that he is in Luisa's presence, he transforms. No longer a confidently clowning hotshot director, he is nervous, unsure of how to approach his own wife. When Luisa turns around and recognizes him, her somber expression transforms into a glowing smile, and Guido, too, appears unabashedly delighted. The couple exchanges pleasantries warmly, each loving contact—the kisses, Guido's guiding arm—soft and slow. Both seem immediately contented by the simple presence of the other. Here and throughout the film, even during quarrels, they are undoubtedly in love with each other.

If Luisa, then, is Guido's true love, she also represents a unique truth amid the whirlwind of deception that wracks Guido's world. The actresses that want parts in Guido's movies speak only to please him, and Guido's mistress Carla is eager to transform herself to suit his immediate sensual desires. Likewise, Guido's production team, excepting Daumier, seems eager to support anything he gives them, no matter its artistic validity, because they expect it to be a success. The press prints whatever he says, only too happy to have recorded his precious words. Surrounded by these legions of yes-men, Guido's tendency to fabricate spins out of control. Only Luisa cares for him enough to tell him the truth—that his movie is a lie. When Guido resolves his creative struggle at the end of the film and convinces Luisa to join his circus line, it appears as if she has resigned

8 1/2

herself to accepting Guido's noncommittal lifestyle. However, considering Luisa's repeated attacks on the veracity of the film, we cannot be sure whether she truly was so easily compliant.

CARLA

Carla, Guido's mistress, reminds us that *8 1/2* is just as much a comedy as a drama. Though her visit to Guido is meant to be clandestine, her presence is never subtle, and Guido's discomfort is hilarious as he watches her flounce off a train wearing a dress of velvet and fur—wholly unsuitable attire for the climate of the spa village—or jingle into a café in a horse-drawn coach. Her lighthearted chatting, punctuated by giggles and gasps, is so genuinely vapid that it is difficult to believe that Guido can endure her. During the scene at the hotel restaurant, Guido's irritation with Carla's insipidity is unmistakable, yet, among countless potential mistresses, Guido chooses her.

Why would the ultra-sensitive Guido choose Carla, a woman who can't begin to understand the subtlety of his genius? Apart from her sumptuous figure and pristine beauty, Guido selects her precisely for the reason that she is so different from the society of his public life. While Pace and the others demand production, Luisa demands commitment, and the pseudo-intellectual crowd demands impossibly abstract discussion, Carla asks for nothing. If she is upset about something—for example, not staying at the grand hotel—her pouting lasts only a few moments, and, like a child, she is contented by the superficial pleasure of eating (she eats a big plate of chicken, gulps red wine, and devours several peaches at a time) and reading comic books. While Carla's attitude is principally childish, she also adopts a maternal tone toward Guido, encouraging him, too, to regress into the capriciousness of youth. Guido's affair with Carla is like his visits to Saraghina as a boy: superficial and embarrassing, but too exhilarating for him to give up.

THEMES, MOTIFS, AND SYMBOLS

THEMES

THE FEAR OF AGING

Guido's first words in the film are "forty-three," his age. The placement of this detail so early in the film indicates Guido's preoccupation with it. A recent onset of health problems (he is ostensibly visiting the spa for a mild liver ailment) causes Guido to worry, like any middle-aged man, that his most productive years are coming to a close. The idea of aging is especially terrifying for a man like Guido, because two of the qualities that he values most—his creative ability and his virility—often rely heavily on youth. Fellini makes some direct references to the physical characteristics of Guido's aging, as when Guido gazes at his wrinkles in his bathroom mirror, when Mezzabotta comments on his gray hair, and when Claudia teases him that he dresses like an old man. Fellini makes a stronger statement, however, with Guido's response to the sickly guests at the spa and to his aging companions, Mezzabotta and Conocchia. Mezzabotta's age is emphasized by his much younger American fiancée Gloria, in whose presence he often comes across as ridiculous or pathetic. When Mezzabotta follows Gloria's lead on the dance floor and performs some vigorous steps, for example, Fellini frames his sweaty efforts from an unbecoming head-on angle to indicate that Guido thinks Mezzabotta is making a spectacle of himself and aging disgracefully. Guido expresses a similar feeling toward Conocchia, his senior collaborator, who embodies Guido's fear that getting old will diminish his professional relevance.

THE TYRANNY OF THE MIND

Fellini's subjective technique of documenting Guido's train of thought from reality to daydream and back again, unburdened from traditional perspective shifts and dramatic convention, seems liberating when we view *8 1/2*. This placement of daydream and reality side by side comes across as a very convincing depiction of the way in which we actually experience life, reminding us of the mind's power to transcend everyday reality. But at the same time, the film makes this process, in which observation alternates with imagination, seem somewhat frightening, as it is something over which we have little control. For example, Guido would never *choose* to have the nightmare of the opening sequence or to imagine his colleagues in the steam baths as hell-bound invalids. His thoughts and daydreams are involuntary. Though this aspect of the mind cannot be consciously controlled, it is interesting to observe the manner in which the subconscious directs it. In the Saraghina sequence, for example, Guido's subconscious alters the memory to make himself seem more innocent. In Guido's fantasies about Claudia, excess sound is silenced so that Guido can focus more closely on her. Guido's dreams seem designed in order to call his attention to his problems. In this way the control of the mind seems constructive, yet the idea of having no free will is frightening.

THE FRIVOLITY OF SOCIETY

Critics applauded Fellini's adept and witty social commentary in *La Dolce Vita,* and the same element exists in *8 1/2* to emphasize the frivolity of bourgeois society. While guests of a ritzy health spa and people in the film industry may seem like easy targets, the elements that Fellini satirizes are relevant to middle- and upper-class society in general. Fellini embeds his satirical references in dialogue that is sometimes off-screen, making it easy to miss. For example, while Guido eyes Carla at the first grand evening at the hotel, we hear the voices of the American reporter and his wife, an American society woman who writes for women's magazines. The American reporter is speaking to the French actress and her manager in French, expressing the simple opinion that a film should have a hero. His wife interrupts him twice with her nasal cawing, first with "What the hell are you talking about" then with "I don't understand a damn bit of that French." After the second interjection, her husband responds in English with "Oh dear, honey, don't drink any more." Fellini's portrayal of the women's magazine writer—the standard-setter for millions of women—as a crass drunk points to the foolish herd mentality of contemporary culture. The American reporter's idle chatting with the French actress in her native tongue makes a subtler point: that reporters will do anything to get their story but really have nothing to say. The couple's American nationality does not indicate Fellini's antagonism to America but rather the quick spread of American pop culture worship into Europe.

8 1/2

MOTIFS

FEMALE SENSUALITY

The most memorable collective body of characters in 8 1/2 is unquestionably its women, who range from a collegiate waif to a movie star to a simple-minded hotel owner. The harem sequence that showcases these women also illustrates the way in which Guido, like many men, is in some way attracted to every woman he's ever known. Guido feels guilty about having extramarital interest and at certain points expresses the wish not to have such temptation. Fellini articulates Guido's incredible difficulty suppressing his desire by emphasizing the sensuality of all of the female characters in the film. Carla, Guido's ever-available, sumptuously beautiful mistress, is the best example, for she personifies sexual temptation itself. Other, more unlikely women also attract Guido, such as the monstrous Saraghina (Guido likes her thick legs and quick hips) and Guido's homely aunts, with whom he associates being nurtured. In any case, every scene in the film includes women with special features— shapely backs, crowns of blond hair, beautiful voices—that taunt Guido's intent to behave.

CATHOLICISM

Though the presence of religion pervades 8 1/2, the film offers no clear religious message—a setup well matched to Guido's ambiguous attitude toward religion. In short, Guido isn't sure how he feels about faith and the church. He began moving away from the church as an adolescent, when he discovered that the rigors of devout Catholicism would not accommodate his emerging libido. Despite this early separation, the middle-aged Guido has a deep respect for Catholicism and yearns to understand it. In his dream involving his parents, he is wearing a clerical robe, and before his appearance at the fountain he is touched by a solemn moment he witnesses between the cardinal and his attendants in the elevator. Guido makes sure to seek the cardinal's advice and approval for the script in his film, but during the interview the cardinal seems distant, commenting on a birdcall and asking Guido questions about his family life. The wisdom of the cardinal seems equally inaccessible in Guido's daydream of their meeting in the steam baths, during which the cardinal recites biblical quotations in Latin and barely acknowledges Guido. Preoccupied with aging, which inevitably leads to

8 1/2

death, Guido makes an earnest effort to understand the religion of his upbringing. Nonetheless, the spirit of Catholicism evades him.

PROFESSIONAL STRESS

Guido's life is fraught with professional concerns. The introductory nightmare sequence during which Guido, blissfully escaping into the clouds, is pulled down by men from the film industry, is a clear symptom of his stress. Although Guido's occupation involves him perhaps a bit more personally than other jobs would—for his artistic production depends on his professional stability—Fellini's description of the interminable nagging and never-tied loose ends of Guido's career is nevertheless universally relevant. For example, during Guido's physical exam, which takes place directly after the nightmare sequence, Fellini depicts the absurdity of society's acceptance of jobs that invade the personal sphere. Guido sits, leaning forward with his pajama top pulled over his head so that the doctor can listen to his breathing, and allows his collaborator, Daumier, who is wearing a robe, to come in to talk about the script. The level of intimacy with his coworkers that Guido is accustomed to accept seems almost ridiculous. Fellini completes the statement with a flourish at the end of the scene: Guido escapes his doctor and Daumier by slipping into his bathroom, where he expects to find privacy, but is afforded only a moment to himself before a phone—a phone in the bathroom, no less—begins to ring.

SYMBOLS

GUIDO'S NOSE

Toward the beginning of the mind-reading magicians scene, right after Gloria and Mezzabotta dance together, Guido wears a funny-looking false nose, fondling and tapping it. Guido, bored with the entertainment and his company, has apparently shaped the false nose from a dinner roll. More than a mere idle gesture, making the false nose contributes to the film's extended Pinocchio metaphor. In the well-known story, when the puppet Pinocchio tells a lie, his nose grows. Guido, thinking of himself as Pinocchio, relates his dishonesty to his nose and taps it with his finger at significant moments. Right before Guido's first daydream of Claudia serving him spring water, for example, Guido taps his nose. He repeats the gesture at the café right before the harem fantasy. In both instances, Guido is uncomfortable before he plunges into his fantasy, and the fabrication seems to be a sort of defense mechanism for him. Guido's glasses, which he touches or pulls away from his eyes before moments of fantasy or dishonesty, have a similar symbolic significance.

THE ROCKET LAUNCH PAD

Since the producers are eager to start shooting Guido's film, they begin construction of a rocket launch pad that Guido designed even before he had completed a screenplay to accommodate it. As it turns out, Guido realizes that science fiction is the wrong artistic direction for him and gives the orders to tear it down before construction is even complete. The launch pad, which consumed two hundred tons of concrete alone, is a prodigious mistake with important symbolic significance. Like the fabled Tower of Babel, the shuttle is a symbol of arrogance, but rather than signifying Guido's attempt to be closer to the gods, the shuttle alludes to his creative pretension. Guido spends much of his professional life among doting admirers, and without proper criticism to temper their praise, he feels an excess of artistic license that allows him to "lie," as he puts it, or to be artistically insincere. The potentially phallic nature of the launch pad apparatus also suggests a reminder of Guido's sexual arrogance and infidelity.

THE ROPE

The traffic jam of the opening sequence represents the suffocating presence of the film industry in Guido's life, which he escapes miraculously by floating into the sky. He is free for only a few moments before two businessmen, the manager and the publicist for actress Claudia Cardinale, yank him back down to Earth with a rope. Guido struggles briefly with the rope before he descends. The rope serves as a symbol of the film industry's control and near ownership of Guido's life. The producers who fund Guido's creative projects nag him, the press never leaves him alone, and Guido himself is tied to his movies by his own concerns about artistic integrity. Toward the end of the film, during the screen tests, Guido takes advantage of a delicious opportunity to reverse the rope's symbolic function when he imagines his producers using it to hang the irritating Daumier.

THE SPRING

Fellini was interested in the work of Carl Jung, the psychologist who wrote that the *anima* (the repressed feminine component of the male unconscious mind) is responsible for the connection to the spring, or source of life, in the unconscious mind. Likewise, the supposedly curative spring in 8 1/2 has symbolic meaning that is at once related to female psychology and youth. The spring, then, is a perfectly appropriate "cure" for Guido's major challenges, which include confusion with women and fear of aging. Claudia Cardinale, whom Guido plans to cast as his lead actress, is a personification of these qualities of the spring. This link between Claudia and the spring is especially clear in Guido's fantasy of her in his bedroom, during which she repeats, "I want to create order, I want to cleanse." The moment when Guido decides not to include Claudia in his film is thus doubly meaningful because while it marks his creative revelation, it also signifies his realization that there is no simple "cure" to his challenges.

FILM ANALYSIS

FILMING INSIDE GUIDO'S MIND

Some passages of *8 1/2*, like the opening scene in which Guido flies away from a traffic jam, obviously are not meant to describe reality. To emphasize the point, Guido wakes up in his bed, and we see that he has been dreaming. In this first example, the exact point at which the dream ends and reality begins is very clear, but in later sequences of dream, memory, or fantasy, the transition to reality is not so distinct. Guido's fantasy often begins by blending itself into his reality, so the shift can be difficult to recognize. These seamless transitions can be confusing, especially upon a first viewing, but their subtlety is essential for what Fellini aimed to achieve: a direct representation of Guido's experience and his response to it. Guido's consciousness acts as a filter between the world around him and the camera lens, and we see the events only as Guido reacts to them. We experience Guido's world from inside his own mind, which explains why reality slips into daydream so smoothly. Guido, like any person, drifts constantly between the world and his thoughts.

Moreover, even the "reality" portions of the film are not quite reality but rather reality as manipulated by Guido's attitude toward it. Consider, for instance, the outdoor sequence at the spa that takes place directly after the phone rings in Guido's bathroom. First, we hear a symphony orchestra playing Wagner's "Ride of the Valkyries." It would be appropriate for an elegant spa to have an outdoor orchestra, and we do see a conductor, but it is unlikely that the spa would hire a full symphony in the daytime, and still more unlikely that the bombastic "Ride of the Valkyries" would be on the program. (Music that is more appropriate for a vacation spa is heard later that evening and on the night that Luisa arrives.) In fact, the reason we hear "Ride of the Valkyries" is that it expresses Guido's thoughts, which at this particular moment are ironic and satirical. Guido is surrounded at the spa by wrinkled, bent, slowly-moving men and women whose features are exaggerated by Guido's focus on them, people so pathetic that Guido mockingly compares them to the heroic warriors of Wagner's opera *Die Walküre*. Guido dramatizes the scene further by imagining the spa guests in fashions from the 1930s rather than contemporary clothing, as if he is blending his boyhood conception of an elegant spa with his current experience. By infusing reality with Guido's reaction to it, Fellini allows us to understand the basic idea of the scene, Guido's first visit to the spring of the health spa, and encourages us to use the peculiarities, incompatible music and anachronistic clothing, to analyze Guido's feelings. This style of filming is consistent throughout *8 1/2*, so it is essential to pay attention to all such details that seem out of place.

If the reality sequences accommodate the reactions in Guido's mind, how can we recognize the shifts from reality to fantasy? In many cases, Fellini nudges us with aural and visual cues. For example, before Guido's first vision of Claudia, he taps his nose with his finger, which is meant to remind us of Pinocchio, another Italian liar, and indicates the incipient fantasy. After the nose signal, the soundtrack falls silent, marking Guido's departure from reality. The fantasy is broken when an insistent voice (in this case, a water-server) invades the silence. Guido's childhood sequences begin more abruptly, as certain elements in his environment yank him into the past with no warning. In retrospect, however, we can recognize why these elements acted as stimuli. The magician reading *Asa nisi masa* at the hotel recalls a scene in which Guido's little cousin told him that the phrase had magical powers, and seeing a woman's stocky legs in the presence of the cardinal reminds Guido of his visit to Saraghina.

The way in which Fellini allows tiny details to orchestrate the trajectory of the plot is, of course, parallel to Guido's experience. Such an absolutely subjective filmic style was a groundbreaking innovation that earned *8 1/2* its place among the most important films ever made. Its novelty, however, is itself delightfully ironic, for the way in which Guido is jerked to and fro between reality and the caprices of his mind is simply a characteristic of normal human consciousness.

MANIPULATION OF CHILDHOOD SEQUENCES

Every scene in *8 1/2* represents Guido's reaction to the world around him. The effect is subtle in the reality sequences, typical in the dream and fantasy sequences (one's dreams, of course, have no objective viewer), and most telling in the memory sequences. There are two memory sequences in the film. The first is set in Guido's grandmother's farmhouse, when Guido is about four or five years old. In the sequence, Guido's aunts make him take a bath and his grandmother puts him to bed. The interior of the farmhouse looks odd: its cavernous rooms are sparsely decorated, and the furniture is too large. Other elements seem exaggerated as well, such as the number of children bathing at once and the intensity of their chants. Did Guido grow up in an abnormally large house, abnormally furnished, with an abnormally large number of similarly aged cousins? Perhaps, but it's more likely that Fellini chose these abnormalities in order to portray the memory as Guido would experience it, distortions and all. Guido knew the farmhouse as a little boy, and any house seems gigantic to a person that small. Many shots in this sequence are filmed from a low point of view, so we see the world at about table-level, as a child would. In the same way, it is likely that the rooms appear bare only because the decorations in them were inessential to the memory. Splashing around with his cousins in the bath is a happy memory for Guido, and, since it is natural to romanticize happy memories, Guido doesn't recall negative details such as soap and scrubbing.

Just as Guido erases negative elements from his happy memory, he alters the facts of a guilt-inducing memory in order to feel innocent. This second childhood sequence shows an adolescent Guido as his school priests catch him watching the gypsy woman, Saraghina. The scene's spatial elements seem less exaggerated than those of the farmhouse episode, as Guido's memory of his preteen years is clearer than those of his early childhood. While its scale seems normal, there is evidence that the content of the sequence is manipulated. We learned from the first memory sequence that Guido is a bright and naughty child who runs away from his aunts and kicks his legs wildly in bed. In this memory, however, Guido is a passive boy who gets into trouble only because his friends are bad influences. His friends beg him to come along to the beach to see Saraghina, and as they arrive Guido keeps hesitating until his friends encourage him to continue. Right before Saraghina begins to dance, Guido remains separated from the other boys, and as they clap and cheer, he remains immobile. Then, it seems as if Saraghina chooses to dance with Guido only because his friends push him into her arms. Again, it is possible that Guido did indeed have an angelic period between the ages of ten and twelve, but it is more likely that Guido was in fact enthusiastic about the trip to see Saraghina and that he remembers it differently only because the result of the episode, the severe punishment given by the priests, was so painful. Rather than remember the trip as a bout of bad behavior, Guido prefers to recall it as a great injustice. Just as Guido's immediate attitude alters his reality, so does his unconscious mind mold his memories to suit his desires.

ASA NISI MASA AND GUIDO'S WOMEN

During Guido's first childhood sequence in the big farmhouse, his female cousin reminds him of a magic spell, *Asa nisi masa*, which she tells him has the ability to make the eyes in a portrait point to a secret treasure. The cryptic phrase makes such an impression on Guido that nearly forty years later it is psychically available to a pair of magicians who read *Asa nisi masa* successfully from Guido's mind. Fellini ostensibly uses the phrase to establish a connection between Guido's past and present, yet it has more significance than a mere bridge between scenes. *Asa nisi masa* is actually only one word, encoded in a children's play language similar to pig Latin. When the second syllable of each word is removed, what is left is the word "Anima." Fellini, who was interested in the work of the psychoanalyst Carl Jung, would have known that Jung used the word *anima* to describe the personification of repressed female characteristics in the male (*animus* describes the personification of repressed male characteristics in the female). *Asa nisi masa*, then, can be interpreted as a reference to Guido's confusion about women.

In the magnificent harem scene, Guido has the ability to control his many women with a few fierce cracks of his whip, yet in reality he is not so powerful. The harem fantasy itself, in fact, is inspired by a humiliating moment during which Rossella and Luisa express their disgust of Guido's affair with Carla. Though Guido enjoys creating the harem fantasy and adores sleeping with Carla, his voracious sexual appetite is a serious problem for him, making his relationship with his wife and his religious impulses painfully tenuous. It may be natural for a man to have some attraction to any woman he meets, but Guido is an extreme case because he wants— even expects—to have them all. This attitude is parallel to Guido's creative demeanor. Just as he doesn't want to commit uniquely to Luisa, he cannot choose a single theme for his film. This irresolution was also a problem for Fellini himself, who made *8 1/2* describe a director's indecision because he himself couldn't commit to a single, more coherent theme. In fact, the original title for *8 1/2* was *La Bella Confusione* (*The Beautiful Confusion*).

Fellini's insertion of the encoded "anima" suggests that Guido's inability to commit, especially to women, is due to the inaccessibility of the part of his mind that comprehends relationships. Jung wrote that the anima is responsible for the connection with the "spring," or source of life, and the "eros," or principle of relationship, both of which are housed in the unconscious. This theory explains why Guido's doctor prescribes spring water for his "cure" and why Guido has difficulty understanding love. The latter problem is referred to several times in the film. When Guido meets Cesarino's two nieces, for instance, one of them tells Guido that he can't make a movie about love, and Guido, upset by the remark, passively agrees. Later in the film, when Guido speaks with Claudia in the street, she teases him that he doesn't know how to love. Guido responds coolly that he doesn't believe in that sort of love, but when Claudia persists, his agitation is undeniable. Poor Guido is deeply upset by his difficulty with women. The difficulty may indeed be due to a faulty connection to his anima, but the magician Maurice, who needs the help of his partner, Maya, to read Guido's mind successfully, suggests otherwise. Guido may think that his problem is psychologically innate, but it is more likely that he needs only a stronger connection with his own partner, Luisa.

Important Quotations Explained

1. DAUMIER: "On first reading it's evident that the film lacks a problematic, or a philosophical premise, making the film a series of gratuitous episodes, perhaps amusing for their ambiguous realism. One wonders what the authors are trying to say."

Immediately after Guido takes his first dose of healing water from the spring, his fellow screenwriter, Daumier, starts critiquing Guido's script of the film. In his characteristically patronizing tone, Daumier dismisses Guido's work as meaningless. The pedantic delivery and exaggerated intellectual language of the speech are a clue not to take Daumier too seriously. He is a caricature of a revered film critic who thinks enormously of himself—the sort of scholarly character that Fellini, a high-school dropout, knew well from his years of working within Italian neorealist circles. Daumier's criticism, however, is not complete nonsense. Though exaggerated, Daumier's objection to the film's lack of clear purpose would be a typical critical response to a film as radically subjective as *8 1/2*.

It was a brilliant gesture for Fellini to create a lifelike film critic in his movie who offers criticism of the very film in which he appears. By accurately anticipating what the real-life critics would say, Fellini kept them from saying it themselves, and as a result, negative reaction to the film was limited. Though Fellini's trick was successful, it does betray his hostility to intellectual types and perhaps his insecurity in their presence. He wickedly makes fun of Mezzabotta's fiancée Gloria, who is a philosophy student, by making her wear ghoulish makeup and limp about cooing ridiculously abstract comments. When the American reporter asks Guido a difficult question about the connection between Catholicism and Marxism, he becomes frustrated, ostensibly because they are in an inappropriate setting for serious conversation, but also because he isn't sure how to answer. Fellini's treatment of intellectual characters in the film may be unfair, but the comic result is delightful.

2.   GUIDO: "I wanted to make an honest film. No lies
        whatsoever. I thought I had something so simple to say.
        Something useful to everybody. A film that could help bury
        forever all those dead things we carry within ourselves.
        Instead, I'm the one without the courage to bury anything at
        all."

After the scene during which Guido and Luisa dance together at the
hotel, Pace leads everyone to the construction site of the rocket
launch pad. Luisa, upset with Guido, begins a tour up one of the
towers with a big group, while Guido and Rossella remain behind.
At first, their conversation is about Luisa, but, typically, Guido soon
turns their discussion to his film. These lines emphasize Guido's preoccupation with telling the truth, but, as we know, this never fails to
keep him from lying on other occasions. That Guido lies so much
seems to be a fault in his nature rather than a result of his choice, and
a major part of his struggle concerns his uncertainty about whether
he has the ability to change.

The abrupt change of subject from his marriage to his film in
Guido's conversation with Rossella seems unbearably selfish, but in
light of Guido's creative crisis, the ways to approach his film and his
marriage are intrinsically related. Guido wants to become more
honest in order to be sincere in his filmmaking and to be a true husband to Luisa. His industrious imagination and voracious sexual
appetite, however, make this a challenge. Guido is better at using
existing elements in reality to create new marvels than working with
what he has to reach a sensible resolution. In this very scene, for
instance, he shows Rossella a mentally disabled sailor whom he's
taught to tap dance. Eventually, Guido realizes that the most appropriate method to complete his film is to explain his indecision. The
original title for *8 1/2*, *La Bella Confusione* (*The Beautiful Confusion*), suggests that Fellini must have had a similar crisis and decided
to describe his problem rather than trying to resolve it. Indeed, Fellini completes Guido's speech to Rossella with "I really have nothing
to say, but I want to say it all the same."

3. LUISA: "Indulge yourself. Stroke your ego. Go make everyone think you're so wonderful. What could you ever teach strangers when you can't even tell the simplest truth to the ones closest to you? To the one who's been growing old with you?"

Luisa, Guido's wife, is the only female character who criticizes Guido's film. When she realizes that the film is autobiographical and that Guido's portrayal of his life is not altogether honest, her frustration with him comes to a head. During the screen tests, when she recognizes that the actresses are meant to represent herself and Guido's mistress, Luisa walks out, and when Guido follows her, they argue. This quotation is especially significant because we know that Guido's film is analogous to 8 1/2 and Guido to Fellini himself. Like the comments of the critic Daumier, Luisa's words apply to the film being depicted and the film actually being watched.

Luisa's criticism of Guido for altering elements in his film to "stroke his ego" suggests that Fellini, too, manipulated certain autobiographical aspects in order to make himself look more attractive. This suggestion is not difficult to believe, because Fellini's analog, Guido, finds himself surrounded by beautiful women and fashionable opulence that seem idealized. Since Luisa's denouncement appears before Guido's ultimate revelation, however, it is possible that Guido (and Fellini) corrected the dishonesty and that Guido's film (and 8 1/2) is more truthful than the version Luisa knew. It is true that Guido's life seems glamorous, but he also experiences a crisis that makes him confused, powerless, and sometimes pathetic. This unbecoming portrait doesn't seem like the result of Guido or Fellini stroking their egos at all, but rather like it might actually be the truth. In any case, if Luisa is trying to convince Guido to be more devoted to her, she makes a mistake here by reminding him that they have been growing old together, for Guido's worry about aging is one of the factors in his hesitancy to commit.

4. CLAUDIA: "A guy like your character, who doesn't love anybody, is not very sympathetic, you know. It's his fault. What does he expect?"

When Guido finally meets Claudia, after having seen her only in photographs and in his fantasies, she drives him to an empty street near the spring. After Guido describes the plot of his film, Claudia laughs dismissively, telling him that he doesn't know how to love. He acts unsurprised and responds coolly that he doesn't believe in love and doesn't feel like telling another bunch of lies. But as Claudia persists in telling Guido about his emotional deficiencies—she clearly understands that Guido's character is autobiographical—he becomes upset. This moment is an echo of the exchange that Guido has with one of Cesarino's nieces in the back room of the production office. The niece tells him that he can't make a love story, and though it is a lighthearted comment, it bothers Guido noticeably enough to prompt Cesarino to try to cheer him up with some clowning.

The fact that these two offhand opinions upset Guido so easily emphasizes his sensitivity regarding his ability to love. Guido is in love with Luisa, but he continues to have extramarital desires and wonders why he can't commit to the woman he loves. It is especially poignant for Claudia to accuse him of not being able to love because she is meant to play a character in Guido's film for whom the hero gives up everything, to whom he decides to devote his life. Immediately after Claudia tells him that he doesn't know how to love, Guido admits to her that he doesn't really have a role for her in his movie, because he knows that he and his hero alike are incapable of perfect devotion. Fellini, too, was confused about love, anxious to know where it is born and where it exists thereafter. Not surprisingly, he also had a famously impressive number of affairs (including one with Sandra Milo, who plays Guido's mistress Carla).

5. GUIDO: "What is this sudden happiness that makes me tremble, giving me strength, life? Forgive me, sweet creatures. I hadn't understood. I didn't know. It's so natural accepting you, loving you. And so simple. Luisa, I feel I've been freed. Everything seems so good, so meaningful. Everything is true."

Guido thinks these words toward the end of the film, immediately after he gives the order to begin the destruction of the launch pad. As Daumier rattles on about the futility of attempting to make a decent film, Guido's magician friend Maurice inspires the director. Guido stops listening to Daumier and begins to think. In the scene immediately preceding this one, Guido imagines that he shoots himself, and judging by his order to destroy his set, it's clear that he has given up his film. This quotation, however, marks Guido's first steps toward a new film without flawless women like Claudia or fantastic themes

8 1/2

like space travel. Guido's decision to be artistically honest immediately moves him to improve his personal life as well.

This moment is a grand one for Guido because he recognizes that he can make his film describe his life truthfully, no matter how confused his life is. He wants to translate the honesty to his personal life and to tell Luisa the truth about his cheating. Moreover, he wants Luisa to accept him as he is. The "sweet creatures" are Luisa and Rossella, and as he addresses them with his internal monologue, he focuses on Luisa and the sad but composed expression on her face. Luisa has always wanted Guido to be honest with her, but Guido's revelation is considerably demanding of her. To admit freely to Luisa that he's been unfaithful and that he has no intention to change seems like a beautiful idea to Guido. However, Luisa's stoically pained expression indicates that Guido's revelation will not be easy for her, no matter how perfectly it solves Guido's troubles.

8 1/2

A CLOCKWORK ORANGE

(1971)

CONTEXT

In 1971, Warner Brothers films released Stanley Kubrick's dark comedy *A Clockwork Orange,* based on a novel by Anthony Burgess, to both critical and popular acclaim as well as to political controversy. A futuristic film about a violent young hoodlum, it scored Kubrick his biggest box office hit at that point in his career. *A Clockwork Orange* was nominated for four Academy Awards, won the New York Film Critics Circle Award for best picture, and found favor with international audiences. It has since gained a cultlike following.

The film's brutality disgusted many viewers, even though most of the violent images in *A Clockwork Orange* are not of the blood-and-gore variety. In this film, Kubrick choreographed gang fights and assaults as graceful dances, and he presented scenes of rape, theft, physical brutality, and murder with a surreal, stylized, and even comic detachment. Even so, the Motion Picture Association of America slapped an X rating on the film's initial American release. After Kubrick deleted thirty seconds of footage, the MPAA revised its rating to R.

Although Kubrick grew up in the United States, he lived much of his adult life in England, and there the film proved even more controversial than in the United States. The British public saw *A Clockwork Orange* as a particularly English film, satirizing English values and manners. For example, the run-down housing complex where Alex, the main character, lives closely resembles London's poorly maintained public housing projects. While many disaffected British teens of the day saw their lives reflected in the film, some adults viewed the film as a celebration of youth violence, one more sign that society had grown too permissive with children. Groups of concerned citizens called for the film to be censored.

A Clockwork Orange had been in theaters for over a year when a bizarre and brutal crime put the movie back in the headlines. In 1974, a gang of British youths attacked a teenage girl. As they raped her, they performed the same song-and-dance number—"Singin' in the Rain," made famous by Gene Kelly in the musical of the same name—that Alex sings as he prepares to rape a woman in the film. Several more copycat crimes followed. The newspapers had a field day with the story, and a British judge declared the film an "evil in itself" and called for it to be censored. Though he defended his film,

Kubrick was appalled at the copycat crimes and feared being sued. He pulled the film from British theaters, and it was not officially screened in full in England again until 2000, after his death.

Kubrick was born in New York City in 1928 and attended public school. His father, a physician, filled the family's home with books of European fairy tales, folk tales, and Greek and Roman mythology. Kubrick read these books extensively when he was a child, and many of his films have the stylized and surreal quality of a myth or a fairy tale. Despite his interest in reading, Kubrick proved a mediocre student. He was an avid chess player and photographer, however, and after high school, he landed a job as a photographer for *Look* magazine. He worked there for four years before turning to filmmaking. He made his first feature-length film in 1953, using money he borrowed from his friends, his father, and his uncle, who was credited as associate producer. Kubrick eventually became a popular success, but for most of his career he avoided the Hollywood spotlight. On the set, he sometimes demanded that a scene be shot as many as seventy or eighty times, which earned him a reputation as a perfectionist. Kubrick died on March 7, 1999, only months before the July release of his thirteenth film, *Eyes Wide Shut*.

A Clockwork Orange was not Kubrick's only shocking film. For years, French authorities banned *Paths of Glory* (1957), one of his early war films, which tells the story of cynical French generals and the soldiers they victimize. The Catholic Church in the United States raised objections to Kubrick's 1962 film, *Lolita*, which is based on the Vladimir Nabokov novel of the same name and details an older man's sexual obsession with a young girl. Kubrick had a keen sense of humor and aesthetic vision, but at the core of his films is a dark vision of humanity. Primitive psychological urges drive his characters, often manifested as impulsive sexual or violent behavior. As his friend Alexander Walker, a film critic, wrote of him, "Kubrick's view of man [is] as a risen ape, rather than Rousseau's sentimental characterization of him as a fallen angel." Kubrick spun out this image of man as the biological and spiritual heir of the apes in his futuristic film *2001: A Space Odyssey* (1968).

Kubrick was fascinated by the dark side of human nature as well as by the dangers of the political systems that humans create to control their own shadowy desires. In 1964, Kubrick released *Dr. Strangelove or: How I Stopped Worrying and Learned to Love the Bomb*, a political comedy about the nuclear arms race between the United States and the Soviet Union. This film satirized the logic of the day, which maintained that the best way to keep the world safe was through an ever-increasing buildup of nuclear weapons. *Dr. Strangelove* is a terrifying and hilarious comedy in which the combination of human irrationality and the overwhelming power of the state manage to destroy the world in a nuclear holocaust. *A Clockwork Orange* offers another look at the dangers of state power, where the power-hungry individual, Alex, and the power-hungry state seem almost equally threatening.

The theme of state power had particular significance in the early 1970s, when *A Clockwork Orange* appeared in theaters. World War II and the rise of the Soviet Union had already shown the world the dangers of fascism, Nazism, and totalitarianism. Before writing the novel *A Clockwork Orange*, Burgess spent some time in Soviet Russia where he saw gangs of violent youths running wild while the police rounded up the government's political opponents. His novel and Kubrick's film, in turn, reflect those experiences.

The 1960s and 1970s also brought about worldwide political upheaval and rebellion against political and social institutions. During those decades, sex and drugs had unprecedented influence on teenagers' lives. This time period yielded drastic ideological alienation between generations, as the young rebelled, politically and socially, and allied against what they saw as the hypocrisy and repression of their elders. Although Alex in *A Clockwork Orange* has no particular political or social motivation for his violence and performs violence simply for its own sake, viewers still took a keen interest in the question of how much power the state should have to control its members, in particular its young.

Many viewers also responded to the film's cynical presentation of science as a tool of state control. In the film, the government chooses Alex to be the subject of an experimental procedure, conducted by government-employed doctors, that attempts to control his violent tendencies by altering his mind. Although the film presents this procedure as a futuristic nightmare, the first half of the twentieth century had seen the rise of psychological and scientific methods of changing human behavior, as well as instances where governments used those methods to control criminals and other members of society they deemed threatening.

In 1971, Zhores and Roy Medvedev, famous Soviet dissidents, published a memoir, *A Question of Madness*, in which they described Zhores's imprisonment in a Soviet psychiatric hospital, where techniques of mind control were practiced on him. In the

United States, lobotomies and electroshock therapy had already been used to treat the mentally ill in the 1930s. Although doctors believed these procedures would truly relieve the suffering of their patients, the government also hoped the procedures would reduce overcrowding in state-run psychiatric hospitals. According to Elliot S. Valenstein, author of *Great and Desperate Cures: The Rise and Decline of Psychosurgery and Other Radical Treatments for Mental Illness*, doctors at the time "were rarely questioned about anything they tried, and institutionalized patients were completely at the disposal of the staff in terms of treatment." In some instances, doctors performed similar procedures in prisons, on inmates judged criminally insane, in the hopes of making them less violent.

In *Clockwork,* a theme of the governmental abuse of power is coupled with the concept of modernity's dehumanization of society, which has filmic roots dating at least as far back as Fritz Lang's *Metropolis* (1927). This film, marking a widespread distrust of the industrial age, portrays an urban society segregated into "thinkers" and "workers," neither group possessing a complete set of human qualities. A similar theme appears early on in *Clockwork,* when Alex's mother wants to see him off to school but is thwarted in her maternal desires by her obligation to her factory job. In this scene, Alex's cheery "Have a nice day at the factory!" offers a comic relief that was more inspired by such films as Charlie Chaplin's landmark *Modern Times* (1936), a slapstick classic set in a factory and featuring Chaplin thrashing about in an effort to keep up with his conveyor belt duties.

Just as *Metropolis* influenced *Clockwork*'s criticism of society, so does Lang's 1931 classic *M* foreshadow *Clockwork*'s theme of irrepressible violence. The murderer in *M,* though guilty of heinous crimes, seems childlike and helpless, his actions only a response to a profound psychosis. Though *Clockwork*'s Alex is a more unforgivable villain, the root of his perverted thrills seems equally innate. The film's more politically oriented satire, apparent, for example, in Alex's rundown community and his state-mandated psychological "cure," preceded that in Milos Forman's mental-hospital drama *One Flew Over the Cuckoo's Nest* (1975), Terry Gilliam's futuristic, bureaucracy-rotten *Brazil* (1985), and Darren Aronofsky's *Requiem for a Dream* (2000), about the horrors of the state welfare system. Like *Clockwork,* these films were all critically acclaimed, praised for their often-shocking explorations of humanity's darkest impulses.

PLOT OVERVIEW

Alex, a young English hoodlum, heads a gang of four other young hoodlums. Instead of attending school, he spends his time performing acts of theft, rape, and violence. During the first night of the film, Alex and his gang members, the Droogs, gather at the Korova Milk Bar, which serves its patrons drug-laced milk from female mannequins. They take a drug that makes them hyperaware and ready for violence, then head out into the night and beat up an old homeless man. Next they come upon a rival gang about to rape a woman, and initiate a gang fight. They steal a car and speed out to the country. There, they don masks, burst into the home of a famous writer, Mr. Alexander, beat him, and rape his wife. As Alex rips off Mrs. Alexander's clothes before the rape, he sings "Singin' in the Rain" and dances like Gene Kelly does in the musical of the same name. During this night, Alex wreaks havoc in such a happy-go-lucky way that his violence seems motivated by pure enjoyment.

As the night comes to an end, Alex returns to his parents' apartment in a decrepit working-class housing complex. Before he climbs into bed, he turns on a symphony by Beethoven. The music conjures up images of bombings, hangings, and other forms of violence. In the morning, Alex's mother wakes him for school, but he says he feels ill. Though he plays the role of dutiful son, his parents clearly don't dare challenge him.

Soon, however, things begin to unravel for Alex. His Droogs have grown tired of his bullying, and they plan to oust him from power. The next night, they drive out to the home of a wealthy lady. Alex breaks in to rob her, but she fights back. In a surreal scene, she seizes a bust of Beethoven, and Alex seizes a statue of a penis. Just as police sirens begin to sound, Alex smashes her in the face with the statue and runs out. Outside, his friends lie in wait. They hit him over the head with a glass bottle of milk and run away, leaving him to the police.

During the night he spends in police custody, the woman dies, and soon the court sentences Alex to fourteen years in prison. For two years, he behaves like a model prisoner, but he has not truly reformed. What he wants is freedom. One day, Alex hears rumors circulating about a new experimental procedure called Ludovico's Technique. The government plans to use it to reduce overcrowding in its prisons and to bring law and order to the streets. Alex doesn't know what the treatment entails, but he is excited to hear that if he undergoes it, the government will release him from prison in just two weeks. When the minister of the interior visits the prison looking for a guinea pig, Alex calls attention to himself and is selected.

Soon, prison officials place Alex in the hands of government doctors, who inject him with a serum, then show him reel upon reel of violent and sexually explicit films. When he sees the films, the serum takes effect, and Alex experiences a horrendous illness, which is brought on by viewing sex or violence. Finally, even without the serum, he automatically becomes ill when he views images of violence or thinks any violent thoughts of his own. His violent impulses are now inhibited by his own physical response. Unfortunately for Alex, one of the films the doctors show him has a soundtrack that he adores: the fourth movement of Beethoven's Ninth Symphony. As a result, Alex becomes violently ill whenever he hears it. Still, he believes he has gotten a good deal when the government sets him free.

When Alex gets home, he finds that his parents have let his room to a lodger, and they tell him he can't stay. Outside, the homeless man Alex once beat up recognizes him, and he and his elderly homeless friends attack Alex. The police come to his aid, but they are his old Droogs, criminals now turned cops, and they drive him out to the country and beat him too. Night falls, a storm kicks up, and Alex drags himself to the nearest house. Once inside the house he realizes it's the home of Mr. Alexander, the writer he assaulted. Mrs. Alexander, whom he raped, had died soon after his attack.

At first Mr. Alexander recognizes Alex only as the boy he's seen in the newspapers for having undergone Ludovico's Technique. Mr. Alexander is a member of an opposition political party, and he believes that if he can show that Alex suffered cruelly at the hands of the government, the public may turn against it. He sees in Alex an opportunity to topple the government and takes Alex into his house. While he plans his scheme, Alex, soaking in a bath, begins to feel a little better and starts to sing "Singin' in the Rain," the same song he sang the night of the attack. Mr. Alexander recognizes the song, and he makes the connection that Alex is his former assailant. Now he not only wants to use Alex to topple the government but also wants revenge. He hatches a plan to drive Alex to suicide. Later in the day, while Alex sleeps, Mr. Alexander and two cronies blast Beethoven's Ninth Symphony into Alex's bedroom. Alex is overcome with illness, but when he tries to flee, he finds his door locked. Desperate to escape his illness, he decides to commit suicide. He jumps from the window.

Alex wakes up in a hospital, after a long time in a coma, in a full-body cast. While he was unconscious, much happened. Public opinion and the newspapers did turn against the government, claiming its cruelty drove Alex to attempt suicide. Mr. Alexander's plan seems to be working—but the government has a plan of its own. While Alex was in a coma, doctors reconditioned him back to his old self. They have undone the results of Ludovico's Technique.

The minister of the interior visits Alex in his hospital bed. Alex is eating his lunch, but because the cast confines his movements, he cannot feed himself. In a saccharine gesture of concern, the minister of the interior feeds Alex himself, while Alex slams his mouth open and shut, enjoying his power. The minister of the interior tells Alex how the government plans to help him, with a good job and a good salary. As a final present, the minister of the interior pipes Beethoven into the room, and Alex does not grow ill. The two sit together as journalists and cameramen rush in to capture the moment. As they wave and smile at the cameras, Alex, inspired by the music, imagines himself having wild sex while proper English men and women stand around and applaud. "I was cured all right," he says as the film ends.

Character List

Alex DeLarge—Played by Malcolm McDowell A young hoodlum and the antihero of the film. Murderously aggressive and also good-natured and innocent, Alex is both horrible and likable. He commits numerous acts of brutality. He speaks in a slang influenced by Russian, Slavic, Gypsy, Shakespearean English, rhymes, and baby talk, and he addresses the audience directly as "my brothers and only friends." He loves classical music, particularly Beethoven, though the music elicits images of violence and depravity for him.

Mr. Alexander—Played by Patrick Magee A famous writer and opponent to the ruling party. Holed up in his ultramodern home, Mr. Alexander writes books, deemed subversive by the government, about the need to protect the rights of the individual from the government. However, his concerns for the rights of the individual seem hypocritical when we see he is ready to use Alex as a pawn to topple the government, even if that means sacrificing Alex's life. In the novel, Mr. Alexander is the character who introduces the phrase "a clockwork orange," which derives from the East London Cockney saying, "as queer as a clockwork orange." This phrase suggests something that looks natural and organic on the outside but that is artificial and mechanical on the inside. Mr. Alexander claims that the government treats human beings as if they were clockwork oranges—creatures who look human but who can be manipulated and directed as if they were robots.

Chief Prison Guard—Played by Michael Bates Sports a small, Hitlerian mustache and walks and talks in a military style. The chief prison guard's manner is so extreme that he becomes a humorous caricature of a prison guard, shouting short commands at Alex like "Shut your filthy hole, you scum."

Dim—Played by Warren Clarke One in Alex's gang of hoodlums. Dim is the biggest, dumbest, and most brutish of the four Droogs, and Alex describes him as a "mindless, grinning bulldog." He becomes a policeman and uses his thuggish brutality to impose law and order.

Dr. Brodsky—Played by Carl Duerring The doctor in charge of Ludovico's Technique. Dr. Brodsky speaks in a calm voice and seems to maintain a scientific detachment at all times, even when Alex is experiencing the horrible illness associated with Ludovico's Technique.

Tramp—Played by Paul Farrell A man beaten up by Alex, who beats Alex up in turn. The tramp represents the youths' lack of respect for their elders, as well as the breakdown of societal order. He calls for a return to law and order, though he himself is homeless and drunk.

Lodger—Played by Clive Francis The young man who moves into Alex's room when Alex goes to prison. The lodger is strapping, healthy, good-looking, and sanctimonious. He tells Alex with self-righteous indignation that he has made his poor parents suffer enough, and that he is not welcome back in his home. He tells him that he himself has become like the good son Alex never was.

Prison Governor—Played by Michael Gover Runs the prison system and believes Ludovico's Technique lets prisoners off too easily. The prison governor believes in an eye-for-an-eye style of punishment and thinks the state deserves to take revenge on violent youths.

Cat Lady / Mrs. Weathers—Played by Miriam Karlin The woman Alex goes to prison for murdering, and the one victim who fights back. When the cat lady sees Alex in her home, she doesn't cower. Instead, she attacks him with a bust of Beethoven. She is wealthy, haughty, and unafraid, and she has filled her home with dozens if not hundreds of cats. Alex finds her in an exercise room, which she has decorated with modern, almost cartoonlike paintings of women in sexual and sadistic poses.

Georgie—*Played by James Marcus* Another member of Alex's gang of hoodlums. Georgie tries to usurp Alex's power within the gang at the beginning of the film. He too becomes a thuggish policeman.

Deltoid—*Played by Aubrey Morris* Alex's parole officer. Deltoid preaches to Alex about reforming his ways but seems to be an unsavory character himself. The first time we see him, he surprises Alex in his apartment. Alex is dressed only in his underwear, but Deltoid encourages him to sit down next to him on the bed while he warns him about not getting himself in trouble. Carried away by his own excitement, he grabs Alex's testicles. He speaks in a whiny, high-pitched voice and ends many of his sentences with "Yes?" His mannerisms and behavior suggest the ineffectiveness of logic in understanding and addressing the causes of violence, as well as the ineffectiveness of adults who try to control rebellious youth.

Prison Chaplain—*Played by Godfrey Quigley* The voice of tradition, he takes Alex under his wing while Alex is in prison. The prison chaplain preaches about good, evil, and freedom of choice, and he opposes the use of modern scientific methods to control human behavior. He is foolish and ineffective, preaching fire and brimstone to the convicts while they burp, fart, and leer. He also mistakenly believes in Alex's act of sincere reform. However, he is one of the few people in the film who speak out against the power of the state.

Mum—*Played by Sheila Raynor* Alex's mother, a well-intentioned but weak and weepy woman. Mum's appearance is very fashionable, and throughout the film she wears leather jumpers of various bright colors, with her hair dyed to match. At the same time, she is old-fashioned, with her hair set in the kind of permanent preferred by older women. She works in a factory, an existence that contrasts with the wild and disorderly ways of her son. Her main response to Alex's trouble is to break into tears.

Dr. Branom—*Played by Madge Ryan* Dr. Brodsky's assistant and the doctor in charge of instructing Alex during his treatment. Like Dr. Brodsky, Dr. Branom tries to maintain a cool scientific detachment. However, her zealousness for reforming the prisoner shows through during some of her speeches about the need to cure him.

Minister of the Interior—Played by Anthony Sharp   A high-ranking government official and the mastermind behind the plan to reform criminals using modern scientific methods. The minister of the interior is a suave politician concerned not with questions of morality but with "what will work" and what will keep his party in power. He dresses in elegant suits and speaks in a calm voice.

Dad—Played by Philip Stone   Alex's father, also well intentioned but weak. Toward the beginning of the film Dad seems as though he might stand up to Alex and ask him how he spends his evenings and whether he is getting into trouble, but then he fails to confront him. When Alex returns from prison, Dad is the one who tells him he can't move back home. Instead of taking responsibility for this decision, he falls back on the excuse that he and Mum have made a contract with their new lodger and couldn't possibly break it. At the end of the film, he comes to Alex full of sorrow and contrition for the way he treated him.

ANALYSIS OF MAJOR CHARACTERS

ALEX

Alex perpetrates gruesome acts of violence for no better reason, it seems, than that he likes to. As Deltoid, his probation officer, says to him, "You've got a good home here, good loving parents. You've got not too bad of a brain! Is it some devil that crawls inside of you?" Alex himself doesn't have a better explanation for his actions. He simply takes pleasure in being evil the way other people take pleasure in being good, he explains. He enjoys seeing blood flow and calls it "beautiful" or "lovely." He enjoys the power he has over people, even his fellow hoodlums. Though at times he feels sad and low, he doesn't appear to feel any empathy with his victims. The violent life is just a feel-good game to him. Somehow Alex's flippant disregard for others gives him an appealing vitality. His extravagant enjoyment of music is contagious, and even his enjoyment of violence makes him seem astoundingly alive. His actions are inherently evil, but his love of life, even an evil life, keeps him from being simply a monster.

Despite being a rapist and murderer, Alex has a strangely innocent, schoolboylike charm. The actor who plays Alex, Malcolm McDowell, also has youthful, even cherubic features, and he speaks in a gentle voice, saying "Yes, sir" and "No, sir" to the officials. This gentleness isn't only hypocrisy. When he first arrives in prison and the prison guards instruct him, in military tones, to do this, do that, stand there, sign here, Alex does it all without much anger. He doesn't like his lot and tries to change it, but when he can't, he accepts it. He may pity himself, but he doesn't wallow in it, which makes him more likable. When he imagines the crucifixion of Christ, he doesn't dwell on Jesus' suffering but rather pictures himself as a Roman soldier taking part in the torture. Compared to the holier-than-thou attitude of the prison chaplain, Alex's sacrilegious response feels refreshingly, almost childishly honest.

Alex does not undergo any fundamental transformation in his personality. In most works of fiction, the main character's struggles with questions of identity or moral choice propel the story forward. In *A Clockwork Orange*, however, Alex undergoes trials and adventures like other characters, but he is essentially the same at the end of the film. Ultimately, *A Clockwork Orange* doesn't ask what Alex should do, but what we as a society should do with Alex. (The novel *A Clockwork Orange* actually includes an additional chapter in which Alex grows up and renounces violence, and so does change and develop, but the novel's American publisher chose to cut that chapter. Kubrick based his film upon that version of the novel, much to the disapproval of its author, Anthony Burgess.)

PRISON CHAPLAIN

Throughout the film, the prison chaplain exhibits a certain blindness to reality, and our first view of him is as a sanctimonious, foolish, and ineffectual man. He preaches fire and brimstone to the convicts, and they ignore and ridicule him. He also consistently underestimates Alex's destructive potential and overestimates his desire for true moral reform. The chaplain believes, when he and Alex study the Bible together, that Alex is contemplating the goodness of Jesus and the evils of sin, but we know he is not. The chaplain believes Alex sincerely wants to reform, but we know he simply wants his freedom. This limitation in the prison chaplain's character doesn't invalidate his argument that even a criminal should not be stripped of his ability to make moral choices, but it does undermine his message to a certain extent.

The prison chaplain is both foolish and authoritarian in his religious outlook, but he speaks eloquently, if not completely convincingly, about protecting the individual's ability to make moral choices. When Alex tells the chaplain he wants to take part in Ludovico's Technique so that he can make the rest of his life "one act of goodness," the prison chaplain responds: "The question is whether or not this technique really makes a man good. Goodness comes from within. Goodness is chosen. When a man cannot choose, he ceases to be a man." After the minister of the interior shows off just how well the state has cured Alex of his violence, the prison chaplain voices an objection to such far-reaching state power. He says: "The boy has no real choice, has he? . . . He ceases to be a wrongdoer. He ceases also to be a creature capable of moral choice." The prison chaplain is an employee of the state, so his speaking out against the state is unexpected. The minister of the interior scornfully dismisses the chaplain's words, but the moral question the chaplain raises complicates Alex's "cure."

MINISTER OF THE INTERIOR

Unlike the prison officials who bark their orders, the minister of the interior wields a quiet power. In all his scenes, he appears pleasant. When he visits Alex's prison to choose a guinea pig for Ludovico's Technique, he is suave, dressed in a good suit and speaking in a calm voice. He uses pretty words, saying that criminals should be dealt with on a "curative basis." In other words, they shouldn't be punished but reformed. However, these niceties belie more sinister intentions. The minister believes the government's goal should be to run society cleanly and efficiently. Ethical and existential questions don't concern him. When the prison chaplain tries to lecture him about the rights of man, the minister tells him that what matters is what works. He wants to maintain law and order in the streets, even if he must hire thugs as policemen. He wants to use their brutality in the service of the state. At the prison, he explains that the government wants to empty the prisons of violent criminals to make space for political prisoners. We don't learn more about these political prisoners, but clearly they are people who oppose the minister and his party. Like any thug, and like the prison officials who seem so high on their authority, the minister of the interior seeks power at any cost.

THEMES, MOTIFS, AND SYMBOLS

THEMES

ORDER IN SOCIETY VS. FREEDOM OF CHOICE

The freedom of individuals to make choices becomes problematic when those choices undermine the safety and stability of society, and in *A Clockwork Orange,* the state is willing to protect society by taking away freedom of choice and replacing it with prescribed good behavior. In Alex's world, both the unfettered power of the individual and the unfettered power of the state prove dangerous. Alex steals, rapes, and murders merely because it feels good, but when his violent impulses are taken away, the result is equally as dangerous, simply because freedom of choice, a fundamental element of humanity, has been taken away.

Thematically, the minister of the interior stands on one side of Alex, supporting an ordered society, and the prison chaplain and Mr. Alexander stand on the other, supporting freedom of choice, even with the negative consequences that go with it. The minister of the interior argues that government should have the power to bring law and order to the streets, and that questions of individual liberty are insignificant compared with the values of safety and order. He cites the suffering Alex causes his victims as evidence for his argument's merit, but the minister's own misuse of power, such as hiring thugs as policemen and imprisoning political opponents, undermines his argument. Mr. Alexander, on the other hand, argues for the protection of individual liberty, but he weakens his own argument with his willingness to sacrifice Alex's life and liberty in order to further his party's agenda. The prison chaplain seems more sincere in his defense of the right of individuals to make moral choices, equating the ability to choose with being human, but his willful ignorance of Alex's true destructive potential makes him seem almost naïve. Throughout *A Clockwork Orange,* the film forces us to weigh the values and dangers of both individual liberty and state control, and consider how much liberty we're willing to give up for order, and how much order we're willing to give up for liberty.

THE NECESSITY OF EVIL IN HUMAN NATURE

The importance of evil as well as good in human nature is a fundamental theme of *A Clockwork Orange*. Alex is despicable because he gives free rein to his violent impulses, but that sense of freedom is also what makes him human. Unlike so many of the adult characters in the film, he, at least, seems exuberantly alive. When Ludovico's Technique eliminates the evil aspects of his personality, he becomes less of a threat to society, but also, the film suggests, less human. He is not truly good because he didn't choose to be good, and the utilization of that choice is vital to being a complete human being.

Alex, with his many evil deeds, isn't a traditional hero, and this is characteristic of and unique to Kubrick's films. The good and bad in Kubrick's characters are almost always inextricably intertwined. Through his characters, Kubrick suggests that dark impulses are a fundamental part of human nature. Human destructiveness and power-lust don't go away with proper conditioning, except when that conditioning is so extreme that it makes us inhuman. Instead, we must decide how to channel those impulses, when to give them free rein, and when to suppress them by force. *A Clockwork Orange* illustrates the extremes of both freedom and suppression.

THE INTERDEPENDENCE OF LIFE AND ART

In *A Clockwork Orange,* characters view and use art in many different ways, creating a complex and conflicted picture of how art and real life interact. Alex uses music, film, and art to express and understand his life. During the two weeks that doctors show Alex reel upon reel of sex and violence, he is amazed that the real world looks even more real on a television screen. He and other characters also use art to detach from life and to cut themselves off from other people. When Alex beats Mr. Alexander and prepares to rape his wife, he sings "Singin' in the Rain" and dances like Gene Kelly did in the musical. By making the violent act into a song and dance, Alex distances himself from the brutality and from his victims' suffering. The cat lady, whom Alex kills, expresses her sexuality through her statues and the paintings on her walls, but when Alex touches her statue of a penis, she screams at him not to touch it because it's a work of art. Through art, she makes sexuality an object not to be touched, rather than an act that is all about touching.

The characters' varied responses to and uses of art in *A Clockwork Orange* suggest that art has within it the potential for both good and evil. Art both expresses and channels human impulses, and it can therefore enhance or deaden life. It can bring people closer to reality or it can distance them from it. Kubrick makes sex and violence look unreal in the film. He directs fight scenes to look like dance, slows down the camera, and distorts images. He plays with our perceptions so that we never forget we are watching a work of art. Some critics have said that the stylized and detached way Kubrick presents violence makes accepting it easier, and that the film even celebrates violence. However, the detachment we experience as a result of the film's artistic elements can also make us reflect more deeply on our own ability to distance ourselves from violence.

MOTIFS

SEXUAL AGGRESSION

Sex in *A Clockwork Orange* is not an expression of love or intimacy, but rather an exhibition of power and violence. The vast majority of sex scenes in the film are violent, including the attempted gang rape of the "weepy devotchka," Alex's rape of Mrs. Alexander, and the on-screen rape scene the doctors show Alex. Other less explicit scenes of sexual repression and aggression appear as well. For example, Deltoid, Alex's probation officer, grabs Alex's testicles. In *A Clockwork Orange,* most human relationships, including sexual ones, revolve around the question of control: who will control and who will be controlled. The minister of the interior sees Alex as a guinea pig for his experiment in law and order. Mr. Alexander sees Alex as an instrument he can use to bring down the minister of the interior and his party. Alex himself wields power not only over the victims of his crimes but also over his other gang members. Even the economy turns people into objects to be controlled or used. Alex's mother goes to work in a factory, presumably functioning as just one piece of the machine. In this depersonalized world of users and used, sex ceases to be an act of intimacy and instead becomes an act of brutality and an assertion of power.

MUSIC

A Clockwork Orange challenges traditional ideas about music's fundamental function, and here music taps into what is most dominant in Alex's nature: violence. Throughout the film, classical music moves Alex to a version of ecstasy, and he imagines hangings, bombings, and other acts of violence. However, music remains valuable as a signal of his freedom of choice. Alex lives violently, brutally, and without compassion, but what initially sets him apart from adults is that he has so much more vitality. While his weary mother trudges off to her factory job, Alex sleeps all day, then wakes up to have sex, take drugs, and perpetrate more violence—only because he wants to and because it is exciting. He also listens to music, which for him is an ecstatic and liberating experience that expresses both the brute and the rebel in him. When the doctors condition Alex's body to become ill from his own violent impulses, they simultaneously condition his body to reject music. Though this is an unintentional result of the conditioning, it is symbolically significant. Music connects to Alex's drives and desires, and stripping him of his ability to enjoy it is equivalent to stripping him of his humanity.

The role music plays in both the novel and the film of *A Clockwork Orange* is Burgess and Kubrick's nod toward history. All governments, particularly totalitarian regimes, have used music to heighten their citizens' patriotic fervor. For example, Adolf Hitler was moved by music and used it as a tool of state control. In Alex's case, the elimination of music from his life is how this control manifests itself, and the consequences are just as dire.

Slang

Alex uses a slang spoken only by young people. Adults don't understand the language, which highlights the emotional and ideological distance between the generations. Burgess invented the language for the novel and called it Nadsat, which is the Russian suffix for *teen*. Nadsat is a language that, like Alex himself and like youth more generally, overflows with energy. Sex, for instance, is called "the old in-out in-out." In contrast, the language the adults speak is far drier and more predictable. Alex's parents speak in clichés. The prison guards speak the language of law and order. The doctors speak in medical lingo. Only the youths' language transcends these linguistic categories and barriers.

In Nadsat, high and low forms of language coexist. Street words, baby talk, and rhyming slang accompany grammar and syntax that sometimes follow formal Shakespearean English. The most dominant linguistic influences on Nadsat besides English are Russian and Slavic. Before Burgess wrote his novel, he spent time in Soviet Russia, where he witnessed youth gangs running wild, just like the ones he'd seen in England. He decided to create a language that incorporated both English and Russian, the two most powerful political languages in the world at that time. The fact that Alex, a completely apolitical youth, speaks it also makes it a language of rebellion. The youths who use the language don't care about the politics that divided the world at the time that Burgess wrote his novel.

SYMBOLS

THE KOROVA MILK BAR

The Korova Milk Bar, where Alex and his gang gather, offers a dual image of innocence and transgression. A mother's milk symbolizes comfort and nurturing. Like mother's milk, the milk in the Korova Milk Bar flows from women—that is, female mannequins, whose bodies are as white as the milk itself. Far from being symbols of innocent motherhood, the mannequins are positioned in provocative sexual poses. They are also plastic, cold, and unresponsive, and drugs taint the milk that flows from them. Some of these drugs bring divine visions, but the drugs that Alex and his friends take heighten their inclination for "ultraviolence." The Korova Milk Bar reflects Alex's own nature, which is childlike and shockingly brutal at the same time. A sexual act lies behind motherhood itself, and the Korova Milk Bar suggests that at humanity's core lie impulses both of nurturance and aggression, innocence and transgression.

SEX AND THE BODY IN ART

In *A Clockwork Orange*, artwork expresses sexual desire, but it also strips desire of human intimacy and individuality. Instead of sex and love cohabiting in representations of the human body, the body in art becomes simply a source of titillation. The film presents a series of such images. Women, in particular, are represented as being less than human, as mannequins, cartoons, and paintings. The first images are those of the female mannequins in the Korova Milk Bar, set in their sexually provocative poses. Because they lack color and individual features, they suggest cold impersonality. Sexual images of women also hang on the walls of Alex's parents' home. For the most part, these paintings are drab, like Alex's parents, and resemble paintings one might purchase at a flea market. Their one striking feature is the women's impressive cleavage. Like the mannequins, these images, too, are at once both sexual and impersonal. The paintings and sculpture in the cat lady's home are modern and overtly sexual. Some are sadistic, with parts of the paintings depicting bondage and dismembered body parts. Like the cat lady herself, the paintings are bold and confrontational, but, like all the other artistic representations of the human body, they are also flat and impersonal.

LUDWIG VAN BEETHOVEN'S NINTH SYMPHONY

Alex loves Ludwig van Beethoven's Ninth Symphony more than any other piece of music, which is ironic because Beethoven meant to express the heights of human goodness rather than depravity. Through the four movements of the symphony, Beethoven traces humanity's ascent. The symphony starts by depicting the plight of offenders in the lowest rungs of hell. In the second movement, humans find happiness in everyday pleasures. In the third movement, they turn to religion. In the fourth movement, the finale, Beethoven aimed to express a vision of humanity that had traveled spiritually from the depths of despair to the heights of fulfillment and glory. What Beethoven hoped the symphony would communicate, however, is quite different from what Alex hears.

In *A Clockwork Orange,* Beethoven's Ninth Symphony punctuates the heights and depths of emotion Alex experiences, just as Beethoven hoped the symphony would express the heights and depths of human experience. The symphony literally drives Alex to his lowest point, when he jumps from Mr. Alexander's window trying to escape the sickness Ludovico's Technique has made him feel whenever he hears it. In turn, he knows he is cured of the effects of Ludovico's Technique when the minister of the interior plays the symphony for him and he no longer feels sick. Unlike Beethoven's vision, for Alex, the glory of the final movement represents simply his own personal glory.

FILM ANALYSIS

THE FILM AND THE FINAL CHAPTER OF "A CLOCKWORK ORANGE"

In 1962, two versions of Anthony Burgess's novel *A Clockwork Orange* were published. One concludes with Alex growing up and turning away from violence, while the second, darker version leaves out that final chapter. Kubrick based his film on this second version. The first version, published first in England, has twenty-one chapters, as Burgess intended it to. Burgess believed that all individuals, even those as violent as Alex, could reform, and in this version, moral growth comes with age. However, Burgess's U.S. editor felt that the twenty-first chapter was "bland" and showed an unwillingness "to accept that a human being could be a model of unregenerable evil." Later, Burgess said he originally agreed to publish the U.S. version without its final chapter only because he needed the money. Kubrick read the U.S. version of the novel and made his film without knowing about the twenty-first chapter. When he eventually read it, he still claimed to prefer the darker version of the story.

Aside from leaving out the twenty-first chapter, Kubrick stayed fairly close to the plot and language of Burgess's novel. However, because film, unlike literature, impacts so many human senses and is so immediately tactile, Kubrick's version heightened the controversy surrounding the novel's violence. Kubrick introduced a number of details not found in the novel that further increased the story's shock value. For example, the most famous moment of the film, when Alex sings "Singin' in the Rain" while preparing to rape a woman, was Kubrick's invention—it's not in the novel. Several other plot differences between the film and the novel make Kubrick's version darker. In the novel, the prison chaplain leaves his post to protest the government, but Kubrick does not include this ethical move in the film. Also, Kubrick makes Alex want to take part in Ludovico's Technique so he can get out of prison quickly, while in the novel, Alex is forced to participate. Kubrick's Alex is an accomplice to the state, while Burgess's Alex, for all his violence, is clearly more of a victim.

Burgess praised the power of Kubrick's film but in later years also complained about Kubrick's omission of his intended ending. Burgess explained that he objected to his work being used to send a message that some humans are simply evil by nature. In an introduction to a revised U.S. version in which Burgess's editor and publisher agreed to reprint the novel with the twenty-first chapter, Burgess wrote: "Much of my later life has been expended on Xeroxing statements of intention and frustration of intention—while both Kubrick and my New York publisher coolly bask in the rewards of their misdemeanor. Life is, of course, terrible." Kubrick, however, continued to believe that the story was better without the final chapter, and the film and novel, though very similar in many ways, ultimately differ greatly in their final verdict on humanity.

DIRECTING

Kubrick was a perfectionist, and his dedication to achieving just the right image, keeping to a low budget, and portraying violence artistically made *A Clockwork Orange* a classic. Kubrick was known to reshoot scenes scores of times, which was often difficult for those who worked with him. However, many of the actors he directed have praised his ability to bring out of them a unique expressiveness. Kubrick began his career as a photographer, and he made himself famous both for his distinctive aesthetic vision and for his technical skill in realizing that vision. His ability did not come only from technical mastery but also from technical creativity. For example, when Kubrick wanted to capture the physical feeling of Alex's fall from the window during his suicide attempt, he wrapped a camera in Styrofoam boxes and threw it out the window. He threw it out the window six times, until he achieved the effect he wanted.

Kubrick made *A Clockwork Orange* on a budget of just $2 million, which is very small for a major feature film. He shot much of the film on location to avoid building sets, and he avoided using expensive lighting by shooting many of the scenes with natural light. Similarly, Kubrick determined that handheld cameras should be used for much of the film. This choice was not just a budgetary decision but also an aesthetic one. Kubrick shot the famous "Singin' in the Rain" rape scene, for instance, with a handheld camera. The handheld camera provides an intimacy that intensifies the savagery of the scene. Also, the visual disorientation we experience as the camera switches perspective increases our own sense of disorientation. Sometimes we see the action from the victim's vantage point, while at other points we see it through Alex's eyes.

Violence is at the center of *A Clockwork Orange,* and it is easy to see Kubrick's signature on these scenes. He distorted and stylized the violent actions, creating an artistic detachment from the violence that seems to match Alex's own detachment. For example, early in the film, Alex's gang fights a rival gang. They meet in an abandoned theater, once a model of classical splendor, now utterly run down. Appropriate to the setting, Kubrick set the fight to soaring classical music. The characters engage in bloody battle, but as the camera pans in and out, offering close-ups and panoramic views of the action, Kubrick has his actors move in ways that make the action look more like acrobatics or ballet than a gang fight.

In scene after scene, Kubrick directs images of violence in a similarly artistic way. Alex prepares to rape Mrs. Alexander while singing "Singin' in the Rain" and doing a soft-shoe. When Alex beats up his two Droogs, Dim and Georgie, Kubrick once again sets the fight to classical music, and this time he slows down the motion. The actors' physical gestures become so exaggerated in this slow-motion scene that the fight again looks like a dance. The exceptions to these artistically rendered scenes are the scenes in which policemen beat Alex. There, Kubrick uses no music, and the blood flows, suggesting that the police are simply brutal thugs, not artists working in the medium of violence. Kubrick uses his directorial vision to offer us an experience of violence as Alex would have experienced it.

Score and Soundtrack

Wendy Carlos was already famous for her album *Switched-On Bach,* an electronic adaptation of some of the famous classical composer's works, before she began her collaboration with Kubrick. The sound she produced playing Bach on her synthesizer was both classical and futuristic, perfect for *A Clockwork Orange.* Carlos had already begun composing a score to the novel when a friend sent her a clipping from a London newspaper saying that Kubrick had begun adapting it for film. Carlos continued to work on her musical composition, and when she saw an article in *The New York Times* announcing that Kubrick had finished shooting the film, she contacted him to suggest that he use her music. Kubrick invited her to London, and the two eventually collaborated on what became the score for the film.

Carlos made electronic recordings of a number of famous classical composers for *A Clockwork Orange,* including Beethoven, Rossini, and Purcell, and Kubrick also included some of Carlos's original compositions in the score. Her adaptation of the choral movement from Beethoven's Ninth Symphony was the first electronic "vocal" piece ever produced. In the film, works by these composers accompany Alex's violent rampages as well as his violent fantasies, lending them an ecstatic and surreal quality that might well match the way Alex feels during them. The film opens with Carlos's own composition, *Timesteps,* a slow, booming, otherworldly piece that sets an ominous tone for the entire film.

Important to note is the fact that the music of *A Clockwork Orange* is credited to "Walter Carlos," even though the composer later became "Wendy Carlos."

IMPORTANT QUOTATIONS EXPLAINED

1.   DELTOID: "We study the problem. We've been studying it for damn well near a century, yes, but we get no further with our studies. You've got a good home here, good loving parents. You've got not too bad of a brain! Is it some devil that crawls inside of you?"

Deltoid, Alex's probation officer, speaks these lines to Alex in an early scene in the film when he visits Alex at home. Deltoid is referring to the problem of youth violence and rebellion. When he says, "We've been studying," he means that science and the social sciences have long tried to understand and control humanity's destructive impulses through rationality. Adults have tried to understand and control youthful rebellion and impulsiveness. Social reformers often suggest that an unstable home produces violence, but Deltoid can't find the culprit here. Ultimately, the film suggests that these violent impulses are irrational and innate and cannot be eradicated by science and rationality. The dark and destructive, the disorderly and the rebellious, are part of who we are. The state cannot get rid of that part of us except by making us inhuman. Alex may be simply an animal, a creature of instinct—but he may also be human, capable of moral choice. The film leaves ambiguous the question of whether or not we as individuals have control over ourselves.

2.   PRISON CHAPLAIN: "Choice. The boy has no real choice, has he? Self-interest, the fear of physical pain drove him to that grotesque act of self-abasement. Its insincerity was clearly to be seen. He ceases to be a wrongdoer. He ceases also to be a creature capable of moral choice."

The prison chaplain speaks these lines after he watches state officials test Alex in order to prove that he has truly been cured of his violent impulses. Alex stands on a stage in front of a room filled with doctors and political figures. To test Alex, a man comes out from behind the curtains and insults him, slaps him, and makes him lick the bottom of his shoe. Alex complies because after the conditioning he has undergone, fighting back would make him too horribly ill. This is the "grotesque act of self-abasement" that the prison chaplain refers to. Then a near-naked woman comes out and tries to seduce Alex, but he turns away in illness at the thought of sex.

While these displays impress most of the audience members, the prison chaplain voices dissent using traditional religious rhetoric. He holds up religious values of good and evil and the importance of moral choice in opposition to the value of ultimate state control. His statement echoes the traditional belief that what makes people different from animals is their ability to make moral choices. Evolutionary science maintains that self-interest and the fear of physical pain drive animals to act, and that this instinct allows them to survive. Religion, however, maintains that people exist on a higher plane than animals and are not driven by their instincts alone, but rather have a divine element in their natures that enables them make moral choices.

3.   MINISTER OF THE INTERIOR: "Padre, these are subtleties. We're not concerned with motives, with the higher ethics. We are concerned only with cutting down crime and with relieving the ghastly congestion in our prisons. He will be your true Christian, ready to turn the other cheek, ready to be crucified rather than crucify, sick to the very heart at the thought even of killing a fly! Reclamation! Joy before the angels of God! The point is that it works."

The minister of the interior speaks these lines in response to the prison chaplain in the scene in which Alex is tested. He voices the ideological position that what matters most in society is law and order and doing what works. He expresses his disrespect for organized religion when he refers to the chaplain as "Padre" instead of "Father." Then he twists the language of religion to express his belief that Alex has been transformed. He says Alex will be ready to "turn the other cheek," as Jesus instructed his disciples to do if they were attacked. He even implies that the government has made Alex a modern-day Jesus, "ready to be crucified rather than crucify." Of course, Alex has been transformed only physically, not morally, but this distinction is not important for the minister of the interior. What concerns the minister of the interior most is the proper functioning of society, and he cares more about Alex's behavior than his motivation. The minister of the interior's words are ironic, since a "true Christian," as he says Alex will be, embraces both responsible external behavior as well as moral motives for that behavior. These words also foreshadow the second half of the film, in which Alex does become the victim of society's violence when his conditioning forces him to turn the other cheek.

4.   MR. ALEXANDER: "The common people will let it go. Oh yes, they'll sell liberty for a quieter life. That is why they must be led, sir, driven, pushed!"

Mr. Alexander speaks these lines on the phone to one of his political accomplices in a scene late in the film. During the conversation, he plots a way to use Alex to topple the government. Mr. Alexander's words suggest that not only is the government willing to sacrifice individual liberty for law and order but that average people, in order to have "a quieter life," will make the sacrifice as well. After all, the government in *A Clockwork Orange* is a democratically elected government, and the people have chosen their own leaders. Throughout the film, Kubrick knocks down precious social beliefs, such as the belief that music can make men moral and that violence grows out of a troubled home. Here, too, the film challenges another idealistic hope of democratic societies: that morality can be found in the common people. Mr. Alexander's words suggest this is not the case. At the same time, the lines show Mr. Alexander's own hypocrisy. He claims to value individual liberty, but he looks on the collective body of individuals as just sheep to be "led, driven, pushed." The verbs he uses to describe the way common people should be treated are indeed verbs someone might use to describe herding sheep.

5.   ALEX: "It's funny how the colors of the real world only seem really real when you viddy them on the screen."

Alex speaks this line while watching a scene in a bloody film the doctors show him as part of Ludovico's Technique. *Viddy* is a slang word that comes from the Russian word meaning "to see." In this quotation, Alex says that art seems more real than life. Throughout the film, Alex seems not to experience the reality of his own violence. His responses to it are at once sinister and childlike, and he sees violence as just a game. When he watches a film, however, images and colors of the real world actually reach him. The color he refers to here is red, the color of blood, which he sees flowing onscreen. "It's funny," he says, and, indeed, irony lies in the fact that life must be turned into art before Alex can truly experience it. This statement expresses Kubrick's own complex attitude toward the arts. In *A Clockwork Orange,* the arts are a way for characters to more clearly understand their world, but they are also a way for them to distance and detach from life.

THE GODFATHER TRILOGY

(1972, 1974, 1990)

CONTEXT

Moviegoers had little reason to expect much from *The Godfather* when it was released in 1972. The film was based on a popular though not best-selling novel, made by a relatively inexperienced director, and performed by mostly unknown actors, plus one, Marlon Brando, who was considered well past his prime—all in all, not exactly the classic Hollywood formula for success. Defying the odds, *The Godfather* went on to become one of the most popular movies of all time. It gave birth to two sequels, the first of which is a masterpiece in its own right, spawned countless clones, launched the film careers of several significant actors, and changed forever what an audience would expect when it entered a theater.

Francis Ford Coppola, the director of *The Godfather* trilogy, was one of many young directors who came to prominence in the 1970s and challenged the old Hollywood system. His contemporaries included Martin Scorsese, Roman Polanski, George Lucas, and Stephen Spielberg, among others. This attack on old Hollywood is announced right at the beginning of *The Godfather* when the lawyer Tom Hagen asks studio owner Jack Woltz to cast the singer Johnny Fontane in a movie. Woltz seems classic L.A.-slick, and we are not surprised when he says no. But we are surprised when we learn why. We expect that Woltz's excuse will be that Johnny is old and washed-up or that he lacks acting talent, but instead, Woltz says that Johnny is perfect for the part, which is precisely the reason he doesn't get it. Woltz blames Johnny for stealing a pretty young actress from him and refuses to do anything that will help him rehabilitate his career. In his exchange with Tom, Woltz comes across as materialistic, crass, bad-tempered, vengeful, and bigoted, but Coppola hints that his greatest crime is that he isn't a real artist. He is in film production only for the sex and the money. Whether he makes a good film is barely a concern.

Coppola's criticism of the Hollywood system goes well beyond this ugly depiction of a Hollywood producer. *The Godfather* trilogy criticizes the content and structure of typical Hollywood films. By the 1970s, moviegoers were more film literate than those of earlier generations and demanded more for the price of their tickets. One way to appeal to an audience of both sophisticated and unsophisticated viewers is through what critic Robert Ray calls a "corrected" genre film. A corrected genre film has its share of action sequences that appeal to naïve viewers, but it also includes new stylistic devices and an irony-laced plot that appeal to a more critical audience. In Ray's analysis of Hollywood films, *The Godfather* is the paradigmatic corrected genre film. To the naive audience, Michael Corleone seems like a heroic outsider battling against the corrupt system—in effect the hero of a Western set in New York City. A more sophisticated audience sees Michael as duplicitous, immoral, and cruel, and will be repulsed by him. But many people would argue that *The Godfather* isn't corrected enough. Subsequent gangster films, such as *Scarface*, *Goodfellas*, and *Donnie Brasco*, as well as the popular TV series *The Sopranos*, all try to further "correct" *The Godfather* by presenting a grittier, less glamorous view of Mafia life. But this process of criticizing the myth of the Mafia really began in Coppola's films. Indeed, the most successful correction of *The Godfather* is probably *The Godfather Part II*. (The analysis section will explore this argument in greater depth.)

In addition to spawning numerous "corrected" gangster films, *The Godfather*'s legacy also includes its amazing cast, with actors such as Al Pacino, Robert De Niro, Diane Keaton, James Caan, and Robert Duvall, who have taken their places among the most successful performers of the past thirty years. No less significant is *The Godfather*'s rehabilitation of the late, incomparable Marlon Brando. Francis Ford Coppola, the director and brains of the entire operation, would himself become a Hollywood fixture, going on to direct classics such as *The Conversation* and *Apocalypse Now*. Certain filmic elements, such as the use of montage in *The Godfather* or of underexposure in the cinematography of *The Godfather Part II*, have proven highly influential in the decades since. Lastly, it should be pointed out that *The Godfather* films took part in the larger social discourse of their times. In 1972 and 1974, when *The Godfather* and *The Godfather Part II* were released, respectively, America was experiencing much turmoil and change. Coming on the heels of the turbulent 1960s, while the Vietnam War and the culture wars raged, the *Godfather* films took part in the New Left critique, exposing the hypocrisy of institutions of power. *The Godfather* highlights police corruption and the questionable morality of politicians who send their citizens abroad to fight wars. Political corruption is a major theme of *The Godfather Part II*. *The Godfather Part III* brings to light the tensions between the worldly and spiritual concerns of the Catholic Church.

The true genius of *The Godfather* films is that they are historically and socially specific genre films and, at the same time, monumental epics exploring universal themes. Their depiction of the experiences of Sicilian-Americans in the twentieth century speaks to the experience of all American immigrant communities. As exciting and suspenseful as any Hollywood action flick, they are also dramas with as much pathos and emotional weight as any film can have. Today *The Godfather* films are classic reference points in American culture, but they startled audiences when they were released because they combined styles and genres in a completely new way. That the films look so familiar to us now is the ultimate proof of their tremendous influence.

Plot Overview

"The Godfather"

During a backyard wedding reception for his daughter, Connie, and his new son-in-law, Carlo Rizzi, Don Vito Corleone, a Mafia boss known as the Godfather, conducts business in his office. With him are his oldest son, Sonny, and his adopted son and family lawyer, Tom Hagen. Several people come to Vito's office to make requests, including Bonasera, an undertaker seeking revenge for a crime against his daughter, and Johnny Fontane, a Frank Sinatra-like singer and actor who wants Vito to help land him a part in a movie. As the wedding reception draws to a close, Vito dispatches Tom to Los Angeles to talk to Jack Woltz, the studio owner. Despite Tom's prodding, Woltz refuses to give Fontane the part, so the Corleones make Woltz "an offer he can't refuse." The day after the meeting with Tom, Woltz wakes up in a blood-stained bed to discover the severed head of his prized horse under the covers at his feet.

Back in New York, a gangster named Sollozzo wants to involve the Corleone family in his narcotics smuggling operation. Two other crime families, the Barzinis and Tattaglias, are already in on the scheme, but Sollozzo wants Vito's protection and financing too. Vito arranges a meeting with Sollozzo. Sonny and Tom support the idea of expanding the family business, but Vito cannot overcome his initial skepticism about the scheme and his distaste for drug trafficking. Vito rejects the offer and orders his bodyguard, Luca Brasi, to investigate Sollozzo. Luca is murdered, and shortly afterward a hit man attempts to assassinate Vito while he shops at a fruit market. Vito survives the shooting but is badly hurt, and Sonny temporarily takes control of the family business.

Vito's youngest son, Michael, a World War II hero, is in town for his sister's wedding, accompanied by his WASP girlfriend from New England, Kay Adams. Unlike Sonny and Tom, Michael is a "civilian" who has vowed never to get involved in the family business. While visiting his father in the hospital, however, Michael discovers that the guards who were supposed to be protecting Vito have disappeared, leaving Vito vulnerable to another assassination attempt. Michael hides his father and pretends to be a gangster holding a gun to scare off the assassins. He grills a crooked cop named Captain McCluskey about the whereabouts of the men who should be guarding Vito, and McCluskey punches him. Michael is knocked unconscious. Days later, after receiving advice and a gun from members of the family, Michael arranges to meet at a quiet Italian restaurant with Sollozzo and McCluskey to negotiate a peace. At the meeting, Michael kills both men. He then flees to Sicily, where Vito was born.

Newspaper headlines announce the slew of Mafia killings that follow. Vito Corleone returns home from the hospital and is disappointed to learn that Michael has participated in a Mafia killing. While Vito recovers from his gunshot wounds, hot-headed Sonny and cautious Tom debate whether to escalate the war with the Tattaglias, Sollozzo's sponsors.

When Sonny sees Connie with a black eye, he learns that Carlo has been beating her, and he attacks Carlo brutally, hitting him with a trash can. After she suffers another beating, Connie calls Sonny, crying. He loses his temper and in a fit of rage drives off to beat, if not kill, Carlo. Unaccompanied by bodyguards, Sonny is an easy target for the Corleones' enemies. When he stops his car at a tollbooth, the car in front of him stops and gunmen hiding in the tollbooth open fire. Sonny staggers out of the car, riddled with bullets, and falls dead.

Meanwhile, in picturesque Sicily, Michael falls in love at first sight with Apollonia, a young Sicilian beauty. He courts her, and they marry, but the marriage is cut short when Apollonia is killed by a car bomb intended for Michael.

Back in New York, Vito assembles a meeting of the five main Mafia families. He announces that he will forgo vengeance for Sonny's murder on the condition that Michael is allowed to return to New York unharmed.

A year after his return, Michael visits his old flame, Kay Adams, whom he hasn't seen in over two years. He tells her he works for his father now, but in the course of their discussion, he promises that the Corleone family will soon become legitimate. He proposes, and Kay agrees to marry him.

Since Sonny is dead, Michael becomes head of the family. He begins planning to move the Corleone family to Las Vegas to enter the casino business. He demotes his adopted brother Tom from the position of *consigliere*, the primary advisor to the don. Vito serves as Michael's advisor, but old age starts to take its toll on him and he eventually drops dead while playing with Michael's young son, Anthony, among the tomato plants in his backyard.

Connie and Carlo have asked Michael to be the godfather to their son. As the baptism is performed, the heads of the other New York Mafia families are killed by Corleone hit men on Michael's orders. When Michael exits the church, he gets word that the killings have been successful. He has become the undisputed Mafia boss of the city.

The Corleones are set to move to Las Vegas, but Michael stays behind to finish up some business. This business consists of taking revenge on two traitors to the family. First, he arranges for the killing of Tessio, his father's old associate who has been dealing in secret with the Barzini family. Second, Michael kills his brother-in-law, Carlo, who tipped off the other families, allowing them to kill Sonny.

A few days later, a hysterical Connie accuses Michael of killing her husband, a charge he denies to Kay with a forceful, if not entirely convincing, "No." Then he retreats to his office, closing his door on his wife, to conduct further business.

"THE GODFATHER PART II"

Note: Two plotlines run through this movie. One continues Michael's story in the late 1950s. The other examines Vito's early years in Sicily and New York. This overview relates the scenes in the order in which they occur in the movie.

The opening shot is of Michael Corleone, now Godfather, having his ring finger kissed.

In the next scene, nine-year-old Vito Andolini walks with his mother through the Sicilian countryside, near the town of Corleone. They are at the head of a funeral procession for Vito's father, who was killed by a local Mafia boss, Don Ciccio. The year is 1901. During the procession, Don Ciccio's men open fire in the surrounding hills and kill Vito's older brother, Paolo. A few days later, Vito's mother takes Vito with her to see Don Ciccio and begs the don to spare Vito's life. When Don Ciccio refuses, Vito's mother puts a knife to his throat and tells Vito to run. When Vito looks back, he sees his mother being shot squarely through the chest by Ciccio's bodyguards. Then he keeps running. Don Ciccio hunts for young Vito, but friends help smuggle him onto a boat bound for America.

Vito arrives at Ellis Island, where he is given the last name Corleone and quarantined for three months until he recovers from smallpox.

The scene shifts to Lake Tahoe, in the 1950s. As Michael hosts a party at his compound to celebrate the communion of his son, Anthony, he conducts business in his office with Nevada Senator Pat Geary. Michael plans to expand his casino empire and rejects the senator's attempts at extortion and his ethnic slurs against Italians. The senator leaves with a smirk. Next, a man named Johnny Ola tells Michael that Hyman Roth, Michael's Miami-based business associate, sends word that he supports the casino move and foresees further opportunities for partnership. Finally, Frankie Pentangeli, an old mafioso from New York, visits Michael. Pentangeli opposes Michael's alliance with Roth. When Michael ignores his protests, Pentangeli leaves the office in a fit of rage.

Michael's sister, Connie, and brother, Fredo, both worry him. Connie visits the office during the party, along with her boyfriend Merle. Connie is overdressed and overly bejeweled and wants money from Michael so that she and Merle can book passage to Europe on the Queen. She also wants Michael's blessing for her engagement to Merle, which Michael refuses to grant. At dinner, Fredo's trampy blonde wife drinks excessively and makes racist comments about his Italian family.

Later in the party, Michael dances with his wife Kay. Kay is pregnant for the third time and is upset that Michael still hasn't made the family legitimate, despite his promises that he would. That evening, Michael enters his bedroom, where Kay is already asleep, and bullets shatter the window. Michael grabs Kay and hurls both of them to the floor, and they both survive the attempted hit. Michael puts his adopted brother Tom Hagen in charge of the family, claiming that Tom is the only one he can truly trust, and decides to investigate what happened.

Back in 1917 New York, young Vito works as a grocery clerk. He sees Don Fanucci, a local Mafia don, prance around town, extorting money from local businesses. One night, as Vito eats dinner with his wife, a neighbor hisses through his window that he needs Vito to hide a parcel. Vito accepts the parcel, opens it, and finds several guns. The neighbor, named Clemenza, introduces himself later in the street. Vito loses his job at the grocery store when the owner is forced to hire Don Fanucci's nephew.

Back in the 1950s, Michael visits Roth in Miami. He tells Roth he knows Pentangeli ordered the hit on him and assures Roth that their partnership will go forward. Michael says he'll visit Pentangeli, and Roth gives his support when Michael says Pentangeli is a "dead man." When Michael visits Pentangeli in New York Michael says he knows Roth was the one who ordered the hit. He asks Pentangeli to help him take revenge. In the middle of the night, Fredo receives a phone call that suggests he was somehow involved in the hit. When Pentangeli meets with the Rosato brothers, he is strangled, but he survives in the custody of the police.

Michael, Roth, and other important American businessmen convene in Havana for a meeting with the president of Cuba. Roth wants to make major investments there, but Michael is concerned about rebel activity. Fredo shows up in Cuba, and Michael tells his brother that he knows Roth was behind the attempt on his life. Fredo denies knowing Roth or Ola, but later that evening, he lets it slip that he knows them both. While Michael celebrates the New Year at the Cuban presidential palace, his orders are executed. A hit man strangles Ola on his hotel balcony. The hit man tries to kill Roth at the hospital by smothering him with a pillow, but he is shot dead before he can finish the job. At the party, Michael kisses Fredo on the lips and then tells Fredo he knows that he was involved in the hit. Later that evening Michael flees a chaotic Havana while the rebels, led by Fidel Castro, take over the city and the Cuban president resigns. When Michael reaches Nevada, Tom tells him that Roth managed to survive and that Kay experienced a miscarriage.

Cut back to New York in the early twentieth century. Young Vito, Clemenza, and Tessio, close friends now, have formed a gang. They steal furniture, clothing, and rugs from homes and then sell them. Don Fanucci tells the young men that he knows what they're doing and demands a cut. Tessio and Clemenza are willing to pay, but Vito tells them to put their faith in him. He says he will take care of the problem with Fanucci but that they must remember the favor he's done them. Vito meets with Fanucci and gives him only a fraction of the requested money. When the meeting is over, Vito follows Fanucci as he strolls through a street festival and then kills Fanucci in the entrance to his apartment. The killing done, Vito returns home and kisses his newborn son, Michael.

In the 1950s, Congress holds hearings in Washington, D.C., investigating the Mafia. A Pentangeli associate testifies against Michael. His testimony isn't good enough to convict Michael of any crimes, because the associate claims never to have taken any orders directly from Michael. Meanwhile, Michael visits his mother and asks her if Vito ever worried about losing his family. His mother says you can never lose your family.

Back in early 1900s New York, young Vito is now a Mafia don. With his new standing in the community, he dresses in fine suits and requests favors on behalf of friends. One woman, a friend of Vito's wife, asks him for help. Her landlord has evicted her without sufficient cause. Vito talks to the landlord and requests that he let the woman keep her apartment, as a favor. The landlord doesn't take Vito seriously. Once he finds out who Vito is, though, he not only gives the woman back her apartment, he lowers the rent.

Testifying before Congress in the 1950s, Michael denies ever participating in any illicit activities. Congress tells him they have a witness who will testify against him, which means Michael could be found guilty of perjury. Back in Nevada, Tom tells Michael that Pentangeli is still alive and will be the one to testify against him. Fredo also admits to tipping off Roth but claims that he never expected Roth to try to kill Michael. Michael responds harshly, telling Fredo that he is no longer a brother to him and that he never wants to see him again. Back in Washington, Michael shows up at the congressional hearings with an unknown older man, and Pentangeli, who spots the man before the questioning, doesn't reveal anything. The old man is Pentangeli's brother, who has come from Sicily to influence him. In the hotel room after the hearing ends, Kay asks Michael why Pentangeli was so afraid of his brother, and Michael says only that it is a conflict between the brothers and has nothing to do with him. Kay tells Michael that she and the children are leaving him. Michael refuses to accept this, and during the ensuing argument, Kay tells him that she didn't have a miscarriage, but an abortion. Michael punches Kay in the face.

Back in the early twentieth century, Vito returns to Sicily with his family, visits old friends, and kills Don Ciccio.

Back to the 1950s. At Mama Corleone's funeral, Connie tries to make up with Michael and says that she forgives him for Carlo's death. She wants to stay closer to the family now. She tries to orchestrate a reconciliation between Michael and Fredo, and Michael reluctantly allows his older brother to hug him. During the hug, Michael shoots an ominous glance to one of his men.

Michael has learned from news reports and his own sources that Roth will return to Miami because no other country will let him stay. Tom tries to dissuade Michael from killing Roth, saying that Roth is a sick man and will die shortly anyway. Michael ignores

Tom and has Roth shot at the Miami airport upon his arrival. Meanwhile, Pentangeli, imprisoned for contempt of Congress, kills himself, after a visit from Tom helps convince him it is the honorable thing to do. Days later, Michael returns home to find Kay, who has been banished from the house, secretly visiting her children. As she leaves the house, he closes the door in her face. Finally, Fredo, fishing on Lake Tahoe with one of Michael's henchmen, is killed as he recites a Hail Mary, praying to catch a fish.

In the movie's final sequence, Michael is left alone in his boathouse to think about all that has happened. He remembers a scene in 1941. He and his siblings sit around the dining room table, waiting for Vito to come home so they can surprise him for his birthday. That morning the Japanese had attacked Pearl Harbor, and Michael announces that he has enlisted in the army, a decision that angers Tom and Sonny, who say that Vito had other plans for him. When Vito enters the house, everyone rushes to greet him and sing "Happy Birthday," except for Michael, who stays at the table alone.

The Godfather Part II ends with Michael sitting alone on a bench.

"THE GODFATHER PART III"

It is 1979. The Corleone compound at Lake Tahoe is abandoned. Michael has returned to New York, where he is pursuing his quest to make the Corleone family legitimate. He creates a charity, the Vito Corleone Foundation. At a ceremony at St. Patrick's Cathedral, Michael is awarded a medal of the Order of St. Sebastian. Kay, who has remarried, sits with her and Michael's children, Anthony and Mary. At the lavish party following the ceremony, Anthony tells his father that he is dropping out of law school to pursue a career as an opera singer. Kay supports his choice, and she and Michael argue in private about Anthony's future.

Vincent Mancini, Sonny Corleone's illegitimate son, shows up at the party. He is embroiled in a feud with a mafioso named Joey Zasa, under whose stewardship the old Corleone neighborhood in New York has become lawless. In a room away from the party, Vincent and Zasa tell Michael about their feud. The discussion grows violent, and Vincent bites off part of Zasa's ear. Vincent asks Michael if he can work for him, and Michael agrees to take his hotheaded, smooth-talking nephew under his wing. That night, two men, sent by Zasa, break into Vincent's home. Vincent kills them both.

Michael wants to buy Immobiliare, an international real estate holding company that is controlled by the Vatican. He negotiates a transfer fee of $600,000,000 with Archbishop Gliday, who has plunged the Holy See into tremendous debt through his poor management and corrupt dealings as head of the Vatican bank. At Vatican City, however, Michael learns that some people oppose the deal. Ratification will be more complicated than he had expected.

Don Altobello, an elderly New York mafioso, tells Michael that his old New York partners want in on the Immobiliare deal. A meeting is arranged in Atlantic City, and Michael appeases most of the mafiosi with generous payoffs from their casino days. Zasa gets nothing. Furious, he declares that Michael is his enemy and tells everyone in the room they must choose between him and Michael. Zasa storms out of the meeting. Minutes later, a helicopter hovers outside the conference room, then sprays a barrage of bullets through the windows. Almost everyone present is killed, but Michael and Vincent escape, with Vincent acting as his uncle's human shield. As Michael considers how to respond to this hit, he suffers a diabetic stroke and is hospitalized.

Vincent and Mary, though cousins, begin a romantic relationship. Vincent plans revenge on Zasa. At a street fair, Vincent and his accomplices murder Zasa and his bodyguards. Michael, still hospitalized, berates Vincent when he finds out, but Vincent insists that he got the go-ahead from Connie, who has become deeply involved in family affairs. Michael insists that Vincent break up with Mary because Vincent's involvement in the Mafia puts Mary in danger. Vincent agrees. However, in Sicily, where the family moves to pursue the Vatican deal and attend Anthony's opera debut, the relationship continues.

Michael tells Vincent to speak with Altobello and, in order to see where the old man's loyalties lie, to pretend that he is thinking of leaving the Corleone family. Altobello supports the idea of Vincent switching allegiance and introduces Vincent to Licio Lucchesi, the man behind the plot to prevent Michael's acquisition of Immobiliare.

Michael visits Cardinal Lamberto, a well-intentioned and pious priest, to speak about the Immobiliare deal. Lamberto convinces Michael to make confession, his first in thirty years, and Lamberto absolves Michael of his sins. Touring Sicily with Kay, who has arrived for Anthony's performance, Michael asks for her forgiveness too. Just as both are admitting that they still love each other, Michael gets word that Don Tommasino, his Sicilian friend, has been killed, signaling that a new round of violence is about to begin. Cardinal Lamberto is elected Pope John Paul I, which means that the Immobiliare deal will likely be ratified.

Vincent tells Michael what he has learned from Altobello: Lucchesi is behind the plot against the Immobiliare deal, and an assassin has been hired to kill Michael. Vincent wants to strike back, but Michael cautions him, saying that if he goes ahead with such a plan, there'll be no going back. Vincent insists on revenge, and Michael relents. He makes Vincent head of the Corleone family, the new Godfather. In exchange for the promotion, Vincent agrees to put an end to his relationship with Mary.

While Anthony performs the male lead of *Cavalleria Rusticana*, Vincent's plans for revenge go into effect. Interspersed with scenes from Anthony's performance are the brutal murders of Lucchesi, Altobello, and their associates, who have, however, already poisoned the new pope. An assassin, sent to kill Michael, lurks at the opera house. The assassin kills several of Vincent's men, but the opera ends before he has the chance to shoot Michael. The assassin retreats to the opera house façade's staircase and tries to shoot Michael there. Mary, upset and trying to speak to her father about the forced breakup with Vincent, steps in front of Michael and takes the bullet. Michael screams in pain and rage on the opera house stairs. Then the scene cuts to a shot of a white-haired and aged Michael, seated in the front yard of his Sicilian villa. He collapses in his chair and dies, alone and forgotten.

CHARACTER LIST

Vito Corleone—Played by Marlon Brando (1) and Robert De Niro (2) Founder and head of the Corleone family and one of the trilogy's two protagonists. As an older man, Vito is a shrewd Mafia boss known as the Godfather. As a younger man, he is a ruthlessly ambitious Sicilian immigrant in New York's Little Italy in the early twentieth century. Vito is a warm and loving father and husband. He wears his hair slicked back and seems incapable of talking without mumbling.

Michael Corleone—Played by Al Pacino The trilogy's other protagonist. Michael is Vito's youngest son. At the beginning of *The Godfather*, he is uninvolved in the Mafia and seems headed for a successful career in politics or another "legitimate" field. Over the course of the film, he abandons these plans. He joins the family business and succeeds his father as head of the Corleone family. A cold-blooded Mafia don with no tolerance for dissent or treachery, Michael is even bolder, more violent, and more ambitious than Vito, and he becomes fantastically rich in the casino business. He proves much less successful in his personal life. Michael seems incapable of relaxing enough to smile, and his tense relationship with his wife, Kay, whom he divorces, is a constant source of anguish.

Kay Adams Corleone—Played by Diane Keaton Michael's girlfriend at the beginning of *The Godfather* and later his wife. Kay is an all-American girl from New Hampshire who falls in love with a decorated World War II veteran and winds up a Mafia don's wife. At first, she plays dumb and chooses to ignore the violence that goes on around her. But eventually, she rebels against the prohibitions on her movement, Michael's cold distance, and the threats to her and her family, leaving Michael at the end of *The Godfather Part II*. By *The Godfather Part III*, she has remarried.

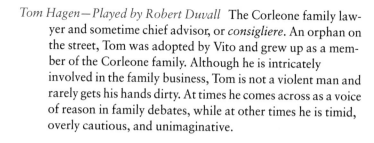

Tom Hagen—Played by Robert Duvall The Corleone family lawyer and sometime chief advisor, or *consigliere*. An orphan on
  the street, Tom was adopted by Vito and grew up as a member of the Corleone family. Although he is intricately
  involved in the family business, Tom is not a violent man and
  rarely gets his hands dirty. At times he comes across as a voice
  of reason in family debates, while at other times he is timid,
  overly cautious, and unimaginative.

(Santino) Sonny Corleone—Played by James Caan Vito's oldest
  son. Sonny is hot-headed, violent, and reckless, a combination that leads him into a death trap set by a rival family. A
  philanderer, Sonny has an illegitimate child, Vincent Mancini, who succeeds Michael as head of the Corleone family in
  The Godfather Part III.

Fredo Corleone—Played by John Cazale Vito's middle son. Weak-
  willed and terribly insecure, Fredo is overshadowed by his
  older brother's reckless passion and his younger brother's
  unshakeable confidence. He briefly finds himself living the
  life of a decadent playboy in Las Vegas, but his comfort with
  women and drink is only a cover for his essential unease.

Connie Corleone Rizzi—Played by Talia Shire Vito's daughter. At
  the opening of *The Godfather*, Connie marries Carlo Rizzi,
  who turns out to be an abusive, adulterous terror. After
  Michael kills Carlo, Connie enters a period of rebellion
  against her brother, behaving like a spoiled, overgrown child,
  pathetic, lost, and very angry. By the end of *The Godfather
  Part II*, however, she regains control of her life, and in *Part III*
  she emerges as the backbone of the family.

Carlo Rizzi—Played by Gianni Russo Connie's abusive husband.
  Carlo betrays the Corleone family, tipping off Sonny's killers,
  and is killed by Michael for his transgression.

Apollonia Corleone—Played by Simonetta Stefanelli Michael's
  first wife. While hiding out in Sicily in *The Godfather*,
  Michael falls in love at first sight with Apollonia, a sixteen-
  year-old beauty. Just days after their marriage, Apollonia is
  killed in a car bomb intended for Michael.

GODFATHER TRILOGY

Clemenza—Played by Richard S. Castellano (1) and B. Kirby, Jr. (2)
A member of the Corleone crime family and longtime associate of Vito. Clemenza is jolly, easygoing, and well-fed, but he is also a vicious killer. He gives Michael lessons in cooking and firing a gun in *The Godfather*.

Tessio—Played by Abe Vigoda (1, 2) and John Aprea (2)   A member of the Corleone family and longtime associate of Vito. Cleverer than Clemenza, Tessio betrays Michael at the end of *The Godfather*.

Don Fanucci—Played by Gaston Moschin   An early-twentieth-century Little Italy Mafia don. Fanucci is a small-time extortionist who dresses like a big-time pimp. Murdering him is Vito Corleone's first step toward gaining power in his neighborhood.

Barzini—Played by Richard Conte   The head of one of the five Mafia families of New York.

Bonasera—Played by Salvatore Corsitto   An undertaker who asks Vito to avenge his daughter's beating.

Johnny Fontane—Played by Al Martino   A famous singer and actor, like Frank Sinatra. Though a successful performer, Johnny Fontane comes to Vito, his godfather, for help with his career on more than one occasion.

Sollozzo—Played by Al Lettieri   A gangster known as the Turk. Sollozzo is involved in the narcotics trade and is backed by Barzini and Tattaglia (another Mafia boss).

Captain McCluskey—Played by Sterling Hayden   A corrupt, bigoted policeman who moonlights as Sollozzo's bodyguard.

Jack Woltz—Played by John Marley   A Hollywood film producer who refuses to give Johnny Fontane a part in his latest war movie. Woltz is crass and materialist, more capitalist than artist.

Hyman Roth—Played by Lee Strasberg An aging Jewish gangster and an old colleague of Vito. Roth partners with Michael in business dealings in Las Vegas and Havana, Cuba, in *The Godfather Part II*. Roth is terminally ill and seems to be dying throughout the film, but he still finds time between doctor's visits to manipulate foreign presidents and plan assassinations.

Johnny Ola—Played by Dominic Chianese Roth's right-hand man.

Frankie Pentangeli—Played by Michael V. Gazzo The head of the New York branch of the Corleone family after Michael moves most of the operation to Las Vegas. Pentangeli is a Mafia traditionalist who feels that Michael isn't running things like Vito did. But despite their differences, Pentangeli refuses to testify against Michael during congressional hearings on the Mafia. While serving out a prison term for contempt of Congress, he kills himself, reenacting the ritual suicide of a failed Roman conspirator.

Senator Pat Geary—Played by G. D. Spradlin A corrupt Nevada senator. One of the least attractive characters in the trilogy, Geary is two-faced, bigoted, and adulterous. He defends Michael in the congressional hearings, but only because Tom caught him in Vegas, unconscious in bed with a murdered prostitute. Geary's presence in the movie is a sign of Coppola's cynicism about politics.

Mama Corleone—Played by Morgana King (1, 2) and Francesca de Sapio (2) Vito's loyal, loving wife.

Anthony Corleone—Played by James Gounaris (2) and Franc D'Ambrosio (3) Michael's son. Rather than joining the family business, Anthony pursues a career as an opera singer.

Mary Corleone—Played by Sofia Coppola Michael's daughter. Closer to Michael than her brother is, Mary is head of the Vito Corleone Foundation for the Poor of Sicily. To her father's dismay, she becomes romantically involved with her cousin, Vincent Mancini.

GODFATHER TRILOGY

Vincent Mancini—Played by Andy Garcia Michael's nephew and successor as head of the Corleone family. Over the course of *The Godfather Part III*, Vincent evolves from a leather jacket-wearing street hood into a silk suit-donning don. Thug or Godfather, he is always a ladykiller.

Andrew Hagen—Played by John Savage Tom Hagen's son and a Catholic priest.

Joey Zasa—Played by Joe Mantegna A smalltime gangster who has become boss of the old Corleone neighborhood in Little Italy in *The Godfather Part III*. Publicity hungry, arrogant, and insecure, Joey challenges both Michael and Vincent.

Don Altobello—Played by Eli Wallach A scheming old-time mafioso who pretends to play the role of peacemaker.

Don Tommasino—Played by Mario Cotone (1, 2) and Vittorio Duse (3) Michael's friend and guardian in Sicily.

Licio Lucchesi—Played by Enzo Robatti The leader of the Vatican conspirators in *The Godfather Part III* who poison the new pope and plot unsuccessfully to kill Michael.

Archbishop Gliday—Played by Donal Donnelly A frail, twitchy-fingered, chain-smoking, corrupt archbishop.

Al Neri—Played by Richard Bright One of Michael's enforcers.

Cardinal Lamberto/Pope John Paul 1—Played by Raf Vallone An earnest, caring, genuinely devout priest who hears Michael's confession. Lamberto is assassinated shortly after his election as pope.

B. J. Harrison—Played by George Hamilton Michael's right-hand man in *The Godfather Part III*. Harrison, a silver-haired, blue-blooded, financial guru, couldn't be more different from the slick-haired (or balding), ring-kissing mafiosi who attend to Michael in the earlier films. Harrison's presence symbolizes Michael's desire to be perceived as "legitimate."

ANALYSIS OF MAJOR CHARACTERS

VITO CORLEONE

The Godfather trilogy presents Vito as the paradigmatic Mafia don. When placed beside him, Barzini lacks class, Don Ciccio looks cruel and petty, and Don Fanucci is smalltime and brutish. Even Michael, despite his tremendous successes, loses in such a comparison, as he appears lacking in warmth and *joie de vivre*. It is unclear whether we are to believe Sollozzo's words about Vito, that "the old man [is] slipping," but even if he is, even if Vito walks right into an assassin's bullets and survives only though sheer luck, he is still the Godfather *par excellence*. He is wise and intelligent, an excellent reader of others' intentions, and a smooth, subtle talker, able to convince with words, not only bullets. The most exceptional thing about Vito, and the way in which he most outshines his son, is the manner in which he conducts his personal life. Though a ruthless, violent criminal, Vito is also a warm, loving father and husband, and the paradox of his character is that it is precisely the warmth of his humanity that makes him appear superhuman. In his later years, Vito comes across as relaxed and playful, even mellow. He has lived a rich, full life and earned a quiet retirement. As a younger man, when he is played by Robert De Niro, he is caring and devoted but also silent and intense. Unlike Michael, he does not let this intensity eat away at him. There is never any tension for Vito between the two meanings of "family" (i.e. blood relations and crime family), and he doesn't feel conflicted about what he's doing. Only when he learns that Michael has killed Sollozzo is he noticeably pained. His intensity is that of a hard-working man, though one who still manages to come home at the end of the workday to spend time with his family. In short, Vito comes across as both the perfect father and the perfect Godfather, making him a difficult model for all of his children, especially Michael, to imitate.

MICHAEL CORLEONE

Michael is cold-blooded, ruthless, smart, and determined. His ability to think clearly under fire, to be decisive, and to command respect makes him an excellent Godfather. Of Vito's children, he is certainly the best candidate to take over the family. But Michael was never supposed to get involved in the Mafia. He was supposed to become a senator, perhaps even president. Even when he does begin working for his father, he doesn't seem fully reconciled to the decision. He promises Kay before they marry that the family will become "legitimate" soon. Over twenty years later, in *The Godfather Part III*, he still seeks this legitimacy. Unlike Vito, who appears at ease in the role of Godfather, Michael is burdened by the responsibility. One senses that he views himself as a sacrificial hero, slaving away for the rest of the family, sacrificing his soul for the well-being of those around him. In many ways, Michael's story is a familiar one in American mythology: that of the immigrant's child. He achieves great heights of success, just as his hard-working immigrant parents hoped for him, but at considerable personal cost. In Michael's case, this cost is to his family life, as he loses his wife and children.

Michael can also be seen as a classical tragic figure. Immensely talented and powerful, he is undone by tragic flaws: his insatiable desire for vengeance, which creates a web of violence and recrimination that he cannot escape; his illusions of omnipotence, which blind him to the fact that achieving legitimacy is impossible; and his sense of being perpetually at war, which never allows him a moment of rest. At the end of *Part III*, Michael dies alone in the yard of his Sicilian villa. The death of his daughter, Mary, has sealed his fate, severing his ties forever with the rest of the family, the family that he tried to save and bring to legitimacy. Instead, he brought them only pain and death. If Vito is an ideal, almost romantic figure who might make the naïve viewer want to live the gangster life, Michael's tale has a corrective effect. His life is tragic and his pain immense.

KAY ADAMS

Of the many Corleone women, Kay is the only one who never accepts the Mafia way of life. Others may fight it for a time, but all eventually give in. Kay moves in the opposite direction. In *The Godfather*, she does not consent to it, but neither does she strenuously object. Instead, she ignores the truth, using her love for Michael as an excuse to avoid seeing the truth that stares her in the face. But at the very end of the film, as the door to Michael's office closes on her, we can sense the awakening of realization. By *The Godfather Part II*, Kay has decided that Michael is a cold, distant, inattentive husband and father, but only after an attempt is made on his life in the family home does she resolve to rebel against him. At first, Kay's rebellion is silent and private: she aborts the child she is carrying. But later, when she tells Michael that she is leaving him and reveals the truth that her "miscarriage" was really an abortion, she challenges him in a way no one ever has before. Kay becomes the first and only battle that Michael loses (until the very end of the trilogy). Michael may appear to get the better of the argument in *Part II*—he kicks her out of the house and keeps the children—but eventually Kay remarries and becomes the children's principal parent. Still, she admits in *Part III* that, even though she has moved on, she continues to love Michael and always will.

Tom Hagen

In the *Godfather* trilogy, men separate themselves and their violence from the innocent world of women, but Tom occupies a middle ground. He is a central figure in family business dealings, but he is kept in the dark about many other matters. Told repeatedly that he is not a "wartime *consigliere*," Tom is never asked to get his hands dirty. Although it appears that he is responsible for the horse's head in Woltz's bed in *Godfather I*, deleted scenes indicate that the thug Luca Brazi did the severing. At times, Tom's lack of involvement may appear strategic, enabling him to remind people that he is "just a lawyer" and allowing Michael to name him interim Godfather in *The Godfather Part II*. But Tom is naturally meek and cautious, qualities associated with women throughout the trilogy—though Connie's aggressive behavior in *Part III* challenges this notion. Tom's ambiguous position in the Corleone crime family mirrors his ambiguous position in the actual Corleone family. Though a valued son, he is not a blood relative and not an Italian. He is aware of his tenuous position and is constantly looking for acceptance from his brothers, particularly Michael. Like Michael, Tom is a perpetual outsider, but he is an outsider of a different sort.

SONNY CORLEONE

If Tom is too cautious to be a good Godfather, Sonny would fail for the opposite reason. He lacks the restraint and sangfroid (self-possession) that make his father and brother so successful. All heart, no brains, he is rash, impulsive, and sometimes just plain stupid. Too often, he acts before thinking. This recklessness gets him killed, as he walks right into a death trap by hurrying out of the house without bodyguards. A man of strong appetites and passions, he cheats on his wife and is barely able to restrain himself from beating his brother-in-law to death when he learns that his sister has been abused. We see a lot of Sonny in Vincent, and we cannot help but wonder how Vincent will lead the Corleones as Godfather—whether he will learn from his uncle or repeat his father's mistakes.

Themes, Motifs, and Symbols

Themes

"It's business, not personal"

This statement, as well as its several variations, is probably the most repeated line in the entire trilogy. At times, it seems like the official slogan of organized crime, an organization-wide mantra. All the mafiosi in the films euphemistically refer to themselves as businessmen. They do this in part to hide from the public the violent reality of what they do, but they also use euphemisms when speaking among themselves. Rather than talk plainly, mafiosi speak about the "family business" and "an offer he can't refuse." Such manipulation of language reveals a basic discomfort with the truth of their actions. The mafiosi not only need to tell policemen, judges, and congressmen that they are businessmen, they also need to tell themselves. They need to hear the lie so that they can look themselves in the mirror without being overwhelmed by guilt. The frequent use of this line also points to the Mafia-wide desire to keep business and personal life separate. The mafiosi may all work in the "family business," but the realms of home and office are never supposed to mix. Violence is supposed to leave the wives and children unharmed, and personal feelings are not to influence business decisions. Of course, all this is much easier said that done. While the separation of family and business may sound good in theory, no mafioso seems capable of forgetting that the guy who killed his son did so only to cement a business deal.

The Different Worlds of Men and Women

Shortly after Michael becomes head of the Corleone family, his father gives him this advice: "Women and children can be careless. Not men." In the world of the Mafia, Vito tells his son, men and women live in vastly different realms. Men should never discuss "business" with women, and women should never question the judgment of the men. Women can be careless, Vito says, they can make mistakes, because if a woman makes a mistake, no one dies. In other words, women can be not only careless but also care*free*. They can live a relaxed life that the men, who must constantly watch their backs, cannot. In *The Godfather Part III*, the barrier between men and women is breached by Connie, who becomes involved in the family business. But never does any woman achieve status in the family hierarchy equal to that of Vito or Michael, nor does any woman ever have to bear such a tremendous burden of responsibility.

THE CONFLICT BETWEEN RESPECT AND LEGITIMACY

Michael is concerned with legitimacy, while Vito cares more about respect. From the moment he takes over the Corleone family, Michael wants to make his family "legitimate." By "legitimate" he means free of criminality and immorality. He is also concerned with assimilation. He doesn't want to kill, bribe, and extort, and he doesn't want to make money through gambling, prostitution, and drug trafficking. Legitimate means being respected by American law and society. Vito's concern, on the other hand, is with respect, rather than legitimacy. As a don, he requires respect from everyone around him, and people respect him out of fear and the desire for Vito's favors. Respect is the backbone of a Mafia family hierarchy, with the top members, such as the don, receiving respect from everyone beneath them. Disrespect, or even inadequate respect, is rewarded with death. Respect establishes power relationships and functions as a method of exchange. For Vito, showing proper respect, kissing the don's ring, exchanging favors, making requests politely—all these formal gestures are more than just show. They are part of the order that keeps the social structure in place.

MOTIFS

RETURN TO SICILY

In *The Godfather* trilogy, there is a direct relationship between how many movies a character appears in and how central he or she is to the plot. Michael, Connie, and Kay, all principle characters, are in all three movies, while secondary characters like Archbishop Gliday or Senator Geary appear in only a single film. Of course, such a structure makes sense. The plot follows the most significant characters, while the less significant die or are forgotten. But every rule has its exceptions. In *The Godfather* trilogy, one such exception is the insignificant, little-known Don Tommasino. Tommasino appears in every movie because he is Vito's and Michael's host and friend in Sicily, the island of Vito's birth to which characters return in every film.

In *The Godfather* films, Don Tommasino may be a minor character, but Sicily is not.

In *The Godfather*, our first view of Sicily is a wide-angle shot of a hilly countryside. The day is sunny and beautiful, and the landscape, though rocky, seems uncorrupted by any signs of modern life. Even the characters, many of them dressed like peasants, appear as if they were from the past. The impression, which is repeated by the initial shots of Sicily in *The Godfather Part II* and *Part III*, is of a pastoral paradise where a life of innocence is possible. Indeed, Sicily is always more than just a quaint Italian island—it is a symbol of a different life, a place of escape. In *The Godfather*, Michael goes to Sicily to escape the Mafia war sure to follow his killing of Sollozzo. In *Part II* and *Part III*, the return to Sicily is associated with more metaphorical notions of escape. In *Part II*, Sicily is the place of Vito's brief innocence, his childhood. In *Part III*, it is a place of art, site of the opera house where Anthony will make his debut.

In all three films, the real Sicily fails to live up to this mythic image. The true Sicily is no paradise, but a place haunted by blood feuds and barbaric violence. In fact, every Sicilian journey culminates in a dramatic act of violence: the killing of Apollonia in *The Godfather*, the death of Vito's entire family at the beginning of *Part II*, the subsequent revenge killing of Don Ciccio later in the film, and the murder of Mary in *Part III*. Ironically, it is the Corleones' failure to escape *from*, rather than to, Sicily that prevents them from leaving their violent past behind. After all, Sicily, despite its rural charms and enticing vistas, is still the ancestral home of the Mafia.

FAMILY GATHERINGS

Family gatherings in *The Godfather* trilogy are just as much about business as they are about pleasure. In *The Godfather* films, the word "family" refers to family in the traditional sense, but also to family in the uniquely Mafia sense (i.e. crime family). For this reason, Mafia family gatherings, whether for a festive party or solemn funeral, always involve backroom schmoozing. Deals are made, hits are ordered, respect is exchanged, honor is shown, and fights are initiated or resolved. All three films open with large gatherings, each of which begins with a large gathering for a formal occasion: *The Godfather* with Connie and Carlo's wedding, *The Godfather Part II* with Anthony's communion, and *The Godfather Part III* with the award ceremony for the medal of the Order of St. Sebastian. In the parties that follow, there is always a good deal of dancing, singing, and drunken revelry, but the mafiosi seem most interested in conducting "business." The plot of each film is determined during these mid-party backroom sessions. Later, subsequent family gatherings are important occasions for resolving plot strands. In *The Godfather*, for instance, Michael learns that Tessio is a traitor at Vito's funeral and has the heads of the five families killed during Carlo and Connie's son's baptism. In *Part II*, Michael and Fredo have a temporary reconciliation at Mama Corleone's funeral. And in *Part III*, the pope and Archbishop Gliday and his associates are killed and Mary is killed by a bullet intended for Michael after Anthony's opera performance.

CORRUPTION IS EVERYWHERE

Michael, Vito, and the rest of the Corleone family may be criminals, but they seem cleaner than many of the public officials they encounter throughout the trilogy. Each of the films presents at least one character in a position of power who is not only thoroughly corrupt, but also ugly, crass, and duplicitous. In *The Godfather*, Sergeant McCluskey is a police officer who doubles as a bodyguard for the drug trafficker Sollozzo. In *Part II*, Senator Pat Geary tries to extort money; spews bigoted, anti-Italian invectives; and frequents whorehouses. In *Part III*, Archbishop Gliday, as head of the Vatican bank, has gotten involved in underhanded dealings with criminal elements and plays a part in their corrupt, illegal activities, including the assassination of the pope. From one movie to the next, these officials occupy more powerful and seemingly respected roles in society, and at the same time they grow uglier, more corrupt, and more sinister. While there are a few examples of well-intentioned public officials, most notably Cardinal Lamberto, who becomes Pope John Paul I, the examples of corrupt public officials are more numerous. By comparison, the protagonists of *The Godfather* trilogy emerge as morally complex figures. Placed beside Senator Geary in a lineup, Michael, even at his most ruthless, would appear a sympathetic figure.

SYMBOLS

WINDOWS

Windows divide the outer, public world from the inner realm of the home. As a boundary, the window is fragile and permeable, and too often windows become an easy entry point for bullets. A shot of a fluttering curtain, a sign of the outer world invading the private space of the home, often anticipates an eruption of violence. In *Part II*, for instance, the window curtains of Michael's bedroom flutter, and moments later a barrage of bullets rains down upon him and Kay. A window can also function as a screen through which a character sees the world, and onto which a character projects his thoughts. When young Vito, upon arriving in America, is quarantined on Ellis Island, he sits on the little chair in his cell and gazes out the window at the Statue of Liberty. For three months, this vista is the closest he will come to American freedom. At the end of *Part II*, Michael, who spends countless hours in his glass-enclosed Tahoe boathouse, stands before the walls and looks out on the water as his brother Fredo is killed. In the case of young Vito, the window looks onto what he desires but cannot have. In the case of the boathouse, the window is an insufficient wall to protect Michael from ugly, painful reality.

Doors

In *The Godfather* trilogy, doors separate women from men. Most of the doors we see are interior doors within houses. They separate one room from another, and they divide the home between the male domain of business and the female realm of family. Whenever men have business to discuss, they close the door to the study and shut the women out. Front doors, entryways to houses, are rarely seen, but when they are, they are even more solid boundaries against female freedom. When Michael discovers Kay visiting the children after she's left him in *Part II*, he closes the door in her face. Similarly, Kay is prevented from leaving the compound in *Part II* when Michael is in hiding. Throughout *The Godfather* trilogy, a woman needs a man's permission to cross through any door.

Chairs

Chairs serve many purposes in *The Godfather* trilogy, but what unites them all is the sitter's solitude. Above all else, the chair is a symbol of isolation. The most obvious function of a chair is that of a throne. The Godfather sits in a chair as suppliants pay their respects and kiss his hand. Remaining seated while others stand is a way of asserting power. Chairs are also places of contemplation. The young Vito sits in a chair to gaze upon the Statue of Liberty from his Ellis Island cell. Michael sits in the chair in his boathouse at the end of *Part II* as his memory leads him back to the day he enlisted for the war. In that memory, he remains fastened to his chair as the rest of the family goes to the door to greet Vito. Chairs are also places of death. A number of characters die while sitting, most notably Michael, who falls dead from the chair on which he'd been sitting in the yard of his Sicilian villa.

FILM ANALYSIS

SEPARATE BUT EQUAL

The Godfather trilogy at once proves and disproves the conventional wisdom that a sequel can never equal the original in a series of films. In the case of *The Godfather Part III*, the dictum holds. Though a good movie, *The Godfather Part III* suffers in comparison to its predecessors for the same reasons that sequels generally fail: surprise is harder to come by because once successful tropes have grown stale. *The Godfather Part II*, on the other hand, is in every way the equal of *The Godfather*. Like its predecessor, it is one of the great movies of the 1970s, indeed of all cinematic history. Ranking the two films is more a matter of taste than artistic merit. Like *War and Peace* and *Anna Karenina*, *The Godfather* and *The Godfather Part II* are each unique and appealing in their own way.

This fact is all the more remarkable considering that, unlike a trilogy such as *The Lord of the Rings*, *The Godfather* and *The Godfather Part II* were not filmed or even conceived of all at once. *The Godfather* is a complete movie, and had Coppola ended his project there, no one would have felt it was incomplete. The ability to generate a second film as fresh and exciting as *The Godfather* is, therefore, the singular achievement of the trilogy. This is possible only because *Part II* is a sequel of an unusual sort. Rather than a continuation of the first film's plot, it is a new take on the themes of the first film and can be classified as belonging to a different genre. *The Godfather* may be classified as an epic, a multigenerational family saga told in an almost mythical way. *Part II*, on the other hand, does contain elements of epic, but feels more like a psychological drama, narrating the making of one don (young Vito) and the personal undoing of another (Michael). Some might even call *Part II* a tragedy. Certainly, this is the element of the film that *Part III* takes up, in the murder of Fredo and the disintegration of Michael and Kay's marriage. As a whole, the trilogy feels more like Michael's tragedy than the Corleone family epic. But regardless of how we decide to classify the *Godfather* films, the fact remains that the first two employ radically different means of storytelling. The principle difference between the two films is in their narrative structures, which are achieved through different modes of editing.

EDITING

Motion pictures can be edited in two basic ways. *Continuous action* presents events in the sequence they occur. Time may lapse between scenes, but the story unfolds chronologically, so that the beginning, middle, and end of the film are also the beginning, middle, and end of the story that the film tells. *Parallel action* cuts back and forth between scenes or narratives. Sometimes parallel action is used to depict events that occur simultaneously, other times to relate multiple narratives, cutting back and forth between them. The primary difference between the first two *Godfather* films is that *The Godfather* employs mostly continuous action, whereas *Part II* uses parallel action. From the opening at Connie's wedding to the final scene in which Michael arrives at Las Vegas, the scenes of *The Godfather* are related in chronological order. The major storylines of the film—the transfer of power from Vito to Michael and Michael's development from youngest son to Godfather—are tales of development, linear in structure. As a result, the characters' actions speak largely for themselves. We see Michael develop from someone who is unable to say "I love you" to Kay into someone who can. We see Vito change from a powerful Godfather into a playful old grandfather.

On the few occasions when *The Godfather* does employ parallel structure, it does so for very specific reasons. The first time is toward the beginning of the movie: as Tom, Sonny, and Vito debate doing business with Sollozzo, we see brief flashes of scenes that show a meeting being arranged. In this case, the parallel structure captures Sollozzo's double dealing, as well as Vito's discomfort about the deal. It should not come as a surprise that Vito rejects Sollozzo's offer at the meeting, nor that shortly afterward Sollozzo tries to have Vito killed. The movie also uses parallel action to relate the Mafia war that directly follows Michael's murder of Sollozzo. Cutting back and forth between shots that depict gangsters going about their daily lives and images of newspaper headlines that chronicle the violent Mafia war they are waging, the editing highlights the disruptive effect of violence on the lives of mafiosi. The most famous use of parallel action is in the baptism scene at the movie's end, which introduces us to Michael's duplicity and the double life he will lead as head of the family.

While *The Godfather* consists of a single narrative whose chronological exposition is interrupted a few times to highlight important moments, *Part II* alternates between two separate stories. Rather than being used sparsely and strategically, as in *The Godfather*, parallel action defines the entire structure of *Part II*. *The Godfather* opens with a scene that culminates in an initially disrespectful suppliant kissing Don Vito's hand in a humble show of respect. *Part II* begins with a parallel shot of Michael, now Godfather, having his hand kissed by a suppliant. But then the movie cuts to an image of the rocky Sicilian countryside. Subtitles state, "The Godfather was born Vito Andolini, in the town of Corleone in Sicily." With this opening, *Part II* announces that it will not simply move forward like *The Godfather*, but back and forth. It also establishes that the film's parallel structure will function crucially, as the display of respect shown to Michael is immediately undermined by the narrator who calls Vito, not Michael, Godfather. Not only will the movie compare the two men, but it will complicate the transfer of power enacted in *The Godfather*. This opening scene shift suggests that Michael has failed to escape his father's mythical shadow.

These questions of succession highlight the problem that *Part II* faces as the sequel to the tremendously popular, critically acclaimed *The Godfather*. The challenge for *Part II* was establishing its own ground. One way that the film resolves this dilemma is by acting as not only a sequel, but also a prequel. By cutting back and forth between a continuation of the narrative of Michael's life, the sequel to his story in *The Godfather*, and the story of Vito's youth, the prequel to his story in *The Godfather*, it solves the problem of succession by complicating it. *Part II* is both the son of *The Godfather* and its father.

Part II performs a critique of *The Godfather* by questioning the morality of the Corleones' actions and by introducing further psychological depth to the family story. In the earliest Sicilian scenes, Vito's father, brother, and mother—his entire family—are all killed over the course of a few days by Don Ciccio, a local Mafia boss. Even though he is only nine years old, Vito is also considered a threat, and so to survive, he runs away to America. As his tale proceeds we see him transform himself from a grocery clerk into a local Mafia don, a classic story of American upward social mobility. Meanwhile, Michael is forced to deal with continual violence, attempts on his life, and treachery within his family. He survives, but only by being more ruthless than his enemies. His survival comes at a cost: Michael winds up losing his family. Kay aborts a child and renounces her love for him, and Michael feels compelled to kill his brother, Fredo, who was involved tangentially in an attempt to kill him. Whereas Vito begins *Part II* alone and then builds a family, Michael moves in the opposite direction, in the end losing much of what his father built. The structure of the film forces us to compare the two men and include moral considerations in the equation. Michael seems less a hero than a villain. Not only does he strong-arm politicians, neglect his family, and murder business associates left and right, he kills his own brother in a vicious display of cruelty and vengeance. The only way for Michael to escape from his father's shadow is to cross over moral and ethical boundaries that his father never would violate.

But more important than *Part II*'s critique of the violence of the Mafia life is its introduction of further psychological depth into its analysis of character. As the movie proceeds, we come to understand that the film's journey backward in time, to Vito's youth, is also a journey inward. The past affects the present, the parallel structure suggests. It explains, for instance, how the Corleones became mixed up in the Mafia and violence in the first place. This equation of backward- and inward-looking isn't complete until the end of *Part II*, where parallel editing is used to take us into Michael's mind as he experiences a memory.

As he sits in his Tahoe boathouse in 1959, Michael recalls December 7, 1941, Pearl Harbor Day and his father's birthday. All Vito's children, Connie, Sonny, Fredo, Tom, and Michael, sit around the dining room table waiting for their father to come home so they can surprise him with a birthday cake. The bombing of Pearl Harbor comes up in their discussion, and Michael announces that he has enlisted to join the army. His brothers are furious. A debate ensues, but it is interrupted by the return of Vito. All the family members run to greet him, except for Michael, who remains alone at the table, deep in thought. This final scene reinforces Michael's isolation from the rest of the family, but also reminds us that Michael fought in a war and knew violence before his killing of Sollozzo in *The Godfather*. He was, in fact, a decorated war hero. If we wonder where Vito learned to be violent, the opening of *Part II* tells us. If we wonder where Michael learned, this scene provides a clue. If violence breeds violence—and *The Godfather* trilogy suggests it does— only the first violent act needs explanation. All the rest follow. The early Sicilian scenes humanize Vito and make us more sympathetic to his violent ways. Michael's flashback at the end of *Part II* suggests that he too may have undergone some sort of traumatic, formative event, but unlike his father's, it will remain hidden to us. Whatever Michael saw in World War II, we will never know. Again, the contrast with his father is reinforced in this last scene, and his isolation and his violence are once again linked.

MONTAGE

Montage, a rapid succession of images that links different scenes, is the most dramatic form of parallel editing. It is used many times in *The Godfather* trilogy, most famously in the baptism scene at the end of *The Godfather*. As Connie and Carlo's son is baptized, the film cuts to images showing the murders of the heads of the five Mafia families, murders that Michael has ordered. The use of montage implies that the murders and the baptism occur simultaneously, and the juxtaposition of the calm, peaceful, and religious church ceremony and the frantic, violent murders gives each unexpected new meaning. The irony between these vastly different scenes is striking. During the baptism ceremony, the godparents must respond to questions such as "Do you reject the glamour of evil?" and "Do you reject Satan and all his works?" by saying "I do." Michael's sincere "I do's" cement his position as Godfather to Connie's baby, but the murders he ordered form a ceremony of their own from which Michael emerges as a Godfather of an entirely different sort.

The duality highlighted by this particular montage captures the nature of Michael's new life. As Godfather, he will be in charge of two very different families. But at the same time that the montage signals Michael's full accession to the title of Godfather, it also shows how he will differ from his father. By carrying out such violence during his nephew's baptism, just as he is declaring his belief in God and denouncing Satan, Michael desecrates the service and brings violence into the sphere of family. Michael's duplicity, his ability to lie, and his ruthlessness are all highlighted by this dramatic sequence of images. But also apparent is his willingness to allow violence into the home, something Vito would have prevented. This distinction between father and son is picked up dramatically in *Part II*.

PERSPECTIVE

The Godfather opens with a shot of Bonasera, a suppliant to Don Vito Corleone. Because we look at Bonasera from Vito's point of view, Vito himself is hidden to us. Only later does the camera pull back, revealing the back of Vito's head and shoulders, then changing angles to show his face. As the movie proceeds, most action is revealed from a more universal, third-person perspective, and Vito becomes a character like any other. But from the opening shot, we know that the story is Vito's and that his is the only perspective that matters. Gradually, as Michael becomes an increasingly important character, we see more and more through his eyes, and at a certain point, the story becomes his. This transfer of perspective occurs during the scene at the Bronx Italian restaurant where Michael kills Sollozzo and Captain McCluskey. This action represents Michael's Mafia initiation and prepares him to eventually succeed his father as the next Don Corleone. Therefore the change in perspective that occurs in this scene anticipates the later transfer of family power from Vito to Michael.

As the Bronx restaurant scene begins, we look at Sollozzo from over Michael's shoulder. The camera stands behind him. We are looking from Michael's vantage, but not from his eyes. As the scene progresses, we move closer to Sollozzo. When Michael's shoulders disappear from the screen, we are seeing Sollozzo through Michael's eyes, just as we saw Bonasera through Vito's eyes in the film's opening scene. Another key to the change in perspective is in the use of subtitles. When Sollozzo and Michael speak in Italian, there are no subtitles. Until this point, the dialogue in Italian has been translated, because Vito was born in Sicily and is fluent. Michael, on the other hand, can barely understand or speak the language. Toward the end of Sollozzo's un-subtitled speech in Italian, Michael tries to respond in Italian, but he is unable and has to resort to English. After killing Sollozzo and McCluskey, Michael goes to Sicily and learns Italian. For this reason, all subsequent Italian dialogue in the trilogy, even when we are seeing things from Michael's perspective, is subtitled.

As Michael retrieves the gun in the bathroom, we enter his head more fully. We hear a din from an elevated subway car passing by. The sound is much louder than that of a flushing toilet, and it is clearly not part of any objective reality. Instead we are in Michael's head, hearing the sound of his anxiety. When Michael returns to the dining area, subtle sounds—a fork clanking against a plate, soft footsteps—are amplified, as Michael's senses are on high alert. Sollozzo again tries to talk in Italian, still without subtitles, but soon the din returns, drowning out the words. The sound of the passing subway car grows and grows, its grating, scratching sound becoming increasingly deafening. At no other moment are we more in Michael's head. Then Michael stands and fires, first shooting Sollozzo, then turning to McCluskey and firing twice. During the shooting and in the first moments afterward, the perspective returns to that of a removed third-person. Once again, we look on Michael and the rest of the restaurant from afar, then the dinner table draped with collapsed, bloody bodies. But the transfer of perspective has occurred. We have entered Michael's head, and now the story is his.

IMPORTANT QUOTATIONS EXPLAINED

1. BONASERA: "I believe in America. America has made my
    fortune. And I raised my daughter in American fashion. I
    gave her freedom, but I taught her never to dishonor her
    family. She found a boyfriend. Not an Italian. She went to
    the movies with him. She stayed out late. I didn't protest.
    Two months ago, he took her for a drive with another
    boyfriend. They made her drink whiskey. And then they
    tried to take advantage of her. She resisted. She kept her
    honor. So they beat her like an animal. . . . Then I said to my
    wife for justice we must go to Don Corleone."

The Godfather trilogy opens with these words. They are said by the
undertaker Bonasera, who requests that Don Corleone render "justice" on two American boys who beat his daughter and got off with
only a suspended sentence. Bonasera's words implicitly link the
boys' crime with the failure of the legitimate American justice system. As such, his statement becomes a strong condemnation of the
society to which he has moved. American justice having failed him,
Bonasera requests Sicilian "justice," by which he means murder. In
his request, we see the first example of what will become a common
occurrence throughout the trilogy: the use of euphemism to describe
the mafiosi's violent, criminal acts. Vito responds by saying, "We are
not murderers." But of course killers is exactly what they are, and
killing, or at least maiming, will be the chosen response. The way the
Mafia uses language to cover up, even excuse, their criminal actions
is another important theme introduced in this opening.

Lastly, Bonasera's words make clear that we are dealing with an
immigrant community. The characters may be rich and powerful,
but they still face the same struggles that all immigrants confront
every day. Assimilation is not easy, and immigrants, when unaware
of local customs, can be taken advantage of, as is Bonasera's daughter. The tragedy that befalls her makes Michael's genuine, loving
relationship with the blue-blooded American Kay Adams seem all
the more remarkable. At the opening of the movie, Michael presents
himself as a totally assimilated Italian-American. Later in the tril-

ogy, when he becomes Godfather, he grows obsessed with the idea of making the family "legitimate," which, in a sense, is a euphemism for "assimilated." Michael wants to de-Sicilianize the family, to take the crime out of it, so that the Corleones will be as American as anyone else.

2.   KAY: I thought you weren't going to become a man like your father. That's what you told me.
      MICHAEL: My father's no different from any other powerful man. Any man who's responsible for other people. Like a senator or president.
      KAY: You know how naïve you sound? Senators and presidents don't have men killed.
      MICHAEL: Oh. Who's being naïve, Kay?

When Michael returns to America after his year of exile in Sicily in *The Godfather*, he decides to track down his old girlfriend, Kay, and propose to her. Years have passed since the beginning of the movie, when the couple dated, and this excerpt of dialogue comes from a discussion in which Michael tries to fill Kay in on all that has happened to him in the interim. Michael has changed significantly since Kay last saw him. Whereas at the beginning the film Michael dressed in an army uniform, now he wears the bowler hat and pin-striped suit of a mafioso. Whereas earlier he been unable to say "I love you," now he is able to tell Kay those words she longs to hear. The most important change, however, is that Michael has begun "working with [his] father," meaning he has become a member of the Corleone Mafia family.

    This excerpt of dialogue is important for a number of reasons. First, it shows Michael unambiguously defending his father and the Mafia life for the first time, signaling that the transformation of Michael from "civilian" to mafioso, a process that began with McCluskey's punch to his face, is complete. Second, it introduces a criticism of broader American culture. By comparing a Mafia don to the president of the United States, Michael may be manipulating language and meaning, but there is no question that Coppola also wants the viewer to seriously contemplate the comparison. *The Godfather* was released in the midst of the Vietnam War, and Michael's cynicism about politicians was common during that time. In *The Godfather*, we learn that Vito hopes Michael would someday become a senator or president, reinforcing the irony of this statement. Third, this dialogue shows that the tension that exists between Kay and Michael goes well beyond Michael's difficulty in expressing love. From the start of their marriage, husband and wife are engaged in a clash of values, and ultimately this, rather than Michael's inability to show warmth, will drive them apart.

3.   MICHAEL: "Fredo, you're nothing to me now. You're not a brother, you're not a friend. I don't want to know you or what you do."

In *The Godfather Part II*, after Fredo admits that he had contact with Hyman Roth, thereby aiding the attack on Michael's life, Michael dismisses his older brother from his life with these words. Fredo insists quite believably that he had no idea that Michael would be attacked, but Michael doesn't care. In dismissing Fredo so coldly, he displays the same ruthlessness with which he has carried out many of his actions. As strong and forceful as these words are, Michael is not done punishing Fredo. At the end of the movie, Michael has his brother murdered. If one had to pick a single climactic moment for the entire trilogy, the murder of Fredo would probably be it. There is a sense in this action that Michael has so internalized the role of Godfather, adopted the mantra "it's business, not personal" so completely, that there is no other way he could act.

Don Ciccio, we learn in the same movie, wants to kill the nine-year-old Vito Andolini, because if he doesn't, Vito will come back one day and kill him. Murdering a young child may seem extreme, but the plot proves Don Ciccio correct. There is a clear logic behind retributive killing: if I don't kill my enemy, he will kill me first. Vengeance is taken not out of any sense of honor, but as a mode of self-protection. It is a rational, rather than emotional, act. At first, the killing of Fredo seems consistent with this logic, but it may not be. Unlike Carlo, Connie's husband, whom Michael also had killed, Fredo appears unlikely ever to intentionally hurt Michael. His carelessness, while dangerous, is probably manageable. But even if Fredo did want to hurt Michael, he probably would not be able to. If Michael were to bide by the words in this quotation and never speak to Fredo again, there would be no way that weak, insecure, fearful Fredo could touch him.

Rather than the prime example of Michael's sangfroid, the murder of Fredo is in fact evidence of Michael's greatest weakness. As much as it appears to be a decision of ruthless efficiency, the perfect business act of the perfect don, the killing is nothing if not personal. Michael cannot tolerate treachery and has a compulsive need for vengeance. This, more than anything else, is his fatal flaw. In *The Godfather*, the peace between the five families is made because Vito forswears his right to vengeance for Sonny's death. But Michael is never able to make a comparable decision. The significance of this quotation is that Michael is unable to abide by what he says. When vengeance becomes emotional, rather than strategic, an unending cycle of violence results. This is the lesson that Michael learns in *Part III*. Despite his great desire and many attempts to become "legitimate," he cannot escape the web of murder that he has played such a large part in weaving.

4. KAY: "Michael, you are blind. It wasn't a miscarriage. It was an abortion. An abortion, Michael. Just like our marriage is an abortion. Something that's unholy and evil. I didn't want your son, Michael. I wouldn't bring another one of your sons into this world. It was an abortion, Michael. It was a son. A son. And I had it killed. Because this must all end. I know now that it's over. I knew it then. There would be no way, Michael, no way you could ever forgive me. Not with this Sicilian thing that's been going on for two thousand years."

Toward the end of *Part II*, Kay announces to Michael that she is leaving him and taking the children with her. He refuses to let them go, they fight, and as their argument escalates, she launches this verbal attack at him. Kay's chilling confession about the abortion is one of the trilogy's most dramatic moments. But Kay's words do more than just reveal the truth behind her "miscarriage." They are a vicious attack on Michael and all he stands for. The attack is personal. Michael is blind, Kay charges, so consumed with his business of being a Godfather that he doesn't even see what is going on in his own family. The attack is also directed at the entire institution of the Mafia, what she refers to as "this Sicilian thing that's been going on for two thousand years." Kay has decided that the Mafia is so destructive that she refuses to participate in it even indirectly. She will not give birth to a child who might in any way become part of this world of killing and retribution. In *Part III*, when she supports Anthony's desire to quit law school and pursue a career in opera, she ensures that their surviving son will never participate, either. She cannot, however, protect their daughter, Mary, from Mafia violence.

In the previous scene, Michael was able to manipulate testimony at congressional Mafia hearings, destroying the state's case against him. Michael had just defeated the United States Congress and seems at the height of his powers, but Kay's words bring him back to earth. She mocks her husband for his powerlessness, both within his family, where he obviously has no control, but also in the larger world of the Mafia. What is his power against two thousand years of history? she asks. She dismisses his desire to become "legitimate" as a pipe dream. "You're caught in something much larger than yourself, something over which you have no control—and there is no way out," she says, taunting him. As if to add salt to the wound, she enunciates the word "Sicilian" with the derisive hiss of a bigot. The abortion is Kay's assertion of control over Michael. At the same time, the fact that she must resort to such a desperate measure is proof of just how powerless she feels. But at least in this one instance, she gets to act as the protagonist, gets to be the victimizer, not the victim. In the twisted logic of the film, the abortion can also be seen as one more link in the chain of retributive killings. Were the son to be born, he might be killed, as Mary will be killed, and Michael would be responsible. Kay exacts preemptive revenge by killing him now.

5. MICHAEL: "Just when I thought I was out, they pull me back in."

In *The Godfather Part III*, Michael utters these words shortly after returning home from a gathering of mafiosi in Atlantic City, where he and Vincent were among the few survivors of a massacre. With this simple sentence, Michael expresses the realization that despite his attempts to become legitimate, he will never be able to escape the Mafia life. Growing up, Michael never expected to be part of the "family business," and his father and brothers didn't want it for him. Their hope was that he would become a politician. When Michael does begin to work for and then take over the Corleone family in *The Godfather*, he has every intention of making its business legitimate. When he proposes to Kay, it is the early 1950s, and he gives himself five years to reform the family. By *Part II*, it is 1959, and Kay, frustrated by his inability to make good on the promise, winds up leaving him. By *Part III*, it is twenty years later, 1979, and

Michael still hasn't completed the transformation. But at the beginning of the film, having been awarded the medal of the Order of St. Sebastian and with the Immobiliare deal seemingly immanent, he believes legitimacy is finally within his reach.

Unfortunately, he quickly loses this illusion. In no time, the tension between Vincent and Joey Zasa, the Atlantic City massacre, and the complications around the Immobiliare deal make clear that going legitimate will not be possible. This sentence is Michael's cry of despair. With it, he acknowledges that he will never be able to escape his past actions. These past actions, as much as other gangsters, are what "pull him back in." Moments after speaking, Michael suffers a stroke, highlighting the statement's importance. For Michael, the failure to make the family legitimate is his principle failure. Indeed, the question of legitimacy has always been about more than crime—it has also been an issue of assimilation. There is a Sicilian way of doing things and an American way, and it was Michael's goal to bring his family into the American mainstream. As such, this quotation touches on the theme introduced by Bonasera in the trilogy's opening statement. With this single sentence, Michael acknowledges that under his watch, the Corleones never achieved full integration into American society. When Vincent, who seems unconcerned with legitimacy, takes over, there is no indication that they will escape the cycle of violence any time soon. Mary's death at the end of the trilogy is a grim signal that the Corleone future looks no less dark than its past.

CHINATOWN

(1974)

Context

Some of film history's most memorable directors created films that were obviously autobiographical—for example, Woody Allen's *Annie Hall* (1977), François Truffaut's *The Four Hundred Blows* (1959), and Federico Fellini's *8 1/2* (1963). The heroes in these films often seem to be simply better-looking versions of the director (with the exception of Woody Allen, who plays himself). *Chinatown*, released in 1974 but set in 1937 Los Angeles and starring Jack Nicholson as a hapless private investigator battling real estate crooks, doesn't seem at first glance to fit into this category. Director Roman Polanski didn't come to L.A. until 1968, never worked as an investigator, and hardly resembles the brash, all-American Nicholson. Nonetheless, *Chinatown* does draw heavily on Polanski's life and experiences. Though the main character, Nicholson's Jake Gittes, is not a stand-in for Polanksi, the director's biography is fragmented and refracted onto many separate elements and characters in the film, which both recalls his life's tragedies and foreshadows the scandals that would subsequently befall him.

Polanski was born in Paris on August 18, 1933, to a Polish father and Russian mother, both Jewish. Some of his first memories, however, would be of Krakow, where the family moved three years after his birth to escape rising anti-Semitism in France. Nazi Germany invaded Poland in 1939, and when Polanski was seven, he witnessed the construction of a wall marking his neighborhood as a Jewish ghetto. His parents were soon sent to concentration camps. Polanski escaped the camps by hiding with a local Catholic family his father had bribed, but he had to manage largely on his own, cowering in barns and, on at least one occasion, dodging the bullets of German soldiers. After the war, Polanski reunited with his father, but his mother had perished in a Nazi gas chamber.

Polanski entered art school in Krakow when he was around seventeen years old, spending his free time with acting groups and in movie theaters, which screened primarily German films. In 1954, the elite state film school in Lodz welcomed Polanski as one of only six accepted students. After graduating in 1959, Polanski made several short films, garnering only lukewarm critical response. In 1962, however, his first feature-length film, *Nóz w wodzie*, was well received and even nominated for an Oscar for Best Foreign Language Film after its American release (as *Knife in the Water*) a year later. Eager to take the international stage, Polanski left Poland for England, where he directed three modest successes: *Repulsion* (1965), *Cul-de-Sac* (1966), and *Fearless Vampire Killers* (1967), the last of which starred American actress Sharon Tate, who soon became his wife. The couple settled in Los Angeles, where Paramount producer Robert Evans invited Polanski to direct *Rosemary's Baby* (1968), based on the novel by Ira Levin. The occult thriller's huge popularity secured Polanski's professional reputation, showcasing his compositional perfectionism, his ability to sustain a suspenseful and gripping narrative, and his strikingly bold artistic flair.

The triumph of *Rosemary's Baby*, however, did not last long. On August 9, 1969, cult leader Charles Manson's "family" attacked the Polanskis' Beverly Hills home, murdering a pregnant Sharon Tate and her four guests. Polanski, who had been abroad the evening of the murders, was devastated. Harassed by the relentless American media, he retreated to Europe to make *Macbeth* (1971). That film's extreme violence reflected aspects of the Manson slayings. After mistakenly trying his hand at comedy with the little known and unsuccessful *What?* (1972), Polanski reluctantly agreed to return to the United States to work with his old friend, producer Robert Evans, on *Chinatown*. Though it was Robert Towne's masterful screenplay that had lured him back to the States, Polanski made many revisions to it. While Towne fought in favor of an optimistic film, Polanski's haunted and pessimistic vision prevailed, marking the picture with a devastating flourish that signified the hopelessness of a world gone rotten.

Chinatown's dark theme is one of the elements that places it in the category of neo-noir, the second generation of the genre known as film noir. Though the precise history of film noir is difficult to define (the term was coined in the journal *Cahiers du Cinéma* by Nino Frank in 1946), this genre evolved through a combination of German expressionistic drama (such as F. W. Murnau's 1922 *Nosferatu*), American gangster film (Mervyn LeRoy's 1931 *Little Caesar*), and popular British mystery novels (by Dorothy Sayers, H. C. Bailey, Agatha Christie, and the like). Several common features characterized film noir pictures, which were popular in the United States during the 1940s and early 1950s: the presence of a beautiful but dangerous woman (known as the *femme fatale*), gritty and generally urban settings, compositional tension (highly contrasting light and dark colors or oblique camera angles, for example), and themes of moral ambiguity and alienation. To prepare for the making of *Chinatown*, Polanski studied John Huston's *The Maltese Falcon* (1941), which is accepted as the first full embodiment of film noir. (Huston himself plays Noah Cross, *Chinatown's* most despicable villain). Polanski also read Raymond Chandler's mystery novels, several of which had been made into film noir classics, such as *Murder, My Sweet* (1944; originally titled *Farewell, My Lovely*) and *The Big Sleep* (1946).

Many scholars insist that film noir is intrinsically linked to World War II and the difficult years of postwar reconstruction (several champion directors of film noir, such as Fritz Lang and Billy Wilder, fled Nazi-occupied territories for Hollywood), and thus Polanski's war-torn history suits him especially well for the genre. *Chinatown*, however, is a *neo*-noir film, and its departures from classic noir elements help to define the newer genre. Most obviously, Polanski shot *Chinatown* with color film, and though his colors do appear especially vivid (Katherine Cross's bright, spotless dress and Evelyn Mulwray's rich, deep eyes, for example), color film precludes the contrast intensity that black and white film offers. In addition, Evelyn Mulwray is emphatically not a femme fatale like the heartless Phyllis Dietrichson of *Double Indemnity* (1944) or the snakelike Kathie Moffat of *Out of the Past* (1947). Though Jake mistakes her for her husband's killer at first, Mrs. Mulwray eventually emerges as the story's most tragic victim. *Chinatown* also exemplifies the neo-noir theme of big-money corruption. Though this theme is also present in classic noir, *Chinatown* and its neo-noir progeny (such as 1997's *L.A. Confidential*) emphasize malignant commercialism and obsession with money to a far greater extent than did their predecessors.

Chinatown was a box office sensation, and after its nomination for eleven Oscars in 1975, Polanski was a darling of the critics. But only two years later, Polanski was charged with the statutory rape of a thirteen-year-old girl, throwing his name into American tabloids once again and connecting him in the public mind with *Chinatown's* child-molesting villain Noah Cross. Nevertheless, Polanski continued directing, having fled to France to avoid standing trial. He was nominated for a Best Director Oscar in 1980 for *Tess* and won his first Best Director Oscar in 2003 for *The Pianist*, which he could not accept in person because he is still a fugitive. Polanski now lives in France with his wife, French actress Emmanuelle Seigner, and their two children.

Plot Overview

Jake Gittes, a former cop who now specializes in divorce investigations, meets a woman pretending to be the wife of Hollis Mulwray, the chief engineer of the Los Angeles Water and Power Company. Claiming that people have seen Hollis with another woman, she asks Jake to investigate her husband's alleged infidelity.

Jake begins his investigation by listening to testimony at a public hearing for a proposed dam and reservoir. Though the city is suffering through a drought, Hollis opposes the project, sending the audience into an angry uproar. One man accuses Hollis of being paid to steal water. Jake then trails Hollis, who spends most of the day checking out the city's water supplies. Later, Jake takes photos of Hollis embracing a blond woman, which he gives to his client. Without Jake's knowledge, the newspaper prints the photographs the next day.

This event brings the real Mrs. Evelyn Mulwray into his office, where she threatens to sue Jake for ruining her husband's name. Jake attempts to find Hollis at his office but is instead escorted out by the chief deputy engineer, Russ Yelburton, and his assistant, Claude Mulvihill. Jake then drives to the Mulwray mansion to convince Evelyn that he was set up along with her husband, and she quickly agrees to drop the proposed lawsuit. When Jake demands to talk to Hollis, Evelyn suggests he look for him at Oak Pass Reservoir. By the time Jake arrives, the police have already discovered Hollis's drowned body in the empty reservoir. Later, Jake investigates a dry riverbed where another drowning death occurred and meets a Mexican boy who tells Jake that he once reported to Hollis about the periodic flooding of the supposedly dry waterway.

That night, Jake returns to the reservoir where the police found Hollis's body. He hears two gunshots—the signal to open the sluice—and jumps into an empty run-off channel for cover. Jake nearly drowns when water comes coursing down the channel but manages to scramble to safety. He then comes across Mulvihill, who threatens Jake for trespassing. Mulvihill pins Jake's arms back while an unnamed hoodlum slices Jake's nostril open with a knife and warns him to stay off the case.

Later, Jake meets with Evelyn and accuses her of hiding something. He tells her that Hollis was murdered because he discovered that portions of the city's water supply were being dumped into run-off channels in order to create a drought and build support for the new reservoir.

The next day, Jake returns to Yelburton's office. There, a secretary tells him that a man named Noah Cross once owned the city's entire water supply, but his business partner Hollis Mulwray persuaded him to turn it over to the city. Jake accuses Yelburton of arranging both the pictures and Hollis's death. Yelburton denies these claims, but suggests that some water is being diverted to irrigate orange groves in the San Fernando Valley, outside of the city limits.. Jake then returns to his own office, where Evelyn officially hires him to find out who killed her husband. Jake also reveals that he knows her father is Noah Cross, a revelation that makes Evelyn visibly nervous. Evelyn explains her nervousness by saying that her father and Hollis had a falling out over the Water Department, but she unintentionally hints that their disagreement may have had something to do with herself as well.

Jake meets with Cross, who abruptly asks Jake if he has slept with Evelyn, which he has not. Cross then probes Jake for information, finally hiring him to find Hollis's missing girlfriend. Later, in the Hall of Records, Jake discovers that farmland is being sold rapidly in the Valley's drought area. Jake drives into the Valley, where a farmer confesses that, rather than secretly irrigating the farm, officials from the city regularly come in to poison his water and blow up his tanks. Jake realizes that Cross and the land speculators have been fabricating the drought in order to force farmers into quickly selling their land at low prices. After the dam Hollis opposed is built, the area will become fertile again and Cross and the other new landowners will be able to sell the land at an enormous profit.

Jake tells Evelyn Mulwray what he has learned about this scheme, and the two discover that Cross and his associates at the Albacore Club, a private association of the wealthy and powerful, are hiding the scheme by purchasing the land in the name of the residents of a local rest home of which they are benefactors. Returning to the Mulwray home, Jake and Evelyn wind up in bed together. While lying there,, Evelyn receives a phone call and leaves the house suddenly. Jake secretly trails her to an unfamiliar house, where the young blond woman he saw earlier with Hollis is lying on a bed, apparently restrained. Jake confronts Evelyn about the woman, and Evelyn says that she is her sister.

The next morning, Lieutenant Escobar of the Los Angeles Police Department finds the fraudulent Mrs. Mulwray (an actress named Ida Sessions) dead and accuses Jake of withholding evidence that proves Evelyn killed her husband. Escobar tells Jake that Hollis was found with saltwater in his lungs, suggesting that his body was moved to the freshwater reservoir. Jake returns to the Mulwray mansion, where he learns that a backyard pool is filled with salt water, and he finds that it contains a pair of broken glasses. Jake deduces that Evelyn drowned Hollis in the pond. He rushes to the house where Evelyn is hiding her sister. There, he sees Evelyn packing hurriedly. Jake calls the police and confronts Evelyn with his theory, showing her the broken glasses.

Evelyn denies everything but finally confesses the secret she's kept throughout the movie: the blond girl, Katherine, is really her daughter *as well as* her sister, the result of an incestuous relationship Evelyn had with her father, Noah Cross. Evelyn claims that Cross had Hollis killed because Hollis and Evelyn tried to keep him away from Katherine. Evelyn points out that the broken glasses were not Hollis's, as Hollis did not wear bifocals, and Jake deduces that they must have belonged to Cross. Jake decides to help Evelyn and Katherine escape, suggesting they hide in Chinatown, his former beat and the site of many bad memories for Jake. After leading the police away from Evelyn's true location, Jake arranges for a former client to smuggle Evelyn and Katherine out of Chinatown and into Mexico.

Jake arranges a final showdown with Cross at the Mulwray mansion, showing him evidence of both the land grab and the murder. Mulvihill, who accompanied Cross, holds a gun to Jake's head and forces him to lead them to Chinatown and the girl. Cross finds the pair on the verge of escaping and pleads with Evelyn to hand Katherine over to him. Instead, Evelyn pulls a gun on Cross, shooting him in the arm before attempting to flee with Katherine in their car. The police, ignoring Jake's claims that Cross is the true criminal, fire on the car and end up killing Evelyn. Cross then takes Katherine away, and Lieutenant Escobar orders the stunned Jake to go home.

CHARACTER LIST

J. J. (Jake) Gittes—Played by Jack Nicholson   A quiet, hard-boiled detective and the movie's protagonist. An intelligent man who alternates between crass jokes and politeness, Jake possesses an inherent honesty that leaves him unable to comprehend the full scope of other people's treachery. He is a former cop whose involvement in the Mulwray case echoes a tragic but largely unexplained incident he was involved in when he worked the Chinatown beat as a police officer.

Evelyn Cross Mulwray—Played by Faye Dunaway   The wife of Hollis Mulwray, daughter of Noah Cross, and major foil for Jake Gittes. A wealthy, elegant woman, Evelyn's cool exterior hides an all-consuming desperation to protect her daughter, Katherine Cross, and hide the truth about Katherine's birth. Evelyn cares for Jake but not enough to tell him the truth.

Noah Cross—Played by John Huston   The father of Evelyn and Katherine and the major antagonist of the movie. A wealthy, well-known man, Cross's affable front masks a sociopath who believes that no law, either legal or moral, applies to him. His crimes range from incest to land fraud to murder, all of which he commits without compunction or remorse.

Hollis Mulwray—Played by Darrell Zwerling   The thin, serious chief engineer of the Los Angeles Water and Power Company. Once Noah Cross's partner, Hollis is concerned about the city's well being and, despite heavy pressure, refuses to build another dam that could injure people. He wants to do what is right, taking care of both Evelyn and Katherine and attempting to unravel the land fraud.

Katherine Cross—Played by Belinda Palmer   The daughter of Noah Cross and Evelyn Cross Mulwray. Katherine is a fragile creature long protected from the outside world. As Evelyn's secret, she is seen only at a distance for most of the movie.

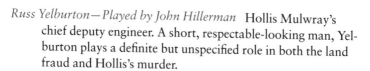

Russ Yelburton—Played by John Hillerman Hollis Mulwray's chief deputy engineer. A short, respectable-looking man, Yelburton plays a definite but unspecified role in both the land fraud and Hollis's murder.

Lieutenant Lou Escobar—Played by Perry Lopez A lieutenant in the Los Angeles Police Department. Lou once worked with Jake in Chinatown and was involved in the tragic incident there that haunts Jake throughout the movie. He fails either to believe or to do anything about the full scope of the corruption Jake uncovers.

Claude Mulvihill—Played by Roy Jenson A large, sloppily dressed man who works as Yelburton and Cross's hired muscle. Mulvihill was once the sheriff of Ventura County, outside of Los Angeles. Jake is convinced that Mulvihill is and was corrupt and insults him at every opportunity.

Ida Sessions—Played by Diane Ladd A red-haired, slightly worn-looking actress hired by Noah Cross to pose as Mrs. Mulwray. Ida is practical-minded and possessed of a strong self-interest. Cross has her killed when the police get too close to her.

Detective Loach—Played by Dick Bakalyan Lieutenant Escobar's partner. A short, slender man who regularly defers to Escobar, Loach dislikes Jake and seems to know something about Escobar and Jake's past in Chinatown.

Man with Knife—Played by Roman Polanski The short, jumpy hoodlum who slices Jake's nose. The character's name is often seen as an allusion to Polanski's first feature film, *Knife in the Water*.

Lawrence Walsh—Played by Joe Mantell An older, bespectacled man working as an associate of Jake's. A careful and thorough detective, Walsh makes few assumptions and in the process often catches details and bits of information that Jake misses.

CHINATOWN

Kahn—Played by James Hong Evelyn Mulwray's butler. A stern-looking Chinese man, Kahn watches over Katherine at the safe house and attempts to help Evelyn and Katherine hide out in Chinatown.

Morty—Played by Charles Knapp A rotund, jovial coroner with a persistent cough. Even when presented with contrary evidence, Morty is willing to accept without question that the drowning deaths were accidental.

Duffy—Played by Bruce Glover Another associate of Jake's. An average-faced man often seen in a hat, Duffy does legwork on the case but has few speaking lines.

Curly—Played by Burt Young A fisherman who hires Jack for an earlier, unrelated case. Curly is an easily influenced man who is losing his hair early. Jake asks Curly late in the film to help smuggle Evelyn and Katherine out of the city.

Mulwray's secretary—Played by Fritzi Burr An older, pinch-lipped woman. Mulwray's secretary is highly disapproving of Jake throughout the movie.

Sophie—Played by Nandu Hinds Jake's young, attractive, and efficient secretary. Sophie's calmness in dealing with both the cases and Jake himself suggests a significant degree of tolerance for the less savory aspects of life.

Analysis of Major Characters

J. J. (Jake) Gittes

Like the film noir detectives that came before him, Jake exhibits some of the common traits of a hard-boiled private investigator. He appreciates crass jokes, shows a willingness to get violent with both men and women who cause him trouble, and never lets physical threats scare him off a case. Unlike the traditional private eye, however, Jake can be disarmingly human. Though he isn't scared by physical threats, he is susceptible to them and spends a good portion of the film wearing a large nose bandage. He starts the movie reluctant to take on a job he feels won't satisfy a client. Unlike most Hollywood private eyes, Jake tends to be wrong more often than he is right, missing important information and putting clues together incorrectly.

The element that brings depth to Jake's character is his odd inability to comprehend the larger picture. Nicholson subtly weaves in this shortcoming as his character develops, mainly through tantalizingly vague references to Chinatown, where the corrupt stay corrupt and everyone is supposed to look away. Jake was never very good at looking away, no matter how much trouble it caused him. Sadly, this also tends to cause trouble for other people, especially Evelyn Mulwray. Jake is a man perpetually in over his head.

Evelyn Cross Mulwray

In the classic tradition of film noir women, Faye Dunaway portrays Evelyn Mulwray as a person defined entirely by the secret she keeps. Her secret dictates the paced, careful precision with which she speaks, suggesting that every word is internally monitored before being let out into the world. It is also the reason Evelyn is so inwardly focused and distant and explains why she is so quick to take offense at even the most casual of personal comments. The moments when this shell cracks move the character beyond the genre cliché. Evelyn does not hide her secret as well as she thinks she does, and she occasionally lets her control slip. Tear-stained and lost, she seems desperate for a guide or protector in place of the father who betrayed her trust. At times, she reflects her fragile, hidden daughter Katherine.

During a brief window of time with Jake, Evelyn transforms into a woman who has had little chance to enjoy life. Through their encounters and brief romance she manages to reveal both quick thinking and a sense of humor. Evelyn craves the intimacy with Jake that she has often denied herself, both through sex and through wanting to hear more about his past. Ultimately, this urge is not strong enough to overcome the secret that dominates her life.

NOAH CROSS

On the surface, Noah Cross appears to be a pleasant, jovial man. His speech is easy and untroubled, and his facial expressions remain open and friendly no matter what he's saying. He has a knowing, faintly chauvinistic charm and a ready smile that manages to avoid any trace of psychosis or cruelty. As we discover, however, this harmless, appealing exterior renders the inner, sociopathic nature that it hides all the more frightening. Cross feels that neither society's laws nor the basic laws of human decency should apply to him, and he treats human life with contempt. When asked about the rape of his daughter, he blames his actions on the depths of depravity people are capable of sinking to, but he gives the explanation with such utter calmness that it's clear he doesn't feel that he's lowered himself at all. If Cross has a basic drive beyond self-interest, it is his need to control everything around him. From the town's water supply to the profitable valley land to Evelyn's and Katherine's innocence, anything he feels might have value must be firmly in his possession.

THEMES, MOTIFS, AND SYMBOLS

THEMES

THE DISHONESTY OF AUTHORITY FIGURES

Chinatown suggests that the very notion of an honest, trustworthy leader is a myth. In *Chinatown*, people in positions of power are never what they seem to be, and their true nature is always harmful to the people beneath them. Cross, who has no official power but who has used his money to essentially run most of the city and the outlying area, uses the people he controls as pawns for his personal gain. The district attorney in Chinatown is legendary for his instruction that the police ignore any crime that is committed. Russ Yelburton, a polite, highly respectable family man, manipulates the public for personal gain and is involved in the slandering and murder of his boss. Even Lieutenant Escobar, a man whom Jake has worked with and respects, is willing to let injustice occur without punishing the people who brought it to pass. In the world of *Chinatown*, anyone with any authority becomes a mere cog in a machine that maintains corruption.

THE CORRUPTION OF THE AMERICAN DREAM

One basic element of the American dream is the idea that common people can move into unclaimed wilderness and transform it into valuable land. Water, and the irrigation systems that provide it, first helped the American West blossom into the rich and thriving area it is it is today. Cross calls Hollis Mulwray a genius for using water to help turn Los Angeles from a wasted patch of desert into an ever growing metropolis. Cross, however, turns this approach into an excuse for murder, killing Hollis when he interferes with Cross's plans for the new reservoir. Similarly, Russ Yelburton is persuaded to betray both the public and a man he admires in order to gain greater control of the water.

Part of the allure of America is its promise of success for the common person, the chance to control one's own destiny with the help of available resources. Cross, however, corrupts the American dream by stealing the most valuable of resources from the struggling farmers, pushing them into bankruptcy in an attempt to further line the pockets of his already rich associates. *Chinatown* shows the promise of America's future betrayed by the desires of its corrupt present.

THE HELPLESSNESS OF COMMON PEOPLE IN THE FACE OF EVIL

No matter how good a character is or how noble his or her intentions are, Polanski is careful to show how impossible it is for the common people to overcome or even escape the corruption that is so pervasive in the world of the film and the world itself. Unlike what Jake and so many other characters tell themselves, corruption isn't confined to just one area. Jake, who years before lost a woman to evil forces in Chinatown, loses Evelyn in nearly the same manner. Evelyn, despite her money and earlier flight from her father, proves unable to run far or fast enough to escape death. Hollis, who tried to free himself from evil by cutting ties to Cross, nevertheless loses his life to his former business associate.

MOTIFS

IGNORANCE

Many of the people in *Chinatown* claim ignorance of the corruption that surrounds them, often with tragic results. Throughout the movie, Jake remains stubbornly incapable of putting the pieces of the case together properly. Evelyn pretends to know nothing about the woman her husband is seeing, in the process keeping information from Jake that may have saved her life. Ida Sessions professes her ignorance to the full scope of the crime she helped commit and therefore cannot see that she is in deep enough to be murdered. At the end of the movie, Jake naïvely tells Evelyn to "[l]et the police handle" it, only to discover that the way they handle it is to kill Evelyn. As Polanski demonstrates, being ignorant of the crime that surrounds you offers no protection from its ravages.

MISIDENTIFICATION

Jake makes several key misidentifications throughout the movie. This inability to see the truth beneath the surface of things serves only to drag him further into the conspiracy. First, he believes Ida Sessions to be Evelyn Mulwray and accepts the case to follow her husband, a decision that leads to his disastrous involvement with Cross and the land conspiracy. Later, he is unable to recognize

Detective Loach as the man who tells him to go to Ida Sessions' house, a mistake that leads to Evelyn's death. Most important, though, he is unable to see Evelyn as the victim she truly is rather than the murderer he believes her to be, a waste of his attention and resources that leaves him unable to solve the case in time.

Haunted Pasts

Most of the characters in the movie have some dark shame or secret haunting their past, a situation that on a larger scale echoes the hidden corruption of the world in which they live. When people live too long in a city with deep-rooted darkness, they will naturally end up with a bit of it in themselves. Some past misfortunes, like the dam Hollis Mulwray built that later collapsed and killed people, show that even innocent mistakes bring about deadly consequences. Others, like Hollis's former partnership with Cross, show that even good people are capable of being involved with corruption, while Evelyn Mulwray's rape and resulting child show how innocent people can be dragged into helping cover up such corruption. Jake's past and his inability to protect the nameless woman in Chinatown repeats itself to show how impossible it is to escape the evil nature, or tendency toward evil, inherent in many people.

Symbols

Chinatown

Chinatown, a place where secret organizations rule, the law is meaningless, and good intentions are brutally suppressed, serves as the symbol for the true nature of every city. Corruption not only exists but has become so much a part of the way societies work that even good men like Lieutenant Escobar do not attempt to fight it. Noble leadership is a lie, civic leaders like Yelburton are willing to do anything to the public in order to line their pockets, and men like Cross are above the law.

Jake's Bandage

The injury Jake sustains at the reservoir serves as a symbol for Jake's limited heroism. While the typical movie hero quickly shakes off an attack, Jake wears the marks of his injury throughout most of the film. The bandage portrays Jake as subject to human frailty and fallibility. Jake deflects questions about the injury with sarcasm, echoing the way he uses his cynicism and occasional crassness to hide his sense of decency. The scene where Jake and Evelyn sleep together begins with Evelyn tending his injury, suggesting that this sign of weakness is in fact what makes Jake appealing.

THE SALTWATER POND

The saltwater pond serves as a symbol of the inherent duality of human existence. On one level, the saltwater pool found in the Mulwrays' back yard is a source of life, a duplicate of an ocean tidal pool that supports a variety of plants and creatures. On another level, the pool brings about death, slowly seeping outward to poison the surrounding grass and any other plant incapable of tolerating the salt. The pool was also used to bring about a much quicker death when Noah Cross drowned Hollis Mulwray in it, filling Hollis's lungs with the deadly salt water. The duality inherent in the water serves as a symbol for corruption, showing it both as the means by which a city lives and grows and as a spreading disease that taints everything it comes in contact with. Like the grass, anything that cannot adapt to the corrupt environment is eventually destroyed.

FILM ANALYSIS

THE ENDING

Chinatown's most innovative scene is its ending. In this final scene, Polanski and the cast use a variety of techniques to make the audience feel as though it is actually experiencing the unfolding tragedy. The night setting serves as an echo of the city's pervasive corruption and creates an odd intimacy as the characters gather in the available light. The camera remains consistently at eye level, with few sudden jumps and no extreme close-ups, mimicking the vision of someone actually standing alongside the characters. Some shots are framed by characters' shoulders and the sides of heads, creating the feeling that we are in the middle of the crowd onscreen.

Jake, whom the audience has come to identify with over the course of the movie, is denied the successful conclusion often expected of a film's protagonist. He is forced to betray the woman he was trying to protect, and when Jake attempts to fulfill his traditional role as the cinematic private detective and explain the case he has just solved to the authorities, he is entirely ignored. Because Jake's attempts to explain the truth are so ineffectual and so frequently interrupted, and because Cross is so effective and composed, the audience momentarily loses its identification with Jake's point of view, identifying instead with the corrupt social structure itself. Jake's arguments are desperate, clearly those of a man who knows he holds the weaker ground, while Cross speaks calmly and warmly, as if his sincerity and truthfulness are givens.

Cross is more implacable than ever in this scene. Even when talking to Escobar, his eyes scan continually for any sign of Evelyn and Katherine, zeroing in on them almost immediately. Cross never raises his voice to Evelyn, even when she shoots him in the arm, because he knows he does not need to. He tells Evelyn that the only way to keep him from getting what he wants is to kill him, a release that Polanski never provides. Instead, the movie ends with Cross gathering Katherine up and spiriting her away, achieving a victory that should have belonged to Jake.

The way Cross finally triumphs is the most devastating part of the scene. Escobar lifts a gun to shoot at Evelyn's car as she drives away and Jake performs the seemingly heroic act of wresting the weapon from him, attempting for a moment to take back the control denied him throughout the movie. Jake's mistake, though, becomes apparent moments later. Escobar shot twice at the sky and even afterward only aimed for the car's wheel, clearly intent on interrupting the getaway in the safest way possible. Loach, however, fires into the car—intentionally or not—and Evelyn is killed, shot through the head and eye. The car rolls to a stop as Evelyn's head falls on the horn, blaring it just as she did earlier in the movie, outside of the safe house with Jake. The image of her destroyed eye is the culmination of the film's assault on the expectations of the viewer.

ACTING

Even those critics who were unimpressed with the film were united in their praise of Jack Nicholson's performance as Detective Jake Gittes. The character's cynicism, world-weariness, and slightly sleazy disposition and habits were drawn straight from classic film noir detectives and the novels that inspired those films. Unlike the constant, cool self-assurance of Humphrey Bogart's Sam Spade in the celebrated film noir *The Maltese Falcon*, Nicholson plays Gittes as a man in over his head.

In fact, much of Jake's anger and determination come from his frustrated realization of just how lost he truly is. Nicholson made the infamous bandage, a disfigurement many actors wouldn't have risked, into a steadying force for Jake. The violence of the knife attack is something he can at least understand and respond to appropriately. Nicholson has a very human approach to the role, the pinnacle of which is his decision to imbue Jake with a stubborn optimism and sense of decency that survive despite his profession and his prior experience in Chinatown. His actions in the final scene are startling and powerfully effective, leaving the viewer with affection for Jake despite his baser tendencies.

Faye Dunaway's portrayal of Evelyn Mulwray is firmly rooted in the film noir tradition of mysterious and beautiful heroines, though the character departs from the femme fatale model. Most of her actions and dialogue are designed to let Nicholson's character know that she is hiding something from him. Dunaway, however, adds surprising shadings to simple lines. Rather than rely on the distance of cool calculation, Dunaway makes Evelyn's reticence that of pure fear: she is a bad liar in a dangerous situation whose only hope of not saying something dangerous is to say nothing at all. Though she continues in the film noir tradition of sleeping with the detective, the oddly tender scene beforehand makes it clear that the sex is the mutual seduction of two lonely people. The discussion of Jake's past that immediately follows is a quest for emotional intimacy that neatly bookends the moment. Dunaway's portrayal suggests that Evelyn hopes to have found a kindred spirit in Jake. The occasional quaver of her voice and the fragile desperation with which she asks him to come back with her hint at a woman who believes she is just as lost as Jake has become.

John Huston's portrayal of Noah Cross is the film's most electrifying performance. He has less screen time than Nicholson and Dunaway, but he still succeeds in giving his character depth. Noah Cross appears to be a faultlessly personable and charming man, a characterization that sets Huston's interpretation of villainy apart from traditional screen villains. Huston's care to keep his pleasantly wrinkled face and friendly smile unmarred by any shades of baser intent makes Cross's character all the more sinister to viewers as they discover his inherently evil nature. How can someone do what Cross has done, believe the things Cross believes, and still look so innocent? What depth of psychosis does that require? Huston's genius is that the viewer's imagination eclipses an entire film's worth of character analysis, turning a character with a mere handful of scenes into a nightmare incarnate.

HISTORICAL CONTEXT

Robert Towne based the plot of his script on the 1904 Owens River Valley "Land Grab," which took place in the early 1900s. William Mulholland, the head of the newly formed Los Angeles Water Department, and Fred Eaton, then mayor of Los Angeles, believed the city would need more water to continue growing and began to look longingly at the distant Owens River as a viable source. The farmers and ranchers who lived in the valley, however, had their own plans for the river, waiting until the Reclamation Service completed its irrigation project there before they could use the water. Knowing they would need to put a stop to the project if they wanted access to the water, Mulholland and Eaton bribed a local Reclamation Service agent into showing them the necessary plans and then began buying up all the pertinent land and water rights in the Owens Valley area.

Mulholland also manipulated Los Angeles residents by portraying acquisition of the river as being vitally important to the city, when in reality he was using much of the water to irrigate the nearby San Fernando Valley and increase the return on the land investments made there by several of Eaton and Mulholland's friends. All in all, the scandal is an almost perfect portrait of corrupt authority figures manipulating the public under the pretense of the common good. Eaton and Mulholland believed that their power placed them and their personal interests above the law.

Other Inspirations for "Chinatown"

Towne based *Chinatown*'s script on a simple equation: he took an infamous incident in California's history and added to it the tough style and tone of great detective novelists like Raymond Chandler and Dashiell Hammett. Polanski prepared for the movie by reading all of Hammett's works, while Towne had read everything written by both Hammett and Chandler before he began writing his screenplay. Both men were inspired by the books, particularly in their portrait of a long-vanished Los Angeles. Even Polanski, despite his insistence that the movie not merely be an exercise in nostalgia, was insistent that the film convey a scrupulously accurate reconstruction of the decade's décor, costume, and idioms.

Another inspiration was the public's preoccupation with corruption. Though it did not provide any actual material for the script or look of the film, the ongoing scandal of Watergate—another incident that began with a seemingly unimportant crime that later revealed manipulation and cover-ups at a much higher level—had a powerful influence on *Chinatown*'s tone. When added to the brutal, senseless horrors of the Manson murders and the muddied, pointless loss of life in the Vietnam War, the America that flocked to *Chinatown* was much less trusting of authority and the idea of a happy ending than the country had been just a few decades before.

Important Quotations Explained

1.   Man with Knife: "You're a very nosy fellow, kitty cat. Huh? You know what happens to nosy fellows? Huh? No? Wanna guess? Huh? No? Okay. They lose their noses."

Theses are the words the Man with Knife speaks before he slices Jake's nose. These lines are a warning to Jake to stop trespassing at the reservoir, but they serve as a broader warning about looking too fervently for the truth behind appearances. Throughout the film, the audience learns that Jake's problems stem from much more than his willingness to climb over fences. Unlike the majority of characters in the movie, Jake cannot ignore all the corruption around him. From shadowy Chinatown to the brighter areas of Los Angeles, authority figures see the public as something to manipulate and control, killing or beating into submission anyone foolish enough to investigate the larger pattern of corruption. Noah Cross murders Hollis Mulwray because Hollis attempted to unveil the corruption behind the new dam project. Ida Sessions, though initially part of the conspiracy, dies when she oversteps her bounds by talking to Jake. The police shoot Evelyn Mulwray, who led a silent yet relatively safe existence during the previous fifteen years, only after Jake intrudes on her life. Jake suffers a more subtle punishment, living with the knowledge that he not only failed to protect Evelyn but, through his *nosiness*, caused her death.

2.   Noah Cross: "'Course I'm respectable. I'm old. Politicians, ugly buildings, and whores all get respectable if they last long enough."

Though Noah Cross is talking about himself during his lunch with Jake at the Albacore Club, the line also pertains to everyone who holds a position of power in the film. The Albacore Club serves as a perfect example. Though the club is a front for large-scale corruption, the public sees only a gentlemen's social club of long standing that gives generously to those in need.. Similarly, the Water Department, which is actually engineering the drought it is supposed to be fighting, is seen as an organization that has helped Los Angeles grow from the desert into the city it is today. The district attorney in Chinatown, a pawn of shadowy organizations who teaches the police to ignore the crimes they're supposed to protect the people from, has become firmly entrenched in a position of power and respect.

This line also addresses the public's willingness to give respect and admiration to organizations simply because they've become used to them. Given enough time and regular exposure, people will let even the most shocking deeds become a part of their landscape, allowing those who practice such activities total freedom from interference. Neither the death of her first boss nor a detective coming to question her second boss makes Russ Yelburton's secretary doubt the practices of a venerable institution like the Water Department. In the final scene, the police immediately believe the older, well-established Noah Cross over the younger, less successful Jake. Even Lieutenant Escobar, a basically honest man, ignores the corruption. He treats power with reverence, not questioning Cross and instead warning Jake to leave for his own good because Escobar knows that corruption has been going on too long for anyone to put an end to it.

3. EVELYN: "She's my daughter."
    [*Gittes slaps Evelyn.*]
    GITTES: "I said I want the truth!"
    EVELYN: "She's my sister. . . ."
    [*slap*]
    EVELYN: "She's my daughter. . . ."
    [*slap*]
    EVELYN: "My sister, my daughter."
    [*More slaps.*]
    GITTES: "I said I want the truth!"
    EVELYN: "She's my sister AND my daughter!"

This exchange, which occurs after Jake confronts Evelyn with what he thinks is the truth, works on several levels. First, the unexpected violence of the scene comes as a shocking payoff for the tension in the film between Jake's frustration and Evelyn's secret. Second, it shows Jake's willingness to use violence against women. In Jake we see a glimpse of the darkness Cross embraces, as well as a sincere remorse when Jake realizes how wrong his actions have been. Third, the dialogue shows the complicated nature of truth. In this scene

Jake is convinced that Evelyn is lying to him, when in fact she has already told him the truth: Katherine is indeed Evelyn's sister. The near desperation with which Jake pushes Evelyn to confess is an expression of his fears and anxieties about being completely lost amidst the lies that surround him. Jake's anger at Evelyn's response comes not just from her reticence, but from the way her answer transforms the exit he has created for himself into another turn in the investigation.

4.   NOAH CROSS: "You see, Mr. Gittes, most people never have to face the fact that at the right time and right place, they're capable of anything."

This is the explanation Noah Cross gives Jake during their final confrontation at the Mulwray mansion. This line suggests there is evil in everyone's heart and that given the right provocation, anyone is capable of committing a heinous crime. But on a deeper level, Cross doesn't mean what he says in the slightest. The calm and even tone of Cross's voice suggests that he sees his actions as reasonable and understandable indulgences—an even more sinister facet of his character.

Cross's words are applicable to many of the conflicted characters in the film. Russ Yelburton, a family man with a good job, is driven to cover up the murder of a man he genuinely liked in the name of greater ambition. Though Ida Sessions swore she didn't know Hollis Mulwray would end up dead, she certainly knew an innocent man would be ruined. Nonetheless, she helped with the scheme for her own financial gain. Evelyn keeps Katherine a virtual prisoner in the name of protecting her, and Jake himself abuses an innocent woman. Lieutenant Escobar, who seems to have as great a dislike for Chinatown as Jake does, helps carry the area's rules beyond its borders by not attempting to question Cross.

5.   WALSH: "Forget it, Jake. It's Chinatown."

This line from the final scene, which Walsh speaks in a sympathetic voice as he leads Jake away from Evelyn's dead body, sums up one of the film's major themes. Throughout the film, several characters suggest that Chinatown is a place to be avoided at all costs. Chinatown is a place where corruption is the status quo and where regular people are forced into silence. Walsh suggests that Evelyn and Jake knew the rules when they went to Chinatown and should have known the story would end as it did. The best Jake can do is regret his foolish mistake and leave as soon as possible.

The spirit of Chinatown is everywhere in Los Angeles. The city's subtly treacherous new chief engineer, Russ Yelburton, is a fair match for Chinatown's more openly corrupt district attorney. Evelyn Mulwray is just as vulnerable to abuse by powerful men as was the woman Jake once knew in Chinatown.

ONE FLEW OVER THE CUCKOO'S NEST

(1975)

CONTEXT

One Flew Over the Cuckoo's Nest (1975) is perhaps the best-known antiauthority film in history. The film's director, Milos Forman, was well acquainted with repressive authority, having experienced it firsthand for much of his life. Born outside of Prague, Czechoslovakia, in 1932, Forman lost both his parents to the Nazi death camps of World War II. When he began making films in the mid-1960s, a brief flourish of Czech political and artistic freedom allowed him to explore daily life through satire, and he helped develop what the French call *cinéma vérité* (truthful cinema), an influential style based on realism and lacking traditional heroes. Forman's *Loves of a Blonde* was nominated for an Academy Award for Best Foreign Language Film in 1966, and his *Fireman's Ball* received the same recognition in 1967. However, communist authorities labeled *Fireman's Ball* as a threat and banned the film. One year later, while Forman was visiting Paris, the Soviet Union invaded Czechoslovakia. Forman never returned to his homeland, but the image of Soviet tanks rolling into his country continued to haunt him and echoes throughout his work on *One Flew Over the Cuckoo's Nest*.

Based on the popular 1962 novel by Ken Kesey, *One Flew Over the Cuckoo's Nest* initially was adapted as a Broadway play. Its star, Kirk Douglas, bought the film rights and tried unsuccessfully for twelve years to generate interest from Hollywood in making the movie. When he felt too old to play the role of the protagonist, McMurphy, Douglas assigned the rights to his son, Michael. After securing private financing, Michael Douglas coproduced the film with Saul Zaentz of Fantasy Records. They went on to earn Oscars as producers—a first for Michael Douglas—when *One Flew Over the Cuckoo's Nest* won the Academy Award for Best Picture of 1975.

The producers chose Forman as director for his ability to capture the concerns of the times. His American film debut, *Taking Off* (1971), was a comedy about the lack of understanding between young people and their parents. The generation gap was a popular theme in the 1960s and 1970s, as the American people, especially young people, began questioning all manners of authority, old-fashioned institutions, and the social status quo. The civil rights movement and the anti–Vietnam War protests of the 1960s morphed into the campus demonstrations, violent antidraft protests, and women's liberation movement of the 1970s. In a particularly transforming event of the times, National Guardsmen opened fire on student protesters at Kent State University in 1970, following a rock-throwing incident, and killed four students. A few years later, American faith in authority was further shaken by the Watergate break-in and subsequent cover-up, which led to the resignation of President Richard Nixon in 1974. *One Flew Over the Cuckoo's Nest,* in its antiauthority stance, resonated strongly with these and other events of the 1970s. Pauline Kael, movie critic for *The New Yorker*, said that the film came along when the right metaphor for the human condition was a loony bin.

Nearly all the top U.S. film critics gave the film positive reviews, heaping particular praise on Jack Nicholson's portrayal of McMurphy. Their reservations related to the film's simplification of themes in Kesey's novel. Kesey, for his part, never wanted to see the film. He was so upset by the film's choice not to use another character, Chief Bromden, as narrator of the story that he sued the producers. Nonetheless, the film succeeded with the public at the box office: made with a budget of $3 million, *Cuckoo's Nest* grossed $112 million after release. At the 1975 Academy Awards, the film won the five top honors—Best Picture, Best Director (Milos Forman), Best Actor (Jack Nicholson), Best Actress (Louise Fletcher), and Best Adapted Screenplay (Bo Goldman and Lawrence Hauben). It was the first film to sweep the top five Oscars since 1934's *It Happened One Night.*

Although Louise Fletcher's portrayal of Nurse Ratched proved Oscar-worthy, many of Hollywood's leading actresses, including Jane Fonda, Anne Bancroft, Ellen Burstyn, Faye Dunaway, Geraldine Page, and Angela Lansbury, had turned down the role. The character of Nurse Ratched may have been unattractive because both Kesey's novel and the Broadway play portrayed her as a castrating female determined to rob men of their masculinity—a stereotype to which the women's liberation movement of the 1970s objected. However, when the film was being made, the screenwriters, producers, director, and actress together altered the portrayal of Nurse Ratched into a broader figure of institutional authority without such sexist overtones. When Fletcher, in her first starring role, earned an Oscar for her portrayal of Nurse Ratched, some of those who declined the role admitted they had made a career mistake. Fletcher furnished one of the award ceremony's most memorable moments when she used sign language to thank her deaf parents.

Although Milos Forman's work is filled with people injured by society, he often relies upon humor to portray the ordinary humanity of these damaged souls. In *One Flew Over the Cuckoo's Nest*, he presents the inmates of a mental hospital as quirky and funny in the midst of outrage. Forman's characters are individual human beings capable of displaying great dignity. He relies upon techniques from his roots in *cinéma vérité* to create the look and feel of reality—an especially noteworthy approach in light of the fact that the novel is quite hallucinatory and the stage play used a surrealistic set design to underscore the madness. Forman set the story in a real mental institution in Oregon, cast the institution's administrator as the doctor in the film, and used actual patients as extras. In the pivotal role of Chief Bromden, Forman cast a nonactor, a full-blooded member of the Creek tribe working as a park ranger near Salem. Through realism, humor and humanism, Forman transforms the story to better express the tenor of its time.

Following his success with *Cuckoo's Nest,* Forman directed the film version of the popular counterculture musical *Hair* (1979), followed by *Ragtime* (1981), *Amadeus* (1984), *Valmont* (1989), *The People vs. Larry Flynt* (1996), and *Man on the Moon* (1999). Although *Amadeus* won eight Oscars in 1984, including Best Picture and another Best Director award for Forman, critics generally acknowledge *One Flew Over the Cuckoo's Nest* to be his foremost work. In November 1977, the American Film Institute voted it into its Top Ten of America's Best Films, along with *Casablanca, Gone With the Wind*, and *Citizen Kane*.

PLOT OVERVIEW

Nurse Ratched, in a black cape, walks into a locked ward of sleeping men. The first order of the day is medication, and the men line up at the nurse's station to take their pills while the phonograph plays a soporiphic waltz. Like a burst of outside air, McMurphy arrives at the institution flanked by two guards. When they remove his handcuffs, he kisses one of the guards in sheer exuberance, cackling and bouncing with joy at being free.

On the ward, Nurse Ratched initially ignores McMurphy while she deals bureaucratically with his paperwork. McMurphy introduces himself to the Chief, a huge deaf-mute man sweeping the hall, then to Billy Bibbit—a stuttering mental patient with a fixation on his mother—and the other patients playing pinochle. McMurphy is loud and rambunctious, luring one patient away from the game with a deck of pornographic playing cards.

Dr. Spivey explores with McMurphy the reason he has been sent to the mental hospital from the prison work farm, where he was held previously. The doctor asks McMurphy whether he is faking mental illness to get out of work, and McMurphy admits slyly that he believes there is nothing wrong with his mind.

At McMurphy's first group therapy session, he riffles his cards while Nurse Ratched speaks—his first gesture of defiance toward her authority. When the session deteriorates into shouting, Nurse Ratched remains straight-faced, impassively reacting at the group's dysfunction. Later, she watches disapprovingly from a window as McMurphy tries to teach the Chief to play basketball. McMurphy also teaches the men to play blackjack. At one point, annoyed with the loud waltz music being played, he invades the nurse's station to turn it down, thereby coming into direct conflict with Nurse Ratched, as patients are not allowed in the nurse's station.

McMurphy's conflict with Nurse Ratched erupts further during the World Series, when McMurphy proposes that Nurse Ratched revise the work schedule so the prisoners can watch the baseball games on television. She argues that the patients would find the change too disruptive. However, she agrees to a vote, knowing that most of the patients lack the courage to oppose her. When only two patients vote on his side, McMurphy is shocked. Later, he boasts to the men that he plans to go downtown to watch the World Series in a bar, betting that he can escape by lifting a marble water fixture and throwing it through the window. When he fails, he says that at least he tried.

The next day in group, Nurse Ratched mercilessly presses Billy Bibbit about a girlfriend, his mother, and his first suicide attempt until Cheswick comes to the hapless Billy's defense. Cheswick joins McMurphy in demanding the World Series, and they force another vote. When all the men in group raise their hands, Nurse Ratched informs them that the "chronics"—the most severe, withdrawn patients—also must vote. McMurphy tries in vain to get any of these catatonic lost souls to respond, and Nurse Ratched adjourns the meeting. Belatedly, the Chief raises his hand to break the tie, but Nurse Ratched refuses to count his vote. Although she appears to have won, McMurphy sits in front of the dark television screen and begins to call the baseball game play-by-play. The other men join him in wonder, cheering imaginary hits and runs under his contagious enthusiasm. Nurse Ratched demands that they stop shouting, but for once she cannot control them.

Dr. Spivey asks McMurphy about his experience on the ward thus far, and McMurphy complains about Nurse Ratched. In response, Dr. Spivey tells McMurphy he sees Nurse Ratched as one of the finest nurses on the ward. Another doctor asks McMurphy how McMurphy's perceptions of Nurse Ratched's unfairness make him feel and what the maxim "moss doesn't grow on a rolling stone" means to him. McMurphy offers his explanation. The conversation ends with McMurphy flippantly showing Spivey a picture of a naked woman from his deck of pornographic cards. He asks Spivey if he knows where the woman lives.

In his frustration at being imprisoned on the ward, McMurphy climbs over the hospital fence with the Chief's help. He hijacks the bus to take the nonrestricted patients on an outing, picking up his girlfriend, Candy, along the way and driving the men to the docks. After boarding a fishing boat, McMurphy introduces the patients to a suspicious harbormaster, claiming that they are doctors from the mental hospital who have chartered the boat for a fishing trip. They motor out of the harbor, and McMurphy teaches Cheswick to drive the boat while the other men learn to fish. Taber catches a monster fish.

When the boat trip is done, the men return to face Dr. Spivey. The doctors decide that McMurphy is dangerous, and although Dr. Spivey wants to send him back to the prison farm, he defers to Nurse Ratched, who thinks McMurphy should stay in the institution.

McMurphy later discovers that this means he is committed for as long as they think he should be—not the mere sixty-eight days left on his prison term.

Nurse Ratched suspends privileges and begins rationing cigarettes. The men question her authority, however, and she starts to lose control of the group. As Cheswick explodes in rage, McMurphy puts his hand through the glass of the nurse's station to retrieve Cheswick's cigarettes. When a fight breaks out between McMurphy and the lead attendant, Washington, the Chief comes to his defense.

In retaliation, Nurse Ratched sends Cheswick, McMurphy, and the Chief to electroshock therapy. As they wait, McMurphy offers the Chief a stick of Juicy Fruit gum, and the Chief thanks McMurphy, proving that he actually can speak and hear. When McMurphy reappears on the ward after his shock treatments, he rolls his eyes back and walks like a zombie to fool the men, then erupts in characteristic laughter to prove once again that he cannot be suppressed or dominated. Privately, however, he confesses to the Chief that he cannot take any more and plans to escape.

McMurphy bribes the night orderly so he can bring his girlfriend, Candy, her friend Rose, and some alcohol into the ward for a party. The men drink, play Christmas music, and dance with the girls. McMurphy removes the keys from the drunken orderly and says goodbye to the men. He invites Billy Bibbit to come with him, but Billy is not ready. Instead, McMurphy arranges for Billy to have sex with Candy, delaying his own escape. Everyone falls asleep, and in the morning Nurse Ratched finds the ward in disarray, with the window hanging open. When she discovers Billy Bibbit naked in bed with Candy, she invokes his mother's name, making him disintegrate with shame. McMurphy tries to make it out the window, but a nurse's scream alerts him that Billy has just committed suicide. McMurphy attacks Nurse Ratched, strangling her until Washington punches him senseless while she gasps for air. The guards take McMurphy away.

The Chief waits for McMurphy to come back to the ward. McMurphy returns in the night, wholly changed: he's become a vegetable with lobotomy scars on both sides of his skull. Saying that he will take McMurphy with him, the Chief smothers his friend with a pillow. Then the Chief lifts the marble water fixture from the floor, throws it through the window, and escapes into the dawn.

CHARACTER LIST

Randle P. McMurphy—Played by Jack Nicholson The cocky convict and rebel-hero of the film. With his wild hair, boundless energy, loud mouth, foul language, pornographic playing cards, ready laugh, and physical courage, McMurphy challenges authority in the mental institution. He encourages the men on the ward to laugh, learn, and stand up for themselves. He gives them playful nicknames: Chezzer, Tabelation, and Hard-on (for Harding). Generosity is his hallmark, and he shares whatever he has—gum, cards, games, fishing, booze, even his girlfriend.

Nurse Ratched—Played by Louise Fletcher The stiff, starched head nurse and antagonist of the film. Nurse Ratched's every physical movement and facial expression is measured and contained: her cap is perfectly white, her voice is polite and controlled, her face is stony, and her expression is unsmiling and cold. Her tightly rolled hairstyle suggests horns, lending a visual weight to her role as McMurphy's enemy. She displays a frightening cruelty, all the more chilling for her calm delivery.

Chief Bromden—Played by Will Sampson The huge Native American mental patient who pushes a broom silently while observing everything that happens in the ward. Everyone thinks the Chief is a deaf-mute, nearly comatose, and unable to interact. His hair is long, his face solemn, and his eyes sad. McMurphy says he is big as a mountain, and he is nearly as silent, solid, and strong.

Billy Bibbit—Played by Brad Dourif A stammering, suicidal young man with a fixation on his mother. Billy is tentative, inhibited, virginal, gentle, and sweet. Long curls fall over his forehead to accentuate his childlike quality. When threatened, he cringes and cowers to make himself smaller, hugging himself into a ball. He attaches himself to McMurphy as a devoted follower.

Harding—Played by William Redfield An intellectual patient who has problems with his wife and his sexuality. The thoughtful, articulate Harding is the leader of the ward until McMurphy appears. He follows the rules, answering Nurse Ratched's questions in group therapy and taking his medication without complaint. He wears a mustache, along with a prissy expression, and loses his self-control only when Taber pokes at him physically or verbally. Nurse Ratched feels especially threatened when even the obedient Harding begins to side with McMurphy.

Cheswick—Played by Sydney Lassick An anxious, fretful patient whose brow is always wrinkled in concern. With thick glasses framing his worried eyes, the diminutive Cheswick sometimes holds his breath and screws up his features until he looks like he will explode. His sense of fairness is easily frustrated, and he comes to Harding's aid even when Harding rejects Cheswick's assistance. McMurphy trusts Cheswick to drive the boat during their unauthorized fishing trip—before Cheswick can panic, McMurphy calms him by evoking the happiness of childhood as he sings "I'm Popeye the Sailor Man."

Martini—Played by Danny DeVito An inmate with a dim, foolish smile and infantile manner. Although Martini is unable to follow even the simplest rules in a game of cards or Monopoly, he loves to play and is always ready for fun. His mouth twitches and grimaces when Nurse Ratched makes him uncomfortable. Martini is fascinated by McMurphy from the moment McMurphy shows him the deck of dirty cards. Martini provides many of the comic moments of the film and is one of McMurphy's most loyal followers.

Taber—Played by Christopher Lloyd A hostile, belligerent, and profane patient. Taber delights in poking at Harding with ridicule and physical jabs. One of the funniest scenes in the film shows Harding finally getting even with Taber by hiding a lit cigarette in his cuff. When Taber begins to shriek and jerk around, the orderlies think he is having a lunatic fit, but actually his ankle is burning. Taber's long face moves rapidly from confusion to amazement to delight, and it is his series of expressions, as well as his laugh, that ends the film.

Dr. Spivey — Played by Dean R. Brooks   The administrator of the mental institution. Dr. Spivey is a calm, mature, gray-haired doctor. McMurphy plays to Dr. Spivey's vanity, as illustrated by a photo of a prize Chinook salmon on his desk. Dr. Spivey expresses doubt that anything is wrong with McMurphy's mind, but he defers to the opinion of Nurse Ratched, for whom he expresses the highest regard.

Candy — Played by Marya Small   McMurphy's pretty, easygoing girlfriend. The good-natured Candy is willing to go along with all of McMurphy's schemes. She asks the patients on the bus whether they are all crazy but does not judge them when they nod yes. She is gentle and understanding with Billy Bibbit and provides him with his first sexual experience.

Nurse Pilbow — Played by Mimi Sarkisian   The nurse who carries out Nurse Ratched's directives. Attractive and young, Nurse Pilbow shadows Nurse Ratched closely and administers the patients' medications. She wears a pink coat in contrast to Nurse Ratched's black one. She seems to believe that the medication she gives McMurphy is good for him. Unlike Nurse Ratched, Nurse Pilbow shrieks at the unexpected, whether it is McMurphy appearing inside the nurse's station or Billy Bibbit lying with his throat cut.

Orderly Turkle — Played by Scatman Crothers   The night orderly in the mental hospital. Turkle accepts McMurphy's bribes of cash, alcohol, and the promise of a blonde, and he willingly lies to the night supervisor with phony respectfulness. He turns a sly, blind eye to McMurphy and Candy in his eagerness to be with Rose. When he gets caught with a woman by the night supervisor, he gives up all hope of controlling the inmates and drinks himself to sleep.

Attendant Washington — Played by Nathan George   The lead attendant. Washington enforces Nurse Ratched's rules and exercises authority through discipline. He does not mind using force, gladly tightening a strap around his knuckles to threaten McMurphy. He enjoys manhandling the patients and pokes McMurphy with a pole simply to emphasize his authority.

Warren—Played by Mwako Cumbuka The second attendant. Warren's physical presence helps keep the patients in line. He does Nurse Ratched's bidding without comment.

Scanlon—Played by Delos V. Smith Jr. A bushy-haired, heavily bearded patient. Scanlon is a speechless presence during most of the film, so it is surprising when, in a group session, he challenges Nurse Ratched about being locked out of the dormitory.

Sefelt—Played by William Duell A short, quiet patient. Sefelt slips his own medications to his buddy and is the first to spread the rumor that McMurphy has escaped.

Frederickson—Played by Vincent Schiavelli Sefelt's tall, quiet companion. Fredrickson has a lost, loony expression in his dark eyes but laughs eagerly at McMurphy's antics.

Bancini—Played by Josip Elic A tall, quiet patient who repeatedly claims he is tired. Bancini allows McMurphy to ride him like a horse in order to teach the Chief how to shoot a basketball.

Colonel Matterson—Played by Peter Brocco A wheelchair-bound patient, presumably the oldest in the ward. The Colonel is one of the "chronics," who do not interact with others. During McMurphy's Christmas party, Martini decorates the Colonel with ornaments, and he has as much fun as everyone else.

Rose—Played by Louisa Moritz A giggling, blowsy friend of Candy's. Rose helps distract Turkle during the party and later dances with the infantile Martini's head on her breasts.

Night Nurse—Played by Kay Lee The supervisor who investigates the ward on the night of McMurphy's party. The night nurse is an older woman with severe gray hair. Her observant eyes and no-nonsense manner serve as one more reminder that authority watches day and night.

CUCKOO'S NEST

Nurse Itsu—Played by Lan Fendors The nurse who administers McMurphy's electroshock therapy. Nurse Itsu has a beautifully soothing voice and gentle manner at odds with the torture she inflicts.

The Harbormaster—Played by Mel Lambert The authority figure on the dock during McMurphy's fishing escape. The harbormaster turns away from McMurphy's fanciful storytelling with suspicious disbelief and alerts the hospital.

Ellsworth—Played by Dwight Markfield A patient who loves to dance alone in the ward. Only at the party is Ellsworth allowed to dance to his heart's content.

Miller—Played by Alonzo Brown The third and beefiest orderly. Miller is always seen with the other two orderlies, which contributes to the sense that they are not individuals so much as a single arm of authority.

Analysis of Major Characters

Randle P. McMurphy

McMurphy bursts into the staid institution from the outside world—he represents freedom, life, joy, and the power of the individual against a repressive establishment. Not totally likable, however, he is something of a rogue, in custody for statutory rape of an underage girl whom he claims was very willing, and he proves to be a literal pirate, commandeering a fishing boat with joyous disregard for the consequences. McMurphy takes risks to feel alive, and he tries to jar the other patients into embracing life as well. His fishing trip is a celebration rather than a serious attempt to escape. When Candy warns him of its potential consequences, McMurphy laughs, unafraid and fully prepared to be recaptured.

McMurphy is wrong, however, that the worst the authorities can do to him is to return him to the institution—and it is a costly mistake. Compounding his error, he wagers that he can get under Nurse Ratched's skin. But he learns that she controls the length of his sentence and that, in opposing her, he has sacrificed his release. Indeed, sacrifice is one of McMurphy's functions as a Christ figure in the film. He performs miracles of a sort, as he makes the Chief speak and causes Billy to stop stuttering briefly at the end of the film. McMurphy also hosts a kind of Last Supper party for the men before he says goodbye. In the end, rather than save himself, McMurphy fights the forces of evil in Nurse Ratched and pays for it with his life. Yet his soul is never conquered and at the end is released through the Chief's love—a triumph of the spirit over repression and death.

Nurse Ratched

If McMurphy serves as a Christ figure, Nurse Ratched is the Antichrist. She represents authority, conformity, bureaucracy, repression, evil, and death. She enters the ward in the morning wearing a black cape reminiscent of a vampire, as if to suck the lifeblood from the patients. She manages to suck out their spirits by medicating them, numbing them with routine, reminding them of their problems, and denying their individual dignity. McMurphy opposes Nurse Ratched's dark power. When she tries to control him, her methods fail: he willfully spits out her medication and violates the sanctity of her nurse's station. He ignores her version of reality in the dispute over the World Series and riles her enough to raise, uncharacteristically, her carefully modulated voice.

As the film progresses, McMurphy rallies the patients to rebel against Nurse Ratched's authority and question the therapeutic value of her rules. In response, and true to her name, she ratchets up the battle between them with increasing viciousness. Hoping to turn the men against McMurphy, she blames him for taking away the patients' privileges and cigarettes. When that tactic fails, she retaliates with electric shock treatments to deaden his mind and break his spirit. Nurse Ratched fights more furiously after McMurphy's party when she finds her starched white cap—the symbol of her authority—dirty and trampled on the floor. In desperation over the ward's defiance and in an attempt to vanquish McMurphy, she shames Billy Bibbit into committing suicide. Having goaded McMurphy to violence, she justifies the surgical removal of the frontal lobes of his brain, which she assumes to be the source not only of his emotions and reasoning but also of his force and power. Yet even after McMurphy is physically subdued, his influence lives on in defiance of Nurse Ratched. The men now play his games, use his deceptions, speak his language, adopt his nicknames, and whisper legends about him. At the end of the film, Nurse Ratched's insidious control is as damaged as her neck in its brace.

CHIEF BROMDEN

At first, the Chief seems almost a caricature of an old wooden cigar-store Indian, but he grows and changes more than anyone during the course of the film. In the beginning, his defense against Nurse Ratched is complete withdrawal. By pretending to be deaf, he need neither speak nor interact with anyone. Even McMurphy's antics do not initially pierce the Chief's protective façade. The first sign of change comes after McMurphy climbs up the Chief's back and arms in order to escape over the fence. McMurphy's getaway brings a smile to the Chief's face, because he sees for the first time that the outside world may be accessible and that rebellion may be an option.

McMurphy's energy continues to work on the Chief, who begins to reengage with life by responding to events on the ward. In an act Nurse Ratched rightly views as insubordinate, the Chief breaks the tie in favor of McMurphy in the World Series vote. He helps the inmates beat the orderlies in a game of basketball. A further breakthrough toward life and health occurs with the Chief's first words, spoken to McMurphy to thank him not just for the comfort of a stick of gum but also for the example of his courage. Although McMurphy tells the Chief he is as big as a mountain, the Chief himself believes he is too small, too damaged, to escape. However, the Chief grows into his physical strength under McMurphy's care, and when McMurphy returns to the ward lobotomized, the Chief decides he is now big enough to escape with McMurphy—this means he has reached sanity. At the end of the film, the Chief goes out into the world much like the biblical Peter, the follower of Jesus who went on to build the Christian church after the death of Jesus.

BILLY BIBBIT

Although Billy Bibbit longs to be like the heroic McMurphy, he is not strong enough to stand up to Nurse Ratched on his own. Billy entwines his arms and legs when Nurse Ratched questions him, virtually tying himself into knots for her. A shine comes into Nurse Ratched's eyes as she makes him suffer by reminding him of his weakness and his previous suicide attempts. Billy is so timid and fearful that he stutters his own name when he first meets McMurphy. However, McMurphy's confidence and strength immediately charm and fascinate Billy, who becomes a devoted disciple. McMurphy tries to get Billy to realize that he should be out in the world, driving a convertible and having fun with girls. Even though Billy is a voluntary patient who can leave the misery of the ward at any time, he tells McMurphy that he is not ready, because he believes he is not strong enough to face the world. McMurphy encourages Billy's natural longing for girls as a healthy appetite for life. By the time of McMurphy's farewell party, Billy is sufficiently self-assured to embrace Candy in a romantic dance. When Billy confesses to McMurphy his attraction to Candy, he is confessing a desire to be the healthy, normal young man McMurphy has encouraged him to be.

The next morning, after Nurse Ratched finds him in bed with Candy, Billy speaks for the first time without stuttering. The men applaud not only for his confidence and manhood but also for his effrontery of Nurse Ratched's control. Using her voice and the threat of his mother to shame Billy back to subservience, Nurse Ratched forces him to cower at her feet, begging for mercy. Rather than continue living under her repressive rule, Billy chooses suicide, relinquishing life, while simultaneously making an independent decision. Billy acts as the catalyst for the final battle between McMurphy and Nurse Ratched, the forces of good and evil in the film.

THEMES, MOTIFS, AND SYMBOLS

THEMES

CONFORMITY AS A THREAT TO FREEDOM

One Flew Over the Cuckoo's Nest is a film with distinct political undercurrents, which are forcefully presented. When men conform to authoritarian rule, the film argues, they jeopardize not only their physical but also their mental freedom. McMurphy learns that the prison where he was held previously offered greater personal freedom than Nurse Ratched's ward. In prison, he could have watched the World Series, served out his sixty-eight days, and then been free to go. Nurse Ratched's authority, however, extends from the television to the term of McMurphy's commitment, and her authority will not bear rebellion. Under her totalitarian control, McMurphy cannot even be sure what the rules are, for she rigs them to achieve the results she wants. When the men side unanimously with McMurphy the second time they vote on watching the World Series, Nurse Ratched announces calmly that the nine men with their hands up represent only half the ward and therefore are not a majority. The unresponsive patients, the "chronics," do not threaten her control. When the Chief surprises everyone by raising his hand, she tells the jubilant McMurphy that his vote does not count, because the meeting is adjourned. Under authoritarian rule, even the appearance of democracy is subverted to maintain the status quo.

THE CONTRADICTION BETWEEN TYRANNY AND SANITY

As head nurse in a mental institution, Nurse Ratched should be promoting her patients' sanity, but instead her tyranny directly subverts their mental health. She keeps the patients docile, medicated, dependent, and childlike. McMurphy tells the patients they are not loonies but men, and he encourages their manhood through fishing and basketball. The men then begin to ask reasonable questions about Nurse Ratched's authority. Scanlon wants to know why the dormitory is locked during the day. She explains, insidiously, that time spent in the company of others is therapeutic. Cheswick demands the cigarettes she has confiscated and informs her that he is not a little child. Nurse Ratched's oppression, however, causes Cheswick to lose control, and she keeps him in place with electroshock therapy. The men do not improve under her domination but rather disintegrate like Billy Bibbit. Nurse Ratched's reason for keeping McMurphy on the ward, she tells the doctor, is to help him. Instead, she robs him of his vivacity and his sanity.

The Sacred Nature of the Individual

Unlike Nurse Ratched, McMurphy honors and loves the sanctity of individual human beings. He talks to the Chief, even though he thinks the Chief is deaf. He is patient with the babyish Martini, even though he cannot grasp the fundamentals of blackjack. He helps Taber catch a fish and teaches Cheswick to drive a boat. He encourages the Chief to grow through playing basketball. He intervenes on behalf of Cheswick by breaking the glass of the nurse's station to get his cigarettes. He shows his affection for all the men, particularly Billy Bibbit, as he gives Billy the gift of his first sexual encounter, even as McMurphy realizes it will cost him his chance at freedom. In all these ways, McMurphy shows love for the unique, individual nature of each man. When McMurphy's lobotomy robs him of the traits that made him an individual, the Chief returns his love through an act of death and resurrection. The Chief frees McMurphy, affirming that the spirit lives on after the body's death in the minds and behaviors of the living.

MOTIFS

Obstacles to Personal Freedom

The film underscores the loss of personal freedom with recurring patterns of barriers, gates, fences, bars, locks, and shackles. We hear the ward door slam ominously behind Nurse Ratched as the first sound of the movie. We see Bancini locked in overnight restraints. McMurphy first appears in manacles. Throughout the film, faces are filmed behind wire mesh and bars to emphasize the hopelessness of captivity. The glass of the nurse's station represents the barrier between the individual and power—a barrier the patients are forbidden to cross, even though it appears more transparent than bars. McMurphy first crosses the barrier when he attempts it to turn down the music so he can think, but Nurse Ratched escorts him out, unwilling to tolerate independent thought. Later he shoves his hand through the glass, shattering the boundaries maintained by the authoritative state, with dire consequences.

GAMES

Games feature prominently in the film, not solely as a simple pastime but also as an affirmation of life, health, and enjoyment. McMurphy teaches blackjack and basketball, games he sees as manlier than the pinochle and Monopoly the patients play prior to his arrival. Under his coaching, the patients have the empowering experience of beating the orderlies in basketball. Enjoyment is important to McMurphy: for him, driving a boat is fun, fishing is fun, sex is fun, and games of all kinds help the patients feel alive. He tells Martini when he teaches him to fish that he is not a loony but a fisherman. In addition, the World Series take on pivotal importance in McMurphy's battle for life against Nurse Ratched: the baseball games symbolize unity, as the ball players work as a team, and also, as a distinctly American pastime, echo the antiauthoritarian strain in American history.

THE REBEL AS SAVIOR

Repeated references to Jesus draw attention to McMurphy's role as a life-giving savior. The men follow him as disciples. When he is exasperated, McMurphy frequently invokes Jesus. He takes the patients fishing on the sea, in a literal representation of Jesus with his followers. He performs the "miracles" of getting the Chief to speak and Billy Bibbit to stop stuttering. He joins the men in the pool, dunking as if baptized. Because of his rebellion against authority, he suffers for them on the electroshock table. Finally, he sacrifices his own flight to freedom to help Billy Bibbit. Sefelt tells legends about McMurphy's mythic escape just as the disciples spread word of Jesus' resurrection in the Bible. When the Chief kills McMurphy out of mercy, the scene echoes the death, the tomb, and the resurrection that leads to eternal life.

HEARING AS A HUMAN CONNECTION

Many of the film's scenes reflect upon the sense of hearing as a means of understanding and connection among the characters. The Chief pretends to be deaf in order to withdraw from his surroundings, but McMurphy talks to him anyway as a means of establishing a human connection. His affectionate chatter begins to engage the Chief in life once again. On the other hand, the numbing music that Nurse Ratched plays is so loud that McMurphy complains he can't

CUCKOO'S NEST

hear himself think. He tells her the men wouldn't have to shout if she would turn the volume down. Nurse Ratched, however, opposes thinking, understanding, and any other activity that would lead to healthy human relationships between the patients.

SYMBOLS

KEYS

Over and over again, the camera focuses upon keys, and their metallic jingle echoes as the overriding symbol of authority. Nurse Ratched wears her keys on a loop over her arm like a decorative bracelet of power. She leads the men in stretches before group therapy, and her keys provide the only sound as she lifts and drops her arms. The orderlies wear their keys clipped to their belts like pistols at their sides. Orderlies control and discipline the men, and they use their keys to lock them down at night and release them in the morning. For McMurphy, keys are the means to escape. He is able to drive the men away for a fishing trip, because the keys to the bus are in the ignition. He gets Orderly Turkle drunk in order to liberate the keys from his pocket while he sleeps, then uses those keys to open the ward's window, the portal to the world of freedom. As the orderlies drag Billy Bibbit away screaming the next morning, Washington flaunts his power by ordering McMurphy to drop the keys. McMurphy, realizing that Washington means to beat him senseless, slowly and carefully places the keys on the windowsill in admission of his failure to escape the institution's control.

CIGARETTES

In contrast to keys, cigarettes represent freedom. The men use cigarettes as chips in blackjack, each cigarette representing a dime—their only money to spend as they wish. Cigarettes provide the men with a makeshift currency, giving them power to place bets, take risks, and feel like men instead of children. In a climactic scene, Cheswick demands to know why Nurse Ratched has confiscated his cigarettes. She blames McMurphy for running a casino in the tub room and winning all the men's money—a form of personal initiative that defies her authority. She does not want the patients to have the powerful feeling of being in control of their own lives. When Cheswick explodes, he makes clear the importance of his cigarettes, yelling that he is not a little child to have his cigarettes doled out like cookies. His desperation leads McMurphy to shatter the glass of the

nurse's station in order to retrieve Cheswick's cigarettes, a symbol of his capacity for individual dignity.

PORNOGRAPHIC PLAYING CARDS

McMurphy's deck of dirty playing cards appears at critical moments of the film to signify his rebellion against authority. He makes Martini his first disciple when he flashes the pictures of naked women in his face, leading him away from the sedate game of pinochle. In his first group therapy session, he shuffles the cards defiantly while Nurse Ratched is speaking. McMurphy uses the cards most effectively during his evaluation by the doctors. As they conclude, Dr. Spivey asks him if he has any questions, and he flashes a card at the doctors, thus undermining their authority over him, openly demonstrating his contempt, and privileging raw, sensual experience over the regular, ordered life in the hospital.

CUCKOO'S NEST

FILM ANALYSIS

THE TRIUMPHANT SPARK

Set in the stark depression of a mental hospital populated by lost souls, this film explores bleak concepts of oppression, cruelty, suicide, and euthanasia, or mercy killing. Yet, remarkably, *One Flew Over the Cuckoo's Nest* celebrates life. From the moment McMurphy enters the institution, he charges it with an unprecedented jolt of vivacity. Both the patients and the staff are accustomed to a world deadened by sedatives and routine. The phonograph in the nurse's station plays numbing waltz music while the patients line up for their medications. During group therapy sessions, the patients and their nurse go over the same ground again and again. The Chief pushes his broom around the floor to no purpose, and the same men play the same card game at the same table day after day.

McMurphy bounds loudly into this setting, irreverent and bold, whooping at the Chief, teasing Martini away from the pinochle game, and generally upsetting the carefully established order with his energy and zest. McMurphy's life force is so strong and compelling that it changes the men on the ward and threatens the authority that has kept them docile and compliant.

Nurse Ratched represents this authority, and she controls all the deadening influences: the drugs administered without question, the rules written on the blackboard, the unalterable work schedule, the music that cannot be turned down. Her therapy sessions have nothing to do with getting well but instead press the group into the same painful and humiliating grooves until she decides it is time to adjourn. Her entire demeanor is in opposition to McMurphy's. Her face is stony and immobile, her voice controlled and modulated, her uniform starched and spotless.

In contrast, McMurphy's expressions change constantly. He shouts, curses, jokes, and cackles with glee, and his hair is wild. After undergoing brutal electroshock therapy, he quips that the next woman to take him on will light up like a pinball machine. Everything about McMurphy threatens Nurse Ratched, and the two are in immediate opposition as the forces of life and death, sanity and insanity, independence and authority.

Even in the setting of a "cuckoo's nest" and under the chilling gaze of Nurse Ratched, McMurphy manages to inspire a spark of life. Games like blackjack, basketball, and the World Series engage the other patients despite Nurse Ratched's disapproval. Under McMurphy's enthusiastic tutoring, the wheelchair-bound Colonel begins to sing as if he were at a baseball game, and the nearly catatonic Chief shoots baskets so the inmates can beat the orderlies in basketball.

Sex is a natural expression of delight for McMurphy, whereas it is a source of embarrassment and shame to Nurse Ratched. McMurphy believes young Billy Bibbit should be out in a convertible with a girl instead of inside the institution, but Nurse Ratched wants Billy to feel ashamed after having sex with a girl in the ward. The most vivid celebration of life in the film occurs during McMurphy's fishing escapade. He teaches Cheswick to drive a boat because it is fun, and he explains to Martini that he is not a loony now because he is a fisherman. McMurphy's infectious joy teaches others to revel in simply being alive, to find identity and meaning in their experiences.

Many of the life-affirming images in Forman's film are taken from the Christian symbolism embedded in Ken Kesey's original novel. Raised in a religious household, Kesey knew Bible stories well. Forman weaved these threads throughout the film to provide additional depth: the patients flock to McMurphy as disciples. They become fishermen. They soak in the pool as in baptism. McMurphy performs the miracle of getting the Chief to speak. McMurphy suffers for the men, and one of them betrays him. Yet he sacrifices himself for them, dying so that his ebullient spirit might live on in each of them, rather than saving himself when he could.

Nurse Ratched believes that she—and the institution—have won when McMurphy undergoes a frontal lobotomy. His body is still alive, but everything that made up his unique spirit is gone. The film's final affirmation of life echoes of resurrection, for the forces of death do not win. Instead, the Chief tells McMurphy, now essentially dead, that they will leave together. He smothers McMurphy's body to free his spirit, then lifts the marble water fixture from the floor and throws it through the window. It is as if he were rolling away the stone from the tomb. As the Chief's white-clad legs run away into the dawn, Taber begins to laugh, and music rises up in triumph.

DIRECTING

Almost no one in the film world believed that a film could be created successfully from Ken Kesey's hallucinatory, nonlinear novel, yet, through Milos Forman's direction, *One Flew Over the Cuckoo's Nest* not only succeeded but garnered significant critical and popular acclaim. Forman brought his unique vision of realism and revelation to the work: he chose actors capable of flexible and spontaneous approaches, including some unknown or nonprofessional actors.

Jack Nicholson, already a star, excelled under Forman's direction. At the beginning of the film, when the prison guards remove McMurphy's manacles, he laughs gleefully, grabs the guard and kisses him. As they rehearsed, Forman did not feel he was getting the response he wanted from the actor playing the guard. Taking Nicholson aside, Forman told him on the next take to kiss the other guard, who was not expecting it. That spontaneous take made it into the film.

Most of the supporting cast members were little-known actors. Some, like Danny DeVito (Martini) and Christopher Lloyd (Taber), went on to long Hollywood careers after their success in this film. Forman coaxed particularly fine work out of the newcomer Brad Dourif as Billy Bibbit, the suicidal stutterer: Dourif won the 1975 Golden Globe award for Best Film Debut. Two key characters were played by nonactors, yet under Forman's direction they gave subtle and believable performances as Dr. Spivey and the Chief. Forman enhanced the real-life feel of the movie by utilizing nonactors.

Forman's use of actual settings and natural light, as well as his emphasis on the human face, also emphasizes the film's realism. He wanted the audience to realize that the mental institution and its inmates are not far removed from the rest of the world. Forman shot locked doors, wire screens, bars, and chain-link fences to underscore the repression of the people caught inside. The hard, white surfaces of the walls, floors, and tiles intensify the contrast between the institution and its human inhabitants. Forman uses close-ups of the characters' faces to tell their stories. In order to increase the tension of the scenes, he uses extremely close shots, cropping out characters' hair or necks. By concentrating on eyes and mouths, particularly expressive features, Forman stresses the men's humanity.

Most of the film occurs in short takes, edited to provide multiple points of view in each scene. During the group therapy sessions, the camera moves from face to face without lingering. Nurse Ratched is smug and controlled as she asks painful, personal questions. Cheswick holds his breath and looks like he will implode. Martini grins and scowls simultaneously. Billy Bibbit folds himself into a near-fetal position. These short takes of varied perspective consistently build tension in the scenes.

Another of Forman's strengths as a director is his ability to use varied camera work to capture the moments at which characters reach important revelations. For example, he sets the moment of McMurphy's epiphany apart through the use of an unusually long take. He cuts quickly back and forth between the doctors and McMurphy at his sanity evaluation, so when he shoots one long, unedited take of McMurphy's face, the importance of the scene stands out. When McMurphy sends Billy Bibbit to sleep with Candy, then sits by the open window, Forman again keeps the camera on McMurphy's face, this time for a full sixty-five seconds. McMurphy in turn becomes troubled, thoughtful, and somber. He shows a hint of a grin as he realizes the cost of his sacrifice, looks up toward the open window, and then closes his eyes in acceptance. Under Forman's tutelage, actors fully inhabit their roles, the hospital becomes an evil institution, and the movie poignantly celebrates the human spirit.

PAGE-TO-SCREEN ADAPTATION

The director, writers, and producers of *One Flew Over the Cuckoo's Nest* faced a formidable challenge in adapting Ken Kesey's novel into a story that would work on the screen. Kesey wrote the novel while working as an orderly in a psychiatric ward and while participating in psychology-department experiments with LSD, mescaline, and other chemicals in order to earn extra money while attending graduate school at Stanford. He began to have hallucinations of a large Native American man sweeping the floors. The Chief became the narrator of his novel, and all the events of the story were told through his eyes. Like Kesey, the character of the Chief suffered from hallucinations: he held a firm belief that Nurse Ratched worked for an evil Combine that twisted and manufactured men. The novel became very popular with the counterculture movement after it was published in 1962, and its paranoia suited the antiwar activism of the era.

Because a film is a very different storytelling medium from a novel, Forman knew that Kesey's story had to be changed to fit the new format, as well as updated to be relevant twelve years later. Equally problematic was the fact that psychedelic illusions of humans changing form or walls sprouting arms would not translate well to the screen, nor would the mythical Combine suit Forman's interest in cinematic realism. The Broadway play of 1963 retained these features of the novel by having the Chief slip to the front of the stage to address the audience in asides, but this approach would look stilted on film.

To adapt the story so that it would work as a motion picture, the filmmakers changed the point of view to an omniscient, all-seeing perspective. The camera focuses upon the characters directly rather than interpreting them through the Chief's eyes. This choice eliminated the need for both the hallucinations and the conspiracy of the Combine. Rather than being controlled by an evil machine, in the film adaptation Nurse Ratched is the ultimate authority-wielding bureaucrat. Forman understood that audiences would better relate to the struggle against a personified, rather than mechanical, enemy. His Nurse Ratched relies upon rules and her power to change them arbitrarily in order to enforce conformity over individualism.

Although Forman elected to retain many of the novel's references to McMurphy as a Christ figure, he chose a more subtle approach for the film. For example, his electric shock table is not in the form of a cross, and McMurphy does not ask whether he gets a crown of thorns, as he does in the novel. The ending of the film, as of the novel, deals with death and resurrection. However, Forman modifies it for the screen: in the novel, by the time McMurphy returns from his lobotomy, most of the patients on the ward have already signed themselves out and managed to escape before McMurphy and the Chief do. In the film, all the characters are still on the ward. Forman's Chief escapes alone, leaving the window gaping open behind him for those who might choose to follow—a visually satisfying image that also underscores the importance of independent thought to a joyful life.

IMPORTANT QUOTATIONS EXPLAINED

1. HARDING: "I'm not just talking about my wife, I'm talking about my life. I can't seem to get that through to you. I'm not just talking about one person, I'm talking about everybody, I'm talking about form, I'm talking about content, I'm talking about interrelationships. I'm talking about God, the devil, hell, heaven."

Early in the film, during the first group therapy session, Nurse Ratched presses Harding about his relationship with his wife until he becomes frustrated and blurts out this clear summary of the film. Harding wants the men in his group to understand he is speaking of issues larger than himself, just as the film's story is meant to transcend the screen. With this speech, particularly since it comes so close to the beginning, the filmmaker signals that the film deals with these same issues. Harding says he is not speaking only of his own life but also of form, the outer appearance of things, and content, their inner meaning; he says that he is talking about everyone and their interrelationships. Both Harding and *One Flew Over the Cuckoo's Nest* address the battle between competing forces—God and the devil, good and evil, heaven and hell, sanity and insanity—within the human soul. In this way, the mental institution stands not just for larger society but for the universe, and the men in the film represent the potential for submission and celebration inherent in everyone.

The ideas in Harding's lines recur throughout the film. The fates of the patients are interconnected, particularly those of Billy Bibbit, McMurphy, and the Chief, who frees McMurphy's spirit. Outward appearances within the film often are deceptive: the Chief, for example, appears to be deaf and mute, but in fact he hears and sees the underlying content and meaning of people's actions on the ward more clearly than the others. In her nurse's uniform and with her calm voice, Nurse Ratched appears to be an instrument of health and sanity, but in fact she prefers weakness and madness. She is a force of destruction who drives Billy Bibbit to commit suicide. The film aligns her with evil by repeatedly linking her with locks, keys, shackles, gates, and other forms of constraint. McMurphy, the former prison inmate, initially appears to be a social misfit, but instead he forms connections with the patients, leading them toward health and sanity. The film aligns him with Jesus and the idea of salvation. The repression of the mental institution refers to hell, particularly as McMurphy is shocked on the electroshock table. McMurphy's spirit escapes with the Chief to an afterlife, a heaven, beyond the hospital's bars. This key speech sets up the film's intention to treat universal issues of human significance.

2. MCMURPHY: "You let me go on hassling Nurse Ratched here, knowing how much I had to lose, and you never told me nothing."

In this session of group therapy, McMurphy accuses the men of betraying him by not telling him how much he was risking with his rebellious behavior. What started as a prank has taken a dire turn. This quote is the only time McMurphy comes close to expressing regret for his choices and actions. It is a moment of pause and reflection in the film as both we as viewers and McMurphy assess whether he can afford to continue his opposition to Nurse Ratched's repression. These lines introduce the concept of betrayal and the fact that McMurphy clearly is saddened by the men's failure to provide him with critical information about the hospital's policies, particularly Nurse Ratched's ability to decide the length of McMurphy's stay. The film suggests that for McMurphy and for humanity, ignorance has devastating consequences. It further suggests that, as interconnected human beings, we have responsibilities to protect one another. With this line, McMurphy publicly acknowledges that he has pitted himself in opposition to Nurse Ratched and admits that he has gone too far to change the outcome. His friends have failed to warn him, and he has lost his physical freedom to Nurse Ratched. An unstated question seems to hang in the air, heightening the tension of the scene. Might there yet be more for him to lose if he continues to fight her? As the scene unfolds, McMurphy must decide whether or not to escalate their conflict despite the magnitude of the risks.

3. MCMURPHY: "Jesus, I mean you guys do nothing but complain about how you can't stand it in this place here and then you haven't got the guts just to walk out? What do you

> think you are for Christ sake, crazy or something? Well, you're not! You're not! You're no crazier than the average asshole out walking around on the streets."

After McMurphy accuses the men of betrayal, they explain that they are almost all "voluntary" rather than "committed" like him. McMurphy is filled with disbelief that any man would choose repression over freedom, particularly a young man in his prime like Billy Bibbit. By exhorting Billy to be out in a convertible, chasing girls, McMurphy extols the virtues of living life to its fullest potential. In these lines, McMurphy expresses three pivotal concepts: courage, free will, and the definition of sanity. When he tells the men they don't have the guts to walk out when they can, he challenges their courage—a characteristic often associated with manhood.

McMurphy himself displays courage every time he opposes Nurse Ratched's authority. Physical courage enables him to jump the fence and hijack a bus to take the men fishing. Mental courage empowers him to invent a World Series game in defiance of Nurse Ratched. His actions consistently demonstrate the importance of courage in the fight against tyranny. By choosing to oppose repression, McMurphy also demonstrates freedom of choice, or free will—a concept important in Christian belief. Free will allows humans to choose between good and evil. When McMurphy discovers that the patients have elected to subject themselves to the institution voluntarily, he reminds them that they have a choice. For emphasis, he invokes "Christ's sake." McMurphy implies that the choice to stay in subjugation is immoral—an act against the free will that God has granted humankind.

He goes on to assert that these men are no more insane than the average man, and indeed the question of sanity is central to the film. This line sets up the quirky individualism of the patients against the rigid conformity of Nurse Ratched. When McMurphy tells the men they are no crazier than the average man on the street, he denies Nurse Ratched's version of normality. Hers is confined to a narrow range of behavior carefully conscripted by rules—her rules. A docile and sedated patient is her ideal. She employs drugs, nighttime restraints, and lullaby-like music to keep her charges in that state. To ensure their compliance, she uses the orderlies to discipline and subdue them. In contrast, McMurphy's definition of normality is as broad as the world and allows for great variation. He makes fun of society's labels for the insane, affectionately referring to the patients as "lunatics" or "mental defectives" and to himself as the "bull goose loony." When they act like men, however, he gives them new labels, as when he tells Martini he's no longer a loony but a fisherman. By denying that the men are crazy, McMurphy refutes Nurse Ratched's definition of sanity. He challenges the men directly to exercise their free will to live fully and with courage, and he dares them to reject the institution's oppression of those aims.

4. CHIEF: "My papa was real big. He did like he pleased. That's why everybody worked on him. The last time I seen my father he was blind in the cities from drinking and every time he put the bottle to his mouth, he don't suck out of it, it sucks out of him. . . . I'm not saying they killed him. The just worked on him, the way they're working on you."

The Chief's warning occurs late at night following McMurphy's electroshock treatments, as McMurphy kneels beside the Chief's bed and confesses that he can't take the institution anymore. The Chief, a physical giant, whispers, making himself small to emphasize his inability to escape with McMurphy. The Chief introduces size as a measure of inner rather than outer reality. By asserting that McMurphy is much bigger than he is, he measures with a different yardstick—that of the heart. The Chief, who speaks very little in the film, says a great deal in these few words. By comparing McMurphy to his father, he makes clear his love and respect. To the Chief, the size of both men he admires is in their ability to do as they please. They behave as men, as individuals, as rebels against institutions of authority.

The Chief implies that society represses such big men when he says that everybody "worked on" his father. His father coped with society's repression by escaping into alcohol. He drank until he was blind, until he no longer had to see the injustice of his situation. Both the cities and the mental institution stand for crowding and oppression, and neither leaves room for such a big man. Alcohol steals more from his father than it gives him: it robs him of his dignity and vision and sucks the soul from his body. Like Nurse Ratched's sedatives, alcohol provides only the *illusion* of killing the pain. McMurphy assumes that drinking killed the Chief's father, but the Chief suggests that something far worse can happen to a man than the death of his body. Repression works on a man and makes him smaller, blinding him and draining the manhood from him. This is what happened to the Chief's father, and it is what the Chief sees happening to McMurphy. The Chief speaks near the end of the film with the voice of prophecy and doom so that McMurphy—and viewers—will heed his lesson.

5.   NURSE RATCHED: "Now calm down. The best thing we can do is go on with our daily routine."

Nurse Ratched ushers the men into the corridor after Billy Bibbit's suicide to deliver this brief line, which encapsulates her entire character and belief system. While the others, including the shrieking Nurse Pilbow and the gasping patients, react with horror to Billy's bloody corpse, Nurse Ratched projects an unnatural discipline. Her cold control betrays her heartlessness. No matter how genuinely appalling the event, Nurse Ratched insists upon quiet, order, and routine. Her need to control every aspect of behavior on the ward extends to a need to direct even how the men should feel. In her tyranny, she tries to strip them of their natural emotions and deaden their sensitivity with routine. In light of the men's affection for Billy, her demand for calm and order is not only grossly inappropriate but also a mad distortion of human nature. With these words, the film portrays her as more insane than the mental patients.

In contrast, McMurphy's selfless rage, which wells up as she delivers this directive, comes from his emotional sanity. He grips her throat with his bare hands as if to choke off the evil of her words. Without regard for himself, McMurphy grapples her to the floor as if wrestling the devil. While he shakes her neck, her carefully arranged hair comes undone, marking her loss of authority and control. The film suggests that McMurphy's attack on Nurse Ratched is far more than revenge for Billy Bibbit's death: he is fighting for humanity, for the individual's right to be loved, respected, and mourned.

TAXI DRIVER

(1976)

Context

Director Martin Scorsese was born in New York City to Italian immigrant parents in 1942. He grew up in an observant Catholic family in Little Italy, and at a young age he wanted to be a priest. His dreams soon changed, however, and he attended New York University film school. After film school, Scorsese moved west to Hollywood. Roger Corman, a pulp movie director and producer, hired him to direct *Boxcar Bertha* in 1972. Scorsese's first collaboration with Robert De Niro, who plays Travis in *Taxi Driver*, was on *Mean Streets* (1974), a film about Catholic Italian-Americans in Little Italy that was rooted in Scorsese's own childhood experiences. The next film Scorsese directed was *Alice Doesn't Live Here Anymore*, for which Ellen Burstyn won a Best Actress Academy Award, the same year that Robert De Niro won Best Supporting Actor for his role in Francis Ford Coppola's *The Godfather Part II*. These Academy Awards helped Scorsese raise the funds to make *Taxi Driver* in 1976. The film received huge critical acclaim, cementing Scorsese's reputation as a major director. In addition to *Taxi Driver*, Scorsese has directed over twenty-five films, including the documentary *Italianamerican* (1974), the highly controversial *The Last Temptation of Christ* (1988), and, more recently, the popular *Goodfellas* (1990) and *Gangs of New York* (2002).

Taxi Driver elevated Scorsese's status as a director, and it assured Paul Schrader's reputation as a major screenwriter. In the mid-1970s, Schrader was an up-and-coming screenwriter whose first screenplay, *The Yakuza* (1975), was considered a success even though the film had not performed well financially. *Taxi Driver's* success bolstered Schrader's career and ensured his place in the Hollywood community. Although some scenes in *Taxi Driver* were influenced by the actors, the film follows Schrader's screenplay closely, more so than Scorsese has followed his other films' screenplays. Many of Schrader's later screenplays deal, like *Taxi Driver*, with one man's loneliness and alienation, including *American Gigolo* (1990) and the more recent *Bringing Out the Dead* (1999), which is in many ways an update and homage to *Taxi Driver*. Like Scorsese, Schrader grew up in a religious household. He did not see a film until his late teens, so his influences are more literary than cinematic. While writing *Taxi Driver*, he was under the spell of existentialist novels such as Albert Camus's *The Stranger* and earlier portraits of loneliness such as Fyodor Dostoevsky's *Notes from Underground.*

Scorsese made *Taxi Driver* in the mid-1970s, a decade famous for its diverse and innovative films. The 1970s produced a group of directors, sometimes called the "film school brats," that included Steven Spielberg, Francis Ford Coppola, Martin Scorsese, George Lucas, and Brian de Palma. These men were young Americans who had studied European filmmakers at film school, and they were also the first generation of filmmakers to have grown up watching television. Their movies feature close attention to technical detail, while demonstrating an encyclopedic knowledge of film and television history. At the same time, their films were not just art house pictures but huge box office successes, funded by Hollywood.

The fall of the Hollywood studio system at the end of the 1950s, combined with the various political upheavals of the 1960s, including the sexual revolution, the anti-Vietnam movement, and the civil rights movement, made predicting the public's taste increasingly difficult. During the early 1970s the largest studios lost over $500 million. They knew their methods of attracting audiences, which included using big name stars, making high-budget musicals, and releasing films based on popular novels, had become outdated. Studios became open to giving money to young and unknown directors who could make more original and risky movies. *Taxi Driver* centers on a racist, sociopathic, and violent protagonist and features a twelve-year-old prostitute, but at the time of its release it was a popular, well-received film. The movie was critically acclaimed in the United States, received four Oscar nominations, and did even better financially in Europe.

Taxi Driver immortalizes New York City in the 1970s, a city vastly different from the New York we know today. The city's filth is exaggerated in the film partly because it is seen through Travis Bickle's skewed perspective, but during 1975, when the movie was filmed, New York was literally a filthy city. New York nearly filed for bankruptcy in 1974, so when the New York City trash collectors went on strike in the summer of 1975, causing the streets to fill with warm garbage, the city didn't have the funds to fix the problem. One of the promises Jimmy Carter made when campaigning for the presidency, which he won in 1976, was that he would make sure New York City wouldn't have to file for bankruptcy. *Taxi Driver* presents a true-to-life portrait of what Manhattan once was. Times Square was filled with peep shows and prostitutes, and during the summer of 1975, when the film takes place, the country was in the middle of a presidential campaign where one of the main issues was moving beyond the Vietnam War, which had officially ended only in 1973. We can easily imagine an ex-marine in New York being disgusted by the filth, finding the politicians who are supposed to help him to be artificial, and feeling that he needs to approach the city as he would a special combat mission.

PLOT OVERVIEW

Ominous music plays as a car emerges out of steam into a dark and threatening urban landscape. The camera flashes on Travis Bickle's eyes, which appear menacing. The first scene after the credits introduces us to Travis as he interviews for a job as a taxi driver. He tells the interviewer that he is twenty-six years old, was honorably discharged from the Marines in 1973 (indicating to viewers that he served in the Vietnam War), and that he can't sleep at night. The interviewer reveals that he had been a Marine as well and tells Travis to come back for work the next day. Travis leaves and begins drinking from a flask in broad daylight.

As Travis's job as a taxi driver begins, so does his diary, which we hear as a voiceover. Travis complains about how dirty New York is and talks about how he does not discriminate against his passengers. We see him driving around on a typical day. When he gets off work in the morning after driving for twelve hours at night, he immediately begins drinking and attends a porn film. At the entrance he tries to be friendly with the concession lady, a young black woman. She quickly rejects his efforts to reach out, so he spends his morning alone in the porn theater. Travis complains about his inability to sleep, even after working all night, and talks about wanting to become more normal. He wishes to have someplace to go and to fit in with other people. Travis hangs out with other cabbies sometimes at an all-night diner. He is clearly made uncomfortable by Charlie T, a black cab driver, and by the other black people in the diner.

One day while driving his cab, Travis sees Betsy, a beautiful blond woman in a white dress. To Travis, she stands out from the rest of the people in the crowded, dirty city. Betsy works at the Palantine presidential campaign headquarters in New York. We see Betsy talking to her coworker, Tom, who also seems to be in love with Betsy, while Travis watches from his cab outside.

Travis finally gathers the courage to ask Betsy out. He dresses up and walks into the campaign headquarters, introduces himself, and asks Betsy out for coffee. Charmed and intrigued, Betsy agrees. Travis and Betsy's date at the diner goes well, and she agrees to go to a movie with him.

Later, coincidentally, Travis gives Palantine, the candidate, a ride in the cab. Travis flatters Palantine, saying he's Palantine's biggest supporter, but when Palantine pushes Travis to talk about an issue, Travis speaks inappropriately, saying that he just wants to see the city rid of all its scum. Travis's next fare is a young prostitute, Iris, who jumps in the cab and tells it to take off. While Travis hesitates, a man pulls the girl out of the cab and throws Travis a twenty-dollar bill, telling him to forget the incident. Travis seems unable to get the girl out of his mind, and he puts the bill in a place separate from the rest of his money.

Travis takes Betsy to a porn film in Times Square. When Betsy realizes what the film is, she becomes disgusted and leaves. After this night, she refuses to take his calls and returns the flowers he sends her. Travis becomes angry and eventually storms into the Palantine office to confront Betsy in public, but there he is humiliated.

The next scene shows Travis, back in his cab, pulling over to let a man out. But the unnamed passenger wants to stay in the cab to watch the silhouette of a woman in a window above. The passenger claims the woman is his wife and that she is sleeping with a black man. He goes on hysterically about shooting his wife with a .44 Magnum. Later, at the diner where the cabbies hang out, Travis pulls Wizard aside and tries to reach out to him, saying he's been feeling down and having bad ideas in his head. The only thing Wizard can tell him is that he is stuck as a taxi driver, that the job will become him. Travis seems to be losing his mind more and more. One day he absentmindedly runs his cab into a young prostitute, the same one who jumped into his cab before.

Travis buys four guns from an underground dealer, saying that he is going to change his life. He wants to turn over a new leaf—to eat and drink more healthily, and to train his body. We see him doing push-ups and holding his fist out over an open flame, as if he is training for combat. Travis begins to stalk Palantine. He goes to his rallies and watches him on television. He arouses suspicion by talking to a Secret Service agent at one of the rallies. Travis's speech becomes more disjointed and repetitive, especially when he is alone. He practices pulling out his gun in the mirror, saying "You talkin' to me?" One night he stops at a convenience store. When a young black man comes in and tries to stick up the store, Travis shoots and kills him. The shooting has no consequences for Travis because the convenience store owner just thanks him and then starts beating the dead man.

Travis continues to stalk Palantine, and he writes a letter to his parents. They know nothing about where their son is or what he does.

Travis finally searches for Iris, the young prostitute he has seen twice before. He tries to pay Sport, her pimp, for time with her. Iris tries to seduce Travis, but he refuses to have sex with her. Instead, he asks her why she doesn't leave her job. He has coffee with her the next day and again tries to convince her to leave Sport. She says she'll think about it, and that she dreams of going to a commune in Vermont. She asks Travis to go with her, but he says he has more important plans. Iris goes back to Sport to tell him she's unhappy, but Sport is seductive and romantic and convinces Iris to stay.

On the final day of the film's action Travis prepares to leave the house. First, he burns all the flowers he bought for Betsy, and then he writes a note for Iris, enclosing $500 so she can go to Vermont. He writes that by the time she reads the letter, he will be dead. He goes to a Palantine rally with his hair shaved into a Mohawk. His intention to assassinate Palantine becomes clear. Soon, though, Secret Service agents spot him and pursue him. Since his plan has failed, he goes instead to Iris's building. There, in a long, bloody shoot-out, he kills Sport, the man who rents out Iris's rooms, and a man who was about to visit Iris. When Travis tries to shoot himself, he realizes that he has run out of bullets. As the police rush in, he puts his hand to his head and pretends to shoot himself.

The film moves forward by a few months. Travis has become a hero of sorts for saving Iris. We hear Iris's father reading a letter he has written Travis, thanking him for sending Iris home. The camera pans across all the newspaper articles that label Travis a hero. In the final scene, which is most likely a fantasy, we see Travis standing around with his cabbie friends when Betsy gets into his cab. She is clearly impressed by Travis's recent success and says she'll see him around. Travis never looks back at her but stares at her reflection in his rearview mirror.

TAXI DRIVER

Character List

Travis Bickle—Played by Robert De Niro The film's protagonist. Travis served in Vietnam as a Marine until 1973, and two years later, he is a taxi driver in New York City. Originally, he comes from an unspecified rural area. Travis is not fully sane when the movie begins, and as the film progresses, his sanity deteriorates. His failed attempt to form a relationship with Betsy pushes him further into insanity, and eventually he succumbs to obsession, fanaticism, and violence.

Iris—Played by Jodie Foster A twelve-and-a-half-year-old prostitute. Iris ran away from her home in Pittsburgh to live in New York, where she does drugs and turns tricks in the custody of her pimp, Sport. She is in love with Sport, and he succeeds in talking her out of leaving him. Travis eventually saves Iris from her corrupt life when he kills the men around her.

Betsy—Played by Cybill Shepherd Travis's ideal woman, blonde and beautiful. Betsy works with the Palantine presidential campaign. Initially she finds going out with Travis to be a fascinating experiment, but she cuts off all contact after he takes her on a date to a porn film.

Sport/Matthew—Played by Harvey Keitel Iris's pimp. Travis believes Sport to be the worst person in the world, but Sport's relationship with Iris is more complicated and ambiguous than Travis thinks. Sport plays the role of father, lover, and pimp for Iris.

The Unnamed Passenger—Played by Martin Scorsese A passenger of Travis's who has perverse ideas about killing his wife. Travis picks the passenger up one evening soon after Betsy rejects him. The passenger directs Travis's attention to the silhouette of a woman in a window. He says the woman is his wife and that she is sleeping with a black man in the apartment. He says he will kill her, describing his plans in gruesome and suggestive detail.

Tom—Played by Albert Brooks   One of Betsy's coworkers on the Palantine campaign. Tom, like Travis, is in love with Betsy, but while Travis is too much of an outsider for Betsy, Tom is too square. His jokes mostly fall flat, and he is cowardly in his attempts to protect Betsy from Travis.

Charles Palantine—Played by Leonard Harris   A senator who is campaigning for President, and whom Travis later tries, and fails, to assassinate. Palantine is a liberal trying to capitalize on the anti-Vietnam youth culture to win the Democratic nomination. His politician's nature comes through when he talks to Travis in his cab, making sure to call him by his name and to shake his hand afterward, even though Travis has unsettled him by swearing and talking like a madman. Palantine may or may not also be the man who gets into the cab early on in the movie with a prostitute, telling Travis to hurry up while pretending he isn't there, a marked contrast to his calm, diplomatic attitude later on.

Wizard—Played by Peter Boyle   An experienced cabby Travis sometimes hangs out with on his break. Travis reaches out to Wizard before he buys his guns, hoping Wizard will have some words of encouragement that will stop his violent plans. All Wizard can say is that once a man has a job, like driving a taxi, he becomes that job. Travis doesn't take him seriously. Wizard's words turn out to be prophetic, as Travis fails to kill himself and so remains a taxi driver indefinitely.

Charlie T—Played by Norman Matlock   A black cab driver who is friendly with Wizard and Doughboy. Charlie T's presence makes Travis uncomfortable, but we know that Travis does have some interaction with him because he borrowed five dollars from him at some point.

Doughboy—Played by Harry Northup   One of the taxi drivers Travis sometimes hangs out with at an all-night diner. Doughboy is the first to suggest that Travis should carry a gun, and for a fee he sets him up with Easy Andy, the underground gun dealer.

Easy Andy—Played by Steven Prince The traveling salesman who sells Travis four guns. Easy Andy offers Travis everything from drugs to cars once Travis makes a purchase. When Travis finally meets Iris, she tells him her name is Easy, unknowingly echoing Easy Andy's name.

Concession Girl—Played by Diahnne Abbott A young black woman with whom Travis tries to make contact before he sees Betsy. This woman works at a porn theater that Travis visits one morning and is not moved enough even to tell Travis her name. However racist Travis may seem, he is threatened only by black men—he doesn't hesitate about approaching this young black woman.

ANALYSIS OF MAJOR CHARACTERS

TRAVIS BICKLE

Although we become well acquainted with Travis throughout *Taxi Driver*, his mental instability makes his actions unpredictable, and although Travis seems sympathetic, we never fully understand him. Travis is never part of the normal world. Though he initially wants to fit in and to be like other people, he is too mentally ill to act normally. Even at his best, at the beginning of the film, he can't sleep, drinks heavily, pops pills, and spends his mornings in porn theaters. After Betsy rejects him, Travis becomes hysterical, violent, and obsessive, and from here descends into madness. He loses all self-awareness and deludes himself into believing that shooting a presidential candidate and then shooting himself is a heroic gesture. Travis changes from a wounded man into a hardened one, testing our sympathies and distancing himself through violence. Young Iris prevents Travis from turning into a monster by giving him a reason to look at the world outside himself. Even as Travis plots his heroic act of violence, he worries about how to save Iris. He believes he has cut himself off from all worldly feelings and that he is just training to be a soldier, but his concern for Iris suggests otherwise. Travis's many contradictions make him one of the great characters in film history.

We never learn exactly what happened to Travis during Vietnam, and the rest of his past remains unexplored, so there's no way to explain why Travis has become the way he is. His war experiences must have influenced his character, acquainting him with violence and helping to turn him into a killer. Travis's anger wouldn't be so frightening if he wasn't able to transform himself into a warrior so efficiently. When Travis goes to kill Palantine, he sports a new Mohawk haircut. The 101st Airborne paratroopers made this a popular haircut for American soldiers to wear into combat when they flew in on D-Day in World War II, and Travis's Mohawk shows the influence of his experience in the army on his character. Travis has also been influenced by his parents and his upbringing, though we never catch any glimpses of this past. His obsession with and disgust for all things sexual are surely rooted in early experiences, and his many comments about destiny or being chosen by God suggest that he may have had a religious upbringing as Scorsese and Schrader did. We know little about Travis outside of his taxi, and he remains a mystery.

IRIS

Iris sees her New York life as glamorous and independent, and although being a prostitute at such a young age is unequivocally damaging, she most likely views Travis's rescue of her as a mixed blessing. In New York, she believes people love and need her, even if those people are her pimp, Sport, and the johns that visit her. She takes pride in being streetwise, as we see during her breakfast with Travis when she asks if he is a "narc" and turns his questions back on him. Though she is willing to entertain the thought of leaving Sport, she is about as likely to go back to her parents on her own as Travis is. Instead, she dreams of moving to Vermont. Though Travis has propriety, morality, and age on his side to justify his actions, his murders would have been more heroic had we not seen Iris dancing with Sport. Though he is her pimp, Sport comes across as comforting and romantic, and Iris clearly cares for him, for better or worse. Travis can neither see nor hear Iris and Sport in this scene. If he had seen it, he may have realized that his so-called heroism is most likely the least heroic in the eyes of the person he saves. After the murders, we don't hear from Iris again. She has disappeared back to Pittsburgh, and the only remaining sign of her is a grateful note her father wrote to Travis.

THE UNNAMED PASSENGER

The appearance of the unnamed passenger and the violent plans he details mark a turning point in the film, and after his ride with Travis, Travis's own violent plans begin to take shape. Halfway through the film, Travis pulls over to a curb and sits with the unnamed passenger, waiting quietly then listening as the passenger reveals his violent and sexually grotesque plans to murder his unfaithful wife. The passenger directs Travis's gaze, as a director might, to the lighted window where his wife is, tells Travis his wife is sleeping with a black man, then describes his plans for murder in gruesome detail. The passenger uses hateful language to describe the black man as well as what he'll do to his wife, giving voice to much of the hate Travis already feels. After this scene, nothing in the movie is the same. The passenger plants the idea of extreme violence in Travis's head. In just a few scenes, Travis will seek out a gun of his own, like the one the passenger has.

Scorsese makes a cameo appearance in *Taxi Driver* as the unnamed passenger, and this is not the first time in film history that a director has acted in the movie in a small role that changes the course of the film. In *Chinatown*, a 1974 film staring Jack Nicholson, the director, Roman Polanski, has a small but influential cameo as well. Halfway through the film, Polanski appears briefly as a thug who slashes the hero's nose, changing the film from a light detective story to a story that takes place in a dangerous underworld. Similarly, Scorsese's part in *Taxi Driver* broaches the idea of twisted violence, which had not been present before. Historical accounts of the making of *Taxi Driver* point out that another actor was slated to play the role of the passenger. When the actor got sick, Scorsese decided on the spur of the moment to play the role himself.

TAXI DRIVER

THEMES, MOTIFS, AND SYMBOLS

THEMES

PREDETERMINED VS. SELF-DIRECTED FATE

Travis frequently changes his view of whether he is in control of his destiny or whether his destiny is predetermined. In the beginning of the film, Travis complains about being lonely and not having any place to go. He tries to control his own fate and change his situation by getting a job and finding a girl. When Travis's plans don't turn out the way he hoped, he shifts the blame away from himself by professing a belief in predestination, claiming he fails because he is meant to be "God's lonely man." By the second half of the movie, Travis has given up on the idea that he has any control over what he does. When he leaves his apartment with the plan of killing Palantine and himself, he notes that this is his destiny and that he never had any choice. Yet he fails in his goal of shooting the candidate, which suggests that Travis's theory about destiny is flawed. Travis creates a new fate for himself by killing Iris's protectors, a decision he makes on his own. Travis, not God, creates this destiny.

Other characters, such as Iris and Wizard, have their own views about how they might change their destinies. Wizard adheres to a more passive philosophy of life, as he tells Travis he'll always be a taxi driver no matter what he does. Travis does indeed remain a taxi driver, which suggests that he may not have as much power over his fate as we might expect. Iris is powerless in many ways, and while her fate may not be predetermined, it is certainly influenced by other people. Sport manipulates and uses her, refusing her the freedom of choice, and Travis forces freedom on her whether she wants it or not. Though Iris came to New York in an act of independence, by the end of the film she has lost control of her destiny.

LONELINESS IN CROWDS

Among the millions of people in New York City, meaningful personal connections can be few and far between, and in *Taxi Driver* we see several cases of such urban isolation. Travis resents that the people in his cab pretend he doesn't exist, and in a way, New York itself is an extension of the little world of the taxi: The city is full of people who don't pay attention to each other and who pretend Travis isn't there. Travis isn't the only lonely character in the film. Tom and Betsy flirt with each other, but they don't seem to share a true personal connection. Betsy is lonely enough to consider a date with Travis, a stranger who approaches her from the street. Wizard and the other cabbies congregate at an all-night diner, hinting that they don't have families or stable home lives. The only true relationship in the film is between Sport and Iris, and that relationship is based on illegal exploitation. *Taxi Driver* contains many shots of crowds, each person going in his or her own direction. To some extent, this view of New York reflects Travis's warped, isolated perspective, but he is not alone in feeling lonely.

THE GLORIFICATION OF VIOLENCE

Taxi Driver's surprise ending portrays society's glorification of Travis's violence. Instead of dying in the shootout, Travis survives and becomes a local hero, despite having murdered several people in cold blood. The film shows several press clippings hanging on the wall of Travis's room as well as a thankful letter written by Iris's parents. Ironically, Travis, the perpetual social outsider, becomes celebrated in society by violating its laws. The law-abiding Travis was invisible, but the murderous Travis is a hero. In a way, this plot twist validates Travis's criticisms of New York society, which tolerates and even praises violent criminal behavior. Only by acting violently could Travis escape the loneliness that seemed to be his fate.

MOTIFS

THE TAXI

The windshield of the taxi is the lens through which Travis views the city, and the taxi itself is a vehicle of loneliness and isolation. As the opening credits role, Travis drives his taxi through the city in the rain. The lights of the city are blurred through the rain on the windshield until the wipers reveal the scene. For the second time, the rain blurs the scene through the windshield, but this time the wipers do not make everything clear again. This blurry view suggests that Travis's view of the city and the world is skewed. Travis never sees the world as it actually is. Because his perspective is warped by mental illness, the taxi, in a way, protects him from the outside world. Inside the taxi, Travis isn't vulnerable to jealous men, beautiful women, and his own angry rages. Outside, the world is full of danger. Within the taxi, Travis is safer, but he must endure isolation even when he has passengers. Passengers often pretend Travis doesn't exist, and personal connections are rarely, if ever, attempted.

RACISM

Though Travis never says anything overtly racist, besides using the word "spook" in his diary, his racism is clear from the way he looks at the black people around him. Travis notices black men everywhere, revealing a deep-seated fear and hatred of black men in particular. The constant shots of groups of black people and black men reveal Travis's obsession. The camera focuses on the black people walking through the streets or sitting in the diner as if they are from outer space. Black people are often shot in slow motion, showing that Travis's gaze lingers on them. He is fascinated with what he hates. Travis's obsession separates him from society, because for the most part the people around Travis accept what goes on. While Wizard and Doughboy are happy to sit around with Charlie T, Travis is uncomfortable. When he leaves the diner with Wizard, Travis looks back at Charlie T, who pretends to shoot Travis with a gun he makes out of his hand. Travis is disturbed by this gesture. Travis also seems jealous of black men. He focuses on the black couple dancing when he watches *American Bandstand*, as if he is not able to believe that they can be happy while he must be alone.

Only two characters in the film share Travis's racism. The first is the unnamed passenger, who wants to kill his wife for having slept with a "nigger." The passenger gives voice to words Travis thinks but did not have the courage to say, which is why the passenger has so much influence over Travis. Some critics argue that the passenger is an object of Travis's imagination, representing the deepest recesses of his psyche. The other racist character is the man who runs the convenience store. When Travis shoots the young black man who is robbing the convenience store, he worries about the consequences of having used an unlicensed gun. The man behind the counter tells Travis not to worry about it, and he beats the dead man with a crowbar. Travis feels justified in his racism because a few other people share it, even though their feelings probably do not resemble his. In the original screenplay, all the people Travis kills at the end of the film were written as black. Scorsese changed this aspect of the story because he believed racism to that extreme would be too controversial.

TELEVISION

Images on television reveal to Travis an alternate reality he himself cannot take part in, where relationships between people are possible. Unlike the actors in the porn films Travis frequents, the people on television seem real to him, and he both envies and resents them. When Travis watches television near the end of the film, he watches it with a gun in his hand, occasionally aiming it at the screen. He watches *American Bandstand* just after he kills the black man who robs the convenience store. The first image he sees on the screen is a close-up of a young and happy-looking black couple. We get an extended view of the dance floor as the camera zooms into the screen. Amidst all the slow-dancing couples there is one pair of shoes without anyone in them. Travis resembles those shoes not only because he is single, but also because he is not even there. He observes other people's happiness through the lens of television.

Later, Travis watches a soap opera conversation between a husband and wife, which, unlike *American Bandstand*, was shot specifically for this film. The wife is leaving her husband for her lover. Instead of pointing his gun at the television, Travis tilts the table it rests on until it topples, and the monitor shatters. When the television breaks, so does what's left of Travis's self-control. He has broken his only window onto outside relationships. He puts his head into his hands and rocks back and forth hysterically. At the end of the film, Travis's room post-shoot out contains a new television to replace the old one, indicating that Travis is trying to make a fresh start.

SYMBOLS

WATER

Travis hates the filth of New York City in the summer, and he wishes for a great rain to wash it all away. His definition of filth includes not only the smell of the city or the garbage, but also the people who live in the city, including the black people in Harlem and the prostitutes and hippies in Times Square. In one of his first diary entries, Travis expresses gratitude for a rain that has left the city slightly cleaner than before, but he adds that someday a "real" rain will fall to clean up the city. By this Travis is imagining an apocalyptic flood, one that will separate the people he thinks should be redeemed from those who are not worthy or clean enough. Water takes on the qualities of a redemptive, baptizing force when Travis gives a ride to a prostitute and a john and goes out of his way to drive his cab through an open fire hydrant. He bathes the exterior and interior of his car, both of which have been corrupted by the passengers.

GUNS

A common lesson for young screenwriters is that a gun that appears in the first scene of a movie must go off before the credits roll. *Taxi Driver* mocks this axiom by giving its hero, Travis, four guns and a knife. The film is full of guns. Travis views them with a certain reverence, and the first and last shots of the .44 Magnum are slow close-ups panning from the handle to the barrel. Guns take on a powerful significance in Travis's emotional life. He buys his guns only after having been rejected by Betsy, and in a way they help him to be potent after his failure at courting her.

Fake guns have significance as well. Travis and other male characters frequently use hand motions to simulate shooting. The hand has the power to insult and offend, but no power to do any physical harm. Charlie T is the first person to make this hand gesture at Travis, accompanied by a verbal shooting noise, even before Travis buys his guns. Later, Sport makes the same motion when Travis visits Iris. These men mock Travis when they pretend to shoot him, and he is put off by their gestures. After the final shootout, when Travis has no bullets left and the police arrive, Travis puts his hand to his head and pretends to shoot himself. In his maniacal state, he seems to believe this gesture will actually work.

THE $20 BILL

When Travis first encounters Iris, she enters his cab and is pulled out by Sport, who tosses Travis a $20 bill to keep him quiet. Travis takes the money, but he leaves it on the front seat, separate from the rest of his cash. Subsequently, whenever Travis sees the folded bill, he remembers Iris, the filth of the city, and his own silence. For Travis, the bill symbolizes the city's corruption, where anyone can be bought, like a prostitute, for the right price. The money serves as a constant reminder of his own complicity in Iris's situation, and it eventually spurs him to action. He is ashamed that he took the money in the first place, and his shame motivates his later actions. When Travis visits Iris in her room, he uses this bill to pay for his time with her. He returns the money to the man it came from in an attempt to atone for his previous inaction, the first step in his new role as Iris's liberator.

FILM ANALYSIS

INSIDE THE MIND OF A LONELY MAN

Taxi Driver is an extended close-up of Travis Bickle, its protagonist, and our proximity to him reveals his loneliness. The camera abandons Travis's point of view only twice, once during the scene between Betsy and Tom in the campaign office near the beginning of the film, and again during the scene between Iris and Sport near the end. Travis watches one of these scenes, but only from afar, in his taxi. He can't hear what the other characters say, but he is involved as a voyeur. By keeping us close to Travis at all times, Scorsese lets us see through his eyes, though we never gain a thorough understanding of who Travis really is. In the diner where Travis relaxes with his cabbie coworkers, the camera is rarely where we would expect it to be. Instead of focusing on the conversation, it lingers on two well-dressed black men for a long time. Travis perceives himself to be surrounded by threatening black men in the diner, yet later in the scene, when the camera shows the whole diner, we see that the tables are filled with innocuous people of many races. When the camera acts as Travis's eyes, we have see the world as he does, and we learn something about Travis in the process. In the same diner scene, Travis drops an Alka-Seltzer into a glass of water, and his gaze lingers again. The camera zooms in until all we can see are the bubbles. Travis's attention is again in the wrong place. We are not likely to share Travis's fascinations, but Scorsese obligates us to partake of them temporarily.

The intimacy with Travis that Scorsese forces upon us wouldn't be so successful if Travis weren't to some extent sympathetic. *Taxi Driver* is, after all, a film about a fundamentally unlikable character. Travis is a racist, murderous, mentally unstable, socially incapable, insomniac war veteran with a deranged hero complex. Yet our intimate view of Travis prevents us from discounting him. We're so close to him that we can feel his embarrassments, paranoia, infatuations, and, most important, his loneliness, as if they were our own. We may not agree with his feelings, and his actions are often surprising and disgusting, but Travis possesses a fundamental loneliness that every human being experiences at some point.

Travis views himself as "God's lonely man," yet the point of "God's Lonely Man," an essay by Thomas Wolfe from which Schrader took this phrase, is that loneliness is a trait that all men possess, even if each man believes his feelings are original and unique. Travis's loneliness, combined with his charisma, makes him fascinating. Travis's racism and violent actions are not endearing, but we can sympathize with his loneliness and with his early attempts to integrate with society. When Travis first asks Betsy on a date, he succeeds at playing the charming young man. His later smiles may seem hysterical or maniacal, but when he walks right up to Betsy's desk and smiles, he is charming. We want him to succeed with Betsy, and we are just as surprised as Betsy is when Travis takes her to a porn film. Like Betsy, we were wrong to believe Travis was innocuous and sympathetic. Travis lives on the extreme outskirts of what is acceptable, but because we know him so intimately, we can sympathize with him even when his actions are unforgivable.

CAMERAWORK

Several styles of camerawork in *Taxi Driver* reveal Travis's loneliness and his distance from society. In general, the shots in *Taxi Driver* are slow and deliberate. After Travis applies to be a taxi driver, he walks out of the dispatcher garage, and as he does so, the camera pans from right to left across the screen as the cabs drive right, in the opposite direction. The other taxis seem to be going forward, in the direction we read and in the direction that picture narratives usually move. Travis walks the other way, and he is moving in the wrong direction even faster than the camera, so it takes a few moments for the camera to catch up to him. The shot indicates that something isn't quite right about Travis. Something about him isn't going the right way.

Much later, when Travis has begun his descent into psychosis, the editing reveals his disjointed state. As Travis turns toward the camera and his voiceover reads a section from his diary ("Listen you fuckers, you screwheads. . . . "), the scene suddenly stops and repeats itself. The cut is so abrupt that it seems like a mistake. The shots are close enough together that we can tell that the two takes are not different, and that the same shot is shown twice in a row. Travis repeats himself obsessively in the "You talkin' to me" speech, and here the film itself adopts that same method. The double shot shows that Travis does not repeat himself for practice, as we might, but that each time he erases what came before. Practice, by definition, involves improving on each additional effort, but Travis acts as if the previous attempts never happened. This editing technique of repetition and replacement gives us a glimpse into Travis's quickly plummeting mental state.

Scorsese has said he believes that the most important scene in *Taxi Driver* is the one showing Travis on a payphone in a hallway, trying to speak to Betsy. As this one-sided conversation takes place, the camera moves from Travis to a shot of an empty hallway around the corner. No people or motion fill the shot, and the hallway has no visual elements to attract the eye. This camera move prevents us from looking at Travis in his shame at losing Betsy, and the fact that neither participant in the phone conversation is visible conveys the fact that no real communication is taking place. The hallway suggests the path the film will take from this point on. Soon after this conversation, Travis changes from any lonely man to "God's lonely man," on a path toward what he views as his destiny—a path as straight and narrow as the hallway.

SCORE

Bernard Hermann's soundtrack, which he wrote shortly before his death, turns Travis's ordinary life into what is sometimes a heroic epic, sometimes a horror film, and other times no more than just another New York story. Two major themes dominate the score of *Taxi Driver*. The first features an eight-bar melodic sighing of a solo saxophone. The theme evokes the lonely melancholy of an individual alienated from his environment. The smooth, jazzy tones of the saxophone also complement New York's urban terrain, which we see as Travis passes through the various neighborhoods of the city in his taxi. The theme varies somewhat, particularly in tempo, but it follows Travis in his taxi as he drives his often sordid passengers around the city.

Travis's psychotic tendencies shine through in a second theme, characterized by an unresolved, dissonant chord played by trumpets over rhythmic snare drums. At various points in the movie, a harp joins the trumpets and snare. At the beginning of the movie, the trumpets punctuate moments that augur Travis's instability, such as when he hits Iris with his car. While Travis descends gradually into psychosis, this theme becomes dominant in the score. The unresolved chords of the blaring trumpets echo Travis's feelings of discord with the city, and the snare drums propel him to action. The unresolved quality of this theme is characteristic of several Hitchcock movie scores, particularly that of *Vertigo*, which Hermann also composed.

These two themes clash with one another in the climactic shootout at the end of the movie, which is originally dominated by the discord of the trumpets playing over an arpeggio in the harp, evoking an atmosphere of surreality around the nightmarish scene. As the camera pans from above across the carnage of the shootout, the trumpets continue to blare, bearing witness to the horror of Travis's actions. They pierce the silence like an alarm, which segues nicely to the imagined sirens of the police cars outside. When the camera pulls away from the upstairs room with the corpses and descends the staircase, the saxophone theme blends with the trumpets, slowed down and played rhythmically out of joint, to emphasize Travis's transformation from a lonely taxi driver into a murderer. This theme serves as a lyric contemplation of Travis's deranged story.

INFLUENCES

One of the benchmarks of 1970s American films is the extent to which they wear their previous influences on their sleeves. Their overt acknowledgement of influences is partly a symptom of postmodernism, a style more interested in portraying copies in a self-conscious and original way than in creating something entirely original. It was also a product of the directors' having grown up in the age of television, where one could watch the same films on re-runs over and over. *Taxi Driver* has a long roster of cinematic, literary, and real life influences of its own, and below is a partial catalogue explaining them. The cinematic influences appear mainly in Scorsese's direction, while the literary influences were written into the screenplay by Paul Schrader. The complex web of influences suggests that *Taxi Driver* is not simply a portrait of random violence and debauched mental illness, but rather a medley of carefully considered responses to previous artistic visions of similar subjects.

FILMS
Taxi Driver's plot pays homage to the 1956 John Ford film *The Searchers,* starring John Wayne as Ethan Edwards. John Wayne was the quintessential hero for children growing up in the 1950s, and *The Searchers* may have been especially influential because Wayne's

character is neither heroic nor admirable. The film's influence was wide-reaching, also inspiring the plot for George Lucas's *Star Wars* (1977), which is surprising given that *Star Wars* and *Taxi Driver* have little else in common.

The similarities between Travis and Ethan are extensive. Both Travis and Ethan are loners who do not quite fit into society. In *Taxi Driver*, Travis appears at the beginning of the film several years after he has been discharged from his service in the Vietnam War. In *The Searchers*, John Ford begins the film several years after the end of the Civil War, a war in which Ethan has fought for the losing side, the South. Ethan makes no explanation for what he's been doing in the intervening years. Society considers both Travis and Ethan heroic, even though they kill many innocent people in the course of their heroic actions. Ethan thinks nothing of massacring Indians and of trying to eliminate their food supply by killing buffalo. Travis kills everyone involved in Iris's life, as well as a black man trying to rob a convenience store. Ethan has an obsessive hatred for Indians, Travis for black people. Ethan is on a mission to rescue his niece from Indians, and Travis devotes his energy to saving Iris from her sexual custody. In both cases the young woman in question has no interest in being rescued, and we are denied her point of view once she is supposedly saved. The Indians have become Debbie's people. Similarly, Iris escaped an unhappy home life to live in the glamorous city where she is the favorite of her pimp, Sport. The styles of these two films, however, are very different. Whereas Ethan is distant and hard to understand, we are uncomfortably close to Travis and his daily habits.

The Searchers influenced *Taxi Driver*'s plot and some of its themes, but this film is only the beginning of Scorsese's references to previous films. Scorsese has stated that Alfred Hitchcock's *The Wrong Man* (1956) inspired his point-of-view shots for Travis. The opening shot of Travis's eyes may come from one of many films, including *The Tales of Hoffman* (1951), *The Conformist* (1970), *In a Lonely Place* (1950), or *Vertigo* (1958). The scene in which Travis stares at his Alka-Seltzer is lifted straight from Jean-Luc Goddard's close-up of the surface of a cup of coffee in *2 or 3 Things I Know about Her* (1967). Scorsese's cameo as the unnamed passenger marks a turning point in the plot just as Roman Polanski's cameo does in *Chinatown*.

LITERATURE

Just as *The Searchers* influenced *Taxi Driver*'s structure, *Notes from Underground*, the 1864 novel by Fyodor Dostoevsky, influenced the development of Travis's character. *Notes from Underground* is told in the form of a diary. The notes that the unnamed protagonist writes are confused and contradictory memoirs that describe his alienation from modern society. Like *Taxi Driver*, *Notes* centers on an unreliable, lonely narrator. Reading spurs the protagonist's disgust and hatred for society, just as driving around the worst areas of the city feeds Travis's hatred. The book even contains a similar plot element to *Taxi Driver*: the protagonist of *Notes* tries to save a young prostitute in the second half of the novel.

Taxi Driver also has more recent literary influences, including the French existentialist novels of the 1950s, such as Albert Camus's *The Stranger* and Jean-Paul Sartre's *Nausea*. Travis resembles an existential hero in that he cannot summon normal emotions about day-to-day occurrences. Unlike the characters from *Nausea* or *Notes from Underground*, whose lives are characterized by an almost obsessive inaction, Travis's crises propel him to violence, which Schrader believes to be a distinctly American reaction to obsession and loneliness.

HISTORICAL

Travis's efforts to save Iris were influenced by *The Searchers* and *Notes from Underground*, but his attempt to assassinate the presidential candidate Palantine was inspired by current events. In 1972, Arthur Bremer tried and failed to assassinate presidential candidate and Governor George C. Wallace. Bremer, a young loner who lived in a rented room, had been following Wallace closely for several weeks. The choreography of his attempted assassination is almost identical to that portrayed in the movie. As Wallace was walking by, Bremer reached into the crowd with a gun and shot at the candidate. Bremer paralyzed Wallace, but security guards prevented him from doing any more damage. Bremer, like Travis, kept a detailed journal, and one of his motivations for trying to kill the candidate was his own failed relationship with a young girl.

Taxi Driver has influenced many subsequent films, but it is more famous for having influenced another would-be assassin, John Hinckley, Jr. Hinkley was obsessed with *Taxi Driver*, and more specifically with Jodie Foster, who plays Iris. After stalking Foster unsuccessfully, Hinkley decided that assassinating the president would get her attention. He tried and failed to assassinate first Jimmy Carter and then Ronald Reagan, whom he shot but did not kill.

Important Quotations Explained

1. TRAVIS: "You talkin' to me? You talkin' to me? You talkin' to me? Well, who the hell else are you talkin' to? You talkin' to me? Well, I'm the only one here. Who the fuck do you think you're talkin' to?"

This is one of the most famous and often imitated soliloquies in film history. It occurs shortly after Travis has bought his guns and has decided to discipline his body, and directly after the scene where Travis gets himself tagged by one of Palantine's Secret Service agents. Travis says these macho lines to a mirror, while drawing his gun as quickly as he can to threaten the imaginary person talking to him. Roger Ebert has noted that the line "Well, I'm the only one here" echoes the central theme of the film, loneliness. Travis is so lonely that he *is* the only one there, forced to speak to his reflection. In the scene, Travis acts as if people commonly talk to him in a manner that merits an aggressive response. However, until this point in the film the only person who has even come close to confronting him is the clumsy and ineffectual Tom. By talking to the mirror, Travis creates a new social situation for himself, one where he is in complete control. He sees himself as a vigilante, but in reality he creates conflict where there is none, becoming his own antagonist.

This defensive soliloquy is not the first time in the film that Travis has a one-sided conversation. When he goes to see Betsy at the Palantine headquarters after she has refused to answer his calls, he is repetitive and accusatory in a way that resembles the "You talkin' to me?" speech. He says, "Why won't you talk to me? Why won't you talk to me? Why don't you answer my calls when I call you? You think I don't know you're here? You think I don't know? You think I don't know?" Instead of faulting someone for talking to him as he does in the mirror, here he is aggressive toward Betsy for *not* calling him. Another version of Travis's soliloquy appears even earlier in the film, when Travis is on his first date with Betsy. Betsy compares Travis to a line of a Kris Kristofferson song, and he asks, "You saying that about me?" She replies, "Who else would I be talking about?" These two questions foreshadow the question-question conversation that Travis has with himself later on. With Betsy, Travis's response is defensive and upset, while she affirms her observation with the rhetorical question, "Who else?" When Travis talks to himself in the mirror, he is the only one asking questions, endowing him with a measure of power he lacked when he talked to Betsy.

2. TRAVIS: "All my life needed was a sense of someplace to go. I don't believe that one should devote his life to morbid self-attention. I believe that someone should become a person like other people."

Travis writes these sentences in his diary and speaks them in a voiceover near the beginning of the film, just before he sees Betsy in her white dress. Betsy is someone to latch on to, someone with the potential to turn Travis into a person like other people. This quotation characterizes Travis during the first half of the film, while he is still half-heartedly trying to fit in, find a girlfriend, and be a hard-working member of society. He tries to "become a person" by chatting up the girl who works at the porn theater, by asking Betsy out, and by starting a conversation with Palantine in his cab. He handles each of these tasks the wrong way: porn theaters are not appropriate places to take girls on dates, and his swearing makes Palantine uncomfortable. Yet Travis does seem to be making an effort to fit in.

The second sentence of the quotation, expressing Travis's scorn for "morbid self-attention," seems particularly misplaced, even at this early moment in the film. By writing obsessively in his diary, Travis reveals that his own self-attention borders on morbidity. Travis might have a chance at becoming "a person like other people" if he could just snap out of his insular world, which consists of porn theaters, driving to dangerous places, and obsessive loathing for blacks and all that is sexually devious. Travis's attempt at dating Betsy by taking her to a pornographic movie is also part of his own "morbid self-attention." Instead of trying to become a social person, he tries to drag Betsy into his anti-social world, one where the only place to go is the intrinsically anti-social porn theater.

3. TRAVIS: "Loneliness has followed me my whole life. Everywhere. In bars, in cars, sidewalks, stores, everywhere. There's no escape. I'm God's lonely man."

Travis says this in a voiceover early in the second half of the movie. The scene takes place after the unnamed passenger talks about shooting his wife and directly after Travis accidentally hits Iris with his cab, and just before he goes to buy his guns. The difference between this quotation and the previous diary quotation, concerning "morbid self-attention," is stark, even though both entries are about loneliness. In the first, Travis knows he is lonely but strives to fit into society, while here he fashions himself as a chosen person, a man who has been predestined to be lonely as part of a special assignment from God. He will no longer try to fit in with the rest of the world, so he fashions himself not only as an outsider but as a vigilante. Travis believes that his subsequent violent actions, including the attempted assassination of Palantine and the final bloodbath, are heroic, suggesting that "morbid self-attention" has become his main motivation.

The phrase "God's lonely man" is the title of an essay by Thomas Wolfe, an American writer from the South who lived at the beginning of the twentieth century. Schrader uses a quote from this essay as the epigraph to the screenplay: "The whole conviction of my life now rests upon the belief that loneliness, far from being a rare and curious phenomenon . . . is the central and inevitable fact of human existence." The ironic relationship between this quote and the moment when Travis defines himself as "God's lonely man" is that while Wolfe was trying to explain that loneliness is what all humans have in common, Travis believes that his loneliness is what makes him special and different from everyone else. Wolfe understands, however, that discovering that everyone is lonely will not help cure loneliness. His point is that although each man feels chosen, no one actually is.

4. WIZARD: " . . . you do a thing and that's what you are . . . Get drunk, you know, do anything. 'Cause you got no choice anyway."

This quotation is part of Wizard's response to Travis when Travis tells Wizard he's down and has been getting bad ideas in his head. Betsy has rejected him, and he has just heard the unnamed passenger's homicidal speech, so he comes to Wizard, who is older and more experienced, for advice. Wizard can offer only this rambling speech, in which he claims a man is what he does. The speech refers to Wizard's own sense of failure for having never moved up in the world. Travis, however, is not feeling down about being a taxi driver, but about being rejected by Betsy and about his burgeoning violent fantasies. Wizard's speech does not speak to Travis's problems, and Travis replies, "That's about the dumbest thing I've ever heard," which puts Wizard on the defensive. Travis in part thinks that the speech is dumb because he doesn't believe his destiny is to be a taxi driver. He wants to rise up above his everyday existence and be heroic. This exchange with Wizard is another of Travis's failed attempts at personal connection.

Wizard's speech, though personal, is also prophetic, since Travis will not be able to escape his fate as a taxi driver. He is praised as a hero after saving Iris, but the newspaper articles all label him as a taxi driver. Travis planned to be a martyr and an important assassin, but since he failed at killing himself, he must return to his old profession, and he seems doomed to be a taxi driver. Although both Wizard and Travis believe the future is determined, they have different ideas about what Travis's fate will be.

5.   BETSY: "'He's a prophet and a pusher, partly truth, partly fiction. A walking contradiction.'"

During her date with Travis, Betsy quotes lyrics from a Kris Kristofferson song to describe Travis. The song is "The Pilgrim: Chapter 33" from the 1971 album *The Silver Tongued Devil and I*. Betsy quotes the lyrics to the song correctly but leaves some words out, and she mixes up their order, so that the "walking contradiction" phrase, which is most important to her, comes last. At first it appears that Betsy does not really understand or appreciate Travis. Earlier in the conversation she underestimates his intelligence by believing that he really thinks "organized" is spelled "organizied." Here, Betsy seems to understand Travis perfectly, and her understanding, as this lyric suggests, is out of character. One might suspect that Schrader, the screenwriter, wanted this line to explain Travis to the audience.

Travis *is* a walking contradiction. He is disgusted by sex and by prostitutes, yet he surrounds himself with pornography and takes prostitutes around in his cab. He wants to be good to his body, yet he constantly takes pills and pours schnapps on his breakfast. Betsy, of course, knows nothing about these quirks. She knows Travis only from the limited and awkward conversation they've had at the diner. Perhaps she is reminded of the song because of its first two lines, which she does not quote: "See him wasted on the sidewalk in his jacket and his jeans, wearin' yesterday's misfortunes like a smile." These lyrics describe Travis's physical appearance perfectly. The Kristofferson lyrics provide an unusual glimpse into Travis's character, though Betsy is not even aware of the elements in Travis's life that make them particularly true.

ANNIE HALL

(1977)

CONTEXT

Largely considered Woody Allen's greatest and best-loved film, *Annie Hall* was released in 1977 to wide critical and commercial success. The film, which Allen cowrote, directed, and starred in, tells the story of a failed romance within the frame of 1970s–era New York City—a romance based loosely on Allen's real-life relationship with actress Diane Keaton, whose given name was Diane "Annie" Hall. *Annie Hall* won four Academy Awards, including Best Picture, and firmly established the comic genius of Woody Allen and the remarkable acting talent of the young Diane Keaton. It is a hilarious but poignant work, remembered as much for its culturally referential wit as for the endearing relationship that unfolds amid the punch lines.

Allen made *Annie Hall* after releasing five previous films, all of them satires of specific film genres or literary canons. These films, which include *Take the Money and Run* (1969) and *Love and Death* (1975), benefited from frequent moments of slapstick. With *Annie Hall,* Allen set out to make a broader film focused less on comedy and more on storyline. Cowritten with Allen's cabaret colleague Marshall Brickman, *Annie Hall* was originally conceived as a murder mystery, but the mystery idea was soon dropped as the quirky romance storyline began to stand out in the script. At the time, the Hollywood movie-making system was in full gear, and the studios were preoccupied with large-scale blockbusters, as well as dealing with some major embarrassments—director Roman Polanski fled the United States to escape a statutory rape conviction, and director Francis Ford Coppola's huge project *Apocalypse Now* (1979) was costing so much time and money that it became a prime target of media mockery. In this cinematic environment, *Annie Hall* stood apart as a refreshing comic masterpiece made entirely outside of the glamorous, profit-oriented Hollywood system.

Making movies seems to serve an almost therapeutic function for Allen. Though relatively reclusive in his personal life—he refused to go to the Academy Awards, where *Annie Hall* took home four Oscars, in favor of playing his weekly jazz gig in a Manhattan club—he has few qualms about exposing his innermost thoughts on screen. Allen's own struggles and complexes, especially in relation to women and sex, saturate many of his films, and it often becomes hard to separate Allen from the characters he writes and inhabits as an actor. Alvy, the protagonist of *Annie Hall,* is, like Allen, a pessimistic, Jewish stand-up comedian who is constantly paranoid. Add to those similarities the fact that the film is based, albeit loosely, on Allen's real-life romance, and it becomes difficult to distinguish autobiography from fiction. Allen uses this confusion to his benefit and experiments with direct address and other self-conscious techniques in the film.

Allen's work is not drawn solely from his own experiences, however. In *Annie Hall*, he takes comic inspiration from the Marx Brothers and cinematic inspiration from filmmakers like Federico Fellini, who gets a tongue-in-cheek nod in a theater lobby scene, and Ingmar Bergman, whose onscreen tricks inform much of *Annie Hall*'s visual invention. But what most permeates the film is the ideology of Sigmund Freud, whose theories about the mind Allen treats both seriously and irreverently within the film. *Annie Hall* uses what could be called a Freudian chronology, as its story is told with a trajectory that seemingly parallels Alvy's stream of consciousness. Allen pays tribute to Freud's influences at several points in the film, perhaps most notably during the second joke he tells in his opening monologue, which refers to both Freud and Groucho Marx. Allen also found a muse in his hometown of New York City, which plays a significant part in *Annie Hall*. Almost as a rule, Allen shoots and edits his films in New York. *Annie Hall* is shot on location, primarily in Manhattan but also with some scenes from Alvy's Brooklyn childhood as well as a handful of scenes in Los Angeles, the butt of numerous jokes.

Annie Hall at once established Allen's reputation as a top American filmmaker and arguably the best comic filmmaker of the latter half of the twentieth century. The film is hilarious to be sure, but its humor never supersedes its story and indeed would dim without it. The combination of endearingly awkward romance and agitated, self-absorbed humor sets *Annie Hall* apart as a different sort of intelligent romantic comedy—one that doesn't end in marriage and one that remains firmly ingrained in its time period and geographical space. And although some of the film's 1970s–specific one-liners might seem foreign to younger viewers, the image of Alvy, nervous and sweaty after a game of tennis, and Annie, decked out in her now-famous vest and tie, is lasting.

ANNIE HALL

Plot Overview

Annie Hall's story unfolds out of chronological order, with events connected to one another by phrases or images rather than cause-and-effect relationships. This jumpiness makes sense within the film, however, as the story is told in retrospect, with Alvy, as the narrator, attempting to make sense of his relationship with Annie within the context of his entire life.

Annie Hall begins with Alvy speaking directly to the camera. He delivers a few key jokes that humorously set up his pessimistic view of life and then adopts a more serious tone as he begins to confront the truth about his relationship with Annie. The question of why the relationship ended is the central question of the film. To find the answer, Alvy looks within himself, and the film flashes back to his visit to a doctor at the age of nine. Alvy is depressed because, as he explains, the universe is expanding and will one day explode. The doctor tells him to enjoy life while he can. The adult Alvy then turns to the schoolroom, where he defends his younger self for kissing one of his female classmates. The story flashes forward to a year or two before the present, when Alvy is heavily involved with Annie, an aspiring singer, who shows up unapologetically late for their movie date.

In line at the theater, the couple bickers: Alvy complains about the obnoxious loudmouth behind him; Annie, about missing her therapy session. After the film, Annie and Alvy go to bed. Uninterested in sex, Annie brings up Alvy's first wife. The film flashes back to Alvy's first encounter with Allison at a fundraiser, and to their sexual problems when married, then returns to a point in time when Annie and Alvy are more fully enjoying each other's company. In a famous scene, Annie and Alvy laugh as they clumsily try to cook some lobsters at a house in the Hamptons. The film flashes back to Annie's previous romantic relationships, with Annie and Alvy physically present in some scenes to provide commentary. Then, the film veers off to examine Alvy's second marriage, to a New York intellectual with whom he is unable to have successful sex. Then, it jumps forward to Alvy's first meeting with Annie on the tennis court. After the game, Annie makes awkward small talk with Alvy and offers him a ride home.

Alvy accepts the ride and then accepts Annie's invitation to go up to her apartment, where they drink wine and talk about Annie's books and family members. On the balcony, subtitles express what each is really thinking throughout their nervous chatter. Alvy asks Annie out and ends up going with her to a nightclub audition, where she sings tentatively to a restless audience. On their way to get dinner, Alvy spontaneously kisses Annie to "get it over with." The next scene is in the bedroom, after they have just finished making love for the first time. Alvy is a mess; Annie smokes pot to relax. The next scene has them at a bookstore, where Alvy buys Annie two books about death in order to school her on his pessimism. Vignettes follow in which Alvy woos Annie in Central Park and Annie stutters her love for him on a waterfront dock. These brief moments of heady romance end with an argumentative scene.

The rest of the film focuses on the relationship's impending breakup. Alvy wants Annie to have sex without marijuana, but she is so distant he gives up. Alvy travels with Annie to her family home in Wisconsin, where he feels alienated by her WASP family and "classic Jew hater" grandmother. Alvy conjures up an imaginary conversation between his family and Annie's, and the film screen splits to illustrate the contrast between the two worlds. Back in New York, Alvy encounters Annie on the street. Annie accuses him of spying on her, and a heated argument ensues. Searching for the secret to a successful relationship, Alvy questions pedestrians on the street. He is left without a solution and blames his failures on his problems in early life, saying he always falls for the wrong women. In an animated scene, Annie is transformed into the evil queen in *Snow White* and Alvy is portrayed as small and childish. A cartoon version of Alvy's friend Rob enters, saying he has a new girl for Alvy.

Some time after splitting up with Annie, Alvy tries dating again. He goes out with Pam, an odd, skinny *Rolling Stone* reporter who describes things as "transplendent." They have bad sex and are interrupted afterward by a phone call from Annie. Alvy goes over to Annie's apartment to find a frazzled Annie, who asks him to kill a spider, then cries about missing him. They reconcile and vow never to break up again.

By this time, Annie's singing talent has significantly improved, and music producer Tony Lacey approaches her at her next gig. In another split-screen scene, Alvy and Annie talk to their respective therapists about their sexual problems. According to Annie, they "constantly" sleep together; Alvy says "hardly ever." After an expensive mishap with cocaine, Alvy and Annie fly out to Los Angeles, where they meet up with Rob and attend a party at Tony Lacey's house in Hollywood. On the flight home, Annie and Alvy decide their relationship is a "dead shark" and no longer works. They split up.

Alvy dates other women with no luck. Lonely and unhappy, he decides to get Annie back and flies out to L.A., where she is living with Tony Lacey. He asks her to marry him. She declines. In the next scene, Alvy is directing a rehearsal of his first play, which dramatizes his relationship with Annie but gives it his ideal ending, with Annie leaving L.A. for Alvy. Turning to the camera and shrugging, Alvy dismisses his revision as no big deal: "You're always trying to get things to come out perfect in art because it's real difficult in life." Alvy and Annie meet once more when they are both dating other people. In brief snapshots, the film flashes back to happier times between Annie and Alvy, summing up his memories and memorializing their relationship. In a brief, distant shot, they are seen shaking hands and parting, Alvy with his head down. Alvy gives a last voiceover about relationships, concluding that they are absurd and futile but ultimately necessary. Annie's song, "Seems Like Old Times," swells up as the credits roll.

Character List

Alvy Singer—Played by Woody Allen An anal-retentive, extremely self-conscious Jewish comedian and the protagonist of the film. Alvy's quick wit is hilarious and often endearingly self-effacing. He claims his adult life is based on the joke "I would never want to belong to any club that would have someone like me for a member." He also claims to be alienated by the "intellectual" climate of New York City of which he himself is so much a part. Obsessed with death, sex, and anti-Semitism, among other things, Alvy has been seeing a psychoanalyst regularly for fifteen years, with little success. He has a wry, pessimistic outlook on life that informs his actions, especially as pertains to his relationships with women.

Annie Hall—Played by Diane Keaton The flighty, giggly woman whose relationship with Alvy is the focus of the film. Although Annie is smart and can keep up with Alvy's wit, she is insecure about her intelligence. She is a photographer and singer and, with Alvy's guidance, becomes increasingly more confident and independent. Originally from Chippewa Falls, Wisconsin, Annie is the antithesis of a "New York girl" and has a positive, fairly healthy outlook on life. She has a generally good-natured, albeit quirky, personality and a kooky but stylish fashion sense. Her trademark expression is "La-dee-da."

Rob—Played by Tony Roberts Alvy's mellow, somewhat superficial sidekick. Rob takes Alvy's anal-retentiveness in stride, his own coolness providing a balance to his buddy's hyperactive aggression. Although Rob often serves as a target for Alvy's venting, he largely lets it roll off his back. Unlike Alvy, he is enamored with Los Angeles and wants a shallower life than is prevalent in New York. In some ways, Rob is Alvy's mirror image, understanding his friend's actions and concerns but reacting in the opposite direction. Alvy and Rob call each other "Max."

Tony Lacey—Played by Paul Simon   A music producer and Svengali figure to Annie. Tony is symbolic of the glamour and self-indulgence of L.A. Tony has hip parties in his house in Hollywood. He is charming and takes an interest in Annie both artistically and romantically. Annie is intrigued by him, and Alvy is repelled.

Allison Portchnik—Played by Carol Kane   Alvy's first wife, whom he reduces to a cultural stereotype: "New York, Jewish, left-wing, liberal, intellectual. . . . " Allison is always willing to have sex with Alvy, but he loses interest, unable to desire a woman who desires him in return.

Robin—Played by Janet Margolin   Alvy's second wife. Pretentious, snobby, and intellectual to the point of coldness, Robin is concerned primarily with academic schmoozing. She refuses Alvy's attempts at lovemaking and blames distractions like street noise for keeping her from reaching orgasm. She cites her analyst when complaining about tension and reaching for Valium.

Pam—Played by Shelley Duvall   A *Rolling Stone* reporter who has a one-night relationship with Alvy after his separation with Annie. The strikingly thin Pam has great interest in spiritual transcendence and tells Alvy at a gathering with the Maharishi (of Transcendental Mediation fame) that she is a Rosicrucian who follows a Christian mystic philosophy. Alvy goes out with her at Rob's suggestion but is underwhelmed by their sexual experience, which Pam describes as "Kafkaesque."

Mrs. Hall—Played by Colleen Dewhurst   Annie's mother. A proper WASP wife and mother, Mrs. Hall does not approve of Alvy and does not get any of his jokes. Polite and gracious, Mrs. Hall steers the dinner conversation around safe topics like Christmas and a swap meet.

Duane Hall — Played by Christopher Walken Annie's disturbed brother. Duane has fantasies of crashing his car into oncoming traffic and does not hesitate to tell Alvy this, with all seriousness, before eventually driving Alvy and Annie to the airport.

Grammy Hall — Played by Helen Ludlam Annie's anti-Semitic grandmother, whom Alvy describes as a "classic Jew hater." Grammy Hall doesn't speak to Alvy.

Mrs. Singer — Played by Joan Newman Alvy's loudmouthed mother. Mrs. Singer is effusive, neurotic, and argumentative. She runs a lively, informal household as a staunchly Jewish matriarch figure.

Mr. Singer — Played by Mordecai Lawner Alvy's father. Like Mrs. Singer, Mr. Singer is argumentative and lives out Jewish traditions. Although he is more rational than his wife, she is the one in control.

Marshall McLuhan — Played by himself A Canadian media theorist whom Alvy pulls onscreen for the benefit of the audience and the obnoxious man behind Alvy and Annie in line for a movie. McLuhan's appearance proves Alvy's point and adds a tongue-in-cheek fantasy layer to the film.

ANNIE HALL

ANALYSIS OF MAJOR CHARACTERS

ALVY SINGER

An insecure, self-reflexive Jewish comedian obsessed with death, Alvy is a clear stand-in for filmmaker Woody Allen. He is introduced in stark close-up, giving a humorous confessional in a tweed getup that mimics Allen's usual style of dress and performance. Alvy's occupation, location, and personal idiosyncrasies resemble those of Allen, making it hard to distinguish the filmmaker/actor from his protagonist. As a fifteen-year veteran of psychoanalysis, Alvy frequently looks to past events to explain his present actions. He became a nihilist at the age of nine after reading that the universe is expanding and suffered criticism as a child for acting on early sexual impulses and kissing a female classmate. These flashbacks set up Alvy as a pessimist who has little luck with sex or relationships. He also almost immediately refers to what he considers the primary joke of his adult life: "I would never want to belong to any club that would have someone like me for a member." All of these themes— Alvy's pessimism, self-loathing, and failure to succeed in love—are established within the first ten minutes of *Annie Hall*.

Although Alvy's self-deprecating quick wit and intimacy with the viewer establish him as an endearing character, his irksome qualities are evident, too. He is anal ("a polite word for what you are," Annie says), neurotic, overbearing, insecure, aggressive, domineering, pretentious, and unusually averse to unfamiliar situations and places. Often, his actions are counterintuitive: he rejects the "intellectual" Manhattan community of which he is a part; he travels across the country to L.A. to participate in a television awards show, and then chickens out; he encourages Annie to sing until she gets noticed; he is not attracted to women who are attracted to him. He is aware and indulgent of his angst, cracking jokes about it constantly. Because Alvy is driven by the notion that art can revise life, he allows fantasy to enter his narrative throughout the film. As Alvy says after directing a rehearsal of his play that is based on his relationship with Annie: "You're always trying to get things to come out perfect in art because it's real difficult in life." Allen, who based the film on his failed relationship with Diane Keaton, clearly would agree.

ANNIE HALL

When Alvy first meets Annie, she is awkward and nervous, somewhat airheaded, and tells herself via subtitles to "hang in there" because she's not smart enough for him. Originally from the Midwest, Annie feels somewhat lost in and intimidated by the intellectual atmosphere of New York City. Nonetheless, she has already hopped on the therapy bandwagon and joined a sports club. Her self-consciousness about her Chippewa Falls upbringing is magnified by Alvy's propensity to make fun of it. Annie allows herself to be steered along Alvy's path, tolerating books on death and four-hour-long foreign films about the Holocaust, but by the end of their relationship, her confidence and independence have grown exponentially. She begins to accuse Alvy of thinking she's not smart enough, thereby suggesting that she knows her intelligence matches his. She becomes so independent, in fact, that upon their split she quickly moves to Los Angeles to pursue a singing career. Annie's transformation is substantial, giving the film a Pygmalion-like storyline in which Annie blossoms under Alvy's influence—so much so that eventually she doesn't need him anymore.

The film plays out much like a tribute to Diane Keaton. Whereas Alvy's idiosyncrasies become tiresome at points in the film, Annie is nearly always a likeable character. When Alvy goes out to California to woo her back with a desperate marriage proposal, Annie is happy and thriving and her polite refusal is practically a relief. Annie has solidified her identity and no longer allows Alvy to push her around in his neurotic fashion. She has struck out on her own and no longer pines for Alvy as she did after their first break-up, when her ego was still fragile and underdeveloped. The last few moments in the film celebrate Annie with vignettes and sweeping music, and the title of course signifies that she is the main figure of the film. Stepping out of the fiction of the film into its reality, it's clear that Allen's romance with Diane Keaton left a lasting impression on him. The film encourages us to fall in love with Keaton just as Alvy falls in love with Annie. It worked—women wholeheartedly adopted the "Annie Hall" look in 1977, and the film has become a classic.

ROB

Rob, an actor, serves as the voice of sanity that balances the turmoil of Alvy's angst. He is Alvy's best friend and his venting ground. The mirror image of Alvy, Rob is refreshingly mellow and superficial, and his presence in the film provides a relief to Alvy's constant paranoia and insecurity. Rob enjoys normal activities like playing tennis, basking in the sun, and dating women and indulges few quirks or psychodramas. Unlike Alvy, Rob seems to have a healthy, optimistic grasp on the world. But while he is amused by and accepting of his friend's idiosyncrasies, he doesn't necessarily understand them. When Alvy and Annie split up for the first time, Rob tries to help the situation by setting Alvy up with Pam, an extremely thin music journalist interested in mysticism who is entirely wrong for Alvy. When Rob moves to L.A., Alvy is appalled that Rob welcomes the glamour and superficiality of L.A., the city that is endlessly battered by Alvy's snide cracks. Nonetheless, throughout the film, Rob is Alvy's loyal sidekick and comes through for him anytime he is in a jam. The two enjoy a comfortable familiarity, calling each other "Max" in a running inside joke, but neither really understands the other. Nonetheless, they don't really need to understand each other to enjoy each other's company.

Themes, Motifs, and Symbols

Themes

The Absurdity and Necessity of Love

Annie Hall follows Alvy as he searches for the secret to successful relationships and ultimately concludes that love is fleeting and ridiculous but absolutely necessary. He begins his narrative wondering out loud what caused his split with Annie. He ends it resigned to the idea that relationships are absurd but that people need them, absurdity and all. In between, he desperately tries to pinpoint what went wrong. Was it that book he read at age nine? His aggressive mother? The cocaine fiasco? After coming up empty, he even asks anonymous pedestrians to identify the key to happiness in relationships. The answers, of course, are unsatisfactory and belie the arbitrariness and absurdity of love. Alvy's relationships with his two ex-wives also underline the dilemma. How can he now feel so underwhelmed by both of these women whom he once vowed to love until death? But despite its eagerness to point out these paradoxes, the film ends by celebrating the romance between Annie and Alvy, though failed, adding weight to Alvy's final monologue about the necessity of relationships. *Annie Hall* simultaneously relishes and dismisses them.

The Transformative Nature of Art

Throughout the film, Alvy emphasizes the capacity of art to transform life into a more ideal version of reality. Narrative control allows him to revisit the past with revisionist intentions, imagine an animated version of his situation, and force geographically and temporally separate scenes and characters to interact. He also gets to call on a famous media expert (McLuhan) on a whim. *Annie Hall* also carries a tinge of regret, as though its narrator's attempt to improve upon life is only halfhearted. Indeed, the fact remains that, regardless of the ending Alvy conjures up in his play, Annie and Alvy in reality do not last as a couple. Although the fantasy elements frequently add a layer of unpredictability and delight to the narrative, the basic elements and conflicts of the story are true to life.

LOCATION AS IDENTITY

Annie Hall places a great deal of emphasis on geographical location as the foundation of personal identity. Alvy is characterized as a New Yorker, fiercely loyal to his city and condescending to all other locations on earth. Annie is a transplant, still getting her bearings in New York after growing up in a WASP household in the Midwest. Alvy criticizes her birthplace and upbringing—and in some ways her character—each time he mocks her "Chippewa Falls expressions." When Alvy and Annie fly together to Los Angeles, Alvy constantly rails against what he sees as that city's cultureless superficiality. Virtually all of the characters in the L.A. party scene are portrayed as vapid and unctuous. The contrast between Alvy's relief at returning to New York and Annie's enjoyment of their L.A. trip is depicted as a distinct personality difference. And when Alvy tries fruitlessly to get Annie back, he criticizes Los Angeles, suggesting that she leave L.A. not just for him, but also for New York. The cities represent two different lifestyles and identities.

MOTIFS

STEREOTYPES

The use of cultural stereotypes in the film pokes fun at the politically correct climate of 1970s New York. As a Jewish comedian, Alvy (like Woody Allen) has a vested interest in labeling himself and others for comedic purposes. The film plays around with stereotypes, treating them both seriously and ironically, using them as a tool to quickly label characters but also revealing the limits and cruelty of such labels. *Annie Hall* invokes stereotypes to reinforce and dispel prevalent cultural stereotypes. Alvy's Jewishness is one example. In a conversation with Rob, he bemoans a remark he heard at lunch that he interprets as anti-Semitic. Later, at dinner with Annie's family, he momentarily transforms into a Hasidic Jew, full beard and all, representing visually the Jewish stereotype that Annie's family seems to hold. The film also uses stereotypes to define Alvy's ex-wives quickly and cleverly and to reinforce the idea that L.A. is full of superficiality, as all Californian characters live up to the stereotype. Interestingly, Annie is the only character in the film who actively resists being stereotyped, defending her Midwestern upbringing and attraction to L.A. when Alvy uses them to attack her character.

TRANSFORMATION

In its heavy reliance on fantastical elements, *Annie Hall* features numerous instances of transformation, both visually and within the narrative. There are obvious examples, such as Alvy's Hasidic Jew experience and the brief cartoon sequence, but other more subtle examples are scattered throughout the film. Annie transforms significantly during her relationship with Alvy, blooming from blushing wallflower to ambitious artist. She is open to new experiences and comfortable with the transformative experiences that drugs allow, using marijuana during sex so that she can, in a sense, perform better. Rob, too, transforms, moving to L.A. and embracing its lifestyle. Alvy, on the other hand, is apparently afraid to change. He refuses to use drugs, claiming they make him "unbearably wonderful," and clings to his city and his life as though an upheaval would drastically harm him. Indeed, even his brief visit to L.A. results in physical illness. Nonetheless, though Alvy is resistant to change in his real life, he adopts it often in his art, riffing on life in his jokes and revising events in his play to fit his desires.

PERFORMANCE

Performance is important to *Annie Hall*, especially in terms of its comedic aspects. The film is framed between two humorous monologues, suggesting that the film itself should be regarded as an entertaining performance rather than taken too seriously. Fundamentally, the film is a comedy and therefore intended to induce laughter; indeed, at its most basic level, it is simply a number of brief comic sketches pieced together. Performance is important not just for the viewer's sake but also for the main characters, who occupy performative roles. Alvy is a comedian; Annie, a singer; Rob, an actor. By emphasizing performance as a career and as the function of the film, *Annie Hall* suggests that all social interaction, particularly as pertaining to romantic relationships, is performance. Surely, Alvy's constant jokes, even in casual conversation, are a form of performance. And of course there are the scenes involving sex, failure to have satisfactory sex, or failure to have sex at all. Alvy avoids having sex with Allison because he simply can't fake it anymore; Robin blames New York noise for preventing her successful performance; Annie needs pot to enjoy sex; Alvy is insecure about his performance generally, and after his first time with Annie, lavishes their coupling with praise. Sex is treated as a performance that can go very well or very, very badly.

SYMBOLS

NEW YORK

New York City symbolizes all that is Alvy Singer: it is gloomy, claustrophobic, and socially cold, but also an intellectual haven full of nervous energy. To Alvy, New York represents home, culture, life, and safety. It is his favorite place in the world, and he will defend it until death. Alvy is not comfortable anywhere else and longs for his city when away. The New York of *Annie Hall* is portrayed as a cultural mecca where Alvy feels free to cross the street without looking and ask strangers about their love lives. Indeed, *Annie Hall* is as much a love song to New York City as it is to the character Annie Hall. The film celebrates New York for its accessibility and intellectual climate. It is also viewed as the antithesis of the cultureless void that Alvy considers Los Angeles to be.

LOS ANGELES

Los Angeles harbors only superficiality, self-indulgence, and empty glamour, according to Alvy and the film. On his visit with Annie, Alvy has a visceral, nauseated reaction to L.A. The city is blindingly bright, but sun is "bad for you," Alvy says. Annie points out the streets' cleanliness, and Alvy jokes that all the trash is put on television. Each overheard conversation at Tony Lacey's party is a jab at Hollywood stereotypes: "All the good meetings are taken"; "I forgot my mantra"; "we're gonna operate together." Alvy views Annie's move to L.A. almost as a personality defect, but it's also a life-changing decision for her, one made entirely without Alvy's input. When Alvy flies out to California to attempt a reconciliation, he makes snide cuts at Los Angeles and glorifies New York. Annie defends L.A., which has become a symbol for her freedom, saying "What's so great about New York? I mean, it's a dying city. . . . Alvy, you're incapable of enjoying life, you know that? You're like New York City." Annie has articulated her realization that Alvy will never change and that their relationship is dead.

DRUGS

Drugs appear in the film several times as a symbol of open-mindedness, youth, escape, and freedom. Annie uses them to enhance sex and for relaxation. She tries to persuade Alvy to smoke marijuana after sex, to no avail. Alvy is uncomfortable around mind-altering substances, saying they generally cause him only embarrassment.

ANNIE HALL

His claim is proven true when he does try cocaine at a friend's apartment and ends up sneezing away thousands of dollars worth of the drug. Alvy feels too old and unhip to use drugs, which points to the profound contrast between Alvy's narrow-mindedness and Annie's interest in new experiences. Alvy views drugs much as he views L.A.: as glamorous and self-indulgent. He doesn't understand Annie's predilection for them. When he persuades Annie to have sex without marijuana, the results are hilarious, with Annie's spirit literally rising up from her body in boredom in a double-exposed scene. While comic, this scene reveals Annie and Alvy's sexual problems and the couple's growing rift.

FILM ANALYSIS

SOCIOHISTORICAL CONTEXT

Annie Hall is a document of its time. Released in the 1970s, it comes dressed in its historical period and geographic setting. As such, the film is an artifact that records the intellectual climate of New York City in the late 1970s. Nearly all of its jokes rely on knowledge of then-current cultural events and figures, as well as prevalent cultural stereotypes. To watch *Annie Hall* is to be plucked from your seat in the twenty-first century and dropped onto a street corner in Manhattan in 1977. The immersion is at once delightful and bewildering, and viewers too young to remember the 1970s are likely to miss out on some laughs without knowledge of how Freud, Fellini, and others factored into the cultural landscape of the time. In a sense, *Annie Hall* is educational, and its name-dropping is often tongue-in-cheek, simultaneously giving glory to and making fun of the pretentious Manhattan intelligentsia that both attracts and repels Alvy Singer.

Freud's ideas exert a great influence on *Annie Hall* and its depiction of relationships. Psychoanalysis as a form of self-help was at its peak in the 1970s, and in New York City, nearly ubiquitous. In both narration and dialogue, Alvy uses his knowledge and experience of psychoanalysis to guide him through current relationships and reevaluate past ones. These experiences inform the story's disjointed retelling, in which one scene is followed by an indirectly related scene, entirely out of sequence and in a stream-of-consciousness fashion. The narration jumps from the present to Alvy's childhood to midway through his relationship with Annie to their first meeting and so on, making for a jagged chronology that could conceivably follow the course of a session between Alvy and his analyst. But while Alvy treats his psychoanalysis sessions with reverence, an ever-present chuckle runs throughout the film at any mention of the technique. Alvy recognizes the failings of psychoanalysis but clings to it nevertheless.

Similarly, Alvy clearly is part of the New York intelligentsia, yet he claims to find that group self-important, elitist, and cold, constantly pointing out the absurdities of its set of social rules. His love-hate attitude is revealed in the film's preface-like opening, in which Alvy paraphrases Allen's idol, Groucho Marx, who himself was paraphrasing Sigmund Freud: "I would never want to belong to any club that would have someone like me for a member." Alvy is eager to be accepted into the artistic, intellectual crowd but finds this same crowd insufferable. To Alvy, Annie is a refreshing alternative to his usual New York scene. He is fascinated by her Wisconsin background and her frequent use of the word *neat* but pokes fun at her at the same time. And while Alvy falls in love with and celebrates Annie's otherness, he attempts to indoctrinate her into the very scene he wants to escape. He mocks Sylvia Plath, whose poem collection *Ariel* he finds in Annie's apartment, and suggests Annie instead read theory-heavy books about death—a concept that profoundly affects the way he views life. He advises her to go back to school, and then gets upset when she establishes a relationship with a professor. He encourages her to improve herself and continue singing, but when she does begin to succeed, he becomes controlling and unsupportive. *Annie Hall* is a Pygmalion-like story, with Alvy shaping Annie in his image until she finds the self-confidence and independence to strike out on her own. Even then, he criticizes her choice of residence. *Annie Hall* is a constant paradox, reflecting Allen's ability to make fun of intelligentsia in intelligent fashion without letting his protagonist off the hook.

FILMIC ELEMENTS

Annie Hall's numerous elements of visual invention supplement the story's main theme that art can reshape life into something more palatable and satisfying. The narrative itself works on this level, as Alvy revises the story to fit his desires. In addition, some of the film's visual techniques allow a different, surprising way for Alvy to go back (literally) and editorialize on the past. Allen appropriates some techniques, such as direct addresses to the camera and a nonlinear timeline, from his own cinematic influences—Ingmar Bergman, Federico Fellini, and the Marx Brothers, among others. Other gags, entirely original and influential in their own right, serve to show that the film is not about the relationship but rather about Alvy's idea of what the relationship was. They gags also reinforce Allen's own image of a self-conscious artist who constantly uses art to revisit and revise his life. With movies, he has the power and control to do so publicly.

ANNIE HALL

One of the most famous techniques used in *Annie Hall* is the double-exposed scene in which Alvy tries to coax Annie into having sex without the assistance of drugs. To display visually Annie's distance and lack of interest, her body is double-exposed so that one Annie is in bed with Alvy while another rises out of bed to search for her drawing pad. Alvy speaks to both Annies, separately and collectively. The visual gag gives humorous emphasis to the conflict of the scene and of course revises what actually would have happened. The visual gag is entertaining and gets a laugh but also demonstrates that Alvy is fantasizing.

Another, similar, visual technique is the addition of subtitles that contradict the onscreen dialogue as Alvy and Annie converse on Annie's balcony. The subtitles ostensibly offer their respective character's thoughts as they chat nervously. This gag adds another layer of awareness to the scene, as well as a bit of humor in exposing the completely unrelated thoughts that most people have while interacting with someone they are attempting to attract. Again, the gag serves as a way to editorialize upon the story's reality and also humorously point out the difference in perspective that two people have while participating in the same conversation.

Time travel and animation are other techniques that emphasize the fantastical aspect of *Annie Hall*. In several scenes, Alvy literally revisits the past and occasionally takes companions with him. He goes back to his childhood to defend his younger self's actions by explaining them in Freudian terms. He takes his friend Rob back to a family party to prove a point about his uncle. He tags along as Annie pulls him along her relationship timeline. All of these moments allow Alvy and, vicariously, Allen, to return to the past, comment on it in terms of what has happened since, and of course slip in some self-reflective jabs at the expense of others, often family members. The animation scene takes this fantastical tack and pulls it in another direction, inserting the characters into a fictional cartoon in which Annie is portrayed as the wicked queen in *Snow White* and Alvy is portrayed as a childish victim. Clearly, Alvy is psychoanalyzing the situation too much. Other visually inventive elements in the film include interactive split screens, sudden physical transformations (such as when Alvy turns into a Hasidic Jew), and the sudden production of a real-life character (Marshall McLuhan) paired with the direct-to-camera comment "Boy, if only life were like this." Together, these techniques support the notion that art can and should be used to reshape life into an easier-to-swallow, more fulfilling version of itself.

Genre

Though *Annie Hall* is a romantic comedy in many respects, it does not fit neatly into this genre. Though the film is indeed about a romantic relationship, and it is comedy, it also disregards several of the genre's conventions, most notably through its lack of a happy ending. Though the protagonists' relationship succeeds on many levels, it does not succeed in the traditional sense—it does not end in marriage. On the other hand, the film does end relatively happily, with only a tinge of sadness. Put simply, the film champions the notion that love fades. People drift apart, but that doesn't mean that what they once had is any less powerful.

The film also pulls no punches in putting both Annie and Alvy's flaws on full display. The confessional, revisionist tone of the narrative pulls us in so that we experience the impending implosion of the characters' relationship as Alvy is remembering it. While Alvy's anal-retentive, neurotic paranoia is endearing, it also becomes irritating to the point at which it's hard to blame Annie for wanting to split. At the same time, Annie's "la-dee-da" habit can be charming, but it becomes apparent why her descriptions of everything as "neat" irk the hyperarticulate Alvy. Although *Annie Hall* clearly contains splendid moments in which Annie and Alvy seem the ideal match, the film doesn't airbrush out the flaws in the relationship. Instead, these flaws—Alvy's domineering nature, Annie's insecurities—are magnified as the film unfolds. Of course, the viewer knows from the start that the relationship will end and spends much of the film anticipating the breakup. Whereas most romantic comedies consist of a couple meeting and overcoming numerous obstacles before eventually realizing they are meant to be together till death do them part, *Annie Hall* comes at love from a different angle, following the storyline of one relationship's bittersweet end.

An argument could be made that *Annie Hall* is less about love than it is about the unending loneliness of the human soul. Alvy's relationship with Annie takes center stage, but the film skirts around his other failed couplings. Much of the narration deals with his sexual frustrations and failure to communicate effectively with women. He seems resigned to a life lived largely alone, with some brief periods in which he is in a monogamous, decently healthy relationship.

ANNIE HALL

Frustrated by his lack of success in love, he stops pedestrians in the streets of Manhattan to ask them the secret to a happy relationship. Their answers are telling: an elderly man suggests, bizarrely, a "large, vibrating egg," and an attractive young couple explains that they're both equally shallow, with "no ideas and nothing interesting to say." The scene supports the idea that the success of relationships depends on factors that are largely arbitrary, and furthermore that most relationships ultimately are not successful. The last mono-logue in the film reiterates this notion, as Alvy concludes that rela-tionships are "totally irrational and crazy and absurd and . . . but I guess we keep going through it because most of us need the eggs." By "eggs" Alvy means all the rewards that come from a relationship, however absurd and troublesome that relationship may be. In focusing on the futility of relationships, *Annie Hall* dismantles many prevalent ideas of love, especially as glamorized and mythol-ogized in typical romantic comedies.

Important Quotations Explained

1.   ALVY: "I would never want to belong to any club that would have someone like me for a member."

Alvy delivers this joke directly into the camera in a stark close-up at the opening scene of the movie, in the middle of an intimate and humorous monologue. It pays tribute to key figures in Allen's life: Groucho Marx, to whom the quote is usually attributed, and Sigmund Freud, in whose *Wit and Its Relation to the Unconscious* the notion originally appeared. From Marx, Allen learned comedy. From Freud, Allen learned about the unconscious and its hold on his present actions. This quotation immediately establishes Alvy's character as riddled with psychopathological hang-ups, especially in the realm of romantic relationships, and sets up the main theme of the film—that love is absurd and in many ways futile. It also sets up the narrative line of the story, serving as a springboard into the memory of Alvy's failed relationship with Annie, as told in retrospect.

The quotation is reinforced throughout the film as Alvy jumps back and forth among his various relationships with women. He avoids sex with his first wife, Allison, because she is willing and therefore unattractive to him. He constantly mocks the New York intellectuals who are his peers. He makes fun of his Jewish family and, of course, makes fun of himself all the time. He also pokes fun at Annie's old boyfriends—a group he eventually joins himself. When Annie wants to make a commitment and moves into his apartment, Alvy pushes her away, yet he attempts a reconciliation with her after she loses interest in him and moves on. Alvy realizes he acts out the conflict articulated in the quotation, but he is unable to stop the pattern and maintain a healthy, lasting relationship. At the end of the film, he concludes that such relationships are virtually impossible and that love itself is absurd.

2.   ALVY: "Boy, if life were only like this . . ."

Alvy turns to the camera and makes this remark after he has gleefully pulled media critic Marshall McLuhan onscreen to tell off the

415

obnoxious loudmouth standing behind him in the ticket line for the movie *The Sorrow and the Pity*. McLuhan tells the man he knows nothing of McLuhan's work and "how you ever got to teach a course in anything is totally amazing." This clearly fanciful exchange provides a visual demonstration of the transformative nature of art—one of *Annie Hall*'s major themes. Alvy is delighted at his control over the narrative, as the quotation indicates. However, the line also signals Alvy's awareness that, despite his control over his memory and the film's storyline, he is helpless to control reality. Within the film, he can time-travel back to age nine and add interpretive subtitles, but in real life there are no such benefits. Alvy's comment indicates his preference of art over life—a preference that filmmaker Allen may hold himself.

Alvy frequently employs fantastical techniques to riff on reality and transform it into his ideal version of what happened between him and Annie. This comment articulates, with humor, the regret that Alvy may feel about some of the choices he has made throughout his life. It also implies that Alvy is more comfortable within the territory of art than he is in reality. Other scenes reinforce this idea: Alvy is hesitant to try new things—drugs, trips, visits to a famous music producer's hotel room—in most areas of his life, but he has no qualms about inserting an animated or double-exposed film into the narrative. Later in the film, while Alvy directs a rehearsal of a play that revises the fate of his relationship with Annie, he reiterates this idea of art being preferable to real life when he says, "You're always trying to get things to come out perfect in art because it's real difficult in life."

3. PASSERBY: "It's never something you do. That's how people are. Love fades."

A passerby makes this response to Alvy's question, "Somewhere, she cooled off to me. Is it something that I did?" The pedestrian's answer encourages Alvy to face reality and chalk up the relationship's end as natural and inevitable. The comment suggests that we, as human beings, are helpless to control what happens to us. Alvy has nothing to do with the cooling of Annie's feelings for him: she has just moved on to a different stage in her life that doesn't include him. People change. Love fades. This idea doesn't make things any easier for Alvy, who seems to want to pinpoint the exact moment and situation in which Annie's feelings tempered. In a sense, it makes things worse, because he is left at a loss, with no one and nothing to blame for his unhappiness. The passerby's remark foreshadows Alvy's final monologue in the film, which sums up his feelings about relationships.

4.   ANNIE: "Alvy, you're incapable of enjoying life, you know that? I mean you're like New York City. You're just this person. You're like this island unto yourself."

Annie makes this remark to Alvy at a sidewalk café in Los Angeles after he flies out in an attempt to win her back with a desperate marriage proposal. The quotation sums up Annie's view of Alvy, whose pessimism has driven her away. She has no hard feelings toward Alvy and wants to remain friends. In this conversation, Annie is finally strong and confident enough to tell Alvy what she really thinks of him, and she compares him to New York. The comment reinforces the parallel between Alvy and his home, New York City, but does so in a negative way. The film has been fiercely loyal to New York until this point, when Annie turns the tables and suggests that maybe New York is not paradise after all. Annie also differentiates herself here from Alvy. He has shaped her in his image in many ways, but this quotation demonstrates her separating herself from him, and from New York City, for good. It becomes clear in this moment that they will not get back together and that their relationship is over for good.

5.   ALVY: "I thought of that old joke. This guy goes to a psychiatrist and says, 'Doc, my brother's crazy. He thinks he's a chicken.' And the doctor says, 'Well, why don't you turn him in?' And the guy says, 'I would, but I need the eggs.' Well, I guess that's pretty much now how I feel about relationships. They're totally irrational and crazy and absurd and . . . but I guess we keep going through it because most of us need the eggs."

Alvy turns to the camera and delivers a final monologue summing up his feelings about his breakup with Annie and relationships in general. For the past ninety-some minutes, Alvy has delved into the psychosexual drama of romantic relationships, trying to figure out the key to making them work. This last remark is akin to Alvy throwing up his hands. There's no secret. He gives up, with the

ANNIE HALL

knowledge that however absurd and ridiculous relationships may be, he still will pursue them. This remark, the last line in the film aside from Annie's song "Seems Like Old Times," is delivered after Alvy is shown meeting Annie by chance on the street. In the brief vignette, Alvy turns away with his head down, signifying that he will always have feelings for Annie and still harbors regret about their breakup. With this last comment, Alvy concludes that there was nothing he could do to prevent the breakup. However, the fact that the relationship ended doesn't mean his and Annie's feelings were any less powerful. He has the "eggs," the memories of the history he shared with Annie. The remark and the film itself pay tribute to those failed relationships that are no less powerful or worthwhile simply because they did not succeed.

STAR WARS
EPISODES IV, V, VI

(1977, 1980, 1983)

CONTEXT

In many ways, Hollywood and the movie business as we now know it were created in the summer of 1977 with the extraordinary success of an unheralded movie by a director named George Lucas, titled simply *Star Wars*. It was a Flash Gordonesque space opera, with ray guns and robots, the kind of "B-movie" item studios used to churn out for children at very little expense—but it was done with "A-movie" production values and an astounding level of technical innovation. The cast was stocked with unknowns (no-names such as Harrison Ford), with the exception of horror-film veteran Peter Cushing and the even bigger exception of Alec Guinness, one of the greatest film actors of all time. Audiences, especially young audiences, were amazed as spectacular scene after spectacular scene flew by at a blazing clip. These audiences would sit through a showing, walk out, and line up outside to watch it again. That summer, many new fans paid to see *Star Wars* on the big screen ten, fifteen, even twenty times.

Soon, the characters in the film, such as Luke Skywalker, R2-D2, and especially Darth Vader, began to pop up in everyday conversation and in jokes on late-night talk shows. The appearance of a sequel in 1980, *The Empire Strikes Back*, helped to keep the craze alive with its revelation of Luke's parentage and its even better effects. By the time the final film of the trilogy, *Return of the Jedi*, was ready in 1983, it was one of the most eagerly anticipated films of all time. The *Star Wars* trilogy shattered box office records, beginning the trend of box office grosses being reported in the paper like baseball scores. Many of the features of the *Star Wars* phenomenon that seemed so novel, such as the eye-popping, special-effects-driven visuals; the epic scale of the sci-fi plot; the abundance of nonhuman characters; and even the massive merchandizing tie-ins (toys, clothes, fast food, etc.), now seem simply a standard part of how movies are made. At the time, though, the "summer blockbuster" was new, not the essential part of the Hollywood economy it was to become.

In the early part of the 1970s, the most acclaimed American film directors included Robert Altman, Peter Bogdanovich, Woody Allen, and the young Martin Scorsese, each of whom worked largely outside the big studio system and, for the most part, outside of California altogether. Many observers felt that big studios such as Paramount, MGM, and 20th Century Fox had become dinosaurs, headed for extinction. Then, beginning in the mid-1970s, a young trio of directors appeared on the scene: Francis Ford Coppola, Stephen Spielberg, and George Lucas. They were all friends, all native Californians, and all perfectly comfortable working within the traditional studio system (and within the generic boundaries preferred by the studios). The three friends bounced ideas off of one another and helped to edit one another's films, and each was spectacularly successful at an early age. Coppola scored with *The Godfather* (1972); Spielberg with *Jaws* (1975), the first of the summer blockbusters; and Lucas with *American Graffiti* (1973), a nearly plot-free evocation of southern Californian hotrod culture in the 1950s.

For his follow-up to *American Graffiti*, Lucas decided to go in a completely different direction: science fiction (though his love of souped-up vehicles is evident in all the *Star Wars* films). Lucas decided to make the kind of science fiction adventure he had always wanted to see as a kid, with the fast pace and slam-bang rhythm of the old, cheesy B-movies, but done with style, class, and a lot more money. Much of Lucas's energy on the first film went into the production design, creature design, and special effects. Lucas has always claimed to have had the overall plot of the *Star Wars* films mapped out far in advance, but there is reason to believe he mostly had a general direction in mind and improvised the specifics of the world he was creating as needed. The actors themselves enjoyed making the films, but they complained about the often stilted dialogue they had to deliver. Harrison Ford famously quipped, as he was looking over his lines, "You can type this shit, George, but you can't say it!" Alec Guinness professed to be mystified by most of what was going on in the movie. In the end, however, many of the lines the actors complained about (such as "May the Force be with you!") became lodged in our collective cinematic memory, and the films have a permanent place in pop culture mythology.

The films as we know them today are different from how they were originally screened. As special effects continued to improve during the 1980s and 1990s, the older *Star Wars* films, once the gold standard for visual and sound effects, began to show their age. Beginning in the late 1990s, Lucas went back and redid many of the original effects, bringing them up to date with the innovations in CGI and digital technology. He and his team reedited many of the space scenes, repainted backgrounds, and edited in more back-

STAR WARS

ground animations and creatures. In a few cases, Lucas added in a scene that had previously been cut, such as the reunion between Biggs and Luke in *A New Hope*, and the encounter between Jabba and Han earlier in the same film. One of the more interesting changes Lucas made involves the scene in *A New Hope* in which Han is cornered by Greedo in the Mos Eisley cantina. In the original scene, Han blasts Greedo from under the table with no warning. In the scene as it exists now, Greedo fires first, missing Han's head at point-blank range. Presumably, Lucas did this to soften Solo's early edginess.

Another inescapable fact about this trilogy is that the *Star Wars* universe has expanded far beyond the original movies. Lucas has licensed any number of novels, comics, and novel series, which have fleshed out the background of most of the characters, even minor ones such as Wedge the X-Wing pilot. Curious about how Han and Chewie met? Or about Lando's early career? Or about Han and Leia's children? The answers are to be found in the so-called expanded universe of novels and comics. And, of course, Lucas has made a new *Star Wars* trilogy, dealing with Obi-Wan and Anakin and the birth of Darth Vader. The release of this new trilogy led Lucas to retitle the original films—as *Episodes IV, V*, and *VI*—to make the sequence of the plotline clearer for first-time viewers.

STAR WARS

Plot Overview

"Episode IV: A New Hope"

Far off in a distant galaxy, the starship belonging to Princess Leia, a young member of the Imperial Senate, is intercepted in the course of a secret mission by a massive Imperial Star Destroyer. An imperial boarding party blasts its way onto the captured vessel, and after a fierce firefight the crew of Leia's ship is subdued. The dark, forbidding figure of Darth Vader appears, brutally interrogating the crew and ordering his stormtroopers to search the ship for the secret documents he believes it is carrying: the technical readouts for the Empire's mightiest weapon—a planet-sized battle station called the Death Star. In the confusion, Princess Leia slips away and hides the secret documents, as well as a recorded plea for help, in the memory of R2-D2, a maintenance droid (robot). Leia is taken prisoner, but R2 gets away in an escape pod, along with his best friend, the protocol droid C-3PO. After crash-landing on the planet below, a barren, desert world called Tatooine, the droids set off in search of civilization but soon quarrel over the way to go. R2 insists that he has a mission to perform, but C-3PO wants no part of such an adventure.

The two droids go their separate ways but are soon reunited when they are both captured by Jawas, child-sized scavengers who trade in droids and technological scraps. The Jawas sell the droids to Owen Lars, a moisture farmer on a remote homestead. Owen's nephew, young Luke Skywalker, cleans the droids and, as he does so, stumbles across a bit of the message Princess Leia had hidden inside R2. The holographic message is addressed to "Obi-Wan Kenobi," and Luke, fascinated by the beautiful princess, wonders if she means Ben Kenobi, a mysterious hermit who lives out in the desert wilds. R2, however, refuses to divulge any more of the message. When Luke asks his uncle about the identity of Obi-Wan, Owen is reluctant to even discuss the subject, but he does drop one tantalizing hint: Obi-Wan was a friend of Luke's father, whom Luke never knew. Luke mentions his desire to leave home to attend the Imperial Academy for starpilots, but Uncle Owen is discouraging, much to Luke's frustration. When Luke's aunt Beru reminds Owen that Luke is too much like his father to stay on the farm, Owen replies that that is just what he's afraid of.

During the night, R2-D2 slips away, intent on finding Obi-Wan and completing his mission. Luke sets out in search of the truant droid the next morning, taking C-3PO with him. They soon find R2 but are waylaid by Sandpeople, barbaric tribal creatures who attack anyone trespassing on their domain. Luke is knocked unconscious but is saved by the timely appearance of old Ben Kenobi, who frightens off the Sandpeople and brings the group back to his humble shelter. There, Ben explains that he was called Obi-Wan back in days when he was a Jedi Knight, one of an ancient order of warriors who fought for peace and justice in the time of the Old Republic, before the coming of the evil Galactic Empire. Further, he informs Luke that Luke's father was also a Jedi, one of Ben's closest friends, and that his father was killed by Darth Vader, a former pupil of Ben's who turned to the dark side of the Force. The Force, Ben explains, is the source of a Jedi's power. It is an energy field created and sustained by life itself, and it flows through the universe, binding it together. Through training, a Jedi is able to tap into the Force and gain great power and wisdom, but, as the example of Vader shows, there is a seductive, evil path to the Force as well.

Ben gives Luke his father's lightsaber, the traditional weapon of a Jedi. After viewing the entirety of Leia's message, Ben says that he intends to join up with the Rebel Alliance challenging the Empire and to bring them the plans hidden in R2's memory. He urges Luke to join him and to learn the ways of the Force, but Luke, echoing his uncle, is reluctant to get involved. Meanwhile, Princess Leia has been taken into captivity on the Death Star. There, Leia is repeatedly interrogated by Darth Vader about the whereabouts of the hidden Rebel base, but she stoutly refuses to crack. When Vader is insolently challenged by the Death Star's Commander, he demonstrates his mastery of the Force by choking the officer into submission merely by raising his finger, until he is restrained by Grand Moff Tarkin, the Imperial governor. Back on Tattooine, Luke and Ben discover that the Jawas have been slaughtered by Imperial troops tracing the droids. Fearing for his aunt and uncle, Luke races home only to find them murdered and the farm in flames. With nothing left to hold him on Tattooine, Luke resolves to join Ben and to become a Jedi.

With the droids in tow, Ben and Luke journey to Mos Eisley spaceport in search of a ship to take them to Alderaan, the Princess's home planet. The Mos Eisley cantina, where the best pilots are to be found, is a rough place, and Ben is forced to act with deadly swift-ness to defend Luke from a couple of toughs. Nevertheless, the pair manages to hire Han Solo, a brash smuggler, and his copilot, the Wookie Chewbacca, to take them to Alderaan without attracting the attention of the Empire. After the deal is struck, Han Solo is cor-nered by Greedo, a lackey of Jabba the Hutt and a gangster angry at Solo for dumping one of his shipments. Solo blasts his way out of the confrontation but is forced to talk his way past Jabba himself when he returns to the hangar where his ship, the ugly-but-fast *Millen-nium Falcon,* is docked. Solo and Chewbacca are surprised when Imperial troops appear and start firing on the ship in an attempt to reclaim the droids, and the *Falcon* barely makes it off Tatooine and into hyperspace on the way to Alderaan.

On the Death Star, meanwhile, Tarkin has decided to break Leia by threatening her home planet, Alderaan, with destruction. Faced with this appalling dilemma, Leia reveals the location of the hidden base, only to have Tarkin proceed with the attack on Alderaan, merely to demonstrate the power of the Death Star. Aboard the *Mil-lennium Falcon,* Ben is stricken, feeling the death of Alderaan as a massive tremor in the Force. Luke trains with his lightsaber, even as Han scoffs at Ben's trust in the Force. Ben replies by having Luke fight blind against a floating target, and Luke is able to defend him-self by sensing the remote with his feelings alone, thereby taking his first steps, as Ben says, into "a larger world." The ship exits hyper-space where Alderaan should be, only to find the planet missing and an asteroid field in its place. Ben realizes the horrible truth when they catch sight of the nearby Death Star, and the *Millennium Fal-con* is quickly captured. The group manages to hide from the guards in Han's smuggling compartments, but Vader senses the presence of his old master, Obi-Wan.

The ship is unable to escape the Death Star as long as the station's tractor beam is operational, so Ben goes off alone to deactivate it. In his absence, the others learn that Princess Leia is aboard the station, and Luke convinces them to attempt a rescue. Han and Luke dis-guise themselves as stormtroopers and, with the droids plugged into the station's computers, break Leia out of her cell. Unfortunately, their activities are soon discovered, and the rescue takes a detour through a massive, monster-infested garbage compactor and several corridors and pitfalls swarming with Imperial troops. Leia is unim-pressed with her rescuers' planning and soon begins to issue the orders, much to Han's chagrin. As the group fights its way back to the *Falcon,* Ben stealthily deactivates the tractor beam. On his way to the ship, Ben is confronted by Darth Vader, who is eager to face his old master. Vader and Ben duel with lightsabers, and the fight draws the attention of the guards. Realizing he is trapped, and not wanting to endanger his friends, Ben allows Vader to strike him down, only to disappear before Vader's stroke hits, merging his consciousness with the Force. Luke is horrified and lashes out, but the others force him onto the *Falcon* and make they their escape.

The fleeing ship is pursued by Imperial fighters but finally escapes, though Leia is convinced that they are being tracked, as indeed they are. The group travels to the Rebel base, with the Death Star right behind. A quick scan of the blueprints provided by R2 offers one slim chance: the Death Star has an Achilles' heel. A direct hit on a small, easily overlooked thermal port will destroy the station, if only a fighter can get close enough to target it. Luke signs up for the desperate assault, but he is disappointed that Han, having received his payment, plans to leave immediately. Watched anxiously by the Rebel command, the fleet of small, single-pilot fighters speeds toward the massive, impregnable Death Star. As the station slowly moves into position to obliterate the Rebels, the pilots maneuver down a narrow trench along the station's equator, where the thermal port lies hidden. Darth Vader leads the counterattack himself and destroys many of the Rebels, including Luke's boyhood friend Biggs, in ship-to-ship combat. Finally, it is up to Luke himself to make a run at the target, and he is saved from Vader at the last minute by Han Solo, who returns in the nick of time and sends Vader spinning away from the station. Heeding Ben's disembodied voice, Luke switches off his computer and uses the Force to guide his aim. Against all odds, Luke succeeds and destroys the Death Star, dealing a major defeat to the Empire and setting himself on the path to becoming a Jedi Knight.

"Episode V: The Empire Strikes Back"

After the destruction of the Death Star, the Empire quickly regroups and begins searching for the new location of the Rebel base. Imperial probe droids fan out across various star systems, and one lands on the surface of the icy planet Hoth. On the surface of Hoth, Han Solo and Luke Skywalker are on patrol near the newly hidden Rebel base. Luke sees the Imperial probe strike the surface and goes to investigate on his own. Before he can identify the probe, Luke is attacked and knocked unconscious by a hulking yeti-like creature. Meanwhile, having returned to the base, Han orders Chewbacca to prepare the ailing *Millennium Falcon* for departure. Han explains to the Rebel general that he feels compelled to leave because of the bounty hunters sent after him by Jabba the Hutt. As Han heads back to his ship, Leia confronts him and tries to convince him to stay for the sake of the Rebellion. Han tries to get Leia to admit that she has more personal reasons for wanting him to stay, but she refuses and the two quarrel.

When Han learns that Luke has still not reported in, he heads out into the deadly Hoth night to find him. In the cave of the creature that attacked him, Luke has been pinioned in ice but is able to use the Force and his lightsaber to fight his way back to the surface. As he wanders blindly in a snowstorm, Luke has a vision of Ben Kenobi, who tells Luke that he must seek out Yoda, the Jedi master who is to train him in the ways of the Force. As Luke collapses, Han appears out of the night to rescue him. Luke recovers after a short stay in the sick bay, and Han and Leia discover that the Imperial probe has located the Rebel base. Aboard his command ship, Darth Vader sees the transmission from the probe and, instantly recognizing the Rebel base, orders his fleet to the Hoth system. However, Admiral Ozzel brings the fleet out of hyperspace in such a way that the Rebels are alerted and have time to prepare an evacuation. Furious, Vader uses the Force to strangle Ozzel and promotes Piett in his place.

Luke leads the counterattack that attempts to hold off the approaching Imperial army of massive armored walking transports, as the Rebels hurriedly flee the base. Leia and C-3PO are forced to go with Han in the *Falcon,* while Luke and R2 head toward the Dagobah system, where Yoda is to be found. Unfortunately, the hyperdrive on the *Millennium Falcon* is broken, and Han and Leia are closely pursued by the Imperial fleet. In a desperate maneuver, Han flies into an asteroid field in order to escape the pursuit and barely avoids being crushed or shot down, ultimately finding shelter in a cave on one of the larger asteroids. Luke crash-lands on Dagobah, a swampy planet teeming with animal life but without any settlements or other signs of civilization. Luke and R2 make camp and are interrupted by the intrusion of an annoying, elderly little creature that pokes around, stealing food and offering to take Luke to Yoda. Luke reluctantly accompanies the creature to his home for a meal but quickly becomes impatient and angry at the delay. At this, the creature, who is of course Yoda himself, sighs and says that he cannot train someone so reckless and angry. To his surprise, Luke hears Ben's voice defending him and urging Yoda to take Luke on as a student. Luke begs Yoda for another chance, and Yoda agrees, warning Luke that what is to come will be the greatest challenge he has ever faced.

Just as he is hiring a group of bounty hunters to find Han and the others, Darth Vader receives a call from the Emperor, who has sensed that Luke has begun his Jedi training. Vader is given the mission of luring Luke to him so that Luke can either be claimed for the dark side of the Force or destroyed. As the Imperial fleet searches the asteroid field, Han and the others work to get the *Falcon* repaired. Han and Leia have a tender moment together, and Leia admits that she is drawn to Han when he isn't acting like a scoundrel, a term with which Han is inordinately pleased. The brief moment of peace is cut short, however, when Han realizes that the "cave" they have taken shelter in is actually the gullet of an enormous, worm-like monster. Han speeds out of the maw of the creature, back into the asteroid field, and back into the sights of the Imperial fleet. Still unable to jump to hyperspace, Han improvises, hiding the *Falcon* by latching directly onto one of the Star Destroyers. The captain of the Star Destroyer assumes that the ship has escaped, apologizes to Vader, and pays for his error with his life. Meanwhile, Han detaches the *Falcon* when the larger vessel dumps its garbage and floats away, unseen, with the debris.

Han decides to travel to the nearby planet of Bespin, where Lando Calrissian, an old friend, runs an independent mining station. However, Han himself fails to notice that his stealthy maneuver has been anticipated by the bounty hunter Boba Fett, who follows close behind. On Dagobah, Luke's training pushes him to the brink of physical and mental exhaustion. As Luke and Yoda rest before a sinister cave, Yoda tells Luke that the place is connected to the dark side and that Luke must go within and see what he finds. Luke enters the cave only to see a vision of Darth Vader approaching. Luke battles Vader and strikes off his head, but the face he sees within Vader's destroyed mask is his own. Later, when Luke is practicing levitating stones, he is distracted by the sound of his ship sinking further into the swamp where he crashed. Yoda encourages Luke to levitate the ship out of the water, but Luke is convinced such a feat is impossible. Luke makes the attempt, but he doubts himself and therefore fails. Luke is frustrated and angry but quickly awed by the ease with which Yoda then draws the ship out of the water.

Han and Leia arrive at Cloud City on Bespin, where they are greeted by Lando, who pretends at first to be angry with Han. Han marvels at the way Lando, once a gambler and rogue, has become a responsible businessman. Leia still does not trust him, sensing something odd about the situation. C-3PO wanders off on his own and disappears, only to be found later, in pieces, by Chewbacca. Before Chewbacca can reassemble C-3PO and find out what happened, Han, Leia, and he are taken to a banquet by Lando. Much to their horror, Lando has betrayed them and Darth Vader is awaiting them in the dining room. The three are taken captive and Han and Chewbacca are tortured, though seemingly without purpose. Back on Dagobah, Luke has another vision, this time of his friends suffering. Yoda tells Luke that what he has seen is may in fact occur, but he warns Luke not to act rashly. Luke insists on going to rescue his friends, though both Ben and Yoda urge him not to face Vader before his training is complete. As Luke and R2 depart Dagobah, Yoda reminds Ben that even if Luke fails, "there is another."

Lando, meanwhile, has come to regret his decision, which he made in order to preserve the independence of his settlement. Clearly, Vader has no intention of honoring his side of the bargain and plans to do just as he pleases. Vader's goal is to lure Luke to him so that he can be captured and brought before the Emperor, but first he needs to test one last part of his plan. Vader orders that Han be placed in "carbon freeze," a sort of suspended animation, so that Vader can be sure that the process he has in store for Luke is not fatal. As Han is lowered into the freezing chamber, Leia at last admits that she loves him, to which he replies, "I know." Han is frozen safely and is handed over to Boba Fett. As Luke arrives, Vader lies in wait and Lando resolves to free the others. Luke is guided into Vader's presence and the two at last stand face-to-face. Lando's men surprise the Imperial troops and free Leia and the enraged Chewbacca, who almost kills Lando with his bare hands. Lando convinces them that there is still time to save Han, and they race off.

Meanwhile, Luke and Vader duel within the depths of the mining complex. Luke is clearly overmatched by Vader, though he fights bravely and avoids the carbon-freeze ambush. Vader is relentless, however, and continues to push Luke, slowly increasing the intensity of his attacks. Eventually, Luke is bloody and desperate, fighting now simply to escape. Vader is too strong, however, and slices off

Luke's hand. Though he is defeated, Luke angrily refuses Vader's offer to join him on the dark side, saying that he could never join the man who killed his father. Luke is devastated by Vader's next revelation: he, Vader, is Luke's father. Unable to deny what the Force tells him to be true, Luke casts himself off of the bridge on which they stand. Leia, meanwhile, has just missed Boba Fett, who has made his escape with Han as his captive. Lando orders the city evacuated, and he, Leia and Chewbacca head to the *Millennium Falcon*, joined by R2-D2 and C-3PO. Clinging to a weather vane below the floating city, Luke calls out mentally to Leia, who hears him and orders Lando to fly back for him. Luke is saved but deeply shaken by what he has learned. The hyperdrive on the *Falcon* is still not operational, as Vader gave orders that it be disconnected. R2, fortunately, is aware of the problem and reconnects it just in time for the friends to escape the pursuing fleet. Once they are reunited with the Rebel forces, Luke is given a cybernetic replacement hand. Luke, Leia, and the droids watch as Lando and Chewbacca head off in search of Han.

"Episode VI: The Return of the Jedi"

C-3PO and R2-D2 approach the imposing compound of Jabba the Hutt. At the gate, C-3PO explains that they have been sent by their master with a message for Jabba. Despite some resistance, the droids are able to talk their way into the presence of the powerful gangster in his throne room, where he wallows in the presence of his monstrous alien cronies. R2 delivers the message from Luke, who now claims to be a Jedi Knight. Luke simply asks Jabba to bargain for Han Solo's life and offers the droids to Jabba as a gesture of goodwill. Jabba accepts the gift of the droids (to C-3PO's dismay) but flatly refuses to discuss Han, whom he uses, still in carbon freeze, as a decoration in the throne room. C-3PO is put to work as a translator and is soon called upon to interpret for a masked bounty hunter who arrives with Chewbacca in tow. The bounty hunter bargains dangerously with Jabba, earning his respect. Chewbacca is taken to Jabba's dungeons, while the bounty hunter joins the ongoing party.

Later that evening, as the others sleep, the mysterious bounty hunter stealthily approaches the frozen Han. The bounty hunter unfreezes Han, who is weakened and temporarily blinded by his hibernation. Just as the bounty hunter reveals herself to be none other than Leia in disguise, Jabba, who has been observing all along, reveals himself and takes her captive. Leia becomes Jabba's personal slave, and Han is reunited with Chewbacca in the dungeons. Soon, Luke appears before Jabba, calmly striding past the guards, whom he immobilizes with a gesture. Luke attempts to use his Jedi powers to influence Jabba, but Jabba's mind is much too strong for such tricks. Jabba uses a trap door to send Luke to meet his pet, the giant rancor, but much to Jabba's surprise, Luke manages to slay the beast. Jabba decides to execute Han, Luke, and Chewbacca together by casting them into the maw of the Sarlacc, a monster something like a cross between a sand lion and a gigantic squid. Luke is unfazed, though Han is less optimistic about their chances. As they hover above the Sarlacc's pit, Luke springs his trap. R2, aboard Jabba's barge, launches Luke's new lightsaber to him, and Lando, who has been undercover as one of Jabba's guards, helps release Han and Chewbacca. Luke uses his Jedi skills to deadly effect, sending many of Jabba's henchmen, including Boba Fett, into the belly of the Sarlacc. Leia makes use of the confusion of the battle to strangle Jabba with her chains. In the end, the friends escape after having destroyed Jabba and freeing Han, Chewbacca, and the droids.

Meanwhile, Darth Vader pays a surprise visit to the new Death Star, where construction is running behind schedule. Vader informs the commander that he intends to put them back on schedule before the Emperor himself arrives to inspect the work. Suitably terrified, the commander redoubles his efforts. Luke journeys back to Dagobah, where Yoda tells him that his training is almost complete. All that remains is for Luke to face his father, Darth Vader, once more. Luke tells Yoda that he felt some spark of goodness still within Vader, and that it could be awakened. Luke watches as Yoda dies, fading into oneness with the Force. Ben appears in his ghostly form, and explains that what he told Luke was true, in the sense that, when he became Darth Vader, the man who had been Anakin Skywalker was killed. Ben then reveals that Luke has a sister as well, and Luke instantly knows that he means Leia.

In the meantime, the Rebel Alliance has received word of the location of the new Death Star, and, further, that the Emperor himself plans to visit the site soon. The Rebel leaders hastily put together a plan: Lando and Admiral Ackbar will lead a direct assault on the Death Star while it is unfinished and vulnerable. At the same time, Han will lead a commando raid on the nearby moon of Endor to knock out the force field generator that is the Death Star's only protection. Leia, Chewbacca, and the droids volunteer for the mission, as does Luke, who arrives at the last minute from Dagobah. As the commando group makes its way to the forest moon, Luke senses Vader's presence nearby, just as Vader senses him. Soon, the Emperor arrives aboard the Death Star and Vader informs him of Luke's presence on the moon below. The Emperor instructs Vader to bring Luke before him, and Vader departs.

The commando group, meanwhile, soon encounters Imperial scouts, who speed off on hoverbikes. Luke and Leia take off after them and become separated after a chaotic running battle through the trees. Luke returns safely, but Leia encounters Wicket, an Ewok—a creature rather like a teddy bear—who helps her defeat the stormtrooper she was chasing and takes her back with him to his village. Han, Luke, Chewbacca, and the droids soon meet Ewoks of their own, when Chewbacca springs a trap and they are all captured. The primitive Ewoks regard C-3PO as a god and begin to prepare to cook the others as part of a feast in his honor. Luke uses his powers, and their mistaken belief that C-3PO is a deity, to frighten the Ewoks into releasing them. Leia soon rejoins the group and they spend the night in the Ewok village. As C-3PO regales the tribe with tales of the group's adventures, Luke tells Leia that he intends to face Vader and that if he is killed, she, his sister, must carry on the Jedi legacy. Luke then departs to seek out Vader. Han sees Luke and Leia deep in discussion and grows jealous. Leia comforts him without explaining.

Luke turns himself in to the Imperial forces and is soon with Vader. Luke tells Vader that he intends to turn him away from the dark side of the Force, but Vader dismisses the notion, though somewhat regretfully. Meanwhile, the Rebel fleet has assembled and moves into hyperspace for the assault. Han's commando team is taken by the Ewoks to a "back door" to the shield generator, where they quickly break in and begin to set their explosives. Luke is soon standing before the Emperor, the master of the dark side. The Emperor explains to Luke that the entire situation was a set-up: he has foreseen the approach of the Rebel Fleet and laid a trap on Endor for Han's group. On Endor, the Emperor's trap is sprung as Imperial stormtroopers appear out of nowhere and overwhelm the commandos. The Ewoks, however, see what is taking place and decide to act themselves, and they suddenly attack the Imperial troops.

The Rebel fleet appears out of hyperspace only to find the shield still up and a fleet of Star Destroyers awaiting them. Lando, aboard the *Millennium Falcon*, convinces Ackbar to stay and fight, trusting Han to get the shield down before they are all destroyed. The Emperor then tells Luke his last surprise: the Death Star, though structurally incomplete, is fully operational. The Emperor gives the order, and the Death Star begins blasting the Rebel fleet apart. Lando and Ackbar take their ships right among the Star Destroyers, hoping to use them as shields against the overwhelming power of the Death Star. Luke, meanwhile, is fighting for self-control as the Emperor tries to goad him into acting out of anger and hatred, which will carry him over to the dark side. Luke springs into action, reclaiming his lightsaber. The Emperor watches with glee as father and son begin to duel before him, knowing that the survivor will remain his servant.

On Endor, the Ewoks fight bravely, using their primitive spears and slings to surprisingly good effect against the heavily armored, well-trained, and vastly technologically superior Imperial forces. Eventually, Han is able to use the confusion the Ewoks cause to lure the Imperial officers out of the bunker and take them captive. They then destroy the shield generator, leaving the Death Star open to attack. Luke masters himself and refuses to fight Vader aggressively, simply defending himself from attack. However, Luke is forced to attack when Vader is able to read his feelings and learns for the first time that Luke has a twin sister. In order to save Leia, Luke attacks and defeats Vader, as the Emperor spurs him on. Luke, however, does not kill Vader when he has the chance. Rather, he throws away his lightsaber and faces the Emperor, fully in control and now a true Jedi.

Lando and several fighters fly directly into the superstructure of the Death Star and blow up the main reactor, escaping just ahead of the resulting blast. Enraged at losing Luke, the Emperor strikes him with purple bolts of pure dark side energy, slowly killing him as Vader watches. At last, something in Vader snaps, and he heaves the Emperor bodily into an abyss where he is torn apart by the Death Star generators. Luke has a last conversation with his father, now Anakin Skywalker again, and sees his shattered face before he dies. Luke escapes with his father's body just before the Death Star explodes. The friends are reunited on Endor, where Luke and Leia's relationship is explained to Han. As celebrations break out across the galaxy, on Endor, Luke sees the ghostly forms of Ben, Yoda, and now Anakin, smiling at him.

Character List

Luke Skywalker—Played by Mark Hamill A courageous, orphaned young farm boy who is eager for adventure and for the chance to prove himself a hero. The chief protagonist of *Star Wars* episodes IV–VI, Luke must learn to control his emotions and desires in order to master the powers of a Jedi Knight, powers that flow from a mystic connection to the Force, an energy field created by life itself. Luke is tutored in the ways of the Force first by Obi-Wan Kenobi and later by Yoda, Kenobi's own master. Soon, however, Luke learns that Yoda and Obi-Wan have concealed from Luke his intimate connection to his greatest enemy, Darth Vader. Vader is in fact Luke's father and a servant of the dark side of the Force. Luke resolves to redeem his father from the evil that controls him, and this fateful decision determines both his own and Vader's fates, as well as that of the evil Galactic Empire.

Darth Vader (Anakin Skywalker)—Played by David Prowse (Vader's body) and James Earl Jones (Vader's voice) A fallen Jedi Knight, now Dark Lord of the Sith and a fearsome evil presence. Darth Vader is the apprentice to the Sith Master, Emperor Palpatine, and serves as his chief enforcer, the iron fist with which the Emperor rules the galaxy. Vader pursues Luke and his friends relentlessly throughout the trilogy, ostensibly in order to crush the Rebellion of which they are a part. Vader's deeper motive, however, is to bring Luke, his long-hidden son, into the Emperor's orbit and to turn him to the dark side of the Force. In the end, Luke succeeds in awakening the good that is dormant within Vader, and Vader turns on his master, becoming, at the very end of his life, Anakin Skywalker once more.

Princess Leia Organa—Played by Carrie Fisher A member of the Imperial Senate and, secretly, one of the leaders of the Rebel Alliance. Leia meets Luke Skywalker and Han Solo when they rescue her from the Death Star and soon becomes close to them both. Courageous, level headed, and sharp tongued, Leia's intense focus on the cause of overthrowing the Empire prevents her from acknowledging her growing attraction to Han Solo until it is almost too late. Early in the trilogy, Leia loses the only home she has ever known, when the planet Alderaan is destroyed by Grand Moff Tarkin via the Death Star, only to find a new family when she learns that Luke is actually her twin brother and, more disturbingly, that Darth Vader is her true father.

Han Solo—Played by Harrison Ford A brash, roguish smuggler who becomes a hero despite his cynicism and his instinct for self-preservation. Solo is captain of the *Millennium Falcon*, a battered hotrod of a starship that, like its pilot, masks a valiant heart in an unprepossessing exterior. Initially Solo joins Luke and Obi-Wan on their quest purely for the money he is promised, but, moved by Obi-Wan's sacrifice and by the courage of his young friend, Solo ends up joining their cause and becoming a leader of the Rebel Alliance. Solo, always careful to preserve his independence, falls in love with Princess Leia but enjoys sparring with her far too much to make his true feelings known. All that changes when Solo is captured by Jabba the Hutt, a gangster to whom Solo owes a small fortune. Luke and Leia lead an elaborate rescue of Solo, after which Solo is more honest about his devotion both to Leia and to the Rebellion they both serve.

Obi-Wan (Ben) Kenobi—Played by Alec Guinness One of the last of the Jedi Knights and Luke's first mentor. Obi-Wan is a steady, wise, reassuring figure who, though old, is still a Jedi, with a Jedi's deadly skill and uncanny powers. Obi-Wan reveals to Luke that his father was once a Jedi Knight and that Luke is meant to follow in his footsteps, but he doesn't reveal the full truth: that Luke's father Anakin is not dead but has become the evil Darth Vader. Obi-Wan also neglects to mention that Princess Leia is Luke's twin sister, in an attempt to preserve her safety. Obi-Wan begins training Luke in the ways of the Force and continues to advise him even after Darth Vader strikes Obi-Wan down in a lightsaber duel. Far from being killed in the duel, Obi-Wan merges with the Force, preserving his consciousness even as he transcends the limits of the flesh.

R2-D2 — Played by Kenny Baker A spunky, trashcan-shaped "astromech droid." R2, along with his friend C-3PO, is swept up into the epic battle for the fate of the galaxy when Princess Leia hides the stolen plans for the Death Star inside his databanks. R2-D2 becomes Luke's robotic copilot and all-around mechanical assistant and always seems to find himself in the thick of the action. Unswervingly loyal, brave, and feisty, R2-D2 is one of the films' most popular characters, as well as a main source of comic relief, all the while communicating only in a series of electronic whistles, beeps, and chirps.

C-3PO — Played by Anthony Daniels A golden, humanoid protocol droid. C-3PO is best friends with R2-D2, though the two often quarrel. Unlike R2-D2, C-3PO has little taste for adventure and is mostly an unwilling participant in the action, convinced all along that he and his friends are "doomed." Though more a diplomat than a fighter, C-3PO always comes through, proving his worth time and again as a translator, a computer hacker (with R2), and a surprisingly quick thinker in a tight spot. Despite all his worries and complaints, C-3PO's saving grace is his strong loyalty to "Master Luke" and his great affection for R2-D2.

Yoda — Voiced and performed by puppeteer Frank Oz The greatest Jedi master and Luke's teacher. At first, Yoda is reluctant to take Luke on as a student, fearing that he is too much like his father, driven by ambition, anger, and a love of adventure. Yoda's fears seem well-grounded when Luke rushes off to face Vader before his training is complete, a reckless decision that nearly costs Luke his life. Later, however, when a more humble, controlled Luke returns to complete his training, Yoda send him back to face Vader again, telling Luke that he must confront his father to become a true Jedi. Despite his elliptical way of speaking, Yoda is the most eloquent spokesman for the wisdom of the Force in the trilogy and represents the moral center of the films. Yoda, then, is the polar opposite of Emperor Palpatine, and it is by staying true to Yoda's teachings that Luke is able to triumph.

Lando Calrissian—Played by Billy Dee Williams A gambler, card player, and all-around scoundrel turned semirespectable businessman. An old friend of Han Solo's, and the previous owner of the *Millennium Falcon*, Lando is the administrator of a floating mining colony (Cloud City) on the planet Bespin. When Han and Leia turn to Lando for help in their flight from the Empire, Lando welcomes them warmly, only to betray them to Darth Vader soon after. Although Lando justifies his betrayal by claiming that he has no choice—he is trying to preserve the independence of the mining colony—he quickly realizes that any deal struck with the Empire is worthless. Lando evacuates the city and has his guards free Leia and Chewbacca, but not in time to prevent Han being taken captive by Boba Fett. After helping rescue Han from Jabba the Hutt, Lando, now thoroughly respectable, joins the Rebellion and leads the direct assault on the new Death Star.

Chewbacca—Played by Peter Mayhew Han Solo's friend and copilot of the *Millennium Falcon*. Chewbacca is a seven-feet-tall Wookie, a creature resembling a cross between a gorilla and an English sheepdog. Despite his intimidating appearance, "Chewie" is something of a softy, affectionate and loyal to his friends. When provoked, however, Chewbacca is truly ferocious, capable of tossing grown men around like rag dolls. A crack shot, skilled mechanic, and daring pilot, Chewbacca is always at Solo's side, deferring to the human's leadership, though the origin of their friendship remains mysterious.

Jabba the Hutt—Operated by puppeteers Tony Philpott, David Barclay, and Mike Edmonds A gangster based on Luke's home planet of Tatooine who places a huge bounty on Han Solo, who owes him for a lost shipment. Jabba is an enormous, sluglike creature, operated by puppeteers and enhanced by digital technology. He delights in his own cruelty and grossness but is strong enough mentally to resist Luke's Jedi mind-control. Jabba manages to capture Luke, Leia, Chewbacca, R2-D2, and C-3PO, as well as the frozen Han Solo, or so he thinks. In truth, Luke has stage-managed the entire captivity in order to get close enough to Jabba to strike him down and free Han. In the resulting struggle, Han is freed, Jabba's henchmen are destroyed, and Jabba himself gets his comeuppance at the hands of Princess Leia.

Emperor Palpatine — Played by Ian McDiarmid and briefly voiced by Clive Revill   The Sith Lord, ruler of the Galactic Empire, and the motivating force behind Darth Vader. Hideously scarred and twisted, the Emperor's own body seems to revolt against the evil it is forced to contain. The living embodiment of the dark side of the Force, the Emperor is driven purely by hatred, anger, and lust for power, and he desires to draw others to the dark side by bringing out these qualities in them as well. The primary focus of his attention is his apprentice, Darth Vader, and Vader's son, Luke Skywalker. The Emperor tries to pit father against son in a fight to the death, in the hope that Luke will destroy Vader and become the Emperor's new apprentice. The Emperor's twisted desire is thwarted, however, when Luke resists the lure of fear, anger, and hatred, becoming at last a true Jedi. Vader's love for his son is awakened by the Emperor's deadly attack on Luke, and he kills the Emperor, though not before sustaining a fatal wound himself.

Grand Moff Tarkin — Played by Peter Cushing   An Imperial governor in *A New Hope*. Tarkin is extremely powerful, unafraid of Darth Vader himself, supremely confident and cold. Tarkin orders the destruction of Princess Leia's home planet, Alderaan, merely to demonstrate the power of the Death Star. Tarkin is destroyed himself, along with the first Death Star, by Luke Skywalker.

Admiral Ackbar — Played by Tim Rose   A fish-headed alien who is the leader of the Rebel fleet that attacks the rebuilt Death Star in *Return of the Jedi*. Lando convinces Ackbar to press the attack, trusting that Han Solo will be able to destroy the shield generator protecting the Death Star.

Admiral Piett — Played by Kenneth Colley   An Imperial commander who rises through the ranks as Darth Vader kills off his superiors as they disappoint him. Piett dies in *Return of the Jedi* when his Super Star Destroyer is brought down by Admiral Ackbar's fleet.

Boba Fett—Played by Jeremy Bulloch A deadly bounty hunter working for Jabba the Hutt and the Empire. Boba Fett shows great skill in tracking and capturing Han Solo in *The Empire Strikes Back,* but he dies ignominiously in the maw of the Sarlacc in *Return of the Jedi.*

Greedo—Played by Paul Blake One of Jabba's flunkies. In *A New Hope,* Greedo corners Han Solo in the Mos Eisley cantina but can't resist gloating, which allows Han to get the drop on him and blast his way out of trouble.

Admiral Ozzel—Played by Michael Sheard An Imperial commander. Ozzel angers Darth Vader through his ineptitude one too many times, and Vader uses the Force to strangle him to death on the bridge of his own ship in *The Empire Strikes Back.*

Owen Lars—Played by Phil Brown Luke's uncle. A stern but loving man, Uncle Owen tries to keep Luke close to home but can't stop him from dreaming of adventure and excitement. Owen worries, with good reason, that Luke is very much like his father. Owen is killed by Imperial stormtroopers seeking R2-D2 and C-3PO in *A New Hope.*

Beru Lars—Played by Shelagh Fraser Luke's aunt. Beru is a kind woman and sees that Luke is not meant to be a farmer. Beru tells Owen that they will have to let Luke go someday. She is killed by Imperial stormtroopers seeking the droids in *A New Hope.*

Wicket—Played by Warwick Davis A fuzzy, forest-dwelling Ewok who befriends Leia in *Return of the Jedi.* Wicket is skittish at first but helps convince his tribe to assist the Rebel commandos led by Han and Leia when they assault the shield generator on the forest moon of Endor.

Wedge—Played by Denis Lawson A Rebel fighter pilot. Wedge is one of the best pilots in the Rebel fleet, surviving the battle on Hoth and the assaults on both of the Death Stars.

Biggs—Played by Garrick Hagon A Rebel fighter pilot and one of Luke's childhood friends. Biggs is shot down by Darth Vader in the attack on the Death Star in *A New Hope.*

STAR WARS

ANALYSIS OF MAJOR CHARACTERS

LUKE SKYWALKER

Luke's quest to become a Jedi Knight is the main engine driving the plot of *Star Wars Episodes IV–VI*. Indeed, all of the epic battles and cosmic events going on around him are in a sense only the backdrop before which Luke's inner struggles are played out. When we first meet Luke on Tatooine, he is a callow youth, dreaming of adventure and escape from the backwater setting in which he finds himself. The classic image from *A New Hope*, in which Luke stands looking out at the horizon as the twin suns of his home planet are setting, captures perfectly this romantic, dreaming quality of his character. Early in *A New Hope*, we also see the reckless, impetuous side of Luke's character as he races off after R2 without telling his uncle and as he spies on the Sandpeople, almost getting himself killed thanks to his immaturity. However, Luke is also motivated by a strong sense of duty and a desire to be a part of something larger than himself. In the person of Ben Kenobi, Luke finds this desire answered, as Ben offers to help Luke become a Jedi Knight.

Through Ben, Luke gets the opportunity to travel, to help the Rebel Alliance against the evil Empire, to feel closer to the father he never knew (who was also a Jedi), and to grow as a person through contact with the Force. In this way, Ben becomes a surrogate father to Luke, replacing Uncle Owen, who mainly wants to keep Luke safe, close to home, and, in that sense, in a state of immaturity. Ben is soon taken from Luke by Darth Vader, the man Luke believes killed his real father, repeating before Luke's eyes the act of parricide for which he already hates Vader. The irony, of course, is that Vader actually is Luke's father, a truth that devastates Luke when he learns it. Disappointed in Ben for hiding the truth from him and horrified at what Anakin Skywalker has become, Luke must learn at last to be his own man, moving out of the shadows of his various father figures and even learning to stand apart from the "grandfather figures" of Yoda and the Emperor, who are also fighting for Luke's loyalty.

In the end, Luke saves his father's soul, gains a sister, and sees Yoda, Ben, and Anakin (his whole paternal set, as it were) united in the afterlife. Much of his success is thanks to Yoda, who encourages Luke to examine himself and to judge how much he has been motivated by a desire for glory and how much by a true devotion to others. Through Yoda's teaching, Luke finally, after many missteps, learns to master his own feelings and gains a deeper insight to the feelings of others. By the end of the trilogy, the eager youth, constantly in over his head, has become the confident Jedi Knight, coolly strolling unarmed into Jabba's palace and, even more challenging, refusing to take the easy, dark path of hatred and anger. Though actor Mark Hamill aged in the role over the course of the seven years it took to make the trilogy, it is impossible to imagine anyone else as Luke Skywalker—and to the detriment of Hamill's later career, it became impossible for audiences to imagine him as anyone else.

DARTH VADER (ANAKIN SKYWALKER)

Darth Vader is one of pop culture's universally recognized figures. His respirator-enhanced breathing, massive frame, and intimidating armored costume, as well as his tendency to enforce discipline in the Imperial ranks by summary execution, combine to make him the baddest of cinematic bad guys. Voiced by James Earl Jones, Vader is a truly awesome presence onscreen, easily one of the most convincing monsters ever to menace a princess and her rescuers. From the beginning, Vader represents the antithesis of the warmly human Ben Kenobi, who is full of wisdom and slow to anger but quick to defend others. Vader, on the other hand, lashes out casually at those who displease him, though he does so as if motivated by a cool, almost rational anger, rather than a raging fury. Vader's conscious goal is to inspire fear wherever he goes and to use the anger and hatred this fear stirs up to control those around him. However, the surprising thing about Vader is that the monster turns out to be human after all.

For all of *A New Hope* and most of *The Empire Strikes Back*, Vader is a static character: the relentless foe of our heroes. At the end of *Empire,* however, comes the revelation that stunned twelve-year-old moviegoers everywhere in 1980—namely, that Vader is Luke's father, whom Luke, up to that point, believed to have been slain by Vader himself. Much of the subsequent drama of *Return of the Jedi* hinges on Luke's efforts to awaken the good that Luke believes, on rather little evidence, to be dormant within Vader's soul. The change finally comes when Vader is at last beaten and spared by Luke, who is then nearly killed by the Emperor. Vader's mask, impassive up to this point, is now lit cleverly in the glow of the Emperor's force-lightning so that pained expressions seem to flit anxiously across Vader's face. Finally, Anakin Skywalker reemerges from within Darth Vader, and he destroys the Emperor and saves his son. His last act is telling: he asks Luke to remove the mask so that he may see Luke with his own eyes—a rejection of the sinister man/machine aspects of Vader's being. In the end, Anakin Skywalker stands, purged of Darth Vader, with Yoda and Obi-Wan, the masters he once rejected.

HAN SOLO

Han Solo, the brash smuggler captain with a heart of gold, is the character that made Harrison Ford Harrison Ford. Before Solo, Ford had appeared onscreen in supporting roles exclusively—after Solo, he was a bona fide star. Ford's Han Solo is charismatic and sexy, the funniest character in *A New Hope*, and likable despite his apparent arrogance and selfishness. A major key to understanding Han's character is the clue provided by his last name. Han is used to looking after only himself, with the Wookie Chewbacca as the lone exception to the rule. If Luke starts out as the romantic dreamer, still immature but eager, Han is the wised-up cynic, willing to fight but only in it for the money. (Ben, with his quiet dedication to the cause of right, stands as a rebuke to both Han and Luke.) Another clue is the connection between Han and his spaceship, the *Millennium Falcon*, a small freighter to which Solo has made extensive modifications in order to boost her speed. Like the *Falcon*, Solo is temperamental, something of a misfit, and distinctly untrustworthy in appearance. But over the course of the trilogy, Han, the quintessential loner, finds himself drawn into friendship with Luke, into a leadership position in the Rebellion, and into a romantic relationship with Leia.

Throughout much of the trilogy, Solo tries to resist commitment, whether to a person or to a cause, but finds his instincts overruled by his affection. For example, Solo initially leaves once he has his reward, but he returns to help Luke take on the Death Star. Later, he is set to leave again, but he delays his departure first to help rescue Luke and then to make sure Leia escapes during the evacuation of Hoth. Similarly, Han constantly needles Leia in order to get her to admit her affection for him but would never dream of being the first to express his feelings. Solo is later captured and held by Jabba the Hutt, giving his friends the chance return his loyalty, and Han is the one rescued. From this point on, Solo is a changed man, still cocky and brash, but now clearly committed to the Rebellion and to the woman he loves.

PRINCESS LEIA ORGANA

Carrie Fisher was still a teenager when she was cast as Princess Leia, and George Lucas gets a lot of mileage, especially early in the trilogy, out of the contrast between Leia's youthful, sweet appearance and her sharp tongue and forceful manner. Leia is a post-feminist sort of princess, equally comfortable firing a blaster or piloting a ship as she is conducting a medal ceremony. Toward the end of the trilogy, we also learn that Leia has the potential to become a Jedi, just like Luke. Leia is a Senator, a princess, and a leader of the Rebel Alliance, and her devotion to duty and to the cause of freedom is one of her defining characteristics. This devotion prevents Leia from acknowledging to Han her growing love for him, and it even prevents her from admitting it to herself. Leia tells Han that he is needed as a leader and a pilot, but never that she needs him herself. Han, of course, tries to goad an admission out of her, but his efforts only cause her to bottle up her feelings even more, though she does make some efforts to inspire jealousy in Han by kissing Luke (before she learns that they are brother and sister). Leia finally tells Han that she loves him, just when it is almost too late and he is about to be frozen alive.

Leia takes part in the rescue of Han Solo from Jabba the Hutt, freeing him from the carbon freeze, only to be taken captive herself by Jabba. Up to this point in the trilogy, Leia has dressed modestly, favoring practical, functional clothing over anything fancy. Now, however, she is forced by Jabba to don a revealing harem outfit, complete with gold bikini, and to wear a chain around her neck. Leia's reaction to the situation is thoroughly in character and reveals the way her character smashes the adventure-fantasy stereotypes about sexy princesses. In the confusion caused by Luke's surprise attack, Leia hops behind Jabba, loops the chain around his massive neck, and strangles him to death. Leia then helps Luke destroy Jabba's barge before escaping with the others. The scene is a perfect summation of the kind of reversal of expectations typical of Leia throughout the trilogy.

Themes, Motifs, and Symbols

Themes

The Mystery and Power of the Force

As Ben and Yoda explain it to Luke, the Force is an energy field created and sustained by all the life in the universe. The Force is omnipresent, binding the universe and everything and everyone in it together. It can be manipulated and controlled by a trained Jedi (and by their evil counterparts, the Sith) and is the source of a Jedi's remarkable powers. The Force can also take a more active role, guiding a Jedi's actions, as when Luke allows the Force to guide his aim and destroy the Death Star. The Force is largely represented as nurturing and benign in nature, but it has a dark side as well. This dark side, the side of aggression, anger, and hatred, empowers the Emperor and his apprentice, Darth Vader. The Force provides a spiritual dimension to the action of the trilogy and has been the subject of much speculation and theorizing by fans of the films. George Lucas is careful *not* to spell out in any specific way what the Force is and what, exactly, the Jedi believe.

As Lucas presents it in the *Star Wars* series, the Force is a rather vague entity, serving primarily as a vocabulary for good and evil and as a way to explain the "magical" powers of the Jedi. Clearly, however, the Force cannot be identified with the God of Christianity, Judaism, or Islam, as it is impersonal, created *by* life and not the creator *of* life. Rather, the Force is a new-agey amalgam of various eastern religious and western philosophical sources. One such source is Taoism, an ancient, nontheistic (without a personal deity) Chinese religion that teaches simplicity and conformity to the Tao, or "Way," of nature. In the concept of "light" and "dark" sides of the Force, there is an echo of Manicheism, an ancient near-Eastern religion that claimed the physical universe was the result of the combat between two equally matched spiritual forces, one good, the other evil. There are also elements of Romantic nature worship (as in the essays of Ralph Waldo Emerson), Pantheism (a belief that the universe itself is God), and Western-influenced Buddhism in the way characters speak of the Force. Yoda's lecture to Luke on the importance of mindfulness in *Empire* is reminiscent of Buddhist teaching, for example. These are just a few interpretations, and though the Force is clearly central to the action of the *Star Wars* films, it ultimately remains mysterious. Lucas seems to intend a general life force with which one can be in harmony or conflict, and the details can be safely left to the imagination.

THE SUPERIORITY OF NATURE OVER TECHNOLOGY

The Jedi strive to live in simplicity and in harmony with nature. They are not averse to technology, but they do not rely on it alone, at the expense of their own senses and feelings. When Luke encounters Ben and Yoda in their homes, he finds these Jedi masters living austere lives, close to the land. And when Luke must destroy the Death Star with one shot, Ben's voice encourages him to shut off his targeting computer, relying on his own senses, his intuition, and his connection to the Force. A stark contrast to the way of the Jedi is the behavior of their dark-side counterparts, the Sith. Darth Vader is, as Ben puts it, "more machine than man," a walking hybrid with robotic limbs and built-in life support. The Emperor's deformed body seems to be in revolt against life itself, and he is seen exclusively in an overwhelmingly manmade, technological environment, the new Death Star. Clearly then, there is something soul destroying in an over-reliance on technology. Significantly, Darth Vader's last request is for Luke to remove his mask, so that Vader may see Luke directly, without the technological filter.

Nature proves to be superior to technology when the Ewoks rise up against the Empire on Endor. Despite the primitive nature of the Ewoks' weapons—sticks, stones, arrows, and spears—they are able to defeat the technologically advanced Imperial troopers, with their walking tanks and laser blasters. Lucas himself has said that he intended this sequence to be reminiscent of the Vietnam War, in which the less technologically advanced side was ultimately victorious. Again, Lucas is not trying to say that technology is bad in itself. Indeed, this would be an odd thing to claim in films that are themselves the product of the most advanced technology available at the time (some characters are completely computer-generated in certain scenes). After all, R2-D2 and C-3PO, two of the best and most beloved characters in the films, are, by their very nature, completely products of technology. Lucas's point is that we must not allow the machines that surround us to make us less than human ourselves, as Darth Vader does but Luke does not.

The Myth of the Hero's Destiny

Joseph Campbell, in his classic study of world mythology *The Hero with a Thousand Faces*, makes the case that all mythology about heroes is really a symbolic retelling of a basic "monomyth" about the growth and personal development of the individual. Drawing on the work of psychologists Carl Jung and Sigmund Freud, Campbell argues that the hero of myth must struggle against society and culture as he finds them in order to define himself both outwardly and inwardly. Outwardly, the hero struggles to find his place and role in society even as he struggles inwardly to understand his own nature. Symbolically, these struggles take the form of an orphaned hero who discovers the secret of his birth (often that he is of royal blood) and must make his way in the world. Along the way, the hero encounters resistance in the form of monsters he must battle (which symbolize his own fears or failings), and he receives aid from wise older counselors. Ultimately, the hero aspires to rise to full maturity by taking his place as a figure of patriarchal authority, often by displacing or destroying a faulty father figure who occupies the hero's rightful place. Classic examples of heroes who fit Campbell's pattern include King Arthur and Oedipus, though in each case the specifics and outcomes of the hero's quest will vary.

The case of Luke Skywalker can easily be seen to fit this mythic pattern. Luke is an orphan, uncertain of his place in the world and even of his own identity. He is cast adrift but is guided along his path by Ben and by Yoda, who share the wise elder counselor function. Luke faces many adversaries, but his greatest challenge is in learning self-mastery, and with each battle Luke grows in wisdom and self-understanding. In the end, however, Luke must face his own father in order to take his father's (abandoned) place as a Jedi Knight and as the symbolic head of his family. Note that Luke fights Vader in the end primarily to defend his sister, Leia. Ultimately, the son overthrows, and saves, the father, achieving the full maturity and goodness that the failed father figure could never achieve himself. In this sense, then, the story of Luke Skywalker is the story of any man's maturation and self-definition, told symbolically through the structure of myth and adventure.

Lucas himself claims to have been influenced by Campbell's ideas as he wrote. However, according to Campbell's theory, such influence would not have had to have been conscious, as he claims that all mythic stories work in essentially the same way. Incidentally, later editions of *The Hero with a Thousand Faces* have featured a picture of Luke Skywalker prominently on the cover.

MOTIFS

COLOR USED FOR CHARACTERIZATION

Certain characters in the *Star Wars* trilogy are closely identified with certain colors, with Darth Vader's all-black outfit being the most obvious example. Vader's black makes a stark contrast with Luke's all-white clothes in *A New Hope*, hearkening back to the serial westerns of the 1940s and 1950s, in which the good guys had white hats and the bad guys wore black. Leia wears an all-white costume in *A New Hope* as well, signaling the goodness of her character and linking her visually with Luke, her (unknown) brother. The Jedi Masters Yoda and Obi-Wan favor brown, a warm color recalling a monk's robes and the earth itself. Han Solo, meanwhile, wears a white shirt with a black vest for much of the trilogy, in an apt reference to the initial ambivalence of his character. Luke's outfits continue to emphasize his characterization in this way throughout the trilogy. In *Empire*, for example, when Luke journeys to Bespin to rescue his friends, his fatigues are a light gray, showing that Luke has traveled a bit from the innocent idealism of his youth and that he has placed himself in peril of straying to the dark side. By the time we get to *Return of the Jedi*, Luke has adopted an all-black wardrobe, though this does not mean that he has gone over to the dark side. Instead, the black robes he wears recall a priest's garb and link him visually to his father, with whose fate he is so deeply concerned.

ORCHESTRAL SOUNDTRACK

John Williams's thematic compositions for the *Star Wars* trilogy have been justly acclaimed, and the films use the soundtrack expertly to heighten the drama and intensify the mood. In many ways, the full orchestral accompaniment provided by Williams and powerfully performed by the London Symphony Orchestra is a throwback to the symphonic scores of classic Hollywood films, at a time when pop music was being used more and more in film soundtracks. There is an intensity and excitement in the *Star Wars* music, especially in the heroic opening theme, with its instantly recognizable fanfare, which contributes greatly to film's overall effect.

STAR WARS

Another dramatic musical moment is the Imperial march introduced in *The Empire Strikes Back* as the theme music for Vader's pursuit of Han and Leia. The march's rhythm is driving and relentless, capturing Vader's own relentless progress through the story. Williams's score can also be delicate and humorous, introducing themes for tender moments and minor characters and mixing in passages from the main themes in minor keys to emphasize crucial moments of dramatic tension.

SPEED

Although it may be hard to believe now, one of the things that set the *Star Wars* movies apart from the very beginning was the speed with which the stories moved and the speed with which certain scenes took place. Each of the films has at least one set-piece moment that is meant to make the audience members grab their armrests to steady themselves. In *A New Hope*, it is the trench runs during the attack on the Death Star—this scene was like nothing else that had come before, and it had theater viewers swaying as if they were on a roller coaster. Though this scene is comparatively slow by today's standards, it is the reason no action movie seems complete now without one super-fast air trip shot from the pilot's point of view. *The Empire Strikes Back* featured Han's vertiginous flight through the asteroid field, while *Return of the Jedi* sent Luke and Leia zooming through the forest of Endor on speeder bikes. Such scenes had many critics comparing the films, disparagingly, to amusement park thrill rides, but for George Lucas, such a comparison was hardly a criticism—more like an indication that he had achieved the effect he was after.

SYMBOLS

LUKE'S CYBERNETIC HAND

At the very end of *The Empire Strikes Back*, Luke's right hand, sliced off by Darth Vader during their duel on Bespin, is replaced by a cybernetic prosthesis that looks, on the surface, just like a real hand. Symbolically, however, Luke's mechanical hand moves him one step closer to being like his father, a full-fledged hybrid of man and machine. Early in *Return of the Jedi*, we are reminded of Luke's hand when it is damaged during the fight on Jabba's barge. Rather than having the hand repaired, Luke simply pulls a black glove over it, and from then on, the glove serves as a reminder of Luke's connection to his father. At the climax of *Jedi*, Luke beats Vader to the ground and slices off Vader's own right hand in a flurry of blows. Vader cries out in pain, but only wires and circuitry dangle from the wound. Luke looks in horror at his own right hand and back to his father, making the connection once again and realizing that he too has the capacity within him to turn to the dark side. With his father's example before him, however, Luke abstains from revenge, becoming a true Jedi Knight.

LIGHTSABERS

The lightsaber is, as Ben teaches Luke, the traditional weapon of the Jedi. In contrast to a blaster, Ben tells Luke, the lightsaber is elegant and precise, an eminently "civilized" weapon. By passing Luke's father's lightsaber on to Luke, Ben is beginning Luke's initiation and symbolically placing him in his father's footsteps. When we add in the fact that the final stage of a Jedi's apprenticeship is the creation of his own lightsaber, the symbolism of the gift becomes even clearer. In order to attain full maturity, Luke will have to release his father's lightsaber and take up his own—symbolically moving from a position of dependence on the father to a position of independence. Of course, Luke doesn't relinquish his father's lightsaber willingly, as it is literally severed from him by Vader, who is, of course, the very father Luke wishes to replace.

A Freudian interpretation would read the lightsabers in this scene as phallic symbols and Luke's amputation as a symbolic castration by his father, but one needn't go quite so far to see the symbolism. Once again, Luke's two father figures are placed in opposition, with Ben as the giving father and Vader as the domineering, taking father. Ultimately, Luke does create his own lightsaber to replace the lost one, and this is a major step on his path to becoming a Jedi and his own man. Note that another example of the expressive use of color involves the lightsabers: Jedi lightsabers are cool blue, whereas Vader's Sith blade is angry red. Luke's own blade is green, perhaps in allegiance to the green-skinned Yoda who trained him.

THE DEATH STAR

The exact symbolic meaning of the Death Star is ambiguous, though it is certainly a symbol of evil. On one hand, the Death Star is a virtually blasphemous instance of the worship of technology over nature. The station is the size of a moon, an artificial world with enough firepower to obliterate a real planet with one shot. When its commander makes the mistake of calling the station "the ultimate power in the universe" in Darth Vader's presence, however, Vader swiftly corrects him, first by reminding him that his "technological terror" is nothing compared to the Force, and then by force-choking the man into submission. On the other hand, Vader himself is something of a "technological terror," and the Emperor, the ultimate voice of the dark side of the Force, seems quite fond of his new Death Star, so the opposition is not complete. In the end, the Death Star represents the innate fragility of even the most potent technology. Just as the Ewoks are unexpectedly able to defeat the Emperor's legion, so are the Death Stars destroyed by unsuspected forces technology could never prepare for.

FILM ANALYSIS

"STAR WARS": A CULTURAL PHENOMENON

The original *Star Wars* films remain some of the most popular movies ever made, having achieved a level of recognition in American and worldwide culture rivaled only by such classics as *The Wizard of Oz* (1939) and *Gone With the Wind* (1939). Indeed, the similarities between these two particular films and the *Star Wars* trilogy go beyond simple popularity. *The Wizard of Oz* was the special-effects masterpiece of its era, showing new ways to bring fantastic vistas to the screen. *Gone With the Wind* was the original blockbuster production, famously over-the-top in its design, scale, and sheer visual sweep. It was, in fact, the box office record holder until the original *Star Wars* dethroned it. In a way, the *Star Wars* films were throwbacks to this earlier era of resplendent production values, epic scope, and the pursuit of sheer entertainment.

After the late 1960s and early 1970s, a period during which the studio system that had made Hollywood into the entertainment capital of the world was in steep decline, George Lucas, along with his friends Francis Ford Coppola and Stephen Spielberg, gave the old studios a new reason for being. No independent production, no matter how dedicated, could produce the kind of effects-laden, flashy, bright, exciting, and simply spectacular creation that Lucas, and Spielberg especially, wanted to create. After *Star Wars* came Spielberg's *Close Encounters of the Third Kind* (1977) and the Lucas-Spielberg co-production *Raiders of the Lost Ark* (1981), starring Harrison Ford, both effects-heavy spectaculars that became international megahits. The race was on: every summer brought the studios' latest attempts to manufacture some of the blockbuster magic—that quality that makes people pay to see a movie again and again—conjured up by *Star Wars* back in 1977.

Another remarkable aspect of the *Star Wars* phenomenon that continues to influence the movie business today is the aggressiveness and pervasiveness with which the films were marketed. Today it is commonplace for every summer film to have its merchandising tie-ins, such as cups emblazoned with a film's characters, for sale in store and fast-food chains. Such marketing schemes had been around before *Star Wars*, such as with the Beatles craze and the 1960s *Batman* television show, but *Star Wars* turned such tie-ins into a major aspect of a blockbuster film's profitability. The *Star Wars* line of toys, especially, remained popular even in the three years that separated each of the episodes of the trilogy, a highly unusual circumstance. Even today, original *Star Wars* toys sell at a premium among collectors. Anyone who was a child in America in the years between 1977 and 1983 can tell you, for example, that the snow monster that attacks Luke on Hoth is called a "wampa" and that the giant lizards the Imperial troopers ride on Tatooine are "dewbacks," even though these terms are never used in the films and don't even appear in the credits—all thanks to the toys and the omnipresent marketing of these films.

Many other examples of the penetration of the *Star Wars* world into our culture spring to mind. When President Ronald Reagan proposed a space-based missile defense program in the 1980s, it was officially called the Strategic Defense Initiative, or SDI—but the program was universally known, to friend and foe alike, as the "Star Wars" program. Reagan also made a famous speech at the height of the cold war in which he identified the Soviet Union as "an Evil Empire," and even if he wasn't thinking of Darth Vader and stormtroopers at the time, everybody else was. "Darth Vader" became an instant synonym for an evil boss or high school principal. Many of Yoda's catchphrases ("Do or do not; there is no try") remain easy laugh-lines after all these years.

With cultural phenomena come cultural myths. The famous line "Luke, I am your father" does not actually exist—the actual line is "No, *I* am your father," and is perhaps the most misheard movie line since the nonexistent "Play it again, Sam" from *Casablanca* (1942).

GENRE

The *Star Wars* films are deeply derivative in terms of plot and character, and they are completely reliant on generic conventions of storytelling—and saying so isn't insulting. After all, the original *Star Wars* film began as a deliberate attempt by George Lucas to capture the feel of the old science fiction and adventure serials that used to run before the feature films in movie theaters. A hallmark of these serials was that the audience usually had not seen the two or three preceding episodes of the story and had to be caught up on the action. So when Lucas begins his film trilogy with *Episode IV: A*

New Hope and with a long, scrolling explanatory text, he is clearly trying to evoke that same sense of being thrown into the middle of the action. However, one problem Lucas faced in trying to do a big-budget science-fiction film was in fact a *lack* of generic models on which to draw for inspiration—there had simply been no similar films made except for the very B-movies whose corny look Lucas was striving to avoid. The only previous respectable science-fiction films Lucas could conceivably turn to for inspiration were Stanley Kubrick's *2001: A Space Odyssey* (1968) and the Soviet director Andrei Tarkovsky's *Solaris* (1972). Both of these films, however, were slow-moving, philosophical art films, not at all the kind of high adventure Lucas was after.

The genre that seemed to offer the best combination of high adventure, expansive setting, and classic characters was the western, a genre that includes both serial shoot-'em-up adventures and epic tales set in a grand landscape. For example, the rowdy cantina at Mos Eisley spaceport is a setting—the frontier saloon full of gamblers and rowdies—that could have been lifted from any number of western films. Han Solo himself bears a strong resemblance to the classic western gun-for-hire, with Chewbacca, perhaps, standing in for the sidekick. And of course there is a strong whiff of the black-hat/white-hat morality of a generic western in the opposed figures of Luke and Darth Vader, especially in the earlier parts of the trilogy. The western isn't the only genre Lucas draws upon. In the end, the *Star Wars* films are in a sense a collage of elements taken from several genres, with the laser guns and rockets of serial sci-fi, the gunslingers and dusty towns of the western, and the dogfights and radio chatter of Hollywood fighter-pilot flicks.

Part of the reason Lucas is so comfortable poaching from these disparate sources is that "originality" in terms of plot and character was, in fact, the last thing he was after. Lucas was going for classic situations and a mythic sort of resonance, and he was able to attain this effect by keeping close to his generic models. He could then place these familiar sorts of characters—the young, unproven hero; the wise counselor; the villain—with their familiar motivations, in incredible, highly unfamiliar settings, while still packing an emotional punch in his story.

STAR WARS

INFLUENCES

Among the more specific influences that guided Lucas as he made the *Star Wars* trilogy, one of the most important was the samurai films of Akira Kurosawa. Kurosawa's classic samurai movies, such as *The Seven Samurai* (1954) and *Yojimbo* (1961), often feature members of the warrior class of samurai who try to live their lives according to the honorable code of *bushido*, the way of the warrior. The samurai of *The Seven Samurai*, for example, are very like Jedi Knights in that they are a separate caste devoted to justice and to protecting others. Obi-Wan's robes (not to mention his Japanese-sounding name) seem to suggest those of the poor samurai of Kurosawa's films, just as the Jedi's two-handed lightsabers seem like a sci-fi version of the samurai's *katana*.

Kurosawa's influence on *Star Wars* is even more specific than that, however. Lucas has said in the past that the inspiration for the characters of C-3PO, R2-D2, Han Solo, and Princess Leia could be found in Kurosawa's *The Hidden Fortress* (1958), in which two bumbling friends help a roguish hero rescue a brave princess from captivity. More specific still, Lucas includes a direct homage to Kurosawa in the scene in which Ben defends Luke in the Mos Eisley cantina. The shot of the ruffian's arm on the floor, severed by Ben's blade, is a reference to a similarly severed arm, filmed in the same way, in Kurosawa's *Yojimbo*.

Another direct influence on Lucas, above and beyond the influence of the genre itself, was John Ford's classic western, *The Searchers* (1956). The scene in which Luke approaches the burned-out farm and finds his aunt and uncle murdered is shot in such a way that it echoes a similar scene in Ford's film, in which the young hero also returns to his family's farm to find the buildings burned and his aunt and uncle murdered. Like Luke, the hero of *The Searchers* is drawn into a relationship with a relentless father figure, bent on evil. And like Darth Vader, the father figure in *The Searchers*, played unforgettably by John Wayne, experiences a last-second moral regeneration. Like the *Star Wars* trilogy, *The Searchers* is essentially a quest story, one in which the son must ultimately redeem the father, and it also approaches the grandeur of myth.

Special Effects

The truly innovative aspect of the *Star Wars* trilogy, in purely filmic terms, was the quantum leap it represented in special visual effects, production design, and sound effects. While most of the techniques used in the trilogy, such as digital matte painting and blue screens (when the actors perform before an empty screen only to be edited into a painted or filmed background later on), stop-motion animation, and computer-generated images, had been used to a certain extent before, never had they been used so extensively throughout the picture. Practically every frame of a *Star Wars* film has some sort of effect added in, whether as part of the main action or merely in the background. Lucas also combined the latest high-tech effects with classic Hollywood techniques, such as elaborate creature costumes and even puppetry. Yoda, for example, is performed and voiced by the master puppeteer Frank Oz, who worked for years with Jim Henson's Muppets.

A typical scene in the trilogy could feature a relatively normal-looking actor interacting with another actor in costume, with another being operated by an off-screen puppeteer, and with yet another who was added in later with a computer—while the scene itself takes place before a matte painting giving the illusion of an alien landscape. With the *Star Wars* films, special effects became a box office draw in and of themselves, as viewers were willing to pay just to see the amazing things Lucas's team at Industrial Light and Magic (including such famous effects wizards as John Dykstra and sound designer Ben Burtt) were able to come up with.

This highly artificial approach to filmmaking has not been without its critics. From the beginning, there have been those who have condemned the films as little more than eye-candy or as coldly technological artifacts with a lot of spectacle but little in the way of true wonder. Lucas himself has been dismissive of such concerns and has often seemed eager to dispense with the formality of having actual human actors. As the technology has improved, Lucas has continued to tinker with the films, adding more creatures and more detail to the backgrounds and even reshooting certain scenes to get them closer to his ideal vision. With the new *Star Wars* trilogy, Lucas again is striving for a quantum leap in what can be done with special effects. Now, the digital revolution has allowed him to create entire landscapes and settings without relying on stage sets or location

STAR WARS

shots at all. Soon the concept of "special effects" will no longer apply, as every aspect of the films will be in some sense an "effect." The irony is that one of the themes Lucas plays with in the original trilogy is of the dangers of surrounding oneself in a completely technological environment—even as he creates just such an environment in his recent work.

IMPORTANT QUOTATIONS EXPLAINED

1. LUKE: "How did my father die?"
   BEN: "A young Jedi named Darth Vader, who was a pupil of mine until he turned to evil, helped the Empire hunt down and destroy the Jedi Knights. He betrayed and murdered your father."

In *Episode IV: A New Hope*, Luke asks Ben Kenobi this question in Ben's home, just after Ben gives Luke his father's lightsaber. Ben's careful reply is technically accurate in all that it says, but it omits the crucial detail, which is that Ben's pupil and the good Jedi, Luke's father, that the pupil "betrayed and murdered" are one and the same. One of Luke's greatest desires is to know his father, and Ben fears that if Luke knew the truth, he would either despair or, even worse, seek to become just like him. Instead, Ben hopes to encourage Luke to emulate the good side of his father's legacy, the side that Anakin betrayed when he turned to the dark side and became Darth Vader. Ben takes a great chance here, risking the loss of Luke's trust should he discover the full truth. And, indeed, Luke is greatly hurt by the revelation when it comes, calling out to Ben in anguish as he speeds away from Bespin aboard the *Millennium Falcon*.

Later, back on Dagobah, Ben explains that what he told Luke was indeed true, if only from a "certain point of view." Luke is frustrated by this response, but Ben maintains that many of the things we believe are true in this sense alone. In part, Ben confesses, he hid the truth out of guilt and shame, since Anakin Skywalker was Obi-Wan Kenobi's greatest failure. Ben, back when he was Obi-Wan, had been in charge of training Anakin but lost him to the Emperor and the dark side. Ben tells Luke that his greatest fear is of losing Luke the way he lost his father. Luke was always meant to know the full truth, but Ben and Yoda had hoped that Luke's deepening understanding of the Force would lead him to see the truth on his own. Luke's anguished resentment of Vader's revelation only shows how unready he was for the truth. Evidence of how much Luke has grown at this point comes when he instantly understands that Leia is his sister, as soon as Ben hints at it.

2. LUKE: "You don't believe in the Force, do you?"
    HAN: "Kid, I've flown from one side of the galaxy to the other, I've seen a lot of strange stuff, but I've never seen anything to make me believe there's one all-powerful force controlling everything. There's no mystical energy field that controls my destiny!"

In *Episode IV: A New Hope*, Han and Luke have this exchange as the *Millennium Falcon* cruises through hyperspace toward Alderaan. Luke is practicing his lightsaber under Ben's tutelage, and Han is amused at Luke's clumsy mistakes. Han claims that a good blaster is worth more than an old-fashioned weapon and a "hokey religion." Han's claim of never having seen evidence of the Force in his travels is clearly self-serving. That is, Han sees no evidence of the Force affecting his life precisely because he does not wish to see such a force affect his life. Han wants to shape his own destiny apart from others, which requires that he be cut off from the Force, which, as we have been told by Ben, penetrates us all and binds us together. Even after Luke is able to defeat the remote with his eyes shielded, Han would much rather trust in his own skill, and even in "luck," than accept that his own fate is contingent on anyone or anything outside of himself.

Han begins to change after Ben sacrifices himself so that the others can escape the Death Star. The clearest sign that the change has begun is when Han calls Luke back in order to say, "May the Force be with you." Still later, Han finds himself in a situation he can't blast his way out of, when he is encased in carbonite and delivered to Jabba the Hutt. Han is rescued by his friends but is still temporarily without his sight. Like Luke aboard the *Falcon*, Han must fight blind, trusting his friends and accepting that he is forced to rely on others. Though he will never be a Jedi Knight, Han develops from a selfish, mercenary loner into a loyal friend and a committed leader of the Rebel Alliance.

3. YODA: "[M]y ally is the Force, and a powerful ally it is. Life creates it, makes it grow. Its energy surrounds us, binds us. Luminous beings are we, not this crude matter. You must feel the Force flow around you. Here, between you, me, the tree, the rock, yes, even between the land and the ship."

This quote appears in *Episode V: The Empire Strikes Back*. This is Yoda's most impassioned exposition of the nature of the Force, and he delivers it just as Luke is doubting his own gifts. When Luke's X-Wing fighter sinks further into the mire of Dagobah, Yoda encourages Luke to use his levitation skills to salvage the ship. Luke is daunted by the task, so much so that when he does try to move the ship, he fails. Yoda then explains that Luke is going about the problem the wrong way: "Size matters not," he tells Luke. Rather than focusing on the relative differential in size between himself and the ship, Luke should open up himself to the Force as it flows around and through him. Once he does so, says Yoda, he will feel connected to the ship in such a way that the relative size of it will not matter. He encourages Luke here to see himself, others, and indeed the entire world in terms of spirit, life, and energy, not "crude" matter. However, Luke becomes frustrated and angrily turns away.

To prove his point, Yoda then extends his arm and, using the force, rather easily lifts the ship completely up out of the swamp and levitates it over to dry land. Stunned by this awesome display of skill and power, Luke stammers, "I don't believe it." "That," Yoda replies, "is why you fail." Yoda's point is that when it comes to mental powers and the horizon of the mind, the only limits we have are those we choose for ourselves. Luke told himself that it was impossible to move the ship, and so it was impossible—for him. Once Luke begins to set aside his ingrained notions of what is possible and impossible, once he begins to "unlearn" what he knows (as Yoda puts it), his powers begin to grow. Eventually the young trainee who fails to move the ship will become a Jedi strong enough to defeat Vader without giving in to hatred and anger.

STAR WARS

4.   DARTH VADER: "Join me, and I will complete your
      training. With our combined strength, we can end this
      destructive conflict and bring order to the galaxy! . . . If you
      only knew the power of the dark side! Obi-Wan never told
      you what happened to your father. . ."
      LUKE: "He told me enough! He told me you killed him!"
      DARTH VADER: "No, *I* am your father!"

This exchange, which occurs in *Episode V: The Empire Strikes Back*
on the catwalk within Cloud City after Vader has thoroughly beaten
Luke, is one of the central moments of the trilogy. The most important thing we learn along with Luke is the Vader's true identity and
his relation to Luke. The loss that Luke experiences in this scene is
profound and multifaceted. He has lost, for one thing, the narrative
that has given his life meaning up to this point: that his father was
killed by Vader and that he, Luke, will someday avenge his death.
Instead, Luke now finds he has a villain, not a hero, for a father. At
the same time, he has, in a way, lost another father in Ben, who not
only was struck down by Luke's real father but now stands revealed
as having been less than honest with Luke. This is the very moment,
the very realization, that Ben had tried to spare Luke, until he was
ready to handle it. As it is, Luke would rather die than face the reality of the situation. He throws himself over the side and is saved
from death only by luck—or perhaps destiny.

   At the same time, Vader's statement here sheds a bit of light on his
own motivations and reveals some of the seductiveness of the dark
side. Vader offers Luke a chance to belong, a chance to seize power,
and a chance to know his father all at once. Vader claims here to be
motivated by a desire for peace, stability, and order, which certainly
doesn't sound all that evil. In truth, however, the only order offered
by the dark side is the order of absolute submission to the will of the
Emperor, and the only peace the peace of surrender, or death. A Jedi,
Luke learns, fights so that others may be free, not to subordinate
others to a specious "order" or "stability."

5. EMPEROR: "Now fulfill your destiny, and take your
    father's place at my side."
    LUKE: "Never. I'll never turn to the dark side. You've
    failed, your highness. I am a Jedi, like my father before me."
    EMPEROR: "So be it, Jedi."

This quote appears in *Episode VI: The Return of the Jedi.* This
moment, which occurs aboard the new Death Star even as the final
assault begins, is the climax of Luke's journey toward heroism. Luke
has just finished beating Vader into submission, having attacked
him furiously in response to Vader's threat to turn Leia to the dark
side. Luke has even severed Vader's right hand, paying him back for
the similar injury Vader had dealt to Luke. Now, the Emperor
descends the steps of his dais toward Luke, encouraging him to kill
Vader and take his position as chief enforcer of the Emperor's will.
In a sense, it is the goal Luke has been working toward all along: taking the position his father once held. Originally, Luke thought this
meant becoming a Jedi, but now a different, sinister possibility is
unfolding before him. Luke could indeed step into his father's place,
but as a Sith, not a Jedi. As Yoda and Ben warned him, Luke finds
the path to the dark side to be easy, quick, and brutally efficient.

However, the Emperor has misjudged Luke's righteous fury in
defense of his sister. Luke has defeated Vader not out of some personal, revenge-driven desire, but in order to protect someone he
loves. As Luke glances from the shattered hulk of Vader to his own
cybernetically grafted hand, he feels pity and understanding for his
father, not hatred. Luke will take his father's place, but it will by following the path of his true father figures, Ben and Yoda, and it will
be Anakin Skywalker he turns to, not Vader. When Luke faces the
Emperor, then, he does so as a true Jedi, one who has faced his own
demons and defeated them, making it impossible for the Emperor to
prey on his weaknesses. The Emperor himself acknowledges his
defeat when he addresses Luke for the first time as "Jedi," rather
than "Young Skywalker" or something similar.

APOCALYPSE NOW

(1979)

CONTEXT

Apocalypse Now (1979), one of the most important films to emerge from the Vietnam War era, took ten years and more than $30 million to make. Director Francis Ford Coppola struggled with setback after setback during production and constantly questioned his work on the film, to the point of threatening suicide. Because the film was shot in the Philippines and financed largely outside of the Hollywood studio system, it acquired a certain mystery among the media. By the time of its release, it had become almost mythical in stature.

Apocalypse Now is based loosely on Joseph Conrad's 1898 novella *Heart of Darkness,* the story of a ship captain's journey up the Congo River during the heyday of European imperialism in Africa. Conrad's novella follows Marlow's quest to find Kurtz, an ivory trader and philosopher whose intentions to enlighten the African natives fail as he gives in to the jungle's savage temptations and ultimately goes insane. Orson Welles worked to adapt the novella for the screen in 1939, but his studio feared the production would go over budget and backed off the project. Welles ended up making *Citizen Kane* instead.

In 1969, Coppola founded American Zoetrope with young filmmaker George Lucas, hoping to create a film company that could be financially and creatively independent from the conservative, restrictive Hollywood studio system. Among the first projects they sought to complete was *Apocalypse Now,* an original screenplay by John Milius based on *Heart of Darkness* but updated to take place in Vietnam during the Vietnam War. Lucas hoped to direct the film, but they were unable to secure financing. At the time, the American antiwar movement was gaining power, as citizens became increasingly bitter and resentful about the United States' role in the war. Executives were reluctant to release a Vietnam-related film amid such a volatile social context.

The project was shelved as Coppola and Lucas put the almost-bankrupt American Zoetrope on hold. Meanwhile, Coppola directed *The Godfather* (1972) and *The Godfather Part II* (1974), which together went on to win nine Academy Awards and make Coppola a multimillionaire. With his new wealth, he revisited his plans for an independent filmmaking company and again chose *Apocalypse Now* to spearhead the reemergence of American Zoetrope. When Coppola took up the film for the second time at age thirty-six, he had seven feature films under his belt and was the winner of six Academy Awards. *Apocalypse Now,* however, was to be his most ambitious film in terms of both vision and scale—he felt prepared to create an epic movie that would capture the totality of the Vietnam War.

The Vietnam War was fought from 1959 to 1975. South Vietnamese independence was at stake, as the war's outcome would determine whether North and South Vietnam would be unified under communist North Vietnamese rule. The United States became involved in the conflict because its policymakers feared the spread of communism. China and much of Eastern Europe were already under communist control, and U.S. leaders felt they could not "lose" Southeast Asia as well. The United States helped install an anticommunist prime minister, Ngo Dinh Diem, in South Vietnam in 1954. When Diem was killed in a military coup in 1963, the United States became more directly involved in the war. The first U.S. combat troops were sent to Vietnam in 1965. With conscription in effect, the U.S. military drafted increasing numbers of young men to serve as the war progressed. The average age of a U.S. soldier in Vietnam was nineteen, and the majority were youths from the poorer sections of American society. By 1968, about 40,000 young men were drafted each month to meet demands for increased troops in Vietnam.

Opposition to the war within the United States developed even before troops were deployed, but its scope was relatively narrow. As the war progressed, an unprecedented antiwar movement emerged in America. Millions participated in protests, teach-ins, and riots. The movement was fueled by public confusion as to the reasons for the U.S. invasion; increasing draft numbers; the Kent State University protest, in which National Guardsmen shot four students dead; and the 1969 revelation of the My Lai Massacre, in which a U.S. Army division killed some five hundred unarmed Vietnamese civilians. Accounts of government deception and secret bombings further aggravated the flame of dissent rippling through America. By 1971, 70 percent of Americans sought the immediate withdrawal of American troops, and a majority thought the war was a mistake. Many U.S. soldiers in Vietnam also opposed the war and the draft, resulting in internal dissension, low morale, and an increasing number of soldiers going AWOL, or absent without leave.

In January 1973, all parties involved in the Vietnamese conflict came together to sign the Treaty of Paris. The treaty's terms pro-

APOCALYPSE NOW

vided for, among other things, a cease-fire between North and South Vietnam and the withdrawal of all U.S. forces from South Vietnam. The last U.S. troops left Vietnam on March 29, 1973, after nearly 58,000 young soldiers had died and more than 300,000 had been wounded.

Filming for *Apocalypse Now* began in February 1976. Coppola was able to secure a large area in the Philippines as the setting for the film shoot. The humid, typhoon-prone climate and dense vegetation provided a convincing substitute for Vietnam's sticky, thick jungles. Coppola made every effort to re-create accurately the atmosphere, character, and action of the Vietnam War. As he said famously in a news conference at the Cannes Film Festival: "My film is not a movie. It is not about Vietnam. It is Vietnam."

Apocalypse Now was released in 1979, after it spent two years in the editing room being painfully whittled down from six hours to two and a half. By its release date, the film had been delayed for so long it had become the butt of many media jokes, spurring headlines that screamed "Apocalypse Never." Upon its highly anticipated release, the film received mostly superlative reviews, and the bulk of critics considered it a flawed masterpiece. It took home the top award at the Cannes Film Festival and won two Academy Awards, for Best Cinematography and Best Sound, out of eight nominations. Coppola, who had never been happy with the final cut of the film, in 2001 released *Apocalypse Now Redux*, which restored forty-nine minutes of scenes deleted from the original film. The new version received mixed reviews, but the original is still widely recognized as Coppola's most ambitious, far-reaching work and the king of Vietnam War movies.

APOCALYPSE NOW

Plot Overview

Apocalypse Now opens in Saigon in 1968. Army captain and special intelligence agent Benjamin Willard is holed up in a hotel room, heavily intoxicated and desperate to get back into action. He has completed one tour of duty in Vietnam, only to go home a changed man, miserable amid the confines of civilization. After agreeing to a divorce, he has returned to Vietnam for a second tour and now waits restlessly for a mission.

Two officers arrive to escort Willard to Nha Trang, where he meets with two military superiors and a CIA operative, who brief him on a rogue Green Beret colonel named Walter E. Kurtz. Willard is ordered to find and "terminate" Kurtz, who has become unhinged and committed murder with the help of a native Montagnard army. Kurtz currently is stationed at an outpost in Cambodia with the Montagnards, who treat him as a god. Kurtz is insane, the officers say, and his methods are "unsound."

To reach Kurtz, Willard joins the crew of a Navy river patrol boat (abbreviated PBR, as in Patrol Boat River), who are to ferry him up the (fictional) Nung River to Cambodia. The boat's crew consists of four men: Chief, Chef, Lance, and Clean. With Willard on board, the crew makes its rendezvous with the Ninth Air Cavalry, who are to escort the PBR to the mouth of the river. The crew members find themselves in the middle of a B–52 bomber strike. Willard encounters the cavalry's commanding officer, Lieutenant Colonel Bill Kilgore, who assures Willard his cavalry will set the PBR safely at the mouth of the river.

At dawn, Kilgore orders an air attack on a Vietcong-controlled village, and one of the film's most memorable sequences begins. The helicopters approach, blasting Wagner's "Ride of the Valkyries" through loudspeakers as the villagers scatter. During the intense air strike, a chopper plunks the PBR down in the river successfully. From this point on, Willard and the crew embark on a journey consisting of a number of episodic encounters connected by Willard's narration.

The first episode takes place in the jungle. Chef's craving for mangoes leads him and Willard to disembark and explore the jungle. Amid mammoth trees and dense vegetation, a tiger lunges out at them from the shadows. Chef and Willard run back to the boat.

Chef has a nervous breakdown as the rest of the crew shoots blindly at the jungle, assuming the danger is Vietcong. Chef's breakdown darkens the crew's mood.

Further up the river, the crew meets a U.S. base supply depot. They dock and collect fuel, cigarettes, and other supplies, then join the throng of men in an amphitheater that has been erected by the river. Soon, a helicopter arrives and drops three *Playboy* Playmates onto the stage to perform in a USO (United Service Organization) show. The Playmates perform to Flash Cadillac's song "Suzie Q" and taunt the sex-starved troops with seductive shimmies and bump-and-grind moves. When some of the soldiers run onto stage in a frenzy, the show is cut short and the Playmates are quickly evacuated.

The crew returns to the PBR, and the boat soon meets other patrol boats coming in the opposite direction, with whom they engage in mock warfare. As the crew continues on and tempers flare up more frequently, Willard obsessively reviews Kurtz's dossier. Lance and Chef are continually under the influence of drugs, and Lance in particular becomes withdrawn, smearing his face with camouflage paint and saying little.

One day, Chief insists on stopping a sampan (a small boat) carrying several Vietnamese peasants and supplies downriver. At Chief's command, Chef boards the sampan and searches it. Chief orders Chef to look inside a rusty yellow can that a peasant woman on the sampan was sitting on; when Chef does, the woman makes a sudden move toward the can. Clean starts shooting at random, killing all the civilians on board except the woman. Once the shooting subsides, Chef looks inside the can and finds only a small puppy. Noticing the woman is still alive, Chief orders Chef to bring her on board, saying the crew will take her to a "friendly" hospital nearby. Willard steps forward, points his gun at the woman's chest, and fires, killing her so that his mission can proceed without a detour. The rest of the crew begins to see him in a different light.

Continuing upriver, the shaken crew reaches an army outpost under fire in a gunfight for an American-held bridge—the last military outpost before the Cambodian border. Willard is unable to find a commanding officer onshore but is given a packet of mail for the boat. One of the letters in the packet informs Willard that the U.S. military previously sent another man on the same mission to retrieve Kurtz but that the man is now operating with Kurtz. As Clean listens to an audiotape letter from his mother, the PBR comes under a surprise attack by Vietcong, and Clean is shot fatally.

The boat continues upriver, only to meet another surprise attack. Primitive natives onshore shoot a storm of arrows at the PBR. Chief is impaled with a spear and dies. With two men gone, the survivors at last reach Kurtz's camp, a macabre site in which countless dead bodies and severed heads are strewn about seemingly at random. A hyperactive American photojournalist, unabashed in his worship of Kurtz, greets the boat.

Willard and Lance disembark to find Kurtz, leaving Chef with instructions to call in an air strike if they are not back at the boat by a specified time. The natives under Kurtz's control drag Willard through the mud and grant him an audience with Kurtz, who imprisons Willard in a cramped tiger cage. During the night, Kurtz throws Chef's severed head into Willard's lap. Willard is freed the next day and given freedom to roam Kurtz's compound. He listens to Kurtz's philosophizing for several days.

In split scenes, Kurtz's natives perform a ritual sacrifice of a caribou, while the film intercuts with images of Willard emerging from the river and approaching Kurtz's quarters. As the caribou is ritualistically slaughtered, Willard slaughters Kurtz with a machete. Kurtz's last words are "the horror, the horror." When Willard emerges, the natives acknowledge him as their new leader and god. He throws down his machete, finds Lance amidst the Montagnard, and returns to the boat. Willard shuts off the radio, and he and Lance pull away from shore as rain begins to fall. Kurtz's last words are echoed again as the film fades to black.

CHARACTER LIST

Army Captain Benjamin Willard—Played by Martin Sheen A U.S. special forces assassin and the protagonist of the film. Willard acts as our eyes and ears, passively observing the surrounding action and rarely participating. He is receptive, not reactive, and identifies increasingly with his target, Kurtz. Willard perceives the futility and insanity of war and its effects on the human soul. He clings to a notion of morality that becomes fainter as the film progresses. As a character, he is not particularly sympathetic and can even be ruthless and alienating, but we relate to his narrated perceptions about the story unfolding onscreen.

Green Beret Colonel Walter E. Kurtz—Played by Marlon Brando The evil genius who is Willard's target and the destination of the film's journey. Kurtz is a brilliant military man whose wartime experiences have unhinged him. Internalizing the primitive values of the Montagnard army he commands, Kurtz has made himself a godlike figure who is judged by no one, not even himself. He speaks in grandiose statements about life and death and represents the unconscious, sinister side of humankind.

Lieutenant Colonel Bill Kilgore—Played by Robert Duvall A lunatic, swashbuckling commanding officer of the Ninth Air Cavalry. Kilgore's methods are senseless and absurd: he plays recordings of Wagner to announce an air strike and orders his men to surf on a Vietcong-controlled beach. In the face of danger, Kilgore is dominating and unflinching. He is a sort of western cowboy, arrogant and heroic and seemingly invulnerable.

Chief—Played by Albert Hall The commanding officer and navigator of the patrol boat that takes Willard upriver. The somber and disciplined Chief follows military procedure to a T, acts as a father figure to Clean, and feels personally responsible for the fate of his crew. Chief blames Willard for his crew's predicament and makes his view on the matter very clear: he is a military man, and although he does not necessarily agree with Willard's mission, he follows his orders—at least, as long as they follow protocol.

Clean—Played by Laurence Fishburne (credited as Larry Fishburne) A seventeen-year-old mechanic from the streets of the South Bronx. Clean represents the young men who fought in Vietnam—those who were still kids and didn't know anything about war. He is basically cannon fodder, like many of the troops drafted into the war. Clean whiles away the time on the boat dancing to music and annoying Willard. He becomes momentarily unhinged during the sampan scene.

Chef—Played by Frederic Forrest A saucier from New Orleans who just wants to go home. Chef seems doomed from the start and escapes mentally by smoking dope. He is prone to emotional breakdowns and has a hot temper, fueled by resentment for the war. An eccentric, Chef appears to be more educated than the rest of the crew. He is also the crewmember with the most anger: he emphatically does not want to be in this strange land.

Lance—Played by Sam Bottoms A cocky young GI and surfer from California. Lance's descent into the primitive nature of the jungle is the most pronounced of the crew. He transforms from an alert young soldier to a spaced-out druggie who masks his face in camouflage and assimilates to the primitive Montagnard lifestyle at Kurtz's compound. Lance has a gentleness in his nature that leads him to withdraw, with the help of drugs, from the war around him.

The Photojournalist—Played by Dennis Hopper A hyperactive American freelance photographer and Kurtz worshiper. In the photojournalist's eyes, Kurtz can do no wrong. The photojournalist has been indoctrinated into Kurtz's philosophy and acts as a connecting character to bring Willard and Kurtz together. He is the fool to Kurtz's king and provides comic relief during the film's dark final scenes.

APOCALYPSE NOW

The Playboy Playmates—Played by Cynthia Wood, Colleen Camp, and Linda Carpenter The Sirens of the film. Costumed as a cavalry officer, a cowgirl, and a Native American, the three Playmates play out a farcical history of America in their performance for the troops. They taunt the sex-starved soldiers by being exactly what they can't have. In the process, they ignite a frenzy that cuts their appearance short. The Playmates also represent empty American values and the absurdity of war.

Captain Richard Colby—Played by Scott Glenn Willard's predecessor. The U.S. military sent Colby to assassinate Kurtz before Willard was given the assignment, but Colby ended up getting indoctrinated into Kurtz's lifestyle and stayed at the compound. The seemingly mute and shell-shocked Colby appears only briefly, surrounded by Montagnard natives and stroking a rifle.

General R. Corman—Played by G. D. Spradlin The military superior who outlines Willard's mission. The grim, no-nonsense Corman is threatened and perhaps even frightened by Kurtz's independent operation in Cambodia. He is convinced of Kurtz's insanity and unpredictable violence and is determined to have him killed.

Colonel Lucas—Played by Harrison Ford Corman's junior officer. Lucas acts as Corman's sidekick and briefs Willard with gravity.

Jerry—Played by Jerry Ziesner A mysterious civilian, possibly an undercover CIA agent. Jerry is secretive and ruthless, and he is the only one calm enough to actually eat during Willard's lunchtime briefing. He has only one line in the film, which is spoken about Kurtz: "Terminate with extreme prejudice."

ANALYSIS OF MAJOR CHARACTERS

CAPTAIN WILLARD

Army Captain Willard is a largely passive character. In fact, Martin Sheen replaced Harvey Keitel in the role after Coppola decided Keitel seemed like too active a screen presence. Sheen brings a more muted presence to the film than the forceful Keitel and, as a result, is more compelling as the audience's guide into Vietnam. Willard's primary action is to kill Kurtz. He spends the rest of the film watching intently and internalizing what goes on in the jungle. In his narration, Willard points out the disturbing ironies of war and attempts to insert a faint notion of morality. As he becomes more alert to the absurdities of war and the darkness of human nature, so do we. Nevertheless, we relate to him slowly, despite his role as the film's protagonist, due to his equivocal and impersonal nature. Willard frequently stares off at a point above our shoulder. The war has shell-shocked him, and the film similarly shell-shocks us.

The first shot of Willard inverts his face and superimposes it over the left side of the screen. His eyes are wide open and disturbingly blank. The subsequent scene introduces him as a man who has reached his breaking point. He is in the midst of a nervous breakdown, a state of dementia induced by alcohol and a sense of alienation from the civilized world. When the scene was shot, Sheen actually was drunk and insisted the cameras keep rolling, even after he bloodied his fist by accidentally punching the mirror. Thus, from the opening scene Sheen portrays Willard as a man changed irreversibly by war. He managed to leave it physically but could not free his mind. Now he is back, abandoning all ideas of home, resigned to and eager for a return to combat.

Willard's behavior is at times infuriatingly passive. He takes the mission—"what the hell else was I gonna do?"—and stays out of events that do not affect that mission directly. He interacts with the PBR crew only minimally. He finds Kilgore and goes along with Kilgore's mass mayhem. He observes the Playmates' show with amusement, barely participating. Most of Willard's time on the river is spent reviewing Kurtz's dossier, understanding and relating to his target more and more. The only action he takes prior to killing Kurtz is his murder of the Vietnamese peasant on the sampan—yet he only takes this action in order to preserve his mission's priority. Even Willard's slaughter of Kurtz is arguably passive: not only is Willard following his orders without judgment, he also is doing exactly what Kurtz wants him to do. While it might be argued that Kurtz's murder is the only action Willard ever takes in *Apocalypse Now,* an argument also could be made that his only real, self-made decision is to leave Kurtz's compound and retreat from the darkness it breeds.

Allegorically, Willard's journey to Kurtz is a metaphor for a journey into the darkness of the soul. His mission is to find and kill Kurtz: ultimately he fulfills his mission, but along the way there is some question as to whether he will kill Kurtz or join him. As Willard increasingly aligns himself with Kurtz, he begins more fully to understand the reasons behind Kurtz's insanity. This understanding is fueled by his own descent into near madness. But Willard is able, in the end, to retreat from his descent's endpoint. Does he return to civilization? The film gives no answer. However, it does imply that Willard at least has given himself the opportunity to reenter the civilized world and its framework of morality—and it leaves the choice to do so up to him.

COLONEL KURTZ

Green Beret Colonel Walter E. Kurtz is the archetypal evil genius. Whereas Joseph Conrad's Kurtz in *Heart of Darkness* was gaunt, his flesh consumed by the jungle, Marlon Brando's weight gain before the shooting of *Apocalypse Now* prevented a similar portrayal in Coppola's film. Rather than portray Kurtz as indulgent, Brando played him as a larger-than-life character with ominous omniscience. He understands war on the deepest of levels—he sees clearly its horror and has implicated himself with helpless resignation. Indeed, he has turned his back on morality and chosen horror as his lifestyle. Whether Kurtz is insane is up to the viewer. The hanging corpses and severed heads flung around his compound attest to madness, but one could argue that Kurtz's methods are perfectly sound in the context of a war that is itself insane. Indoctrinated into the methods of the U.S. armed forces, Kurtz did everything right until he got in trouble for killing some Vietnamese intelligence agents. His career was ruined. Bitter at what he considered hypocrisy within the military, Kurtz chose the path of subversion and created his own colony and army, where he now plays God and makes decisions outside the subjective stain of morality.

As Kurtz is Willard's endpoint, so Willard is Kurtz's. Kurtz sees Willard as a receptacle for the philosophy that he has lived out in Cambodia. Kurtz wants to die but must first impart his knowledge to Willard so that the assassin will be able to denounce the war after he completes his mission. Kurtz sees no hope in the world, only the darkness that he himself has fostered. He speaks in lofty, grandiose statements about "the horror" of war, yet he is fully, willingly complicit in these horrors. He has given himself full reign, freeing himself from all moral judgments—after all, what place does morality have in war? Thus, Kurtz has become a dark, godlike figure. No one holds him accountable for his actions, not even himself. Brando's baldness gives his character a monklike, spiritual physicality that emphasizes his godly posturing. While Kurtz accepts and indulges the darkness within the soul, this darkness is what eventually breaks him down. His last words, "The horror, the horror," suggest that he is seeing clearly for the first time and that he has greeted death so willingly because only death can liberate him from his hopelessness.

Coppola cloaks Kurtz in shadows for all of his scenes. His face is shown in full light only twice, and fleetingly both times: as he calls Willard an "errand boy," and as he throws Chef's head into Willard's lap. (Brando's face is camouflaged in the second scene.) This shadowy portrayal adds to the surreal quality of the film and the character. The poetry of T. S. Eliot, specifically "The Hollow Men" and "Love Song of J. Alfred Prufrock," figures in Kurtz's dialogue, as well as in the photojournalist's blathering. All of this combines to create a character that is out-of-bounds mentally, spiritually, and physically. Despite his grandiose physicality and manner of speaking, Colonel Kurtz's humanity has withered away. He has faced, and egged on, his demons, and they have won. He can go now, and Willard is his way out.

APOCALYPSE NOW

THEMES, MOTIFS, AND SYMBOLS

THEMES

THE HYPOCRISY OF WESTERN IMPERIALISM

Apocalypse Now continually spotlights the ironies that accompanied the Vietnam War in particular and western imperialism in general. The film is not overtly antiwar, but it takes pains to reveal the atrocities of a war fought by the United States in the name of democracy and freedom. In the air strike, sampan, and bridge scenes, Coppola clearly depicts the death and destruction that result directly from U.S. involvement. Instead of helping innocent civilians, American troops kill them. They are strangers in a strange land, yet they act as if they own it, staking out territory and firing without provocation.

The film characterizes Willard's mission as the epitome of hypocrisy: in the midst of scores of senseless killings, the U.S. military is wasting energy and lives on killing one of its highest-ranking military officials. While Kurtz may well have gone insane, it's not clear why killing him is a priority when U.S. troops and Vietnamese civilians are dying. Moreover, since the military seems to encourage assassination in war, as evidenced by Willard's assignment, we may question why Kurtz is demonized for killing two people who may have been working against the United States. Willard points out a number of other hypocrisies in his narration. For instance, after killing the Vietnamese peasant in the sampan, he reflects, "We'd cut them in half with a machine gun and give them a Band-Aid. It was a lie." When Willard kills the woman, the others' perception of him changes, yet Clean is not criticized for shooting preemptively and killing an entire family—because he was following protocol.

MADNESS AS A RESULT OF WAR

The film is a metaphor for a journey into the self and shows how the self, in the face of war, darkens beyond recognition. As they move upriver, Willard and the PBR crew become more agitated and separated from reality. Each experiences his own kind of mental breakdown. Chef enters the jungle, has a run-in with a tiger, and is no longer the same—his temper becomes shorter, and he withdraws further into drugs. Lance turns to drugs too, but he also camouflages his face, signaling a changed self. When Clean is killed, Chief breaks down emotionally and becomes a changed man. Willard, already broken from his first tour in Vietnam, becomes obsessed with his target. What originally is a mysterious, exciting voyage morphs into a descent into hell, and the characters respond by hardening themselves, withdrawing, and transforming. The cinematography reflects their impending madness by cloaking the journey in darkness and fog, creating an increasingly hallucinatory atmosphere.

THE EMPTINESS OF AMERICAN VALUES

While the Vietnamese are fighting for their homes, American troops are fighting to go home—and home, to them, is a combination of surfing, *Playboy* Playmates, and psychedelic rock. These values are what the soldiers in *Apocalypse Now* live for, and Willard often reflects upon their emptiness and absurdity. Kilgore's introductory scene also features a team of American journalists ridiculously filming the soldiers and telling them not to look at the camera. The film crew essentially converts the war into popular entertainment, much as actual footage of Vietnam once dominated the airwaves, exacerbating the antiwar movement. After a senseless air strike, Kilgore orders his men to surf or fight. The priorities of the American officers seem confused, to say the least.

Perhaps the biggest absurdity appears when Willard and the PBR crew happen upon a military supply post where a USO show is about to take place. In showing the Playmates in Vietnam, the film highlights the contrasts between American and Vietnamese values. Frenzied U.S. soldiers drool over the women they can't have while Vietnamese villagers eat rice calmly. Willard reflects on the contrast: "[Charlie's] idea of great R and R was cold rice and a little rat meat. He had only two ways home: death or victory." Meanwhile, as he speaks, American soldiers continue hooting loutishly.

MOTIFS

DARKNESS

The omnipresent darkness in the film emphasizes the absence of civilization. Much of the film is shrouded in shadow, and it gets progressively darker as the PBR ventures farther into the jungle. The cinematography transforms the river from a broad, gleaming waterway to a dark, narrow stream overpowered by dense vegetation.

APOCALYPSE NOW

The scene of the arrow attack is bathed in blinding fog, while the bridge scene is bathed in darkness, lit only by flares and what appears to be a searchlight. The erratic light adds to the sense of confusion and conveys the idea that the crew is now totally beyond the comforting glow of civilization. The dark/light contrast is heightened when Willard reaches Kurtz's compound. Kurtz's face is almost always hidden in shadow; only rarely is it seen in full, and it is never filmed in daylight. The climax of the film heightens the contrast to an extreme, as Willard slaughters Kurtz in a scene backlit so that the figures are silhouettes. While the action takes place in darkness, the presence of light suggests a way out of madness.

ESCAPE

The intensity of war leads the characters in *Apocalypse Now* to seek escape. For some, escape comes in the form of drugs or alcohol. When we are introduced to Willard, he is intoxicated to the point of delusion—he practices martial-arts moves as if he were fighting some imaginary enemy—and his intoxication is his mask against the world. Chef and Lance also seek solace in intoxication, with marijuana and LSD. The photojournalist's mania suggests he too is hopped up on something. Escape figures in the film not only through drugs but also through frenetic lighting schemes and surrealistic sets. Often, lighting schemes, especially in the slaughter scene, suggest that despite the cloying pervasiveness of darkness, there is a bright light somewhere, always some way out.

HOME

The soldiers' longing for home permeates the film, and several scenes depict troops seeking reminders—any reminders—of life in America. At Kilgore's camp, Kilgore strums a guitar by the fire. Willard reflects that "the more they tried to make it just like home, the more they made everybody miss it." Music and women, especially, serve as symbols of home. Clean dances around to psychedelic rock blasting through the radio. The Playmates shimmy and strut to an emblematically American 1960s song, "Suzie Q," reminding the troops of home and how far they are from it. The PBR crewmembers get mail at the bridge site, and they read their letters out loud. The film emphasizes that home exists as a faraway paradise for the troops. They are constantly missing it. Invariably each reminder of home makes them miss it even more but also serves to harvest further resentment for the forces that keep them in this strange, dangerous place, rather than enjoying the comfort and safety of the places they know best.

Symbols

Masks

Masks are used at key points throughout the film to symbolize the anti-self—the new identity each character assumes in order to deal with the war, an act that requires a symbolic killing of the old self. Willard's smashing of his reflection in the first scene suggests such an act of self-destruction. By the end of the movie, numerous characters have donned masks or painted their faces with camouflage, signs that they are no longer themselves. When Lance seems finally to reach his breaking point, he drops acid and hides his face in camouflage paint. Kurtz's face is often obscured by shadow or darkness, and when Kurtz throws Chef's severed head into Willard's bamboo cage, he does so wearing face paint. Finally, when Willard prepares to kill Kurtz, he covers his face in mud. These masks underscore the dramatic transformation of the human self during wartime.

The River

The fictional Nung River is the setting of a literal and metaphorical journey. As the river takes the boat up to Cambodia and Kurtz, the crew moves beyond civilization to the heart of darkness within themselves. After Chef and Willard venture into the jungle, Chef screams that he should not have left the boat. "Never get off the boat," Willard muses in narration, for the river is a sanctuary from the primal darkness that lies in the jungle. The river also symbolizes transformation, as when Willard, hidden in the water, rises up from it as the new Kurtz before the assassination scene. While the river leads Willard to a place of death and despair, in the final scene it is also Willard's escape route.

Fog

Fog suggests confusion and alienation for Willard and the rest of the crew, as they journey upriver into the unknown. By cloaking scenes in fog and mist, Coppola emphasizes the fear of the unknown, the perils of venturing too far into the subconscious, and the supremacy of the wilderness. The PBR is an easy target for anyone or anything hiding in the depths of the jungle, and fog makes this vulnerability and dislocation even more evident.

APOCALYPSE NOW

Film Analysis

Depicting the Psychology of War

Apocalypse Now illustrates the horror, the absurdity, and the futility of war, but most important it portrays war's damaging psychological effects. As it charts the characters' descents into literal and metaphorical darkness and fog, the film suggests that war indulges the darkest, foggiest parts of human nature. The protagonist, Willard, is introduced as a man already pushed off-kilter by his first tour in Vietnam. His unsettling behavior in the opening hotel room scene marks the beginning of his descent and immediately raises questions as to his sanity. He can barely stand up. He punches a fist into a mirror, destroying himself symbolically. He wails. He cannot wait to get back to the jungle. This scene, as well as its preceding narration, illustrates war's capacity to change a person's psyche substantially. Willard can no longer lead a normal life within the confines of civilization. He has tried and failed, and now he feels compelled to return to combat.

When the film begins, Willard is already psychologically damaged by the war, and his crewmates are about to experience similar damage. If one were to take "before" and "after" snapshots of the PBR crew, the changes that take place during their participation in Willard's mission would be clearly evident. When Willard first boards the boat, its crew members seem excited by and perhaps somewhat naïve about the journey ahead of them. Lance, particularly unaffected by the war around him, occupies himself with his tan. Young Clean, clueless in combat, still gets a thrill out of the radio, and Chef is so much in denial that he thinks it perfectly safe to go on a mango hunt in the middle of the jungle at nightfall. Chief too seems overly calm and optimistic. But the crew's morale plummets quickly as the journey progresses, and each character's sanity becomes less certain. Lance moves further inward, helped by various drugs, and by the film's end he is seen frolicking in a loincloth and face paint. Clean loses control during the inspection of the sampan, firing at will with little provocation. Chef reaches his breaking point after a run-in with a tiger, and Chief experiences an intense emotional breakdown when Clean is killed by enemy gunfire.

Meanwhile, Willard becomes increasingly infatuated with his elusive target, Kurtz. He obsessively reviews Kurtz's dossier, ultimately aligning himself strongly with the philosophy therein. In narration, Willard reads aloud a letter written by Kurtz to his son, and momentarily the voice of the "I" is unclear—are the words those of Willard or Kurtz? Willard's sense of self has become confused. He feels a strong admiration for and connection to Kurtz, while at the same time he harbors vague suspicions about Kurtz's "methods"—even though he has yet to encounter the man or the methods first-hand.

Upon meeting Kurtz at last, Willard realizes that Kurtz has experienced a break from reality and is indeed insane. Kurtz has given into the primordial temptations of jungle life, killing at random and leaving dead bodies and severed heads as testament to his omnipotent mayhem. He has indulged himself and become a godlike figure, worshiped by many, answering to no one or nothing. He justifies his unconscionable behavior by declaring moral judgment a liability in wartime: "It's judgment that defeats us."

Such an extreme characterization of Kurtz's appalling lifestyle implies that freedom from all societal constraints results in insanity. Kurtz's last words are "the horror," a phrase that conjures up the darkest parts of the human soul, where Kurtz has resided since he "got off the boat." Despite Willard's identification with Kurtz, he does not take up Kurtz's throne. He leaves the compound, rejecting that darkest part of himself and presumably heading back into the civilized world. A descent too far inward thus becomes a descent into hell—a hell brought on by the metaphorical journey upriver. The atrocities of war have caused the each character to lose all sense of self and to become an other, an empty shell that can no longer recognize itself or, like Kurtz, discriminate along moral lines. But while *Apocalypse Now* implies that war effectively displaces the self and the rights and wrongs of morality, its conclusion suggests that the soul is capable of rejecting such darkness.

PAGE-TO-SCREEN ADAPTATION

John Milius's original screenplay moved Joseph Conrad's 1898 novella *Heart of Darkness* from colonial Africa to the heart of the Vietnam War in the late 1960s. Although Milius made drastic changes, he left the basic structure intact: a man travels upriver to face an evil genius and, along the way, must face his fears, his mortality, and the possibility that he will go slowly insane. Director

Francis Ford Coppola in turn embellished Milius's screenplay to make it more closely mirror Conrad's book, cutting scenes, adding others, and demanding a great deal of improvisation from his actors. Milius and Coppola therefore shared the film's screenwriting credit. Author Michael Herr, who wrote a notable collection of Vietnam War articles entitled *Dispatches,* also received a writing credit for penning the film's narration.

In addition to switching the setting, Milius renamed or modified nearly all of Conrad's characters (aside from Kurtz). Conrad's protagonist, Marlow, a pensive sailor on a quest to meet the ostensibly great, multitalented thinker Kurtz, becomes Milius's Army Captain Benjamin Willard, an emotionally scarred Special Forces operative on a classified mission to terminate Kurtz. Milius's Kurtz was an outstanding military officer who has apparently gone crazy. As the film opens, he leads a small colony in Cambodia, relying on "unsound methods" for imperious control. Moreover, Kurtz as portrayed by actor Marlon Brando is drastically different from the Kurtz of Conrad's novella. Brando's portrayal was influenced by his own corpulent, imposing physical presence, which contrasted greatly with the appearance of the emaciated Kurtz in *Heart of Darkness.* Conrad's Kurtz withers away in the jaws of the jungle; Brando's Kurtz is broad and large, with an imposing, sinister presence. Coppola decided to shoot Brando from the waist up to give him the appearance of being enormous and superhumanly tall without out seeming fat.

As both Marlow and Willard make journeys up their respective rivers, they witness unthinkable atrocities. In Marlow's case, the scenes of torture and slavery can be attributed to European imperialism. Willard's story, on the other hand, requires him frequently to participate in the atrocities himself, as they are part of the war he is fighting. *Heart of Darkness* is a searing indictment of imperialism. *Apocalypse Now* similarly indicts the American presence during the war in Vietnam, which is seen by its critics as yet another version of western imperialism. In both stories, operating beyond the constraints of civilized society for an extended period leads to insanity. Reality in the novella and film is transformed into a cloudy surreal landscape where what is moral is gapingly unclear, moral judgment is no longer possible, and the very nature of humanity is challenged.

Coppola and cinematographer Vittorio Storaro translate the updated novella beautifully onto the screen, playing out the novella's titular darkness visually through shadows and light-dark contrast. Joseph Conrad's vivid descriptions of the Congo jungle jump into the film in the tiger scene, as Chef and Willard cower under mammoth trees. The fog that pervades the novella also features prominently the film, most notably when Willard emerges from the river at the film's climax.

Milius's original screenplay was structured with narration, but this narration was discarded during filming. Sound engineer Walter Murch, however, added his own voiceover during sound editing, because he felt the film lacked structure. Eventually, Michael Herr, a journalist who spent a year in Vietnam, later publishing his writing as *Dispatches,* was brought on to replace Murch's narration. Herr's work tells the story through Willard's eyes and gives the film an intimacy and organization that otherwise would not exist. This narration humanizes Willard, making him more sympathetic and the story more comprehensible.

Score and Soundtrack

In *Apocalypse Now*, music primarily sets a psychedelic, hallucinatory tone that both places the film in its historical period—America in the late 1960s—and mirrors the surreal events depicted onscreen. The opening sequence fades in to "The End," an atmospheric song by the Doors that sounds as exotic as the Vietnamese jungle looks. With this eerie, moody song as his backdrop, Captain Willard tumbles into a downward spiral that continues throughout the film. Immediately, the music links image to place and time: with its frenzied rhythms, the song prepares us for the odyssey that is about to begin. Music from the Doors appears again near the end of the film, when Willard emerges from the river and shots of Kurtz's slaughter are interwoven with shots of the caribou slaughter. The murder scene is the most hallucinatory of the film, thanks to the combination of the Doors' rock, cinematographer Storaro's surreal lighting scheme, and the back-and-forth cuts between Kurtz and the caribou.

In other instances, the soundtrack is used to reinforce the notion of war's absurdity. The most obvious example occurs as Kilgore blasts Wagner's "Ride of the Valkyries" to announce a senseless, unnecessary air strike. To pair such a bombastic composition with the atrocities that unfold below is absurd nearly to the point of comedy. But the comedy dissipates as soldiers are wounded and a Vietnamese woman throws a grenade into a helicopter, killing all on board. Soon, the combination of triumphant music and deadly combat creates a sense of madness that is reinforced by Kilgore's unconventional "surf or fight" methods.

Elsewhere, the soundtrack symbolizes home. Kilgore strums a guitar around the campfire as his troops sing along during a gathering akin to an American beach party. Clean frequently listens to the radio, which blasts comforting American rock in the midst of a strange country and climate. The USO show features Flash Cadillac's "Suzie Q," a song popularized by the band Creedence Clearwater Revival. In the Playmates scene, the pairing of American women and American pop music becomes too much for some of the soldiers to bear, and several cannot control themselves. A few soldiers even cling to the Playmates' helicopter as it ascends. Eventually, these men let go and fall into the river. What was meant to be a patriotic reminder that America still cares about them turns into a sad reality check. As the songs remind the soldiers of home, they also serve to remind us that the film is not just fiction but *historical* fiction.

Coppola used music to anchor the film to its specific social context. The songs' recognizability lends the film another layer of authenticity, particularly to those who lived through the Vietnam War and, like the characters, can instantly relate to the sounds that characterized this era of American cultural history.

Important Quotations Explained

1.   Kilgore: "I love the smell of napalm in the morning."

Lieutenant Colonel Bill Kilgore delivers this line to Captain Willard on the beach after ordering a destructive helicopter strike on a Vietcong-controlled coastal village. Kilgore delivers the line in an uncharacteristic, matter-of-fact tone, but characteristically he doesn't flinch when a bomb explodes loudly behind him. This chilling quotation adds to the uncanny and invulnerable quality of Kilgore's character while signifying the far-reaching effect war has had on his mentality. The quote also speaks to the idiosyncrasies of war by describing and even celebrating the unique smell of napalm. Kilgore also says the smell is like "victory." In typically absurd fashion, the havoc-wreaking Kilgore follows up his napalm-glorifying remark by leaving the film on a bright note. However, since we are aware that the Vietnam War did eventually end but that it is known historically as a great failure for the United States, the optimistic tone and the use of the word *victory* are ironic.

2.   General Corman: "In this war, things get confused out there—power, ideals, the old morality, and practical military necessity . . . because there's a conflict in every human heart between the rational and the irrational, between good and evil. And good does not always triumph."

Over lunch in the intelligence compound at Nha Trang, General Corman explains Kurtz's descent into insanity as he briefs Willard on his mission to terminate Kurtz. The quotation delineates the basic premise of the film by aligning war with madness. Willard's journey thus becomes both an actual journey upriver and a metaphorical journey through philosophical terrain. Corman relates the confusion inherent in war to the adoption of an irrational and ultimately evil path. According to Corman, participation in war requires a certain readjustment of morality, and sometimes that readjustment swells until morality is completely skewed. The human heart deals with moral conflicts every day, but war, with its haunting atrocities, exaggerates such conflicts until they easily over-whelm the heart to the point of intense confusion—and sometimes madness. Kurtz, Corman says, has allowed himself to go the way of madness.

The quotation foreshadows the rest of the film, forecasting the dark and difficult choice that Willard will have to make when he reaches Kurtz. Corman's words resonate throughout the film, as Willard sees the conflicts described played out before him, within himself, and within the other soldiers. Willard struggles with his own internal conflict between good and evil, rationality and irratio-nality. In Kurtz, his double of sorts, Willard can understand what happens when evil triumphs over goodness and morality. While he relates to Kurtz and even goes so far as to admire and respect him, he must decide his own path. In the end, he chooses the path of ratio-nality, and in doing so he implies that the outcome is indeed a choice—a difficult one but one that every soldier must make. Perhaps good doesn't always triumph, but evil can win only if one lets it.

3.   WILLARD: "It was the way we had over here of living with ourselves. We'd cut them in half with a machine gun and give them a Band-Aid. It was a lie—and the more I saw of them, the more I hated lies."

Willard narrates these words after fatally shooting the Vietnamese peasant woman on the sampan. With this act, he makes himself complicit in the atrocities of war and aligns himself more closely with Kurtz. In his narration, Willard details the hypocrisy of the U.S. military: just before Willard shoots the woman, Clean sense-lessly and without provocation opens fire on Vietnamese peasants. Although Clean kills several innocent civilians with no conse-quences, Chief makes no mention of it but instead makes a big deal of following orders by trying to take the woman to a nearby hospi-tal. Willard shoots her, because he does not want to waste more time and because he reasons that she likely would have died before receiving medical attention anyway. After all, the other peasants have been killed, so why spare this woman's life when it interferes with his mission? Willard's action and subsequent reflection upon it possess a disturbing logic that makes sense only in the morally skewed frame of war. Yet, although his crew members are also com-plicit in the atrocity, they see him differently after the shooting.

Whether or not U.S. military protocol makes sense, it's the only way they know how to live. Willard, on the other hand, has breached the code, and the other soldiers cannot condone such a breach. Willard's Kurtzlike transformation accelerates as a result of this incident.

4.   KURTZ: "It's judgment that defeats us."

Here, Kurtz, in his quarters, attempts to indoctrinate Willard with his ideas. Willard, freed from the tiger cage and allowed to roam throughout the compound, internalizes Kurtz's philosophy. This quotation is part of a longer monologue in which Kurtz compares the Vietcong's combat methods to those of U.S. troops, explaining why the Vietcong will inevitably win the war. Their victory is sealed because they use their primordial instincts to murder without emotion or judgment. Kurtz believes that moral judgment is out of place in war and serves only to thwart victory. Accordingly, only the ruthless can win. With this quotation and its encompassing monologue, Kurtz also explains to Willard why he himself chose to give in to the temptations of the jungle, to deify himself among the Montagnard tribe, and to practice behavior devoid of moral constraints. His justification for this lifestyle is that judgment "defeats us." It prevents soldiers from winning the war, and it prevents humans from realizing their full potential to live as one with the primitive nature both outside and within them.

5.   KURTZ: "The horror, the horror."

These are Kurtz's last words, uttered after Willard brutally slaughters him with a machete and repeated as the film fades to black at its end. The words revisit a monologue Kurtz delivers to Willard earlier in the film, intimating that if horror is not made to be one's friend, it becomes "an enemy to be feared." Kurtz's last words—also spoken by Kurtz at the end of Conrad's novella *Heart of Darkness*—are enigmatic and can be taken to indicate several different outcomes. Critics generally agree, however, that these words signify Kurtz's final acceptance of the horrors in which he has participated through the Vietnam War, as well as the horrors he has produced independently of the U.S. military machine. He dies a broken, conflicted, tormented man, ready to give his life away. His last moments become moments of clarity, and his tone is one of shock: while he acknowledges his actions, he is appalled by the atrocities he has committed. With these final utterances, Kurtz at last accepts the evil present in his soul and welcomes the promise of some semblance of peace in death.

SCHINDLER'S LIST

(1993)

CONTEXT

In 1933, Adolf Hitler and the National Socialist German Workers' (Nazi) Party assumed power in Germany and began plans for war. The party wanted to rid Germany, and eventually the world, of "impure" groups: Jews, Gypsies, homosexuals, and the handicapped, among others. Thus began a period of genocide.

In 1935, the German government passed the Nuremberg Laws, which defined individuals as Jews based not on their religious practices but on bloodlines. In other words, a person raised Christian who had at least three Jewish grandparents was considered Jewish and therefore impure. These laws also called for the separation of the "pure" Aryan race from the Jews. In 1938, in an event called Kristallnacht (Night of Broken Glass), the Nazis broke windows and tore apart Jewish businesses and synagogues, foreshadowing the eventual attempt at comprehensive destruction of the Jewish race.

When Germany invaded Poland in 1939, the policies of racial hatred already in place in Germany were adopted in the new German-occupied territories. Jewish people could no longer own businesses in Poland and other German-occupied territories and eventually were forced to wear armbands or patches emblazoned with the Star of David so they could be easily identified as Jews. They were forced out of their homes in the city and countryside and into ghettos, concentrated and separated from rest of the population. The Kraków ghetto, featured in *Schindler's List*, covered sixteen square blocks and was populated by approximately 20,000 Jews. In time, Jews were forced to work in labor camps, and some were murdered by mobile killing units.

Around 1941, the "Final Solution" was implemented in order to exterminate all the Jews, Gypsies, and other "impure" groups in Europe. Today, it stands as one of the darkest periods in human history. The Nazis evacuated Jews violently from the ghettos, sending them to Auschwitz, Treblinka, and other death camps to face the gas chambers. Bodies of the murdered were cremated in large ovens, often making the sky above the death camps and surrounding towns black with smoke, with human ashes raining down like snow.

During this bleak and terrifying period in Kraków, Oskar Schindler, a war profiteer and womanizer, saved the lives of about 1,100

Jews who worked for him. These people would come to call themselves Schindlerjuden (Schindler Jews). Given that the Nazis killed millions of people during the Holocaust, 1,100 might seem an insignificant number. However, this number represents 1,100 unique human lives, all of which would have ceased to exist if not for Schindler, and those 1,100 produced some six thousand descendants. Despite the overwhelming scale of the Holocaust as a whole, the powerful story of the Schindlerjuden and the man who risked his life and wealth to save their lives has endured.

In 1983, Australian author Thomas Keneally published his fact-based novel *Schindler's Ark,* which chronicled, through first-person accounts, the amazing story of the Schindlerjuden. American film director Steven Spielberg read the book about the same time he was filming his movie *E.T.* He was struck by the story, particularly by the book's powerful rendering of the Holocaust through individual accounts. Spielberg was driven to adapt the book into a film, but it was ten years before he was emotionally ready to embark on the project.

Spielberg, born on December 18, 1947, in Cincinnati, Ohio, was raised by Jewish parents in the suburbs of Phoenix, Arizona. There, he was dismayed to find he was the only Jewish person most of his classmates had ever met. He went on to study English at California State University, Long Beach, when his grades were not good enough to get him into film school. Nonetheless, he managed to land a job on the Universal Studios lot and, after starting out directing television shows, eventually moved to films. By the age of thirty, he had directed two of the highest-grossing films of all time: *Jaws* (1975) and *Close Encounters of the Third Kind* (1977). Spielberg went on to become one of the most popular, prolific directors in history, with blockbuster films such as *Raiders of the Lost Ark* (1981), *E.T.* (1982), *Jurassic Park* (1993), and *Saving Private Ryan* (1998).

The story of the Schindlerjuden greatly affected Spielberg. He has said that he had fallen out of touch with his Jewish identity as an adult but that he learned a great deal about his own heritage while researching *Schindler's List.* After visiting Auschwitz, the enormous responsibility of his project became clear. Spielberg understood that in order to help people digest and understand an event as huge and incomprehensible as the Holocaust, he had to make the stories personal.

The director's intentions for the film were to educate people about the Holocaust, to silence those who deny that the Holocaust ever happened, and to make sure people never forget so that history does not repeat itself. Moreover, he filmed the movie in the early 1990s when genocide against Serbs, Bosnian Muslims, and ethnic Albanians was taking place in Yugoslavia. The fact that another genocide could happen in the present day strengthened Spielberg's desire to educate.

When *Schindler's List* opened in 1993, it received widespread critical acclaim. Spielberg expected a decent number of people to see the movie in theaters but primarily hoped the film would be adopted by schools in order to educate students about the Holocaust. To his surprise, more than fifty million people saw the film in theaters, and more than sixty-five million people watched it during a special airing on national television.

Schindler's List transformed Spielberg from the king of high-budget action-adventure movies into a director capable of creating moving human drama. The film finally earned him the Academy Award for Best Director—a prize that had eluded him in the past. In addition to Best Director, *Schindler's List* won six more Academy Awards: Best Art Direction (Set Design), Best Cinematography, Best Film Editing, Best Music (Original Score), Best Picture, and Best Writing (Screenplay Based on Material Previously Produced or Published). The film also won three Golden Globe awards, for Best Director, Best Motion Picture (Drama), and Best Screenplay (Motion Picture).

PLOT OVERVIEW

Schindler's List opens with a close-up of unidentified hands lighting a pair of Shabbat (Sabbath) candles, followed by the sound of a Hebrew prayer blessing the candles. This scene, one of only a handful of color scenes in the film, closes as the flames flicker out. The wisp of smoke from the dying flames fades into the next scene, now in black and white, and becomes a plume of smoke from a steam engine. A folding table is set up on a train platform, where a single Jewish family registers as Jews. The single table becomes many tables, and the single family becomes a large crowd. Close-up images of names being typed into lists provide a sense of the vast number of Jews arriving in Kraków.

Oskar Schindler appears in his Kraków hotel room. His face is not shown, and the focus is on his possessions. He puts on his expensive watch, cuff links, and Nazi Party pin, and takes a large wad of bills from his night table. Schindler then enters a nightclub. Once he is seated, a high-ranking Nazi official at a nearby table catches his attention. Attempting to ingratiate himself with the local Nazis in order to secure lucrative war contracts, Schindler sends drinks to the table. Before long, he is treating a large table of Nazis and their friends to expensive food and fine wine. Schindler has his picture taken with everyone important at the table, as well as with dancers at the club.

Schindler next visits the Judenrat, the Jewish council charged with carrying out Nazi orders in Kraków. He walks directly to the front of a seemingly endless line of Jews, where he finds his accountant, Itzhak Stern. Schindler tells Stern that he needs investors, "Jews," to help him buy an enamelware factory. Since Jews, by law, cannot own businesses, Schindler tells Stern that he will pay the investors in product, not money. A profiteer, Schindler knows that he will maximize his profit if he does not have to pay the Jewish investors in cash. He also wants Stern to run the business, but Stern initially refuses the offer, telling Schindler that the Jews will not be interested in investing.

Schindler, however, does not give up. Next, he visits a church where Jewish smugglers conduct business. All of the smugglers, except one named Poldek Pfefferberg, are scared off. Schindler tells

Pfefferberg he will need lots of luxury items in the coming months, and Pfefferberg promises to procure them.

The scene then changes to one of masses of Jews walking over a bridge. Their armbands stand out starkly. It is March 20, 1941—the deadline for Jews to enter the ghetto. A little Polish girl in the street shouts, "Good-bye, Jews," over and over again. While Schindler arrives at his new luxury apartment, recently vacated by the Nussbaum family, the Nussbaums themselves arrive in the ghetto with thousands of other uprooted families.

Schindler finally secures money from the Jewish investors, who agree to accept goods as payment, because, as Schindler points out, money will be worthless in the ghetto. Schindler sets up his factory with Stern's help and hires Jews, rather than Poles, because they are cheaper to employ. Workers at the factory will be deemed "essential"—a status that saves them from removal to death camps. Stern recognizes this fact immediately and fills the factory with many Jewish workers whom the Nazis would otherwise have deemed expendable.

At this point, Schindler is unaware that Stern is using his position in the factory to save people. His awareness grows, however, when Stern brings to see him a one-armed man who wants to thank Schindler for saving him by making him "essential." Schindler dismisses the gratitude and chastises Stern for bringing the man to see him. Shortly after the scolding, Schindler has to rescue Stern himself from a train bound for a death camp.

Meanwhile, construction on the Plaszów labor camp begins, and Amon Goeth appears. Goeth, a sadistic Nazi, is charged with building and running the camp. When Plaszów is completed, the Jews are evacuated from the Kraków ghetto and sent to the camp. From a hill high above the ghetto, Schindler and his girlfriend watch the destruction. He sees a little girl in a red coat—the only color in the otherwise black-and-white scene—walking through the carnage. Schindler's girlfriend tearfully begs him to go home, and Schindler is obviously moved by what he sees. Schindler convinces Goeth to allow him to build his own subcamp to house his factory workers.

Schindler begins to participate actively in saving Jews when Regina Perlman, a Jewish girl passing as a gentile, visits his office. She begs Schindler to hire her parents because she has heard that his factory is a haven. He refuses to help and sends her away. Later, he yells at Stern and tells him he is not in the business of saving people. But when Schindler finishes his tirade, he gives Stern his gold watch and tells him to bring the Perlmans over. With this decision, he begins to actively save Jews. Over time, Schindler gives Stern more and more of his own personal items to use for bribes to bring people to his factory.

Some time later, Goeth is charged with evacuating Plaszów and exhuming and burning the bodies of 10,000 Jews killed there and at the Kraków ghetto. Schindler realizes that his workers, Stern included, face certain death at the hands of the Nazis, so he decides to spend his fortune to save as many Jews as he can. With that, Schindler begins to make his list. He persuades Goeth to sell him his workers, as well as Goeth's maid, Helen Hirsch, to work in his factory in Czechoslovakia. The men and women are transported to Czechoslovakia on two separate trains, however, and the women are inadvertently diverted to Auschwitz, where Schindler is forced to buy them again. The men and women are reunited at the factory, where they remain until the war's end.

When the war ends, Schindler tells his workers they are now free but that he will be hunted as a war criminal and must flee at midnight. When he bids his Schindlerjuden good-bye, they give him a ring made from the gold tooth work of a factory worker, engraved with the Talmudic phrase, "Whoever saves one life saves the world entire." Schindler breaks down, crying that he could have sacrificed more, saved more lives. He and his wife then flee.

The next morning, a single Russian soldier enters the camp and tells the Jews they are free. As they walk toward a nearby town, the scene dissolves into full color and reveals a group of real Holocaust survivors walking across a field. They line up, many accompanied by the actors who play them, and place rocks on Schindler's grave. The last person at the grave is Liam Neeson (Oskar Schindler). He places a rose on the tombstone.

CHARACTER LIST

Oskar Schindler—Played by Liam Neeson The protagonist and eventual savior of approximately 1,100 Jews. The film follows Schindler's progression from a callous, greedy war profiteer to a man willing to sacrifice his fortune to save the lives of his Jewish factory workers. Schindler is a womanizer and con artist who never hesitates to do something outside the law, such as placing bribes, to get what he wants. His metamorphosis into a hero is slow in coming. Initially, he is indifferent to the plight of the Jews and has little concern for the moral issues at stake. However, he develops compassion for the Jews and begins to see his factory workers as humans deserving of life. His compassion ultimately compels him to save them at great personal risk. Schindler's motives are never directly stated in the film, and the real-life Schindler never offered an explanation.

Itzhak Stern—Played by Ben Kingsley Schindler's Jewish accountant and conscience. Stern is an intelligent man who never loses his pride in the face of the violent and dehumanizing conditions the Jews face under the Nazi regime. He is able to influence the good, moral side of Schindler. Stern is the first to recognize that Schindler's factory can be a haven for Jews. His paternalistic attitude toward his fellow Jews in the ghetto leads him to take advantage of his position to save those who would otherwise be exterminated. He initially expresses contempt for the materialistic Schindler but gains respect for him as the profiteer changes. Stern's relationship with Schindler contributes greatly to Schindler's decision to save the Schindlerjuden.

Amon Goeth—Played by Ralph Fiennes A Nazi soldier in charge of building of Plaszów work camp. Goeth is a cruel, sadistic man deeply entrenched in Nazi philosophy. Goeth exhibits a true hatred for the Jews, at times shooting them randomly from his balcony high above the labor camp. He and Schindler share many common traits, such as greed and callous self-centeredness, but Goeth gives himself totally to evil and hatred. He is also deeply conflicted, torn between feelings of attraction and disgust for his Jewish maid. Goeth represents the all-consuming hatred of the Nazi Party.

Emilie Schindler—Played by Caroline Goodall Oskar Schindler's wife. Emilie is a good and patient woman who loves Schindler unconditionally, even as he cheats on her continually. She expresses only exasperation upon finding another woman in Schindler's apartment but is visibly hurt when she finds that the doorman does not even know Schindler is married. Emilie has pride, however, and leaves Schindler in Poland because he cannot promise to be faithful to her. She tells him to "send chocolate" to her at home in Czechoslovakia.

Poldek Pfefferberg—Played by Jonathan Sagalle A Jewish smuggler and Schindler's black-market connection. Pfefferberg, whom Schindler first approaches in a church, becomes Schindler's provider of black-market luxury items. Pfefferberg is enterprising and determined to survive. During the liquidation of the ghetto, he plans to escape through the sewers. Though his wife, Mila, refuses to go in the sewers, he reassures her and goes to see if they are clear. When he returns for her, she is gone. He uses his quick wit to save himself in an encounter with Amon Goeth by pretending to be working under Nazi orders.

Helen Hirsch—Played by Embeth Davidtz Amon Goeth's Jewish maid, who lives a tortured life as the object of Goeth's desire and disgust. Helen Hirsch is a strong woman lost in despair, forced to work for Goeth, whom she despises. She faces brutal, unpredictable beatings at Goeth's hands and begins to lose hope, accepting the probability of her own death. She is representative of victims who experienced psychological abuse under the Nazi regime.

Marcel Goldberg—Played by Mark Ivanir A friend of Poldek and a ghetto policeman. Goldberg is an opportunist and black marketer and becomes a policeman after striking a deal with a Nazi. The job pays well, which is all he cares about. Goldberg continues to be opportunistic throughout the film, accepting bribes from Schindler via Stern to move Jews into Schindler's factory.

Julian Scherner—Played by Andrzej Seweryn An SS officer whom Schindler bribes in order to gain the necessary permits for the sale of his enamelware factory. Although Scherner is a member of the Nazi Party and buys into all the beliefs of that party, he is not a sadist like Goeth. Scherner's total disregard for the plight of the Jews comes from indifference and latent anti-Semitism. He represents the institutional evil that was the Third Reich.

Chaja and Danka Dresner—Played by Miri Fabian and Anna Mucha A mother and daughter who epitomize family bonds and loyalty. Chaja and Danka are inseparable throughout the film. During the liquidation of the ghetto, Chaja makes the ultimate sacrifice, forcing Danka to take the last hiding spot left in a building. Danka, however, exhibits the same loyalty as she leaves the hiding spot to find her mother. This mother and daughter represent the loyalty and devotion of family.

Mr. and Mrs. Nussbaum—Played by Michael Gordon and Aldona Grochal A wealthy couple forced to vacate their apartment, which later becomes Schindler's. The Nussbaums are rich and snobbish, initially disgusted with not only their ghetto quarters but their country neighbors as well. However, they quickly lose their snobbery as they realize that all the Jews in the ghetto are in the same boat.

Rabbi Menasha Lewartow—Played by Ezra Dagan A man who serves as a rabbi prior to the Nazi invasion. Rabbi Lewartow, whom Schindler saves, escapes execution at Goeth's hands, and his inability to lead religious ceremonies represents the oppression of the Jewish faith. The rabbi is grateful and redeemed when Schindler, in the Czechoslovakian factory, tells him to begin performing prayers again.

Regina Perlman—Played by Bettina Kupfer A woman who attempts to convince Schindler to save her parents. Regina lives in Kraków and passes as a gentile in order to avoid Nazi capture. She is desperate to save her parents and risks detection by dressing up and going to Schindler's office to beg him for help. She is crushed when he refuses her, but her spirit is redeemed as she later sees her parents enter the factory gate.

ANALYSIS OF MAJOR CHARACTERS

OSKAR SCHINDLER

Oskar Schindler, war profiteer, womanizer, and Nazi Party member, becomes the unlikely hero and savior of about 1,100 Polish Jews during the Holocaust. He is essentially a con artist and moderately successful businessman who recognizes the potential for profit in wartime. He buys a formerly Jewish-owned enamelware factory and uses bribery and ingratiation to procure military contracts to make war supplies. At the beginning of his quest to become rich, he is indifferent to the Jewish situation, which he sees as merely an unfortunate result of war. A playboy with a large ego, Schindler routinely cheats on his wife and joins the Nazi Party not for ideological reasons but because it will help him make more money. Although he purchases the factory after it has been confiscated from Jewish owners and is given an apartment appropriated from wealthy Jews, Schindler feels no remorse and does not consider the origins of his good fortune.

Schindler, initially concerned only with himself and the success of his moneymaking scheme, undergoes a change that prompts him to spend his fortune to save the lives of those he once exploited. His motive is never completely clear—and indeed, the real Schindler never revealed his motivations. However, the film does suggest that at least one of his incentives was obvious: Schindler simply could not sit by and watch people he knew be sent to death. His metamorphosis from a man of indifference to one of compassion takes place gradually over a number of scenes. His respect for his Jewish accountant, Itzhak Stern, probably has a great deal to do with his transformation, as does his witnessing of the Kraków ghetto evacuation, when he sees the little girl in the red coat. However, Schindler's motivations may also be less altruistic: it is possible that his own ego and narcissism led him to be a savior. He initially reacts angrily to the idea that his factory is a haven, but perhaps became enamored of the idea of being a hero. The needs of his ego may, in some capacity, have surpassed his material needs. The film does not propagate such a harsh stance, but Schindler's boorish behavior makes this speculation plausible. Nevertheless, whatever the results of an analysis of Schindler's motivations, the good effects of his choices are undeniable.

ITZHAK STERN

Itzhak Stern, bright, proud, and determined, brings out the moral side of Schindler, and Stern's attitude toward Schindler reflects Schindler's change throughout the film. Stern recognizes immediately Schindler's callousness and greed. Early on, he expresses disdain for Schindler and controlled outrage at his original offer to have Stern run the factory and secure Jewish investors. He refuses to drink with Schindler, making clear he does not approve of Schindler's morals. But Stern's attitude softens as Schindler becomes an active participant in saving the Schindlerjuden, and he eventually sees the good in his employer. He finally does have a drink with Schindler when the two say good-bye after they learn of the closing of the Plaszów labor camp and realize Stern will almost certainly be sent to his death. By accepting a drink, Stern demonstrates his respect for Schindler, and Schindler accepts the finality of Stern's probable fate.

Stern, like Schindler, is an opportunist, and he is the brains behind the rescue of the Schindlerjuden. Stern is the one who discovers a way to channel his essentially forced labor for Schindler into a way to help his fellow Jews. Schindler does no work, leaving Stern to run the factory, and Stern immediately begins to give factory jobs to Jews who otherwise would be deemed "nonessential" and would most likely be killed. He forges documents to make teachers and intellectuals appear to be experienced machinists and factory workers. Stern's motivation—to help his people—is abundantly clear. Ben Kingsley plays him as a proud man with a mission and a palpable desperation to help all those he can. These traits are absent from Schindler, the film's protagonist and hero, until late in the film. Although Schindler ultimately makes the rescue possible by using his connections and monetary resources, Stern plays just as large a role by driving Schindler gently from behind the scenes. Stern sets the wheels in motion, making the factory a haven for the Kraków Jews before Schindler even notices what is occurring.

AMON GOETH

Sadistic and ruthless, Amon Goeth represents the evil of the Nazi Party. Goeth finds a sanctioned outlet for his cruelty in the Nazi military and is representative of the mindless evil of the Third Reich and its "final solution." He views Jews as vermin, creatures unworthy of possessing basic human rights. He kills often and without hesitation or provocation. Unlike Schindler, Goeth never strays into goodness. However, the lack of change in his basic nature does not render him a one-dimensional character; Goeth is a complicated and conflicted man, as well. He lusts after his Jewish maid, Helen Hirsch, and actor Ralph Fiennes skillfully conveys both the strength and ambivalence of this passion. Goeth attempts to seduce Helen, and when she shows no reaction, he turns on her, blames her for trying to tempt him, calls her names, and beats her savagely. Later, when Schindler wants to buy Helen to put her on his list, Goeth refuses. He tells Schindler he will never let her go, that he wants to bring her back to Vienna and grow old with her. Schindler tells him it can never be, and Goeth, exhibiting his conflicting feelings, replies that he would never subject Helen to Auschwitz, but would shoot her in the head, "mercifully," instead. Goeth's twisted idea of a merciful end for Helen epitomizes both his inner conflict and essential cruelty.

THEMES, MOTIFS, AND SYMBOLS

THEMES

THE TRIUMPH OF THE HUMAN SPIRIT

In the face of overwhelming evil, the Jews in *Schindler's List* exhibit an unbroken spirit and will to survive. Mrs. Nussbaum, trying to make the best of the situation just like all the other Jews forced into the ghetto, tells her husband their ghetto apartment could be worse. Schindler's factory workers believe they may be safe in his factory and continue to hope for survival. The event that perhaps best illustrates this triumph of spirit is the wedding in the Plaszów labor camp. Even though the Jews in Plaszów live in constant fear of death, including random shootings from a hilltop villa by camp overseer Amon Goeth, two people manage to fall in love. With possibly no future to look forward to, they marry in the hope that they will survive. A woman in the barracks apologizes to God for performing the ceremony when she is not a rabbi, but explains that desperate times call for desperate measures, and that the union of the couple is ultimately what counts. The groom crushes a light bulb—an improvised substitution for the traditional wineglass—with his foot at the conclusion of the ceremony. Not only does the couple wed, but they stay true to Jewish traditions, which symbolizes hope for the survival of the Jewish race.

THE DIFFERENCE ONE INDIVIDUAL CAN MAKE

The more than six thousand descendants of the Schindlerjuden might never have been born had one man not chosen to take a stand against evil. The Third Reich sanctioned and encouraged violence against the Jews and sought the ultimate destruction of the Jewish race, and millions of citizens of the Third Reich either stood idly by or actively supported this persecution. In *Schindler's List,* as the Jews in Kraków are forced into the ghetto, a little girl on the street cries out, "Good-bye, Jews," over and over again. She represents the open hostility often shown the Jews by their countrymen. After all, the little girl did not contain this hatred naturally—she learned it. Through her, Spielberg sends the message that the evil of the "final solution" infected entire communities. Although some people tried to help their Jewish friends and neighbors, far more refused to help, fearing reprisal, and some even turned on their Jewish neighbors. Any one of these people could have made a difference in the lives of Jews, but almost none did. Oskar Schindler risked his life and stood alone against the overwhelming evil of the Nazi Party. The powerful idea that one man can save the life of another underlies the entire film.

THE DANGEROUS EASE OF DENIAL

The Jews in *Schindler's List*, even as they are forced into the ghetto and later into the labor camp, suffer from a denial of their true situation. This denial afflicted many European Jews who fell victim to the Holocaust. They leave their homes in the countryside and move to Kraków and later to the ghetto because the Nazis force them to. Once in the ghetto, however, they believe the bad times will pass. Their denial of their situation continues in the labor camp, even as killing surrounds them. A prime example of denial occurs in the scene when Mila Pfefferberg tells the other women in her barracks about the rumors she heard of the death camps like Auschwitz. She tells the women how Jews are being gassed to death en masse, their remains cremated. The women respond with an almost angry dismissal, saying something like that surely could not happen. However, the actors manage to convey the fact that deep down, the women suspect the truth. They have suffered enough horror already to know mass extermination is possible.

MOTIFS

LISTS

Lists dominate the lives of the Kraków Jews in *Schindler's List*. Early in the film, close-ups of name upon name being typed into the list of Jews registering in Kraków demonstrate the vast number of Jews forced into the city. But this first list only scratches the surface of danger and destruction. The lists become increasingly ominous during sorting exercises to determine who is fit to work or who is "essential" and who is not. Those deemed "unessential" are placed on the list to be evacuated to extermination camps. Stern's name appears on a list sending him to Auschwitz. When Schindler saves him, an SS officer mentions that it doesn't matter which Jew gets on the train, and that keeping track of names just means more paperwork. This disregard for names and particularity symbolizes the extent to which the Nazis dehumanized Jews. Schindler's list is one that saves lives. The Nazis' lists represent evil and death, but Schindler's list represents pure good and life. In an ironic twist, the final list in the film is a list that Schindler's workers give to him—a list of their signatures vouching for Schindler as a good man, to help him if Allied soldiers catch him. The saved in turn become saviors.

TRAINS

Trains were an integral logistical component of the Holocaust. Jews were loaded into actual cattle cars of freight trains, which carried them to death camps. In *Schindler's List,* the first Jews arrive in Kraków by train and register as Jews on the platform. When Stern is rescued from a crowded train bound for Auschwitz, thousands of other Jews are visible on the train, packed into the cars like sardines. In one scene, Schindler implores Goeth to spray water into the cars on a hot day to help the dehydrated Jews inside. Goeth tells him that to do so would give false hope—a clear implication that the trains deliver Jews to their deaths. When the Schindlerjuden are transported to Schindler's new factory in Czechoslovakia, the men travel in one train, the women in another. In this case, the trains signify hope and life, since they are taking their occupants to a safe haven. But the women's train becomes a death train when it is diverted to Auschwitz, where Schindler's intervention saves the women from extermination. The women board a train to safety, but as they depart, more trains arrive at the camp. The cycle of death seems never-ending.

DEATH

Death and fear of death govern the lives of the Jews in *Schindler's List.* Images of death pervade the film, usually in the form of executions, as people are shot in the head, often indiscriminately. This method of execution is used again and again. The one-armed man who thanks Schindler for employing him and making him "essential" is shot in the head by an SS officer as he shovels snow the next day. Blood flows from his head, staining the surrounding snow. In a later scene, Goeth orders the execution of a Jewish woman engineer who tells Goeth of a fatal construction error. Her blood, too, pours from her head and darkens the snow around her. The blood pouring from the victims' heads is both literally and metaphorically the life-blood being bled out of the Jewish race. In yet another scene, Goeth attempts to execute a rabbi working at the Plaszów labor camp. The rabbi stays kneeling as Goeth again and again attempts to shoot him in the head. But the gun jams, and the rabbi is spared, symbolizing the tenuous protection the Schindlerjuden had and the fine line between life and death.

SYMBOLS

THE GIRL IN THE RED COAT

The girl in the red coat is the most obvious symbol in *Schindler's List*, simply because her coat is the only color object, other than the Shabbat candles, presented in the main body of the film. To Schindler, she represents the innocence of the Jews being slaughtered. He sees her from high atop a hill and is riveted by her, almost to the exclusion of the surrounding violence. The moment Schindler catches sight of her marks the moment when he is forced to confront the horror of Jewish life during the Holocaust and his own hand in that horror. The little girl also has a greater social significance. Her red coat suggests the "red flag" the Jews waved at the Allied powers during World War II as a cry for help. The little girl walks through the violence of the evacuation as if she can't see it, ignoring the carnage around her. Her oblivion mirrors the inaction of the Allied powers in helping to save the Jews. Schindler later spots her in a pile of exhumed dead bodies, and her death symbolizes the death of innocence.

THE ROAD PAVED WITH JEWISH HEADSTONES

The road through the Plaszów labor camp, paved with headstones torn up from Jewish cemeteries, is a replica of the actual road that existed there. The road adds to the historical accuracy of the film but also symbolizes the destruction of the Jewish race. The removal of the headstones from the cemeteries represents the enormity of the Holocaust. Unsatisfied with simply wiping out existing Jews, Goeth, by planning the road, denies acknowledgement of many Jews' final resting places. By removing the grave markers, Goeth in effect erases the existence of the dead. Moreover, Goeth forces the Jews in the camp to build the road, rubbing in their faces the fact that they, too, will soon be erased. The message is clear: the Nazis view the Jews as not worth even grave markers and want only to erase them from history.

PILES OF PERSONAL ITEMS

In one of the most jarring scenes in the film, Jews are loaded onto cattle cars as a recorded voice tells them to leave their luggage on the platform, as it will follow on a separate train. The luggage, however, will not follow them. Instead, Nazis bring it to a back room, where they dump out and sort the contents. This room holds huge piles of personal belongings, including photographs, shoes, hairbrushes, and clothing, all separated for processing. At a table sits a group of Jewish jewelers, forced to sort and determine the value of the gold, silver, and jewels belonging to those on the train. These piles symbolize the millions of lives that were lost—not just the physical lives but the very essence of the victims, who are stripped of their identity. One thousand hairbrushes represent one thousand victims and one thousand lives.

FILM ANALYSIS

COMPREHENDING THE HOLOCAUST ONE NAME AT A TIME

In the face of an evil like the Holocaust, making a true connection with the victims can be overwhelming. Separating the victims from the numbers in order to comprehend the scope and horror of the Holocaust is nearly impossible. Museums, books, and pictures help to educate people, but more than six million Jews alone were slaughtered, which is a tremendously difficult reality to grasp emotionally and intellectually. The enormous number of victims and the many ways in which they were tortured and murdered are so vast that one could get lost in these statistical masses without ever really understanding the plight of individual victims. Only the victims themselves were truly able to feel the horror of the Holocaust. Steven Spielberg hoped to address this difficulty with *Schindler's List*. Since it is easier for people to make connections on a personal rather than an abstract level, Spielberg tried to replace the vast numbers with specific faces and names. He tried to ensure that viewers would make personal connections with the characters in the film and thus begin to digest the events on a smaller scale.

Spielberg manages to convey the horror the Schindlerjuden faced by making the viewers feel as if they are participating in the events, not just watching. Viewers meet characters and follow their plights closely, developing a connection to these individual victims who are themselves representative of all Holocaust victims. This connection is Spielberg's main goal in *Schindler's List*. He wants the viewer to identify with the characters, to feel their pain and fear. This individualization forces viewers to confront the horror on a personal level and to realize that every victim had a story, loved ones, a home, a business, and a life. To look at the Jews of the Holocaust simply as a group or race dehumanizes them a second time, removing their individuality and uniqueness. The Nazis dehumanized Jews in the camps by tattooing numbers on their arms in order to identify them by number rather than name, and Spielberg makes an effort to recognize individuals' names in his film.

Oskar Schindler himself embodies this idea of recognizing and caring for the individual. He is unable to stand by and watch his Jewish workers perish, for he makes a personal connection with them and does not want to see them killed. This relationship between Schindler and the Schindlerjuden parallels the connection the viewers make with the latter. In a sense, the viewer knows and cares about these people, wants them to survive, and feels triumphant when they do.

Spielberg personalizes the Nazis as well, however. The character of Amon Goeth allows an intimate glimpse into the mind of a Nazi officer corrupted by anti-Semitism. He shoots Jews from his balcony for target practice. He sees the Jewish people as a mass, not as individuals with thoughts and feelings. However, he is intoxicated by his Jewish maid, Helen Hirsch, and struggles with his conflicting feelings of attraction to Helen and pure hatred of Jews. Unlike Schindler, Goeth denies his connection to an individual. He cannot overcome his hatred, just as the Nazi Party in general could not overcome its wholesale hatred of Jews.

Spielberg carries the idea of individualism through to the powerful final scene in the film. Here, in full color, the real surviving Schindlerjuden appear. Lined up as far as the eye can see—many with their actor counterparts in the film—they place rocks on Oskar Schindler's grave. Spielberg's decision to show the actors accompanying the actual survivors serves two purposes. First, the scene drives home the point that the characters in the film are real people rather than just invented figures. Viewers can feel a great sense of satisfaction in seeing the actual survivors who triumphed over evil. Second, Spielberg is sending a message to all those who doubt the reality of the Holocaust that human proof of the tragedy exists and that what happened can never be erased. Witnesses to the horror are still alive to tell their tales and to make sure we never forget.

The Impact of Black-and-White Film

In movies set in modern times, a director's choice to use black and white might seem trite and artistically showy. In *Schindler's List*, however, the black-and-white presentation effectively evokes the World War II era and deepens the impact of the story. Black and white also presents the filmmaker with the opportunity to use sparing color to highlight key scenes and signal shifts in time. For example, the opening full-color scene, one of only a handful of color

SCHINDLER'S LIST

scenes in the movie, fades into the next scene, in black and white. The shift plunges viewers into 1939, bringing them symbolically closer to the events and characters in the story. This artistic and psychological convention of bringing the audience back in time works well partly because it captures the way many people visualize World War II—through black-and-white images and film footage of the 1930s and 1940s. Although contemporary viewers are accustomed to full-color images and tend to consider such images to be more realistic than those in black and white, the black and white in *Schindler's List* conveys an alternate but no less realistic version of life. The movie presents an eclectic mix of styles, such as film noir, which is associated with the great detective stories of the 1940s. The style links the film to that time period and serves to deepen viewers' immersion in the historical setting.

The artistic advantage of black and white is that it heightens the impact of the film's violence and highlights the duality of good and evil. The lighting and contrast in the film noir style enhance the brutality of each violent scene. For instance, when the one-armed man is shot in the head in the snowy streets of Kraków, his seemingly black blood spreads through the pure white snow, and the stark contrast in colors emphasizes the split between life and death, good and evil. In some terrifying scenes, such as the evacuation of the Kraków ghetto, the lighting is kept dark, conveying a sense of panic and confusion. The white faces of the dead in the streets contrast starkly against the murky background. The same contrast marks the pile of burning bodies in the Plaszów work camp: the white skulls stand out in the pile of ashes. The women's faces in the shower scene at Auschwitz are bathed in white light as they stare up in terror at the showerheads. The contrast of light and dark also marks Schindler's face, which is often half in shadow, reflecting his selfish dark side. His face becomes more fully lighted as he makes the transformation from war profiteer to savior. *Schindler's List* might not have had the same visual and emotional impact had Spielberg made the film in color.

PARALLEL EDITING

Spielberg uses parallel editing, or crosscutting, a cinematic convention in which two or more concurrent scenes are interwoven with each other, throughout *Schindler's List*. Parallel editing illuminates the stark difference between the hardships of the Jews and the comfort and optimism of Schindler and the Nazis in Poland. In the broadest sense, it demonstrates the powerful contrast between happiness and sadness. Two scenes in particular demonstrate the powerful impact of parallel editing that a linear presentation of the story could not have produced. In the first scene, Schindler moves into his luxury apartment in Kraków soon after the Jewish owners are evacuated by the Nazis and sent to the Kraków ghetto. In the second and perhaps most compelling example, three scenes are interwoven: Schindler celebrates his birthday, a wedding takes place in the Plaszów labor camp, and Goeth beats Helen Hirsch.

These expertly edited scenes leave an indelible impression on the viewer for several reasons. Early in the film, Mr. and Mrs. Nussbaum, under the watchful eye of SS officers, grab everything of value they can fit into a suitcase as they are chased from their luxury apartment and forced to join the Jews marching to the Kraków ghetto. These wealthy people are obviously outraged at their treatment. As they make their way to the ghetto, the scene cuts to Schindler entering the very same apartment seemingly moments after the family left. He tours the expansive, richly furnished apartment, admiring the luxurious furnishings and decorations. As he does so, the family arrives in the ghetto to find a tiny, dark, dirty room waiting for them. Sprawled on the Nussbaums' bed, Schindler says, "It couldn't possibly be better." The scene then cuts back to the Nussbaums. Mrs. Nussbaum, with unconvincing optimism, remarks to her husband that "it could be worse." Mr. Nussbaum responds, "How could it *possibly* be worse?" By interweaving these moments into a single scene, Spielberg forces the viewer to confront the bitter irony of the situation in which Schindler benefits from the Nussbaums' misery. In addition, Schindler at this point in the film takes no notice of and has no remorse for the evacuated couple. The tremendous impact of his callousness is intensified in light of the family's suffering.

Perhaps the most powerful crosscut scene in the film occurs when Schindler celebrates his birthday with a group of Nazis in a nightclub. Here, Schindler's wantonness rises to new heights as he and the Nazis hold a party in the midst of the evil of the Holocaust surrounding them. But even in dire situations, a celebration proves that hope persists, as Spielberg shows us by splicing this scene with the wedding in the labor camp. But yet a third line of action is cut into this scene, its brutality contrasting with the hope and joy of the wedding and birthday celebrations: Goeth brutally beats Helen Hirsch in her basement room after attempting to seduce her. The contrast between Helen's desolation and the happiness of the participants in the two celebrations forces viewers to confront the reality of the Jewish situation during the Holocaust, when violence and death were always just around the corner.

IMPORTANT QUOTATIONS EXPLAINED

1. STERN: "... The Jews themselves receive nothing. Poles you pay wages. Generally they get a little more. Are you listening? ... The Jewish worker's salary, you pay it directly to the SS, not to the worker. He gets nothing."
   SCHINDLER: "But it's *less*. It's *less* than what I would pay a Pole. ... Poles cost more. Why should I hire Poles?"

This exchange takes place as Stern helps Schindler set up the enamel-work factory. The men are talking about hiring workers, and Stern explains that the Jewish salaries are paid directly to the Reich Economic Office, not to the Jews. Stern, disdainful of Schindler, is trying to call Schindler's attention to the Jewish situation. He is feeling Schindler out and presents the Jews as the cheapest labor option. The comment is also a dig at Schindler, since Schindler has not yet shown Stern that he is anything but an ignorant member of the Nazi Party. Stern's speech also supplies the viewer with the kind of information a narrator would usually supply. If viewers have not realized the immense restrictions Jews endure, this quote serves to educate them.

Schindler's response reveals the greedy, callous, solely self-interested character he exhibits in the first half of the film, before his transformation. He seems, especially to Stern, to be a complete egotist. Schindler shows no compassion whatsoever for the Jews. In fact, he is not even interested enough in their plight to care. He can see only the potential to line his pockets with more profit. Jewish workers are cheaper than Poles, so he doesn't care where the money goes, as long as he pays less of it. Schindler cements himself as amoral—a characterization that sets up his conversion to a caring person later in the film. At this point, he shows no hint of the goodness to come, but Stern is anxious to exploit the opportunity Schindler is offering the Jews.

2.   STERN: "The list is an absolute good. The list is life. All around its margins lies the gulf."

Stern makes this pronouncement as he and Schindler complete Schindler's list. The two men have been working all night, adding as many names as possible—everyone Schindler can afford to buy. The list stands on its own as unadulterated good, unaffected by the mystery behind Schindler's motives and any other mitigating factor. It represents the life of the Jewish race. Stern is perhaps stating the obvious when he says this, but symbolically, the list is the essence of life itself and stands in stark contrast to the Nazi death lists. The completed list stands as a testament not only to Schindler's newfound kindness but also to the hard work of Stern, who now sees the results of his original desperate attempt to save his fellow Jews. Schindler dictates the lists, and Stern types. The names flow though Stern's own hands. But in the end, it is Schindler who holds the lives of approximately 1,100 people in his grasp.

In the second half of the quotation, Stern mentions more than the life the list represents. He mentions the "gulf" that surrounds the list. The gulf is the millions of Jews who will not be saved but rather are left in a real-life purgatory, held prisoner, awaiting either freedom or death. The goodness of the list does not cancel out the evil that befalls the Holocaust victims, but even a small goodness is total goodness. Acknowledging all those who cannot be saved intensifies the impact of the good of the list, impressing upon the viewer the power of Schindler's deed. The quote as a whole also signifies Stern's final acceptance of Schindler's goodness and an appreciation for the metamorphosis Schindler has undergone. Stern has seen the beginnings of change in Schindler and slowly gained respect for him as Schindler accepted his role as a savior. Until the list is actually made, however, and the plan to save lives becomes real, Stern does not fully give himself over to his faith in Schindler.

3.   GOETH: "Is this the face of a rat? Are these the eyes of a rat? 'Hath not a Jew eyes?' I feel for you, Helen. No, I don't think so. . . . You nearly talked me into it, didn't you?"

This quote is part of a monologue that Goeth delivers to Helen in her basement room. She does not respond to him at any point, but he carries on a conversation as if she does. She just stands there, arms at her sides, shaking with fear. He tells her he wonders what it would be like to be with her, even though it is forbidden. Jews are vermin in his mind. But he does not see Helen that way: he chose her to be his maid and does not allow her to wear the Star of David because he does not want anyone to know she is Jewish, lest someone catch him admiring her. Although he seems as if he is trying to reach out to Helen, he is doing nothing but satisfying his own needs. He is not trying to be kind to Helen but rather trying to convince himself that it is permissible to be attracted to a Jewish woman.

These few sentences present Goeth's inner conflict in stark fashion. Goeth almost gives in to his impulse to force himself on Helen and loathes himself for it. He changes his mind at the last instant and turns his self-loathing into aggression, blaming her for trying to seduce him although it is clear she has not. He then beats her savagely for this imagined transgression. His sudden changes in thought and his brutal response illustrate clearly how unpredictable and sociopathic he is.

4.   HOSS: "I have a shipment coming in tomorrow. I'll cut you three hundred units from it. New ones. It's yours. These are fresh. The train comes, We turn it around. It's yours."
SCHINDLER: "Yes. I understand. I want these."
HOSS: "You shouldn't get stuck on names. That's right. It creates a lot of paperwork."

This conversation takes place between Schindler and Rudolph Hoss, the commander at Auschwitz, in Hoss's well-appointed office. The train on which the Schindlerjuden women are being transported has been diverted mistakenly to Auschwitz on the way to Schindler's factory in Czechoslovakia. Schindler hears of this mishap and rushes to Auschwitz to try to save the women. He sits in Hoss's office with a pouch of diamonds that he plans to use as a bribe to have the train redirected—the second time he has purchased the women's freedom.

Hoss's quotation summarizes perfectly the Nazi attitude toward Jews: they are less than human and do not deserve life or even the smallest acknowledgement of their humanity. The commander does not understand why Schindler wants these particular women and in his speech presents clearly the dehumanization of the Jews. Hoss calls the Jews "units," never referring to them as human beings. They are just numbers or bodies to him, the source of needless paperwork. They have already been processed into Auschwitz, and

Hoss sees no reason to do extra paperwork or to maneuver for those whom he knows will end up dead anyway. Moreover, Schindler's attitude is a mystery to Hoss, who does not understand why Schindler wants specific Jews. When he tells Schindler that he "shouldn't get stuck on names," he is almost challenging Schindler to come up with an explanation for why these women are important enough to warrant extra paperwork when they are only Jews, objects that have no value. Schindler prevails, however, and the next day the women are put on a train to his factory.

5. STERN: "Whoever saves one life saves the world entire."

In one of the last scenes in the film, as Schindler prepares to flee from the Allies, the Schindlerjuden give Schindler a gold ring made from gold fillings, engraved with the above quotation from the Talmud, the book of Jewish law. After the Allied victory, Schindler is a hunted war criminal. When the workers hear he must flee, they make him the ring as a small token of their appreciation, knowing that there is no way to repay the gift of life. Stern presents the ring to Schindler, telling him the quotation is from the Talmud. The Jews want Schindler to know that by saving them, he has saved humanity.

The quotation supports the theme that one man can make a difference. If even one man shows humanity to another, he demonstrates the continuing existence of humanity in society—something utterly void in the actions of the Nazis during the Holocaust. For society to continue, selflessness and kindness must exist: as long as one good person exists, good still exists in the world. The Schindlerjuden want Schindler to have a constant reminder of the goodness in him and understand that he now needs their help. They give him, with the ring, a signed statement swearing to his good actions, hoping to help if the Allies capture him. These eight words—one of the tag lines for the film in its marketing—capture the sentiments of the entire film.

THE MATRIX TRILOGY

(1999, 2003, 2003)

CONTEXT

In early 1999, strange posters appeared throughout the United States, advertising an enigmatic movie created by a little-known writer-director team with only one movie to its credit. The mystery extended to the film's unusual name, *The Matrix*. When *The Matrix* finally appeared, over Easter weekend of 1999, the anticipation created by this campaign paid off. The film earned $460 million worldwide, and became one of the most iconic and imitated films in recent memory. Along with a number of other special-effects innovations, *The Matrix* introduced "bullet-time" photography, in which the action slows down or freezes as the camera seems to circle 360 degrees around the characters. This effect in particular was so stunning that it was spoofed or emulated in *The Simpsons*, *Shrek*, *Scary Movie*, *Charlie's Angels*, and at the Super Bowl. Cowriters and codirectors Larry and Andy Wachowski—a.k.a. the Wachowski brothers—became famous overnight.

The Wachowskis are notoriously private. They rarely grant interviews to the media, and their contract with Warner Brothers for *The Matrix Reloaded* and *The Matrix Revolutions* actually stipulates that they are required not to do so. The essentials of their biographies, though, are well-known. The brothers were born in the 1960s and raised in Chicago. In the 1980s, the two of them dropped out of college, Larry from Bard and Andy from Emerson, and became high-end carpenters and house painters before landing jobs writing for Marvel Comics. In the early 1990s, they sold a script to Warner Brothers studios, which would emerge, dramatically altered, as the 1995 movie *Assassins*, starring Sylvester Stallone and Antonio Banderas. The film was a flop, and the Wachowski brothers vowed never to cede artistic control again.

Rebounding from their disappointment, the brothers wrote and directed *Bound* (1996), a noir-thriller with lesbian heroines that starred Jennifer Tilly, Gina Gershon, and Joe Pantoliano, who plays Cypher in *The Matrix*. Even as the Wachowskis were making *Bound*, they were already planning *The Matrix*. After fourteen drafts, they showed the script to Warner Brothers—in the form of a comic book—and ultimately received a budget of nearly $70 million to make the film.

To prepare for filming, the Wachowski brothers required their actors to undergo as much as fourteen months of martial arts training, along with a course of required readings. The intense preparation paid off, and *The Matrix* was so popular that the Wachowskis quickly received permission to create the next two installments of the trilogy, with a much bigger budget. The films were skillfully rendered cross-genre spectacles with ground-breaking special effects and Keanu Reeves in a starring role, Warner Brothers gave them all wide releases. Critics praised *The Matrix*, but support waned with each of the next two films, a surprising phenomenon given that the trilogy maintained its internal story logic more rigorously than most other film series in recent memory. Nonetheless, audiences worldwide flocked to all three films, which together grossed over $1.5 billion. *The Matrix Reloaded* set box-office records for its opening days of release.

The Matrix films abound with references to pop culture, philosophy, religion, classic literature, myths, and other films. In making the *Matrix* trilogy, the Wachowski brothers drew on imagery and ideas from Greek mythology, Gnosticism, Buddhism, Hinduism, Nihilism, Taoism, comic books, the works of René Descartes, Homer's *Odyssey*, Jean Baudrillard's *Simulacra and Simulation*, Kevin Kelly's *Out of Control*, and Dylan Evans's *Introducing Evolutionary Psychology*. Actors from all over the world contributed their efforts to the films, and the cast is meant to represent a wide cross-section of humanity. In this mishmash of ideas, cultures, religions, and nationalities, cultural theorists of every stripe, religious scholars of all religions, and sci-fi fans all over the world have seen their own pet ideas reflected. The Wachowski brothers insist that the trilogy is not meant to reflect one consistent set of symbols or any single religious or philosophical system. Instead, they claim, the films draw upon an eclectic array of sources in order to forge a new, universal mythology.

While *The Matrix* films have also been remarkably influential in their own right, they have spawned several collections of philosophical essays, semester-long college courses, and endless debates and discussions. The "bullet-time" special effect pioneered by visual effects supervisor John Gaeta was instantly mimicked in television advertisements for cars and other products and has been spoofed in parodic films, both animated and live action. *The Matrix* films inspired an onslaught of commercial products, including video games, clothing, and comic books. *The Matrix* DVD became the

THE MATRIX

first release to outsell its VHS copies and was instrumental in fueling the development of a burgeoning DVD industry. The Wachowskis were attuned to the cross-market potential of their films, and between *The Matrix Reloaded* and *The Matrix Revolutions* they created a series of animated shorts called *The Animatrix*, some of which give important background information for the films, and a video game called *Enter the Matrix*.

With its countless references, cross-references, riddles, and enigmas, the trilogy seems to raise more questions than it answers, creating a sense of frustration that the filmmakers gleefully acknowledge. The Wachowskis have said that one of their primary goals was to make an action movie that would make people think, and because the movie is based on the idea that knowledge frees us, we are left to figure much of it out for ourselves. The directors are careful not to produce clear-cut answers to the problems they raise. Sometimes understanding *The Matrix* films is less about knowing exactly what's going on and more about knowing what questions you're supposed to ask. As Trinity tells Neo when she first meets him, "It's the questions that drive us."

PLOT OVERVIEW

"THE MATRIX"

The Matrix opens with a shot of a computer screen, indicating that a phone call is being traced, as we overhear the voices on the phone line discussing whether they have found "the One." Policemen enter a motel room and confront one of the parties to the phone call: Trinity, a leather-clad, renegade computer hacker. Trinity dispatches them all with gravity-defying kung-fu moves. Reinforcements arrive in the form of Agents, men in business suits with ear radios and sunglasses, who commandeer the scene and try to capture Trinity. They pursue Trinity through a nameless city, and both the Agents and Trinity reveal themselves to be more than human. They sprint over abandoned rooftops and leap over city blocks, and Trinity dives through a window across streets. The chase ends inside a phone booth on a secluded street. Trinity answers a ringing phone and disappears. The Agents remark on her mysterious disappearance and discuss the next target, Neo. Next, a garbage truck, driven by an Agent, destroys the booth.

We next see Keanu Reeve's character asleep at his computer desk. He wakes up to messages flashing across his computer screen. The messages, from an unknown source, call him by his hacker name, Neo. Neo sells illegal software, and just before a client knocks on Neo's door, Neo receives a message on the screen saying "Follow the white rabbit" followed by "Knock, knock, Neo." Delivering his goods to the client, a confused Neo notices a tattooed rabbit on the shoulder of the client's girlfriend, and so, heeding the message, he follows them to a techno Goth club. There, Trinity approaches Neo. Neo doesn't know who she is, but Trinity explains that she knows all about him. She knows he's searching for something called the Matrix and that he's suspicious of what it is. Abruptly, the club scene gives way to a ringing alarm clock. Neo wakes with a start, back in his own bed. He's late for work.

At work, Neo's boss reprimands him and reveals some vital information—Neo's real name is Mr. Anderson, and he's a successful computer programmer. A cell phone is delivered by FedEx to Neo's cubicle and rings immediately. On the line, a deep-voiced man

THE MATRIX

identifies himself as Morpheus. Morpheus tells Neo that Agents are after him and, directing him by cell phone, helps him navigate through the labyrinth of cubicles in his office and escape to a ledge outside the building. Neo doesn't have the courage to walk across the ledge to some nearby scaffolding, and Agents capture him, then take him for interrogation. Neo demands his rights from the creepy lead Agent, Smith, who renders Neo mute by magically sealing over his mouth so that it nearly disappears. Agents hold Neo down and forcefully insert a metallic insectlike device into his stomach.

Neo jolts awake at home. Soon after, he receives a phone call from Morpheus, who explains his belief that Neo is "the One" he's been searching for all his life. Morpheus and Neo arrange a meeting. Trinity, along with two other renegades named Switch and Apoc, pick Neo up under a bridge on a stormy night. Unsure of what's happening, Neo decides he wants to get out of the car, but Trinity calmly empathizes with his confusion and his desire to know more, so he stays. Trinity then removes the bloody, wriggling, mechanical "bug" from Neo's stomach with a terrifying spike and tube instrument, and Neo is shocked to realize that the episode with Agent Smith actually happened.

In an old room in an abandoned building, Neo finally meets Morpheus. Morpheus tells Neo that Neo has always been a slave and offers to reveal the Matrix to him. Morpheus presents two pills, red and blue. If Neo selects the blue pill, he'll wake up again at home and remember nothing. If he selects the red pill, Morpheus will allow him to see the truth. When Neo chooses the red pill, a mirror near him liquefies. When he touches it, its mercury-like substance oozes over him, threatening to envelop him. His world dissolves in front of him, and he panics. Neo wakes up naked and hairless in a vat of jelly, with plugs connecting him to the vat. Millions of similar vats, each with a human inside, stretch around him in all directions. Flying robotic insects drill a hole in the back of his neck. Then the jelly drains from Neo's vat, and Neo slips through pipes down into a pit full of water. A metal claw rattles down from a spaceship and plucks him up into the light.

In the true real world, Morpheus and his crew rehabilitate Neo's body, for Neo has never actually used it. His muscles have atrophied, and his eyes have never actually seen. After this rehabilitation, Morpheus tells Neo that the year is actually closer to 2199 than to 1999, and Neo meets the crew of Morpheus's hovering ship, the *Nebuchadnezzar*. Besides Trinity, Switch, and Apoc, whom he's already seen, Neo meets the brothers Tank and Dozer, the snake-skin-jacketed Cypher, and Mouse, the youngest crew member. Tank works as the Operator of the ship, staying in the real world, guiding those who are plugged into the Matrix, and helping them find exits. These exits are pay phones through which the hackers can escape the program of the Matrix and return to the real world. Neo settles into a chair, and Tank thrusts a sharp spike into his head, via a hole at the back of Neo's brain. Neo enters a computer program.

Morpheus explains that, years ago, humans developed Artificial Intelligence but lost control of it. In desperation, humans chose to create a nuclear winter, thinking that by blocking out the sun, they could eliminate the solar power the robots needed to survive. But the robots adapted, and now they run the ravaged world and har-vest humans for bioelectric food. The Matrix is a computer-gener-ated dream world designed to keep these humans under control. Humans are kept sedated, effectively living a virtual life. Neo awak-ens in a bed back on Morpheus's ship, and Morpheus further explains that one man was born into the Matrix with the power to change anything in it. This man freed the first human minds. An Oracle has prophesied his return, and Morpheus believes Neo is the reincarnation of the One.

Tank tells Neo about his homeland, Zion, the only city of free humans left. Zion lies deep underground, near the warmth of the earth's core. Neo begins training with Tank, who downloads pro-grams into Neo's head that teach him martial arts. Instantaneously, Neo becomes a jujitsu master. His training carries on for ten hours, as Neo absorbs all martial arts. Morpheus tests Neo with a Kung Fu fight in a virtual computer world, emphasizing that Neo can bend or break the rules of whatever world he's in. The crew eagerly watches their fight, which includes ultrafast punching, artful dodging, wall-cracking punches, and gravity-defying leaps.

Morpheus speaks in koans, or paradoxes, and tells Neo that he can show Neo the door, but Neo will have to open it himself. He plugs Neo into a test program in which he must leap from the top of one skyscraper to another. No one ever has enough faith to succeed on a first jump, yet the crew hopes that Neo might, since they believe Morpheus's predictions that Neo is the One. Neo fails to clear the jump, however, and emerges from the program with a bleeding mouth. He learns that though the program world is virtual, his mind itself is real, and it affects his body. In other words, he can die in the Matrix, even though the Matrix isn't real. Another training program demonstrates that the Agents work as a part of the Matrix and can immediately transform themselves into anyone in it. Therefore, no matter how innocuous he or she seems, every person in the Matrix is a potential enemy. Morpheus explains that no one has ever defeated the Agents, yet at some point Neo will have to fight them.

Back in the real world, robotic sentinels, which the crew refers to as "squiddies," pursue the ship. The sentinels, which resemble metal octopi, can detect the electricity expended by humans. Their only function is to destroy. The *Nebuchadnezzer* hides out in an abandoned server port and switches its power offline to avoid detection. The ship's one weapon against the sentinels, an EMP (high-voltage electromagnetic pulse), renders all the objects currently using electromagnets useless within a certain radius, but it can be used only once, requiring a long time to recharge. The *Nebuchadnezzer* escapes detection by the sentinels.

Cypher explains to Neo that from the Operator's chair he understands the Matrix by reading its computer code, not by seeing any images. Cypher also offers him moonshine and explains his doubts about the whole journey. When Neo leaves, Cypher covertly enters the Matrix to make a deal with Agent Smith over a virtual steak dinner. Cypher, answering to his Matrix name, Reagan, promises to deliver Morpheus to Agent Smith in exchange for a safe return to the blissful ignorance of the Matrix, accompanied by an increase in socioeconomic status. Agent Smith wants Morpheus because, as the captain of the *Nebuchadnezzar*, Morpheus has access codes to Zion, which Smith wants to destroy.

In sharp contrast to the rich steak dinner, the crew eats foul, nutrient-rich gruel in their cold, functional mess hall. Mouse chatters about the human need for sex and ponders the question of real taste in the simulated Matrix. Morpheus decides to take Neo to see the Oracle, and the crew knows the meeting will be meaningful. In the Matrix, Morpheus, Trinity, Cypher, and Neo drive to see the Oracle, with Switch, Apoc, and Mouse covering. Unseen, Cypher drops a cell phone in a trash can, allowing the Agents to discover their location. Neo watches his old city pass by in a new light. The Oracle appears in the form of a black grandmother in a tenement house. Young telekinetic prodigies fill her apartment's waiting room. Neo encounters a young monk, who teaches him to bend a spoon using only his mind.

The Oracle speaks confidently and tells Neo that he's not the One. Instructing him to "know thyself," she reveals that soon he'll make a choice to decide between his own life and Morpheus's life. She claims that Morpheus will willingly give his life for Neo. Neo notices a black cat moving forward, then seemingly rewinding and moving forward again, as though he's seeing the same thing twice. Such experiences of déjà vu indicate that a glitch has occurred in the Matrix, and this time, the Agents have set a trap with Cypher's help. The group hides in the walls of the building, but dust triggers a cough from Cypher, and Smith's Agents discover their location. Morpheus and Neo leave the Oracle, but Agents ambush Mouse, who dies with his guns blazing. Morpheus blasts through the drywall onto Smith so the others can escape, despite Neo's protests. Smith and Morpheus fight in a rusted-out bathroom. A host of officers eventually overpower Morpheus and capture him, despite his valiant efforts.

Cypher mysteriously splits from the rest of the group and returns first to the *Nebuchadnezzar*. There, he shoots Tank and Dozer and assumes control of the board. When Trinity and the rest of the group find an exit, Cypher answers the Operator's call. Trinity perceives Cypher's betrayal immediately, watching helplessly as Cypher unplugs Apoc and Switch, who collapse to the ground, their life support severed. Cypher doesn't believe Neo is the One and argues that if Morpheus were really right, then a literal miracle would have to occur immediately to save the lives of both Trinity and Neo. Cypher believes he holds their lives in his hands. The miracle happens. Tank turns out not to be dead, but only grievously wounded. He manages to kill Cypher, thus saving Neo and Trinity.

Agent Smith, along with his subordinates, Brown and Jones, transports Morpheus to a secure skyscraper for interrogation, where he is hooked up to electrodes and given drugs. Smith hopes that this torture, combined with the wear from the beatings, will force Morpheus to reveal Zion's access codes. Morpheus remains silent. Smith begins to explain the history of the Matrix. A previous version existed in which the machines created an entirely perfect world for humans, but the program failed. Smith believes the failure relates to humanity's definition of itself through misery and its inability to handle happiness. Thus, the second, intentionally flawed Matrix was developed.

Back on the *Nebuchadnezzar*, the survivors discuss the option of pulling Morpheus's plug. They reason that, despite their love for Morpheus, all of the humans in Zion together are more important, and they can't risk him breaking and giving up the access codes. Just

THE MATRIX

as Tank solemnly prepares to kill their leader, Neo remembers something the Oracle said to him. He begins to have faith in himself and believes he can save Morpheus. Although what he wants to attempt has no precedent, Neo believes he can do it. He plans to enter the Matrix and rescue Morpheus. Trinity accompanies him.

As Neo and Trinity outfit themselves with numerous firearms, Agent Smith describes his theory of humanity to Morpheus, who is beaten, bloody, and drugged. Smith reasons that humans are not mammals but viruses, since they spread exponentially, using up every resource they have then moving on to devour the resources of another place. When Morpheus refuses to break, Agent Smith asks the other two agents to leave him alone with Morpheus. This decidedly unmachinelike behavior alerts us to Smith's anomalous position in the Matrix. Removing his glasses and disconnecting himself from his earpiece (the earpiece that connects him to his machine superiors), Smith admits to Morpheus that he despises the Matrix. He views himself as superior to it, and he wants Zion's access codes to destroy humanity and free himself from the Matrix forever.

Meanwhile, Tank places Neo and Trinity at the lobby of the skyscraper, and the pair proceed to shoot their way through it, killing a team of security guards in the process. Agents Brown and Jones return, surprised and confused to see Smith without his earpiece. Because the earpiece was out, Smith didn't hear that Neo and Trinity are trying to save Morpheus. Neo and Trinity drop a bomb down the elevator shaft and ride the elevator cable up to the skyscraper's roof, where they battle a host of soldiers. The bomb cuts the building's power, and the sprinklers come on, drenching the Agents and Morpheus. An Agent shifts into a helicopter pilot's body, and a showdown begins between him and Neo. The Agent dodges all of Neo's bullets at superhuman speed. Neo, with increasing confidence, manages to dodge most of the Agent's shots. His skills aren't yet perfect, though, and he gets nicked by a bullet. Just as the Agent stands over him, ready to finish him off, Trinity appears and shoots the Agent in the head. Before the body falls, the Agent shifts back out of it, leaving only a human soldier dead on the roof. The Agent himself is gone.

Tank downloads a B-212 helicopter flying program into Trinity, and she and Neo lower the helicopter right outside the room where Smith holds Morpheus. In an explosion of glass, bullets, and water, Neo empties the copter's cannon, forcing the Agents to hide. Morpheus breaks his chains and runs toward the copter. Just as he's ready to leap, an Agent's bullet catches him in the leg. Realizing Morpheus won't make it, Neo, tied to the copter, jumps to meet him in midair, sixty stories or so above the ground. He catches Morpheus as Trinity flies the copter away. The Agents empty their weapons, piercing the copter's fuel tank.

Neo and Morpheus drop onto a roof. The helicopter crashes spectacularly into a nearby building, with Trinity leaping out just in time, grabbing onto the rope bound around Neo. Neo lets himself be dragged to the edge of the building, stands upon the edge calmly, and reels Trinity to safety, after which Morpheus proclaims that Neo is the One. Neo protests that the Oracle told him differently. Morpheus counters smoothly that the Oracle told him all he needed to know.

Tank finds an exit for the trio in an abandoned subway. Morpheus exits first. Trinity, worried, stops to confess something to Neo that the Oracle had told her. Soon after, Smith shifts into the body of a homeless man in the corner. Smith shoots at her just as she exits. He misses her but succeeds in slicing the phone line, which removes any possible exit for Neo. A final showdown between Neo and Smith begins. Although everyone has told him to run when an Agent arrives, Neo, starting to believe in his own abilities, turns to face Smith. Tank, Morpheus, and Trinity watch the code at the *Nebuchadnezzar*'s board. A colossal fight ensues with spectacular special effects, and Neo heroically bounces back many times from seemingly certain defeat. Smith refers to Neo by his Matrix name, Mr. Anderson, but just before a subway car crashes through, Neo fully assumes his new identity, saying forcefully, "My name is Neo."

The subway appears to crush Smith, but even this collision proves insufficient to stop an Agent. The subway screeches to a halt, and Smith emerges for more fighting, but Neo finally runs. Back at the *Nebuchadnezzar*, sentinels close in. Multiple Agents chase Neo through crowded streets, shifting into any body that can get a good shot at him. Aboard the *Nebuchadnezzar*, the crew charges the EMP but can't fire it until Neo finds an exit and joins them. Neo steals a cell phone, and Tank directs him through the streets and alleys back to the motel where we first saw Trinity. The sentinels land on the ship and begin to slice it open, but Morpheus believes Neo can make it and holds off from discharging the EMP. Neo opens the door to Trinity's room, only to find Smith right in front of him. Smith empties his gun into Neo, who falls to the ground, dead. On the ship, as the sentinels approach the deck, Trinity whispers her revelation into Neo's ear: the Oracle told her she would fall in love with a dead man, and that he would be the One. She kisses him. With this, Neo is resurrected.

With his newfound realization and acceptance of his role, Neo rises and assumes even greater powers. Three agents empty their guns at him, but with a quiet "No," Neo stops all the bullets with his mind, holding out his hand and causing the bullets to drop harmlessly to the floor. Through his point of view, we suddenly see that everything around him is covered with green computer code. Neo is finally able to see the code that creates the Matrix. The agents are now powerless against him. Neo flies into Smith's body, and in a blinding glow, explodes outward from within him. The other Agents run, Trinity screams at Neo on the ship as the sentinels pierce the deck, and Neo picks up the phone and exits the Matrix. With Neo safely back on the ship, the crew discharges the EMP. The sentinels drop away. Neo and Trinity kiss.

The Matrix ends with Neo talking to someone on a pay phone. He warns that he's going to expose the truth of what's really out there. He flies straight up into the sky.

"THE MATRIX RELOADED"

Trinity flies through the night air on a motorcycle, crashes into a building, and kills a host of security guards. Suddenly we see an image of her falling out of a skyscraper, shooting bullets upward at an Agent, who falls down with her. The Agent strikes Trinity with a bullet, something crashes hard into the ground below, and Neo wakes up from this nightmare, in bed next to Trinity. She tries to calm him. The *Nebuchadnezzar* sits and waits, the crew members hoping the Oracle will summon them. Morpheus speaks with the ship's new Operator, Link, telling him that if he wants to volunteer for this mission, he has to trust Morpheus completely. Neo has accepted his new role as the One, but doesn't know what to do. He, too, sits and waits.

The captains of all the humans' ships, both the *Nebuchadnezzar* and others, meet inside the Matrix, in an underground bunker. Niobe, captain of Zion's ship, the *Logos*, reports that the machines have begun drilling toward Zion. A quarter million sentinels are ready to attack the remnants of humanity once they reach the core. Commander Lock requests that all ships return to Zion and prepare to defend it. Morpheus resists, wanting at least one ship to stay in case the Oracle calls. During this meeting, Neo senses something is amiss. Agent Smith has pulled up outside and asks a young guard to deliver a package and a message to Neo: "He set me free." The package contains Smith's earpiece. Neo orders the guards to leave, warning that Agents have arrived. The Agents refer to Neo as the "anomaly." After an intense battle, Neo escapes, but something has shifted. Two identical Agent Smiths speak to each other, agreeing that things continue to go according to plan. Neo flies to visit the Oracle, but she's not home.

Having left another ship behind, the *Nebuchadnezzar* enters Zion dramatically. A vast cylindrical city burrowed deep into the earth, Zion maintains central axes for defense and has living quarters around its perimeter. Humans guard it by sitting in the rib cages of large anthropomorphic robots that respond to each driver's every move. Captain Mifune, a severe military patriot, greets Morpheus and his crew and escorts Morpheus to Lock's office. We discover that Niobe used to work with Morpheus until the Oracle made a certain prophecy and has since been loyal to Lock. A teenager excitedly greets the *Nebuchadnezzar*'s crew and offers to help Neo with anything. Apparently, Neo once saved the Kid's life. The Kid wants someday to become a crew member of the *Nebuchadnezzar*.

Morpheus and Lock clash in their beliefs concerning the best way to defend Zion. Lock is angry at Morpheus for leaving one ship behind, blatantly disobeying Lock's direct order to bring all ships back to Zion. Lock puts little stock in the Oracle's prophecies. Zion's inhabitants notice that more ships are docked at one time than ever before, and rumors flood the city. People fear the coming of the Armageddon between Good and Evil, Man and Machine. Councilor Hamann, a senior member of Zion's Council of Elders, wants to assemble Zion's population that night and speak to them, but he is unsure what to say. Lock advocates discretion in delivering information. Morpheus advocates telling the complete truth and hoping inspiration will deliver them from fear.

Link and the Kid leave Neo and Trinity alone in an elevator, where they begin to kiss. They look forward to a few hours alone together. When the doors open, Neo finds that the sick and destitute of Zion have come to him for guidance and salvation, treating him as a Christ figure. Trinity leaves Neo to do his work. Link returns to his wife, Zee. Zee, sister of Tank and Dozer, worries about Link's volunteer status with Morpheus, but Link reassures her that he's starting to believe in the acts he's seen Neo perform.

At a nighttime assembly in a great cave of Zion, Morpheus tells the people the truth about the impending attack from the machines but immediately inspires them with his fearlessness. The Zionites celebrate with a sweaty, pulsing, underground rave. Simultaneously, Neo and Trinity consummate their relationship under an arch in private quarters away from the assembly. As Neo and Trinity make love, Neo again has his nightmare vision of Trinity falling from the skyscraper and being pierced with a bullet. Trinity attempts to reassure him by telling him she'll never let go. Finally, Zion sleeps.

Meanwhile, in the Matrix, two renegade hackers flee from Agents. One man makes his exit, but another, Bane, is intercepted by one of the two Agent Smiths. Smith slices his hand into Bane's chest, infecting Bane's body with the same type of fluid Neo first saw after he took the red pill. Smith exits the Matrix into Bane's body, aboard Bane's ship, in the real world.

Neo walks outside his room overlooking the sleeping city of Zion restlessly, knowing that something isn't right, but unsure what to do. Hamann, the aging Elder of Zion, also wandering, joins Neo for conversation. Hamann takes Neo down to the engineering level of the city, the part no one thinks about. Hamann claims that people don't want to know how things work, as long as they keep working. They converse about the symbiosis between man and machine, then discuss the nature of control. Hamann admits he has no idea how Neo does the things he does.

Someone knocks on Trinity's door. Neo is there. Finally, the Oracle has summoned him. The *Nebuchadnezzar* prepares to leave. As Link readies to once again risk his life, Zee offers him a good luck charm. Link doesn't believe in it, but Zee does, so he willingly takes it and promises to return. Bane/Smith has returned with his ship to Zion and can't take his new human body, so he slashes himself. As Neo readies to board the *Nebuchadnezzar*, Bane/Smith approaches from behind with a knife, but Neo turns at the last minute when the Kid calls him. Though puzzled at Bane's presence, Neo accepts a gift that someone instructed the Kid to deliver—a spoon. Neo understands. Lock doesn't want the ship to leave and expresses his frustration to Hamann.

In the Matrix, Neo wends his way through a Chinatown and enters a door into a wood-and-paper templelike structure. An angel named Seraph awaits him politely, then begins to fight him. Neo and Seraph fight throughout the temple, knocking over wooden bowls. Seraph, the Oracle's benevolent protector, insists that he had to be sure Neo was the One, and that the only way to do that was to fight him. Leading Neo down a white hallway full of doors, Seraph opens a door onto a city playground, where the Oracle sits on a bench.

Neo begins to realize that Seraph and the Oracle are not humans, but parts of the machine program that constitutes the Matrix, a fact that the Oracle confirms. Wondering aloud how he can then trust her, she replies only that he has to choose for himself what to believe in. She suggests he's already made major choices and is presently only trying to understand them. She explains the anomalous programs a bit more. Everything in the Matrix is a program, but the noticeable ones are the ones that aren't working. They're either rebellious, failing, or resistant to being replaced. When a program faces deletion, it can either hide itself or return to the Source, the machine mainframe, where, she suggests, the path of the One ends. The Source, the Oracle reveals, comprises only light. She affirms that Neo can now see outside of time. He naturally wonders why he can't see the end of his frightful vision of Trinity. The Oracle says he can't see beyond the choices he doesn't yet understand. As their time together ends, she tells Neo he must see the Keymaker to gain access to the Source. If he can't, Zion will fall.

Agent Smith arrives as soon as the Oracle leaves, implying a connection between himself, Neo, and the Oracle. Smith and Neo discuss this idea explicitly. Smith maintains they're both anomalies in the system, no longer part of it. However, both are still imprisoned and must play out their purpose, a purpose Neo has yet to discover. Smith tries to replicate himself inside Neo as he did with Bane, but Neo resists it, beginning a colossal street fight that pits Neo against Smith and dozens of replicated Smiths. Smith has departed from the strictures of the program, but he is still a machine. He has no free will and can't escape his program. Neo eventually escapes again.

Back at Zion, Lock addresses the Council and emphasizes the seriousness of the machine threat, requesting them to hold all ships in port, as nothing has been heard from the *Nebuchadnezzar*. The Council overrules him and asks for two volunteers to search for the *Nebuchadnezzar*. Captain Soren from the *Vigilant* answers the call, as does, to Lock's surprise and disappointment, Captain Niobe from the *Logos*.

In an effort to find the Keymaker, Morpheus, Trinity, and Neo visit the Merovingian, a haughty Frenchman, at his upscale restaurant in the Matrix. The Merovingian dines with his wife, Persephone. In their conversation, the Merovingian suggests that the three don't understand why they've come, or why they need the Keymaker—they simply obeyed the Oracle's order automatically. To demonstrate his power over the program, the Merovingian sends a coded slice of cake over to a gorgeous woman. The cake slowly affects her erogenous zones, a subtle process that the Frenchman narrates in appreciative detail. He observes that we are all similarly out of control, slaves to causality. He refuses to make a deal for the Keymaker. The Twins, a pair of white-suited, powder-skinned, dreadlocked enforcers, escort Neo, Trinity, and Morpheus to the elevator.

Unsure exactly what the Oracle intended to happen, the three ride the elevator. It opens onto a floor where they are surprised to be greeted by Persephone. She escorts them into a fancy bathroom and rants against the Merovingian, whom she says used to be like Neo but has since changed. Explaining that she can see true love written all over the stoic faces of Neo and Trinity, she requests that in exchange for the Keymaker, she wants to receive one kiss from Neo. She orders Neo to kiss her just as he kisses Trinity so that she can experience real love again. Trinity draws her gun. Persephone insists, saying that if she lies to them, Trinity can kill her where she stands. Neo kisses her chastely, then realizes the gravity of the situation. He removes his sunglasses and kisses Persephone passionately, with Trinity standing by. Persephone leads them through the restaurant's basement into an impossibly large hall, then through the hall to the Keymaker, who grinds away making keys in a key-lined closet, waiting for Neo.

As they leave, the Merovingian and his henchmen confront the group. Persephone accuses the Merovingian of cheating on her with the girl from the cake episode. Though plainly guilty, he denies it. Seeing the Keymaker freed, the Merovingian orders an attack on all of them. The Twins disappear into the floor and come up on the other side of the room. The Keymaker flees, and Morpheus and Trinity run to help him. Neo stays to handle the rest in the great hall. He stops all their bullets, as well as the thrusts of the swords they pull from the great staircase. An extended battle and chase sequence ensues.

The Twins, occasionally shifting into matterless ghosts, chase Morpheus and Trinity into a parking lot, where they battle. Trinity gets into a car and drives it around, leading the chase onto city streets. Just as Neo defeats the henchmen in the great hall and aims to catch up with the others in the parking lot, the Twins close the door. When Neo forces it open, he's suddenly miles away, high up in a mountain range. Careening onto city streets, the chase pits the Twins against Morpheus and Trinity, who attempt to protect the Keymaker. Agents arrive on the scene and also try to catch the "exile." Link guides them onto the freeway.

During the chase, numerous cars crash, Agents shift into multiple drivers, and the Twins bleed into whatever car they want. At one point, Trinity and Morpheus split up, and Trinity grabs the Keymaker, leaps off an overpass onto a trailer carrying motorcycles, and drives the Keymaker down the wrong side of a crowded highway. Morpheus slices the gas tank of the Twins' SUV with a sword and fights an Agent atop a speeding eighteen-wheeler. At one point, while defending the Keymaker, who has been passed to him, he's knocked off the truck and crashes onto the front of a car driven by Niobe, who has arrived just in time.

Finally, Trinity escapes. Morpheus knocks an agent off an eighteen-wheeler and stands there helplessly with the Keymaker. An Agent drives the truck directly toward another eighteen-wheeler, also driven by an Agent. Morpheus pleads quietly for Neo's help. The trucks smash into each other, erupting into balls of flame. In midair, Morpheus and the Keymaker are caught by Neo, who has flown in from the mountains. Watching the Matrix at his board, Link cheers.

In Zion, sentinels relentlessly grind away into the earth. The Keymaker explains to Soren's, Niobe's, and Morpheus's crews that one door in the primary skyscraper leads to the Source. To access it, the units have to work together and knock out power in a massive grid as well as disable the emergency power system. They will then have only 314 seconds to access the door. They strike at midnight, during a shift change of security guards. Morpheus gives an inspirational speech in which he affirms his belief that this night will bring the Oracle's prophecy of the end of the war to fruition. Neo, worried about Trinity, asks her to stay behind. Reluctantly, she agrees. During their attack, sentinels discover Soren's ship and disable it, killing Soren and all his crew. Therefore, the emergency power system remains engaged. Link can't contact Neo, so the only option left is for Trinity to enter. Otherwise they would miss their only chance. She has only five minutes.

We return to the beginning and witness the playing out of Neo's vision: Link patches Trinity near the skyscraper, and Trinity flies in on a motorcycle, taking out a group of guards. At the same time, the

Keymaker leads Morpheus and Neo down a white hallway with countless doors. As they turn the final corner, they meet Smith and hundreds of replicated Smiths. During the fight, Morpheus is nearly absorbed and replicated by the penetrating hand of Smith, but Neo saves him. The Keymaker hides. Trinity finds Soren's lifeless crew and hacks into the emergency backup system, disabling it grid-by-grid. Just as the system finally falls, the Keymaker sneaks out and opens the correct door. At the sound of the click, all the fighters stop and turn. Neo grabs Morpheus and flies him through the crowd of Smiths, diving through the door just as the Keymaker closes it. The Smiths empty their guns as the door shuts, striking the Keymaker. As he dies, he affirms that he has fulfilled his purpose and gives Neo the key to the correct door from around his neck. Neo inserts it, and blinding light immediately surrounds him.

Neo finds himself in an all-white room ringed by monitors. He meets the Architect, the creator of the Matrix. The Architect reveals that his original, perfect Matrix failed because he didn't understand the frailty and flawed nature of the human mind. His increased understanding spurred the creation of the second Matrix, in which a certain percentage of people did not believe. The Architect allowed Zion to exist so the disbelievers could congregate there. Once the instability in the system could be contained, the rebels, conveniently assembled all in one place, could be periodically destroyed. The Architect tells Neo that Neo represents the sixth cycle of these growths and extinctions. One of the earlier "Neo"s was the Merovingian, but Neo has been built much differently from his predecessors. With increased efficiency, the machines have this time created a "savior" who has direct experience and knowledge of the humans in the Matrix. The idea is to manipulate his capacity for love and thereby cause him, effectively, to choose to eliminate all of humanity.

The Architect gives Neo two choices, which explain Neo's visions of the falling Trinity. Walking through one door will lead to the death of Trinity but the salvation of humanity for yet another cycle. Zion will be rebuilt from scratch and, essentially, the program will repeat with its previously acceptable levels of instability. Walking through the other door will give Neo the chance to save Trinity, but doing this will likely lead to the permanent elimination of all humanity. The Oracle and her prophecies of the One, then, were also intentional inserts into the program, further systems of control to manipulate the One into following his predetermined path. The

One's function is to return to the Source. Neo now has the potential to stop the cycle of mass extinctions. Possessing no humanity themselves, the machines are unable to predict what will happen if Neo chooses the door allowing him to save Trinity, selecting love over saving the human race. In the end, Neo chooses to save Trinity.

Trinity finds herself fulfilling the nightmarish visions Neo has been having of her. Trying to escape after disabling the emergency system, she's met by an Agent at an elevator. As they fight, she is forced to leap out of the building. As she falls down in a hail of bullets and broken glass, shooting unsuccessfully at the Agent, who dives after her, Neo flies through the city in a blaze unlike anything seen before. Fire trails behind him, and cars and street matter are swept up behind him in his tumultuous, tornado-like wake. As in Neo's vision, a bullet strikes Trinity, but just before she hits the ground, Neo swoops in and catches her. The Agent smacks into a car at street level, and Neo's blazing wake destroys the entire block.

After soaring carefully to the top of a building, he reaches inside of Trinity's body and removes the bullet. Nevertheless, Trinity dies in Neo's arms. He reaches inside of her and massages her heart, resurrecting her as she did him. They kiss. Morpheus and Link look on at the board.

Back on the *Nebuchadnezzar*, Neo reveals the falsity of the prophecy to Morpheus. Though Morpheus doesn't want to believe it, the fact that the war has not ended remains undeniable. Sentinels show up near the ship but stay out of EMP range. Neo senses that they're building a bomb, so the crew evacuates the ship—just in time. The *Nebuchadnezzar* explodes as Morpheus watches, confused and despondent. The crew ventures out onto the mechanical wires of the real world, becoming utterly vulnerable. The sentinels attack, but something has changed—Neo can feel their presence. He stops running from them and disables them all with his own self-generated EMP. Then, exhausted, he collapses and enters a coma. Captain Roland's ship, the *Hammer*, swoops in to pick up the crew of the *Nebuchadnezzar*. The crew of the *Hammer* relates a pointless tragedy in which five ships were lost by an improperly discharged EMP.

The only survivor, Bane/Smith, lies in a coma, right next to Neo, in the *Hammer*'s medical bay.

"THE MATRIX REVOLUTIONS"

Captain Roland's ship, the *Hammer*, drifts through the real world, trying to establish contact with Captain Niobe's ship, the *Logos*. Trinity sits patiently by Neo's bedside. The health monitor, Maggie, tells Trinity about the suspicious conditions surrounding Bane's survival and Roland's desire to interrogate him when he wakes up. On the *Hammer*'s deck, Morpheus asks Roland to search for Neo in the Matrix, even though Neo is not jacked in. Roland doesn't see anything, but Morpheus's suspicion—that Neo no longer needs to be jacked in—proves to be correct. The people of Zion believe that the city has approximately twenty hours left before the sentinels' first drill pierces the upper dome of the city. Seraph calls the *Hammer*, and the Oracle beckons Morpheus. Trinity accompanies him.

Neo wakes up in a pure white train station. A small Indian girl, Sati, hovers over him. Sati, who is a program, not a human, explains that the Trainman will soon come to take her away. Seraph, Morpheus, and Trinity meanwhile meet the Oracle in her new shell. She explains to them that the Trainman, who smuggles programs between the Matrix and the real world and who works for the Merovingian, eventually will hold Neo hostage. They have to save Neo or Zion will be lost, but the Merovingian has set a bounty on their heads. Neo remembers seeing Sati's father, Rama-Kandra, who reminds him that they met at the Merovingian's restaurant. Rama-Kandra and his wife, Kamala, both of whom are programs, have made a deal with the Merovingian to smuggle Sati away from the coming battle to safety in the custody of the Oracle. Neo wonders how these programs can feel such human emotions. Rama-Kandra says love is only a word and what matters is the connection the word implies and the actions that follow based on that connection.

Seraph, Morpheus, and Trinity approach the Trainman on one of his subway cars to try to make a deal for Neo, but the Trainman refuses to make a deal without the approval of his boss. The three chase him through a station, making the Trainman late to pick up Sati. The Trainman narrowly escapes their pursuit by jumping in front of an oncoming train and disappearing into it from the opposite side of the tracks as it rushes by.

Back at Neo's station, as the Trainman's train finally arrives, Rama-Kandra explains that the Oracle has agreed to care for Sati. Neo tries to carry Sati's luggage onto the train but doesn't fool the

Trainman, who created the station and all its rules. Laughing, he punches Neo into the wall, suggesting ominously that Neo's prospects for escape are dim, since his freedom depends on the Merovingian. Neo tries to run after the train out of the frame, but he loops back to the other side. The program has trapped him in a closed circuit.

Seraph, Morpheus, and Trinity fight their way down into the Merovingian's Dantean S&M club, Hell. They kill the bouncers and then the guards at the gun check. They move through the crowd of Hell's latex- and leather-clad revelers by covering themselves in triangle formation. The amused Merovingian, wearing a bright red shirt, agrees to talk with them above the dance floor, amid masked thugs with guns. Sitting next to his wife, Persephone, who also wears red, and the grungy Trainman, the Merovingian licks two olives provocatively. Seraph, Morpheus, and Trinity try to make a deal for Neo, whom the Merovingian will return only in exchange for the eyes of the Oracle. Trinity refuses that deal and knocks away the nearest guns. The brief fight concludes with guns drawn all around, but no one dares shoot, since Trinity has hers pointed directly at the Merovingian. Powered by her willingness to die for Neo, Trinity revises the deal. Either the Merovingian returns Neo, or she pulls the trigger, sparking a chain reaction that will inevitably result in the deaths of everyone present. Persephone and the Merovingian both understand that her threat is sincere.

Meanwhile, at the station, Neo concentrates in an attempt to envision a means of escape. He has a vision in which he sees three heavy cables, but doesn't know what this image means. A train finally pulls up, and Trinity, who has persuaded the Merovingian to release Neo, gets out. The two embrace and kiss. Morpheus, Seraph, and Trinity take Neo to visit the Oracle, who is baking cookies with Sati. Neo sees the Oracle from a new perspective and decides it's time for him to learn more. The Oracle agrees and helps him realize he has no choice but to go back to the Source, and that the fate of Zion lies with him. She explains to Neo that Smith represents Neo's programmatic opposite, "the equation trying to balance itself" in the face of instability, passion, and the fight for free will. Finally, she says cryptically that "everything that has a beginning, has an end."

Smith, in Bane's body, finally wakes up aboard the *Hammer*. Seraph takes Sati from the Oracle and tries to lead her to safety, but they are cornered by many Smiths. Eventually the Smiths enter the Oracle's apartment. Waiting calmly, the Oracle sits at the kitchen table, smoking. Frustrated, Smith can't figure out how much she knows or why she's staying if she knew he'd come. The Oracle allows him to do what he came there to do, so he replicates himself into her. However, something doesn't go quite right with the replication. The first Agent Smith steps back in confusion as the new Agent Smith stands up and laughs.

The crew of the *Hammer* interrogates Bane/Smith, but he claims he doesn't remember anything. He agrees that his arm scars are suspicious but insists he has no recollection of the events he's being questioned about. The health monitor, Maggie, notes his unusual neural activity and try to figure out a way to force him to remember. Alone in his quarters, Neo again envisions the three cables winding up through some dark, ravaged land. Finally, the *Hammer* locates Niobe and the *Logos*, which is damaged but reparable.

Lock delivers a bleak outlook of Zion's chances to the Council and asks for volunteers to help his grossly outnumbered forces hold the dock. The city is evacuated, but Zee stays behind to volunteer. She grinds handmade artillery shells in her metal bunker apartment. The Kid offers himself as a volunteer to Captain Mifune, who realizes that though the Kid may be young, every available volunteer is needed.

As the crews repair the *Logos*, both ships' Operators note something unusual taking place in the code of the Matrix. The three captains, Roland, Niobe, and Morpheus, try to figure out a way to sneak their ships back to Zion to assist in the city's defense. At Niobe's insistence, they decide to risk flying through a little-used, extremely narrow mechanical channel. Neo enters and announces that he must take one of their ships to the Machine City. Roland strenuously resists this idea, pointing out that no one in a century has ever made it even close to the city. Niobe offers to give up the *Logos*, claiming that she doesn't believe in the prophecies, but does believe in Neo.

Alone in the medical bay with Maggie, Bane/Smith pretends to slowly regain his memory, admitting that he did blow the EMP. Maggie tries to sedate him, but he stabs her to death before she can warn anyone. In a quiet moment in a bunk, Neo tells Trinity he doesn't know what's going to happen at the Machine City, and that he's probably not coming back. She tells him she'll accompany him anyway. Neo and Morpheus say goodbye warmly, as do Link and Trinity. Niobe pilots the *Hammer*, which takes off for Zion. Just as Trinity and Neo get set to launch the *Logos*, all the power shuts off. Trinity investigates the fuses below the hatch.

As they fly off, Roland's crew discovers Maggie's body and notices that Bane has disappeared. Realizing that Bane must have stowed away on the *Logos*, the crew know they cannot go back, because Bane may have gained control of another EMP. On board the *Logos*, Trinity fights with Bane/Smith, letting Neo know via intercom that he's on the ship. Neo emerges from the cockpit with a gun and finds Bane/Smith holding a knife to Trinity's throat. Though Trinity urges Neo to shoot, Bane/Smith notes with disgust the emotions of love that spur Neo to lay the gun down. Bane/Smith calls Neo "Mr. Anderson" and throws Trinity down a hatch, grabbing the gun.

Slowly, Neo realizes that Smith has concealed himself in Bane. Just before Bane/Smith can fire a fatal shot at Neo, Trinity manipulates the fuses and kills the lights. In the ensuing fight, Bane/Smith blinds Neo by jamming a work light into his eyes, burning them out. He taunts Neo by slipping into the shadows of a stairwell as Neo waves his arms helplessly. Bane/Smith picks up a massive crowbar and prepares to smash Neo's head. As Bane/Smith swings, Neo ducks, and we see from Neo's point of view that Neo can still see machines and programs. In the ensuing fight, Neo gains the upper hand and knocks Bane/Smith's head off. He frees Trinity from the fuse room, and they embrace.

At Zion, the dock prepares for battle. The Kid loads ammunition into the anthropomorphic robots, but because he is inexperienced and too eager, he spills the ammunition, costing the soldiers valuable time. Mifune and his men strap themselves into their robots, and Mifune delivers a rousing speech. Zee and a volunteer friend promise to stand and fight with each other. Niobe approaches Zion slowly, creeping quietly through the tiny mechanical line. Despite her skill, she nicks an outcropping, and the sentinels instantly sense her. Demanding full power, she orders Roland and Ghost to man the turrets and Morpheus to work as her copilot. She races down the line.

The machines finally breach the dome. A monstrous corkscrew splits the upper sphere and falls through the city, causing massive damage. Hundreds of sentinels swarm into the opening like a plague of locusts. Zee and her friend load rocket launchers with their handmade shells—Zee loads, her friend shoots—and they take a leg off a drill. At the dock, bullets fly. To reload the oversize robots, the men have to wheel ammunition onto the dock while under attack and then elevate the ammunition awkwardly into the robot as the battle continues. Sentinels swarm over a command center. Zee's friend shoots again, as another massive drill drops through the dome. Niobe races toward Zion, covered by sentinels and driving recklessly but successfully. Zee and her friend climb up a few levels and try to shoot down into a drill's core, but they accidentally hit a sentinel. In response, several sentinels try to squeeze into their narrow opening. They kill Zee's friend, but Zee escapes.

The crew members see the *Hammer*'s signal on Zion's radar and tries to open the city's gate to let the ship in. The gate jams, but Zee and the Kid together manage to fight off the sentinels and open it manually. Niobe blasts through the half-open gate and slams into the city wall. The *Logos* discharges its EMP, and thousands of sentinels, suddenly disabled, stream down through the sky and cylinder to the pit of the city. The people greet the disembarking crew as heroes, and Link and Zee reunite. Lock, though, is furious, for the EMP disabled all of Zion's hardware, leaving the city completely vulnerable to another wave of sentinels. Lock blows up a shaft, sealing the city off for a couple of hours from the incoming sentinels, which have already arrived in a mushroom-cloud-like plume. The three captains report to the Council, explaining their decision to give a ship to Neo, a decision Niobe and Morpheus defend.

Trinity and Neo slowly approach Machine City, hovering over a vast crop of humans awaiting harvest. Neo, using his second sight, directs Trinity toward a mountain range, where he sees the three power cables he saw earlier in his vision. Massive city-sized ships emerge from the landscape and unleash hundreds of pods at the *Logos*. Neo wards off as many as he can but is unable to deflect them all. Sentinels attach themselves to the ship. Neo and Trinity's only option is to fly directly up, straight over the city. As they rise, sentinels fall away, and for a brief, beautiful moment, Neo and Trinity peek up above the black post-nuclear clouds into a brilliant pink and orange skyscape. Just as quickly, they descend back down into the dark, flying behind the city, straight toward the heart of a tower. They crash.

Neo crawls over to Trinity, who has been impaled by many twisted rods. Through the wreckage, Neo is amazed at what he sees—nothing but light all around. Trinity reassures him yet again that this is her time to die and that nothing's going to bring her back this time. She wants to say goodbye the right way. They express their love and kiss, and she dies.

At the now defenseless Zion, another drill breaches the hull of the dome. The city's people gather at the temple and wait. In the machine city, Neo climbs through the wreckage and walks across beams of light. Little mechanical spiders and other tiny insectlike machines creep around him until he gets to an outcropping at the end of the wreckage. A spirit—the Deus ex Machina—rises, assembling a giant face made up of many tiny machines. Neo shows no fear and speaks quietly, asking only to be allowed to say what he came to say. The face grants its permission. Neo points out that the Smith program has gotten out of control and will eventually take over the real world as well as the Matrix. The face resents this and spits a swarm of robot bees all around him. Neo doesn't flinch, and he tells the face he wants only peace. The robot bees calm. Neo allows himself to be jacked in to the Matrix.

The final battle between Smith and Neo occurs in the Matrix on a rainy highway at night. Smith has apparently replicated himself onto every inhabitant of the Matrix, which is now entirely full of Smith replicas rather than people. Neo fights a representative Smith as countless other Smiths look on. The fight ranges from the street to the sky to empty warehouses, and the two strike each other with enough force to send shock waves through the atmosphere, breaking glass all over the city. Neo gets up every time he gets knocked down. Smith says that the purpose of life is to end, as he drives Neo deep into the ground, forming a crater filled with rain and green liquid sewage. Smith demands to know why Neo keeps getting up. What is the cause? Freedom? Survival? Truth? Peace? Love? Neo answers that he gets up because he chooses to. Strangely, Smith says that "everything that has a beginning has an end," revealing that a bit of the Oracle lurks inside him. Neo allows Smith to replicate himself into Neo; the Deus ex Machina gives Neo a bit of a jolt; and Neo, in a flash of light, explodes out of Smith's body. The nature and cause of Neo's triumph remain somewhat mysterious, but Neo has apparently purged the Matrix of Smith and restored it to its former state.

Precisely where Smith had been only a moment before, the Oracle lies in a puddle of water—the Smith that fought Neo was the replica that had originally been the Oracle. Neo lies on the wreckage in the Machine City, exhausted. At that moment, the sentinels suddenly withdraw from Zion. The Kid delivers the good news to the city, and the people rejoice. Link and Zee embrace, as do Niobe and Morpheus. Neo is slowly pulled into the Source, with no clear indication of whether he's alive or dead. The real world Matrix remakes itself. The Architect and the Oracle meet on a beautiful expanse of lawn and confirm that all those who want to be freed will be freed.

Seraph and Sati arrive, and Sati embraces the Oracle. They both admire the brilliant, multicolored sunrise that Sati made for Neo. Seraph wants to know if the Oracle knew all along that it would work out this way. The Oracle assures him that she didn't know anything, but she believed.

CHARACTER LIST

Neo (a.k.a. the One, a.k.a. Thomas A. Anderson) — Played by Keanu Reeves   The protagonist of the trilogy, a hacker who eventually liberates humanity from the Matrix. Soft-spoken and reclusive, Neo is initially confused when he is torn out of the Matrix by strangers. Morpheus and his followers look up to Neo, thrust major responsibility onto him, and seem to know all about him, but he has little idea why he has been chosen as the object of their admiration. As the trilogy progresses, Neo becomes more sure of himself as he accepts and nurtures his newfound abilities. Neo is a unique kind of superman: healthy, but not overmuscled; strong, but not especially masculine. He assumes responsibility but gives no lectures on moral goodness, and he doesn't shy away from violence when it's necessary. His character develops gradually from passivity toward action, until he finally initiates conflict in order to bring about resolution.

Trinity — Played by Carrie-Anne Moss   The underground hacker who first contacts Neo and later becomes his lover. Trinity is a force of quiet intensity and utter confidence. She plays a crucial role in the first *The Matrix*, when she resurrects Neo from the dead. Trinity is extremely loyal, and she is ready to die for Neo not long after meeting him. Her physical fighting skills are top-notch, and she tends to pilot the helicopters, drive the luxury vehicles, and speed on the motorcycles when in the Matrix. In the Matrix, she always wears black leather or latex, and with her closely cropped hair she appears both androgynous and attractive.

Morpheus — Played by Laurence Fishburne   The brooding and mysterious leader of the *Nebuchadnezzar*, a renegade ship. A tall, strong presence, Morpheus leads his crew bravely, delivering inspiring speeches and exhibiting utter calm in the face of every challenge. His physical size and rock-solid confidence make him an anchor for the ragtag crew of the *Nebuchadnezzar*. Morpheus is one of the first people to believe Neo is the One, and, since his faith in Neo has always been strong, Morpheus will go to any lengths to protect him. Morpheus is willing to die for Neo, but Neo is determined not to let this happen. Morpheus sports stylish sunglasses in the Matrix that consist only of lenses and a nose bridge.

Agent Smith—Played by Hugo Weaving The most important Agent, who proves to be Neo's foil. Able to inhabit any body in the Matrix, Agents Smith, Brown, and Jones are literally no one and everyone. Smith is the most dangerous and powerful, and he proves to be much different from the other Agents. Over the course of the trilogy he develops humanlike anxiety that becomes increasingly desperate and egocentric. Initially he represents only inevitable death, but eventually he develops a personality, a blend of sarcasm and incomprehension of the program in which he's an anomaly. Smith, like the other Agents, wears a standard gray business suit, sunglasses, and a white earpiece through which he assimilates the information of the Matrix's code. Smith manages to replicate himself a million-fold, rendering himself Neo's toughest, most persistent enemy.

The Oracle—Played by Gloria Foster (The Matrix, The Matrix Reloaded) and Mary Alice (The Matrix Revolutions) The gentle seer who guides the freed minds through the complex world of the Matrix. In a trilogy filled with stereotyped characters, the Oracle takes on the most stereotypical form of them all, that of the wise and kindly grandmother who bakes cookies in a tenement apartment. The Oracle moves slowly around her cozy green kitchen, drags pensively on her cigarettes, and conducts conversations that are alternately circuitous and direct. She often roots through her purse for hard candy to suck on. She is a source of faith and belief for Morpheus, and of maternal guidance for Neo. The Oracle doesn't determine Neo's fate, but she helps him realize for himself what his path should be.

Sentinels (a.k.a. Squiddies)—Created by the special effects team Computer-generated, squidlike robots programmed to seek and destroy humans. The Sentinels are all eyes, slithering pads of searching, red, electromagnetic sensors. Their many surveillance mechanisms make them highly sensitive. Their responses are terrifyingly fast, and their aerodynamic tentacles can either entangle a helpless victim immediately or extend back into a cometlike tail for pursuit. When they appear en masse through the dome of Zion, they resemble plague of locusts, intent on bringing extinction.

Cypher—Played by Joe Pantoliano   The mustached, snakeskin-jacket-clad, traitorous crewmember of the *Nebuchadnezzar*. The anxious Cypher accepts his role as a traitor over a last supper in the Matrix, savoring his juicy steak. He can no longer tolerate the depressing grind and tasteless gruel aboard the *Nebuchadnezzar*, and in exchange for betraying Morpheus, he expects to be granted a happy return to the Matrix, with no memory of the real world. He prefers the illusion to reality. His name suggests both the number zero and the act of making or breaking codes. His reptile-skin jacket hints that he is a serpent or tempter, but unlike the serpent in Genesis, he covets blissful ignorance rather than knowledge.

The Merovingian (a.k.a. the Frenchman)—Played by Lambert Wilson   The pompous and refined computer program who was a previous incarnation of the One. A very campy and entertaining character—and a bit of a ham—the Merovingian deliberately overemphasizes his French, delivers portentous lectures on causality, and professes to have lost all faith in all things human. He dresses impeccably in tight, expensive suits and sits as if on a throne, next to his voluptuous wife, Persephone, whom he treats as a trophy. His wife's name, among other things, suggests that he corresponds to the lord of the underworld in Greek mythology. Having failed in other realms and given himself over to the thirst for power in his own, he is interested only in exploring poetic, subtle exploitations of that power, and in maintaining it. His name refers to a seventh-century Frankish dynasty of suspicious kings who stayed within their own kingdom, distributed power in a hierarchy, and believed themselves to be descendants of Christ. Neo attempts to persuade the Merovingian to help him find the Keymaker.

THE MATRIX

The Keymaker (a.k.a. the Exile) — Played by Randall Duk Kim
The apron-wearing entity imprisoned by the Merovingian who holds the key to the Source. Believing that his only purpose is to deliver this key to the One, the humble, big-hearted Keymaker grinds away in a small closet filled with keys, waiting for the day of his calling. When it comes, he fulfills that purpose with serenity, conveying necessary information and organizing the renegades with acumen. Short and hunched, he contrasts with the muscular figures and sleek styles of the rest of the warriors in the Matrix. The keys to practically anything that needs to be started or opened are tangled somewhere around his waist, though he wears the most important key around his neck.

Commander Jason Lock — Played by Harry Lennix The hardened military chief in charge of Zion's home defense. An exasperated, tight-shouldered man, Lock believes in Zion and attempts to defend it the way he was trained, with as much fortification and as clear a plan as possible. He always pursues the proper channels when relaying his orders and voicing his opinions, but he has little room for creativity or hope in his desperate plans. Jealousy over Captain Niobe eventually starts to eat away at his normally confident demeanor.

Niobe — Played by Jada Pinkett Smith An expert pilot and captain of Zion's ship, the *Logos*. Niobe, whose name refers to a mortal who suffers a tragic fate in Greek mythology (she was a queen of Thebes who had to watch all her children and her husband die), embodies intensity, individualism, and courageousness more successfully than the other captains. She makes her decisions based on her own beliefs and instincts, and she allies with, and is swayed by, no one. She is both a skilled military asset and a source of contention between Morpheus and Lock.

The Architect — Played by Helmut Bakaitis The dignified, white-suited, and white-bearded creator of the Matrix. A nonhuman figure of vast intelligence, the Architect cannot completely hide either his slight disgust for the weaknesses of humanity or his intense interest in investigating its behavioral patterns. He is so powerful that the mere clicking of a pen completely transforms the wall of monitors behind Neo in his room. As the creator of the Matrix, he strikes a Godlike figure, but the Architect operates on a different plane of morality. In Gnostic theology, Satan, rather than God, created the world and formed its sufferings and burdens to shackle humanity. Since the Architect provokes the coming Armageddon, he likely represents the Gnostic Satan instead of God.

Seraph — Played by Collin Chou   The tranquil, angelic spirit who protects the Oracle. Seraph first appears in a flowing white shirt, sitting cross-legged in meditation upon a wooden table in a sparse temple room. Seraph is a martial arts expert and tests Neo when he comes to visit the Oracle. His name refers to the seraphim of Christian theology, the highest order of angels. Composed of pure light, the seraphim communicate directly with God, since they are the caretakers of God's throne. Seraph always wears sunglasses.

Tank — Played by Marcus Chong   The initial Operator of the *Nebuchadnezzar*. A friendly and muscular man, Tank serves Morpheus loyally and believes in his leadership.

Dozer — Played by Anthony Ray Parker   Tank's more muscular brother and fellow *Nebuchadnezzar* crew member. When Dozer and Tank appear together, they may obliquely recall James and John, the brothers who were both apostles of Christ.

Link — Played by Harold Perrineau   Tank's replacement as Operator aboard the *Nebuchadnezzar*. Initially a doubter, Link serves as a register of burgeoning faith as he personally witnesses Neo's increasingly unbelievable achievements. As a volunteer from Zion, Link suggests a connection to the human homeland. He fights for the love of his wife, Zee.

Zee — Played by Nona Gaye   Link's strong and careworn wife in Zion, and the sister of Tank and Dozer. Essentially stuck in a small, dreary compartment, the winsome Zee exudes a quiet integrity and inner strength after having survived trial after trial. She is superstitious and gives Link a good luck charm when he reboards the *Nebuchadnezzar*.

Sati—Played by Tanveer K. Atwal The young Indian child who escapes the Matrix through a deal her parents make with the Merovingian. Sati is a program, not a human. Wide-eyed and clear-speaking, she represents the future of humanity after Armageddon. Her parents' love for her surprises Neo, who had assumed programs were incapable of human emotions such as love. Sati's name perhaps refers to an Indian widow who bears the burden of following her husband in death at the funeral pyre, forced by the pressures of society or hallucinogenic drugs. At the end of the trilogy, Sati creates a stunning sunrise for Neo.

Rama-Kandra—Played by Bernard White The father of Sati. Rama-Kandra, a program, makes a deal with the Merovingian to save his daughter's life.

Kamala—Played by Tharini Mudaliar The mother of Sati. Kamala, a program, makes a deal with the Merovingian to save her daughter's life.

The Trainman—Played by Bruce Spence The grungy creator and operator of a limbo world in between the Matrix and the real world. Sporting a dirty jacket, long, unkempt hair, and an angular sunken face, the Trainman looks like a homeless derelict but actually reveals himself to be an ingenious programmer who loses himself in his invisible world of subway trains. He sometimes smuggles programs between the Matrix and the real world. His decisions are always contingent on those of his boss, the Merovingian.

Persephone—Played by Monica Belluci The Merovingian's curvaceous, alluring wife. Mostly silent around her devilish and loquacious husband, Persephone wallows in the loss of his human passion and their true love. Jealous of her husband's attention to a virtual woman, Persephone betrays him by leading Neo, Trinity, and Morpheus to the Keymaker in exchange for a kiss from Neo. In Greek mythology, Persephone became the goddess of the underworld when Hades kidnapped her and took her below. The Merovingian's Persephone also lurks beside her husband in Club Hell, and she is thrilled by Trinity's commitment to die for Neo.

Captain Roland—Played by David Roberts The captain of Zion's ship the *Hammer*. A gray-haired, drawn-mouthed officer, Roland seems more human than the rest of his inspired captains. He thinks logically, makes mistakes, and changes his mind. He behaves like a kindly career military official.

Mouse—Played by Matt Doran The young techno-whiz who creates the *Nebuchadnezzar*'s training programs. Mouse was an original member of Morpheus's crew, and his excitability justifies his name. An incredibly intelligent philosopher-savant, he enjoys bringing up human concerns appropriate to his age level, such as sex and the taste of cereal.

Councilor Hamann—Played by Anthony Zerbe The aging Elder of Zion, fond of prattling good-naturedly. Hamann is a kind of wild card on the Council. His approach to issues balances the wisdom of his age and experience with the irrationality of hope and faith.

The Twins—Played by Neil and Adrian Rayment The powder-skinned, white-suited, white-dreadlocked bodyguards of the Merovingian. The shape-shifting Twins remain almost wordless through much of *The Matrix Reloaded*, but when they do speak, their calm British accents attest to their solidarity with the Merovingian in terms of smooth style and haughty decorum. The Twins look and act like something out of *Ghostbusters*, and they exemplify the Oracle's claim that the ghosts and monsters of legend are actually anomalous programs.

Bane—Played by Ian Bliss The crewmember of a Zion ship whom Agent Smith replicates himself into to enter the real world. With a goateed, shady face, Bane/Smith speaks with Smith's considered affect but maintains Bane's physical exterior. Bane/Smith lurks around the cabin and appears suspicious right from Smith's first infiltration. His face lends Smith a new mask of terror late in the trilogy.

Deus ex Machina—Voiced by Kevin M. Richardson The ultimate spirit at the heart of the Machine City, which takes the form of swarms of metallic insects. A face of light rising above the thick cables of the City, Deus ex Machina, sets up Neo's final

THE MATRIX

confrontation with Agent Smith when Neo has the courage to address him. Latin for "god from the machine," the name is likely used ironically in the credits, since the entity is never addressed by name during the film. In Greek and Roman theater, a god would often suddenly emerge from the rafters to resolve a plot that had tangled itself impossibly or save characters who were in hopeless situations. In more recent works, it refers to any contrived or artificial device that ends a story in a manner that doesn't follow logically from the plot.

Captain Mifune—Played by Nathaniel Lees The extremely intense Zionite patriot who battles with his men on the front lines of the dock. With a seemingly bottomless pit of passion, Mifune screams and yells and ripples his biceps throughout much of *The Matrix Revolutions*.

The Kid—Played by Clayton Watson The eager youngster passionate about Zion's dock defense. Initially nervous and excitable, the Kid learns to stay calm and get the job done in battle, in the face of dying comrades and swarms of sentinels.

Captain Soren—Played by Steve Bastoni The stolid captain of Zion's ship the Vigilant. Captain Soren admirably volunteers with Niobe to ascertain the fate of the *Nebuchadnezzar*.

Switch—Played by Belinda McClory An original crewmember of the *Nebuchadnezzar*. In contrast to the rest of the *Nebuchadnezzar*'s crew, Switch wears crisp, clean, all-white suits and sports a spiked blond hairdo.

Maggie—Played by Essie Davis The red-haired medical advisor on the *Hammer*. Maggie is murdered by Bane/Smith.

Councilor Dillard—Played by Robyn Nevin The regal and authoritative director of Zion's Council of Elders. Dillard's poise speaks to years of experience, and the respect she commands on all sides is a further testament to the central position she holds in deciding Zion's future.

Councilor West—Played by Dr. Cornel West, author and Princeton University Professor of Religion and African-American Studies The funkiest, most soulful member of Zion's Council of Elders.

Apoc—Played by Julian Arahanga An original crewmember of the *Nebuchadnezzar*.

Ghost—Played by Anthony Wong An expert gunner and member of Niobe's crew.

ANALYSIS OF MAJOR CHARACTERS

NEO (A.K.A. THE ONE, A.K.A. THOMAS A. ANDERSON)

Early in *The Matrix*, Neo learns that his life as he knows it has been an illusion, a computer-generated world beyond anything even his own computer-hacker sensibilities can comprehend. He gets over his shock swiftly and undertakes the task of liberating others from the virtual fate that's been forced on them. Neo's path to enlightenment is quick and smooth. He is sought out by those who already understand the truth and given the choice to learn the truth or return to a life of falsity. He chooses the red pill—the choice that opens his eyes and changes his direction from lazy hacker to hero of the universe. Neo never shows much emotion, and we get a sense of his growing self-confidence mainly by watching his increasingly shocking and skillful fighting moves.

As he embraces his role, Neo becomes a Christ figure in the trilogy. Morpheus, the Oracle, and other characters in the Matrix trilogy call Neo "the One," and they are certain he is the man who will liberate and save them. Several parallels exist between Neo and Christ. Neo is resurrected from the dead at the end of *The Matrix*, a feat that cements his role as savior of the human race. Christ was both earthly and godly, and Neo, once he fully understands who he is, can see the Matrix's code covering everything around him, which demonstrates his own ability to transcend the division between realms. Even Neo's Matrix name, Thomas Anderson, suggests a parallel with Christ. "Anderson" literally means "son of man," a phrase used to describe Christ in the Gospels. "Thomas" suggests the New Testament figure of the disciple Thomas who won't believe in Christ's resurrection until he sees proof with his own eyes. Neo makes this same connection between believing and seeing, and he doubts himself and his abilities until he begins to actually accumulate experience. Neo is not meant to actually represent Christ, but these suggested connections elevate his status in the films and underscore the important role he plays in the battle to save the human race.

MORPHEUS

Morpheus serves as a leader in the real world, steadfast and courageous in the face of great danger and difficulty. He is the one who plucks Neo out of his comfortable life in the Matrix and shows him the truth, and he believes immediately that Neo is the One. Morpheus's faith in Neo remains consistent even when Neo proves to be less than perfect, and his loyalty to Neo is so deep that he is willing to die so Neo can continue his work. Morpheus is a kind of father figure for Neo, Trinity, and the rest of the *Nebuchadnezzar*'s crew, and though Neo eventually eclipses him in terms of fighting skill and power, Morpheus remains the epicenter of wisdom and guidance. Morpheus represents the best kind of leader and teacher: He teaches Neo what he knows and guides him to the right path, then steps aside and lets Neo proceed on his own. Morpheus does not seek glory, and his selflessness makes him heroic in his own way.

The many philosophies and religions alluded to in the Matrix trilogy suggest that Morpheus has multiple roles and meanings. The name Morpheus itself suggests the Greek god of dreams, whose name literally means "he who forms." The god Morpheus has the ability to change his own shape and manipulate reality, as well as the power to bewitch other people's minds with dreams and fantasies. He also has the power to wake people up, and in *The Matrix*, Morpheus wakes Neo from the world of illusions. The root of the name Morpheus, "morph," which means "form," appears in words such as morphine, a drug known for its sleep- and dream-inducing qualities.

TRINITY

Once a computer hacker, Trinity was freed from the Matrix by Morpheus and is now one of a band of rebels living in Zion. Tough, leather-clad Trinity is a kind of super-woman in the Matrix. Master of kung fu fighting and a skilled shooter, Trinity can take out a roomful of gun-wielding enemies without tousling a hair out of place. She isn't made entirely of steel, though, and when she meets Neo, she proves to be a loyal partner, willing to follow him into danger and chase after him when he's in trouble. Her love for Neo is powerful, and she brings Neo back to life at the end of *The Matrix* by declaring her love. Trinity is also a martyr, and though Neo does everything he can to keep her alive, she accepts her death as a necessary part of Neo's work to save the world. This willingness to die for Neo is not the mark of a weak will or a yearning for victimization. Rather her death demonstrates her total commitment to the cause she believes in. She's just as determined to save the world as Neo is—her role in the quest is just different.

The name "Trinity" carries with it a host of Christian connotations. The Trinity, in Christian theology, represents the unity of God, Jesus Christ, and the Holy Spirit (Father, Son, and Holy Ghost). According to a Christian view of salvation, we can receive eternal life through the Trinity. Just as the Holy Trinity acts as the center of Catholic religion, *The Matrix* trilogy is in many ways united by the relationship that develops between Trinity and Neo. God is the only savior who offers us salvation, and he offers it through Jesus Christ, whom we can only come to know through the power of the Holy Spirit. In *The Matrix* trilogy, Trinity serves as a uniting force, the one who gives us access to Neo.

AGENT SMITH

Smith is a computer program with a particular purpose to serve within the Matrix. When programs die in the Matrix—as the Keymaker does, for example—they are deleted because they have fulfilled their purpose. When Agent Smith fights Neo at the end of *The Matrix*, something unexpected happens to him. His program evolves or becomes corrupted, and increasingly Smith finds himself at odds with the Matrix world, where all the other Agents remain at ease. He is a program, but somehow he also demonstrates an evolution of character and purpose.

Hugo Weaving portrays Smith as a confused, complex entity. Smith is a program, but he also seems to possess human qualities. We see his desperation, for example, when he faces the Oracle and tries to figure out what she knows and how she knows it. Smith's style of speech evolves as the trilogy progresses. Initially, Smith is smug, slow, and methodical in his questions, assured that whatever programs he is a part of will run smoothly. Slowly, though, doubt creeps into his voice, and his facial expressions become less controlled. He shows anger. The tone of his voice grows more varied. At crucial moments, Smith takes off his sunglasses and reveals his eyes. Smith blurs the line between man and machine, and though ultimately humans prove more powerful, his resilience suggests that victory was never certain, and that machines have more influence and potential than it might seem.

THE ORACLE

Like Morpheus, the Oracle is a trusted figure of wisdom and guidance who helps Neo make sense of his mission, but the actual scope of her powers is never quite clear. At times, she seems to be able to control the future, while at other times she seems able only to predict it or offer possibilities. In either case, her prophecies suggest that the future is predetermined and, therefore, that Neo and the others have no free will. However, her powers and her role evolve throughout the trilogy, as does our understanding of her. Eventually, we may question whether she truly knows anything about the future, or if she is instead simply a good judge of character. The discovery that the Oracle is actually a program, part of the Matrix itself, complicates our understanding of her abilities even further. Ultimately, her calm and comforting demeanor may help Neo and the others with their mission almost as much as an actual prophecy would or does.

The Wachowskis adapted their Oracle from the mythical Oracle at Delphi, who, according to legend, once declared Socrates the wisest man in the land. Socrates responded that if he was wise, it was only because he knew nothing. Neo, too, is aware of his own ignorance, and the inscription over the Oracle's door, "Know Thyself," suggests that self-knowledge is of the utmost importance. The Oracle in *The Matrix* films isn't as grand or as awe-inspiring as the Oracle of ancient Greece, however. Where the ancient Oracle sat over a chasm in a three-pronged seat, inhaling hallucinatory vapors from the depths of the earth that were believed to be the breath of Apollo, here the Oracle sits on a three-legged stool in her tenement apartment and breathes in the smell of cookies baking in the oven.

THE MATRIX

THEMES, MOTIFS, AND SYMBOLS

THEMES

THE BLURRED LINE BETWEEN HUMANS AND MACHINES

The films of *The Matrix* trilogy pit man against machine in a clearly drawn battle, but they also reveal that the humans are more machinelike than they think, and that the machines possess human qualities as well. The humans, for their part, are as relentlessly driven as machines. Morpheus's faith in the Oracle's prophecy, and in Neo, is unwavering and unquestioning, and his own followers follow him automatically. Trinity's loyalty and attachment to Neo have machinelike constancy. Her actions suggest her love, but her love expresses itself not so much as passion or emotion than as ceaseless, frenzied activity. As Neo, Keanu Reeves exudes an almost robotic calm, and both he and Carrie-Anne Moss wear sleek, androgynous clothes. Their incredible fighting skills and superhuman strength seem to put them in the machine category, and their fluid movements are the result of programs that have been downloaded into them. The Agents, by contrast, are fluid, adaptive, and creative. They shift seamlessly throughout the programs and listen intently to human speech, responding accordingly and sensitively. When Agent Smith removes his glasses and orders the other Agents out of the room in a decidedly unmachinelike manner so he can confess something personal to Morpheus, he infuses his speech with human emotions such as disgust and horror. Indeed, Smith seems to become almost desperately human, and his endless replication of himself is decidedly egocentric.

With the line between man and machine blurred to the point almost of disappearing, *The Matrix* trilogy raises the complicated question of how interdependent man and machine actually are, or might be. One fear of artificial intelligence is that technology will entrap us in level upon level of dependence, and in the trilogy Neo discovers more and more about the thoroughness and subtlety of the Matrix. Technology threatens to become smarter than humans, but one larger point of the trilogy is that technology doesn't have to be smarter than us to enslave us. As long as humans turn to technology to solve human problems, humans and technology are interdependent. In the trilogy, the machines are dependent on the humans for life, and they grow and harvest humans so they can continue to exist. Though the reverse doesn't necessarily follow—humans don't rely on the machines for their existence—the trilogy's entire story hinges on the fact that at one point humans needed artificial intelligence for something, and so created A.I. to fulfill that need.

FATE VS. FREE WILL IN THE MATRIX AND THE REAL WORLD

When Morpheus asks Neo to choose between a red pill and a blue pill, he essentially offers the choice between fate and free will. In the Matrix, fate rules—since the world is preconstructed and actions predetermined, all questions already have answers and any choice is simply the illusion of choice. In the real world, humans have the power to change their fate, take individual action, and make mistakes. Neo chooses the red pill—real life—and learns that free will isn't pretty. The real world is a mess, dangerous and destitute. Pleasure exists almost entirely in the world of the Matrix, where it's actually only a computer construct. Cypher, who regrets choosing the red pill and ultimately chooses to return to the Matrix, views any pleasure, even false pleasure, as better than no pleasure at all. Neo, Morpheus, Trinity, and the others in Zion, of course, value free will and reality no matter how unpleasant they may be. *The Matrix* trilogy suggests that everyone has the individual responsibility to make the choice between the real world and an artificial world.

Though Neo is the exemplar of free will, fate plays a large role in his adventure. Neo relies on the Oracle, and everything she says comes true in some way. If she can see around time and guide Neo to the right decision at each encounter, he doesn't have to exhibit much, if any, free will. Morpheus tries to describe the Oracle as a "guide," not someone who knows the future, and at the end of the trilogy she tells Seraph that she actually knew nothing, she only believed. Nonetheless, the Oracle is always right, raising doubts about how much free Neo actually has. In another way, as an integral part of the Matrix, the Oracle's intelligence and composure lead her visitors to believe what she says, a trust that perhaps renders her prophecies self-fulfilling. In this sense, she shares the same final goals as Morpheus, Neo, and Trinity, and together they actively shape the future.

THE RELATIONSHIP AMONG BODY, BRAIN, AND MIND

The Matrix trilogy explores the interconnection among the body, the brain, and the mind, especially how that connection changes when the world turns out to be an illusion. Two different kinds of humans populate the world of *The Matrix* films: ordinary humans and those who, thanks to a port in their head, can be jacked into the Matrix. People in the Matrix can feel physical sensations, which are created by the mind, and *The Matrix* trilogy makes it clear that the body cannot live without the mind. If skills, such as fighting skills, are downloaded into the brain, and if the mind is free, a person can control his or her body as if he or she actually has had these skills all along. The trilogy suggests that humans need the body, brain, and mind working together simultaneously to stay awake in the world, which, in a way, is a declaration of the power of individuality and humanity. The existence or absence of all three elements separates Neo, Morpheus, and Trinity from not only the Agents but also the Architect, the Oracle, and all the other Matrix-bound entities.

MOTIFS

SEXUALITY AND SENSUALITY

In *The Matrix*, all references to sex occur only in the Matrix—that is, in the mind. Mouse, the young techno-whiz, creates a fantasy woman dressed in red as part of a simulation of the Matrix. *The Matrix Reloaded* shows an earthier version of sex in the real world, in the human city of Zion. Neo and Trinity, whose passion was previously much colder, make love under an arch, a traditional symbol of heavenly blessing. The film interrupts their lovemaking with scenes of the earthy, sensual Zionites celebrating their community to the beat of tribal drums. They're loosely garbed in earth-toned clothing and are muscular, tattooed, and sweaty. The vast population jumps up and down, undulating in a sweep of ecstasy that seems to serve as a connection to the earth. Sex and sensuality are concrete in the real world, while in the Matrix, they are illusions like everything else.

The Matrix Revolutions portrays the Merovingian's underground club, Hell, as an S&M paradise, full of latex, whips, chains, masks, and muscular bodies. The club suggests Dante's circles of hell, in which sinners receive various tortures and punishments. Here, the Wachowskis present the idea that the simulation of punishment, the sensations of various materials, bindings, and masks, and the assumption of various roles of domination and submission can be a liberating and sensual experience. What the Christian Dante condemns as debauchery, the Merovingian presides over as an entertaining party.

SUNGLASSES, EYES, AND MIRRORS

The renegades and the Agents always wear sunglasses in the Matrix. Sunglasses hide the eyes and reflect those who are being looked at. The removal of sunglasses signals that a character is gaining a new or different perspective, or that he or she is vulnerable or exposed in some way. When Neo removes his glasses to kiss Persephone in *The Matrix Reloaded*, he looks deeply into her eyes, indicating both the precariousness and gravity of the moment. When Morpheus offers Neo his crucial choice between the pills, the blue pill is reflected in one shade of his sunglasses, the red pill in the other, an overt reference to the two different ways of seeing that Neo must choose between. When Neo enters his new world, his sunglasses serve as protection for him, keeping him invulnerable to the dangers and surprises he encounters.

Mirrors reveal how we see the outside world, but also, crucially, how we see ourselves and our own world. When Neo takes the red pill, he enters the real world, and the mirror he touches infects him slowly with metallic goo, suggesting the fraying of all his illusions as he enters a new realm of perception. Other reflective materials are shattered throughout the trilogy. Skyscraper glass rains down, water rains from above and pools below, and anything transparent continually shifts forms and locations, transforming whatever it reflects.

BIBLICAL REFERENCES

The films in *The Matrix* trilogy frequently employ biblical references to augment character development and suggest a significance greater than the mere actions taking place. On the plaque of Morpheus's *Nebuchadnezzer*, for example, as part of its identifying numbers, is the notation *Mark III, No. 11*. In the Gospel of Mark in the New Testament, Mark describes large crowds who follow Jesus and are healed of their diseases. Chapter 3, verse 11 (King James Version) reads, "And unclean spirits, when they saw him, fell down before him and cried, saying, 'Thou art the Son of God!'" In some ways, Morpheus parallels a Gospel writer delivering news of a savior. He is, after all, the first person to believe and declare that Neo is the One. When Neo disembarks at Zion for the first time in *The*

Matrix Reloaded, afflicted crowds await him and treat him as a messiah, begging for his healing touch just as the crowds in Mark's Gospel do. Though Neo isn't necessarily a messiah, the biblical reference here suggests he embodies the qualities of one and presents a possible interpretation of his role.

Just before Agent Smith's first appearance in *The Matrix Reloaded*, we see the license plate on the luxury car he drives: IS 5416. In the Old Testament, Chapter 54, Verse 16, of Isaiah, reads "Behold, I have created the smith that bloweth the coals in the fire and that bringeth forth an instrument for this work; and I have created the waster, to destroy." In this chapter, Isaiah refers to the Lord's assurances that Zion, the promised land for the Israelites, will be victorious in future glory. He reminds his people that he created everything and goes on to reassure them that "no weapon forged against you will prevail." Though we don't necessarily need to recognize and understand the biblical reference in order to understand *The Matrix* trilogy, references like this one add a second layer of meaning to the films. They augment what we do know about the characters and add depth to the conflict, giving the films hidden meanings and reinforcing the idea that what we're seeing isn't all that's there—more lurks beneath the surface, if we just know where to look, much as those who take the red pill discover an alternate universe just beyond what they know.

Symbols

Zion

The meaning of the human city of Zion changes throughout *The Matrix* trilogy. In *The Matrix*, the city is discussed but not seen and works mostly as a metaphor for a promised land of sorts, and a goal that makes the fighting worthwhile. The Zion in the films recalls the biblical city of Zion. In the Old Testament, Zion is Jerusalem, the heavenly city God promised to the Israelites. The city sits on the top of a hill, commanding a distant view of the kingdom—both for meditative purposes and for safety. The people in Zion live in harmony and are unified in their faith. The word Zion suggests safety, since the city became a religious haven for the Israelites after years of wandering and enduring torture. In *The Matrix* trilogy, Zion is still a promised land as well as a safe haven, but the parallels end there. The Zion of the Matrix commands not a vast view of land, but is instead buried within the heart of the earth, and though it offers the illusion of safety, in *The Matrix Revolutions* the enemy infiltrates that safe haven and crashes violently through its borders.

The Zion in *The Matrix* trilogy contrasts with the illusory program of the Matrix. The Matrix represents a system of control that operates completely in the mind. As a complex, machine-driven program, it appropriates any personal, political, or ideological leanings and renders them wholly false. It allows illusions but no action. Zion, as a promised land, represents a real, tangible, human place fought for, worked for, and died for. Zion is a living sanctuary and a memorial to the efforts and faith of a chosen people. When Zion appears in *The Matrix Reloaded* and *The Matrix Revolutions*, its symbolic connotations intensify as its inhabitants fight for a true human community.

THE GREEN LIGHT OF THE MATRIX

Everything in the Matrix is bathed in a green light, as if the camera were capped with a green-tinted lens. (The green in question is the color that characters on computer screens used to be before the advent of Windows and word-processing programs that used black-on-white color schemes to make the computer world look more like the "real" world of paper and ink.) This color suggests that, unlike in the real world, what we see in the Matrix is being shown, or filtered, through something else. When Neo finally develops the ability to see the Agents as code rather than as their fake human shapes, he sees them in the same menacing green color that saturates the rest of the Matrix. In all three of the movies, when something is evil, green light is involved—Club Hell, for example, is bathed in green light, and green flames surround Bane/Smith just before Neo kills him. We might expect, then, that Neo will see nothing but green when he approaches the supposedly evil Machine City. Instead, with his second sight, Neo sees golden spires of light reaching toward the sky—no hint of green. Whatever the machines are, they're not only embodiments of evil indulgence and selfishness as are the Merovingian and Smith.

THREE/THE TRINITY

The Matrix trilogy itself is, of course, three films, and arrangements of threes and references to threes saturate the films. The number three has strong spiritual significance, which appears in the character of Trinity. The name Trinity suggests the holy trinity of the Father, Son, and Holy Spirit, which represents the divine nature of God. In *The Matrix* films, Morpheus, Neo, and Trinity form their own trinity, as do Agents Smith, Brown, and Jones. Three ships' crews, another trinity, try to access the door of the Source: Soren's, Niobe's, and Morpheus's. The reappearance of the number three perpetuates and emphasizes the idea of the trinity. *The Matrix* begins and ends in Room 303 at the Heart O' the City Motel. Without the zero, the number becomes 33, which recalls the purported age of Christ at the time of his crucifixion and resurrection. Neo also has visions of three thick cables bound together in *The Matrix Revolutions*, and these power cables lead to his penetration of the heart of the city.

Film Analysis

Philosophical Influences

Many precedents exist for the idea that the real world is an illusion, and *The Matrix* trilogy is riddled with specific references to philosophers who have entertained this idea. Although the films are meant to stand on their own and create their own set of philosophical questions, the Wachowskis pay homage to these precedents through both obvious and subtle references. Four of the most striking philosophical precedents for *The Matrix* trilogy are Jean Baudrillard's *Simulacra and Simulation*, Plato's allegory of the cave, Socrates' visit to the Oracle of Delphi, and the work of Descartes. The films refer to all four of these at various points.

Jean Baudrillard's "Simulacra and Simulation"

One of the most overt philosophical references occurs near the beginning of *The Matrix* when Neo stashes his illegal software inside a hollowed-out copy of a book by French postmodern philosopher Jean Baudrillard entitled *Simulacra and Simulation*. Originally published in 1981, Baudrillard's book argues that late-twentieth-century consumer culture is a world in which simulations or imitations of reality have become more real than reality itself, a condition he describes as the "hyper-real." For example, walking and running are not nearly as important as they were in premodern societies, but jogging is a recreational pastime, replete with special shoes, clothes, books, and other gear. To take another example, we no longer live in communities where food is produced locally and whole grains are a necessary dietary staple, but we have health food that enables us to replicate the experience of a peasant's diet. (Admittedly, terms such as "jogging" and "health food" show that the book is somewhat dated, but the point still holds.)

Baudrillard argues that consumer culture has evolved from a state in which we are surrounded by *representations* or imitations of things that really exist, toward a state in which our lives are filled with *simulations*, objects that look as if they represent something else but have really created the reality they seem to refer to. In such a situation, the world of simulations increasingly takes on a life of its own, and reality itself erodes to the point that it becomes a desert.

Morpheus introduces Neo to the real world by welcoming him to "the desert of the real," a phrase taken from the first page of *Simulacra and Simulation*. Thus, the entire concept of *The Matrix* films can be interpreted as a criticism of the unreal consumer culture we live in, a culture that may be distracting us from the reality that we are being exploited by someone or something, just as the machines exploit the humans in the Matrix for bioelectricity.

Baudrillard's greatest philosophical influence is Karl Marx, and while the Matrix films do not refer to Marx explicitly, the fact that the inhabitants of the Matrix are exploited by means of an illusion that they all inhabit renders the films closer in spirit to Marx than to any other philosopher. Marx argued that the working class is exploited by the ruling classes, but the working class's exploitation is only possible because it does not perceive itself as being exploited. The working class misunderstands its own position because it is confused and distracted by social messages that give workers a distorted explanation of how they fit into the world—for example, religion, school, and ideologies such as nationalism and patriotism. (According to Baudrillard, consumer culture is what misleads us.) Marx's partner, Friedrich Engels, coined the term *false consciousness* to describe the working class's ignorance. Of course, the argument that average people are ignorant of their own best interests and exploited by rulers who create and capitalize on that ignorance is still common today. The documentary films of Michael Moore, for example, have sought to demonstrate that politicians and the news media exploit Americans' fears of violence and terrorism to distract us from our true economic and political best interests. Nevertheless, the original source of all such "false consciousness" arguments, including that of *The Matrix* trilogy, is Marx.

PLATO'S ALLEGORY OF THE CAVE

Plato explores the idea that the real world is an illusion in the allegory of the cave in *The Republic*. Plato imagines a cave in which people have been kept prisoner since birth. These people are bound in such a way that they can look only straight ahead, not behind them or to the side. On the wall in front of them, they can see flickering shadows in the shape of people, trees, and animals. Because these images are all they've ever seen, they believe these images constitute the real world. One day, a prisoner escapes his bonds. He looks behind him and sees that what he thought was the real world is actually an elaborate set of shadows, which free people create with statues and the light from a fire. The statues, he decides, are actually the real world, not the shadows. Then he is freed from the cave altogether, and sees the actual world for the first time. He has a difficult time adjusting his eyes to the bright light of the sun, but eventually he does. Fully aware of true reality, he must return to the cave and try to teach others what he knows. The experience of this prisoner is a metaphor for the process by which rare human beings free themselves from the world of appearances and, with the help of philosophy, perceive the world truly.

Neo is pulled from a kind of cave in the first *Matrix* film, when he sees the real world for the first time. Everything he thought was real is only an illusion—much like the shadows on the cave walls and the statues that made the shadows were only copies of things in the real world. Plato insists that those who free themselves and come to perceive reality have a duty to return and teach others, and this holds true in the *Matrix* films as well, as Neo takes it upon himself to save humanity from widespread ignorance and acceptance of a false reality.

THE WORK OF RENÉ DESCARTES

Yet another philosophical precedent for *The Matrix* films is the work of René Descartes, the man responsible for Cartesian coordinates and the phrase "I think, therefore I am." In his 1641 book *Meditations on First Philosophy*, Descartes poses the question of how he can know with certainty that the world he experiences is not an illusion being forced upon him by an evil demon. He reasons since he believes in what he sees and feels while dreaming, he cannot trust his senses to tell him that he is not still dreaming. His senses cannot provide him with proof that the world even exists. He concludes that he cannot rely on his senses, and that for all he knows, he and the rest of the world might all be under the control of an evil demon.

Descartes' evil demon is vividly realized in *The Matrix* films as the artificial intelligence that forces a virtual reality on humans. Just as Descartes realized that the sensations in his dreams were vivid enough to convince him the dreams were real, the humans who are plugged into the Matrix have no idea that their sensations are false, created artificially instead of arising from actual experiences. Until Neo is yanked from the Matrix, he, too, has no idea that his life is a virtual reality. Like Descartes, Neo eventually knows to take nothing at face value, and to question the existence of even those things, such as chairs, that seem most real.

SOCRATES' VISIT TO THE ORACLE OF DELPHI

Ancient Greeks considered Delphi to be the center of the world and revered the wisdom of the Oracle who resided there, in the Temple of Apollo. This Oracle's prophecies were always cryptic. When Socrates visited the Oracle, he claimed that he knew nothing, and the Oracle replied that he was the wisest man on earth. Socrates disagreed, but he eventually discovered her ironic meaning. By claiming to know nothing, Socrates truly was the wisest because all others were under the false impression that they knew more than they actually knew. The phrase "Know Thyself" was inscribed on the walls of the Oracle's temple, suggesting that true wisdom lies in recognizing one's own ignorance. Neo, like Socrates, is willing to admit to his own ignorance, and the Oracle in *The Matrix* films maintains her confidence in him and his abilities despite his often visible confusion and doubt.

FILM AND LITERARY REFERENCES

Film and literature buffs have identified countless film references in *The Matrix* trilogy. Some of these are mere in-jokes for fans of certain film genres, such as sci-fi or *anime*, but others are more significant. A small sampling of the most obvious film references includes 2001, *The Wizard of Oz, Star Wars*, *Alien, Men in Black*, *The Terminator* films, and *The Truman Show*. Some of the most apparent literary references include George Orwell's 1984, Jules Verne's *Twenty Thousand Leagues Under the Sea*, William Gibson's *Neuromancer*, and Aldous Huxley's *The Doors of Perception*. The film employs *Alice in Wonderland* explicitly to help set the plot in motion with the White Rabbit.

FAITHS AND RELIGIONS

Released on Easter weekend in 1999, *The Matrix* suggested a parallel between Neo and Christ, both of whom are resurrected. Neo is referred to throughout *The Matrix* trilogy as the One, that is, the chosen one, which also describes Christ—a messiah, sent to deliver salvation. References to Christianity proliferate in the films, and *The Matrix* films are an allegory for the Christian faith and that Neo is a modern-day Jesus. This interpretation is only one of the many possible readings of the films' symbolism and references. *The Matrix* trilogy is remarkable for the breadth and depth of its religious references, not just its references to Christianity. Though pervasive and often thorough, none of the religious references build into a cohesive allegory, and many of them appear and disappear quickly. The trilogy refers not only to Christianity but also to Judaism, Eastern religions, Hinduism, and others. Two of the more detailed spiritual frameworks *The Matrix* films frequently incorporate are Gnosticism and Buddhism.

GNOSTICISM

Though Neo is undoubtedly a messiah figure, the messiah he resembles most is not really a Christian messiah. Christians believe Christ was a sinless man who, through his death and resurrection, brought people salvation from sin. Judeo-Christian scripture traces human sinfulness back to the myth of Eve and the forbidden fruit, pointing to her disobedience of God as the source of that sinfulness. The problem for the humans in *The Matrix* is ignorance, not sin. They need liberation from their illusions, not necessarily salvation. Furthermore, Neo doesn't die for others' sins, but for his own: not coming to terms with his identity. After all, Neo is mostly human, with all the attendant physical needs, and conducts his affairs with incredible violence. His risky goal for Zion and all humanity is to reveal the truth at the risk of losing all people, rather than preserve them in the illusory web of the Matrix. Neo, a liberator rather than a savior, is a Gnostic Christ.

The Gnostics were a loosely connected set of religious dissidents who persevered in various sects throughout history. The Gnostics were originally an offshoot of the Christian church, and we can see how their fundamental beliefs differ from those of Christians through the allegories in *The Matrix* and *The Matrix Reloaded*. Gnostics believe that they alone truly understand Christ's message, and that they alone are an enlightened few. Their name derives from the Greek word *gnosis*, meaning knowledge. For Gnostics, knowledge is the true basis for spirituality. Rather than blind faith, knowledge and the perpetual quest for knowledge liberate individuals and help them break free from their natural state of bondage to the world. In fact, some early Gnostic sects worshipped the mythical serpent for bringing knowledge to Adam and Eve and allowing them to become fully human. Neo becomes a liberator by coming to understand himself. He discovers faith in himself, not in an all-powerful, unknowable God. "Know Thyself," says the Oracle's mantelpiece, and Neo eventually does.

THE MATRIX

The Gnostic God operates on two levels. The Supreme God knows all but remains remote from human affairs, almost in a state of irrelevance because it is so impossibly unknowable. A lesser god, the Creator God, exists, the son of a virgin who was herself created by the Supreme God. This Creator God sculpted the earth. The Creator God of the Gnostics is called the Demiurge, a Greek word meaning "public craftsman," and is paralleled in *The Matrix* films by the Architect. The Demiurge is inherently evil, without compassion or other human emotions except for pride and strict adherence to laws and disciplines. His cold logic often results in massive natural disasters or genocides. He thinks he's the real creator, and he's responsible for the painful condition of the world. *The Matrix* postulates that suffering in the real world is preferable to a life of pleasure in blissful ignorance, and this idea matches the Gnostic life perfectly. Knowledge prevails over blind faith. This overcoming of blindness is explicitly rendered in *The Matrix Revolutions* when Bane/Smith burns Neo's eyes, rendering him physically blind.

The Gnostics believe that a select few people have within their bodies remnants of the divine virgin daughter of the Creator God. They believe that by learning about one's self, one's world, and one's spiritual essence one may reveal these divine sparks of original spirit. At the end of *The Matrix*, Neo actually seems to glow, making his image resonate with both the Christian resurrection story and Gnostic theology. Knowledge of the self is the true faith.

BUDDHISM

The Matrix itself parallels *samsara*, an illusory state of reality that is not what it appears. *Samsara* refers to revolving worlds that develop, reach heights, collapse, are eliminated, and then ultimately are replaced by other worlds. The goal of some Buddhists is to escape from this cyclical pattern of doom and eternal pain, which they believe is possible. Many of the freed humans choose to accept the Buddhist state of *karma*, which suggests that whatever state they are in, it is the result of their own doing. Their condition is self-created, and this idea emphasizes the importance of choice. *Karma* allows people to shape their next life. If they choose actions that are virtuous in this world, they'll be more contented now and in the next life. But if they choose nonvirtuous acts, they get what they deserve. Buddha's Four Noble Truths suggest that life is suffering, an idea *The Matrix* supports. Practicing Buddhists of all sects are rigorous meditators, practicing their faith by disciplining their minds. Morpheus trains Neo with the programs to free his mind and realize his potential based on freeing himself from laws. The training is not intended to teach new skills, since these skills can be easily downloaded, but to liberate Neo from the bondage of rules and to free him from the trappings of the world.

The most accessible and most popular elucidation of these beliefs relates to the spoon parable a young boy tells Neo in the Oracle's waiting room. The story is specifically contrary to Christian belief systems and refers to an old Zen Buddhist koan (paradox) about freeing yourself from the logical mind and entering the "Buddha-mind":

> *The wind was flapping a flag at the temple. One monk said the flag was moving, the other monk said it was the wind that was moving. They argued and pondered, but could not come to a conclusion. An elder passed by and they asked him which was moving. "It is neither the flag nor the wind that moves, but your mind."*

When Neo visits the Oracle for the first time, she jokingly gives him a cursory doctor's exam. Even this action has a mythic dimension, as a certain sect of Buddhism believes that the reincarnation of the Dalai Lama will be proven by a set of markings on his body.

The Matrix trilogy refers knowledgeably to certain aspects of Eastern religions while ignoring or contradicting others. Not many practicing Buddhists would carelessly fire any type of automatic machine gun. Similarly, true Buddhists, practicing proper virtues, have no enemies, though Morpheus clearly tells Neo that not only are the Agents enemies, but since Agents can turn into anyone in the Matrix, *everyone* is a potential enemy.

No one religion or spiritual discipline forms the backbone of *The Matrix* trilogy. Instead, parts of many religions are fused into a patchwork quilt of ideas and references that deepen and enrich the films.

VISUAL STYLE

The visual style of *The Matrix* draws on its creators' love for the comic book and Japanese animation traditions, as well as reflecting an affinity with video game culture. These stylistic elements include certain modes of framing and lighting, along with an emphasis on violence. Clearly the bulk of the films, and the bulk of their budgets, went into choreographing fight sequences. Over the course of the trilogy, fights take place in subway stations, in grand halls, on speed-

THE MATRIX

ing eighteen-wheelers, in empty warehouses, in spaceships, in the ravaged real world, and even in the sky above the city as Neo and Agent Smith take to flying. Although the *The Matrix* films reference a dizzying variety of philosophies and religions, the genre conventions of science fiction and action films tend to meld large questions about the human condition with the pure entertainment of fantastic spectacles.

The "bullet time" effect, for which *The Matrix* films are famous, gives the audience the vicarious visual thrill of omniscience, of being able to stop time and see an event from several points of view at once. This technique offers the audience a feeling of power over the temporal world of the film, as well as over the characters, since the audience experiences the luxury of seeing the most phenomenal events in slow motion and from more than one point of view. The characters are fantastically fast and powerful, and this method of presenting the action, rather than blinding or confusing the audience with too much speed, imparts a feeling of control to the audience, as if we have superpowers too.

The *mise-en-scène* (physical environment of a film) displays the strong sense of metaphor throughout the trilogy. The repetitive blandness of the grid in Thomas Anderson's plain, cubicle-laden corporate office symbolizes the Matrix's stifling system of control, and it visually illustrates the Matrix's latitudinal/longitudinal web-like code that Neo finally sees at the end of *The Matrix*. The cylindrical Zion emphasizes the city's communal nature, and the dark sweep of the Machine City suggests the strange and massive presence that might emit anything. The cold halls of the *Nebuchadnezzar* and the decks strewn with wires emphasize the ragtag, underdog nature of the crew, who build and repair the ship while on the run.

Finally, the world of *The Matrix* is appealing because it is a world of shortcuts. Scenes change at a dizzying pace. Cameras swoop in from every direction, cutting from the ground to the sky and piercing walls and panes of glass. Thousands of guns appear in an instant, summoned by a computer keystroke. Amazing skills are downloaded instantly, instead of learned through a long process, and philosophical ideas are suggested and referenced but not fully developed. Though comic books tend to emphasize serialization and multiple plotlines that gain depth and breadth over time, the books can also be flipped through and a new episode started on a whim. The quick, bite-size, transient spirit of comics matches the production philosophy of *The Matrix* trilogy at every level.

Important Quotations Explained

1.   TRINITY: "You know the question, just as I did."
   NEO: "What is the Matrix?"
   TRINITY: "The answer is out there, Neo. It's looking for you. And it will find you if you want it to."

This exchange takes place in a techno Goth club near the beginning of *The Matrix*, before Neo understands what the Matrix is and before he ever meets Morpheus. These lines set Neo's adventure in motion. Not long after this exchange takes place, Neo will decide to let the Matrix find him, and he will discover that more than one person has been counting on him to find and understand an important answer to a cryptic question. From the very beginning, the film suggests that more than one real world exists, if we can just open our minds to it. Trinity suggests that Neo can't avoid this other world, and that it's open for him if he knows how to look for it. Trinity's final sentence foreshadows the tension that will arise between fate and choice, a tension that will reappear throughout the trilogy.

This exchange reveals the true extent of Neo's double life. As the everyman Thomas Anderson, he holds a day job as a respectable computer programmer and works at night as a renegade hacker, nicknamed Neo. Now he is also a chosen one, someone selected to find the cryptic answer to which Trinity refers. Though Neo is thrust into this strange world with no explanation, he doesn't seem entirely surprised—when Trinity refers to the question, Neo knows instantly what question she means. On some level, Neo may have expected to one day be taken to task for his suspicions and speculations about reality. That an everyman like Thomas Anderson could be plucked from ordinary life and chosen to search for an answer suggests that anyone in the audience might one day be chosen to be a messiah as well.

2. MORPHEUS: "You take the blue pill, the story ends, you wake up in your bed and believe whatever you want to believe. You take the red pill, you stay in wonderland, and I show you how deep the rabbit hole goes."

In *The Matrix*, Neo meets the enigmatic and imposing Morpheus for the first time in an empty room in an abandoned building in the Matrix, when he still has no idea what's happening to him. With little time available, Morpheus gives Neo the famous choice between the red and blue pills. The blue pill will let Neo keep control over his story, but his story will have no basis in truth. The red pill will throw Neo headlong into a world he has no basis for understanding. Neo takes the red pill, of course, setting the trilogy in motion, and this moment with Morpheus marks a clear before and after in both the film and Neo's life. Nothing, after this decision, will ever be the same.

The "wonderland" and "rabbit hole" references come from Lewis Carroll's *Alice's Adventures in Wonderland*. At the beginning of the story, young Alice follows a white rabbit into a deep rabbit hole. By entering the rabbit hole, she leaves the real world behind and enters a strange new world where the usual physical laws don't apply. In this new world, for example, she can change the size of her body, from abnormally big to unusually small. During her adventure she bends and breaks the rules of reality just as Neo will when he enters the Matrix. The rabbit hole for Alice, like the mirror for Neo, marks the transition from one world to the next.

3. YOUNG MONK: "Do not try and bend the spoon—that's impossible. Instead, only try to realize the truth."
NEO: "What truth?"
YOUNG MONK: "There is no spoon."

When Neo visits the Oracle in *The Matrix*, he sees a young boy in the Oracle's living room who is bending a spoon in mid-air. The boy, dressed as a Buddhist monk, bends the spoon just by looking at it. When Neo approaches him to learn the secret, the boy tells him that in order to bend the spoon, Neo must bend only his mind. In the Matrix, the spoon doesn't exist—it's just a code or a program that tells Neo's brain that he's looking at a spoon. Neo's mind, on the other hand, does exist. What he sees before him is not a spoon, but rather an idea his brain has created of a spoon—his own perception. He can change reality by changing his perception.

Neo remembers this exchange as he becomes more confident in his ability to break the rules of the Matrix. All he has to do is remember that the rules he breaks aren't actual rules. Just as there is no spoon, there is no gravity, there is no time—all these things are lies the machines tell his brain. Neo can fly, for example, because he can see gravity is a false construct. Once Neo understands that "there is no spoon," he gains more power in the Matrix.

4. SERAPH: "You do not truly know someone until you fight them."

In *The Matrix Reloaded*, the Oracle calls Neo away from Zion to give him crucial guidance about the path of the future. When Neo arrives at the address the Oracle gives, he encounters the Oracle's guardian, Seraph, who proceeds to fight him as a way of certifying that Neo is who he says he is. Seraph then delivers this cryptic comment to explain his unprovoked physical attack. His words suggest a philosophical theme of sorts that runs throughout the trilogy: fighting is not only a combat but also an almost spiritual process of discovery. Therefore, the fighting in the film is elevated to a more spiritual plane. Seraph's tone makes his proclamation seem profound, even divine. In a way, by giving the line such weight, Seraph justifies the exorbitant glut of action sequences that occur in *The Matrix* films. Instead of fight scenes simply being par for the action-movie course, Seraph suggests that they have a more noble purpose, an idea that sheds a different light on Neo's many battles with Smith.

5. AGENT SMITH: "You can't win, it's pointless to keep fighting! Why, Mr. Anderson? Why do you persist?"
NEO: "Because I choose to."

This exchange between Neo and Agent Smith takes place during their final battle in *The Matrix Revolutions*. Smith has replicated himself onto the entire Matrix, populating it completely with copies of himself, and the Smith that is battling Neo was once the Oracle. Smith and Neo have beaten each other nearly to a bloody pulp, and they're in a crater created by the impact of their bodies hitting the ground. Smith thinks he has beaten Neo, but Neo has once again summoned the strength to keep fighting. Though Smith absorbed some of Neo's powers when Neo almost destroyed him in *The Matrix*, he has never absorbed the ability to fully understand what it means to be human. He doesn't understand love, freedom, or truth, and so he dismisses them as something humans made up to help them endure their short, pointless lives. Smith has ruined the Matrix, and he's made everyone in it into himself. Smith knows that Trinity is dead, and that Zion is under attack. He can't understand why Neo won't just give up, and Neo's answer infuriates him.

When Neo and Morpheus first discuss fate, Neo says he doesn't believe in it and that he likes to be in control of his own life. Here, when Neo says that despite the destruction of everything he loves he'll continue fighting because he chooses to, he means he fights for the right to continue making choices. Neo understands that freedom and the ability to make choices are better than the blissful ignorance that comes from being plugged into the Matrix. His initial choice in *The Matrix*—between the red and blue pills—was Neo's first experience with true free will, and this final choice, to keep fighting, suggests that Neo has come full circle. When he chose the red pill, he chose to discover free will, and here, he actually embraces and uses that free will to fulfill his mission.

THE MATRIX

THE LORD OF THE RINGS TRILOGY

(2001, 2002, 2003)

CONTEXT

Peter Jackson, the director of *The Lord of the Rings* trilogy, was born in New Zealand in 1961, on Halloween. When Jackson was eight years old, his parents bought an 8mm camera, and in just a few years he was making short movies with his friends. He often used innovative special effects techniques for his very low-budget films, paving the way for his work with special effects later on in his filmmaking career. He began making his first feature film, the low-budget *Bad Taste* (1987), when he was twenty-two, and it became a cult classic. Eventually, he made a name for himself as a director of gory horror movies, including *Meet the Feebles* (1989) and *Dead Alive* (1992), then branched out a bit with *Heavenly Creatures* (1994), a film based on a real-life murder perpetrated by two young girls in New Zealand.

Jackson had been a longtime fan of J. R. R. Tolkien's *The Lord of the Rings,* and he first approached Miramax with the idea of making two films based on the novels. Despite the studio's initial support of the project, the budget proved too daunting for them, and Jackson brought his idea to New Line Cinema in 1998. Jackson's plan to film the movies in New Zealand and employ his own special effects studios pleased New Line, and they increased the project to three films. In an unprecedented move, they agreed to let Jackson direct all three films at one time. His budget was $270 million, and filming took nearly fourteen months.

In 2004, *The Return of the King* (2003), the third film in *The Lord of the Rings* trilogy, won the Oscar for Best Picture. The award was hardly a surprise. The first two films in the series, *The Fellowship of the Ring* and *The Two Towers,* had both been nominated but lost, and the trilogy seemed to be due an award. Few critics, however, considered the third film better than the first two, and, like its predecessors, the film was praised but not celebrated. However, the fact that *The Return of the King* concluded the trilogy seemed to make it more worthy of an Oscar than the previous two installments had been. Unlike the films that make up other famous trilogies, such as *The Godfather, Star Wars,* and *Indiana Jones,* the films in *The Lord of the Rings* are not complete in and of themselves. *The Fellowship of the Ring* might as well have a To Be Continued . . . sign before the credits, and *The Two Towers* actually has neither a real beginning nor a real end. Even *The Return of the King*, though it indeed has an ending, starts in media res, and anyone who has not seen the first two films will be a bit lost. The Best Picture award is, in effect, a single award for the entire trilogy, which itself might be more accurately described as one very long movie than as three separate films.

The trilogy's unity is perhaps its most distinguishing characteristic. Its consistency is largely due to the circumstances of its production. For two years, from 1999 to 2001, Jackson filmed in New Zealand, creating the footage used in all three films. Though the movies were edited and released separately, the fact that the entire trilogy's footage was filmed at one time and in one place goes a long way toward explaining the unity of the entire trilogy. The congruity of the trilogy can also be ascribed to the fact that the films closely follow Tolkien's novels. Movies, which are collaborative, tend to be influenced by many different people—writers, directors, producers, cinematographers, and actors—while books tend to represent the vision of one writer. Because the films stay close to the novels, they benefit from the consistency of Tolkien's vision.

While critics generally praised the films, few considered them to be anything more than very well-done big-budget extravaganzas, but the films' popularity has made them very influential in the film-making world. For example, *The Lord of the Rings* trilogy has influenced the length of motion pictures. Each of the three films is approximately three hours long, and the entire trilogy lasts well over nine hours. For many years the standard Hollywood film length was an hour and a half. The average feature film had already begun to grow before the release of *The Lord of the Rings*, but the trilogy's success partly explains the increasing number of two-and-a-half to three-hour movies, as well as multifilm epics, such as Quentin Tarantino's two-part *Kill Bill*.

The trilogy also helped to reintroduce a forgotten genre: the war epic. For many years, most war films concerned the Vietnam War, and these films invariably approached the war with cynicism and aimed to present a balanced picture that documented the human suffering on both sides. Even war films, such as *Glory* and *Saving Private Ryan*, which seem to celebrate the heroism and sacrifice of common soldiers fighting just wars, never hide the fact that war is hell. Even if a war is just, these films suggest, it is still pure hell for the soldiers fighting it. *The Lord of the Rings* trilogy, however, seems to have helped reintroduce the notion of war as an aspect of coming of age, one way that a man can mature and make his name.

Neither Tolkien nor Jackson intended their work to be classified as "fantasy," and instead viewed their work as a form of history-making. Many aspects of Jackson's films, however, are indeed fantastical and follow a line of other films that portray worlds far different from the one we know. Movies have always taken place in both recognizable and alternative worlds, and for many years, the dominant genre in this alternate tradition was science fiction. Films like *The Terminator* portray futures in which cyborgs walk the earth and space travel is common. Science fiction eventually produced cyberpunk, a subgenre that includes such films as *The Matrix,* in which the virtual world of the computer becomes the new frontier. Fantasy, like science fiction and cyberpunk, portrays worlds that differ radically from both the present and the past, but the alternate world in works of fantasy is not defined by technology. Science fiction and cyberpunk most often concern an imagined future, while fantasy generally concerns an alternative past. Middle-earth, the setting of *The Lord of the Rings,* resembles a legendary, rather than historical, conception of the Middle Ages, where warriors wear shining armor and ride off to battle on horseback. Moreover, Middle-earth is a world of mystery, populated by elves, dwarves, magicians, and evil spirits, a fantastic land in keeping with the religiosity of the Middle Ages. Science fiction and cyberpunk are rooted in both the modern and the futuristic worlds, and to some extent, *The Lord of the Rings* signals a return to more conservative Hollywood films, a step back from the technology-centric, socially critical movies that have been the norm for the better part of the past thirty years.

PLOT OVERVIEW

"THE FELLOWSHIP OF THE RING"

The film begins with a summary of the prehistory of the ring of power. Long ago, twenty rings existed: three for elves, seven for dwarves, nine for men, and one made by the Dark Lord Sauron, in Mordor, which would rule all the others. Sauron poured all his evil and his will to dominate into this ring. An alliance of elves and humans resisted Sauron's ring and fought against Mordor. They won the battle and the ring fell to Isildur, the son of the king of Gondor, but just as he was about to destroy the ring in Mount Doom, he changed his mind and held on to it for himself. Later he was killed, and the ring fell to the bottom of the sea. The creature Gollum discovered it and brought it to his cave. Then he lost it to the hobbit Bilbo Baggins.

The movie cuts to an image of the hobbits' peaceful Shire years later, where the wizard Gandalf has come to celebrate Bilbo's 111th birthday. The party is an extravagant occasion with fireworks and revelry, and Bilbo entertains children with tales of his adventures. In the middle of a rambling speech, however, he puts on the ring, which makes him invisible, and runs to his house to pack his things and leave the Shire. Gandalf meets Bilbo back in his house and tells him he must give up the ring. Eventually Bilbo agrees to entrust it to his nephew Frodo. Gandalf senses that the ring is gaining power over Bilbo. We see a flash of Mordor, and hooded horsemen, the ringwraiths, leave its gates. The scene shifts to Gandalf, who rushes to a library to sift through ancient scrolls. As the ringwraiths begin to close in on Bilbo's house, Gandalf returns to Frodo and throws the ring into Bilbo's hearth. Mysterious letters appear on the ring's surface. Only then does Gandalf realize that this ring is actually Sauron's ring. Gandalf explains to Frodo that the ring and Sauron are one. He longs to find it, and it longs to find him. Gandalf has learned that Sauron has kidnapped Gollum and that Gollum has revealed that Bilbo has the ring. The ring must leave the Shire or it will endanger all the hobbits. Gandalf cannot take it himself, since as a wizard he will wield too much power with the ring. He determines that Frodo must take it. Gandalf explains that if Frodo puts on the ring, it will draw Sauron's agents to it. Suddenly, Gandalf discovers that Frodo's friend Sam has been hiding outside and listening to Gandalf and Frodo. At first, Gandalf is furious at Sam's eavesdropping, but then he recruits Sam to be Frodo's travel partner and protector.

Sam and Frodo leave Bilbo's house, and in very little time they have ventured further from the Shire than ever before. Merry and Pippin, two mischievous hobbits who are fleeing a farmer from whom they've stolen, encounter Sam and Bilbo and join their party. The ringwraiths ride by, and the hobbits narrowly escape detection. Frodo is tempted to put on the ring, but Sam stops him. This urge is Frodo's first insight into the power and temptation of the ring.

The hobbits arrive at the town of Bree and enter the inn known as the Prancing Pony, where they are supposed to meet Gandalf, but the wizard isn't there. The ring accidentally slips onto Frodo's finger, alerting the ringwraiths to his whereabouts. A ranger named Strider introduces himself to the group of hobbits and urges them to be more careful. The wraiths arrive at the hotel, but the hobbits, thanks to Strider, are well hidden. Strider explains to them that the wraiths were formerly the nine human kings who had the nine human rings. They are hunting the ring because finding it is the only way they can come back to life.

Meanwhile, Gandalf has approached another wizard, Saruman, for counsel. Saruman already knows about the ring and Sauron's attempts to regain power. He declares that Mordor cannot be defeated and that the two wizards must join with Sauron. Gandalf protests, and the wizards battle. Saruman wins and imprisons Gandalf atop Saruman's giant tower, Isengard. At Isengard, Saruman is constructing a terrifying army with the intention of waging war on Middle-earth. A butterfly rouses Gandalf and takes a message from him, and a giant eagle comes and saves him.

Strider and the hobbits head for Rivendell, home of the elves. They stop at a hill called Weathertop, where Strider hands the hobbits weapons and suggests they make camp for the night. The hobbits foolishly light a fire at their campsite, and the ringwraiths spot them. The ringwraiths stab Frodo, but Strider fights them off and saves Frodo's life. Arwen, an elf princess, finds the party and hurries to Rivendell with Frodo, barely evading the wraiths. Frodo is cured and wakes up to discover Gandalf by his side. Bilbo, who has aged significantly, is also at Rivendell, having just completed the book of his adventures, *There and Back Again: A Hobbit's Tale*. Elrond, the king of the elves and Arwen's father, tells Gandalf that the ring cannot stay in Rivendell but must go further. Pessimistic about the future of Middle-earth, Elrond claims that the time of the elves is over, the dwarves are too selfish to help, and men are weak. The ring survives because of Isildur's weakness. Moreover, the line of human kings is broken, though the heir of Gondor, who has chosen exile, can reunite them.

Shortly after this declaration, we learn that Strider's true name is Aragorn and that he is the heir of Gondor. We also learn that Aragorn and Arwen are in love and have been for many years. However, this love requires that Arwen sacrifice her immortality, one of the chief attributes of elves.

Elrond convenes a meeting and announces that the races must come together to defeat Mordor. Frodo presents the ring, and Elrond insists that it must be destroyed in the fires of Mount Doom, where it was made. There is some disagreement as to who will undertake this arduous task, and eventually Frodo emerges. Others step forward to accompany Frodo, forming a fellowship of the ring. The fellowship includes the hobbits Frodo, Sam, Merry, and Pippin; one elf, Legolas; one dwarf, Gimli; one wizard, Gandalf; and two humans, Aragorn and Boromir. Boromir is the son of the steward of Gondor, who has ruled the kingdom in the absence of the rightful king.

The fellowship sets forth from Rivendell. Saruman causes an avalanche of snow to block the group's attempt to cross the pass of Caradhras, and they decide to enter the realm of the dwarves, the mines of Moria. Inside Moria, the party discovers that all the dwarves have been killed, and soon the fellowship is surrounded by an army of orcs, inhuman creatures that are also brutal, ruthless warriors. The orcs disperse, however, at the approach of a Balrog, a demonic creature from the underworld. The fellowship flees this creature as the mines collapse. Gandalf stays behind to battle the Balrog, which he sends collapsing to the depths of the mines. However, as the Balrog falls, it grabs hold of Gandalf's legs and drags the wizard down with it. The fellowship emerges from the mines saddened by the loss of Gandalf, but Aragorn insists they have no time to mourn and must press on.

Coming to a forest, the Sylvan elves, led by Galadriel, the Lady of Woods, meet the fellowship. That evening, the Lady and Frodo speak in private. She asks him to look into a mirror, which is a basin of water, and tell her what he sees. He sees visions of the Shire destroyed, of his companions surrounded by orcs, and of the huge, fiery eye of Sauron. The Lady tells him he has seen visions of what will happen if his mission fails. She warns him that the fellowship is breaking and that one by one the ring will destroy them all. Frodo doubts his ability to accomplish his task on his own, but she says that as the ring-bearer, he is already alone. If he does not accomplish the task, no one will. The Lady encourages Frodo and gives him a parting gift, a star of light that will illuminate his path when all other lights go out. The next day, the fellowship departs in boats down the river. Meanwhile, Saruman has dispatched Uruk-hai, unusually large and powerful creatures whose sole mission is to destroy the world of men, after the party, with the instructions to kill everyone but bring the hobbits back alive.

After docking on dry land, Frodo wanders off, and Boromir follows. Frodo is determined to go off alone, but Boromir wants the ring. He is about to attack Frodo for it when Frodo puts on the ring and disappears. This is the longest period of time that Frodo has ever worn the ring, and he has his longest look yet at the fiery eye of Sauron. When Frodo takes the ring off, Aragorn is beside him. Frodo distrusts him, too, but Aragorn passes the test that Boromir failed. He tells Frodo to run off and turns to face the approaching army of Uruk-hai. Boromir also fights valiantly but is badly wounded. The Uruk-hai capture Pippin and Merry. Aragorn wins an epic battle with an Uruk-hai, then rushes to the fallen Boromir, who confesses that he tried to steal the ring from Frodo. Boromir says he has failed the group, but Aragorn tells Boromir he has fought bravely. Boromir swears allegiance to Aragorn, his rightful king, as he dies. Back at the river, Frodo regrets having the ring but remembers Gandalf's words about his destiny. He departs in a boat, but Sam insists on coming along. Though he can't swim, Sam jumps in the water, and Frodo is forced to rescue his flailing friend and pull him aboard. Once safe, Sam reminds Frodo that he made a promise never to leave him. On the water's opposite side, Sam and Frodo climb a mountain and spot Mordor in the distance.

"THE TWO TOWERS"

The movie begins with Gandalf falling into the mine with the Balrog. As he falls, he catches his sword, which is dropping beside him, and stabs the Balrog. Then he lands in a body of water. This vision is just a dream of Frodo's, however, not reality. Frodo and Sam seem to be going in circles, not making any progress on their way to Mordor.

Frodo has a vision of Sauron's fiery eye—the ring is beginning to take hold of him. Frodo and Sam smell something swampy, then stumble upon Gollum, a pale, hunched creature who used to be a hobbit. Gollum calls the hobbits thieves and accuses them of stealing his ring from him. After a brief fight, the hobbits subdue Gollum and place a leash around his neck. Sam doesn't trust him, but Frodo pities him. In exchange for Gollum's leading them to Mordor, they agree to remove the leash from his neck.

Meanwhile, Legolas, Gimli, and Aragorn pursue the Uruk-hai, which carry Pippin and Merry. In the castle of Rohan, Éowyn and Éomer, the niece and nephew of King Théoden, tell the elderly, incapacitated king that Saruman's army has severely injured his son the prince; he will soon die. Wormtongue, the king's evil advisor, has Éomer banished. The Uruk-hai carrying Pippin and Merry are attacked by horsemen of Rohan, led by the banished Éomer, and Pippin and Merry escape in the confusion. Aragorn, Legolas, and Gimli reach the scene of battle shortly afterward. At first they fear there are no survivors, but then they find footprints leading into the woods, which indicate that the hobbits escaped.

In the forest, they come upon a white wizard, who turns out to be Gandalf. Gandalf says that a new stage of the war of Middle-earth is upon them: war has come to Rohan. He leads the others back to the edge of the forest and whistles for his horse, and then the four set off for Rohan. Asked to disarm before going to see the king, Gandalf holds onto his staff, which he uses to release Théoden from Saruman's controlling spell. Théoden is transformed from elderly to middle-aged and from weak to strong, and he banishes Wormtongue. Soon villagers arrive at the castle, telling of an oncoming orc and Uruk-hai army. Théoden elects to move Rohan's entire population to the fort at Helm's Deep, which is what Wormtongue, who arrives at Isengard, tells Saruman will happen.

Meanwhile, Pippin and Merry have discovered Treebeard, a giant walking tree, or Ent, which has promised to keep them safe. Sam, Frodo, and Gollum, having arrived at the gates of Mordor, are about to enter Sauron's kingdom when Gollum suggests that they take a back entrance. Frodo defends Gollum to Sam. Frodo feels sympathy for the former ring-bearer, while Sam says that the ring is beginning to take over Frodo.

One night, as Frodo and Sam sleep, Gollum has the first of what will become a series of internal debates. Sméagol, his good side, wants to be obedient to Frodo, who has treated him so nicely. Gollum, his bad side, desperately wants the ring. Sméagol temporarily wins out, and the next day Gollum/Sméagol presents Frodo with a gift, a rabbit he's hunted, which Sam cooks as a stew. As they eat, they see thousands of troops marching to Mordor, part of the army Sauron is assembling. These arriving soldiers are attacked by a group of humans led by Faramir, Boromir's younger brother, who come upon Frodo and company and capture them.

In a dream, Arwen encourages Aragorn to stay the course and not falter. Her father wants her to go off with the other elves to eternal life. Aragorn tells her that their love is over and she should go. As his people head to Helm's Deep, Théoden leads an army to fend off the approaching orcs. Aragorn appears to die as he falls over a cliff in the clutches of a hyenalike creature. However, he actually falls into a body of water, and dreams of Arwen kissing him. Aragorn's horse resuscitates him and carries him to Helm's Deep. Arwen's father, Elrond, tells her that the time has come to leave Middle-earth. She wants to wait for Aragorn, but her father insists that Middle-earth can offer her only death. Even if Aragorn does manage to return, he is mortal and will eventually die. However, the Lady of the Woods tells Elrond that Faramir, who has taken Frodo captive, will seize the ring and then all will be lost. Do we elves leave Middle-earth to its fate? she implores Elrond. Do we abandon the fight and let them stand alone?

Faramir questions Frodo and Sam. He wants to know of his brother's death. That evening, Faramir captures Gollum, who's been following the troop. Faramir wants to kill the creature, but Frodo insists on sparing him. Later, Frodo tries to help Gollum escape, but Gollum misunderstands and thinks Frodo is complicit in his capture. He undergoes another round of Sméagol/Gollum debates, and Faramir comes to understand that Frodo has the ring. Sam explains that their task is to destroy the ring in Mordor, but Faramir says the ring will go to Gondor.

An army of 10,000 marches on Rohan, and Helm's Deep prepares for battle. Aragorn says they must call upon their allies, but Théoden says they have none and that Gondor cannot be counted on. Things do not look good for Rohan, since the fighters are few and of generally low quality, but all try to be hopeful. Then an elf army of bowmen led by the warrior Haldir arrive. Sent by Elrond, they come to honor the ancient alliance between men and elves. The orcs and Uruk-hai arrive at the walls of Helm's Deep beneath a pouring rain. The two armies face each other, and the combat begins when a single human lets an arrow fly. After that, a ferocious battle rages. The Uruk-hai raise ladders and scale the walls of Helm's Deep. The elf-human army fights bravely, but the oncoming Uruk-hai are difficult to withstand. They pierce the castle walls and force the defending army deep within the castle. Haldir is killed in battle. Gimli and Aragorn fight bravely on the drawbridge, buying time for the rest of the defending army to regroup.

Meanwhile, the Ents have gathered to debate whether to go to war. They speak incredibly slowly and take a long time to make decisions. Eventually, despite Merry's entreaties that they participate in the world, the Ents decide against going to war and encourage the two hobbits to return to the Shire. As Treebeard carries the two hobbits to the edge of the forest, however, he comes across a stretch of gutted forest and burnt trees. He blames Saruman for the destruction and decides to rally the other Ents to war.

Women and children flee Helm's Deep for the safety of the mountains as Aragorn rallies the remaining soldiers to continue to fight. When all hope seems lost, Gandalf appears in the distance along with the riders of Rohan, led by Éomer, who charge the Uruk-hai. The Ents attack Isengard and destroy its defenses. They open a dam and the rushing water floods the entire plain surrounding the tower. The battle of Helm's Deep is won, but Aragorn and Gandalf see Mordor in the distance, buzzing with activity. The battle for Middle-earth, they know, has just begun.

Meanwhile, back in Gondor, where Faramir has brought his captives, Frodo stands face-to-face with a wraith riding a dragon and is about to hand him the ring when Sam intervenes. Angered, Frodo almost attacks his friend, then apologizes and begins to doubt his own strength. Sam encourages him with a stirring speech about heroism and fighting for good. Moved by Sam's words, Faramir releases the hobbits.

"The Return of the King"

In a flashback, we see Sméagol, a hobbit, happily fishing with a friend. The friend falls into the water and reemerges holding a ring. Sméagol wants the ring and strangles his friend to death. After this, Sméagol slowly decays into the dirty, green, raw-fish-eating swamp creature Gollum. He says he forgot what life was like outside his cave. He even forgot his own name. Back in the present, Gollum awakens Frodo and Sam and hurries them along. Sam says he's begun to ration the little food they have left.

Meanwhile, Aragorn, Gimli, Legolas, and Gandalf come upon Merry and Pippin celebrating on the flooded plain of Isengard, which Treebeard now seems to control. Saruman is still alive, but he is powerless and isolated in his tower. Pippin spots a seeing stone in the water, and Gandalf grabs it and covers it up. At a memorial service and victory celebration at Rohan, Éowyn shares wine with Aragorn, with whom she is falling in love. That evening, Pippin steals the seeing stone from Gandalf and sees the fiery eye of Sauron. The stone nearly kills Pippin, who is revived by Gandalf. In the stone, Pippin saw a vision of Minas Tirith, the capital of Gondor, destroyed. He also saw Sauron but refused to give the Dark Lord any information about Frodo. Gandalf says this vision proves that Sauron plans to attack Minas Tirith, where he and Pippin head.

About to depart Middle-earth for immortal life, Arwen has a vision of a child that she and Aragorn will have. Quickly, she turns around and returns to Rivendell, where she beseeches her father, who has the gift of foresight, to tell her everything he has seen. She says she knows that death is not the only thing that awaits in her future, but also a child. She says that if she leaves now, she'll regret it forever. She asks her father to reforge Narsil, the sword with which Isildur cut off Sauron's finger, thereby releasing the ring.

Meanwhile, Gandalf and Pippin arrive at Minas Tirith, where Lord Denethor, who rules Gondor as steward in the absence of the king, already knows of the death of his son Boromir. Pippin offers his fealty in payment for Boromir's life, claiming that Boromir saved his own. Gandalf calls upon Denethor to raise an army and call upon his allies. Denethor, however, knows about Aragorn and is afraid of losing power. Gandalf says he cannot resist the return of the king, but Denethor insists that Gondor belongs to him. Disobeying Denethor but following Gandalf's instructions, Pippin lights the Beacon of Minas Tirith, with which Gondor calls its allies to help. Soon, beacons all across Middle-earth are lit, and Théoden decides that Rohan will answer the call.

Faramir and his men are gathered at Osgiliath, an outer fortress of Gondor, but lose a battle to an approaching orc army. Escaping to Minas Tirith, Faramir tells Gandalf he has seen Sam and Frodo. Denethor, who clearly favors the deceased Boromir over his surviving son Faramir, beseeches Faramir to retake Osgiliath. Faramir agrees, even though it is clearly a suicide mission. He and his men are promptly slaughtered as they ride into battle.

Gollum leads Sam and Frodo to a secret staircase that leads into Mordor. Frodo is pulled toward the front gates, and Sauron's giant eye burns, sensing the nearness of the ring. Gollum tells Frodo that Sam will turn on him and come after the ring. As the hobbits sleep, Gollum throws away their remaining food after sprinkling crumbs on Sam to make it look like Sam ate the food himself. When they wake up, Sam discovers that the food is gone and accuses Gollum, who points to the crumbs on Sam's cloak. Sam beats up Gollum and then asks Frodo if he needs help carrying the ring, which triggers Frodo's doubts about Sam. Frodo decides that Sam, not Gollum, is the problem and decides to continue on with only Gollum.

At camp with the horsemen of Rohan, Aragorn dreams that Arwen has chosen immortality, thereby breaking her promise to him. He is roused by a messenger, who informs him a stranger has come. Aragorn follows the messenger into a tent where Elrond reveals himself and relates very different news about Arwen: she is dying, and her fate is tied to the ring. For Aragorn, saving Middle-earth is now bound up with saving the life of his love. Elrond also tells Aragorn he needs to enlist those who dwell in the mountain to fight against Sauron. These mountain-dwellers are crooks, murderers, and traitors, but they will respond to the king of Gondor. In an act that functions as a kind of coronation, Elrond presents Aragorn with the sword Anduril, which was forged from the shards of Narsil. Éowyn confesses her love to Aragorn, but he tells her he is committed to another. He rides into the mountain with Legolas and Gimli. The men of the mountain swore an oath to a previous king of Gondor but reneged, and Isildur put a curse on them, decreeing that they would never rest until they had fulfilled their obligation. Aragorn and company enter a cave in the mountain and come across a ghost king who says that the dead do not suffer to let the living pass. Suddenly, swarms of ghostly warriors appear. Legolas's arrows are powerless against them, but Aragorn's sword can stop their thrusts. He asks them to fight for him and regain their honor, marking the first time that he asserts himself as king of Gondor.

Dragged behind a horse, Faramir's body arrives at Minas Tirith. The orc army catapults the heads of his dead companions into the city. Denethor bemoans the end of his line, but Pippin insists that Faramir is still alive. The attack on the city begins, but Denethor commands the soldiers to abandon their posts. Seeing that the king is losing his mind, Gandalf takes over command and orders the sol-diers to prepare for battle. While the battle rages outside Minas Tirith, Denethor plans to burn Faramir and himself on a pyre. Pip-pin insists that Faramir is not dead, but Denethor is unconvinced. He lights the pyre, but Gandalf and Pippin rescue Faramir, and Denethor burns alone.

Gollum and Frodo arrive at a cave full of skeletons and giant spi-der webs. With his plan to steal back the ring falling into place, Gol-lum seems to disappear, and Frodo is suddenly alone and lost. Meanwhile, Sam, descending the stairs out of the mountain, comes upon the bread that Gollum dropped. He understands Gollum's deceit and turns around. In the cave, Frodo gets stuck in a web. Using the gift given to him by the Lady of the Woods, he lights the cave and sees Shelob, a giant spider, coming toward him. Frodo cuts his way out of the web and escapes the cave, but Gollum attacks him. They struggle, and Gollum falls over a cliff. The Lady of the Woods reappears to Frodo and encourages him to complete his task. Frodo continues to Mordor on his own. However, Shelob creeps behind him, stings him, and spins a thick web around him. Sam arrives and fights off the creature, but Frodo is wrapped tight in a cocoonlike bundle of webbing, and Sam fears he is dead. Sam aban-dons the body when a few orcs come down the path. They pick up Frodo's body and carry it off with them.

Giant elephants, carrying numerous reinforcements from Sauron, arrive on the battlefield of Minas Tirith. Having recently arrived at the battlefield, the riders of Rohan fight bravely, using their speed and agility to confront the elephants. Still, the battle appears to be going in Mordor's favor. Pippin and Gandalf, within the castle, begin to philosophize about death. On the battlefield, the witch-king is about to kill Théoden, but Éowyn and Merry intervene. Merry distracts the creature, and Éowyn kills it. Théoden dies from his wounds, but he is proud of Éowyn and goes gladly into the after-life. Meanwhile, a ship carrying Aragorn and his army of ghost men arrives, and the group overwhelms the orc army. The field is calm, and the battle seems won. Aragorn releases the men of the mountain, and they disappear. Pippin and Merry reunite on the battlefield.

Frodo awakes in Mordor. He is chained and half naked. His things have been taken from him, including the ring. Sam enters the orc stronghold where Frodo is held captive and rescues Frodo. When they are free, Sam tells Frodo that he, not the orcs, has the ring. He took it when he thought Frodo was dead. Though a little reluctant to return it to Frodo, he agrees to. The two friends dress in orc armor and go onto the plains of Mordor. They spot Mount Doom in the distance, Sauron's fiery eye raging at its peak.

Back at Minas Tirith, Gandalf despairs about Frodo's ability to complete the mission, but Aragorn says they must not give up hope. He suggests they march upon Mordor to distract Sauron. As Aragorn's army approaches the gates of Mordor, Sauron's orcs are drawn from the plains of Mordor to its front gate, and Sam and Frodo cross the plain unhindered. Nevertheless, the passage is far from easy. They have little water left. They drink the last drops and accept that there will be no return journey. As they struggle up Mount Doom, Sam encourages his friend with talk of the Shire and has to carry the weakened Frodo a good distance on his back. Gollum reappears, and Sam fights him as Frodo runs to the top of Mount Doom on his own. Standing above the fiery inferno of Mount Doom just as Isildur did years earlier, Frodo holds the ring above the volcano, but, like the former king, he cannot let it go. Instead, he declares the ring his and puts it on. Gollum has also managed to get to the top of the mountain and attacks Frodo. In the ensuing struggle, Gollum bites off the finger on which Frodo is wearing the ring and falls, clutching the ring, over a cliff and into the lava below, while Frodo survives by holding onto the cliff. Sam pulls him up as the ring disappears into the sea of fire. With the ring destroyed, Sauron's eye burns out. The tower of Mordor begins to collapse and then explodes. Mount Doom erupts, flooding the plain with lava. Sam and Frodo are stuck on top of a giant boulder, with lava flowing all around. They prepare for their deaths, but Gandalf swoops by on a giant eagle and picks them up.

Frodo awakens in a luxurious bed with Gandalf by his side. The remaining fellowship is there, too. Aragorn is crowned king at a ceremony in Gondor. Placing the crown on his head, Gandalf announces the return of the king. Legolas and the elves arrive, along with Arwen. She and Aragorn kiss. Then the whole crowd bows before the four hobbits. The fellowship is declared over, and the fourth age of Middle-earth begins. The hobbits return to the Shire, and the four friends drink at a pub. Sam sees the girl he used to have a crush on and talks to her. Shortly thereafter, they are married. Frodo writes his adventures in the same manuscript in which Bilbo wrote his. It is called *The Lord of the Rings*. He finishes four years to the day after receiving his wound from the ringwraith, but he still hasn't healed from the experience, and he, along with Bilbo and

Gandalf, head off with the elves to eternal life. As he boards the ship that will carry them off, Frodo hands Sam his book. "The last pages are for you, Sam," he says. Then the boat sails off. Returning to the Shire, Sam joins his wife and two children.

CHARACTER LIST

Aragorn—Played by Viggo Mortensen   The heir to the throne of
    Gondor. Though Aragorn is the rightful king of Gondor, he
    travels under an assumed identity at the beginning of the tril-
    ogy: he is a ranger, known as Strider. The fact that he is not
    upon the throne reveals the weak state of the kingdoms of
    men. As the trilogy proceeds, Aragorn shows himself to be a
    noble leader with a pure heart. He is relatively unaffected by
    desire for the ring and routinely throws himself in harm's way
    to ensure the fellowship's survival. In love with the elf prin-
    cess Arwen, he fights for her survival and for the successful
    return of the ring to Mordor. He becomes increasingly com-
    fortable asserting his royal identity, but only when he
    addresses the men of the mountain in *The Return of the King*
    does he actually declare himself king of Gondor. By the time
    he is crowned king at the end of the final film, he has proven
    himself to be a worthy leader.

Arwen—Played by Liv Tyler   An elf princess and Aragorn's future
    queen. Like many characters in the trilogy, Arwen must make
    a sacrifice. She must choose between the immortal life of the
    elves and a mortal life with Aragorn, whom she loves. Not
    only does she choose the latter path, which goes against her
    father's wishes, but she also encourages Elrond to stay in
    Middle-earth until its future is secure. At the end of the tril-
    ogy, she marries Aragorn and becomes queen of Middle-
    earth. Based on a vision Arwen has of the future, we know
    the couple will eventually have a child.

Bilbo—Played by Ian Holm   Frodo's uncle, who possesses the ring
    at the beginning of the trilogy. Bilbo is a playful old hobbit,
    but he is restless and covetous of his ring. His unsettled feel-
    ings suggest how great a burden it is to carry the ring and
    foreshadow the great travails that await Frodo. Bilbo never
    realizes that his ring is the one ring of power. Like Gandalf
    and Frodo, he is invited to depart with the elves at the end of
    The Return of the King.

Boromir—Played by Sean Bean The heir to the steward of Gondor. More than any other member of the fellowship of the ring, Boromir is the victim of desire for the ring. At the end of *The Fellowship of the Ring*, he attacks Frodo to try to take it from him. Later, Boromir attempts to make up for this slip by fighting the oncoming army of Uruk-hai. He is killed in battle, but his bravery allows the other members of the fellowship to survive.

Denethor—Played by John Noble The steward of Gondor. The ruler of Gondor in the absence of the proper king, Denethor has grown corrupt and weak-minded. He is reluctant to give up power should the real king return. Lamenting the death of his oldest and most beloved son, Boromir, he is cruel to his second son, Faramir, and sends him off into an unwinnable battle. When Faramir returns unconscious but alive, Denethor insists that his son is dead and builds a funeral pyre. Gandalf and Pippin save Faramir, and only Denethor burns.

Elrond—Played by Hugo Weaving Ruler of the Rivendell elves and Arwen's father. Though Elrond is sympathetic to the goals of the fellowship, his primary concern is the safety of his elf subjects. The elves face a choice: they can leave Middle-earth for immortal life, or they can delay their departure and contribute to the fight against Sauron. Elrond has a low opinion of men, as he was with Isildur when the king failed to destroy the ring of power. For this reason and because of his concerns about Arwen's life, he is reluctant to aid in the fight against Sauron. Eventually, he commits himself to the ancient alliance of men and elves, sends an army to defend Rohan, and reforges Isildur's sword for Aragorn.

Éomer—Played by Karl Urban Théoden's nephew and the leader of the riders of Rohan.

Éowyn—Played by Miranda Otto Théoden's niece. Éowyn falls in love with Aragorn, but he cannot return her love. Though Théoden has commanded her not to, she rides into battle with Merry and kills the witch-king.

Faramir—Played by David Wenham Younger son of Denethor, the steward of Gondor. Faramir is forever living in the shadow of Boromir, his older brother and Denethor's favorite. When he learns that Sam and Frodo have the ring, he wants to bring them to Gondor, thinking the ring will help protect the kingdom. Eventually, he reconsiders his plan and sets the two hobbits free. Faramir fights bravely against Sauron's army, even riding into an impossible battle in order to impress Denethor. He manages to survive, but only barely, and Denethor comes close to burning him alive on a funeral pyre.

Frodo—Played by Elijah Wood The ring-bearer and protagonist of the trilogy. A young hobbit, Frodo is chosen by the wizard Gandalf to return the ring to Mordor. The ring offers terrible temptation to anyone who comes near it, and though Frodo on occasion succumbs to its power, he generally shows remarkable strength before its siren call. However, when it comes time to drop the ring into Mount Doom, he is unable to simply let the ring go. Only because the ring is torn loose in Frodo's struggle with Gollum does it fall into the fiery pit of lava below, which suggests that Frodo is a very fallible hero. Unlike the three other hobbits, Sam, Merry, and Pippin, Frodo is unable to readjust to life in the Shire upon his return. In this way, he resembles his uncle Bilbo, a former owner of the ring who is forever restless. The ring has a great effect on Frodo, changing him from an ordinary hobbit of exceptional qualities into someone extraordinary. He becomes a legend and eventually leaves the land of living mortals for immortal life with the elves. Despite Frodo's success in returning the ring to Mordor, in some ways he is the least memorable character in the trilogy. In three epic films full of battles, he is a reserved, physically small, and ineffective fighter.

Galadriel—Played by Cate Blanchett An elf queen known as the Lady of the Woods. Galadriel is the leader of the Sylvan elves. She offers spiritual aid to Frodo, giving counsel and encouraging him during the dark moments of his quest. She gives him a star of light that proves essential to Frodo when he is betrayed by Gollum and trapped in the spider Shelob's webs.

Gandalf—Played by Ian McKellen A grandfatherly wizard. Gandalf is the first to understand the dangers that Bilbo's ring poses, and his knowledge sets the whole trilogy in motion. Gandalf selects quiet Frodo to carry the ring and the bumbling Sam to be Frodo's protector, and these hobbits seem unlikely choices for such a dangerous mission. Here and elsewhere, Gandalf exhibits a remarkable wisdom and insight into hobbits and men alike, and he seems to see potential and ability where others do not. Gandalf is affable, slow, and deliberate, but he is also a skilled fighter. His battles with Saruman and in the mines of Moria are heroic, and the Moria fight in particular provides the others in the fellowship with a model for the sacrifice their quest may require of them. The others assume Gandalf has died in this battle, but he returns, transformed from a gray wizard into a white one. Gandalf is often playful, but he is also deeply concerned about the fate of Middle-earth and always prepared to fight for its safety. At the end of the trilogy, he leaves with Bilbo, Frodo, and the elves for immortal life. Though this wizard seems human, he has always been a little different and a little better than any man could possibly be.

Gimli—Played by John Rhys-Davies A bearded, ax-wielding warrior dwarf. Gimli is a brave and loyal member of the fellowship of the ring.

Gollum—Played by Andy Serkis A wretched swamp creature who covets the ring. Before becoming obsessed with the ring, Gollum was a hobbit named Sméagol. His transformation into the disgusting, raw-fish-eating Gollum serves as a cautionary tale about the evil effects of the ring. Both Gollum and Sméagol are vastly different from Frodo. Gollum is a living reminder of a possible alternate life for Frodo, and, while Frodo is incorruptible, Sméagol is weak-willed and criminal. From the moment he first laid eyes on the ring, Sméagol was obsessed with it, and years later it is still Gollum's sole reason for living. Gollum leads Frodo and Sam to Mordor, and his intentions are constantly suspect. Usually he seems to be waiting for an opportunity to steal the ring, but at times he appears to be a faithful servant, won over by Frodo's generous spirit. His desire for the ring eventually wins out, and this desire ultimately leads to the destruction of the ring and his own death at Mount Doom. As is Sauron's, Gollum's identity is tied up with the ring. Whereas Sauron is pure evil, however, Gollum is pure weakness. He is always the ring's victim.

Haldir — Played by Craig Parker An elf leader. Haldir is killed defending Rohan, which suggests the larger sacrifice the elves have made by choosing to defend the human kingdom.

Isildur — Played by Harry Sinclair The former king of Gondor. Isildur once defeated the forces of Sauron and came to possess the ring of power. He went to Mount Doom to destroy the ring, but at the last moment decided to keep it, a fateful decision that breathed new life into Sauron, allowing him to wage war on Middle-earth a second time.

King of the Dead — Played by Paul Norell The ruler of the men of the mountain. The men of the mountain reneged on a pledge to the king of Gondor and were cursed to suffer eternal servitude for their transgression. The King of the Dead listens to Aragorn when he requests their help. Aragorn succeeds in enlisting the ghostly army for his battle and says they will be free of their pledge when the battle for Middle-earth is over. When the forces of Sauron are defeated, the men of the mountain simply disappear.

Legolas — Played by Orlando Bloom A boyish elf. Thanks to Legolas's skill with a bow and arrow, his kill number is consistently higher than Gimli's. Like his dwarf friend, he is a brave and loyal member of the fellowship of the ring.

Merry — Played by Dominic Monaghan A mischievous and courageous hobbit. Like Pippin, his best friend, Merry is a rabble-rouser and troublemaker. However, he proves himself to be a fearless fighter at the great battle of Minas Tirith, when he helps Éowyn slay the witch-king.

Pippin — Played by Billy Boyd A mischievous hobbit. If Sam and Frodo are necessary members of the fellowship, chosen to carry the ring because of their essentially incorruptible spirits, Pippin and Merry are the accidental fellowship members, who come on the journey because they happen to bump into the other two. Pippin is playful and enjoys a good party, but his carelessness also causes many problems. When he steals the seeing stone from Gandalf, he alerts Sauron to the party's whereabouts. He tries to atone for this error by pledging fealty to Denethor.

Sam—Played by Sean Astin Frodo's best friend and constant companion. If Frodo's burden is to carry the ring, Sam's is to carry Frodo, which he literally does as the two finally struggle up Mount Doom. Sam is Frodo's loyal friend, as committed as Frodo is to returning the ring and keeping the Shire safe. Considering his proximity to the ring, Sam is remarkably immune to its call. Sam himself carries the ring for a short time, and, if necessary, could probably have completed the mission on his own. When the four hobbits return to the Shire at the end of *The Return of the King*, Sam emerges from Frodo's shadow. He approaches the woman he's been dreaming about, and soon they are married. Within little time he is a father of two, with a nice house and garden. Back in the Shire, Frodo suffers, but Sam thrives. Sam is no less pure a soul than Frodo, but his purity is one rooted in his own world, not in a world beyond. His life represents the mortal life lived to the fullest. Immortality holds no charm for him, and he wants nothing more than to thrive in the present.

Saruman—Played by Christopher Lee A wizard who joins forces with Sauron. A former friend of Gandalf, Saruman has been tempted by evil and has allied with Sauron. At his mighty tower, Isengard, he creates countless Uruk-hai, monsters that terrorize Middle-earth.

Théoden—Played by Bernard Hill The king of Rohan. Initially, Théoden is an elderly, decrepit king nearly out of his mind, doing the bidding of his evil advisor, Wormtongue. His insanity and decrepitude, however, are both symptoms of his being under the spell of Saruman. When Saruman's spell is overthrown and Wormtongue, Saruman's disciple, is banished, Théoden becomes a strong, gray-bearded leader. He bravely leads his people in defense of Helm's Deep and shows his true mettle when he answers Gondor's call for help, despite the bad feeling between the two kingdoms of men. Théoden dies in battle but proves himself a worthy king.

Treebeard—Voiced by John Rhys-Davies A friendly Ent who becomes Merry and Pippin's protector. Ents are walking, talking trees who are well intentioned but generally pacifist. The Ents decide to join the battle against Sauron's forces when they come upon a patch of scorched forest, which they blame on the orcs. The Ents defeat Saruman and flood the fields around his tower, Isengard.

The Witch-king—Played by Lawrence Makoare One of Sauron's most feared warriors. Unable to be killed by men, the witch-king is eventually felled by Éowyn, a woman, with the help of Merry, a hobbit.

Wormtongue—Played by Brad Dourif A disciple of Saruman. The frightfully pale Wormtongue is evil but weak. He serves as advisor to the ailing Théoden and uses the king's weakened state to advance his own agenda. When he wields power in Rohan, he banishes Théoden's nephew, Éomer. Soon thereafter, he himself is banished when Saruman's spell on Théoden is broken and Théoden sees Wormtongue's true evil.

ANALYSIS OF MAJOR CHARACTERS

ARAGORN

The descendent of Isildur, Aragorn is the heir to the throne of Gondor, but at the beginning of the trilogy, he hides this identity and pretends to be a ranger named Strider. That Aragorn does not claim his throne, and that the steward Denethor rules Gondor, show the disunity and weakness of man at the beginning of *The Fellowship of the Ring*. However, Aragorn is not king because he is not yet ready. As much as the trilogy tells of Frodo's inner steadfastness before constant temptation, it also tells of Aragorn's transformation from ranger to king. He must grow into his position as king, and his own journey proves vital not only for his rightful coronation but for the very survival and growth of the kingdoms of man. He gains confidence and self-awareness through his courageous support of Frodo and the rest of the fellowship, as well as from his love of Arwen.

Four main points mark Aragorn's path to becoming king. When he publicly pronounces his identity during the initial meeting of the fellowship, he rouses the jealousy of Boromir, who is heir to the steward of Gondor. Aragorn's pronouncement and its effects show that the human race does not yet accept Aragorn as king. Aragorn demonstrates his increasingly strong leadership role when he shows conviction and strength before the leaders of Rohan, a second human kingdom he will someday rule. Elrond's gift to Aragorn of the sword Anduril shows that the elves recognize that Aragorn is king and is ready to lead the battle against Sauron. Finally, and most important, Aragon fully embraces his role as king when he demands the fealty of the men of the mountain, who will obey only the king of Gondor. With this act, Aragorn commits himself to the role of king and gains his first followers. When Aragorn is finally officially crowned, the ceremony is only symbolic—Aragorn has already proven himself to be the true and rightful king.

FRODO

Though in many ways Frodo is an ordinary hobbit, happy to live among his friends and family in the Shire, his pure, incorruptible heart sets him apart not only from other hobbits but also from the other races of Middle-earth and makes him the ideal candidate to deliver the ring of power to Mordor. Frodo's mission to destroy the ring involves a treacherous journey and countless dangers, such as orcs, volcanoes, and wraiths, and in facing these obstacles he is no different from the other eight members of the fellowship. However, his task involves much more than this perilous journey to Mordor. His real challenge is to bear the ring without giving in to its temptations. This resistance is Frodo's inner journey, in which his pure heart is constantly under assault by his darker yearnings for power. The ring tempts others in the fellowship, however good and pure they are. Gandalf, Aragorn, Sam, and Bilbo all have their eyes widen when the ring is before them, and their own weaknesses, despite their often remarkable physical strength, prove how difficult a task for Frodo carrying the ring really is. The difficulty makes his success all the more impressive.

Though the ring is eventually destroyed at Mount Doom, Frodo does not let the ring go on his own, and the destruction of the ring is more an act of chance than an act of will. At the last minute, Frodo is overcome by the ring and gives in to its power, and only in a final struggle with Gollum is the ring torn away from him. In this sense, Frodo fails in his task. However, since no one in Middle-earth was better equipped to carry out the mission than Frodo was, perhaps Frodo's final struggle suggests that the task would have been impossible for any individual to accomplish without the intervention of luck or providence. Frodo is a hero, certainly, but in many ways the entire fellowship is as responsible for the victory as Frodo himself is.

Frodo carries himself throughout the trilogy with composure and calm, hardly ever flagging in his optimism and dedication to the task at hand, and only when he returns to the Shire and fails to readjust to life there does he reveal how traumatized he has been by the journey. Frodo's journey took him beyond the point of no return, and though the memory of the Shire was what kept him going in the darkest moments, he cannot actually go back. Like Bilbo, Frodo feels compelled to write down his adventures, but even this does not put him at ease. Ultimately, he departs Middle-earth with the elves, a final gesture that suggests that although Frodo did not actually die during his efforts, he did pay for his journey with his life in the Shire.

GOLLUM/SMÉAGOL

While most of the main characters in *The Lord of the Rings* are either good or evil, the wretched creature Gollum constantly struggles between the two. Gollum was once a good hobbit named Sméagol, and this past identity comes to represent Gollum's good side, the part of him that loves and wants to help his "master," Frodo. However, Sméagol the hobbit had a glaring weakness. During a fishing trip, his companion found the ring in the water, and Sméagol wanted it so much that he killed the other hobbit to get it. This heinous act eventually transformed Sméagol into the slimy, hunched Gollum who follows Frodo. Gollum, the dark side of Sméagol, covets the ring, which he calls "my precious," so much that he is willing to kill for it again. Gollum and Sméagol struggle with each other, often arguing about what course of action to take and how far to go to gain possession of the ring. The evil Gollum side usually wins, and in the trilogy, Gollum serves as a symbol of how the ring can transform a basically decent person into a dirty, smelly, swamp creature.

Gollum serves as a foil to Frodo, his physical presence implicitly emphasizing the younger hobbit's strength and purity. However, Gollum is not pure evil—that distinction goes to Sauron. Instead, Gollum is pure servility, and this characteristic unites both his good and dark sides and allows him to function as a guide for Frodo. The opposite of servility—strength of character and individual will—become those qualities that a good ring-bearer must have, qualities that Frodo clearly has in abundance.

SAM

Sam views Frodo much as Frodo views the ring, as something to be protected and guided to a final destination, and Sam's dedication makes him one of the most important members of the fellowship. While Aragorn is the star fighter of the group, it is Sam who proves the most indispensable to Frodo, and the two are so isolated in their journey that they usually don't know what the other members of the fellowship are doing or facing. Though the other members make it possible for Frodo and Sam to continue on their journey, Sam himself makes it possible for Frodo to carry on. Sam takes his responsibilities as Frodo's companion very seriously, and he upholds his vow never to leave Frodo even when circumstances are at their most dangerous. When an exhausted Frodo falters near the end of *The Return of the King*, Sam literally carries his friend the rest of the distance to Mount Doom. Sam is loyal as well as pure, and this purity helps him resist the power of the ring. Sam has countless opportunities to steal the ring from Frodo, but he takes it only when he believes Frodo is dead. He returns the ring with little hesitation, a selfless act that suggests that had Frodo actually died, Sam would have had the strength to carry out the destruction of it on his own.

Frodo's strength at times seems almost otherworldly, but Sam's is very much of the world, and this distinction becomes clear at the end of *The Return of the King*. While Frodo struggles to readjust to normal life in the Shire, Sam thrives. He bravely approaches the woman he has always loved, marries her, and soon is a father of two. The journey to Mordor gave Sam new confidence and maturity, and our final glimpse of him shows him to be on his way to a long, happy life. Frodo, however, has been changed by the journey in a way the Shire can no longer accommodate, and his only option is to leave.

Themes, Motifs, and Symbols

Themes

The King vs. the Steward

At the beginning of *The Lord of the Rings,* Middle-earth is weak and disunited, with little trust existing among the various races. Dissension plagues the different human kingdoms, and one of the main problems is that the true leaders are not in their rightful positions. In *The Return of the King,* Théoden of Rohan proves himself to be a good, noble leader when he heeds Gondor's cry for help, but he was not always so effective. For a while, a spell cast by Sauron incapacitated him, and his kingdom was effectively ruled by the evil wizard Saruman. Even after Théoden's strength is restored, he is incapable of uniting all humanity. Only the king of Gondor can do that.

Until the conclusion of the trilogy, Gondor is without a king. The throne is instead occupied by the steward Denethor, a weak-willed man who seems to be losing his mind. The perilous state of Denethor's sanity suggests the weakness of Gondor when it is ruled by a steward rather than a king. Boromir, Denethor's son and heir to the stewardship, also displays considerable moral weakness when he attempts to steal the ring from Frodo. Aragorn, the true heir to the throne and the future king of Gondor, is able to resist the temptation of the ring. Just as Saruman had to be cast out of Rohan to restore that kingdom to strength, the real king of Gondor must assume his throne for that kingdom to thrive. Throughout the trilogy, this tension between true leader and acting leader means the difference between life and death, success and defeat, and unity and dissent among the people of Middle-earth.

The Limits of Fellowship

Though the fellowship is integral to the success of Frodo's mission, it cannot make the entire journey with Frodo or help him at the journey's end. The fellowship serves as a kind of backup for Frodo, keeping enemies at bay and Middle-earth as calm as possible so he can fulfill his mission. Frodo must ultimately make the journey with only the company of Sam. The entire fellowship is committed to

Frodo's success, but their roles are ultimately limited by the nature of the task at hand. The journey is such that only the two small hobbits are capable of making it successfully.

The nature of the ring itself puts its own limits on fellowship. The ring is a heavy burden for whoever carries it, and it forces its bearer into tremendous isolation. Gollum was a victim of the ring, and his peaceful life as a hobbit ended when he gave in to its temptation. He retreated into a cave and became isolated from the world. The ring isolates Frodo, too, even though Sam accompanies him. While the entire fellowship is in great danger, only Frodo is haunted by visions of Mordor and Sauron. He is unable to share this torment with the others, so it becomes the very basis of his isolation. At the end of *The Fellowship of the Ring*, Galadriel tells Frodo that bearing the ring is a solitary task, prompting him to leave the others. Though Sam refuses to leave Frodo alone and gives him much comfort, he remains blind to his friend's inner torment. Even after the ring is destroyed, Frodo remains isolated. He is unable to readjust to life in the Shire and eventually leaves the other hobbits behind. His experience as ring-bearer has permanently isolated him from his peers.

THE SHIRE AS A FANTASY OF HOME

At the very start of their journey, Sam notes to Frodo that they have just passed the spot that marks the farthest he's ever before been from home, the first of many thoughts the hobbits will have about home and their distance from it. Nostalgia for home, even to the point of homesickness, plagues Frodo and Sam throughout their journey, and Sam speaks of it most often. When Sam and Frodo travel to Mordor, Frodo's intense focus on the journey to Mount Doom is balanced by Sam's focus on the return journey. The Shire is a lush, happy place untouched by the tumult disturbing much of Middle-earth and, compared to the rocky, dangerous terrain Frodo and Sam face on their journey, seems for them a kind of paradise. However, their talk of returning to the Shire is rooted in more than the physical Shire itself. The Shire suggests a childlike innocence, which the hobbits left behind with the very first step of their journey. It also suggests a different kind of life, where hobbits live simply, unworried, and free from war, greed, evil, death, and all the other vices and hardships that complicate life in much of Middle-earth. In Frodo's and Sam's memories, the Shire becomes a sort of Eden, where life was perfect and could be perfect again, if they can only get back. The thought of returning animates them and gives them strength in their darkest moments.

The paradise of the Shire, however, is an illusion. Though the Shire remains lush and the hobbits who live there remain happy and joyful, especially when Frodo and Sam return, the innocence and ignorance Frodo and Sam once enjoyed in the Shire are gone forever. They have seen and experienced too much, and they have become adults now, with many painful memories. Though Sam adapts to his new status in the Shire and thrives in the happiness it offers, Frodo cannot regain a sense of equilibrium even being back at home. Returning to the Shire had seemed to promise the end of fear and worry, but Frodo must journey on.

MOTIFS

MORDOR

Frodo and Sam's destination is Mordor, specifically the volcanic Mount Doom, in which they intend to destroy the ring of power. Though their journey is hard, their destination is almost always in sight, at the edge of the horizon. However, actually reaching Mordor proves to be extremely difficult. The hobbits frequently find themselves going in circles. When they finally arrive at Mordor, Faramir captures them and brings them back to Osgiliath. Later, Gollum leads them back to the gates of Mordor, only to propose a different way in. Sam and Frodo seem to be always on their way to Mordor, but they never quite arrive. Mordor is the place that drives their every action and the goal they hold above all else. The closer they get, the further off Mordor seems, and their journey takes on epic proportions, outlasting two tremendous battles.

The journey to Mordor is fraught with setbacks not only because Mordor is located in difficult terrain and guarded by dangerous monsters, but also because this journey represents another journey, a spiritual quest that Frodo, as well as Sam and other characters, must undertake. This journey takes Frodo to a private Mordor, the dark core of his soul, where even his pure heart is no match for the temptations of the ring. The many delays in the journey to the actual Mordor suggest the many trials and tribulations Frodo must face in confronting his internal Mordor. The hobbits eventually reach Mordor, and Frodo faces his inner darkness. Though he returns to the Shire, the Mordor he's seen within himself precludes his journey coming to a completely peaceful end.

THE TEMPTATION OF THE RING

The temptation of the ring is the motivating force behind every action in *The Lord of the Rings*, whether characters are fighting the temptation, nurturing it, denying it, or preventing someone else from giving in to it. Characters of every race pursue the ring. The ringwraiths and Sauron seek it constantly. Gollum attacks Frodo several times to try to take it from him. The sons of Denethor, Boromir and Faramir, both try to take it from Frodo. The ring tempts Gandalf and Galadriel, each of them drawn to the thought of the immense power it could give them. Even pure-hearted Sam briefly wonders how it would be to possess the ring. No one, apparently, is immune to its temptation, and Frodo is no exception. Though he is chosen as ring-bearer because he is most resistant to the ring's lure, Frodo must constantly fight his desire for it. He is sometimes tempted to hand it over to his more powerful friends, while at other times he wants to keep it for himself. When he finally arrives at Mount Doom, Frodo elects to keep the ring, despite the tremendous anguish it has caused him. At no other moment in the trilogy is Frodo more tempted by the ring's power. Frodo gives up the ring only because Gollum appears and fights him for it, a fight that leads to its destruction. The ring that has possessed so many and that has served as a kind of connective tissue among all the races of Middle-earth is ultimately destroyed by its own power.

JOURNEYS

The Lord of the Rings is a trilogy about a journey, but this large journey consists of many smaller journeys that advance the greater one. Individuals and groups are constantly setting off for someplace, to pursue a goal of their own, rescue someone, or escape. Merry and Pippin engage in an unintentional journey when they join forces with Frodo and Sam early in *The Fellowship of the Ring*. Aragorn takes many dramatic journeys across Middle-earth on his horse, a Lone-Ranger-type figure taking the brave and necessary steps to save his people. Gollum journeys with Frodo and Sam and also within his own conflicted soul. The elves journey to their land of immortality, though Arwen elects to remain behind—her own journey will be one that leads her to Aragorn and a mortal life. The last time we see Frodo in *The Return of the King*, he is embarking on yet another journey, this time with the elves, to pursue his next adventure. A constant feeling of movement stretches through all three films, and, though the destinations are always clear, the journeys often seem to have no end in sight.

SYMBOLS

WATER

Throughout *The Lord of the Rings,* water serves as a lifesaving force for the good beings of Middle-earth. Gandalf and Aragorn are saved from death after long falls when they land in bodies of water. When Arwen races to Rivendell on horseback with a badly injured Frodo, she escapes the pursuing ringwraiths when they are flooded by water. Similarly, Isengard loses its power when its plain is flooded. Water also suggests the afterlife. The elves depart Middle-earth on a boat and sail out to a great body of water. When Boromir dies, his dead body is placed on a pyre and sent down a river. Although he is dead, this journey suggests that he will live on in the memory of others.

THE RING

The ring is the center of the trilogy, and it gains multiple, changeable meanings as Frodo's journey proceeds. Created by the evil Sauron, it is at first synonymous with its maker's evil power. Those who encounter the ring are overcome with longing for power over others, and the ring could give more power to Sauron. For all, the ring suggests the dangerous urges that lurk even in the most pure-hearted beings of Middle-earth. It also suggests slavery and weakness, since whoever gives in to the temptation of the ring becomes a slave to it. Gollum is an example of what happens physically when one succumbs to the ring. Man, too, is weak, and Isildur failed to destroy the ring in Mordor. The fact that weakness affects every race of Middle-earth shows the extent of the ring's power.

As the trilogy proceeds, new symbols emerge to counteract the temptation of the ring. The sword Anduril suggests good and unity, rather than evil and disunity. When Elrond presents the sword to Aragorn, he says that the fate of Arwen has been linked to the fate of the ring: as the ring grows stronger, she grows weaker. Arwen, therefore, serves as a kind of symbol herself, the very opposite of Sauron: the anti-ring, the symbol of hope and good.

MOUNT DOOM

Mount Doom is both the birthplace of the ring and the place where it can be destroyed. This is Frodo's ultimate destination, and it also presents him with his greatest challenge. Destroying the ring is in many ways more difficult than reaching Mount Doom, and twice we see characters fail when faced with the task. Isildur, after defeating Sauron's armies, enters the fiery mountain intending to destroy the ring, but at the last moment he turns back and decides to keep it for himself. When Frodo brings the ring to Mount Doom, he, too, intends to destroy it, but like Isildur, he decides at the last minute to keep it. Though the ring is ultimately destroyed after Frodo and Gollum's struggle for it, Frodo did not let it go on his own. Though he passes many tests on his journey, Frodo fails in this final test at Mount Doom. Mount Doom in this case suggests the darkness and weakness that exists even in the most pure-hearted, a lure so powerful that even the most determined voyager needs additional help to resist temptation. Mount Doom also marks the furthest Frodo gets from the security and familiarity of the Shire. He is as out of place at Mount Doom as the ring was in the Shire, and this is the place where Frodo comes closest to actually giving himself over to evil.

Film Analysis

"The Lord of the Rings": From Novels to Films

One of the most remarkable aspects of Peter Jackson's *The Lord of the Rings* trilogy is its faithfulness in spirit and detail to the J. R. R. Tolkien novels on which the films are based. Books and movies tell stories in vastly different ways, and one of their primary differences is length. Novels often tend to contain more information than a two- or three-hour movie can possibly cover, and short stories are frequently used as the basis for film adaptations instead. When a director chooses to turn a novel into a movie, he or she must often eliminate or de-emphasize important subplots. Clocking in at over nine hours, *The Lord of the Rings* trilogy is much longer than the usual feature film, but Tolkien's trilogy, plus the related novels *The Hobbit* and *The Silmarillion*, is itself long, spanning thousands of pages. Jackson's ability to capture the diversity and richness of Middle-earth's lands and peoples is therefore a substantial achievement. Jackson is evidently a reverential reader of the original books and did not want to deviate too much from Tolkien's vision. In a sense, Jackson's faithfulness to the books was necessary for the trilogy's success. Dedicated readers of *The Lord of the Rings* are the book world's equivalent of Trekkies: they are archivists of obscure, trivial details, even protective of these details. If Jackson had disappointed them, he would have lost a crucial audience and perhaps even caused a public relations mess. Tolkien fans, however, generally love the films.

Despite Jackson's careful dedication to the novels, some differences do exist between the books and the films. In order to turn thousands of pages into roughly nine hours of film, Jackson had to simplify the original story by eliminating or changing certain characters. For example, Tom Bombadil, a significant character in the novel version of *The Fellowship of the Ring*, is absent from the movies. As a hard-to-classify godlike creature, he may have required more explanation than a fast-paced film could make time for. Crucial scenes involving Bombadil are therefore missing, including one in which the four hobbits come across a cache of elf weapons, weapons that prove important when Merry uses an elf sword to slay the witch-king, which cannot be killed by a human, in *The Return of the King*. Jackson works around Bombadil, however, to get the same information across. He gives the hobbits their weapons more directly: Aragorn gives the hobbits a sack of weapons on the hill called Weathertop in *The Fellowship of the Ring*.

The book-to-movie adaptation also affects the elf princess Arwen, but instead of dropping out of the film altogether, she actually takes on the characteristics of two characters from the novel. Arwen appears in the novels but plays a less significant role than she does in the films. The movie Arwen is a combination of the novel Arwen and an elf warrior named Glorfindel. In the film version of *The Fellowship of the Ring*, Arwen rescues Frodo after he's been stabbed by a wraith and whisks him safely on horseback to Rivendell, with the wraiths in close pursuit. By giving Arwen this role, which Glorfindel carries out in the novel, Jackson does much more than simplify his story: he portrays Arwen as a heroine. This rescue is our first impression of her, and her bravery and strength in this scene balance out the more subdued role of delicate princess that she plays later, as she idles in Rivendell wondering whether to choose a mortal or immortal life. Her courage in saving Frodo puts her in the same league as the warrior-princess Éowyn.

Despite these changes, the essence of Tolkien's novels remains intact. Jackson's decision to forgo the obscure, extra details that round out the author's trilogy didn't lessen the thematic and narrative meat of Tolkien's work, and the conflation or elimination of characters from the novels ultimately does not change the story very much. The films and the novels are not interchangeable, but the films prove as faithful as they can be to the novels without testing the limits of viewers' patience and attention.

THE ENDING OF "THE LORD OF THE RINGS"

Though Peter Jackson had to change certain aspects of certain characters to smoothly create films from Tolkien's novels, no change he made to a character affects the general spirit of Tolkien's work. However, Jackson did make one major change to his trilogy that differs vastly from Tolkien's novels. This change concerns what happens at the end of *The Return of the King*, when the hobbits return to the Shire. In the films, Frodo and Sam return to find the same green, peaceful countryside they left, exactly how they'd imagined it throughout their journey. In the novels, however, they return to a land ruled and terrorized by the evil wizard Saruman. In the films, Frodo looks into Galadriel's mirror and sees visions of a burning Shire and hobbits marching in chain gangs. Galadriel says that this is what awaits the Shire in the future, if Frodo fails in his mission. In the novels, these visions are of the actual future, even though Frodo succeeds.

Throughout the trilogy, the Shire is a peaceful idyll far from the horrible wars of Middle-earth. While the trilogy's human heroes, such as Aragorn, thrive in the wars and political intrigue of Middle-earth, hobbits seem to prefer to be far from the center of action. This separation engenders in hobbits a kind of innocence, and Frodo's pure spirit enables him to be a successful ring-bearer. When the four hobbits first depart from the Shire, they leave a small world of innocence for a larger world of unknown mystery, where both adventure and terror await them. This journey from peaceful home to mysterious larger world suggests the journey from childhood to maturity, with the hobbits cast as young adolescents venturing into the adult world. However, except for those hobbits, such as Bilbo, who have ventured beyond its boundaries, the Shire is populated by adults who seem as innocent as children. The Shire, therefore, suggests a kind of Eden, where a hobbit can live an entire lifetime far from cruelty, greed, and war.

In Jackson's films, the hobbits return to the Shire after the great battle of Middle-earth has been fought, the evil forces of Sauron have been defeated, the ring has been destroyed, and the various human kingdoms have been united under Aragorn's rule. In other words, all of Middle-earth has become much like the Shire, a place free from strife. In the novels, however, precisely the opposite has happened: the struggles of Middle-earth have come to the Shire. Even though Frodo has destroyed the ring of power, war and hardship have not ceased to exist. In the novels, the destruction of the ring marks an important victory against evil, but the world has somehow changed irreversibly nonetheless, signaling an end of innocence.

Tolkien's version of the return to the Shire allows for further exploration of the differences between Sam and Frodo. In the novels, Frodo, exhausted by his journey to Mordor, barely participates in the ensuing rebellion against Saruman. Sam, meanwhile, leads the rebellion and eventually becomes mayor of the Shire. This final confrontation sheds new light on what Frodo says as he departs Middle-earth with the elves. Handing the memoir of his adventures to Sam, he says, "The last pages are for you, Sam." In the film, this line suggests that Sam will go on to live happily ever after in the Shire. In the novel, Sam will be forced to display courage and heroism in the rebellion in the Shire as Frodo did on the journey to Mordor.

Jackson's rosier conclusion simplifies the story, certainly, since a Shire-based battle would probably have added another thirty minutes to the film, but it serves another purpose as well. By allowing the hobbits to return to an idyllic Shire, Jackson has lightened Tolkien's much darker vision and opted to conclude the trilogy with a classic Hollywood ending. In a way, however, by presenting such a simple version of good and evil, a version in which the worst evil is vanquished and no new evil rises to take its place, Jackson renders his films even more fantastical than Tolkien's original novels. In a world as tumultuous as Middle-earth, evil is sure to one day return.

NARRATIVE STRUCTURE

The Lord of the Rings films progress chronologically, following Frodo and the other members of the fellowship on their journey. A narrator relates the history of the ring at the very beginning of *The Fellowship of the Ring*, which is the only background information we need to understand the urgency of the upcoming journey. From there, events happen in order, from Gandalf's arrival in the Shire at the beginning of the first film to Sam and Frodo's return at the end of the last. While Tolkien's trilogy relies on appendices and companion books to augment the story with historical minutiae and tangents, Jackson elects to stay close to the central narrative—incorporating such obscure details into the films would have been all but impossible. After the fellowship breaks up at the end of *The Fellowship of the Ring*, individual characters and smaller groups pursue their own journeys, and the scenes move back and forth between them. However, their stories take place more or less simultaneously and are related in the order in which they occur. Dreams, visions, and psychic messages occasionally appear and reveal images of past or future events, but since these occur within specific characters' minds, they still follow the chronology of the action taking place.

Only one scene in the trilogy appears out of chronological order: the opening scene of *The Return of the King*. In this scene, the hobbit Sméagol kills his friend to acquire the ring of power and eventually becomes the withered creature Gollum, whose singular obsession is the ring. As a freestanding scene, this episode is unique in the trilogy. In a way, the scene reveals nothing new, since Gollum's internal debates in *The Two Towers* reveal enough information for us to speculate about his history. Other background information may have been equally or more useful, such as the history of Saruman and Gandalf's relationship or the story of Aragorn's being raised by elves.

The Sméagol scene, however, has two important effects on *The Return of the King* and on the trilogy itself. Though the power of the ring has been evident from the very beginning, Sméagol's transformation shows exactly how dangerous that power is. In a way, the story of Sméagol serves as a cautionary tale or a dire prediction of what could happen to Frodo if he gives in to the power of the ring. The scene also gives new edges and layers to the character of Gollum. Gollum is a complex combination of good and evil, and this ambiguity sets him apart from other characters in the trilogy, who are usually completely good or wholly evil. Gollum's history provides a window into his psyche, and, with him more than with any other character, we can see what motivates both his actions and his anxiety. Gollum's utter helplessness in the presence of the ring renders him, to some extent, an object of sympathy.

IMPORTANT QUOTATIONS EXPLAINED

1. GALADRIEL: "You are a ring-bearer, Frodo. To bear a ring of power is to be alone. This task was appointed to you. And if you do not find a way, no one will."

Galadriel, the Lady of the Woods, says these words to Frodo near the end of *The Fellowship of the Ring*. The fellowship has just barely escaped from the mines of Moria, where they believe Gandalf has been killed. The experience has made them all uneasy. As the others sleep, Galadriel makes Frodo look into a mirror, in which he sees visions of what will happen if his mission fails: among other trage-dies, the Shire will be overrun by orcs and his friends will be impris-oned. She tells Frodo that the fellowship has broken and that one by one the others will come after the ring, a statement that anticipates Boromir's attempt to steal the ring at the end of the film. Frightened by the awesome responsibility before him, Frodo offers Galadriel the ring, which she refuses.

When Frodo says he cannot accomplish his task on his own, Gal-adriel responds with the quotation above. She means to encourage him but also to let him know that his journey has just begun. The fel-lowship has given him a start, but the task ahead is his and his alone. He no longer needs the others, and, indeed, he separates from them at the end of the film. These words also serve as a warning for Frodo, alerting him to the solitude he'll struggle with as long as he has the ring. Frodo will wrestle with solitude even after he's destroyed the ring and returned to the Shire. When Galadriel tells Frodo, "To bear a ring of power is to be alone," she demonstrates her understanding of exactly how enormous Frodo's task is, and how separate he is from the rest of the fellowship. His task is completely solitary, and it will consume his life.

2.   SAM: "I made a promise, Mr. Frodo. A promise. Don't you
leave him, Samwise Gamgee. And I don't mean to. I don't
mean to."

When Frodo breaks off from his companions at the end of *The Fellowship of the Ring*, all except Sam willingly let him go, understanding his decision to travel alone. As Frodo rows away from shore,
Sam, who cannot swim, runs into the water after him. Sam quickly
starts drowning, and Frodo reaches into the water to save him. Once
aboard the boat, Sam uses these words to explain his refusal to let
Frodo go on alone. The promise he refers to is the promise he made
to Gandalf when Gandalf recruited him to be Frodo's traveling partner. Sam may seem like just a bumbling hobbit, but his steadfastness, even in the face of Frodo's willful determination, shows him to
have a tough inner core that will prove invaluable to Frodo as the
journey continues.

Sam's affirmation of his promise to stay with Frodo suggests how
fully interdependent the two friends are. From this point on, Sam
will be Frodo's protector, but here, Frodo protects Sam's life. As
harsh and solitary as Frodo's task is, Sam is always right beside him,
providing as much support as possible. As pure a heart as Frodo
must have to bear the ring and destroy it in Mount Doom, Sam must
have a similarly pure heart to support his friend so completely and
never desire the ring for himself. With his actions and these words,
Sam shows that his relationship with Frodo is different from everyone else's, and he contradicts Galadriel's message about the breakup
of the fellowship of the ring. The fellowship, Sam's actions and
words suggest, has merely been reconstituted from a group of nine
to a group of two. With these words, Sam shows that he, like Frodo,
understands the nature of his mission.

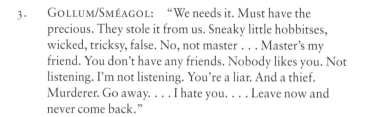

3.   GOLLUM/SMÉAGOL: "We needs it. Must have the
     precious. They stole it from us. Sneaky little hobbitses,
     wicked, tricksy, false. No, not master . . . Master's my
     friend. You don't have any friends. Nobody likes you. Not
     listening. I'm not listening. You're a liar. And a thief.
     Murderer. Go away. . . . I hate you. . . . Leave now and
     never come back."

Though this passage from *The Two Towers* appears to be a dialogue,
it is actually a monologue, and it exemplifies the internal debate that
consumes Gollum. In *The Two Towers,* Gollum has agreed to lead
Sam and Frodo to Mordor. This particular internal argument occurs
one night as Sam and Frodo sleep, but it is not the only passage of its
kind, and we might assume that this is only part of an ongoing
debate in Gollum's mind. Whenever Gollum has a quiet moment,
this debate overtakes him. The conflict is between his good and bad
intentions, and these intentions manifest themselves in his double
identity, Gollum/Sméagol. Sometimes the doting, kind Sméagol
seems to genuinely like Frodo, who has shown him pity and kindness, and to want to help him. Gollum, however, seems to be merely
biding his time with the hobbits, waiting for the perfect moment to
steal the ring of power, by force if necessary.

This particular debate between Gollum and Sméagol bodes both
good and ill for Frodo and his mission. It shows clearly the anguish
the ring causes its bearer, and Gollum's pathetic existence is a constant reminder of what may be in store for Frodo. However, this
debate also shows clearly how different Frodo and Gollum are. As
Gollum understands it, his choice is between the ring, which he calls
his "precious," and Frodo, his "master." In other words, he must
choose between two things of value, both of which are worth more
than he himself is. Whatever he chooses, Gollum will remain inferior and subservient, and he hints at the reason for his low opinion
of himself in the penultimate line, in which Gollum accuses Sméagol
of being "a liar. And a thief. Murderer." We don't understand until
The Return of the King that Sméagol killed his friend to get the ring.
Because of the guilt Gollum continues to feel about this act, he'll
never be free from his need for the ring. Frodo, on the other hand,
who has acquired the ring in a much more innocent way, might not
have to undergo a similar struggle. Frodo has never been reliant on
or covetous of the ring, and, if he completes his mission successfully,
he never will be. For Gollum, it's too late.

4.   SAM: "It's like in the great stories, Mr. Frodo, the ones that
       really mattered. Full of darkness and danger, they were. . . .
       Those were the stories that stayed with you, that meant
       something, even if you were too small to understand why.
       But I think, Mr. Frodo, I do understand. . . . There's some
       good in this world, Mr. Frodo, and it's worth fighting for."

Sam makes this speech to Frodo at the end of *The Two Towers*, when
the hobbits have reached a low point. They'd been close to the gates
of Mordor when Faramir captured them and took them and the ring
to Gondor. Just before Sam makes this speech, a weakened, hypno-
tized Frodo nearly hands the ring to a wraith. Success in the mission
seems unlikely. However, as Sam gives this inspiring oration, we see
images of Rohan's victory over the forces of Saruman and the Ents
wreaking havoc on Isengard, good signs that suggest Sam and
Frodo's fortune is about to turn. Indeed, Faramir is so moved by
Sam's words that he sets the hobbits free, rather than hold them and
the ring in Gondor.

   Sam's words inspire those who listen, and they also reveal Sam's
growing wisdom. Frodo is not the only one undergoing a difficult
journey—Sam is as well. He no longer speaks as a fresh-faced youth
but with the wisdom of age and experience. He refers back to childhood stories, another component of the innocence of the Shire, now
a thing of the past for Sam and Frodo. Here, Sam finds a way of
looking back without regret, and in the Shire's innocence he finds
the inspiration he and Frodo need to push forward. The Shire is
never far from Sam's mind, and he draws his strength from his memories of it. Frodo, on the other hand, will never be able to go back to
the Shire. The answer Sam claims to have found will never come to
Frodo. This passage does, however, anticipate the fact that Frodo
will turn his adventures into a story. When his journey is over, composing this story will be as close as he comes to finding the peace of
mind that Sam does.

5. ELROND: "As Sauron's power grows, her strength wanes. Arwen's life is now tied to the fate of the ring. . . . The man who can wield the power of this sword can summon to him an army more deadly than any that walks this earth. Put aside the ranger. Become who you were born to be."

Elrond delivers this message to Aragorn in *The Return of the King*, as the fellowship travels with the riders of Rohan to Minas Tirith to defend Gondor against the forces of Sauron. One evening, Aragorn dreams that Arwen chooses immortal life and cannot marry him, and he wakes up to find Elrond, king of the elves and Arwen's father, waiting for him. Elrond tells Aragorn that, contrary to Aragorn's dream, Arwen has chosen mortal life, and her survival now depends on the defeat of Sauron's army. Aragorn has been motivated all along to protect Middle-earth and restore balance and peace to all its realms, but Elrond's news of Arwen gives Aragorn another reason to fight. Arwen has risked her life for the chance of being with him, and Elrond is entrusting Aragorn with the task of protecting her. Elrond gives Aragorn a sword, a sign that he now commits himself fully to supporting the human cause.

The sword Elrond gives Aragorn is Anduril, which was forged from the shards of the sword Narsil. Isildur used a shard of Narsil to fight Sauron and cut the ring from Sauron's finger, and legend claimed that the sword would not be reforged until the ring was found and Sauron returned. By giving Aragorn this gift, Elrond anoints him as Isildur's heir, finally ready to take over Isildur's role as king of Gondor. This moment marks the final step in Aragorn's embracing his status as king, and he uses his status to recruit the men of the mountain to join his army. Elrond says that Anduril can gather an army as great as any "that walks this earth." In other words, at this moment, the forces of good finally have a weapon as powerful as Sauron's ring, and final battle can begin. With the support of Elrond firmly behind him, Aragorn has no choice but to accept his destiny as king of Gondor and set out to save both Middle-earth and his love.

SPIRITED AWAY

(2002)

CONTEXT

In 2003, *Spirited Away* was the first *anime* film (Japanese animated movie) to win the Oscar for Best Animated Feature. For many Americans, the director, Hayao Miyazaki, was an unknown despite the fact that his seven previous full-length animated features had made him a household name in Japan. Disney Studios had tried in the past to expand Miyazaki's American audience, and in 1996 negotiated with Miyazaki and his animation company, Studio Ghibli, to bring nine of their films into wide release for English-speaking audiences. The first film to be distributed was *Princess Mononoke*, which succeeded critically but failed at the box office. Disney was reluctant to release any more Studio Ghibli films—until the success of *Spirited Away*. The film's fine storytelling and breathtaking animation made it the highest grossing movie of all time in Japan, and Disney hoped it would create wider appeal for Japanese *anime* in the U.S.

Born in Japan on January 5, 1941, Hayao Miyazaki grew up in the shadow of World War II. Miyazaki's father, Katsuji, headed the family's airplane factory, which produced wingtips for Zero fighters. The factory made his family wealthy, but Miyazaki was ashamed that his family profited from the war when so many others suffered. In 1944 the entire family was forced to evacuate the city and flee to the country, and after the war Miyazaki's family moved several more times. Miyazaki started school in 1947, the same year his mother was hospitalized due to spinal tuberculosis. In spite of her illness, she had a strong influence on Miyazaki, who rarely saw his busy father.

Miyazaki's interest in art and animation grew from two major influences: Japanese comic books, called *manga*, and his schooling at Gakushuin University. *Manga* were a profound cultural phenomenon when Miyazaki was growing up, embracing complex themes and often targeting an older audience. Miyazaki decided he wanted to draw *manga* for a living when he was in high school. Later, inspired by the full-length Japanese animated features that were becoming increasingly popular, he changed his mind and decided to become an animator. At Gakushuin University, Miyazaki's economics and political science studies shaped the cultural, artistic, and political sensibilities that influenced his later works. As part of his economics major, Miyazaki researched Japanese industry and the war's effect on his country. He later incorporated this and other material into movies such as *Princess Mononoke*, where a city of women produces nothing but weapons and iron. He also joined the children's literature research society, a club for aspiring *manga* writers and illustrators.

Shortly after graduating in 1963, Miyazaki landed a job as an inbetweener—helping to create seamless frames—at Toei Douga, Japan's leading animation studio. But just as important to Miyazaki's career was his role as chief secretary of Toei Douga's labor union. His involvement with the union, and the union itself, deviated from Japan's cultural programming, which insists on absolute subordination to one's employer. As a labor leader, he made many valuable career connections and met his future wife, animator Akemi Ot. In 1971, Miyazaki left Toei Douga for A-Pro, an animation studio owned by two of his former Toei Douga colleagues. At A-Pro and subsequent studios, Miyazaki honed his skills as a storyteller and animator in both television and film. He also became a popular author and creator of *manga*.

In 1984, Miyazaki released his first full-length feature, *Nausicaä of the Valley of Wind*, which was based on his popular *manga* series. It was so successful that he was able to establish Studio Ghibli. More importantly, the success of the movie revived feature-length animation in Japan. For some time, television *anime* had threatened to render animated movies obsolete. Miyazaki's films helped to reverse this trend, and the success of each new Miyazaki film has surpassed its predecessors. *Princess Mononoke* received the Japanese Academy Award for Best Film and was the highest-grossing domestic film in Japan's history until *Spirited Away* supplanted it.

Now in his sixties, Miyazaki shows no sign of slowing down. His films are still not commercially successful in America, possibly because American audiences have difficulty identifying with the Japanese culture he explores. However, his influence on the art of feature-length *anime* has given it a quality unrivalled in American animation.

Plot Overview

Chihiro, a ten-year-old girl, sulks in the back seat of her parents' car. The family is on its way to a new home in a new town, and Chihiro doesn't want to move. When her father gets lost taking a short cut, they discover the entrance to an abandoned theme park. The parents investigate and find a deserted stall piled with food. They start eating, and soon, they're both pigging out. They try to make Chihiro eat, but she has a bad feeling about it and refuses the food. Chihiro wanders away by herself. While she explores, a boy appears and warns her to leave before dark. She runs back to the stall, only to find that her parents have turned into pigs. As night falls, shadowy spirits fill the park, and Chihiro starts becoming transparent. The boy appears again and coaxes her to eat food from the spirit world, which will keep her from disappearing. He then leads her to a busy bathhouse, negotiating her safely through a phalanx of spirits who aren't happy about having a human among them. After getting her to safety, he gives her detailed instructions on how to get a job in the spirit world, which he says is the only way to survive. He says his name is Haku, and that he has known her since she was very small.

Chihiro first goes to the boiler man, Kamaji, for a job. Kamaji tells her that the enchanted soot creatures provide him with all the help he needs. As they talk, Chihiro rescues one of the soot creatures. A girl named Lin arrives and is shocked to discover the human everyone is looking for. Impressed with Chihiro's tenacity and kindness, Kamaji lies and tells Lin that Chihiro is his granddaughter. He bribes Lin to take Chihiro to Yubaba, the witch who runs the bathhouse, to ask for a job. Yubaba initially refuses, but gives in when Chihiro persists. After Chihiro signs a contract for the job, Yubaba steals several of the characters that make up Chihiro's name, renaming her Sen.

The next morning, Haku takes Sen to see her pig-parents, who no longer remember they were once human. Sen tries to remember her real name, and almost can't. Haku warns Sen that he no longer remembers who he used to be and that if she forgets she'll never be able to get home. Returning to the bathhouse, Sen looks back and sees a white dragon in the air. She knows the dragon is Haku.

On Sen's first day of work at the bathhouse, she encounters a silent, white-faced spirit called No-Face, for whom she kindly leaves a door open. She also cleans a stink spirit, which turns out to be a polluted river spirit. The river spirit rewards her job well done with a magic herbal cake. No-Face becomes obsessed with getting Sen's attention. The next day, Sen awakens to find everyone gone, and No-Face, who has gained a voice by eating a frog worker, is causing an uproar by creating gold out of thin air.

Outside of the bathhouse, Sen sees the white dragon, Haku, being attacked by birds. She opens a door for him and he flies through, followed by the birds, which are made of paper. In agony, Haku flies to Yubaba's rooms on the upper level. Knowing he'll bleed to death without help, Sen runs to find him. One of the paper birds hides on her back. As Sen runs through the bathhouse, No-Face sees her and tries to give her gold. She refuses it and runs away. Angered by her refusal, No-Face starts swallowing the staff and causing a panic. Arriving at Yubaba's quarters, Sen finds Haku unconscious. The paper bird that has been hiding on Sen's back seems to turn into Yubaba, but actually it's her twin sister, Zeniba. Zeniba has followed Haku because he stole her gold seal. Disgusted by Boh, Yubaba's giant baby, Zeniba turns him into a small mouse and turns Yubaba's pet bird into a fly. Thrashing around, Haku smashes the paper bird, and Zeniba disappears.

Haku and Sen fall down a dark shaft into the boiler room. Kamaji tells Sen that Haku is bleeding from the inside, so Sen gives Haku part of the herbal cake the river spirit gave her. Haku vomits up the gold seal and a slug, which Sen squashes. Haku turns back to his boy form, but he is still very ill. Sen decides to go to Zeniba in an attempt to convince her to cure Haku. Kamaji gives Sen train tickets to get to Zeniba. On her way to the train, Sen confronts No-Face, who is still terrorizing the bathhouse. She gives him the rest of the herbal cake that she's been saving for her parents. He begins to vomit and becomes angry at Sen, chasing her through the bathhouse. As he runs he vomits up all the people and things he's eaten, getting smaller and smaller until he's back to his normal size and meek demeanor. Sen, the Boh-mouse, the Yubaba-fly, and No-Face leave together for the train. As the group makes its way to Zeniba's, Haku recovers. He leaves the group and goes back to Yubaba, promising to return Boh to her if Yubaba will send Sen and her parents back to their world.

When Sen arrives at Zeniba's, she asks Zeniba to forgive Haku for stealing the seal and apologizes for killing the slug. Zeniba explains that Yubaba put the slug in Haku to control him, and that

Sen has already healed Haku with her love. Haku arrives in his dragon form, and Sen climbs on his back so he can fly her, the Boh-mouse, and the Yubaba-fly back to the bathhouse. Sen remembers that when she was very young she fell in a river. Instead of allowing her to drown, the river carried her to safety. She had forgotten the river's name, but now remembers that it was called the Kohaku River. Sen tells Haku she thinks he was the river. Upon hearing his true name, Kohaku River, Haku's dragon scales fall away and he turns back into his boy shape. They arrive at the bathhouse, and Haku reminds Yubaba she promised to free Sen and her parents. Yubaba says Sen must first identify her parents from a group of pigs. Sen looks over the pigs and declares, correctly, that none of them are her parents. Her contract dissolves and she again becomes Chihiro. Free at last, Chihiro finds her parents, and, as they drive away, Chihiro assures her parents that she can probably handle a new home and school.

Character List

Chihiro/Sen — Voiced by Daveigh Chase   A gangly, ten-year-old human girl, heroine of the movie. At first Chihiro is sullen, whiny, and afraid, with an annoying voice and sulky face. After her name is changed to Sen, she becomes brave and self-sufficient enough to free herself and her parents from the spirit world. As Sen evolves, her voice becomes less grating and her expression lifts and glows. By the end of the movie, when she becomes Chihiro again, her features appear much more mature. She is notable for her lack of greed, her respect for her elders, and her kindness toward others. These qualities cause those she meets to respect, love, and help her.

Haku/White Dragon — Voiced by Jason Marsden   A mysterious, secretive boy of about sixteen who can take the form of a flying dragon. He works for Yubaba, doing rather underhanded deeds such as stealing magic from others, but also has his own agenda. Haku helps Chihiro find an inner strength to survive in the spirit world. Alternatively gruff and gentle, he recognizes Chihiro when he meets her. However, he doesn't remember why he knows her, nor does he remember why he can't leave the bathhouse. Later, we learn he is a river spirit who once saved Chihiro's life and that his real name is Kohaku River.

Yubaba — Voiced by Suzanne Pleshette   A witch who runs the bathhouse and gives Chihiro a job. Yubaba is strict, greedy, and quick to anger, but she's also fair and a stickler for following the rules of the spirit world. She understands the power of identity and changes her workers' names as a means of control, such as when she changes Chihiro's name to Sen. Yubaba is perfectly groomed and heavily bejeweled, and her head is huge in proportion to her body. As befits her station in life, she lives in opulent rooms at the top of the bathhouse.

Zeniba — Voiced by Suzanne Pleshette   Yubaba's kinder twin sister. She helps Sen recognize what was inside her all along. Zeniba is the only one with power equal to Yubaba's, and she's an important key to the conclusion. She explains the other characters' previous lives to Sen, who then confides to Zeniba that her real name is Chihiro. Zeniba critiques Yubaba's lifestyle and misguided parenting style. In contrast to Yubaba's luxurious quarters, Zeniba lives in a modest cottage far from the bathhouse.

Boh — *Voiced by Tara Strong*   Yubaba's giant, spoiled baby. Yubaba keeps him isolated in a luxurious room, surrounded by soft pillows. Boh knows only what his mother chooses to tell him, until Sen expands his world. Although Boh is huge, he's completely helpless. Boh is, in fact, what Chihiro might have turned out to be if she hadn't come to the spirit world. Later, Zeniba turns Boh into a mouse, which allows him to escape his isolated state.

Kamaji — *Voiced by David Ogden-Stiers*   A spider-like spirit that runs the boiler room. He's the first to witness the humanity that makes Chihiro special.

Lin — *Voiced by Susan Egan*   The main female bathhouse worker. Lin is initially gruff with Chihiro but comes to admire her and act as her big sister.

No-Face — *No voice credit*   A sad, voiceless spirit. When No-Face tries to repay Sen for her kindness to him, the results are disastrous. He takes on a frog/worker's voice after he eats the worker.

Yubaba Bird — *No voice credit*   One of two birds with Yubaba's head. This one is Yubaba's pet, and the other is Yubaba herself. Yubaba turns herself into a bird to monitor the village. Her pet is turned into a fly by Zeniba.

Chihiro's Father — *Voiced by Michael Chiklis*   His arrogance begins the chain of events that binds Chihiro in virtual slavery.

Chihiro's Mother — *Voiced by Lauren Holly*   Strong enough not to give in to Chihiro's whining, but follows her husband in spite of her misgivings.

Stink Spirit—No voice credit   An ancient river spirit that has been polluted. To thank her for cleaning him, he gives Sen a food reward that enables her to purge others of what ails them.

Traveling Soot—No voice credit   Enchanted soot works for Kamaji and haul coal in the boiler room. Chihiro's kindness to the soot makes Kamaji her first ally.

The Three Heads—No voice credit   Three disembodied heads that act as attendants for Yubaba. They move by bouncing around on the floor and make odd ponging noises, like video game characters.

The Spirits—No voice credit   Important in Japanese folklore. Traditionally, the Japanese believed that everything had a spirit, even something as humble as a radish.

ANALYSIS OF MAJOR CHARACTERS

CHIHIRO/SEN

Chihiro is a typical ten-year-old girl, spoiled and overprotected. When we first meet her she is angry because her parents are moving the family to a new town and she doesn't want to go. Her parents want her to think of the move as an adventure, but she stubbornly refuses. Beneath Chihiro's childish behavior, however, is a well of maturity and wisdom that Chihiro isn't yet aware of. One sign of this maturity is that she instinctively values and follows rules that she knows are important, even when authority figures tell her to break them. For example, when Chihiro's father decides to explore the abandoned theme park, Chihiro's instincts tell her it's not a good idea. Once inside the park, her parents gorge themselves on the food they find, and she refrains from eating anything. Chihiro's wise respect for rules will prove important in the spirit world.

When Yubaba changes Chihiro's name to Sen, Chihiro seems to lose her true identity. Chihiro desperately holds on to her former self because if she forgets who she used to be, she'll be trapped in the spirit world forever. She believes that resisting her new identity as Sen is necessary to survive. Yet Chihiro's time spent as Sen is when her true self develops. Chihiro has always been instinctively kind and respectful, but as Sen, she relies on these qualities. She doesn't allow scary circumstances to dim her optimism and trust. Chihiro's kindness toward others isn't just a façade to help her escape, and she forms true friendships with several of the bathhouse inhabitants. She helps Haku, Boh, and several needy spirits, even though doing so means she may get stuck in the spirit world. Chihiro leaves the spirit world a more self-sufficient and self-reflective young girl. She realizes that the problems of moving to a new school are nothing compared to the real challenges of growing up.

HAKU/WHITE DRAGON

Haku first appears as a boy of about sixteen, but he is actually a lost river spirit that also can take the form of a white dragon. In his guise as a white dragon his appearance suggests a river: flowing and graceful. As Haku, however, he is not always so composed, and he exhibits both bravery and real sadness. The river he once represented, the Kohaku River, was drained and paved over to build an apartment complex, and Haku is truly a lost soul. Though he has made a home of sorts at the bathhouse, he knows he once had another home, and the loss of it haunts him. Haku's treatment of Chihiro is sometimes kind and sometimes gruff, and Chihiro later learns that Yubaba controls him through a slug she planted inside him. Haku may seem powerful at times, but he is also weak—he cannot remember his name, which means he can never leave the spirit world, and he is under Yubaba's control.

Haku's initial kindness toward Chihiro serves him well. Sen pauses in her quest to rescue her parents to save Haku when he is hurt, as Haku once saved her from drowning in the Kohaku River. He and Sen develop a loyal and deep friendship, and love each other like brother and sister. Since Haku cannot remember who he really is, he must rely on Sen to remember, and his kindness makes her determined to do so. Sen eventually does find Haku's true identity, which gives Haku the power to free himself from the spirit world and Yubaba's control. Although we never learn Haku's ultimate fate, by the end of the movie he has at the very least found a measure of freedom and peace.

YUBABA/ZENIBA

The twin sisters Yubaba and Zeniba teach Chihiro that good and evil both exist in the world, and often exist within the same person. While Yubaba represents evil and can be quite scary, she also honors her word and is scrupulously honest in her business dealings. She recognizes that everyone needs to feel useful and gives a job to anyone who wants one, which is a way of acknowledging the dignity of every individual. Yubaba trusts no one and assumes that everyone is as sly and greedy as she is, but she adores her baby, Boh, beyond all reason. She literally almost smothers him with love, filling his room with pillows, keeping him safe from the world by keeping him away from it. Yubaba has a big, warty head and a huge nose, features that make her evil seem inevitable.

At first Zeniba seems as unscrupulous as her sister, but Zeniba leans more consistently toward good. At one point she notes that she and Yubaba are complete opposites even though they are identical twins, but their differences aren't always so black and white. While Zeniba threatens to kill Haku for stealing her seal, she later forgives him with no strings attached. She also critiques greed and overconsumption, and she insults Yubaba's indulgent parenting. Zeniba is still no saint, but her wisdom helps everyone to discover their true identities and abilities. By the end of the film Sen addresses both Zeniba and Yubaba as "Granny," which suggests not only that both twins are wise in their own way, but that they are merely two sides of the same coin.

Themes, Motifs, and Symbols

Themes

The Power of Words and Names

Words play a role in both Chihiro's initial enslavement at the bath-house and her eventual escape from her contract. Haku and Yubaba understand the power of words from the beginning, and Haku repeatedly warns Chihiro not to allow Yubaba to distract her from her goal of requesting a job. If Chihiro begins to talk about other subjects, Yubaba can take control of her, and Chihiro will have no further recourse. Chihiro has to choose her words carefully and say only what is important for her to get what she wants from Yubaba. Ultimately, this advice saves Haku as well: Yubaba tries to distract Chihiro from her job request by tricking her into revealing who helped her. Lin's and Kamaji's lives would have been in danger too if Chihiro had said the wrong thing or said too much.

Names are equally important in the characters' quest for free-dom. After Yubaba steals part of Chihiro's name, Haku warns Sen not to forget her former name or she will be trapped in the spirit world forever. Sen must remember the qualities that make her who she is and remain true to them, even though her name, the one word that defines her, has changed. Sen succeeds in keeping her identity and also helps Haku regain his, ultimately freeing them both. Haku is living proof of the dangers inherent in forgetting one's true iden-tity. Names are of fundamental importance in the spirit world, and those in power keep their control by stealing and changing names. Only those characters with the inner strength to hold onto their names and identities can free themselves.

The Blurred Line Between Good and Evil

In *Spirited Away*, every character is a mix of good and bad qualities and actions. Even those who seem good at first, such as Haku and No-Face, have their share of evil qualities. By the same token, those who seem bad in the beginning, such as Zeniba, Kamaji, and Lin, become instrumental in Chihiro's escape. Chihiro herself is extremely unpleasant at first, and she reveals her better nature only after she becomes Sen. *Spirited Away's* blurred line between good and evil is a much more accurate reflection of the real world outside the film. In the end, evil is not vanquished but pushed aside as characters make choices that weaken bad influences. These choices have a ripple effect: Sen's acts of goodness bring out the latent good in those she encounters. The only character who seems to remain unchanged by Sen's example is Yubaba, but even Yubaba has qualities, such as her love for Boh, that keep her from being an absolute villain. This theme is unusual for an animated film, as most films in the genre clearly divide good and evil.

THE SHOCK OF ENTERING ADULTHOOD AND THE WORLD OF WORK

Entering the adult world is a substantial and shocking transition for some of the characters in *Spirited Away*. Idleness is a luxury of childhood—Chihiro lies in the backseat while her parents drive, and Boh lolls among soft pillows while his mother goes about her daily business. Neither Chihiro nor Boh is capable of doing anything independently, nor does either know how to effectively ask for what they want. Whining and complaining are the methods they know best, but, for Chihiro at least, these have no place in the spirit world. When Chihiro becomes Sen and starts her job at the bathhouse, she works idly and ineffectively. Lin correctly suspects that Sen has never worked a day in her life. Sen gradually learns to keep up: she works diligently and even undertakes the monumental task of washing the stink spirit until it's true river spirit form emerges. Though hard work is not the only element of the spirit world that transforms Sen into a stronger, more capable person, it certainly helps her learn to deal with problems maturely. The shock of entering the working world is a theme rarely dealt with at this age level, which gives *Spirited Away* one more mark of distinction.

MOTIFS

GREED

Both humans and spirits are greedy in *Spirited Away*, and their greed is always destructive. At the beginning of the film, Chihiro is greedy for her parents' attention. She whines and complains, and covets the familiarity of her own town and home. Chihiro's parents' greed leads them to eat the food that turns them into pigs. The bathhouse workers' greed blinds them not only to the goodness in their midst, in the form of Chihiro, but also to present dangers, such as No-Face. Even Haku is greedy for power to match Yubaba's. Human greed is the reason that Haku can't go home—humans filled in his river to build apartments. Yubaba is the greediest of all. Her greed leads her to serve those who ultimately cause destruction, such as when No-Face rampages throught he bathhouse. She's so preoccupied with gold she initially overlooks the kidnapping of baby Boh, ostensibly her most precious possession. In every case, greed makes characters oblivious to what is truly important, preventing them from reaching their full potential as people and spirits.

FOOD

Food has enormous power in *Spirited Away*, and it can be a force of either good or evil. At the beginning of the movie, food sets Chihiro's entire adventure in motion. When Chihiro's mother and father gorge themselves on the food they find in the abandoned amusement park, they turn into pigs, and Chihiro must save them. In the spirit world, gluttonous No-Face can't fill himself up no matter how much he eats. Food and greed are always a bad combination, but food is also a source of comfort and community. For example, Haku urges Chihiro to eat food from the spirit world so she doesn't disappear, and he gives her food he's put a spell on to restore her strength. Later, as Sen, Chihiro feeds both Haku and No-Face a magic cake to cure them of illnesses brought on by what they have consumed. No-Face knows well the comfort food can offer, and he uses it as a substitute for companionship.

ENVIRONMENTALISM

Spirited Away examines the consequences of actions that alter the natural world in destructive ways. Haku and the ancient river spirit represent these consequences most dramatically. Haku lost his home because his river was paved over to build an apartment complex, and the ancient river spirit at first seems to be a stink spirit because it's so polluted. The abandoned amusement park at the beginning of the movie is linked to the issue of land management. Chihiro's father notes that many theme parks were built in Japan during the boom times, and they were abandoned when the economy tanked. As a result, unsightly, false landscapes dot the countryside. Self-pollution, a more personal aspect of environmentalism, occurs through No-Face's and Chihiro's parents' over-consumption of food. Haku, too, is polluted by Yubaba's slug. Environmentalism is a familiar motif in Miyazaki's films, and critiquing the consequences of development and pollution through animated characters sheds new and unusual light on these issues.

RULES

Rules give structure to the spirit world, and all who live there are bound to them. Chihiro knows that rules permeate the spirit world from the very beginning of her residence there. When Haku leads Chihiro across the bridge to the bathhouse, he warns her not to breathe or she'll be spotted. As Sen, Chihiro has to carefully watch what she says and what she eats. If she doesn't, she risks putting herself or others in danger. Even the most powerful spirits, Yubaba and Zeniba, must follow rules. Despite her fondness for Sen, Zeniba can't help her in the end because doing so would be against the rules. Even though Haku has returned Boh to Yubaba, Yubaba can't allow Sen to go without one final test because Haku has agreed to that condition. A sense of helplessness almost always accompanies the characters' inability to bend the rules, but no one attempts to cast them aside. The final rule Chihiro must follow again comes from Haku: He tells Chihiro not to look back. She knows by now that she must adhere to the rule, and she does as he says despite.

SYMBOLS

WATER

Just as food plays contradictory roles in *Spirited Away*, water represents entrapment and freedom, life and death. When Chihiro tries to escape the abandoned theme park, she discovers that the previously dry ground is now a huge body of water she can't cross. In order to survive in the spirit world, Sen works at the bathhouse, which depends on water for its livelihood. In the course of Sen's work, she rescues a polluted river spirit by pouring liberal amounts of water over him. Sen nearly drowns in the process, but the spirit places her in a protective bubble that keeps her from harm, and this and other acts of kindness play a role in her liberation. Later, Sen releases Haku from his imprisonment when she realizes he is really a river spirit. Her assistance is a kind of repayment, as years before Haku saved Chihiro from drowning after she fell into a river.

FLIGHT

Flight usually has ominous purposes in *Spirited Away*. Yubaba turns into a bird to keep a close watch on her dominion, and when she flies, she resembles a military plane. Haku flies primarily to carry out secret missions for Yubaba. On one of these missions he is attacked by Zeniba's paper birds, which bring him down and nearly kill him. Only one flight promises liberation and hope: when Haku transports Sen from Zeniba's house to the bathhouse so she can identify her parents and return home, Sen remembers Haku's true name, which restores his identity and frees him.

GOLD

Most of the characters in *Spirited Away* obssess greedily about gold, and it almost always brings misery. No-Face can make gold out of thin air, but those who take the gold find that it brings them no happiness. Yubaba is so enamored with her gold that she thinks of it first, even before her baby Boh, when Haku warns her that something precious has been taken from her. The gold eventually disappears, rendering the pursuit of it pointless, even for Yubaba. Though not all of the characters are evil, how they respond to gold in some cases determines their fate. For example, Sen, who turns down the gold, ends up with a much richer life than those who accepted it.

FILM ANALYSIS

THE DEATH OF AN ART FORM

Spirited Away stands apart from other animated movies because it is hand-drawn—not computer-generated—a method of animation that is nearly extinct in the United States. In early filmmaking, all animation was hand-drawn and was almost as simple as the flip books from which animation evolved. Because moving pictures were in their infancy, animated films of this time often looked jerky. The characters bobbed along awkwardly, and backgrounds were jumpy or nonexistent. As film and filming techniques became more sophisticated, so did animation. However, the basic technique of drawing animation has remained the same. Artists draw and paint single pictures, called frames, which are then filmed in order. The work is tedious, time consuming, and tends to be expensive because of its high labor costs. Just as with other labor-intensive industries, technology seemed an answer to the rising costs of production.

In the early 1980s, filmmakers began to use computer animation to fill in backgrounds and add special effects. One of the first animated features to effectively combine a roughly equal measure of computer generated images (CGI) and hand-drawn animation was Disney's *Beauty and the Beast*, released in 1991. Then, in 1995, *Toy Story* became the first movie created wholly on computer. CGI now dominates American animation. In fact, in early 2004 Disney closed its hand-drawn animation studio, signaling a complete shift from hand-drawn animation to CGI. While most recent CGI films have done well at the box-office, other films, featuring either hand-drawn animation or a combination of CGI and hand-drawn animation, have fared poorly. Two films relying on hand-drawn animation, *Atlantis: The Lost Empire* and *Spirit: Stallion of Cimarron*, were box-office flops; Disney reasoned the failure was due to the fact that young American audiences, who have grown up on video games, have no interest in non-CGI films.

While CGI can be impressive because the image it produces is three-dimensional rather than two-dimensional, its look is very different from hand-drawn animation. In fact, the two are actually different mediums. The difference between them is comparable to the difference between hand-drawn illustrations and Clip Art, or between oil paintings and photographs. Japanese animation studios have begun using some CGI technology, but hand-drawn animation remains the primary medium of *anime*.

CHARACTER AND SETTING

The artists behind *Spirited Away* paid close attention to the consistency of setting and character and the relationship between them. Yubaba has a sense of richness about her even when she's just sitting in a towel with a simple white turban wrapped around her head. Chihiro, even when she is Sen, always appears plain and straightforward, from her ponytail to her humble clothing. She works in the elaborately appointed bathhouse, but the background always suggests simplicity and quiet. In spite of the lushness of the bathhouse, Sen must clean the big tub that sits alone in a nearly bare room. In that room she transforms a huge, ungainly, polluted spirit into the essence of simplicity: First he appears as a skeletal head, then as a sleek serpent. Even her meals are simple affairs. She nibbles a dumpling on her balcony far from the multi-course hubbub of the main house. The scenery, which tends to be of secondary importance in animated films, is as impressive as any exquisitely filmed landscape in a live-action movie.

The minor characters are rendered just as flawlessly as the setting, with expressions and movements that range from the subtle to the garish. The different techniques the characters use in trying to reach No-Face in the bathhouse make for a powerful contrast. After No-Face becomes the rich, gold-making spirit, the assistant manager uses exaggerated songs and dances, including a fan dance, to ingratiate himself to No-Face. Later, after No-Face has practically wrecked the bathhouse, Sen confronts him with a still, silent dignity that is profoundly effective.

DIRECTING

After releasing *Spirited Away* in 2001, Hayao Miyazaki hinted that it would be his final picture, much to the dismay of Japanese movie-lovers. Miyazaki is a revered figure in Japan, and his movies are wildly popular. Miyazaki's success is linked to his level of involvement in his films, which goes far beyond his position as director. Not only was *Spirited Away* based upon an original Miyazaki story, but

Miyazaki gave the final approval for every piece of key animation in the film. At 24 frames per second in a 124-minute movie, it was an overwhelming job. In addition, Miyazaki helped choose the voice cast. He personally attended every voice taping session and every recording session for the background music. He often worked until two or three in the morning for months on end.

When the hubbub over his feared retirement died down, Miyazaki explained that he was not planning to quit but merely to delegate more duties to his younger staff members. Delegation had been difficult in *Spirited Away* because of the sheltered upbringings of many of his young staffers. Miyazaki could explain what he wanted, but they couldn't adequately picture what he requested because of their limited life experiences. For example, Miyazaki wanted the white dragon to have a snout like a dog's, and to react as a dog would when something was forced into its mouth. However, none of his young artists had ever owned a dog, and they had no idea what he meant. Miyazaki took them on a field trip to a veterinarian's office and had them videotape a dog being handled by a veterinarian's assistant so they could watch it back at the office until they captured Miyazaki's vision.

Miyazaki's difficulty with his staff is ironic because Miyazaki critiques exactly this type of sheltered upbringing in *Spirited Away*. Chihiro and Boh are both brought up in a bubble, separated from the real world around them. Although Miyazaki may want to step back and be less involved in his films, the cultural gap between his generation and the younger generation of animators will clearly make doing so almost impossible. Miyazaki is part of a generation of Japanese animators who made *anime* an important mirror of Japanese culture, both past and present.

Historical Context

The Westernized look of *anime* is rooted in the post-World War II occupation of Japan by the American armed forces. Inspired by the American adventure-based comic books that appeared during the occupation, an artist named Osamu Tezuka created the first commercially successful *manga* (the Japanese name for comic books) in 1947. The *manga* was called *New Treasure Island* and featured highly Westernized characters with big eyes, small noses, and a variety of hairstyles. It was based upon an English novel, Robert Louis Stevenson's *Treasure Island*. After *New Treasure Island* became a hit, imitators began churning out *manga* featuring characters inspired by Tezuka, and *manga* went on to become hugely popular in Japanese culture. Eventually, these comic books were put on film and the medium of *anime* was born. Like most creators of *anime*, Miyazaki got his start drawing *manga*. His first film was based on a successful series of *manga* that he created.

Spirited Away is the second of Hayao Miyazaki's *anime* to win the equivalent of the Academy Award for Best Picture in Japan. While it would be almost unheard of for a comic-book-based movie to achieve this honor in America, the historical significance of *manga* in Japan makes it possible there. *Manga* is a medium that crosses both gender and generational boundaries. *Manga* exist to fit every interest, from politics to pornography to violence, and the Japanese read *manga* much the same way that American adults read novels. However, *manga*'s readers do not draw the same distinction between animation and live action that Americans do. In fact, *Spirited Away* is one of Miyazaki's few feature-length films intended for children. Most of his other movies, such as *Princess Mononoke*, which also won Best Picture in Japan, contain violence and adult concepts that could frighten a child.

Animation may be starting to cross generational boundaries in America the same way it does in Japan. The audience for *anime* in America is growing. As children who cut their *anime* teeth on Pokémon get older, they can begin to appreciate higher quality *anime* such as *Spirited Away*. Some filmmakers already credit *anime* for influencing their cinematic style, such as the Wachowski brothers with *The Matrix*. The influence of *anime* can only increase as today's young *anime* fans become tomorrow's filmmakers.

INFLUENCES ON THE FILM

Spirited Away has been aptly compared to both *Alice in Wonderland* and *The Wizard of Oz*. Like both Alice and Dorothy, Chihiro gets lost in a fantastical world where she meets odd characters, who alternately help and hinder her adventure. Food constantly changes Alice's body, just as it changes bodies in *Spirited Away*: It turns Chihiro's parents into pigs and it saves Chihiro's life. Words and word games confuse and enlighten Alice, and words play a big role in Chihiro's adventure as well. Thematically, *Spirited Away* most resembles *The Wizard of Oz*. While Alice goes looking for adventure to escape the boredom of a lazy day with her sister, Chihiro and Dorothy are thrust unwillingly into their strange new worlds and want only to go home. Unlike Alice, who encounters other characters only briefly, Chihiro forms deep friendships in her new world, just as Dorothy does in Oz with the Scarecrow, the Tin Man, and the Lion. At the end of *Spirited Away*, Chihiro finds that what she needs to get home has been inside her all along. She summons her inner strength just as Dorothy does when she clicks the heels of her ruby slippers.

Important Quotations Explained

1.   Chihiro's father: "Don't worry, you've got Daddy here. He's got credit cards and cash."

Chihiro's father reassures Chihiro with these words early in the film, when the family explores the abandoned theme park. Chihiro's parents find a food stall and begin eating, even though no one is present to give them permission, to serve them, or to accept their payment for the food. Although Chihiro's father brazenly asserts that Chihiro shouldn't worry, Chihiro follows her own instincts and refuses the food. Her instincts, not her father, keep her from being turned into a pig like her parents. Chihiro's father claims to be her protector, but his greed and thoughtlessness suggest that Chihiro is perhaps even more adult than her parents are. She will eventually save them, not the other way around.

    Chihiro's father's pride in his credit cards and cash, and his certainty that they can act as a kind of shield, foreshadows the spirit world's rampant greed. Chihiro's father thinks wealth can compensate for a lack of respect and good manners and that just because he has the money his hungers should be instantly gratified. Chihiro soon learns that money can't solve every problem, and she wisely chooses duty over gold while working in the bathhouse. Those who give in to their greed are enslaved by it. In the end, both the food and the gold fail to satisfy.

2.   Yubaba: "You humans always make a mess of things. Like your parents who gobbled up the food of the spirits like pigs. They got what they deserved."

Yubaba uses these words to insult Chihiro when Chihiro asks for a job. Yubaba doesn't have much respect for the way humans have handled their world, and she doesn't want them messing up her well-run spirit world. This disdain permeates *Spirited Away* as a whole, and an important theme in the movie is how humans change the landscape of the natural world with their arrogant interference and ignore the consequences. Like pigs, humans gobble up what is in front of them without considering the effects of their actions or acknowledging that the natural world might sometimes be more important than humans themselves. Pollution, land misuse, and unsightly abandoned buildings are just a few of the negative consequences of irresponsible actions. When humans bring natural or not-so-natural disasters upon themselves, they whine and complain. Yubaba expects Chihiro to take this same position. She is counting on it, in fact, because then she won't have to give Chihiro a job. However, Chihiro is different from her parents, and she stays focused on her goal.

Yubaba's words call into question what people do and do not deserve. Chihiro's father and mother are accustomed to taking things as their due, and they pass this attitude on to Chihiro. However, Chihiro now finds herself in a world where everything has to be earned through hard work. The bitterness in Yubaba's comment suggests that not everyone gets what they deserve, or that people don't always deserve what they get. For example, Haku and the ancient river spirit didn't deserve to be displaced and polluted. The humans who displaced and polluted them deserve to be punished, but they probably won't be. Chihiro's well-off parents have always given her everything she wants or needs, whether she deserves it or not. Only through her work at the bathhouse does Chihiro learn the connection between work, accomplishment, and reward. Eventually, Chihiro earns her way out of her situation through a combination of hard work and good character. Ultimately, she gets what she deserves.

3.   HAKU: "You still haven't noticed that something precious to you has been replaced."

Haku says this to Yubaba after Chihiro heals him and takes off for Zeniba's with baby Boh. Yubaba doesn't realize Boh is missing because Zeniba has made Yubaba's attendants, three disembodied heads, look like Boh. Haku understands that greed has blinded Yubaba to what she truly values, and his words suggest that without this hint Yubaba will remain interminably oblivious to what is missing. Though she usually smothers Boh with attention, Yubaba is distracted by her work and doesn't realize that Boh is definitely not acting like himself. When Haku tells Yubaba that something precious has been replaced, the first thing Yubaba looks for is the pile of gold beside her on the table. Only when she sees that the gold is safe does she understand he's talking about another precious thing, and when she refocuses her attention on Boh, she discovers he isn't Boh at all. A few seconds later, the gold turns to dirt. Her greed has left her with nothing, and now, with no material objects to protect or covet, she wants only her baby. Boh becomes an important bargaining chip in obtaining Sen's freedom, while Yubaba learns a lesson about what really matters in the world.

Almost every major character in *Spirited Away* has experienced replacement in some way. Shortly after this scene with Yubaba, Sen remembers Haku's real name, which is Haku's own precious thing that has been replaced. Sen's memory of the Kohaku River reminds us that humans constantly replace precious parts of nature with more transient things. Haku's true identity, Kohaku River, was replaced by an apartment complex. The stink spirit replaced the ancient river spirit because his river was polluted. Pigs replace Chihiro's gluttonous parents. Even Chihiro's real name is replaced with the name Sen, a smaller and presumably less important name. Ultimately, Chihiro survives because she recognizes what is precious and tries to preserve it.

4.   CHIHIRO: "I knew you were good!"

Sen says this to Haku as they're returning to the bathhouse near the end of the movie. She has agonized about Haku's true motives and character since the moment she met him, and she now remembers that he saved her from drowning when she was very young. Suddenly, all of her decisions are justified, and her doubts about her abilities disappear. She has trusted her instincts, and her instincts have proved trustworthy. She has come into her own. When Sen returns to the bathhouse and takes on Yubaba's last challenge, she completes her transformation from a hesitant little girl to a self-confident young woman. She has no hesitation in her voice when she answers Yubaba's question. She trusts her instincts once again and tells Yubaba that her parents are not among the pigs before her, thus freeing herself and her parents from their slavery.

Throughout the movie, Sen has doubts about Haku, but she nonetheless stands by him. Her loyalty reveals her understanding that a person's character is multi-layered and that appearances can be deceiving. Although both Haku and Lin initially treat her gruffly, they quickly become her biggest allies. While the rest of the bathhouse workers seem to hold fast to the first impressions they have of their customers, Sen treats everyone equally and finds out what's beneath the surface. The bathhouse workers try to scare away the Stink Spirit, but Sen treats him as she would any other customer and discovers that he isn't as nasty as he appears to be. Sen gives people and spirits a chance to prove their goodness even if that goodness is hidden, and her acceptance helps to free her.

5.   BOH: "If you make Sen cry, I won't like you anymore."

Boh says this to his mother, Yubaba, when they return to the bathhouse. His impertinence is surprising, since Yubaba has sheltered and pampered him for his entire life. Boh learns much about the world when he is transformed into the Boh-mouse. His more manageable size enables him to accompany Sen on the greatest adventure of his life, and Sen shows him there is more to life than mindless luxury. He observes how she rejects greed for good deeds and sees how her devotion and honor affect those around her. He finds joy in making something for a friend and participating in the real world, as opposed to the virtual reality in which his mother imprisons him. He eventually respects Sen so much that he rejects his mother to help her, even though it means Sen will become Chihiro again and leave him behind. While Chihiro's parents may not be the best role models for her, and Yubaba may not be a great role model for Boh, Chihiro and Boh draw from their own wells of good judgment and kindness to make the right choices.

Boh's statement also reveals the transforming power of loyalty and strong friendships in *Spirited Away*. Throughout her ordeal, Chihiro never wavers in her loyalty to her parents, but as she makes friends in the spirit world and becomes committed to those friendships, her loyalties expand. She must make fast decisions and figure out her priorities. As Sen, Chihiro ends up risking her chance to save her parents by saving No-Face and Haku with the herbal cake she received from the ancient river spirit. In return, Kamaji sacrifices his long-treasured train tickets to send Sen to see Zeniba. He does so because of the loyalty Sen shows her friends, a loyalty Kamaji calls love. Sen's loyalty inspires loyalty in others, even in the spoiled, selfish Boh.